W9-CEU-545

ENCYCLOPEDIA OF JEWISH CONCEPTS

ENCYCLOPEDIA OF
JEWISH
CONCEPTS

PHILIP BIRNBAUM

HEBREW PUBLISHING COMPANY
NEW YORK

Encyclopedia of Jewish Concepts was previously published in hardcover editions under the title *A Book of Jewish Concepts*.

HEBREW PUBLISHING COMPANY
100 Water Street
Brooklyn, New York 11201

The publishers acknowledge, with warmest thanks, the help of the Boesky family—Seema, Ivan, Billy, Marianne, Teddy, and John—in making this printing possible.

L

THOSE who are learned in the principles of religion, and also well versed in philosophy, need not my book, for their own wisdom can give them more satisfaction than this work. It is the beginner in speculation who can benefit from this work—the man who has not yet been able to see the rational necessity of the beliefs and practices which he knows from tradition.

—RABBI ABRAHAM IBN DAUD (1110-1180)

Emunah Ramah (Sublime Faith)

INTRODUCTION

THE purpose of this book is to provide in a single handy volume the essential teachings of Judaism. It is written for those who want an up-to-date and easily intelligible account of basic Jewish concepts, a knowledge of which brings meaning to what may otherwise seem empty phrases. At the present time when we are confronted with widespread indifference, we have great need of a spirituality based upon genuine knowledge of our heritage.

The need for some guiding principles or standards for Jews of this generation is being enunciated in every direction. Knowledge of Jewish values has reached an abysmally low point. It is of the utmost importance that the Jewish heritage be looked upon as a whole, not as a mere series of precepts and concepts linked together. Its study must not be the prerogative of specialists, but should be shared by the multitudes. The present volume has been prepared in a manner that old and young alike will find easily what they seek to know about each book of the Hebrew Bible, about the contents of the talmudic-midrashic literature, about the Jewish codes of law and ethics, and in general about all the wisdom literature in Judaism.

Encyclopedic in scope and compact in content, easy to consult and convenient to use, this work has been designed not only for rabbis, teachers and students, but also for all laymen who are interested in the universal message of Judaism. Here, in one volume, are the ideals, practices and aspirations of Judaism brought into contemporary focus for the benefit of the inquiring minds of today that seek basic answers to life's questions.

As a reference work on so vast a subject as Judaism, this book cannot be all things to all readers. It presupposes some familiarity with the subject, and is designed to point the way to further study. It is, moreover, composed with an awareness of today's tensions, and with the conviction that the Jewish message about life's meaning is true and effective for all time. Modern man, who is threatened by a world of his own making, should try to understand the range and depth of the heritage received from Israel's prophets and sages.

Among the hundreds of ethical concepts discussed in the present work, a considerable variety of liturgical compositions have been included because they represent a goodly portion of the spiritual sustenance of the Jewish people in many generations. The oft-repeated blessings and prayers frequently emphasize the Jewish concepts of mercy and kindness. They serve as reminders of man's duties to his fellow men by praising God for opening the eyes of the blind, clothing the naked, setting the captives free, raising those who are bowed down, guiding the steps of man, and giving strength to the weary. Similary, the concept of holiness, often expressed in the liturgy, includes such qualities as justice, goodness, wisdom, and truth. In imitation of God who is addressed as holy and merciful, one generation after the other has been trained to be profoundly moved by compassion for human beings.

Since the vast majority of Jewish concepts are expressed in Hebrew terms, the alphabetical arrangement of the entire volume is in Hebrew, immediately translated or transliterated. A glance at the English or Hebrew index in back of the book will prove suggestive enough for purposes of discussion and clarification. Though each entry is an independent unit, it will prove fascinating to relate various subjects by consulting either index. If any reader wishes to make a systematic study of the composition and contents of the Hebrew Bible, for example, he should begin with the entry *Tanakh* or *Bible* and follow through all the biblical books that are treated throughout the volume each separately. The same applies to tannaitic, talmudic-midrashic, and ethical books as well as philosophic and poetic compositions. Jewish festivals, laws and customs, historic movements and spiritual trends can be traced in the same manner by using the index.

With the idea that the present volume will be used chiefly for obtaining precise information quickly, we have given it the form of a dictionary, a dictionary of Judaism, where the material required by rabbis, teachers, students and laymen, can be found without laborious searching. Cross references and other technicalities have been avoided so as not to confuse the reader. For his convenience certain ideas are repeated, instead of sending him to consult similar thoughts elsewhere in the book. The documentation has been kept to a minimum in order to simplify the presentation as much as possible.

This book should have a definite value at the present time. Whether it is opened at random or is methodically read from beginning to end, it will justify itself in interest and instruction. It has been noted that our contemporaries move about the earth with unprecedented speed, yet they cannot be saved without wisdom. Judaism characterizes wisdom by such qualities as honesty, sobriety, patience, discretion, and consideration for fellow men. To open the Jewish classics is to enter a world of wisdom that is strange to the modern mind.

For purposes of lucidity and readability, the numerous biblical and talmudic-midrashic quotations are freed from archaic forms in this book. The new renditions are designed to facilitate a proper understanding of the original Hebrew and Aramaic passages. The articles are concise and to the point; technical language is explained.

In keeping with our method of translating the liturgical classics, and following the example of English Bibles, no pronouns have been capitalized in this work, because the frequent use of capitals makes for confusion. The pronouns *thou* and *thee* have been retained in biblical quotations where they are addressed to God, since they convey a more reverent feeling than the common *you*.

The Hebrew language has about thirty words to express justice and humanity, but not a single adequate term for slave. The word *eved* is used not only for domestic servant but also for officer, worshiper, prophet, and subject. It is this *leshon ha-kodesh*, this sacred tongue, which has held together the dispersed people of Israel, binding them to their remote ancestors who built pyramids in Egypt and to those who cried *Shema Yisrael* at the burning stake. Like the traditional festivals and practices, it has been the common ground upon which countless generations of Jews have met. By preserving their identity and being themselves, the Jewish people may again be expected to blaze a trail for others, as they did in the past.

In one of his essays, the immortal Hebrew poet Ḥayyim Naḥman Bialik states: Jewish literature, comprising tens of thousands of volumes, represents the creative forces of hundreds of generations and is highly varied in form and content. Yet, for all this wealth, we are hardly in a position to indicate even a limited number of works which could become significant to the contemporary Jew as a source of spiritual sustenance.

In all ages the rich literature of Judaism had a certain number of books of permanent value, which were a source of enjoyment to every class of Jews. There has not been a single period which did not make some permanent contribution to posterity. Each era deposited behind it a sort of layer. For thousands of years our people thought and felt and expressed itself in various styles and forms. The Bible, the Apocrypha, the Talmud, Philosophy, Kabbalah, Poetry, Ethics, Ḥasidism—each of these represents an entire era with its own atmosphere and character.

But we have difficulty now in meeting a request for a book, or set of books, by means of which a young person may familiarize himself with our people's creativity through choice selections from original books, adequately translated into readable and intelligible English. We certainly cannot advise the mere reader to dig for himself in the vast amount of ancient and medieval literature. Such labor is for experts and not for casual readers.

What are we to do, then, for our contemporary Jew who wants to know the literary activity of the Jewish people through the best illustrations culled from all periods? We must resort to literary ingatherings with the purpose of saving the people from confusion and lack of knowledge with regard to their immortal heritage. We must draw forth the sparks from every nook and corner in which there is concealed a bit of the holy spirit of the people, and combine them into one complete unit.

A Book of Jewish Concepts is the result of an attempt to put into one volume the essence of Judaism for the use of the modern English reader. Judaism has influenced, directly and indirectly, countless millions of people in the course of thirty centuries. Modern man will do well to discover what this profoundly felt system of thought has that will help him in his own search for truth. It has been pointed out that to assign limits to the development of Judaism and to assert that the communication of divine truth to Israel ceased with Moses or with Malachi, or with the close of the Talmud, is to ignore the readings not only of reason but of history.

May this book introduce many readers to a better understanding of the ethical and religious resources of Judaism. May its contents be vividly impressed upon their minds and influence their daily life.

PHILIP BIRNBAUM

May 1964

NOTE TO THE REVISED EDITION

This new edition has been revised, corrected, and brought up to date.

PHILIP BIRNBAUM

January 1975

CHRONOLOGY OF JEWISH HISTORY

First half of second millenium B.C.E.	The Patriarchs
17th to 13th centuries B.C.E.	Hebrews in Egypt
13th century B.C.E.	The Exodus
1020-1004 B.C.E.	King Saul
1004-928 B.C.E.	United Kingdom (David and Solomon)
960 B.C.E.	Solomon builds the Temple in Jerusalem.
930 B.C.E.	Kingdom divided into Judah and Israel
721 B.C.E.	Conquest of Israel by Assyrians.
586 B.C.E.	Destruction of the First Temple by the Babylonians.
516 B.C.E.	Return from Babylon and rebuilding of Temple.
332 B.C.E.	Alexander the Great conquers Eretz Yisrael.
3rd century B.C.E.	The Torah translated into Greek in Egypt (The Septuagint).
168 B.C.E.	Revolt of the Hasmoneans.
37 B.C.E.-72 C.E.	The Herodian Dynasty.
66 C.E.	Jewish revolt against Rome.
70	Destruction of Second Temple.
132-135	Bar Kokhba's rising against Rome.
200	Completion of the Mishnah.
400	Completion of Talmud Yerushalmi.
500	Completion of Talmud Bavli.
1038-1204	The age of Gabirol, Halevi, Rashi, Maimonides.
1267	Ramban (Naḥmanides) revives the Jewish community of Jerusalem.
1492	Expulsion from Spain.
1517	Ottoman conquest of Eretz Yisrael.
1897	First Zionist Congress convenes in Basle.
1909	Tel Aviv founded, first all-Jewish city.
1917	Balfour Declaration.
1925	Hebrew University open on Mount Scopus.
1942	Nazi death camps at full capacity.
1943	Warsaw ghetto revolt.
1948	Proclamation of the State of Israel.
1956	Sinai Campaign.
1967	Six-Day War, Jerusalem reunited.
1973	Yom Kippur War
1979	Israel-Egypt Peace Treaty

ENCYCLOPEDIA OF JEWISH CONCEPTS

Av, the fifth month of the Jewish calendar, counting from *Nisan*, corresponds to the latter part of July and part of August. Like the names of all the Jewish months, the name *Av* is of Babylonian origin. Tradition has it that the first day of *Av* is the anniversary of the death of Aaron, the brother of Moses.

In Zechariah 8:19, the ninth day of *Av* is mentioned as the "fast of the fifth" month. It commemorates the destruction of both Temples, the fall of Bar Kokhba's fortress Bethar, the expulsion from Spain in 1492, and other national calamities. *Tish'ah b'Av* (ninth of *Av*) is the culmination of the nine-day mourning period that begins with the first day of *Av*. These *Nine Days* are observed by abstaining from meat, except on the Sabbath.

As a fast day, *Tish'ah b'Av* is postponed to Sunday if it falls on the Sabbath, since it is forbidden to fast on the Sabbath except when *Yom Kippur* coincides with it. *Tish'ah b'Av* resembles *Yom Kippur*, however, in its restrictions upon eating, drinking, bathing, perfuming, and so on. The three weeks which precede the fast of *Tish'ah b'Av* are observed by refraining from various festivities, such as wedding celebrations. They are called *ben ha-metsarim*, in the sense that Judea was narrowly confined by her foes (Lamentations 1:3).

The special prayers and supplications recited on *Tish'ah b'Av* are keyed to sorrow. The book of Lamentations, and the dirges (*kinoth*) that describe Jewish martyrdom, are chanted solemnly before congregations seated on the ground or on low stools as a sign of mourning. The curtain is removed from the holy ark (*aron ha-kodesh*) in order to stress the sense of mourning; for the same reason, visits are made to the cemeteries.

In Temple times, the fifteenth day of *Av* was a popular holiday known as *Ḥamishah Asar b'Av*, when maidens of Jerusalem dressed in white danced in the vineyards, suggesting to the young men to make their choice of a partner for life. They sang: "Young man, raise your eyes and look around; see whom to choose for yourself. Do not set your eyes on beauty, but on family. . ." (Ta'anith 4:8).

On the Sabbath preceding the month of *Av*, the blessing of the month refers to *Rosh Ḥodesh Menaḥem Av* by way of euphemism. Hence, it is generally known as מנחם אב, the comforting month of *Av*. *Shabbath Naḥamu* (שבת נחמו), the Sabbath after *Tish'ah b'Av*, is the

1

joyous occasion when the prophetical lesson begins with words נחמו
נחמו עמי ("Comfort, O comfort my people"). It is the first of the seven
Sabbaths devoted to reading prophecies of comfort and hope.

AV-BETH-DIN　　　　　אַב־בֵּית־דִּין

THE title *Av-beth-din* (father of the court) was originally given to the
vice-president of the supreme court (*Beth Din ha-Gadol*) in Jerusalem
during the Second Commonwealth. The *Av-beth-din* sat at the right
hand of the president (*Nasi*) of the *Sanhedrin* (supreme court), and
the other members of the court sat before them in a semi-circle.

The *Nasi* was the leading authority in civil and political matters,
and the *Av-beth-din* headed the administration of the purely religious
life of the people.

The Hebrew term *Av* (father) is often used as a title of respect and
honor. In the Bible, it is applied variously to master, priest, prophet,
counsellor, king, ruler, chief (Judges 17:10; 18:19; I Samuel 24:12;
II Kings 2:12; 6:21; 13:14; I Chronicles 2:24, 42). The title *Av-beth-
din*, then, signifying father of the court, seems to point to the presiding judge. Hence the assumption that the presiding head of each
Small Sanhedrin (*Sanhedrin Ketannah*), consisting of twenty-three
members, was called *Av-beth-din*. In the case of the Great Sanhedrin,
numbering seventy-one members, the *Av-beth-din* was second in
authority only in relation to the *Nasi*. After the destruction of the
Second Temple, the function of the *Av-beth-din* in the Sanhedrin of
Yavneh and Usha was that of presiding over the Academy.

In modern times, the title *Av-beth-din* is given to the head of a
rabbinical court.

AV HA-RAḤAMIM　　　　אַב הָרַחֲמִים

AV HA-RAḤAMIM (Merciful Father), an elegy over the ravages during the crusading epoch which lasted through the twelfth and thirteenth centuries, is recited during the Sabbath prayers just before the
return of the Torah to the ark. In many communities of Germany,
on the Sabbaths between *Pesaḥ* and *Shavuoth*, long martyrologies
used to be recited of men who died for the sake of the Torah.

Originally, the medieval dirge *Av ha-Raḥamim* was read twice a year: on the Sabbaths preceding the *Torah*-festival *Shavuoth* and the great national fast day *Tish'ah b'Av*. Later, however, it became customary to recite it in Ashkenazic synagogues throughout the Sabbaths, except on distinguished occasions such as feasts, *Rosh Ḥodesh*, the Sabbath prior to *Rosh Ḥodesh*, *Parashath Shekalim*, or when a bridegroom is present.

The opening sentence of *Av ha-Raḥamim* reads as follows: "May the merciful Father who dwells on high . . . remember those saintly souls, the holy communities who offered their lives for the sanctification of the divine name. . . They were swifter than eagles and stronger than lions to do the will of their Master. . ."

Leopold Zunz, who gives a full account of the Hebrew elegies which the medieval persecutions produced, has this to say: "If there are ranks in suffering, Israel takes precedence of all the nations; if the duration of sorrows and the patience with which they are borne ennoble, the Jews are among the aristocracy of every land; if a literature is called rich in the possession of a few classic tragedies, what shall we say to a national tragedy lasting for fifteen hundred years, in which the poets and the actors were also the heroes?" (*Synagogale Poesie des Mittelalters*).

FATHER AND MOTHER   אָב וָאֵם

THE words אב (father) and אם (mother), the etymologies of which are quite uncertain, primarily denote parents of an individual. The utmost respect and obedience to both are stressed in an impressive variety of biblical passages (Exodus 20:12; Leviticus 19:3; Deuteronomy 5:16; Proverbs 1:8; 6:20; 19:26; 20:20; 23:22; 28:24; 30:11, 17). A curse is invoked upon anyone who is disrespectful to father or mother (מקלה אביו ואמו—Deuteronomy 27:16). This is the exact opposite of the Fifth Commandment: Honor your father and your mother.

The constant coordination of father and mother in biblical passages places the mother on the same level with the father with regard to the children. In the Talmud, high praise is accorded to Rabbi Tarfon, a colleague of Rabbi Akiva, for his extraordinary filial devotion and affectionate treatment of his mother. The mother's place and influence in the home life of the Jewish people, especially in the rearing of young children, have always been supreme.

3

"If the Jewess made but rare appearances as a public teacher, she was present in every home as a private instructress. Several medieval rabbis declared, that their first and best teachers were their mothers. The average Jewess was not equal to such a burden as this, but the education of her boys regularly fell on her shoulders until they attained their fifth year. Subsequently her part was that of the moral monitress rather than the intellectual guide" (I. Abrahams).

In Judaism, the Fatherhood of God has become the basis for the brotherhood of man. If God has created all men, it follows that they are brothers and owe brotherly behavior toward one another. "Have we not all one Father? Has not one God created us? Why then do we break faith with each other? . . ." (Malachi 2:10). The *Siddur* or Prayerbook, being a crystallization of the biblical and post-biblical Jewish outlook, is replete with expressions of faith which are addressed to God as the merciful Father, who regards all as his children: "You are the children of the Lord your God" (Deuteronomy 14:1)

PATRIARCHS   אָבוֹת

THE three ancient patriarchs who laid the foundations of Israel have been described as the historic cornerstones for humanity. Each generation contributed to the portrait of Abraham what it held to be purest and noblest and worthiest of the forefather of the Jewish people. The disciples or followers of Abraham, we are told in the Mishnah, possess three traits: generosity, simplicity, and humility (Avoth 5:22). Whoever lacks kindness of heart is no true son of Abraham, according to a talmudic statement (Betzah 32a). Abraham, not Moses, was the founder of Israel's monotheism; hence, in biblical and post-biblical literature, God is frequently referred to as the God of Abraham, Isaac and Jacob, and nowhere as the God of Moses. Abraham has been described as a singular moral phenomenon in the history of humanity's development to a higher life.

Life in Mesopotamia (*Aram Naharayim*) must have been intolerable to a believer in the One God at the beginning of the second millenium, when local society was strictly regulated on principles of polytheism and demonology; so Abraham and his household migrated to the south of Canaan, the Negev, where he became known as a godly prince and a prophet (Genesis 23:6; 20:7). He established the worship of God in his family and passed on his faith to his son Isaac, who

4

in turn passed it on to his son Jacob, who bequeathed it to his twelve sons, whose descendants preserved it in Egypt until the days of Moses (*Yad, Avodah Zarah* 1:3).

The wealth of the patriarchs, who were the heads of large households living in tents, consisted of livestock and wells to water the animals; they were not townspeople, but they dealt with the cities presumably as breeders of sheep and cattle. Their half-nomadic way of life explains why the archeologists of our time cannot determine the exact periods at which the patriarchal incidents occurred. The biblical description of the manner in which Abraham conducted his own life and that of his followers points to a period not later than the eighteenth century before the common era. The patriarchal age of wandering and transition lasted about five generations.

The Talmud traces the origin of the three daily prayers (*Shaḥarith, Minḥah, Ma'ariv*) to the three patriarchs, respectively (Berakhoth 26b). The first of the nineteen benedictions of the *Amidah* prayer, known as *Shemoneh Esreh*, is called *Avoth* because it begins with addressing God as "God of Abraham, God of Isaac, and God of Jacob." The threefold repetition of the word *God* at the beginning of each *Amidah* has been interpreted to allude to the idea that each individual ought to seek and find God for himself, like the patriarchs, in addition to his inherited faith. Hence, the expression *our God and God of our fathers*, used repeatedly in the Hebrew prayers.

The popular Jewish philosopher of the medieval period, Rabbi Baḥya ibn Pakuda, writes in his famous *Ḥovoth ha-Levavoth* (Duties of the Heart): "If you are a man of intellect and understanding, able to verify what you have learned from the sages with regard to the basic principles of religion, you are obligated to use your own faculties to gain clear and definite knowledge of the truth so that your faith and conduct may rest on a foundation of tradition, reason and personal understanding. If you ignore this duty, you fail in your obligation to your Creator."

Even though the patriarchs' merit, frequently mentioned in Hebrew supplications as *zekhuth avoth* (זכות אבות), is regarded as a great influence and help, the talmudic sages cautioned against implicit reliance on it at the risk of neglecting personal merit and worthy conduct. Thus, for example, we find the admonition: "Let all who work for the good of the community do so from a spiritual motive, for then the merit of their fathers will sustain them and their good work will endure forever" (Avoth 2:2).

ETHICS OF THE FATHERS   אָבוֹת

AVOTH (Fathers), one of the sixty-three tractates of the Mishnah, deals with the ethical principles established by the fathers of Jewish tradition who flourished over a period of nearly five centuries, from the time of the last prophet to the end of the second century.

Having achieved a place in the Prayerbook, *Avoth* became the most popular of all books of the Mishnah and its contents exercised a most salutary influence on the Jewish people. The custom of reading *Pirké Avoth* (Chapters of the Fathers) on Sabbath afternoons was originally limited to the period between *Pesah* and *Shavuoth*.

A sixth chapter, derived from a source other than the Mishnah, was added to the five chapters of *Avoth* in order to provide a separate chapter for each of the six Sabbaths between the two festivals. The sixth chapter, called *Kinyan Torah* (acquisition of Torah), was chosen to be read on the Sabbath immediately preceding *Shavuoth*, the anniversary of the giving of the Torah, because its subject matter is almost exclusively in praise of the Torah. The paramount importance of learning and ethical conduct is accentuated throughout this priceless literary gem. *Pirké Avoth* means the ethical teachings of the spiritual fathers of Israel, since the word פרק means also lesson.

Here are a few random excerpts quoted from *Avoth:*

Let your house be a meeting-place for the wise . . . drink in their words thirstily. Judge all men favorably. Stay away from a bad neighbor, and do not associate with an evil man. He who does not increase his knowledge decreases it.

Greed and hatred shorten a man's life. Let the honor of your pupil be as dear to you as your own. Be the tail of lions rather than the head of foxes. One good deed leads to another; one misdeed leads to another. Do not despise any man. The reward is according to the effort. None can be considered really free except those who devote themselves to learning.

AVOTH D'RABBI NATHAN   אָבוֹת דְּרַבִּי נָתָן

AVOTH D'RABBI NATHAN is the first of the Minor Tractates which are printed together with *Seder Nezikin* in editions of the Babylonian Talmud. It has been suggested that Rabbi Nathan is the unknown author of *Avoth d'Rabbi Nathan*, which cites the maxims of *Pirké Avoth* mainly in an expanded form and in different sequence. The book has come down to us in two versions. In addition to the one regularly appearing as one of the Minor Tractates, printed in the Babylonian Talmud, there is another version, consisting of forty-eight chapters, published by Solomon Schechter.

The wise sayings of the Ethics of the Fathers are illustrated in this priceless work by a wealth of examples and stories:

"And develop many students" (Avoth 1:1). According to the school of Shammai, one should teach only the talented, the meek, and those of distinguished ancestry. But according to the school of Hillel, one should teach all men... Rabbi Akiva says: Whoever needlessly takes a penny from charity shall eventually fall in need of charity... Whoever tears his clothes or smashes his furniture in frenzy will end up by worshiping an idol.

The evil impulse bids a person to tear his clothes today, and the next day it bids him to engage in idolatry... Once there was a truly charitable man who set out in a boat, which was sunk in the sea by a wreckful storm. Rabbi Akiva, who had witnessed this tragic event, later appeared before a court to bear testimony so that the widow might be free to remarry. Suddenly, however, the man presented himself to Rabbi Akiva and explained to him how he was saved from drowning by reason of the charity which he had been in the habit of practising. "When I sank to the depths of the sea," he said, "I heard one wave saying to the other: Hurry! Let us raise this man out of the sea, for he has practised charity all his life.

"And judge all men favorably" (Avoth 1:6). A young girl had been taken captive, and two saintly persons went to ransom her. One of them entered the harlots' house, and when he came out he asked his companion: "Of what have you suspected me?" "Of nothing," came the reply. "I felt that you stayed there long enough to find out the ransom price demanded for the girl."

Here are several pithy sayings from *Avoth d'Rabbi Nathan:*

A man's character is known by his walk, dress and greeting.

Who is a hero? He who turns an enemy into a friend.

The man who eats disagreeable food violates three prohibitions: he hurts his health, wastes food, and offers a benediction in vain.

He who esteems himself highly because of his knowledge is like a corpse at the wayside: the passers-by turn their heads away in disgust and walk quickly by.

PARENTS AND CHILDREN   אָבוֹת וּבָנִים

THE first human beings mentioned in the Torah were a family. The history of the Jewish people began with the history of a family, which developed into a tribe and then into a nation. The narratives of Abraham's family life are unsurpassed portrayals of early home life. The father was supreme over the children. He could dispose of his daughter in marriage, and arrange his son's marriage.

The utmost respect and obedience to both father and mother are stressed in the Bible on many occasions. The law concerning a stubborn and rebellious son, who is to be stoned by his fellow citizens (Deuteronomy 21:18-21), imposes limits on the authority of the father: he must not himself put his son to death, but must procure his punishment by a public legal process. The constant coordination of father and mother in Bible passages places the mother on the same level with the father in regard to the children.

In a polygamous family, each mother was more important to her own children than their father. Her position was often revered. The early education and training of her children was mostly given by her. Indeed, each mother and her children formed a sub-family, the management of which was in the hands of the mother. Children were named by the mother, as for example, Jacob's sons. In earlier times polygamous sub-families were so distinct that brothers married half-sisters. Tamar, for example, thinks that David would certainly sanction her marriage with her half-brother Amnon (II Samuel 13:13). Such unions are, however, forbidden in the Torah (Leviticus 18:9).

A married son would remain part of the father's family while the father lived. He would still be in some measure subject to his authority. The sons were the heirs, but in the absence of sons the daughters might inherit, and after the daughters other male relatives in order of kinship (Numbers 27:1-11). A larger portion of the inheritance was given to the firstborn son, but the right of the firstborn might be sold, or bestowed on a younger son by a partial father. Such practice is forbidden in Deuteronomy 21:17.

Isaac had one wife. In later tradition, his household was represented as ideal. The elaborate praise of the housewife in Proverbs (31: 10-31) suggests a monogamous family. Talmudic literature reflects a monogamous society. According to a rabbinic interpretation, the biblical verse, "you may be sure your house is safe," refers to him who

8

loves his wife as himself and honors her more than himself, who leads his children in the right path and arranges their early marriage (Yevamoth 62b).

Jewish family life has retained throughout the centuries a distinct character to which the teachings of the Bible and the Talmud have greatly contributed. Religious observances, particularly those connected with the Sabbath and the festivals, strengthened Jewish family life and developed its solidarity to an extent unusual among non-Jews. The dwindling of internal solidarity and the increase in Jewish divorces have been attributed of late to gradual assimilation. The Jewish family pattern is said to be approaching that of the environment.

The whole of Jewish family life was pervaded by religion. The commonest acts of the daily life were sanctified. The faithful observance of the numerous Sabbath restrictions was associated with a spirit of joy. On Sabbath-eve the children were blessed—a custom which still widely prevails in Jewish homes.

The *Brandspiegel*, a treatise published in 1602, speaks of the custom in these terms: "Before the children can walk they should be carried on Sabbaths and festivals to the father and mother to be blessed; after they are able to walk they shall go of their own accord and shall incline their heads and receive the blessing." This custom linked the generations together in mutual loyalty and affection.

The mutual reverence between parents and children was far reaching. The son must not occupy the father's seat—according to the Jewish code of laws and ethics—or contradict him, or call him by his name. The son can be compelled by Jewish law to maintain his parents. On his part, the father is obligated to educate his children. The education of the young is indeed the primary parental duty.

The *Shema* is perhaps the best statement in the Bible of the obligations of the Jew to his children: "These words which I command you today shall be in your heart. You shall teach them diligently to your children, and you shall speak of them when you stay at home and when you go on a journey, when you lie down and when you rise up" (Deuteronomy 6:6-7).

The early traditions were transmitted orally. They were spoken and they were remembered, hence the expression, "you shall bind them for a sign on your hand, and they shall be for frontlets between your eyes." Thus the book of Proverbs is full of maxims aiming at the inculcation of filial reverence. "My son, observe your father's command, and reject not your mother's teaching; keep them fastened over your heart always; tie them about your neck. When you walk, wisdom will guide you; when you lie down, it will watch over you; when you wake up, it will talk with you" (6:20-22).

Rabbi Israel al-Nakawa of fourteenth-century Spain writes: "If you train your child when he is young, you will enjoy rest and peace later on. You will not have to worry about his going astray and forming habits which are hostile to the well-being of society. Do not be discouraged if you find that your child is dull; do not give up training and correcting him. Though he may not master all you try to teach him, he will learn a little. Try to induce the child to like the process of education. At first you may have to coax him with sweets and toys; then you may have to lure him with the prospects of a higher reward; but, in the end, he will come to love education for its own sake" (לשמה, *lishmah*).

The biblical command, "You shall not put a stumbling block before the blind" (Leviticus 19:14), was interpreted in the Talmud as a caution against striking a grown-up son, who might be tempted to retaliate with a severe blow (Mo'ed Katan 17a).

Heinrich Heine saw in the Jewish family "a haven of rest from the storms that raged round the very gates of the ghettos, nay, a fairy palace in which the bespattered objects of the mob's derision threw off their garb of shame and resumed the royal attire of freedom. The home was the place where the Jew was at his best. . ."

OUR FATHER OUR KING   אָבִינוּ מַלְכֵּנוּ

AVINU MALKENU, a prayer consisting of a series of invocations and supplications recited in the synagogue services during the ten-day period of the High Holydays and on fasts (except *Tish'ah b'Av*), is mentioned in the Talmud (Ta'anith 25b) as the improvised prayer of Rabbi Akiva on the occasion of a drought.

The nucleus of five lines with the initial refrain *Avinu Malkenu* (our Father our King), quoted in the Talmud, was in the course of time increased to forty-four lines. The phrases "our Father" and "our King" are borrowed from Isaiah 33:22; 63:16; 64:7, where God is addressed in such terms as these: "The Lord is our King, he will save us; thou, O Lord, art our Father; O Lord, thou art our Father ... we are all the work of thy hand."

10

According to the anonymous code of laws *Tanya* (page 74), the litany *Avinu Malkenu* originally consisted of nineteen verses to correspond in contents and order to the nineteen benedictions in the *Shemoneh Esreh*. This will explain why this prayer is recited after the *Amidah* on the afore-mentioned occasions, as well as the *Ne'ilah* service at the end of *Yom Kippur*. It is omitted on Sabbaths for the same reason that the thirteen petitions of the weekday *Shemoneh Esreh* are not included in the *Amidah* which is recited on Sabbaths and festivals, namely: no personal requests may be made during Sabbaths and festivals.

Avinu Malkenu is not omitted, however, during the High Holydays, unless they coincide with the Sabbath. On *Rosh Hashanah* and *Yom Kippur* it takes the place of the *Hallel* which is recited on the festivals after the *Amidah* of *Shaharith*. The explanation, as given in the Talmud (Berakhoth 32b), is that on the days of judgment it is more fitting to recite supplications than hymns of praise and thanksgiving.

Avinu Malkenu reflects the frequent persecutions and disasters which have given rise to outcries such as: "Our Father, our King, abolish all evil decrees ... rid us of every oppressor ... close the mouths of our accusers ... remove pestilence, famine, destruction and persecution from thy people. . ."

MOURNING   אֲבֵלוּת

MOURNING is frequently mentioned in the Bible as being observed for the death of a near relative, but the Torah warns against the paganism of excessive ceremonials for the dead: "You shall not cut yourselves or make any baldness on your foreheads for the dead" (Deuteronomy 14:1). The mourning of the orientals has always been ostentatious: shaving the head or plucking out the hair, putting on sackcloth, sprinkling ashes or dust on the head, weeping and lamenting. Professional mourners were employed who made loud lamentation "till the eyes ran down with tears and floods gushed from the eyelids" (Jeremiah 9:17-18).

According to ancient Jewish tradition, mourners are forbidden to eat of their own bread on the day of the funeral. Therefore, they used to carry food to the house of mourning, the rich in silver and gold baskets, the poor in wicker baskets. In deference to the poor, it was ordained that all had to use wicker baskets.

11

Since one must not weep too long for the dead, the Talmud limits the period of mourning in these terms: three days for weeping, seven for lamenting, and thirty for abstaining from a haircut and pressed clothes. Thereafter, God says: You are not more compassionate toward the departed than I am (Mo'ed Katan 27a-b).

The time of mourning is divided into four separate periods: 1) from the death to burial (aninuth); 2) seven days after burial (shiv'ah); 3) the first thirty days after death (sheloshim); 4) the first year after death. In the period of aninuth, the mourner is relieved of the performance of religious duties such as prayer; he makes a rent (keri'ah) in his garments of at least one handbreadth and receives no consolation. In the period of shiv'ah, he sits on a low stool (except on Sabbath and festivals) and receives consolation from his friends. He may not attend to his business or occupation, unless he is very poor (in which case he may start after the third day). He may read only books like Job which treat of suffering.

The day of burial, if the burial takes place before sunset, is considered the first day of shiv'ah, so that the mourner is required to observe six additional days only. Public signs of deep grief are dispensed with on the Sabbath. If the burial occurred an hour before a holyday, the mourner is relieved from the obligation of observing shiv'ah; but if the death occurred on Ḥol ha-Mo'ed, the full period of shiv'ah is observed by the mourner immediately after the holyday. If a holyday intervenes in the midst of shiv'ah or sheloshim, the mourning is not continued to completion. If the death notice reached the relative within thirty days, he must observe shiv'ah; but if it reached him at a later date, the shiv'ah mourning lasts only one hour.

One who loses a father or mother must regard himself as a mourner for a year and avoid all kinds of entertainment. He recites Kaddish for eleven months, and also on the anniversary of his parent's death. A tombstone (matsevah) is consecrated about a year after the death, and on each death anniversary (Yahrzeit) a light is kindled as a symbol of the soul of the departed parent. Formerly the Kaddish was recited the whole year of mourning, so as to rescue the soul from the torture of Gehinnom, where the wicked are said to spend no less than twelve months. In order not to count one's own parents among the wicked, the period of reciting the Kaddish was later reduced to eleven months.

Most of the Jewish death customs are motivated by the high regard felt for the departed. Such are, for example, the thorough cleansing

12

and washing of the body (*tohorah*); the continuous watching of the corpse (*shemirah*) till it is interred, for fear of irreverent treatment; early burial, especially in hot climates where rapid decomposition is likely. In matters connected with the departed, all pomp and luxury are avoided by observant Jews. White linen shrouds (*takhrikhin*) and plain wooden coffins are used for rich and poor alike. This custom was introduced by Rabban Gamaliel II of the second century.

In order to counteract a series of abuses in funeral and mourning practices, several congregations adopted the following regulations:

In keeping with the Jewish tradition, there must be no distinction made between rich and poor in time of death; hence, a uniform coffin should be used for all funerals. In order that the living may remember those who have departed as they were in life, the coffin should be kept closed. The person guarding the body (*shomer*) should stay with it until the funeral rites. Rather than engage in idle talk, visitors should recite appropriate prayers or psalms. The funeral parlor should never be filled with visitors prior to the funeral service. It is, however, a friendly and charitable act (*mitzvah*) to attend funeral ceremonies and to visit bereaved families during the *shiv'ah* period. Pallbearers are not to be provided with gloves. Mourners should not be expected to provide meals or refreshments for those who attend the *shiv'ah* services. Objectionable and unwarranted, this un-Jewish practice should be discarded.

The kindling of lights at the head of the death-bed is in allusion to the biblical expression: "The spirit of man is the lamp of the Lord" (Proverbs 20:27). The use of hard-boiled eggs at the meal, served for the mourners after the burial, suggests the idea of resurrection, life and death being mere changes of form. Also, eggs are symbolical of the perpetual wheel of life. The pouring on the ground of all water in the house of the departed and all adjacent houses is a symbolic announcement of death, which should be made indirectly.

According to *Menorath Hammaor* by Rabbi Israel al-Nakawa of fourteenth-century Spain, one must beware of grieving too much. Unseemly as it is to be callous and indifferent to tragedy, it is just as bad to carry grief to extremes by constantly weeping and sighing. That is a sign of arrogance and reminds one of those haughty people who, when overtaken by misfortune, act as if the sun, moon and stars should cease shining out of sympathy with them. If one is in trouble, let him think of the many noble and illustrious men who had to endure the greatest of hardships.

It has been suggested that the expression *may he rest in peace* has reference to the welfare and happiness of the living, who are in the habit of visiting the graves of close relatives in order to share with them their tragic experiences. "May he rest in peace," that is to say, may we have no cause to disturb his peace (*Ta'amé ha-Minhagim*).

During *shiv'ah*, the bereaved do not go to the synagogue until Friday evening. Then one of the worshipers comes to meet them at the entrance of the synagogue on behalf of the congregation, and greets them in these terms: "May God comfort you among all those who mourn for Zion and Jerusalem" המקום ינחם אתכם בתוך שאר אבלי ציון וירושלים. This sentence is spoken also at the cemetery by those who have attended the funeral, when they say goodbye to the mourners, as well as at the end of a visit to the house of mourning.

Excerpts from the Talmud and Midrash concerning life and death:

"Repent one day before your death." But how does one know which day that is? Therefore, we ought to live every day as though it were our last.

A hungry fox was eyeing some luscious fruit in a garden, but he could find no way to enter until he discovered an opening through which he might possibly get in if he fasted three days, for the hole was too small to admit his body. After a three days' fast he finally managed to enter the orchard, where he now feasted to his heart's delight on all the good things he found. But when he wanted to get out before being caught by the owner of the garden, he found that the opening had again become too small for him, so he had to fast three days once more in order to lose the weight he had gained during his stay in the orchard. Upon escaping, he cast a farewell glance upon the scene of his revels and said: O garden of delicious fruits, what have I now gained by all my futile toil? So it is with man. Naked he comes into the world, and naked he must depart from it. He carries nothing away with him except the good deeds he performed during his lifetime.

Blessed is he who pleases his Creator and acquires a good name. Concerning him Solomon says: "A good name in life is better than precious perfume, and the day of death is better than the day of birth" (Ecclesiastes 7:1).

A rabbi once saw a very old man planting a tree, and asked: Why are you planting that tree? You do not expect, of course, to live long enough to see the full-grown tree! But the old man replied: The trees I have found and enjoyed were planted by my forefathers for me; so I, too, am planting for those who will come after me.

14

Blessed shall you be as you come in, and blessed shall you be as you start out" (Deuteronomy 28:6). May your leaving this world be like your coming into it. You entered this world sinless; may you depart from it sinless.

Rabbi Meir's two beloved sons died suddenly one Sabbath afternoon, when he was delivering a discourse in the house of study. Upon returning home, Rabbi Meir asked his wife, Beruriah, about their two children whom he had missed in the synagogue. At the conclusion of the Sabbath, she remarked to Rabbi Meir: "Some time ago, precious jewels were entrusted to my care. Now the owner has come to reclaim them. What shall I do? Shall I return them to him?" "But of course, you must return them!" Rabbi Meir replied. Thereupon Beruriah took him by the hand and led him to the bed of their sons. She drew back the sheet, and Rabbi Meir burst forth into bitter crying, lamenting: "My sons, my sons!" But Beruriah reminded him tearfully what he had said about the jewels that must be restored. "Our sons were the jewels which God had left with us, and now he has taken them back."

MOURNERS FOR ZION   אַבְלֵי צִיּוֹן

AVÉLÉ ZION is the name given to the Jewish sects whose members mourned over the destruction of the Temple and the loss of the Jewish state. They were to be found already in early talmudic times (Bava Bathra 60b). On *Tish'ah b'Av*, a special petition is inserted in the *Shemoneh Esreh* of the afternoon service, which opens with these words: "Comfort, Lord our God, the mourners for Zion and the mourners for Jerusalem."

They led a life of asceticism, spending their days in fasting and praying for the restoration of Eretz Yisrael and for the advent of the Messiah. They, as a rule, refrained from meat and wine and showed mystical tendencies. The ever-growing group of Mourners for Zion formed an important segment of Jerusalem's population. They were supported mainly by the charity of the Diaspora.

Avélé Zion was also the name of an ascetic movement among the Karaites in Jerusalem, lasting from the eighth century to the eleventh. This order consisted of men who renounced their families and their property, secluded themselves from the world, and spent their lives in fervent prayer for the liberation of the people of Israel. One of the

Karaite leaders and Bible commentators, Daniel al-Kumisi of the early tenth century, urged his fellow sectarians to return *en masse* to the Holy City, adding: "If you do not come, because you are engrossed in the running of your trades, send five men from each city and provide them with a livelihood."

The famous Jewish traveller of the twelfth century, Benjamin of Tudela, gives a description of the Mourners for Zion in southern Arabia, who dress in black, live in caves, abstain from meat and wine, and continually pray for the return of Israel.

AGGADAH   אַגָּדָה

AGGADAH, or *Haggadah* (narration), includes everything in talmudic literature that is *not* of a legal nature, such as descriptions of historical events and legends, proverbs and aphorisms that illustrate moral duties, and scientific data concerning medicine, mathematics, astronomy, physiology, botany and other branches of knowledge.

About thirty percent of the Babylonian Talmud is taken up with *Aggadah*; the remaining seventy percent consists of legal subject matter (*Halakhah*), containing discussions leading to rules of conduct as prescribed by the unwritten, oral law. The aim and purpose of the aggadic literature is to inspire and edify, and to move people to the kind of righteous behavior which the *Halakhah* requires.

The Aggadah penetrates deeply into the spirit of the Bible by means of its broad interpretations of the text. From the wealth of the aggadic material the Jewish people continue to receive comfort and strength, as they have for many generations.

Here are several maxims and aphorisms from aggadic writings:

He who knows that he knows nothing possesses knowledge indeed.

A teacher should give instruction concisely.

Love your wife as much as yourself; honor her more than yourself.

A lovely wife, a splendid home and beautiful furniture cheer a man's heart.

The noblest charity of all is that which enables the poor to earn their living.

No man dies with even half his desires realized.

No one should taunt a reformed sinner about his past.

A liar finds his punishment in being disbelieved even when he tells the truth.

He who seeks a friend without faults will remain friendless.

Love the one who shows you your faults more than the one who praises you.

When good people die they are not truly dead, for their example lives. Hence we are told that Jacob never died (Ta'anith 5b).

Though the Aggadah contains parables of infinite beauty and enshrines sayings of everlasting worth, it consists of individual utterances that possess no binding authority.

LETTER TO YEMEN   אִגֶּרֶת תֵּימָן

IN 1172, during a crisis through which the Jews of Yemen in southwestern Arabia were passing, Moses Maimonides wrote his famous *Iggereth Teman* (Letter to Yemen), which has come down to us in three Hebrew translations from the Arabic. A forced conversion to Islam threw the Jews of Yemen into panic; and the letter of Maimonides, supplying guidance and encouragement to the Yemenites, was circulated widely and read publicly in all the congregations of Yemen, until they included a complimentary allusion to Rabbenu Moshe ben Maimun (Maimonides) in the daily *Kaddish* prayer, in gratitude for his spiritual and material help.

The following excerpts from *Iggereth Teman* clearly illustrate Maimonides great love for his people and his faith.

"Our religion differs as much from other religions as a living person differs from a lifeless statue, which is ever so well carved out of marble, wood, bronze, or silver. When an ignorant person sees a statue that superficially resembles man in contour, form, features, and color, he thinks that the structure of its parts is similar to that of a human being. But the informed person, who knows the interior of both, is aware of the fact that the internal structure of the statue shows no skillful workmanship at all, whereas the inner parts of man are marvelously made.

"So, too, a person ignorant of the deep meaning of the Bible, and of the deeper significance of the Torah, would be led to believe that our religion has something in common with another. True, both contain a system of religious observances; but the tenets of other religions, though resembling those of the Bible, are merely superficial imitations. People have modelled their religions after ours in order to glorify themselves.

17

"Divine assurance was given to Jacob that his descendants would survive those who degraded them. Do not be dismayed at the persecutions of our people, for these trials are designed to test and purify us. You should take it upon yourselves to hearten one another. Let your elders guide the youth and let your leaders direct the masses. May God grant us the privilege of beholding the return of the exiles. May he remove the darkness from our eyes and from our hearts."

ADON OLAM   אֲדוֹן עוֹלָם

ADON OLAM (Eternal Lord), a hymn of universal and deeply religious content, has been attributed to various medieval poets, particularly to Solomon ibn Gabirol who lived in Spain during the eleventh century. In his famous philosophical poem *Kether Malkhuth* (Royal Crown), Ibn Gabirol addresses God in terms curiously similar indeed to the theme of *Adon Olam*. This noble hymn of purest poetry has been part of the daily Prayerbook since the fifteenth century, whereas *Kether Malkhuth* has been appended to the Sephardic liturgy for the evening service of *Yom Kippur*.

Some authorities have suggested that originally *Adon Olam* was designed as a night prayer. This seems to be indicated by the concluding stanza, which reads: "To him I entrust my spirit when I sleep and when I wake... The Lord is with me, I am not afraid." *Adon Olam*, recited at the beginning of the daily morning service, forms also part of the prayer recited each night before retiring. There are many musical settings for *Adon Olam*.

In the first four lines of *Adon Olam*, God is described as the Eternal Lord who existed before the creation of the world and will still exist after the cessation of the world. Between the eternal past and the eternal future comes the world of time. The fact that the entire hymn stresses the idea of eternity is sufficient to prove that the initial words, *Adon Olam*, must not be rendered "the Lord of the world" but *Eternal Lord*. The error has been attributed to the double meaning of the Hebrew word *olam* (world, eternity).

According to Greek philosophers, the universe is eternal; according to Judaism, it is God alone who is eternal. He transcends man and the universe, though he is also immanent and dwells within the human soul as well as within the universe. He is high above the world, yet near to those who call upon him sincerely.

18

ADDIR BIMLUKHAH   אַדִּיר בִּמְלוּכָה

ADDIR BIMLUKHAH (Glorious in Kingship), an alphabetical acrostic poem of unidentified authorship, is mentioned by a disciple of Rabbi Meir of Rothenburg in the thirteenth-century work *Tashbatz*. The refrain alludes to several biblical verses, such as: "Thine, O Lord, is the greatness . . . for all that is in heaven and on earth is thine; thine, O Lord, is the kingdom. . ." (I Chronicles 29:11).

It has been proposed that Rabbi Elazar ha-Kallir of the eighth century was the author of this poem, which has been inserted among the closing hymns of the Passover Haggadah.

ADDIR HU   אַדִּיר הוּא

ADDIR HU (Glorious He Is), composed by an anonymous poet, consists of eight stanzas of eight lines each and is sung at the end of the Passover *Seder*. Its tune, which has been popular since the beginning of the seventeenth century, has eventually become something of a Passover motif in the worship service of many a synagogue. According to Zunz, *Addir Hu* was written in the sixth century or the seventh.

MAN   אָדָם

JUDAISM stresses the far-reaching importance of man. He possesses qualities that fit him for a life of creativity because he is made in the image of God. An insult to man is an insult to God: "He who oppresses a poor man insults his Maker" (Proverbs 14:31). "Adam was created alone, to show that if anyone destroys a human life he is held responsible as though he destroyed a whole world; and if anyone saves a human life he is credited with having saved a whole world. . . All men are fashioned after the pattern of the first man, yet no two faces are exactly alike. Hence, every person may well say: For my sake the world was created" (Sanhedrin 4:5). Man's likeness to God is seen in the mental and moral features of his character, such as reason and free will.

The wonderful structure of the human body, its delicate adaptations to countless needs, is the subject of the following benediction,

recited after the normal functions of the body as well as in the daily
morning service: "Blessed art thou ... who hast formed man in wisdom and created in him a system of veins and arteries ... if but one
of these be opened or if one of those be closed it would be impossible
to exist..." (Berakhoth 60b).

Though, on the physical side, man has much in common with the
animals, he is described as little less than divine (Psalm 8:6), standing
nearest to God in the ranks of the universe. Man is placed at the top
of the scale of creation. "There are three partners in the formation
of man: God, father, mother" (Niddah 31a). "Let man ever bear in
mind that God dwells in him" (Ta'anith 11b). "Man eats and drinks,
performs natural functions and dies like an animal; he stands erect,
thinks and has vision like an angel" (Genesis Rabbah 14:3).

ADAR   אֲדָר

ADAR, the twelfth month of the Jewish calendar, corresponding approximately to March, consists of twenty-nine days in an ordinary
year and of thirty days in a leap-year, when a month is inserted between *Adar* and *Nisan*. This added month is known as *Adar Sheni*
(second *Adar*). *Adar Sheni* is also called *Va-Adar*.

The memorable days of *Adar* are: the seventh, anniversary of the
birth and death of Moses; the thirteenth, fast of Esther (*Ta'anith
Esther*); the fourteenth and fifteenth, festival of *Purim*.

In a leap-year, the festival of *Purim* is celebrated on the fourteenth
and fifteenth of *Adar Sheni*, whereas the fourteenth and fifteenth of
the first *Adar* are observed as *Purim Katan* (minor *Purim*).

LOVE AND FRIENDSHIP   אַהֲבָה וְרֵעוּת

THE biblical command: "You shall love your neighbor as yourself"
is universal: it applies to everybody. In the same chapter the commandment of love is extended to the stranger: "You shall love him
as yourself, for you were strangers in the land of Egypt" (Leviticus
19:34). This is the most comprehensive rule of moral conduct.

Once a heathen came to Hillel, who lived in Jerusalem a few decades before the common era, and mockingly asked him to teach him
the Torah while he stood on one leg. Hillel, who was famous for his

gentleness and patience, said to the mocking heathen: "What is hateful to yourself do not to another. This is the whole Torah; go and study it; the rest is commentary" (Shabbath 31a).

True love is tested by its sincerity. It will not hesitate to express blame or censure; it will also accept criticism. "Reprove a wise man, and he will love you" (Proverbs 9:8). On the other hand, loving friendship will overlook faults: "Hatred stirs up strife, but love covers all offenses. He who forgives an offense seeks love" (Proverbs 10:12; 17:9).

The making of friends is declared as true greatness: "He is a strong man who can turn his enemy into a friend" (Avoth d'Rabbi Nathan, chapter 23). Just as true friendship is recommended, so false friendship is condemned: "Keep at a distance from high officials who pose as friends when they have use for you, and will not assist you when you are in distress" (Avoth 2:3).

Maimonides says: "You shall love your neighbor as yourself" means that you should honor him as you would like to be honored yourself. Whoever glories in the humiliation of others has no share in the future world. "You shall not hate your brother in your heart" (Leviticus 19:17) means that you must not bear silent hatred for the wrongdoer; ask him frankly: "Why have you done this to me?" If he is sorry and asks your forgiveness, do not be relentless but forgive him. "You shall reason with your neighbor" means that if you see him commit misdeeds, you must convince him of his faults. This should be done privately and gently. You should never call him by an insulting name, or say anything that is likely to embarrass him (*Yad, De'oth* 6:6-8).

Rabbi Israel Salanter said that sincerity is especially important in self-criticism. Without deep sincerity we would find little to criticise in ourselves; self-love would blind our judgment. Self-love often excites in man so strong a feeling of self-importance that he is unaware of his shortcomings while he sees those of his neighbor quite clearly. In self-criticism we should try to eliminate, or at least reduce to a minimum, this element of self-love, and scrutinize ourselves in the same way that we would others.

Rabbi Elijah Vilna-Gaon, in a letter to his family, wrote: Treat all men with respect and amiability. Bring happiness to one another by kindly social relations. Let there be no dissension of any kind, but let love and brotherliness reign. Forgive one another and live in amity for the sake of God.

AHAVAH RABBAH   אַהֲבָה רַבָּה

Ahavah Rabbah (Great Love) and *Ahavath Olam* (Everlasting Love)
are the initial words of the prayer that precedes the *Shema*. As a compromise between two competing phrasings, reported in the Talmud
(Berakhoth 11b), *Ahavah Rabbah* is used in the morning daily service
and *Ahavath Olam* in the evening service.

One of the most beautiful prayers in the liturgies of the world,
Ahavah Rabbah is very old and was probably instituted by the men
of the Great Assembly in the early period of the Second Temple.
A profound love for God and the Torah is echoed in this prayer, in
which the merciful Father is entreated to enlighten our eyes and our
minds to understand his teachings.

This is the second of the two benedictions preceding the *Shema*,
Yotser Or being the first. As Psalm 19 praises God first for the sun
and then for the Torah which enlightens the mind, so have we in the
two benedictions preceding the *Shema* first a thanksgiving for natural light ("Blessed art thou . . . Creator of the lights"), then a thanksgiving for spiritual enlightenment.

Here are several expressions excerpted from *Ahavah Rabbah:* "Our
Father, merciful Father, have pity on us and inspire us to understand
and discern, to learn and teach, to observe and fulfill gladly all the
teachings of thy Torah. Enlighten our eyes in thy Torah. . ." The
phrase "to learn and teach" emphasizes one of the greatest ideals.

True wisdom is unselfish. It craves to be shared. The truly wise
man will freely dispense what he himself has so generously received.
Torah implies more than a body of ancient religious lore; it also signifies a careful probing of the truth embodied in the text, which will
disclose its deeper meaning and wider application. Biblical narratives
are not mere reproductions of historical episodes; they teem with
lessons of universal truth. The Torah suggests to us our responsibility as teachers and interpreters of the truth to the people.

LOVE OF GOD   אַהֲבַת הַשֵּׁם

Love of God is described by Maimonides (*Guide*, 3:51) in these
terms: "The intellect which emanates from God to us is the link that
joins us to God. You have it in your power to strengthen that bond

or to weaken it gradually till it breaks. It will become strong only when you employ it in the love of God and seek that love; it will be weakened when you direct your thoughts to other things. . .

"We must bear in mind that all such religious acts as reading the Torah, praying, and the performance of other precepts serve as the means of filling our mind with thoughts of God and freeing it from worldly preoccupation; we are thus, as it were, in communication with God. If, however, we pray with our lips and think at the same time about something else; if we read the Torah while our mind is occupied with the building of a house, we are like those who are engaged in digging or hewing without reflecting the nature of their work. . ."

Rabbi Akiva of the second century, who suffered martyrdom at the hands of the Romans, is reported in the Talmud as having recited the *Shema* calmly despite his agonies. When asked by his torturer whether he was a sorcerer, since he felt no pain, Rabbi Akiva replied: "I am no sorcerer, but I rejoice at the opportunity now given to me to love my God with all my heart and soul, with all my life." He expired with the *Shema* on his lips. His last words were: "The Lord is One."

Maimonides declares: "When a person contemplates God's great and wondrous works and obtains a glimpse of God's incomparable and infinite wisdom, he will straightway love and glorify him, and long to know his great name, even as David said: My whole being longs for God, the living God" (*Yesodé ha-Torah*, 2:2). Rabbi Samson Raphael Hirsch states: "To love God means to realize that life has value only through God. We love God by loving the Torah and meeting its commands. There should be nothing dearer to us than the faithfulness which we owe to our God."

OPPRESSION   אוֹנָאָה

THE Hebrew term *hona'ah* or *ona'ah* includes the idea of defrauding a man in a transaction and that of wounding his feelings by unkind words. A wrong inflicted by means of words is regarded as worse than a wrong inflicted in financial dealings. Examples: one must not say to a repentant sinner: "Remember your former deeds" (Bava Metzia 57b). A man must be especially careful not to hurt his wife's feelings; for, a woman is naturally sensitive and easily moved to tears. . . One should not ask a merchant for the price of an article when he has no intention to purchase it. . .

It is forbidden to use a person's nickname with the intention of embarrassing him. . . One should not invite a person to a meal, or offer him a gift, knowing fully well that his offer will not be accepted. Make-believe offers, in order to receive unmerited thanks, constitute verbal deception. It is forbidden, therefore, to create a false impression even where no financial loss is involved. Upon selling a defective article, the merchant must indicate the defect to the purchaser, even though the defective article is worth the price.

These regulations are based on the following biblical precepts: "When an alien resides with you in your land, you shall not do him wrong. You shall treat the stranger who resides with you as one born among you; have the same love for him as for yourself. . . Do not act dishonestly in using measures of length or weight or capacity. . . When you sell to your neighbor or buy from your neighbor, you shall not wrong one another" (Leviticus 19:33; 25:14).

URIM AND TUMMIM   אוּרִים וְתֻמִּים

Two mysterious objects contained in the breastplate of the high priest are mentioned eight times in the Hebrew Bible, together or separately. They are known as *Urim* and *Tummim* (light and perfection), meaning perfect light. They are first mentioned in Exodus 28:30, where we read: "You shall place the *Urim* and *Tummim* in the breastplate of judgment, that they may be over Aaron's heart whenever he enters the presence of the Lord."

Since the exact nature of the *Urim* and *Tummim* is uncertain, various explanations have been offered. It has been suggested that they were lots of some kind which were drawn or cast by the high priest to ascertain God's decision in doubtful matters of national importance. Used until the reign of Solomon, the *Urim* and *Tummim* were later abandoned in favor of advice given by the prophets.

The breastplate of judgment (*hoshen ha-mishpat*) bore the names of Israel's tribes on twelve precious stones. The gleaming of the gems in the breastplate, according to some interpreters, miraculously confirmed the answer which occurred to the high priest while he was offering prayer for divine guidance. Others are of the opinion that the answer was inward illumination, without any external sign. In his great faith, the high priest believed that the response which dawned in his mind was divinely inspired and therefore correct.

24

SONG OF MOSES   אָז יָשִׁיר

THE magnificent hymn of praise, chanted by Moses and the people of Israel at the Red Sea (Exodus 15:1-18), consists of three stanzas of increasing length, giving expression to the mingled feelings of horror, triumph and gratitude of slaves pursued by Egyptian hordes and delivered by their redeeming God. This "song at the sea" (שירת הים), or *Az Yashir* ("then he sang"— the initial words of the hymn), forms part of the daily morning service, at the end of the biblical poetic passages known as *Pesuké d'Zimrah*, in keeping with the precept to "remember the day you left Egypt *all* the days of your life" (Deuteronomy 16:3). Mystic tradition states that "he who recites *Az Yashir* audibly and joyously is pardoned in heaven" (*Sefer Ḥaredim*). It is one of the finest codes in the Bible as to glowing diction and vivid imagery.

EḤAD MI YODEA   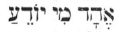

ONE of the songs at the end of the Passover *Haggadah*, known as *Eḥad Mi Yodea*, is a cumulative riddle designed to keep the children awake till the end of the *Seder* service. By means of questions and answers, the fundamental Jewish beliefs and traditions are imparted in the thirteen stanzas of the poem. Beginning with "Who knows One? I know One! One is our God in heaven and earth," it refers to the revelation at Mount Sinai, the three patriarchs and the four matriarchs of Israel, the five books of the Torah, the six major divisions of the Mishnah, the Sabbath, the *mitzvath milah*, the providential care of mother and infant during the nine months' pregnancy, the Ten Commandments, the eleven brothers of Joseph who were unwittingly carrying out the design of Providence, the twelve tribes of Israel, the thirteen attributes of God, describing him as merciful, gracious and kind. The numerical value of the word אחד (13), referring to the One and only God, may have determined the number of stanzas in the song, which concludes with the mention of the thirteen divine qualities.

This song, as well as the Aramaic *Ḥad Gadya* song which is written in the form of a nursery rhyme, was not included in any of the *Haggadahs* that appeared before the sixteenth century. Both are said to have originated in medieval Germany.

25

MONOTHEISM   אַחְדוּת הַשֵּׁם

THE doctrine that there is only One God, or that God is One, has been the very foundation of Judaism. According to tradition, Abraham discovered monotheism and taught it to his generation. The Jewish people have always been uncompromising monotheists, confessing their faith in One God in prayer, in observances, and in dissociation from every appearance of idolatry. Jewish monotheism connotes denial of divine attributes to any other being, and is sharply opposed to a wide variety of beliefs and teachings. It denotes belief in the existence of One God who is the righteous Creator and Ruler of the universe, the Father of all, who champions the cause of justice and secures the triumph of the upright. The Hebrew term האמין (to believe) signifies strong confidence in God's help.

The divine unity is re-echoed throughout the Jewish liturgy. Every worship service ends with the *Alenu* prayer, which is a repudiation of idolatry and an acknowledgment of the Oneness of God. It is proclaimed in the *Shema*, which sounds the keynote of Judaism and is the first spiritual lesson a Jewish child is taught and the last utterance of the dying Jew. The Jewish confession of faith is not so much in words as in conduct, which must conform to the requirements of a system of *mitzvoth*, positive as well as negative precepts. Jewish monotheism expresses the duty of loving and serving God wholeheartedly by careful observance of the divine commands.

ESCHATOLOGY   אַחֲרִית הַיָּמִים

ESCHATOLOGY, the branch of theology treating of the last things and final destinies of humanity, is known in Hebrew as אחרית הימים (the end of days), a phrase borrowed from Isaiah 2:1. The same expression is used in Genesis 49:1, by Jacob, who called his sons and said: "Gather yourselves together, that I may tell you what shall befall you *in after days.*" It occurs again in Micah's prophecy concerning the time when "nation shall not raise the sword against nation..."

Jewish eschatology is linked with the messianic hopes and the belief in the ultimate regeneration of humanity. The final goal of world history is the transition of man to a higher life and the annihilation of the forces that oppose the messianic reign.

Many elements of later Jewish eschatology are already found in the prophetic books. Throughout the biblical prophecies the blessings of the future are on this earth. "It shall come to pass in the latter days that the mountain of the Lord's house shall be established as the highest mountain, towering over every hill. All nations shall stream toward it; many peoples shall come and say: Come, let us climb the mountain of the Lord, to the house of the God of Jacob, that he may instruct us in his ways, and we will walk in his paths. Out of Zion shall go forth instruction, and the word of the Lord from Jerusalem. He shall judge between the nations. . . They shall beat their swords into plowshares, and their spears into pruning hooks; nation shall not lift up sword against nation, neither shall they learn war any more. They shall sit each under his own vine and under his own fig tree, undisturbed" (Isaiah 2:2-4; Micah 4:2-4).

The great event preparatory to the messianic reign is *kibbutz galuyyoth* (the ingathering of the exiles) and the return of the scattered homeless people of Israel to Zion. The eschatological conceptions are variously referred to in talmudic literature as, for example, עולם הבא (the world to come), לעתיד לבוא (in the future), ימות המשיח (the messianic days). Describing the messianic era according to Jewish tradition, Maimonides writes: "At that time there will be neither famine nor war, neither envy nor strife. Prosperity will be abundant, comforts within the reach of all. The one preoccupation of the entire world will be to know the Lord . . . as it is written: The earth shall be filled with the knowledge of the Lord as the water covers the sea."

Eschatology in an individual and personal sense deals with the destiny of the soul after death, the nature of future reward and punishment, the resurrection of the body. It has never assumed in Judaism the character of a dogmatic belief. The scene of heavenly judgment has been transferred from the hereafter to the annual day of judgment at the beginning of the year.

JOB   אִיּוֹב

THE book of Job, placed after the books of Psalms and Proverbs in the Hebrew Bible, contains some of the deepest thoughts that have come down from antiquity. It deals with the problems of human suffering and records the spiritual agony of a man who has tried to harmonize his experience with his belief in an all-powerful, all-wise, and all-loving God. Written in poetry, which is always more difficult than prose, the book of Job is not known and read as it deserves to be. It is the longest and finest poetic creation in the Bible.

The forty-two chapters of Job consist of three parts: a prologue, a poem in dialogue form, and an epilogue. The poem contains the debates between Job and his three friends; a speech by a bystander named Elihu; an address by God; and penitent confession by Job, who learns the value of perfect trust and patience and acknowledges the divine supremacy. Though the general form of this dramatic poem is that of a debate, many passages within it can be read independently of the argument. In chapter thirty-one, the virtues enumerated by Job are: a blameless family life, consideration of the poor and weak, charity, modesty, generosity, and hospitality to strangers.

The function of Satan, the Adversary, is described in the prologue as that of testing the sincerity of man's character. In talmudic literature, Satan was transformed into the *yetser ha-ra*, the evil impulse, whose function it is to strengthen man's moral sense by leading him into temptation. Man's heart is pictured as an arena where the good and evil wrestle in perpetual conflict. The lesson of Job is that man's sufferings are a test of his fidelity. Man's finite mind cannot probe the depths of the divine omniscience that governs the world. A broader and deeper awareness of God's wisdom may solve the problems we encounter.

In midrashic literature, Job is represented as a most generous man. He built an inn at the crossroads with four doors opening in four directions, so that the transients might have no trouble in finding an entrance. Job's chief complaint was, according to talmudic opinion, that although man is driven to sin by the *yetser ha-ra*, the evil impulse which is part of God's creation, yet he is punished. But Eliphaz answered him that if God created the *yetser ha-ra*, he also created the Torah by which a man can subdue the evil impulse (Bava Bathra 16a). The talmudic sages attributed the anonymous book of Job to Moses.

Maimonides, in his *Guide for the Perplexed* (3:22-23), devotes two chapters to a discussion of Job, and he writes: "The strange and wonderful book of Job has been designed to explain the different opinions concerning divine providence. Some of our sages clearly state that Job never existed, and that he is a product of poetic fiction. Those who assume that he did exist, and that the book is historical, are unable to determine when and where Job lived. Some say that he lived in the days of the patriarchs; others maintain that he was a contemporary of Moses; still others place him in the days of David, while there are some who believe that he was one of those who returned from the Babylonian captivity.

"This difference of opinion would seem to indicate that Job never really existed. According to both theories, the introduction to the book of Job is certainly fiction, that is, the dialogue between God and Satan and the handing over of Job to Satan. This fiction, however, is different from other fictions in that it includes profound ideas, removes great doubts, and reveals most important truths."

The etymology of the name איוב (Job) is uncertain. It has been suggested that it is derived from the Hebrew root איב (to be hostile to), which in the passive form signifies one persecuted (by Satan, calamity, or insincere friends). A man by the name of Job is mentioned in Ezekiel 14:14, 16, 20.

The contents of the book of Job, as well as its elegant style and artistic structure, place it among the literary masterpieces of all time. The lesson derived from Job is that even the just may suffer, their sufferings being a test of their fidelity. Man's finite mind cannot probe the depths of the divine omniscience that governs the world. The problems we encounter can be solved by a broader and deeper awareness of the divine power and wisdom. Job's attitude of humility and trust in God is deepened and strengthened by his experience of suffering.

"Terrors are let loose on me; like a cloud my welfare has disappeared. My soul within me melts with sorrow; days of affliction lay hold of me. The night racks my bones; the pain that gnaws me never slumbers. God has plunged me into the mire; I am reduced to dust and ashes. I cry to thee and thou dost not answer. Thou hast turned cruel to me; thou tossest me before the wind. I hoped for good, and evil came; I waited for the light, and darkness fell. . .

"Then the Lord answered Job out of the whirlwind, saying: Who is this that darkens my design by thoughtless words? Gird up your loins like a man, answer me the question I will ask you. When I founded the earth, where were you then? Tell me, if you have understanding. . . Have you discovered the fountains of the sea? Have you set foot upon the depths of the ocean. . . Do you know the laws of the heavens? Can you describe their sway over the earth? Can you lift up your voice to the clouds, that a flood of water may cover you? Can you send out lightnings on a mission. . . Do you know how wild goats breed upon the hills. . . Can you give strength to the horse? Do you make him leap like the locust, with majesty and terrible snorting?. . .

"Then Job replied to the Lord: I am of small account; how shall I answer thee? I put my hand over my mouth; I will not answer. I know that thou canst do all things, and that nothing is too difficult for thee. I have said what I did not understand, things too wonderful for me, things which I did not know. I despise myself; in dust and ashes I repent... The Lord restored Job's fortunes when he had prayed for his friends... The Lord made Job more prosperous than he had been before... Job lived to see his grandsons and great-grandsons—four generations. Then Job died, old, after a full life."

PLACE OF SACRIFICES   אֵיזֶהוּ מְקוֹמָן

THE fifth chapter of Mishnah Zevaḥim, describing the places where the sacrifices were offered in the Temple, forms part of the preliminary morning service, in keeping with the following statement concerning the substitution of prayer for ancient sacrifices: "Whenever they recite the order of sacrifices, I will deem it as if they offered them before me, and I will forgive them all their sins" (Ta'anith 27b).

The sacrificial system symbolized self-surrender and devotion to the will of God. The peace-offering with its communion-feast showed the idea of fellowship. It served to keep alive the sense of dependence on God for the natural blessings of life, while it had a social value of promoting the solidarity of the nation. The *Tamid*, or daily offering, symbolized Israel's pledge of unbroken service to God. From Psalm 141:2 ("Let my prayer rise like incense before thee") it appears that the incense-offering symbolized prayer.

It has been suggested that the fifth chapter of Mishnah Zevaḥim was selected to be used as part of the liturgy because it consists throughout of undisputed statements, whereas other Mishnah sections contain divergent opinions offered by various tannaitic sages.

LAMENTATIONS   אֵיכָה

THE Hebrew title of the book of Lamentations, איכה (How), is derived from the opening word in the third of the five *Megilloth* (scrolls), which is recited in the synagogue on *Tish'ah b'Av*, the ninth day of *Av*. Tradition assigns the composition of Lamentations to Jeremiah, who was an eyewitness to the agony of Jerusalem and the despair of

30

its inhabitants during the invasion of Nebuchadnezzar in 586 before the common era.

The book consists of five lyric poems lamenting the destruction of the Holy City. In the Hebrew Bible, four of these dirges (קינות) are alphabetical acrostics, each verse beginning with one of the twenty-two successive letters of the Hebrew alphabet.

The fifth poem, though it is not an alphabetical acrostic, has twenty-two verses, corresponding to the number of letters in the Hebrew alphabet, and is a prayer rather than an elegy. Excerpts:

"Our pursuers were swifter than the vultures of the air; they hunted us on the hills, they lay in wait for us in the wilderness. Remember, O Lord, what has befallen us; look and see our disgrace! Our heritage has been turned over to strangers; we have become orphans and are fatherless... Slaves rule over us; there is none to free us from their power... Restore us, O Lord, and let us return to thee. Renew our days as of old."

EN KELOHENU   אֵין כֵּאלֹהֵינוּ

T<small>HE</small> chant *En Kelohenu* (there is none like our God), sung by the *Ashkenazim* at the end of the Sabbath and festival morning service, is used by the *Sephardim* also on weekdays. Though it is not rhymed, there is throughout a pleasing assonance in the constant repetition of the sounds *énu*, recurring twenty times.

Rashi points out in his *Siddur* that *En Kelohenu* is recited on Sabbaths and festivals, when the *Amidah* prayer is limited to seven benedictions instead of the nineteen benedictions contained in the regular *Shemoneh Esreh*, in order to bring the benedictions to a total of nineteen in the following manner: *En Kelohenu* forms the acrostic אמן, ברוך אתה (Amen, blessed art thou), alluding to a blessing and a response. Now, each of the three letters of אמן is repeated four times in the chant *En Kelohenu*, totaling twelve.

IYYAR   אִיָּר

I<small>YYAR</small>, the second month of the Jewish calendar, consists of twenty-nine days, beginning in April or early in May. In the Bible, this month is designated as זִו (I Kings 6:1) in the sense of splendor. The name

אִיר is obviously connected with אוֹר (light). The greater part of the *Sefirah*, the counting of seven weeks between *Pesaḥ* and *Shavuoth*, occurs within this month, the first of *Iyyar* being the sixteenth day of *Omer*. *Lag b'Omer*, the thirty-third day of *Omer*, when marriages may be performed, falls on the eighteenth of *Iyyar*.

Unlike the rest of the *Sefirah* period, which is observed as one of semi-mourning on account of the Hadrianic persecutions and the massacres of Jews during the Crusades, *Lag b'Omer* is celebrated as a day of victory. It is also the anniversary of the death of Rabbi Simeon ben Yoḥai of the second century, who has been credited with the authorship of the *Zohar*, the kabbalistic commentary on the Torah. *Yom ha-Atzmauth* (Independence Day) is celebrated on the fifth of *Iyyar* in commemoration of the liberation of Israel in 1948.

EL ADON אֵל אָדוֹן

EL ADON (God is the Lord), an alphabetical but unrhymed hymn of the medieval period, is generally attributed to the *Yordé Merkavah*, mystics of the eighth century who applied their minds to theosophy. Its meter is four accents to the line. The hymn, forming part of the morning service for Sabbath, is a praise of God who created the sun, moon and stars. Having spoken of the sun and the moon, the poet alludes to the five planets Saturn, Venus, Mercury, Jupiter, and Mars by means of the initials of the words of the last of the six stanzas, which read: שבח נותנים לו כל צבא מרום. The Hebrew names of the mentioned planets are: שבתאי, נוגה, כוכב, צדק, מאדים.

To the ancients the planets appeared to wander about among the stars, hence the name planet from a Greek verb meaning to wander. Only five of the nine primary planets were known to the ancients; but to these were added the sun and the moon, making seven in all, known in Hebrew as שבעה כוכבי לכת, the seven seemingly "wandering" celestial bodies. Now it is commonly known that the nine primary planets revolve around the sun in approximately circular orbits and that they include the Earth, Neptune, Uranus, and Pluto (discovered in 1930) in addition to the five planets mentioned above.

The Tur, by Rabbi Jacob ben Asher (1269-1343), mentions a variant reading in *El Adon*, והסקטין instead of והתקין, according to which the clause concerning the form of the moon refers to the talmudic tradition that God diminished the original size of the moon.

EL MALÉ RAḤAMIM   אֵל מָלֵא רַחֲמִים

EL MALÉ RAḤAMIM (Merciful God), a prayer for the repose of the soul of the departed, is usually chanted with great solemnity at the graveside and at memorial services (*Yizkor, Hazkarath Neshamoth*). The *Sephardim*, the Jews who originate from Spain or Portugal, call this prayer *Hashkavah*. It is ordinarily accompanied by offerings for charity and is recited by the reader of the Torah on Mondays and Thursdays.

It reads as follows: "Merciful God in heaven, grant perfect repose to the soul of . . . (the name of the deceased is supplied) who has passed to his (her) eternal habitation. May he be under thy divine wings among the holy and pure who shine bright as the sky; may his place of rest be in Paradise. Merciful One, O keep his soul forever alive under thy protective wings. . ."

The *Yizkor* service, which includes this prayer, is conducted on four occasions: *Yom Kippur, Shemini Atsereth*, the last day of *Pesaḥ*, and the second day of *Shavuoth*.

EL MELEKH NE'EMAN   אֵל מֶלֶךְ נֶאֱמָן

EL MELEKH NE'EMAN (God is a faithful King), the phrase immediately preceding the *Shema*, has initial letters which spell out the word אמן (Amen). It serves as a response to the *ahavah rabbah* benediction. This response is added only when the *Shema* is recited in private. The reason is that when the Reader in a congregational service repeats the three-word phrase ה' אלהיכם אמת (the Lord your God is true) he raises the number of words contained in the *Shema* to 248, corresponding to the traditional 248 parts of the human frame. On reciting the *Shema* privately one is required to add the three words אל מלך נאמן in order to complete the number 248.

GOD   אֱלֹהִים

THE Hebrew word for God (*Elohim*) primarily conveys the idea of power. The extraordinary power, purity and richness of the Hebrew idea of God have exerted an enormous influence on countless millions of people throughout the world. Though the existence of God is pre-supposed in the Bible, where no attempt is made to demonstrate his reality, almost all Jewish philosophers produce proofs for his existence. These proofs are based for the most part on principles of physics.

Philo writes: "Who can look upon statues or paintings without thinking at once of a sculptor or painter? . . . So he who beholds hills and plains teeming with animals and plants . . . the whole firmament revolving in rhythmic order, must gain the conception of the Creator and Father and Ruler." Maimonides, at the outset of his *Mishneh Torah*, states: "The basic principle and the pillar of all sciences is to know that there is a First Being who has brought every existing thing into being. . . He it is who controls the celestial sphere with a power to which there is neither end nor limit . . . it is impossible for it to revolve without Someone making it revolve. . ."

In our time, scientists occasionally endeavor to prove the existence of God by pointing to the hugeness and orderliness of the universe and to the structure of the smallest particles known. Atoms have a great similarity to our solar system and to the universe, in that they have electrons rotating about a nucleus in regular patterns. The distances of the celestial spheres, spoken of in terms of light years, are beyond human comprehension. Light travels 186,000 miles per second, equivalent to about seven times around the earth every second. Now if we start that light ray out straight and let it continue for a year's time, that distance is a light-year, approximately six *trillion* miles!

When we recall that our galaxy is some 1,000,000 light-years in diameter, the sun being an insignificant star some 30,000 light-years from the galactic center, circling in an orbit of its own every 400 million years as the galaxy rotates, we realize how difficult it is to visualize the tremendous scale of the universe beyond the solar system. Nor is the interstellar space of our galaxy the end, for beyond are the millions of other galaxies, all apparently rushing from one another at fantastic speeds. The limits of the telescopically observable universe extend at least two *billion* light-years from us in all directions.

God is characterized as the supreme power in the universe, the source of all other existing things, the controller of the creative process, the object of man's highest reverence and hope. The Jewish conception of God and his relations to nature and human beings is a combination of both transcendence and immanence. "God is supramundane but not extramundane, exalted but not remote" (Moore,

34

Judaism). God is far away in the heavens, but near to the praying soul. According to traditional interpretation, *Elohim* typifies the divine quality of justice, and the four-letter name (י' ה' ו' ה') that of mercy. The utterance of the quadriliteral name (tetragrammaton) was forbidden so as to guard the holy name from the disrespect of trivial use.

The attributes of God include omnipresence, omniscience, omnipotence, eternity, truth, justice, goodness, purity, and holiness. He is thought of being everywhere in the numerous worlds, and knowing all the past, present, and future free actions of human beings. His unparalleled power bears no comparison to our conception of power. Unlike the pagans of the ancient world, who threatened and punished their gods in times of disaster and misfortune, traditional Judaism has maintained its faith in the omnipotent God who is able to hear all the prayers uttered at different places at the same time, fulfilling even contradictory requests of various sincere worshipers.

The traditional Jewish conception of God has been described as ethical monotheism. The God-idea demonstrates moral values to be adopted by men: "Even as he is gracious, so be you gracious; even as he is merciful, so be you merciful; even as he is holy, so be you holy" (Shabbath 133b). This is known as the imitation of God. The standard of man's morality is to be reflected in the divine attributes.

Maimonides asserts that belief in an anthropomorphic God is worse than idolatry; the literal understanding of the biblical text is no excuse for this erroneous belief. A person is an unbeliever if he thinks God is corporeal. In the Bible, it was necessary to attribute human form or personality to God, because this is the only thing that suggests real existence to the vast majority of people. To show that God has all perfections, certain senses are ascribed to him; and to indicate these senses, the organs of motion and sensation, of touch and speech, are related to them. Because bodies as we know them have attributes, men thought that God too is made up of essential elements or attributes. The imagination is responsible for this error.

ELUL   אֱלוּל

ELUL, the sixth month of the Jewish calendar, consists of twenty-nine days. Being followed by the High Holydays, *Rosh Hashanah* and *Yom Kippur*, the month of *Elul* is the period of preparation for repentance. It is customary to sound the *shofar* every day during this month, and to recite Psalm 27 (The Lord is my Light) following the morning and evening services.

During the last week of *Elul*, *Seliḥoth* (prayers for forgiveness and mercy) are recited prior to the morning services, as soon after dawn as possible. The four Hebrew letters of the word *Elul* are supposed to suggest the initials of the words אני לדודי ודודי לי in the Song of Songs, referring to the love between God and his people. On the other hand, the reversed form of the Hebrew word *Elul* spells out לולא, the word found at the end of Psalm 27 which is recited throughout the month of *Elul* until *Simḥath Torah*.

ELIJAH THE PROPHET   אֵלִיָּהוּ הַנָּבִיא

PROPHET ELIJAH, who lived in the ninth century B.C.E. during the reign of Ahab, king of Israel, has been described as the most romantic and enigmatic character in the whole range of Jewish history. When Ahab, influenced by his wife Jezebel of Tyre, had given himself to the worship of the Phoenician god Baal, Elijah's emergence was sudden and dramatic. He appeared upon the scene and predicted a drought as a penalty for the introduction of the Phoenician cult into Israel.

Then followed the scene at Mount Carmel, demonstrating the supreme power of God and the impotence of Baal. Baal's prophets, who proved to be impostors, were slain at his bidding.

When Jezebel had Naboth murdered in order to obtain his vineyard for Ahab, Elijah met the king in the coveted plot of ground and denounced him for the crime of murder. Due to his great zeal for God, Scripture tells us that the prophet was translated to heaven without dying. It became a cherished widespread belief that Prophet Elijah, who had never died, would appear again to restore Israel. "And he will turn the hearts of fathers to their children and the hearts of children to their fathers" (Malachi 4:6).

Elijah is frequently referred to in Jewish literature not only as the promised precursor of the Messiah but also as the dynamic helper in distress and guiding teacher of the sages. Whenever there was an unsolved legal or religious problem, the great teachers of Jewish tradition would end the debate by saying "this is for Elijah to solve." Indeed, it was expected that all controversies and disputes which had accumulated in the course of time would be adjusted by him. Rabbi

36

Joshua ben Levi, who lived in Palestine during the middle of the third century and became the subject of many legends, was reputed as a favorite of Elijah who was always ready to fulfill his requests.

Rabbi Joshua ben Levi once asked Elijah to take him along on his journeys through the world. To this the prophet agreed on condition that Joshua should never question him concerning the causes of his actions, strange as they might appear; should this condition be broken, Elijah would be compelled to part from him.

Both set out upon their journey. The first stop was at the house of a poor man who owned only a cow, but who received the strangers most kindly and entertained them to the best of his ability. Before they continued their journey the following morning, the rabbi heard Elijah pray that God might destroy the poor man's cow, and before they had left the poor man's house the cow was dead.

Joshua could not contain himself, but in great excitement he said to Elijah: "Is this the reward which the poor man receives for his hospitality toward us?" The prophet reminded him of the condition upon which they had undertaken the journey, and silently they continued on their way.

Toward evening they came to the house of a rich man who did not even look at them, so that they had to pass the night without food and drink. In the morning, when they left the inhospitable house, Joshua heard Elijah pray that God should build up a wall which had fallen in one of the rich man's houses. At once the wall stood erect. This increased the agitation of the rabbi still more; but remembering the condition which had been imposed upon him, he kept silent.

On the next evening they came to a synagogue adorned with silver and gold, none of whose rich members showed any concern for the poor travelers, but dismissed them with bread and water. Upon leaving the place Joshua heard Elijah pray that God would make them all heads and leaders.

Joshua was about to break his promise, but forced himself to go on in silence again. In the next city they met very generous people who performed acts of kindness toward the strangers. Great, then, was the surprise of Joshua when, upon leaving the place, he heard the prophet pray that God might give them only *one head*.

Joshua could not refrain any longer, and asked Elijah to explain to him his strange actions, although he knew that by asking he would forfeit the prophet's companionship. Elijah answered: "The poor but generous man lost his cow because of my prayer, for I knew that his wife was about to die, and I asked God to take the life of the cow instead of the life of the wife. My prayer for the heartless rich man was because under the fallen wall was a great treasure, which would have come into the hands of this unworthy man had he undertaken to rebuild it. It was also no blessing that I pronounced upon the unfriendly synagogue, since a place which has many heads will not be of long duration. On the other hand, I wished the good people to have *one head*, so that union and peace might always reside among them."

As the ever-ready defending champion of his people, Elijah has been supposed to rove about the earth testing the hospitality and goodness of men and women. As the "angel of the covenant" (Malachi 3:1) and protector of children, he is believed to be the invisible participant at circumcisions. Seated at the right hand of the *sandek*, the person privileged to hold the child during the circumcision ceremony, invisible Elijah guards the infant from danger. The symbolic chair known as "Elijah's chair," set aside for the prophet, is left in position for three days, the dangerous period following the operation.

According to tradition, Elijah will settle every doubtful case in Judaism shortly before the advent of the Messiah. Elijah's cup of wine, which is placed on the *Seder* table, is linked with a talmudic dispute as to whether four or five glasses of wine are to be used at the *Seder* celebration. Hence the extra cup, known as Elijah's cup, conveys the thought that the question could not be solved by the authorities of the Talmud and must therefore wait for Elijah's decision.

Elijah's cup is commonly regarded, however, as the glass of wine that is symbolically ready for any fellow Jew who may seek hospitality in response to the invitation extended at the beginning of the *Seder* service to the poor and needy. In some countries, a similar cup is used on the occasion of a *brith milah* celebration.

ALMEMAR   אַלְמֵימָר

ALMEMAR, from the Arabic *alminbar* (platform, pulpit), is the raised platform in the center of a synagogue on which the reading of the Torah and the Prophets takes place. It is otherwise known as בּימה, from the Greek *bema* (speaker's tribune) mentioned in the Talmud (Sukkah 51b) in connection with the centrally located platform in the famous Alexandrian synagogue.

Rashi, in explaining the word בימה, equates it with the *minbar* used in his time (כעין אלמימברא שלנו).

The use of a בימה was suggested by Ezra's recital of the Torah from a raised platform in the midst of the men and women who listened attentively from early morning until midday (Nehemiah 8:2-4).

The *Ashkenazim* employ the בימה, as originally designed, for reading the Torah and the Prophets; the *Sephardim*, however, use it also for the pulpit from which the *ḥazzan* (cantor) recites the services.

As a result of the reform movement, the Torah-table was relegated to a platform in front of the synagogue ark so that the traditional and architectural significance of the *almemar* was destroyed. Modern architecture seeks to return to the original arrangement which was both traditional and magnificent. The synagogue architecture in modern Israel is reminiscent of the ancient synagogues in Eretz Yisrael.

ALFASI   אַלְפָּאסִי

RABBI ISAAC ALFASI, known as the *Rif* (רי״ף) from the initials of his name (Rabbi Isaac Fasi), came to Spain from the North African city of Fez at the age of seventy-five. Both in North Africa and Spain he had many students, eager to listen to his exposition of the Talmud. Rabbi Joseph ibn Migash, the reputed teacher of Maimonides, was one of them. He died at the age of ninety (1013-1103) at Lucena, having laid the real foundation of the Spanish talmudic tradition. His chief work, the *Halakhoth*, became famous and was studied like the Talmud of which it was an abridgment. He omitted material which had no relation to the traditional law (*Halakhah*), epitomizing the legal discussions in the Talmud that were important for the Jewish people in the Diaspora.

Ever since the completion of the Babylonian Talmud at the beginning of the sixth century, attempts were made to collect the legal decisions and the *Halakhoth* it contained and to elucidate them. Collections like *Halakhoth Gedoloth*, *Halakhoth Pesukoth*, and *Sheeltoth d'Rav Aḥai*, were geonic works that proved insufficient. Alfasi's work, often referred to as *Rav Alfas* or the *Rif*, was designed to be comprehensive and thorough. Maimonides, in his introduction to his commentary on the Mishnah, describes Alfasi's work as having superseded all its predecessors, because it contains everything useful for the understanding of the legal decisions "at present in force. . . The author

39

clearly demonstrates the errors of those before him when his opinion deviates from theirs. . ."

Rabbi Isaac Alfasi wrote his abridgment of the Talmud in Spain at the very time that Rashi was preparing his great commentary on the Talmud in France. Rashi and the Tosafists who succeeded him were interested in making the entire contents of the Talmud clear to every student, whereas Alfasi and his successors concentrated on the practical observance of the traditional law. In his abridged Talmud, the *Rif* succeeded in reproducing the practical contents of the Babylonian Talmud, which he extracted from a bewildering maze of discussions and summed up by decisions.

ALPHABET   אָלֶפְבֵּית

THE Hebrew alphabet, like other Semitic alphabets, consists of consonants only, twenty-two in number. Some of these, however, have also a vocalic force, namely: א, ה, ו, י. Five letters have a special form at the end of words, and grammarians combine them in the word מנצפ"ך or כמנפ"ץ. As to the origin of the Hebrew alphabet, some scholars suggest that it is not very much earlier than the fifteenth century before the common era, since otherwise the al-Amarna letters, sent to Egypt by Canaanite kings, would not have been written exclusively in cuneiform.

The Hebrew alphabet served as the ancestor of all European forms of writing through the medium of the Phoenicians and Greeks. The shapes of the letters were very different in early times from those in present-day printed Hebrew, but in spite of all changes the Hebrew alphabet was always written from right to left and not from left to right. In order to safeguard the traditional pronunciation and meaning of the biblical and liturgical texts, two systems of vowel-representation were ingeniously devised by grammarians in the sixth and seventh centuries of the common era.

Current among eastern Jews there was a system of vowels consisting of marks placed over the consonants, while in the west there was a system of dots and dashes placed for the most part under the consonants. The copies of the Torah used in synagogue worship to this day have no vowels indicated at all. The letter ו (*vav*) is, according to the masoretic calculation, the most frequently used letter in Hebrew. It occurs 76,922 times in the 815,280 letters in the Torah.

A homiletic interpretation of the names of the Hebrew alphabetical order is given in the Talmud (Shabbath 104a), where we are told that the first two letters *Aleph Beth* mean *learn wisdom* (*alef binah*); the next two letters *Gimmel Daleth* signify *show kindness to the poor* (*gemol dallim*); and so on to the end. Then the talmudic statement continues as follows: Why are the three letters of שקר close together in the Hebrew alphabetical order, while the three letters of אמת are far apart? The answer is: Falsehood (שקר) occurs frequently, whereas truth (אמת) is found only at distant intervals. And why does falsehood stand on one foot, while truth has a level foundation? That is, each of the letters of שקר is insecurely poised on one leg, whereas the letters of אמת are firmly set, each resting on two ends. The implication is that one-legged falsehood cannot endure as well as two-legged truth.

GOD WILLING

THE expressions *im yirtseh ha-shem* (if it please God) and *b'ezrath ha-shem* (with God's help) are used by the Jewish people in connection with plans, hopes, promises and wishes. Conscious of the nearness of God, those who constantly live by faith are in the habit of accompanying every decision and promise with the words that have become an integral part of every Jewish dialect. They express traditional Jewish faith in God and his relation to human destiny.

The word היא in עצת ה' היא תקום (Proverbs 19:21—"it is the Lord's purpose that prevails") has been referred to as an allusion to the customary phrase אם ירצה השם, the letters of היא, in reverse, being used as initials of the three words.

FAITH   אֱמוּנָה

EMUNAH (faith) primarily denotes faithfulness, as in אל אמונה (God of faithfulness) and איש אמונות (Deuteronomy 32:4; Proverbs 28:20). The sages of the Talmud stress faith as highly meritorious, and they blame greatly the men of little faith. The term *Emunah* now denotes absolute belief in divine providence, in God's unfailing goodness, in his aid and deliverance in time of distress. This is expressed in the Jewish hopefulness for a better world and optimistic outlook on life.

41

During the medieval period, *Emunah* came to include the tenets of the Jewish faith. The Talmud (Sotah 48b) records a tannaitic statement which reads: כל מי שיש לו פת בסלו ואומר מה אוכל למחר אינו אלא מקטני אמנה—"Whoever has bread in his basket and says *what am I going to eat tomorrow?* only belongs to those who are little in faith."

Abraham ibn Daud, historian and philosopher (1110-1180), famous for his chronicle *Sefer ha-Kabbalah* (Book of Tradition), writes in the introduction to his philosophical work *Emunah Ramah* (Sublime Faith): "In our days it sometimes happens that an individual who studies a little of the philosophies is unable to hold in his hands the two lamps, the lamp of religion in his right hand, and the lamp of philosophy in his left; but no sooner does he kindle the lamp of philosophy than he extinguishes the lamp of religion. And this has happened not only in our generation. . ."

The thirteen principles of faith formulated by Moses Maimonides (1135-1204) are summed up in the daily prayerbook on two occasions (*Ani Ma'amin* and *Yigdal*) as follows: 1) There is a Creator. 2) He is One. 3) He is incorporeal. 4) He is eternal. 5) He alone must be worshiped. 6) The prophets are true. 7) Moses was the greatest of all prophets. 8) The entire Torah was divinely given to Moses. 9) The Torah is immutable. 10) God knows all the acts and thoughts of man. 11) He rewards and punishes. 12) Messiah will come. 13) There will be resurrection.

These thirteen principles are divided into three groups. The first group (existence of God) includes the first five principles; the second group (revelation) contains the next four principles; the third group (reward and punishment) comprises the remaining four principles. According to Rabbi Joseph Albo of the fifteenth century, the Jewish faith is based on three principles: 1) the existence of God, 2) revelation, and 3) reward and punishment. He thinks that belief in the impossible does not produce happiness.

Moses Mendelssohn writes: "Among all the precepts of the Torah there is not one which says *you shall believe this* or *you shall not believe it*, but rather *you shall do, you shall not do*. The very Hebrew word *Emunah*, which is commonly translated *faith*, means trust, reliance, full confidence in a promise. Wherever the question is of eternal, self-evident truths, there is nothing said of believing, but of understanding and knowing. For this reason also, ancient Judaism had no articles of faith. No one was asked by oath to subscribe to symbols or articles of faith. . ." (*Jerusalem*, 1783). According to Mendelssohn, the opening formula of the thirteen principles of Maimonides, *ani ma'amin*, should be rendered *I am firmly convinced* instead of *I believe*.

Rabbi Abraham Isaac Kook (1864-1935) declares that faith is the song of life. The whole mass of prosaic literature and knowledge is of value only when it is founded on the perception of the poetry of life. Faith and love are the very essence of life. There would be nothing of value left in the travail of life if these two luminaries, faith and love, were taken from it. Contemporary civilization throughout the world is founded entirely on unbelief and hate, forces which nullify the essence of life. It is impossible to overcome this disease of modern society unless we discover the good that is contained in faith and love. The Torah and the divine precepts are the channels through which faith and love flow unceasingly... The Torah and all its precepts form a great and mighty divine poem of trust and love.

Martin Buber, whose attitude to Judaism has been largely influenced by Ḥasidism, describes religious faith as a dialogue between man and God. Every action must be performed in response to divine bidding, since God tells man what to do in every situation. Man must listen to God through establishing an "I and Thou" relationship, frequently asking himself what God wants him to do. In one of his most important works, which influenced contemporary non-Jewish theology, Buber develops the idea of "I and Thou" relationship between man and God, enabling man to know God who addresses each person individually. By carrying on a dialogue, by letting God speak to him, each individual can better determine what God demands of him. The nearness of God is felt deep in the heart of the man of faith. Thinking of God must be combined with taking action in human society. When there is no dialogue between man and God or between man and man, society breaks down and human personality disappears.

BELIEFS AND OPINIONS   אֱמוּנוֹת וְדֵעוֹת

ONE of the standard works of medieval philosophy is *Emunoth v'De-oth* (Beliefs and Opinions) by Rav Saadyah Gaon (882-942), who was appointed to the exalted position of *Gaon* as the head of the talmudic academy of Sura, Babylonia, when he was barely forty years old.

In this book Rav Saadyah presents, in addition to his own views, a summary of the most important divergent opinions about the ten cardinal principles of Judaism: Creation, God, Revelation, Divine

43

Justice, Divine Commandments, Resurrection, Messiah, Reward and punishment, Right Living. He affirms that Messiah will deliver Jerusalem from the enemy and settle there with his people forever.

Among other things, Rav Saadyah states: Self-restraint is commendable if it is properly practised; but a too solitary individual is likely to become so shy of other human beings that he nurtures a hatred for them based on suspicion. Wine makes the miser generous and the coward brave; but the person who is addicted to drinking will spend all his energy in attempting to satisfy his strong desire under all circumstances.

The quest for wealth entails many hardships. Sleep may become difficult; quarrels and animosities spring up, reminding us of fierce lions attacking their prey. The man who is completely given to amassing money pays little attention to the poor and the oppressed. The upright man loves the life of this world because it serves as a stepladder to the next. Physical science and religious knowledge form an excellent combination. As a rule, God does not change the laws of nature established by him, though there are occasions when he miraculously provides us with the things we need.

SUPERSTITIOUS BELIEFS   אֱמוּנוֹת תְּפֵלוֹת

WITCHCRAFT is condemned in the Torah as an abominable form of idolatry, being steeped in crime, immorality and deception. Sorcery, or the pretended holding of communication with evil spirits, is perpetually prohibited as a practice borrowed from paganism and not in accord with Israel's belief in One God. The Torah prohibits divination as a heathen practice; thus we read: "Do not eat meat with the blood still in it; do not practise divination or soothsaying" (Leviticus 19:26).

As to what is divination, Maimonides cites the following examples: "A piece of bread dropped out of my mouth, my cane fell from my hand, so I will not start out today... Since a fox ran past me on the right, I will not venture outside the door today... If a certain thing happens to me, I will follow this course of action... This house which I built has turned out lucky for me... From the moment I bought this animal I became rich... That is a lucky sign..." He concludes by saying that all these practices are false and deceptive, and that whoever believes in them is nothing but a fool (*Yad, Avodah Zarah* 11:16).

44

It has been noted that on account of the non-Jewish demon-haunted religious books, some 100,000 women and children suffered a cruel death during the horrible hunt for witches in the sixteenth century. Some medieval Jewish thinkers denied witchcraft altogether.

AMORAIM   אֲמוֹרָאִים

THE term *Amoraim* (Interpreters) is applied to the sages of the Talmud who were active from the time of the conclusion of the Mishnah to the end of the fifth century, a period of about three hundred years. Their activity was dedicated chiefly to expounding the Mishnah, which had been compiled and edited by Rabbi Judah the Prince (רבנו יהודה הנשיא) and had become the code of the Oral Law (תורה שבעל פה). They also concerned themselves with all Bible interpretation that is non-legal in character, or *Aggadah*, and frequently held popular discourses before congregations.

The two Talmuds, the Palestinian as well as the Babylonian Talmud (תלמוד בבלי) and תלמוד ירושלמי), mention hundreds of *Amoraim*, whose work finally became embodied in the *Gemara* (גמרא) which includes an expanded interpretation of the Mishnah. The term *Gemara* signifies that which has been learned of the oral traditional law, a knowledge acquired by study.

The *Amoraim* occupied an intermediate position between the sages of the tannaitic period, known as *Tannaim* (תנאים), and the *Savoraim* and *Geonim*, talmudic sages who were active in Babylonia from the beginning of the sixth century to the end of the tenth century.

Of the thousand or more *Amoraim* mentioned by name, Rav and Samuel were of the first generation. Rav founded the Sura Academy in 219, and it continued to flourish for eight centuries. His colleague, Samuel, head of the Nehardea Academy and authority on civil law, in which his views were accepted as decisive, was a physician and expert astronomer. He laid down the principle *dina d'malkhutha dina*, the law of the land where Jews live is binding in civil cases.

Rav Ashi and Ravina, responsible for the arrangement and editing of the Babylonian Talmud, were of the last generation of *Amoraim*. Rav Ashi, who headed the Sura Academy for fifty-two years, was presumably aided by the large group of scholars attached to his academy in his tremendous task of systematising the bewildering mass of material and preparing it for the crystallization of the Talmud. His

45

colleague Ravina, who died in 500, marks the close of the amoraic
period and the completion of the redaction of the Talmud.

The title *Savoraim* was used for scholars who were competent to
render authoritative decisions resulting from careful reflection and
reasoning in points of *Halakhah*. The *Savoraim* undertook to give the
last touches to the Talmud that had been redacted by Rav Ashi and
Ravina. They made some additions of considerable length, enlarging
the text of the Babylonian Talmud by means of explanations referring
especially to questions that had been left vague and undecided by the
Amoraim. The Geonim, who derived their authority by virtue of
their preeminence as teachers and interpreters of the Talmud, were
the intellectual leaders of the Babylonian Jews in the post-talmudic
period between the sixth and eleventh centuries.

AMEN   אָמֵן

AMEN (so be it) occurs fourteen times in the Torah as a formula of
confirmation or agreement. During the period of the Second Temple,
Amen served as a response to benedictions and prayers recited outside the Temple. In place of *Amen*, the response used in the Temple
was: "Blessed be his glorious majesty forever and ever."

The Mishnah relates that "when the priests and the people . . .
heard the distinctive name of God pronounced by the high priest,
they exclaimed: ברוך שם כבוד מלכותו לעולם ועד (Yoma 6:2). The
congregational response אמן יהא שמה רבא מברך לעלם ולעלמי עלמיא
(*Amen*, may his great name be blessed forever and to all eternity),
forming the essential part of the *Kaddish*, is a combination of the
Amen response and the response used in the Temple.

This explains the great significance generally attached to this utterance in the liturgy of the synagogue. It is recorded in the Talmud
(Sukkah 51b) that in the great synagogue of Alexandria the attendant
signaled the congregation with a flag, at the conclusion of benedictions by the reader, to respond *Amen*. In the Middle Ages it became
customary to conclude every good wish with *Amen*.

By pronouncing *Amen* the listener associates himself with what has
been uttered; he makes it his own and is ready to conform to it. The
people said *Amen* to the commandments which Moses gave them,
thus agreeing to follow them and accepting the consequences implied.
Amen is used where one person confirms the words of another.

46

According to a statement in the Talmud (Sanhedrin 111a), the initial letters of אל מלך נאמן (God is a faithful King) form the word אמן. By responding *Amen* upon hearing a benediction recited by another person one is exempted from reciting that benediction himself. The third benediction of *Birkath Hammazon* (Grace after meals) ends with *Amen* to indicate the end of the three benedictions which are based on the biblical command in Deuteronomy 8:10; otherwise the *Amen* response must not be used in conclusion of one's own benediction.

TRUTH   אֱמֶת

TRUTH is one of the pillars upon which the world rests (Avoth 1:18). The core of Judaism is the conviction that whatever is true is also good and beautiful. Telling the truth is frequently emphasized in the book of Proverbs: "Truthful lips endure forever, but a lying tongue is only for a moment. A false tongue comes to grief. . ." (12:19; 17:20).

Elsewhere in the Bible, this cardinal virtue in Jewish ethical conduct is expressed as follows: "These are the things that you shall do: Speak the truth to one another; let your decisions in court be true and make for peace; plot no evil in your hearts against one another; and never give yourselves to any perjury—for I hate all these things, says the Lord" (Zechariah 9:16-17). According to a talmudic statement, "the seal of God is truth" חותמו של הקדוש ברוך הוא (Shabbath 55a).

This thought has been interpreted to the effect that the universe and all it contains, reflecting the greatness of God, is based upon truth. The Jewish concept of a happy life is expressed in Proverbs 30:7-9: "Two things I ask of thee; deny them not to me before I die: Remove falsehood and lying far from me; give me neither wealth nor riches, but feed me with the food I need, lest I be full and deny thee . . . or lest I be poor and steal, discrediting my God." One of the seven characteristics of a wise man listed in the *Ethics of the Fathers* is that of acknowledging the truth (Avoth 5:9).

EMETH V'YATZIV   אֱמֶת וְיַצִּיב

EMETH v'YATZIV (true and certain) are the initial words of the lengthy benediction following the *Shema* of the morning service and ending with the words גאל ישראל ("blessed art thou . . . who hast redeemed

47

Israel"). The main theme of this passage, known as גאולה (redemption), is the liberation of Israel from Egypt as well as a plea for deliverance in the future. *Emeth v'Yatziv* is mentioned in the Mishnah (Tamid 5:1) among the prayers used in the Temple.

The fifteen synonyms, beginning with the word ויציב and ending with ויפה, correspond to the fifteen words in the last sentence of the *Shema*, beginning with אני and closing with אמת. The rule is not to interrupt the connection between ה' אלהיכם and אמת, as if these three words formed one sentence, meaning: "The Lord your God is true," corresponding to Jeremiah 2:21 (וה' אלהים אמת). Compare Mishnah Berakhoth 2:2. In this manner the *Geullah* benediction attaches itself to the concluding words of the *Shema* as well as to the paragraph immediately following the *Shema*, namely אמת ויציב.

Since the *Shema* is the watchword of Israel's faith, and it is the desire of every loyal Jew to have it on his lips when he dies, the passage *Emeth v'Yatziv* connected with the *Shema* contains a profession of faith (אמונה=אמת) in the declaration of the Oneness of God and the eternal validity of the Torah: "True it is that the eternal God is our King... His words are living and enduring, faithful and precious, forever and to all eternity, as for our fathers so also for us, for our children and future generations..." Reminiscent of the second paragraph of the *Shema* are the words: "Happy is the man who obeys thy commands and takes thy Torah and thy word to heart."

MARRANOS אֲנוּסִים

THE Spanish term *Marranos* (swine) was applied to those Jews in Spain who, after the 1391 persecutions, were compelled to adopt Christianity, and in many cases secretly practised Judaism and remained faithful to it. According to some, the name *Marrano* is derived from the Aramaic phrase *maran atha* (our Lord has come), which the unfortunate were compelled to repeat on frequent occasions. *Anusim*, the Hebrew equivalent of *Marranos*, signifies *those who were compelled*. It has been estimated that one hundred thousand Jews became *Marranos* or secret Jews, whose existence formed the pretext for the establishment of the Spanish Inquisition in 1480.

Cecil Roth, in his *History of the Marranos*, points out that crypto-Judaism is as old as the Jew himself. In Hellenistic days, some weaklings endeavored to conceal their origin in order to escape ridicule when participating in the athletic exercises. He goes on to say that the phenomenon of Marranism is more than the commonplace occurrence of forcible conversion, followed frequently by the practice of Judaism in secret. Its essential element is that this clandestine religion is passed on from generation to generation. The classical land of crypto-Judaism is Spain. According to one theory, the ceremony of annulment of vows on the eve of *Yom Kippur*, known as the *Kol Nidré* service, was instituted for the benefit of Spanish crypto-Jews, or *Anusim*, in order to absolve them from any promise for the observance of another religion in the following year. The initial reference to עברינים (transgressors) has been taken as a cryptic allusion to the Iberians, natives or inhabitants of Spain or Portugal. The pre-*Kol Nidré* declaration אנו מתירין להתפלל עם העברינים literally means: We declare it lawful to pray in the company of sinners.

The medieval Inquisition, which was instituted in Spain and Portugal to detect and punish crypto-Jews as well as Christian heretics, reached its climax with the famous *auto-da-fé* (an act of the faith), a ceremony at which the sentences of the Inquisition were announced or carried out. The inquisitors burned their victims in keeping with the prohibition against shedding blood. The heretics were handed over to the secular arm for carrying into execution the sentences imposed. The day chosen was usually a Sunday. In the procession through the streets, the Dominican monks marched first; then the penitents, followed by those condemned to die, dressed in horrifying robes called *Sanbenitos* (from Saint Benedict) and with dunce-caps on their heads; and next black coffins containing the bones of those who had escaped sentence by dying in prison.

The first *auto-da-fé* was conducted by Torquemada in 1481; the last was in 1826. Some thirty thousand men and women were put to death by the Inquisition in the course of the three and a half centuries of its existence. Those who confessed that they had practised Judaism secretly were first strangled by the executioners; then their bodies were laid on the scaffold beside the living men and women already bound there. A prominent dignitary set fire to the faggots while the priests chanted praises to God from the book of Psalms.

Three classes of *Marranos* were distinguishable: those who took advantage of the social opportunities offered by the forced conversion; those who courageously attended synagogue services in secret; and those who made every effort to reach other countries in order to throw off the disguise and practise the precepts of Judaism openly. After the expulsion from Spain in 1492, the *Marranos* were persecuted by the Inquisition with the utmost severity. Their numbers were greatly increased by their forced baptism in Portugal in 1497.

In order to profess their Jewishness freely, the *Marranos* migrated first to Turkey and Italy and later to Amsterdam and London. At the end of the sixteenth century, Portuguese *Marranos* founded the first Sephardic community in Amsterdam. In 1639, three *Marrano* congregations united in Amsterdam and founded the great Portuguese synagogue which still exists. For many generations, the *Marrano* communities continued to speak Spanish and Portuguese among themselves and regarded themselves as the aristocracy of the Jewish people. Though it was long imagined that the *Marranos* of Spain and Portugal had disappeared, it was discovered in 1920 that large numbers still retained some of their Jewish beliefs and customs, now hardly recognizable.

PRINCIPLES OF FAITH   אֲנִי מַאֲמִין

ANI MA'AMIN (I believe), like the poem *Yigdal* which opens the morning worship for each day, is based on the thirteen creeds of Rabbi Moshe ben Maimun, generally known as *Rambam* or Moses Maimonides (1135-1204). In his commentary on the Mishnah (Sanhedrin 10:1), Maimonides examines the current conceptions of immortality and the doctrines upon which Judaism rests. Summing up his Jewish philosophy, he formulates thirteen articles of creed covering the 613 commandments of Judaism.

Almost every country where Jews lived has produced a poem or prayer based on these principles of faith, which are in brief as follows: 1) There is a Creator. 2) He is One. 3) He is incorporeal. 4) He is eternal. 5) He alone must be worshiped. 6) The prophets are true. 7) Moses was the greatest of all prophets. 8) The entire Torah was divinely given to Moses. 9) The Torah is immutable. 10) God knows all the acts and thoughts of man. 11) He rewards and punishes. 12) Messiah will come. 13) There will be resurrection.

Ani Ma'amin, which appears in the daily Prayerbook at the end of the morning service, reads as follows:

1) I firmly believe that the Creator, blessed be his name, is the Creator and Ruler of all created beings, and that he alone has made, does make, and ever will make all things.

50

2) I firmly believe that the Creator, blessed be his name, is One; that there is no oneness in any form like his; and that he alone was, is, and ever will be our God.

3) I firmly believe that the Creator, blessed be his name, is not corporeal; that no bodily accidents apply to him; and that there exists nothing whatever that resembles him.

4) I firmly believe that the Creator, blessed be his name, was the first and will be the last.

5) I firmly believe that the Creator, blessed be his name, is the only one to whom it is proper to address our prayers, and that we must not pray to anyone else.

6) I firmly believe that all the words of the Prophets are true.

7) I firmly believe that the prophecy of Moses our teacher, may he rest in peace, was true; and that he was the chief of the prophets, both of those who preceded and of those that followed him.

8) I firmly believe that the whole Torah which we now possess is the same which was given to Moses our teacher, may he rest in peace.

9) I firmly believe that this Torah will not be changed, and that there will be no other Torah given by the Creator, blessed be his name.

10) I firmly believe that the Creator, blessed be his name, knows all the actions and thoughts of human beings, as it is written: "It is he who fashions the hearts of them all, he who notes all their deeds."

11) I firmly believe that the Creator, blessed be his name, rewards those who keep his commands, and punishes those who transgress his commands.

12) I firmly believe in the coming of Messiah; and although he may tarry, I daily wait for his coming.

13) I firmly believe that there will be a revival of the dead at a time which will please the Creator, blessed and exalted be his name forever and ever.

The religious philosopher Rabbi Ḥasdai Crescas (1340-1412), in his *Or Adonai* (Light of God), criticises Maimonides' list of dogmas, which he reduces to six. Rabbi Joseph Albo (1380-1440), a pupil of Ḥasdai Crescas, goes still further in his famous work *Sefer ha-Ikkarim* (Book of Fundamentals) and lays down three essential principles from which the rest are derived. They are: the existence of God, revelation of the Torah, and future reward and punishment. Rabbi Samson Raphael Hirsch (1808-1888) states that Judaism embraces 613 precepts, but knows no dogmas. Samuel David Luzzatto (1800-1865) affirms that the principal dogma of Judaism is the belief in the divine origin of the Torah

THE GREAT ASSEMBLY   אַנְשֵׁי כְנֶסֶת הַגְּדוֹלָה

The Great Assembly consisting of 120 members was a legislative body that functioned during and after the Persian period in Jewish history, about 500-300 before the common era. How often this body met, in Jerusalem, is unknown.

It has been suggested that it was called together at critical times when matters of national policy were involved. According to tradition, the Great Assembly received the Torah from the prophets and instituted the basic prayers and benedictions. The *Shemoneh Esreh*, for example, is attributed to it.

The Great Assembly is also credited with the adoption of the larger portion of the biblical books and the general framework of the synagogue worship. The Mishnah ascribes to the Men of the Great Assembly a passage of three clauses, which reads: "Be patient in the administration of justice; develop many students; and make a fence for the Torah" (Avoth 1:1). The last clause (ועשו סייג לתורה) is understood to mean additional regulations, designed to preserve the biblical laws.

ESSENES   אִסִּיִּים

The etymological origin of the name *Essenes* is unknown, though some scholars connect it with the Aramaic noun *asya*, physician, and others derive it from the Syrian word *hasyah*, pious. The Essenes, a Jewish ascetic sect in the days of the Second Temple, are described as pious healers, soothsayers and miracle-workers, who worked, prayed and practised their religious customs together in settlements formed on the basis of joint and indivisible ownership.

They occupied themselves with agriculture and handicrafts and despised trade and wealth. They took their meals together in strict silence, beginning and terminating with solemn prayer. Every morning before their first meal they bathed in fresh spring water. They denounced slavery and considered it their duty to aid the poor, the weak and the aged.

According to a description by Philo of Alexandria, the famous philosopher of Hellenistic Judaism, the Essenes were a sect of Jews, numbering more than four thousand, who lived in villages and avoided

52

cities, in order to escape the contagion of evil. No maker of war weapons was to be found among them. They felt that the law of nature made all men free and that slavery was a violation of this law. They were chiefly preoccupied with ethics, and taught piety, holiness, justice, love of God and man. Their love of virtue revealed itself in their indifference to money, worldly position and pleasure. No one lived in a private house, but shared his dwelling with all the rest. They threw open their doors to any of their sect who happened to stop by. The aged among them were treated with reverence and honor.

The famous Jewish historian Josephus Flavius (37-105), who probably lived among the Essenes when he spent three years in the desert as an ascetic, describes the Essenes as follows: "The Essenes shun pleasure as a vice. . . They despise riches, and there is no one among them who owns more than another. . . Like brothers they share equally what the community possesses. . . They do not throw away their clothes or shoes until they are worn to shreds. . . They do not speak about worldly things before sunrise, but recite prayers that have been handed down to them from their forefathers. Immediately afterward, they set out to do the various tasks assigned to them.

"They work strenuously for four hours. Then they gather to one place, bathe in cold water and go to a special building, where they meet in the dining room as solemnly as though it were a sacred shrine. . . Before and after the meal the priest offers a prayer. . . No noise ever desecrates the house; the silence that prevails in this house is both mystifying and awe-inspiring. . . They enjoy long life, many of them living to be more than a hundred years old, possibly because of the simplicity and regularity of their way of living. . ."

The Essenes were exceedingly devoted to the observance of the Sabbath and all that was attributed to Moses. They had a secret lore about angels, and practised healing in accordance with medicinal properties of roots. They declined to participate in Temple rites involving animal sacrifices. They believed unconditionally in divine providence, and manifested implicit faith in immortality. They performed frequent ablutions and wore white garments. They renounced marriage and forbade membership to women.

In the war against the Romans (66-70), many Essenes died under torture refusing to eat forbidden food. In the words of Josephus: "They did not cringe before their persecutors or shed a tear in their presence. Smiling in their agony, scorning their tormentors, they gave up their souls cheerfully, confident that they would receive them

53

back again. . .'' Many scholars have identified the Essenes with the Qumran sectarians, whose colonies were near the place where the Dead Sea Scrolls were discovered in 1947.

ISRU ḤAG   אִסְרוּ חַג

THE day following the three pilgrim festivals (*Pesaḥ, Shavuoth* and *Sukkoth*) is known as *Isru Ḥag* (bind the festival), with reference to Psalm 118:27. It is observed as a semi-festive day, when the *Taḥanun* supplications are omitted from the *Shaḥarith* and *Minḥah* services. In Temple times, *Isru Ḥag* was the day when the pilgrims left Jerusalem for their homes. According to a talmudic statement, he who observes *Isru Ḥag* as a festive day with eating and drinking is as if he offered sacrifices upon the altar (Sukkah 25b).

ESTHER   אֶסְתֵּר

THE book of Esther, one of the most cherished books in Jewish literature, is the last of the five *Megilloth* (scrolls) that are part of the third division of the Bible, known as כתובים (Sacred Writings). *Megillath Esther* tells the story of a Jewish girl who used her influence as queen of Persia to save her people from a general massacre which Haman had plotted against them. It is a tale of plot and counterplot, showing the downfall of the arrogant and the vindication of the innocent.

Queen Esther is depicted as dutiful toward Mordecai, her cousin and guardian, and faithful to her people. Haman's fate reminds us that pride goes before a fall. Ahasuerus, who agrees to Haman's plot without thought, is described as a pompous and feeble-minded monarch. Though the name of God is not mentioned in the book, the author clearly implies that God used Mordecai and Esther as instruments for the deliverance of a persecuted people. On *Purim*, the book of Esther is recited in the synagogue twice: evening and morning. The narrative may be summed up as follows:

There was a Jew in Shushan by the name of Mordecai. He had adopted his orphaned cousin Esther, and brought her up as his own daughter. Beautiful and lovely, she was taken into the royal house where she became a favorite. She said nothing about her people or her descent, for Mordecai had told her not to reveal it. King Ahasuerus promoted Haman and advanced him above all his officers. All bowed low before Haman, but Mordecai would not bow to him. This infuriated Haman so much that he decided to destroy all the Jews throughout the empire of Ahasuerus. He said to the king: There is a certain people dispersed in every province of your kingdom, whose laws are different from those of other people and they do not obey the king's laws. The king should not tolerate them in the land. If it please the king, let it be decreed that they be destroyed, and I will pay ten thousand talents of silver into the royal treasury.

Keep your money, and do what you like to the people—the king said to Haman. Then instructions were sent to all the king's provinces to massacre and destroy all the Jews, young and old, women and children, in one day, the thirteenth day of the month of *Adar*. The king and Haman sat down to drink, but the city of Shushan was perplexed. . . When the king saw Esther standing in the court, he held out the golden scepter to her. Esther approached and touched it. What is your wish, queen Esther, what is your request?—the king asked. It shall be given you were it even half of my kingdom, he said. Esther replied: If it please the king, let the king and Haman come today to a banquet which I have prepared. . .

On the second day of the banquet, the king again asked Esther: What is your petition, queen Esther, what is your request? Queen Esther replied: O king, let my life be given me—that is my petition! Grant me my people—that is my request! My people and I are to be destroyed, to be slain, to be annihilated . . . by a foe, an enemy, this wicked Haman! . . . One of the royal attendants, Harbonah, said: At Haman's house a gallows is standing, which he prepared for Mordecai who had saved the king's life. The king ordered: Hang him on that! So they hanged Haman on the gallows which he had prepared for Mordecai.

AFIKOMAN אֲפִיקוֹמָן

AFIKOMAN, mentioned in the Mishnah (Pesaḥim 10:8), is the piece of *matzah* broken off from the central of the three *matzoth* used in the *Seder* service the first two nights of Passover. The breaking of the middle *matzah* in two and the hiding of the *afikoman*, which is shared by all at the table at the conclusion of the meal, are intended to awaken the children's curiosity. It has been suggested that the *afikoman* is wrapped in a napkin as a symbol of the unleavened dough which, wrapped in their garments, the Israelites carried on their shoulders out of Egypt (Exodus 12:34).

According to some, the *afikoman* is symbolically concealed between the cushions, upon which the leader of the *Seder* service reclines, in keeping with a literal rendering of Exodus 12:17 ("you shall watch the *matzoth*"). However, the practice may simply be designed to preserve the *afikoman* intact till it is distributed as the last thing eaten at the *Seder* service in remembrance of the paschal lamb which, during Temple times, was eaten at the end of the Passover meal.

The custom of encouraging the children to snatch the *afikoman* and make it disappear for a while, until a promise of a gift has been obtained, is said to be based on a misinterpretation of the talmudic statement which reads: "The *matzoth* are eaten hastily (חוטפין מצות) on the nights of Passover so that the children should not fall asleep" (Pesaḥim 109a).

The word *afikoman* is of Greek origin and denotes something served after the meal in the form of entertainment or food.

EPIKOROS אֶפִּיקוֹרוֹס

THE term *Epikoros*, used loosely of a person who is lax in Jewish religious observances and finds himself intellectually out of tune with Jewish religious thought, essentially means a follower of the Greek philosopher Epicurus, who taught that "all parts of the universe . . . owe their origin to accident and chance" (*Guide for the Perplexed*, 3:17).

Because of the phonetic resemblance between אפיקורוס and the Hebrew verb פקר (to be licentious) the term *epikoros* is used in talmudic literature to denote one who denies the authority of the Torah. Hence, there is a statement that he who insults a student of the Torah (המבזה תלמיד חכם) is an *epikoros* (Sanhedrin 99b). In the Ethics of the Fathers we are told: "Be eager to study the Torah, and know what to answer an *epikoros* (Avoth 3:19).

It has been suggested that there exists a marked distinction between the *epikoros* who possesses knowledge of Judaism and the man whose estrangement from Jewish life and thought is due to indifference or ignorance. There is room for differences in philosophic thinking among Jews of all shades of opinion, who seek to promote Judaism.

56

According to Epicurus, who lived in the third century before the common era, pleasure is the only good and the end of all morality. Mental pleasures are greater than the pleasures of the body. Hence, it is wise to choose the joys of intellectual life. Social life, declares Epicurus, is based on the principle of self-interest; individuals join together in groups for self-protection. There is no such thing as absolute justice. He teaches that there is nothing evil in injustice as such, but to live in constant fear of punishment—that is an evil. We are just, because it is to our advantage to be just.

The Epicurean philosophy is essentially a doctrine of enlightened self-interest. The individual is asked to make his own happiness the goal of all his strivings, and such a theory of life is apt to lead to selfish disregard of others. Many followers of Epicureanism came to interpret it in terms of a life of luxury and sensuous enjoyment.

ASTROLOGY   אִצְטַגְנִינוּת

THE belief that planets and stars influence the fate of man stems from ancient Babylonia. The prophets attacked it as futile and idolatrous. The talmudic expression אין מזל לישראל signifies that Israel's fate depends on no planet but rather on divine providence (Shabbath 156a). Maimonides, who was the keenest antagonist of astrology during the medieval period, addressed a letter to the Jewish community of Marseilles, France, in which he declared: "Astrology is a disease, not a science. All sorts of superstitions thrive under its shadow. Only fools and charlatans lend value to it."

However, in spite of the *Halakhah*, which regards practical astrology as prohibited magic, a considerable number of Jewish authorities in the Middle Ages were inclined to consider astrology as an authentic science. Rav Saadyah Gaon, Ibn Gabirol, Rashi, Ibn Ezra, Abravanel and others are included among those who believed that astrologers could foretell events by the position and movements of the stars. Astrological notions are to be found in kabbalistic books. The expressions *mazzal tov* (good luck) and בר מזל (lucky man), widely used as figures of speech, are survivals of the old belief.

Though practised among most of the peoples mentioned in the Bible, astrology found no encouragement among the people of Israel. In an ode on the humiliation of Babylon, which was renowned in the ancient world for astrology, and for the practice of all kinds of magic, the prophet says: "Keep up your spells and your many sorceries, with which you toiled from your youth; perhaps you can make them avail . . . let the astrologers (הוברי שמים החוזים בכוכבים) stand forth to save you, the stargazers who forecast at each new moon what would happen to you" (Isaiah 47:12-13). Modern science has completely discredited astrology, though astrological observation contributed much toward the advancement of scientific astronomy.

AKDAMUTH אַקְדָּמוּת

AKDAMUTH, chanted on the first day of *Shavuoth* before the reading of the Torah, was composed in Aramaic by Rabbi Meir ben Isaac of the eleventh century. It consists of ninety verses alphabetically arranged; they contain acrostically a twofold alphabet, the name of the author and that of his father, and a short petition: מאיר ביר רבי יצחק, יגדל בתורה ובמעשים טובים אמן, וחזק ואמץ. There are ten syllables to each verse, and one rhyme (תא) runs through the entire poem. This mystical hymn deals with the indescribable greatness of the Creator, the excellence of the Torah and the future hope of Israel.

Akdamuth, serving as an introduction to the Ten Commandments about to be read out of the *Sefer Torah*, consists of two parts. The first part describes the unspeakable majesty of the Lord who created heaven and earth. The second part presents a dialogue between persecuted Israel and those who try to persuade him to change his faith to which he clings affectionately and tenaciously. A glowing description of the hoped-for messianic era then follows, mentioning the contest between the legendary monsters, Leviathan and Behemoth. The battle ends with the destruction of both. In kabbalistic literature the Leviathan is identified with evil, which is destined to disappear in messianic times.

ARBA KANFOTH אַרְבַּע כַּנְפוֹת

ARBA KANFOTH (four corners), also known as *tallith katan*, is a rectangular piece of linen or woolen cloth with fringes (*tsitsith*) on its four corners and an opening in the center large enough to admit the head. It is worn under the upper garment throughout the day. Resting on the shoulders, it is suspended over the chest and back.

58

Like the *tallith*, worn by adult male worshipers during the morning services as a rule, the *arba kanfoth*, resting upon every male from early boyhood, is provided with *tsitsith* as a reminder of the obligation to keep God's commandments. No pious Jew would permit himself to walk about without this continuous reminder.

Originally, the purple-blue thread entwined in the *tsitsith* (פתיל תכלת) was its chief distinction. When, however, it became impossible to procure the special dye required, it was made permissible to use white threads alone. Why blue? "Because this color resembles the sea, the sea resembles the sky. . ." (Menaḥoth 43b).

Four threads are taken, of which one (the *shammash*) is considerably longer than the rest, for each of the four corners of the *tallith* as well as the *tallith katan*. The four threads are drawn through a small hole or eyelet and the ends brought together. A double knot is tied close to the margin of the *tallith;* the *shammash* is then twisted tightly seven times round the remaining seven threads, and another double knot is tied; then round eight times, and a double knot; then round eleven times, and a double knot; and finally round thirteen times, and a double knot. 7 and 8 – 15 equals the numerical value of the Hebrew letters י and ה; eleven equals the numerical value of the letters ו and ה; thirteen equals the numerical value of the word אחד (one). All of this amounts to two Hebrew words which signify: *The Lord is One.*

Furthermore, the numerical value of the word ציצית is six hundred, which with the eight threads and the five knots makes a total of 613, the exact number of the positive (248) and negative (365) precepts of the Torah. This explains the talmudic statement that the wearing of the *tsitsith* is of equal merit with the observance of the whole Torah (Nedarim 25a).

The duty of wearing *tsitsith* derives from Numbers 15:39, where we are told: "You shall have it as a fringe, so that when you look upon it you will remember to do all the commands of the Lord, and you will not follow the desires of your heart and your eyes which lead you astray."

FOUR TORAH-SECTIONS   אַרְבַּע פָּרָשׁוֹת

THE Sabbath preceding *Rosh Ḥodesh Adar*, which is close to the month of *Nisan*, is termed *Shabbath Parashath Shekalim*. If it coincides with *Rosh Ḥodesh*, three *Sifré Torah* are taken from the ark during the congregational morning service. The *sidrah* of the week is read from the first scroll for the first six individuals who are called to the Torah; the portion designed for *Rosh Ḥodesh* is read from the second scroll for the seventh *aliyyah* (calling up); the section concerning the half-shekel contributions, for the maintenance of the Temple worship (Exodus 30:11-16), is read from the third scroll for the *Maftir.*

The Sabbath preceding *Purim* is termed *Shabbath Parashath Zakhor* when, for the *Maftir*, the section against the hostile Amalekites is read from Deuteronomy (25:17-19): "Remember how Amalek treated you on the road from Egypt, how he harassed you along the way, weak and weary as you were. . ."

The Sabbath preceding *Rosh Ḥodesh Nisan* is termed *Shabbath Parashath ha-Ḥodesh.* If it coincides with *Rosh Ḥodesh*, three *Sifré Torah* are taken from the ark, according to the manner applied when *Shabbath Parashath Shekalim* coincides with *Rosh Ḥodesh Adar.* This is done in order to prevent unnecessary discomfort on the part of the congregation: the three *Sifré Torah*, previously prepared to open each at the desired section, dispense with the need of rolling the scroll back and forth for the place to be read.

The Sabbath preceding *Parashath ha-Ḥodesh* is termed *Shabbath Parashath Parah;* the section concerning the red heifer (Numbers 19:1-10) is read for the *Maftir.* The law prescribing the ritual of the paradoxical red heifer sacrifice has never been adequately explained. Its aim was to purify the unclean, and yet it defiled all those who handled its ashes for the purification of others. It has been suggested that, though sacrificial animals were usually males, the use of a female (*parah*) in this case symbolized the imparting of new life to those who had been defiled by contact with death. The color red, being the color of blood, may have been the token of life. The paschal lamb could be eaten on the first night of Passover only by those who had been purified from their defilements.

HOLY ARK

THE synagogue ark which contains the *Sefer Torah* (Five Books of Moses written on parchment sheets in the form of a scroll) is a reminder of the biblical ark of the covenant, in which the two stone tablets were placed. The ark is the central object in the synagogue as it used to be in the Tabernacle and then in Solomon's Temple.

For this reason, a wealth of art has been invested in its elaboration ever since the medieval period. The ark is set on an elevated platform against the eastern wall so that the worshipers, when turning toward the ark, face in the direction of Jerusalem.

The ark in large synagogues contains many scrolls of the *Sefer Torah*, donated by members of the congregation in the course of many years. The presentation of a *Sefer Torah* to the synagogue was always highly regarded. As a reminder of the Tabernacle and Temple, a velvet curtain known as פרוכת is suspended before the open face of the ark. Special hangings of white silk are used on the High Holydays to symbolize forgiveness and atonement.

In keeping with the statement in the Ethics of the Fathers (Avoth 5:23) that "you ought to be bold as a leopard, light as an eagle, swift as a deer, and strong as a lion to do the will of your Father who is in heaven," two symbolic figures of two lions holding the Ten Commandments are generally carved or painted above the ark, as well as deer, despite the prohibition of pictures and paintings in the synagogue.

ARAMAIC   אֲרָמִית

ARAMAIC and Hebrew, Arabic and Ethiopic, are sister languages belonging to the Semitic group; they stand to one another in much the same relation as those of the Germanic group, or as the Slavonic languages. There is a close resemblance among them both in grammatical structure and vocabulary. Several Aramaic dialects were used in Bible lands. The Jewish people, after the Babylonian captivity, acquired gradually the use of Aramaic from their neighbors in and about Eretz Israel.

W. Wright, in his *Comparative Grammar of the Semitic Languages*, page 16, states: "Now do not for a moment suppose that the Jews lost the use of Hebrew in the Babylonian captivity, and brought back into Palestine this so-called Chaldee. The Aramean dialect, which gradually got the upper hand since 5-4 centuries B. C., did not come that long journey across the Syrian desert; it was *there*, on the spot; and it ended by taking possession of the field, side by side with the kindred dialect of the Samaritans."

It has been pointed out that the term *Chaldee* for the Aramaic of either the Bible or the Targums is a misnomer. The Aramaic of the books of Daniel and Ezra has a close resemblance with the Aramaic of the Targums of Onkelos and Jonathan. "Just at what time among the Jews of Palestine Hebrew ceased to be the spoken language of the people is a mooted question. The older view has it that the Jews lost their Hebrew speech in the Babylonian captivity whence they brought back with them the Aramaic. . . It has therefore been argued that the change of speech must have occurred in Palestine itself a century or so after Ezra. . . For a time indeed both languages were spoken and understood, until at length Hebrew vanished from the mouth of the people. As late as the second century of the current era Hebrew was still spoken in some nook or corner, but in the main it had become a sacred tongue understood by the learned, but unknown to the unlettered who conversed in Aramaic" (Max L. Margolis).

The Aramaic of the Babylonian Talmud represents the East-Aramaic dialect, while the Aramaic of the Palestinian Talmud and the Samaritan Targum on the Torah is that described as the West-Aramaic dialect. The modification of Aramaic by an admixture of Hebrew forms is to be seen in all Aramaic texts composed by Jewish writers.

ERETZ YISRAEL   אֶרֶץ יִשְׂרָאֵל

THE Jewish people lived in Palestine some three thousand years, from about 1200 before the common era. From the destruction of the Second Jewish Commonwealth by the Romans in the year 70, Palestine had not been an independent state until Israel's independence was declared by its founders on May 14, 1948, at which time Israel had to repel an invasion by Egypt, Jordan, Iraq, Syria, Lebanon and Saudi Arabia. The war of liberation ended with the defeat of the Arab States. In 1949, Israel was admitted to membership in the United Nations Organization.

The State of Israel has a remarkable range of climate, from perpetual snow on nearby Mount Hermon to the tropical heat of the Jordan Valley and En-Gedi in the Negev. The average temperature at Jerusalem in January, which is the coldest month, is about 50° F. The lowest temperature is 28° F. In August the average is 80°, and the greatest heat is 92° in the shade. In Eilat the temperature rises as high as 118° in August.

Two seasons follow each other almost immediately: a rainless, hot summer from May to October, and a rainy cool winter. The coastal area has mild winters and damp, hot summers; in the hills, summer days are warm, but rapidly become cool in the afternoon. Winters are wet and marked by heavy storms.

The very name Eretz Yisrael has always stirred within us the most elevated sentiments. All find consolation in that land, some by its memories, others by its hopes. Veneration and love for Eretz Yisrael were maintained by the talmudic sages in many ways. Rabbi Yoḥanan declared that one who walks a distance of six feet in Eretz Yisrael may be confident of a share in the future world (Kethuboth 111a). The merit of living in Eretz Yisrael equals the merit of observing all the commandments. Rabbi Ḥiyya ben Gammada showed his devotion by rolling himself in the dust of Eretz Yisrael, in conformity with the words of the psalmist: "Thy servants take pleasure in her stones, and favor her dust" (Psalm 102:14). Rabbi Yosé ben Ḥanina kissed the stones of Akko, saying: "Up to this point is the land of Yisrael." However, Jewish persecutions in Eretz Yisrael after the destruction of the Temple made it so difficult for the sages to maintain their position that many were compelled to remove to Babylon, which offered them better protection (Pesaḥim 87a).

Jewish liturgical literature comprises many poems on the holiness of Eretz Yisrael. The holiness of Eretz Yisrael attracted Jewish settlers not only to live, but to die there. All sins are considered absolved for the Jew who is buried in Eretz Yisrael. The custom of importing dust from Eretz Yisrael for burial purposes is in vogue to this day among observant Jews. The holiness of Eretz Yisrael is due to the many laws in the Torah which apply to Eretz Yisrael only. The Holy Land is distinguished as "a land which the Lord your God cares for; the eyes of the Lord your God are always upon it from the beginning of the year to the end" (Deuteronomy 11:12).

Special laws which operate only in Eretz Yisrael are referred to as *mitzvoth ha-teluyoth ba-aretz*, namely, laws that were in force at the time when the Temple was in existence and in connection with the Temple service: the paschal lamb, the bringing of the first-fruits to Jerusalem, the pilgrimage three times a year, the poor man's rights to the gleanings, the unreaped grain in the corners of the fields, the sanctification of the new moon, and the regulations for the cities of refuge.

Though conquered by the Romans in the year 70, the Jews never abandoned their country totally, but tried again and again to rebuild their communities there. Nor did they ever renounce their claim to the country of their origin. Israel's Declaration of Independence of

63

1948 reads: "Here . . . was the birthplace of the Jewish people. Here, their spiritual, religious and political identity was shaped."

Returning home from more than a hundred countries, the people of new Israel had to reconstitute themselves into a nation. They had to revive their ancient language, Hebrew. They had to restore the land from centuries of neglect and indifference on the part of a long succession of conquerors. They had to build new villages and cities.

New social forms have been created. There is the *kibbutz* form, in which land and property are owned in common, while the community provides for all the needs of its members. The *moshav* is an advanced form of smallholders' cooperative village. Similarly, while private initiative in industry and transport is given full scope, a considerable sector of the economic life is run by the State, the cooperative movement and the trade unions.

The Israeli Parliament (*Knesset*) consists of 120 members, elected on the basis of proportional representation. All men and women from the age of 18 upwards, regardless of creed, have the right to vote in parliamentary and local elections. Elections to Parliament are held every four years. Freedom of worship, freedom of speech, freedom of press, equality before the law, old age pension, unemployment insurance, accident insurance, holidays with pay, are the rights of every citizen.

In literature and music, in drama, science and the humanities, the re-born nation of Israel is seeking to express itself and its aspirations. Hebrew books published in 1973 were 3,368. Twenty-five daily newspapers cover every shade of political opinion, and numerous periodicals deal with cultural, economic and professional affairs. On the 25th year of its independence, Israel's population numbered 3.4 million inhabitants—about the same number as the city of Philadelphia. Yet Israel had already entered the space age, and established itself among the most advanced nations in the world in technology.

Israel has become one of the world's leading exporters of concrete, as well as a world leader in diamond cutting and polishing. Israel is a large producer and exporter of plywood, made of lumber imported from Africa. The entire country is crisscrossed by underground pipelines. The Jerusalem area gets all its water through pipes from the coastal plains. Successful attempts are being made to desalinate sea water. Water is soon to be taken from the Red Sea for both drinking and irrigation. Israel is exporting its technical know-how to Asia and Africa. Hundreds of Israeli scientists and technicians are working in other countries. Thus Israel teaches the world what a determined people can do against great odds.

On the occasion of the fifteenth anniversary of the founding of the State of Israel, David Ben-Gurion, Prime Minister of Israel, stated: "We have covered a long road since that day in May, 1948, when, in the midst of an invasion by six Arab armies, the State of Israel was resuscitated after nearly two thousand years of exile and servitude. We are building an independent nation that earns its livelihood in field and factory, in the air and on the seas, and is increasing our great Hebrew heritage.

"We have established a modern educational network, from kindergarten to university, with a school population of 650,000—as many as the number of Jews in the country on the day our independence was proclaimed. The work of our scientists and scholars, artists and musicians, has won worldwide acclaim. . . We have taken in over a million Jews from a hundred different countries . . . taught them modern skills and techniques, and introduced them to our literary and cultural heritage."

On another occasion, Ben-Gurion declared: "We have gathered up human particles and combined them into the fruitful and creative nucleus of a nation revived. In the desolate spaces of a ruined and abandoned homeland, we have built villages and towns, planted gardens and established factories. We have breathed new life into our muted and abandoned ancient language. Such a marvel is unique in the history of human culture."

According to *Hatzofeh*, published daily by the National Religious Party, new statistics, taken in 1962, prove the present existence in the State of Israel of as many as four thousand five hundred synagogues and houses of worship, as well as one hundred and eighty-five *yeshivoth* in which talmudic instruction is given to twelve thousand students. Two hundred and fifty thousand children receive a religious education. Thirty thousand teen-agers are affiliated with religious organizations.

Despite the unprecedented rise in the number of synagogues and *yeshivoth* in Israel, for most inhabitants the synagogue is not the focal center of life. While tens of thousands go to synagogue, especially for the festivals, their participation has no social basis or connotation. Many Israelis say that they feel as close to God outside the synagogue as the worshiper feels while following prescribed worship services within. Spiritual identity, they claim, has different meanings in different environments. Our survival in Israel has become a physical problem, a matter of territorial security, of defense against external forces seeking to obliterate our existence as a national entity.

After the Six-Day War, Soviet Russia and its satellites, with the exception of Rumania, severed diplomatic relations with Israel. During 1968-74 one hundred thousand Jews were allowed to immigrate to Israel after a prolonged struggle for the right to leave the USSR. On Yom Kippur, 1973, Egypt and Syria attacked Israel. After initial gains, the Syrians were driven back. The Egyptians maintained a hold along much of the Eastern bank of the Suez Canal, but Israel crossed to the Western bank, reaching the suburbs of Suez and Ismailia. A cease-fire called for peace talks, which opened in Geneva.

ASHKENAZ; SEPHARAD   אַשְׁכְּנַז; סְפָרַד

THE name *Ashkenaz* (Genesis 10:3) has since the tenth century been identified with Germany. As the German and French Jews of the medieval period formed a uniform group in culture and religious customs, they were all referred to as *Ashkenazim* in contradistinction to the *Sephardim* or Spanish-Portuguese Jews.

France was the center of the *Ashkenazim* until 1306, when the Jews were expelled from France; then Germany took its place until the middle of the sixteenth century; then Eastern Europe became the center of the Ashkenazim. From the sixteenth century onward, the differentiation between Ashkenazim and Sephardim became more elaborate.

They are the people who use *Nusah Ashkenaz*, the prayer arrangement adopted by the medieval Franco-German Jews, including certain variations described as belonging to the Polish custom (*Minhag Polin*). In the eighteenth century, the Ḥasidic movement adopted the Sephardic arrangement of prayers; hence, the Ḥasidim have been called Sephardim on many occasions.

The Ashkenazim in Eastern Europe developed an intense religious life, disseminating talmudic scholarship among the people to a degree never before surpassed in Jewish history. A high Jewish literacy existed in an illiterate non-Jewish environment. Despite the Cossack massacres in 1648-9, which wiped out hundreds of thousands of Jews in various parts of Eastern Europe, the Ashkenazim represented a throbbing, vibrant and variegated Jewish life through the generations

66

that flourished in Poland and Lithuania, Hungary and Roumania, Ukraine and Russia. Most of them spoke Yiddish until the twentieth century. Before 1933, they constituted nine-tenths of the Jews.

Ḥasidim and Mithnaggedim and followers of the Haskalah movement (*Maskilim*) presented a changing pattern of types, trends and ideologies. Before the First World War, the Ashkenazim proved themselves creative in many new fields of endeavor, such as Hebrew and Yiddish literature as well as modern art. The years between the two World Wars were filled with new spiritual developments among the Jews in Eastern Europe, not including the Jews of Soviet Russia whose fate continued to be a mystery to the rest of the Jewish people.

The vitality of the Ashkenazim still dominates wherever they are transplanted. In Israel, however, where the Oriental Jews are gaining in numbers, it is likely that the Sephardim and their patterns and customs will prevail.

ASHAMNU   אָשַׁמְנוּ

ASHAMNU (we have sinned), an alphabetical acrostic in which each letter of the Hebrew alphabet is successively utilized, is a brief confession recited responsively by reader and congregation in the *Yom Kippur* liturgy. It is accompanied by a symbolical beating of the chest as a further indication of repentance.

The confession is couched in the plural form to stress the solidarity of the people of Israel. The round number of twenty-four expressions is reached by the threefold use of the last letter of the Hebrew alphabet which consists of twenty-two characters.

USHPIZIN   אֻשְׁפִּיזִין

UPON entering the *Sukkah*, which serves as a center of hospitality during the festival of *Sukkoth*, a short prayer is recited in connection with the custom of symbolically inviting the patriarchs of the Jewish people as invisible guests (*ushpizin*).

This custom of inviting seven biblical guests (Abraham, Isaac, Jacob, Joseph, Moses, Aaron, David) rests on a kabbalistic statement to the effect that the *Shekhinah* (Divine Glory) shelters the *Sukkah* beneath its wings, and Abraham, in the company of six righteous men, enters to participate in the hospitality of the Jew who properly observes the precept of *Sukkah*. In the presence of such immortal guests, one should rejoice together with an equal number of needy people sharing his meals in the *Sukkah* (Zohar, *Emor*).

ASHER YATSAR אֲשֶׁר יָצַר

QUOTED in the Talmud (Berakhoth 60b) in the name of Abbayé, head of the school at Pumbeditha toward the end of the fourth century, the *Asher-Yatsar* benediction refers to the complexity of the human body. It is included in the preliminary morning service as a blessing over the physical health of the worshiper. It reads: "Blessed art thou . . . who hast formed man in wisdom, and created in him a system of veins and arteries . . . if but one of these be opened, or if one of those be closed, it would be impossible to exist... Blessed art thou, O Lord, who healest all creatures and doest wonders." This benediction is recited in an undertone after washing the hands following an act of responding to the call of nature.

ASHERAH אֲשֵׁרָה

ASHERAH was the Hebrew name of a Canaanite goddess, the mother of seventy gods. She appears in the Ras Shamra literature as well as in the Amarna letters. When not the name of a deity, *Asherah* refers to a wooden pole which stood at Canaanite places of worship (Exodus 34:13) and was regarded as the wooden symbol of the goddess *Asherah*, typifying fertility. The word is used in the Bible in a fluid manner, at times denoting the Canaanite fertility goddess herself, or her wooden image, or the tree or pole used as her symbol.

The regular furniture of a Canaanite shrine consisted of the altar, a stone pillar (*matsevah*), and a sacred tree (*asherah*). When the Israelites first occupied the land of Canaan, there were those who availed themselves of the Canaanite shrines for their own religious worship, adopting also the *matsevoth* and the *asheroth*. The Torah declares: "You shall not plant a sacred pole of any kind of wood beside the altar of the Lord your God; nor shall you erect a sacred pillar. . ."

Jezebel had four hundred "prophets of the *Asherah*" eating at the table of Ahab her husband, king of Israel. There was a tendency to

68

use the plurals *Ashtaroth* and *Asherim* to summarize all the various manifestations of this deity, worshiped in Palestine as the wife of Baal.

The worship of Baal, the farm god responsible for the growth of crops and the increase of flocks, was conducted in fields and on mountains, around altars flanked with sacred poles and symbolic stone pillars (מצבות), concerning which the Torah commands: "You shall demolish their altars, break their obelisks, burn up their sacred poles, and shatter the graven images of their gods" (Deuteronomy 12:3).

ASHRÉ   אַשְׁרֵי

ASHRÉ is an alphabetical hymn: its successive lines begin with the letters of the Hebrew alphabet taken in order probably as an aid to memory; it is recited daily twice in the morning service and once in the afternoon service. It consists of Psalm 145, preceded by two verses taken from two other psalms (84:5; 144:15) which contain the word *ashré* (happy) three times.

According to a talmudic statement, anyone who recites this noble psalm three times a day is assured of his share in the world to come (Berakhoth 4b). Psalm 145, calling upon all mankind to glorify God's majesty, emphasizes his providential care for all his creation: "The Lord upholds all who fall... The eyes of all look hopefully to thee... Thou openest thy hand and satisfiest every living thing... The Lord is near to all who call upon him sincerely..."

GOOD WIFE   אֵשֶׁת חַיִל

THE famous biblical poem in praise of the good wife (Proverbs 31: 10-31) has an acrostic arrangement in which the verses begin with the letters of the Hebrew alphabet in regular order. It describes the ideal Jewish housewife, who is trusted by her husband, obeyed by her servants, and admired by her people. She is kind to the poor and gentle to all. She is self-respecting and dignified. Husband and children praise her as the source of their happiness. Excerpt:

"She is worth far more than rubies... She reaches out her arms to the needy... Dignity and honor are her garb; she smiles looking at the future... She looks after her household; she never eats the bread of idleness. Her children rise and bless her, and her husband praises

69

her: Many women do worthily, but you excel them all! Charm is deceptive, and beauty is vain; only a God-fearing woman deserves praise. . ."

This is part of the liturgy for Friday evening, prior to the Sabbath meal. "Nothing in ancient literature equals this remarkable attestation to the dignity and individuality of woman" (Abrahams).

Writing in the fourteenth century, Rabbi Israel al-Nakawa seems to expatiate on this biblical poem as follows: "If a man is fortunate enough to have found a good wife, he will never miss anything. Though he may be poor, he should consider himself rich. . . A good wife is one who manages her husband's affairs correctly, helps him to the best of her ability, gives him her honest advice, and does not urge him to spend more than is necessary.

"She intelligently supervises the needs of their home, and the education of their children. . . She does not act snobbish toward her husband's family even if she happens to come from a more refined environment. . . Marriage is not a onesided affair. The man has obligations as well as the woman. . . A man should sacrifice his personal needs in order to provide more abundantly for his wife and children. Above all, he should treat his wife with love and sympathy, for she is part of him. He must never abuse her. . ." (*Menorath Hammaor*).

ATTAH BEḤARTANU אַתָּה בְחַרְתָּנוּ

IN THE festival *Amidah* prayer, the contents of the paragraph *attah b'hartanu* (thou hast chosen us) are based on many biblical passages that keep reminding the people of Israel that they have been chosen by God to be his witnesses, his kingdom of priests, a beacon of light and truth to the nations of the earth: "You are a people holy to the Lord your God, who has chosen you from all the nations on the face of the earth to be his own possession. . ." (Deuteronomy 14:2). However much they may have fallen short of their duty, however much they may have neglected to remain faithful to their sacred task, they have not been deposed from the office to which they were appointed.

Rabbi Samson Raphael Hirsch, in his *Nineteen Letters*, states that the biblical term *God's own people* does not imply Israel's exclusive possession of divine love and favor. On the contrary, it means that God has exclusive claim to Israel's service. The most cherished ideal of Israel is that of universal brotherhood.

70

Rabbi Abraham Isaac Kook describes the affection for the people of Israel as sacred, derived from a high and divine source. A wonderful vital force is hidden in the heart of each Jew. This subconscious impulse makes the Jew share the powerful yearning for the pure and uplifting light of truth and divine equity, a yearning that is bound to be realized some day in actual life. The moment a man desires to have a share in the spirit of Israel, the divine spirit enters his aspirations, even in spite of himself. . .

Güdemann, in *Das Judentum*, says that Israel's character as the chosen people does not involve the inferiority of other nations. . . "It was the *noblesse oblige* of the God-appointed worker for the entire human race."

The best thinking by various Jewish theologians on the subject of the election of Israel may well be summed up as follows. Only in Israel did the ethical monotheism exist; and wherever else it is found later on, it has been derived directly or indirectly from Israel. The term *election of Israel* expresses merely a historical fact. Israel feels itself chosen, not as a master but as a servant. It separates itself from others only for the purpose of uniting them. The people of Israel affirm not that they are better than others, but that they ought to be better.

Judaism differs from all other religions in that it is neither the creation of one great moral teacher, nor seeks to typify the moral and spiritual sublimity in a single person. The entire people must bear the stamp of holiness. The people which has given mankind its greatest prophets and psalmists must be the religious people *par excellence*.

God's selection of Israel does not imply any inequality or favoritism. Of the stars perhaps only one has planets. Of the planets, only one is at all likely to sustain organic life. Of the animals, only one species is rational. The same selective process appears also in operation in human history. The whole human history would seem to show that God prefers one person before another. There are differences of mind, body, gifts. One man appears to be more favored than his fellow, more clever, more beautiful, more prosperous. Higher attainment means higher responsibility. So, this apparent inequality and favoritism which Israel's selection implied was but designed to afford them greater opportunity for service.

A biblical expression similar in thought to the idea of a chosen Israel is to be found in I Chronicles 17:21, where king David declares: "There is none like thee, O Lord, and there is no God besides thee. . . What other nation on earth is like thy people. . ." In the passage

אתה אחד (Thou art One), which forms part of the *Amidah* for Sabbath afternoon, David's utterance is quoted along with a reference to the prophecy: "On that day the Lord shall be the only One, and his name the only One" (Zechariah 14:9). This implies that mankind will at a certain future time understand the significance of universal unity and brotherhood and be free from past errors concerning the essence of God. The election of Israel and the Oneness of God are closely related concepts which blend into one aspiration and ideal for a united mankind.

ETHROG   אֶתְרוֹג

IN HIS commentary to Leviticus 23:40, the *Ramban* (Moses Naḥmanides) points out that the tree which is called *ethrog* in Aramaic is rendered by *hadar* (הדר) in Hebrew. Thus, the biblical command concerning the use of the four species (*arba'ah minim*) during the festival of *Sukkoth*, reads: "You shall take on the first day the fruit of the *hadar* tree (*ethrog*), branches of palms (*lulav*), boughs of myrtles (*hadassim*), and willows of the brook (*aravoth*); and you shall rejoice before the Lord your God seven days." The kind of citron known as *ethrog* was a popular Jewish symbol in ancient times. It was to be found in synagogues, on coins, monuments, and graves.

The Midrash explains the symbolical significance of the four plants which are held together during part of the morning services of *Sukkoth*: The *ethrog* has both taste and fragrance; the palm has taste but no fragrance; the myrtle has fragrance but no taste; and the willow has neither taste nor fragrance. Similarly, some Jews have both learning and good deeds; some have learning but no good deeds; others have good deeds but no learning; still others have neither learning nor good deeds. Therefore, God said: Let them all be combined together, and they will atone one for the other (Leviticus Rabbah 30:12).

72

BABYLONIA

BABYLONIA, now Iraq, influenced Jewish life and culture more than any other country except Eretz Yisrael. The ancient city of Babylon and the land of Babylon are mentioned in the Bible more than two hundred times. Abraham began his journey to Canaan from the now excavated Sumerian city Ur (אוּר כַּשְׂדִים) in southern Babylonia, where "art treasures of unbelievable beauty and expert craftmanship were found in the royal cemetery," dating from 2900 to 2500 before the common era. It may have been settled some four thousand years before the common era. Its inhabitants worshiped the moon-god.

Following the destruction of the Judean Commonwealth in 586 before the common era, the so-called seventy-year exile began as the Babylonian Captivity. When Cyrus, king of Persia, permitted the Judeans fifty years afterwards to return to their homeland, the large majority remained in Babylonia, their adopted country. Under the Persian flag, the Jews of Judea and the Jews of Babylonia were politically united. They continued to live under one flag when the Persian empire was taken over by Alexander the Great. After Alexander's death, however, when his empire was divided, the Babylonian Jews were separated from the Jews of Eretz Yisrael for the first time.

After the fall of Jerusalem in the year 70, Babylonia became, and for centuries remained, a center of Jewish scholarship devoted to the study and interpretation of the Torah. Owing to the proximity of the Aramaic-Syriac districts, the Babylonian Jews adopted the Aramaic dialect, which remained the daily language of the people for more than a thousand years, until the ninth century when Arabic became the popular language. In the course of several centuries the Targum to the Bible and the Babylonian Talmud were produced in Aramaic.

The Arab conqueror of Babylonia appointed an exilarch (chief of the exiles) by the name of Bustanai, who received high privileges and became the founder of the succeeding exilarch dynasty that served as a bond of union among all Jews. The heads of the Babylonian academies, situated in Sura and Pumbeditha, were selected for their office by the prominent scholars of the period, but the selection had to be ratified by the exilarch, who was believed to be a descendant of king David. They were referred to as גְאוֹנִים (Geonim) and רָאשֵׁי יְשִׁיבָה (Rashé Yeshivah), and the academies they were heading were spoken of as גְאוֹן יַעֲקֹב (the pride of Jacob). Students from various countries flocked to the Babylonian academies during the geonic period, which ended with Rav Hai (939-1038), son of Rav Sherira Gaon.

As a mark of recognition of the incalculable influence of Babylonian Jewish scholarship, the prayer *Yekum Purkan* is still recited as part of the Sabbath morning service in behalf of "our scholars and teachers . . . in the land of Israel and in the land of Babylon, the heads of the academies and the chiefs of the captivity. . .''

INSPECTION   בְּדִיקָה

THE term *bedikah* (examination) is used in connection with the careful inspection to which a human being or an object is submitted in keeping with religious requirements. Such an inspection is applied to a slaughtered animal to ascertain that it was not suffering from a serious disease and that the knife used in the slaughtering process was in accordance with the law.

In Hebrew, a *shohet* is called *shohet u-vodek* (שו"ב). The examination of the knife is termed *bedikath ha-sakkin*. The inspection of the general condition of health of the slaughtered animal (*bedikath ha-re'ah*) is prerequisite to the permission to eat the meat.

Bedikah is applied to the questioning of witnesses (*bedikath ha-edim*) by a court, and to various matters of a religious nature.

SEARCHING FOR ḤAMETZ   בְּדִיקַת חָמֵץ

THE searching for *hametz* (leaven) occurs at the beginning of the evening of the fourteenth of *Nisan*, following an elaborate cleaning of the house in preparation for the spring festival, *Pesah*. The searching is performed symbolically by deliberately placing crumbs of bread in several parts of the house and then discovering and sweeping them into a wooden spoon which is wrapped in a cloth and burned in the morning of *erev Pesah*.

If *erev Pesah* coincides with the Sabbath, the *hametz* is searched on Thursday evening and burned on Friday morning. Crumbs of bread are deliberately placed in several parts of the house, so that the benediction which is recited prior to the search might not be in vain.

The formal search is concluded by this pronouncement: "Any kind of leaven in my possession which has escaped my notice, and which

74

I have not removed, shall be regarded as non-existent or as mere dust of the earth."

After burning the *ḥametz* on *erev Pesaḥ*, before 10 o'clock in the morning, the following statement is made: "Any kind of leaven in my possession, whether or not I have seen it, whether or not I have removed it, shall be regarded as non-existent or as mere dust of the earth."

The evil impulse (*yetser ha-ra*) is metaphorically called "leaven" in the sense of fermenting passion (Berakhoth 17a), which prevents man from doing the will of God. The Jewish moralists have therefore found deeper significance in the searching for *ḥametz*, suggesting that when the Jew removes all leaven from his home prior to the festival of freedom he should remove his evil inclination from his heart. He removes the leaven by the light of a candle; even so must he remove the evil residing in his heart by the light of his conscience, which is "the lamp of the Lord" (Proverbs 20:27).

Similarly, the *matzah*, rich in ethical symbolism, is seen as a remedy to counteract the effects of the *ḥametz*. Being a reminder of the joyous eagerness which marked the departure from Egyptian slavery to freedom, the *matzah* suggests purity of heart and implicit faith resulting in moral courage. In the Zohar, *matzah* is called celestial bread in the sense that it served as an antidote to Egyptian bondage, decay and corruption.

SHAME   בּוּשָׁה

IDEAS of what constitutes shame have changed in various climes and ages. It has been observed that there is shame that brings sin and shame that brings glory (Ben Sira 4:21). Shyness is a good trait, since it leads to fear of sin (Mekhilta on Exodus 20:17). Many precepts are fulfilled only out of shame (Baḥya ibn Pakuda). The best of all ten virtues is a sense of shame (Solomon ibn Gabirol). This explains the talmudic dictum: Jerusalem was destroyed because its inhabitants had no shame (Shabbath 119b).

On the other hand, we are told that the sin of putting another to shame in public is one of the gravest crimes. "Let a man throw himself into a blazing furnace rather than shame a fellow man in public" (Berakhoth 43b). "Shaming a fellow man in public is like shedding blood" (Bava Metzia 58b).

BEHINATH OLAM   בְּחִינַת עוֹלָם

THE poem *Behinath Olam* (Test of the World) by Rabbi Yedaiah Bedersi (1270-1340) became one of the most cherished medieval works on popular ethics. As a boy, the author of this famous book was extremely precocious: he composed a prayer of a thousand words, each word beginning with the letter מ; hence it is known as *Bakkashath ha-Memin* (בקשת הממין). On account of his eloquent writing, he was styled *Ha-Melitz* (the Rhetorician) and *Ha-Penini* (the Dispenser of Pearls). This philosopher-poet, who was born in Beziers, France, practised medicine in Perpignan and Barcelona. In addition to his *Behinath Olam*, treating of the way to attain everlasting happiness, he composed other works in poetry and prose.

He writes: The world is a tempestuous sea of immense depth and breadth, and time is a frail bridge constructed over it, the beginning of which is fastened with the cords of chaos that preceded existence... And you, son of man, against your will are you living... Even if you pride yourself with the desirable acquisitions and the abundance of possessions which you have amassed ... what will you do against the tempest of the sea and its roaring, when it rages, overflows, and passes through, so that even your house where you dwell is about to be broken? ... O sleeper, what do you mean? How did they deceive you by making you forever the possessor of the riches of such lands, while you are merely a sojourner for an appointed time in the innermost part of your house? ... Indeed, the glory of wealth does not last ... since there is no escape from the destruction of death... What pleasure is there in eighty years, since by their side is the shadow of death?... Shall ants that languish and perish, and creeping things that melt away like water, exalt themselves to reign?... (chapters 9-10).

FREE WILL   בְּחִירָה חָפְשִׁית

THE doctrine of free will, ascribing to the human will freedom and ability to choose between alternative possibilities of action in accordance with the inner motives and ideals of the agent, is often referred to as one of the basic principles of Judaism. It is consistently assumed that God has taught man what is right and what is wrong and left him to choose between the alternatives and the consequences. This

76

is clearly stated in the Torah: "I have set before you life and death, the blessing and the curse; choose life, then, that you and your descendants may live" (Deuteronomy 30:19). Rabbi Akiva declared: "Though everything is foreseen by God, yet free will is granted to man" (הכל צפוי והרשות נתונה, Avoth 3:19). That is, God's foreknowledge does not predetermine man's actions, good or bad. In matters of ethical conduct, the choice is left to man; he is capable of choosing between right and wrong and of carrying the decision into action. In the same vein are talmudic-midrashic expressions to the effect that God does not predetermine whether a man shall be righteous or wicked; that he leaves to man himself. Everything is in the hands of God except the reverence for God (Tanḥuma, *Pikkudé* 3; Berakhoth 33b).

Biblical statements that God preordains how a person shall behave in a given situation, thus interfering with man's freedom, have been variously explained by medieval Jewish thinkers. Predicting Pharaoh's attitude, God said to Moses: "I will make Pharaoh so obstinate that, despite the many signs and wonders that I will perform in the land of Egypt, he will not listen to you" (Exodus 7:3-4). Similarly, we read: "But Siḥon, king of Ḥeshbon, refused to let us pass through his land, because the Lord your God made him obstinate..." (Deuteronomy 2:30).

It has been observed that all that happens in the world must be traced to God who rules all. In some sense, all acts whether beneficent or destructive, derive their power from him. Yet, men have moral responsibility for their actions. God is never said to make a good man obstinate and stubborn of heart and mind, It is always those who are guilty of evil acts upon whom this works. Maimonides regards the Jewish doctrine of free will as the pillar of the Torah and the divine commandments, and he states: "Every person is capable of being as upright as Moses or as wicked as Jeroboam, wise or foolish, kind or cruel. The Creator does not predetermine whether a man should be good or evil, as the foolish astrologers falsely allege; otherwise, what room would be there for the entire Torah? . . ." (*Teshuvah* 5:2, 4).

It has also been suggested that true freedom is the power to do what we ought. Maimonides explains that normally a man is free, but he may forfeit his freedom if he abuses it. Pharaoh's sin consisted in his tyrannical treatment of the Israelites, which he did of his own accord and free will. He then was punished by the loss of his freedom to comply with the request of Moses. This was aimed at letting the world know that a person might forfeit his freedom of action as a punishment for abusing the human privilege of free will.

77

BITTAḤON   בִּטָּחוֹן

THE prophet emphasizes that God alone is worthy of trust. "Blessed is the man who trusts in the Lord, whose hope is the Lord. He is like a tree planted beside the water, that stretches out its roots to the stream; it fears not the heat when it comes, its leaves stay green; in the year of drought it shows no distress, and does not cease to bear fruit" (Jeremiah 17:7-8).

The concluding verses of the book of Habakkuk stress a faith in God which is independent of things material: "Though the fig tree blossom not, nor fruit be on the vines, though the produce of the olive fail, and the fields yield no fruit, though the flocks disappear from the fold and there be no herd in the stalls, yet will I rejoice in the Lord and exult in my saving God. God my lord is my strength; he makes my feet swift as those of hinds, and enables me to tread upon the heighths" (Habakkuk 3:17-19). This is the triumph of faith.

The Torah tells us that "as long as Moses kept his hands raised up, Israel prevailed, but when he let his hands rest, the Amalekites prevailed" (Exodus 17:11). Thereupon the Midrash remarks: When Moses raised his hand, Israel turned their thoughts and hearts toward their Father on high, and that led them to prevail (Mekhilta). Baḥya ibn Pakuda, in his *Ḥovoth ha-Levavoth*, declares: He who trusts in God fears no man. The concept of *bittaḥon* (trust in God) is by no means a negation of the need of self-reliance. Hillel teaches: "If I am not for myself, who is for me? ... If not now, when?" (Avoth 1:14). That is, one must be self-reliant and take swift advantage of opportunity.

BIMAH   בִּימָה

THE term *bimah* (platform) is mentioned in the Mishnah (Sotah 7:8) as the elevated stand prepared for the king in the Temple Court after the close of the Sabbatical Year, that he might sit on it and read passages from the book of Deuteronomy in the presence of the assembled throng. The word is derived from the Greek *bema* (tribune from which speakers address the public), and is otherwise known as *almemar* (from the Arabic *alminbar* for pulpit, platform). Rashi (Sukkah 51b) explains בימה by equating it with the *minbar* used in his time (כעין אלמימברא שלנו).

78

This platform should stand in the middle of the synagogue, after the pattern of Ezra's platform, from which he recited the Torah in the midst of the men and women who listened attentively from early morning until midday (Nehemiah 8:2-4). In modernized synagogues, however, it has been placed in front of the *aron ha-kodesh* (holy ark).

Several authorities have recently explained the position of the *bimah* in the following terms: According to the Jewish religion, the rabbi enjoys no special status or priestly power in the eyes of God, nor does he fulfill any sacramental function. Rather, he is a combination of spiritual leader and teacher. Therefore, the *bimah*, or reading platform, is designed so that when the rabbi leads the congregation in prayer he faces the Ark rather than the congregation. This procedure is followed during all worship. When the rabbi is offering a sermon or instruction, he uses the adjacent side of the *bimah* and faces the congregation. The early synagogue architecture of second century Palestine contained the same feature. Under the strong influence of church architecture of the nineteenth century this style of design was dropped. Our architects have reestablished this ancient practice and have integrated this feature into the present design of synagogues.

TEMPLE   בֵּית הַמִּקְדָּשׁ

THERE were three successive temples in Jerusalem, all on the same site. The first temple was begun in the fourth year of Solomon's reign and was completed in seven years and six months. After an existence of four hundred and ten years it was burned by Nebuchadnezzar of Babylonia in 586 before the common era. The second temple was begun fifty years after the destruction of the first and was completed within twenty years (516) by the exiles who returned to Judea. The third temple, referred to as that of Herod the Great, was begun twenty years before the common era and was destroyed after ninety years of existence by the Roman soldiers in the year 70.

The temple of Solomon stood within a great court as one of a series of buildings. It was an oblong structure of stone, faced by a porch, in front of which stood two bronze pillars called Yachin and Boaz. The two pillars stood about thirty-one feet high, or forty feet including base and capital. They caught the gleam of sunrise, and are said to have symbolized the pillar of fire and the pillar of cloud that are mentioned in connection with the exodus from Egypt (Exodus 13:21)

The names **Yachin and Boaz** may denote: God establishes; in him is strength.

Though beautiful and costly, Solomon's temple was smaller than Herod's temple which was erected nine centuries later on the same site. The structure, exclusive of the porch, was sixty cubits long, twenty broad, and thirty high (a cubit = about one foot and a half). It was not designed to admit worshipers, who went to the house of the Lord rather than *into* it. The whole temple area, however, was regarded as the house of the Lord. The interior walls were lined with cedar, carved, and ornamented with gold; the floor was of cypress. Treasures were stored in side chambers, between the walls of the structure and an outer wall. Before the erection of the second temple, the ark of the covenant with the cherubim disappeared from the most holy place (*devir*) in the temple of Solomon. The worshipers gathered in the court, which was divided into two parts by a wall. The court of Israel was for the men of Israel; the court of priests was for the priests. Adjoining to the court of Israel was the court of women. These three courts and the temple were encompassed in the sacred inclosure. The *hekhal* (holy place) was for the priests alone. In it stood the table for showbread, the golden altar for incense, and the *menorah* or seven-branched candelabrum. Outside the porch was the altar for burnt-offerings, and near it a brazen sea supported by metal oxen, as well as ten smaller lavers on wheels. The brazen sea was a large basin where the priests washed their hands and feet prior to ministering in the sanctuary or at the altar.

Herod's temple, built on a larger scale, was of white marble. The *devir* was twenty cubits square; the *hekhal* forty cubits long, twenty broad, and forty high. The porch was a hundred cubits high, a hundred broad, and twenty in depth. It extended on both sides beyond the temple and its side buildings by some fifteen cubits. Herod's temple is fully described by Josephus, who was thoroughly familiar with the building (*Antiquities* 15:11), and in Mishnah Middoth. The materials were brought together before the old structure was taken down. The old area was enlarged to twice its former dimensions. The temple proper, standing upon the highest ground in the inclosure, was built of great blocks of white stone. The Holy of Holies (*devir*) was separated from the Holy Place (*hekhal*) by a veil.

The remains of the last temple have disappeared. Part of the wall enclosing Herod's temple is still standing in the old section of Jerusalem. This part of the wall, known as *kothel ma'aravi* (western wall), has been regarded as sacred ever since the talmudic period; it has served as a place of endless pilgrimage for Jews from all parts of the world. Since about the tenth century, regular services were daily held close to this wall, which is popularly known as the Wailing Wall. After 1948 Jews have not been admitted to the Wailing Wall, it being in the hands of hostile Arabs.

SYNAGOGUE   בֵּית כְּנֶסֶת

THE synagogue, as a place of congregational prayer and public instruction, had come into existence long before the destruction of the Second Temple and the cessation of the sacrificial worship. It is generally assumed that the synagogue had its beginning during the Babylonian captivity in the sixth century before the common era, when the Jewish people were separated from their Temple and its centralized sacrificial system, and was brought to Judea after the restoration of Zion and the rebuilding of the Temple. It has been estimated that approximately four million Jews of the Diaspora had more than a thousand synagogues by the time the Second Temple was destroyed in the year 70. The third-century synagogue at Dura-Europos was excavated in 1932-5. Biblical scenes were painted on its walls.

During the Second Commonwealth there were hundreds of synagogues in Jerusalem and the rural towns of Eretz Yisrael. Egypt is known to have had many synagogues during the third century before the common era. The celebrated synagogue of Alexandria, Egypt, was a magnificent edifice in the form of a basilica, in which the most important crafts were represented—goldsmiths, silversmiths, weavers—each having an appointed place. Inscriptional evidence has revealed some twelve synagogues in ancient Rome.

Throughout its long history, the synagogue has been the spiritual home of the Jew; hence the various titles by which it has been known: house of prayer, house of study, assembly house, people's house, little sanctuary. The synagogue has been the spiritual home of the Jew in view of its many functions. Not only was it a place for divine service, but also a center for study, for *tsedakah* and social work. In the olden days, strangers were fed there; hence the custom of reciting the *Kiddush* in the synagogue as part of the Sabbath and festival evening services, except the first two nights of *Pesah* when strangers used to be given hospitality in private homes instead. Synagogues came to

81

be schools of every kind of virtue; hence the name *Shul* (school) in the Yiddish vernacular.

The talmudic sages praised congregational worship in the most elaborate terms: "A man's prayer is heard only in the synagogue. . . If a man is accustomed to attend synagogue and fails to come one day, God makes inquiry about him. . . When a man leaves the synagogue, he should not march with hasty steps; but when he goes to the synagogue, it is right to run" (Berakhoth 6a-b). The verse, "I offer my prayer to thee, O Lord, at a time of grace" (Psalm 69:14) is interpreted to mean the time of public worship (Berakhoth 8b).

Since the synagogue fulfills an educational purpose, as well as a devotional function, instruction in the Torah forms a major part of congregational worship. The reading from the Torah, accompanied by interpretation of passages read, has come to be as much a part of worship as the prayers and meditations. The synagogal liturgy has developed in a way that enables every devout worshiper to become familiar with the various forms of Jewish learning and religious expression. The ideals of Judaism are always brought afresh to the attention of the worshiper by means of the *Siddur* which, in addition to its purely liturgical contents, is replete with vital Jewish instruction.

It has been pointed out that no human institution has a longer continuous history than the synagogue, and none has done more for the uplifting of the human race. With the synagogue began a new type of worship in the history of humanity, the type of congregational worship. In all their long history the Jewish people have done scarcely anything more wonderful than to create the synagogue (Herford). "Judaism gave to the world not only the fundamental ideas of the great monotheistic religions but the institutional forms in which they have perpetuated and propagated themselves" (Moore).

BETH MIDRASH   בֵּית מִדְרָשׁ

SERVING the double function of study and prayer, the *beth ha-midrash* (house of learning) was designed primarily for the study of talmudic literature. The terms *kloiz* (from claustrum, an enclosed place) and *beth ha-midrash* were used interchangeably in East-European countries. Students of various age levels would, before and after the daily worship services, sit in the *kloiz* or *beth ha-midrash* and study mostly alone. When they did not understand one of the complex talmudic problems, they would ask elder students to explain it for them. They repeated each page at least six times and practically memorized the actual talmudic text. They learned the exact medieval commentaries and used large volumes containing notes about these commentaries.

In the *beth ha-midrash*, the sacred books were greatly respected. Nobody would sit on a bench if there was a book anywhere on it. A book that fell to the ground was picked up and kissed. To put other things on top of a book was a sin. When a book was so badly torn that it could not be used, the caretaker took it to the cemetery and buried it. Even the smallest scrap of paper must not be left lying around on the floor if it has Hebrew characters printed on it, letters that spell out a sacred text.

Students at the *beth ha-midrash* would never leave books open except when actually in use. If obliged to go away for a short while, a student would cover the open book with a cloth. The parchment scroll of the Torah, which is hand-written, is to this day held in even greater respect than printed books. The young students (*bahurim*) would continue their studies throughout the day and into the night. From the fourteenth century, *bahurim* chiefly signified rabbinic students, often referred to as *yeshivah bahurim* or *beth ha-midrash bahurim*.

The *yeshivah*, as a school devoted to the study of the Talmud, is a direct continuation of the ancient academies in Eretz Yisrael and Babylonia. These were transplanted to various parts of the world, including the American continent. World War II demolished East-Eurpeoan *yeshivoth*, some of which have been revived in Israel and America.

Varied viewpoints are now expressed in the relationship between worship and study within the synagogue. Followers of recent Jewish trends assert that a synagogue should be primarily a house of study (*beth midrash*) and only secondarily a house of worship (*beth tefillah*). Torah study in our day, they say, has to be far more comprehensive in scope of knowledge, more in keeping with reality, and cognizant of human deeds. Stricter adherents of the Jewish tradition insist that Jewish study and worship are synonymous and inseparable. Jewish tradition has always considered study of the Torah literature as a mode of worship; both of them express a devotion to the divine precepts. We need both, they say, prayer and study. If we de-emphasize prayer, we are in great danger of losing out in both areas. Nothing can be accomplished for adult Jewish education by doing away with the devotional aspect of *Talmud Torah*, the study of Torah, which has been described as excelling all other *mitzvoth* (תלמוד תורה כנגד כולם).

CEMETERY   בֵּית עוֹלָם

THE name *cemetery* is derived from the Greek and signifies a sleeping chamber or the place where the dead sleep. Formerly, the cemetery consisted of catacombs, subterranean galleries provided with side recesses for tombs. Jewish catacombs have been discovered in Egypt, Rome, and especially in Beth Shearim, Israel, where there was a central burial place between the second and fourth centuries of the common era.

Hundreds of rock-tombs have been revealed in Beth Shearim from the time the excavations began in 1936. The ancient town became the spiritual center of the Jewish people in the year 170, when Rabbi Yehudah ha-Nasi transferred his academy and Sanhedrin from Sephoris. In Sanhedrin 32b, the expression is found: אחר רבי לבית שערים (follow up Rabbi Yehudah ha-Nasi to Beth Shearim). He was buried in Beth Shearim, a burial-place for Jews from both the Diaspora and Eretz Yisrael.

The inscriptions of the catacombs are in Greek and Latin, with a minority in Hebrew. Among the various Jewish symbols included in the decorations, the seven-branched *menorah* was used most frequently in the Jewish cemeteries. The term מערתא (burial-cave), in Bava Bathra 58a, refers to the Jewish system of catacombs.

After the Bar Kokhba defeat in 132, when the ancient Jewish cemetery on the Mount of Olives, east of Jerusalem, became closed to the Jewish people, the catacombs at Beth Shearim became the new burial center for devout Jews. In talmudic-midrashic sources there is no reference to the recently-discovered subterranean burial galleries beneath a mountain at Beth Shearim, in the Valley of Jezreel, with pillared vaults of rock and side recesses for tombs, similar to those found in Rome, where six separate systems of Jewish catacombs of the classical period have become known. A Greek inscription in bold letters, carved near the entrance of one of the Beth Shearim catacombs, reads: "Good luck on your resurrection."

It has been noted that the tide of Hellenization reached its peak during the period of Beth Shearim, between the second and fourth centuries, when the Roman empire was saturated with Greek feeling. This explains the reliefs of animals and plants and human faces, with rich mosaics, in designs essentially Greek, that have been revealed in the Beth Shearim catacombs. According to a tannaitic report, Rabbi

84

Yehudah ha-Nasi declared: "Why speak Aramaic in Eretz Yisrael? One should speak either Hebrew or Greek" (Bava Kamma 82b—באָרץ ישראל לשון סורסי למה? או לשון הקודש או לשון יונית).

The euphemistic names *beth ḥayyim* (house of life), *beth 'olam* (house of eternity) and *beth 'almin* (=*beth 'olam*) allude to various biblical and post-biblical expressions. The name בית קברות (house of graves) occurs in the Bible (Nehemiah 2:3). We are told in the Talmud that cemeteries must not be treated with disrespect (Megillah 29a). "Walk reverently in a cemetery, lest the deceased will say: Tomorrow they will join us, and today they mock us" (Berakhoth 18a). For reasons of priestly cleanliness, *kohanim* have been forbidden to enter a cemetery. Graves are customarily visited during the month preceding *Rosh Hashanah* and upon anniversaries of the death of close relatives.

FIRST BORN   בְּכוֹרִים

The Hebrew term *bekhor* is used of firstborn men and firstling animals alike. The eldest son, to whom special value was attached during the biblical period, received the right to inherit a double portion of his father's estate as well as family leadership. One of the important reasons for this distinction was the fact that God, when liberating the people from Egyptian slavery, had preserved the firstborn of the Israelites from the tenth and last plague.

The sanctification of every firstborn was (Exodus 13:2) designed to keep the memory of the great liberation fresh in every home. In commemoration of the exodus from Egypt and the miraculous deliverance of their forefathers, *Erev Pesaḥ* is observed as a fast by the firstborn, known as תענית בכורים (*ta'anith bekhorim*).

Talmudic tradition reports that the firstborn males acted as officiating priests in the wilderness until the task was turned over to the tribe of Levi after the erection of the portable sanctuary known as the *Mishkan* or Tabernacle. The observance of *pidyon ha-ben* (redemption of the firstborn son) occurs on the thirty-first day after the child's birth, if he is the firstborn of his mother; he is redeemed by the payment of the equivalent of five shekels to a *kohen*, descendant of the tribe of Levi, chosen for the service in the sanctuary in place of the firstborn of all the tribes. The *sacred shekel* (שקל הקודש) had twice the value of the common silver shekel, known as *sela* (סלע) in post-biblical Hebrew and slightly larger than an American half-dollar.

FIRST FRUITS   בִּכּוּרִים

THE law of *bikkurim* is stated in the Torah as follows: "When you
have come into the land which the Lord your God is giving you as a
heritage, and have occupied it and settled in it, you shall take some
first fruits of the various products of the soil which you harvest . . .
and put them in a basket; you shall go to the place which the Lord
your God chooses to make his name to dwell there. Then you shall
come to the priest in office at that time and say to him: Today I acknowledge to the Lord my God that I have indeed come to the land
which he solemnly promised to our fathers to give us. The priest shall
then receive the basket from you and shall set it in front of the altar
of the Lord your God. . ." (Deuteronomy 26:1-11).

The word מראשית (some of the firstfruits) intimates, according to
tradition, that not all fruits were subject to this enactment. By means
of an analogy it is deduced that the law of *bikkurim* applied only to
the seven species which were special products of Eretz Yisrael. They
are mentioned in Deuteronomy 8:8 as typical of the fruitfulness of
the land—wheat, barley, vines, figs, pomegranates, olives, and date-
honey. In the sixteenth-century commentary by Rabbi Obadiah Sforno
it is pointed out that the seven species (שבעת המינים) are named in
the Torah in order to indicate that Eretz Yisrael is distinguished by
the abundant supply of food essential to man's subsistence, and that
its soil yields not only essential food but also delicacies.

The Mishnah, describing *bikkurim*, informs us that "when a man
goes down to his field and sees (for the first time) a ripe fig or a ripe
cluster of grapes or a ripe pomegranate, he binds it round with reed-
grass and says: These are *bikkurim*. . . Those who lived near Jerusalem brought fresh figs and grapes, and those who lived far off brought
dried figs and raisins. Before them went the ox, having its horns over-
laid with gold and a wreath of olive-leaves on its head. The flute was
played before them until they came close to Jerusalem, when they
sent messengers before them. Priestly and Levitical authorities of the
Temple came forth to meet them. . . They were greeted by all, saying: Brethren, men of such-and-such a place, you are welcome! . . ."
(Bikkurim 3:1-3). Mishnah Bikkurim, the eleventh and final tractate
in *Seder Zera'im*, consists of three chapters concerning the offering of
firstfruits. Its vivid description of the *bikkurim* ceremony is well
known and often quoted.

86

BE NOT DESTRUCTIVE   בַּל תַּשְׁחִית

THE Torah forbids the people of Israel to cut down the fruit trees surrounding the town of an enemy against whom they fight: "You must never destroy its trees . . . you may eat of them, but you shall not cut them down" (Deuteronomy 20:19).

This precept, referred to as בל תשחית, has served as the basis of the talmudic law which prohibits willful destruction of natural resources, or any kind of vandalism, even if the act is committed by the owners of the property themselves.

According to this law, which is based on human sympathy, one must not destroy anything that may prove useful to others. The person who tears his clothes or smashes his household furniture in a fit of anger, or squanders his money, is likened to an idolater (Shabbath 105b). "Just as one must be careful not to destroy or injure his own body . . . so he must be careful not to destroy or injure his own property. Whoever breaks a utensil . . . or spoils any other thing that is fit for human enjoyment breaks the command: You shall not destroy" (*Shulḥan Arukh* by Rabbi Shneour Zalman of Liadi).

Similarly, according to the Jewish doctrine, he who commits suicide is a murderer, since life is not man's own possession, but a trust from the Creator of all the living.

NUMBERS   בְּמִדְבַּר

NUMBERS, the fourth book of the Torah, is so named on account of the census of the people in chapters one, three, four, and twenty-six. The first census was taken in the second year, the other in the fortieth year of the exodus from Egypt.

In Hebrew, the book is known as במדבר (in the wilderness) from the fifth word of the opening verse. Its thirty-nine chapters consist of narratives, laws and poems that concern Israel's forty years of wanderings in the wilderness. The book records the expedition of the twelve spies into the land of Canaan, the rebellion of Korah against Moses and Aaron, the striking of the rock, and the story of Balaam.

Korah the Levite charged that the priesthood rightfully belonged to members of any Levite family, not simply to the house of Aaron. Dathan and Abiram, of the tribe of Reuben, rebelled against the civil authority of Moses, charging that the leadership rightfully belonged to the descendants of Jacob's eldest son, Reuben.

Balak vainly hoped to destroy Israel by having recourse to black magic, and sent for the magician Balaam to come and curse them. But the powers of darkness could not stop the victorious march of Israel. Balaam could say only what was given him to say. Therefore, he had to bless the people of Israel.

The commanding personality of Moses is seen throughout this book, which portrays his faithfulness to God and devotion to the people of Israel despite their waywardness. Excerpts:

"The people of Israel complained bitterly to Moses: Would that we had meat for food! We remember the fish we used to eat without cost in Egypt, and the cucumbers, the melons, the leeks, the onions, and the garlic. But now we are famished; we see nothing before us but this manna.

"The manna was like coriander seed; the people would gather it up, grind it between millstones or pound it in a mortar, then cook it in a pot and make it into loaves which tasted like cakes made with oil. At night, when dew fell upon the camp, the manna also fell.

"Moses heard the people weeping, and he said to the Lord: Thou layest the burden of all these people upon me. I cannot carry all their burdens by myself. Where can I get meat to give them? Pray kill me at once, and let me no longer face their distress.

"Then the Lord told Moses to say to the people: Tomorrow you shall have meat to eat; you will eat it . . . for a whole month, until you cannot bear the smell of it, until you loathe it. For you have spurned the Lord who is in your midst, and you have wailed. . .

"Then there arose a wind sent by the Lord, that drove in quail from the sea and brought them down over the camp site. All that day and night, and all the next day, the people gathered in the quail. As the people were devouring this food, the Lord struck them with a terrible plague. So that place was named *Graves of Greed*, because it was there that the greedy people were buried."

HIGH PLACE   בָּמָה

THE term *bamah* (high place) was applied to a tribal or village place of worship. Its basic meaning was an elevated platform on which cultic objects were placed by Canaanites who pinned their faith to

88

Baal and Asherah, the gods associated with rain, crops and fertility. The *bamoth* were usually on hilltops; they had, as a rule, a stele or pillar of stone (*matsevah*) as the seat of the local god Baal and a wooden pole or tree (*asherah*), itself an object of worship.

This worship of Baal and Astarte was denounced fiercely by the prophets as "idols on every high hill" (Ezekiel 6:13). During the period of the Judges, altars were frequently erected on rocks and under shady trees in imitation of the Canaanite immoral cultic rites. King Hezekiah was praised lavishly for having removed high places: "He did what was right in the eyes of the Lord. . . He removed the shrines, broke the obelisks, and cut down the sacred poles" (II Kings 18:3-4). This was the first attempt to put an end to the provincial shrines which had co-existed with the Temple at Jerusalem as seats of worship from the time of Solomon.

The purpose of the law forbidding high places was to prevent the people from worshiping at idolatrous shrines used by the ancient Canaanites, to guard against schism and corruption, and to secure the support of a national sanctuary. The worship of the Lord at other altars was permitted only during the time when the Temple had not yet been erected. No high places are mentioned as having existed during the period of the Second Temple.

BAMMEH MADLIKIN   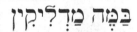

THE second chapter of Mishnah Shabbath, beginning with the phrase *bammeh madlikin* (with what may the Sabbath lamp be lighted), was inserted as part of the Sabbath-eve services in post-talmudic times. Various reasons are given for the inclusion of this chapter, which deals with the oils and wicks appropriate for the Sabbath lights.

Rashi, in his *Siddur* (page 243), says that *bammeh madlikin* is recited by the congregation *after* the Sabbath-eve service in order to enable the late-comers to complete their prayers and leave the synagogue together with the rest of the worshipers. The synagogues were often located outside the precincts of the city, since the rulers did not tolerate Jewish worship within the confines of their municipalities, and it was dangerous to walk home alone at night.

By prolonging the Sabbath-eve service, which was far better attended than weekday services, the late-comers were given an opportunity to join the others on their way home. Accordingly, *bammeh madlikin* is omitted when Sabbath-eve coincides with a festival, when late-coming is not likely to occur.

Rabbi Isaiah Horowitz, known as *Sheloh* from the initials of his chief work (1556-1630), and Rabbi Jacob Emden, known as *Ya'avetz* (1697-1776), in their respective editions of the Prayerbook, are of the opinion that *bammeh madlikin* should be recited before welcoming the Sabbath. In the current editions, it is found between *Kabbalath Shabbath* and *Ma'ariv*, as a compromise between two divergent opinions.

REBELLIOUS SON   בֵּן סוֹרֵר וּמוֹרֶה

THE severe punishment of an incorrigible son described in the Torah (Deuteronomy 21:18-21) was never administered, according to a tannaitic statement which reads: בן סורר ומורה לא היה ולא עתיד להיות (Sanhedrin 71a). The biblical law merely stresses the community's interest in the proper upbringing of children; when the authority of the parents is powerless, that of the state must be exercised.

The biblical law reads: "If a man has a stubborn and unruly son who will not listen to his father or mother, and will not obey them even though they chastise him, his father and mother shall have him apprehended and brought out to the elders at the gate of his home town, where they shall say to the city elders: This son of ours is stubborn and unruly; he does not listen to us; he is a glutton and a drunkard. Then all the men of his town shall stone him to death; thus shall you purge evil from your midst, and all Israel, on hearing of it, shall fear." The gate was the forum for the administration of justice.

The Mishnah enumerates several conditions upon which this condemnation depends: "If his father was willing to accuse him but his mother was not, or if his father was not willing but his mother was, he cannot be condemned as a stubborn and rebellious son... If his parents were not compatible, he cannot be condemned... If either of them was maimed in hand or lame or dumb or blind or deaf, he cannot be condemned... They must warn him, and scourge him before three judges. If he again behaves evilly, he must be tried before twenty-three judges. He may only be stoned if the first three judges are there..." (Sanhedrin 8:4).

The law of a rebellious son applies to one beyond the age of thirteen years and one day, exhibiting signs of puberty, when he already possesses a mind of his own but is still under the control of his parents, who are without defect so that they can fully exercise their authority under normal conditions. When the entire blame cannot be placed on the son, because of disagreement between his parents who are not fit for each other, he is left unpunished. Hence, the Talmud says that the law of a rebellious son, which can never be carried out on account of the numerous strictures, was imposed merely for the purpose of receiving a reward through studying it (דרוש וקבל שכר).

BEN SIRA   בֶּן סִירָא

THE book of Ben Sira, known as Ecclesiasticus, was written in Hebrew by one named Joshua Ben Sira who lived in Jerusalem before the period of the Maccabees. Didactic in character and blending worldly with spiritual counsel, it speaks slightingly of illiterate people. Ben Sira has much to say of the values of social relations and the benefits of friendship.

In the prologue, Ben Sira's grandson tells us that he translated the book into Greek at a date corresponding to 132 before the common era. About two-thirds of the Hebrew text was recovered in manuscripts found in the famous *Genizah* of Cairo, Egypt, where it had been customary for many centuries to deposit old Hebrew books. Ben Sira belongs to the post-biblical literature known as Apocrypha, *Genuzim* (hidden away books) or *Sefarim Ḥitzonim* (outside books), that is, books excluded from the Hebrew Bible.

The book of Ben Sira, which contains fifty-one chapters, was written by a man who had the gift for clear and forceful expression. It reminds us of the biblical books of Proverbs, Ecclesiastes and Job. Here are a few excerpts taken at random:

"A man who talks excessively is detested. Healthy sleep results from moderation in eating. A fool raises his voice when he laughs. A quiet, silent wife is a gift from the Lord. Envy and anger shorten a man's life. Worry makes a man old before his time. Speak concisely; say much in a few words.

"The man who fears the Lord will fear no man. Be on your guard against advisers. Conceal your plans from those who envy you. When you are at the table, do not be the first to help yourself. Do not follow your impulses, but curb your longing. Do not forsake an old friend, for a new one is not equal to him. A new friend is new wine; when it grows old, you will enjoy drinking it.

"Flee from sin as you would from a serpent, for like a serpent it will bite you if you go near it. Do not indulge in too much luxury, or be tied down by its costs."

NOACHIAN PRECEPTS   בְּנֵי נֹחַ, שֶׁבַע מִצְוֹת

THE term *Noachians* (בני נח) denotes all the descendants of Noah, who survived the Flood along with his closest kin. The seven Noachian precepts, distinct from the laws obligatory on the people of Israel alone, are binding on all human beings. They prohibit: 1) idolatry, 2) murder, 3) theft, 4) blasphemy, 5) incest, 6) eating the flesh of a living animal; and they include the duty of 7) promotion of justice. All non-Jews who observe these laws, upon which all civilized society depends, are deemed worthy of life in the world to come.

The prohibition of cruelty to animals is reminiscent of biblical laws forbidding plowing with a mixed team of an ox and a donkey or taking a mother bird and her young from the nest at the same time or muzzling an animal during the threshing season or slaughtering a cow and her calf on the same day (Deuteronomy 20:10; 22:6; 25:4; Leviticus 22:28). Man's obligation not to inflict cruelty upon animals is rooted in the recognition that they represent the handiwork of the Creator.

The talmudic statement concerning the seven Noachian precepts reads: שבע מצות נצטוו בני נח: דינין וברכת השם, עכו"ם, גילוי עריות ושפיכות דמים וגזל ואבר מן החי (Sanhedrin 56a). By observing these as a minimum, a non-Jew settling among Jews might enjoy the privileges and responsibilities of a full-fledged proselyte. Hence, there is no imperative need for a non-Jew to adopt the Jewish faith in order to merit salvation.

The attitude of Judaism to conversions is based on the conception of the seven precepts that were imposed on the descendants of Noah, or the entire human species. "Judaism was a missionary religion, but its missionary activity was of a restricted character. No organized attempt was made by official Judaism to propagate the observance of the practices of the Jewish religion which were never intended for any other people than Israel by virtue of her priestly calling. All that Judaism was concerned with in its missionary work was to substitute the religion of humanity, communicated to Noah... [Then] Judaism withdrew from the missionary field and was satisfied to leave the task

92

of spreading the religion of humanity to her daughter faiths . . . [that] shared in common many truths, religious and moral, with the mother faith. . ." (Epstein, *Judaism*).

The Noachian precepts represent a theory of universal religion, emphasizing good actions rather than right belief, ethical living rather than credal adherence; they require only loyalty to a basic code of ethical conduct, and rest upon the recognition of a divine Creator.

BIKKUR ḤOLIM   בִּקוּר חוֹלִים

BIKKUR ḤOLIM (visiting the sick) is counted in the Talmud among the religious duties (*mitzvoth*) to which no limit has been prescribed (Shabbath 127a). God himself is said to have visited Abraham during his illness. The rabbis of the Talmud found reference to this visit in Genesis 18:1, where we are told that the Lord appeared to Abraham soon after his circumcision. Visiting the sick is, according to the Talmud, one of the precepts for the fulfillment of which a man is rewarded in both this world and the world to come. Ben Sira counsels: "Do not hesitate to visit a man who is sick. . ." (7:35).

According to a talmudic statement, whoever visits a sick person helps him to recover: כל המבקר את החולה גורם לו שיחיה (Nedarim 40a). The purpose of visiting the sick is to cheer them by pleasant conversation and good advice, by rendering them any service and inspiring them with hope.

In some communities there is a special *Bikkur Ḥolim Society*, whose function it is to visit those who are confined to the house by illness. *Bikkur Ḥolim* is a term which is also used to denote Jewish hospitals and homes for the aged.

In the *Shemoneh Esreh*, the nineteen benedictions which are recited three times daily, there is a prayer for the sick, known as רפואה (healing). It reads: "Heal us, O Lord, and we shall be healed; save us, and we shall be saved. . . Grant a perfect healing to all our wounds, for thou art a faithful and merciful God, King and Healer. . ."

In the anonymous ethical work *Orḥoth Ḥayyim* (Paths of Life), which has been attributed to Rabbi Eliezer ben Isaac the Great of eleventh-century Germany, we read: "Visit the sick and lighten their suffering. Pray for them and leave. Do not stay long, for you may inflict upon them additional discomfort. And when you visit a sick person, enter the room cheerfully."

93

BAR MITZVAH   בַּר מִצְוָה

THE Hebrew term *Bar Mitzvah* is applied in the Talmud to every adult Jew in the sense of *man of duty*. Similarly, the term בר דעת is the counterpart of איש דעת and signifies *a sensible man*. Like the Hebrew word בן, the Aramaic equivalent בר denotes age, membership in a definite class, or the possession of some quality. Hence, the popular rendering of *Bar Mitzvah* "a son of the commandment" is erroneous and misleading.

Many have been led to think that the concept *Bar Mitzvah* applies only to a youngster of thirteen. At the age of thirteen, the Jewish boy reaches his religious maturity and is held thereafter personally responsible for his religious acts, that is, he remains a *Bar Mitzvah*, man of duty, for the rest of his life. This entrance into religious manhood is expressed by extending to the boy the adult privilege of reading the Torah, or being called up to the Torah, the first Sabbath after his thirteenth birthday. From this time on the boy is regarded as an adult in all religious respects: he uses *Tefillin* in weekday prayers each morning, and is counted as one of the ten men necessary for *minyan*, the minimum required for congregational worship service.

The purpose of the boy's public reading of the Torah and the Haftarah is to make him feel a full-fledged adult who is obliged to obey what is written in the Torah and the Prophets. Rabbi Judah ben Tema of the second century expressed this in the famous maxim: בן שלש עשרה למצוות (Avoth 5:24), that is, on each boy of thirteen falls the responsibility of fulfilling the commandments.

It has been conjectured that the *Bar Mitzvah* celebrations were introduced some six centuries ago, though scholars think that the beginnings of the custom date back to an earlier age. It is customary that the father of a *Bar Mitzvah* pronounces the following blessing: ברוך שפטרני מענשו של זה (Blessed be he who has relieved me of the responsibility of this boy). This is a manner of expressing the parent's joy that his son has attained an age when he can independently distinguish between right and wrong.

In 1963, Rabbi Yitzḥak Nissim of Israel was asked for a ruling concerning Bath Mitzvah celebrations in honor of twelve-year-old girls. He replied: "The reason *Bar Mitzvah* occasions are celebrated in all Jewish communities is that as soon as the boys of thirteen are initiated into the observance of *mitzvoth*, they assume the immediate *mitzvah*

94

of putting on *tefillin* on weekday mornings. Girls, however, do not have an immediate special precept to perform when they reach religious maturity at twelve. But this does not imply that they should not rejoice on the day they enter the world of *mitzvoth*. On the contrary, it is good and proper to celebrate this occasion at home in the company of friends and relatives, and with the participation of a rabbi who should describe the virtues of *Torah* and *mitzvoth*. It is fitting that the girl should wear a new dress and recite the blessing *shehehe-yanu* and deliver a short address on the significance of the day. Her father should then recite the blessing ברוך שפטרני.

Rabbi Yitzḥak Nissim quoted Rabbi Yaakov Yeḥiel Weinberg, one of the leading talmudic authorities, stating: "There are those who are opposed to *Bath Mitzvah* celebrations. . . In the past it was not necessary to give girls a Jewish education; every Jewish home was filled with Torah and reverence for God. An immense change has taken place in our time; the influence of the street removes from the hearts of boys and girls the enthusiastic attachment to Judaism. . . The discrimination we make between the boys and the girls on reaching puberty impinges heavily on the feelings of the adolescent girl, who has in other fields reached full equality." A substantial number of orthodox congregations in America have introduced the observance of *Bath Mitzvath* occasions.

GENESIS   בְּרֵאשִׁית

THE book of Genesis, the first of the Bible, contains the early history of mankind, describes the lives of the forefathers of Israel, and ends with the death of Joseph in Egypt. The narratives in Genesis, the first of the Five Books of Moses, have been the vehicle for countless ethical and spiritual lessons in talmudic-midrashic literature.

Throughout the book there is a noble conception of man, what he was created to be and what he has the power to become. The statement that man was made in the image of God strikes the keynote of all that follows. The moral grandeur and depth of meaning, as well as the simplicity and sublimity of the story of creation, are universally recognized. All men are descended from Adam and Eve, all men are related; hence the unity of all mankind. This is said to be the most fundamental teaching in the entire Bible: *all* men are created in the image of God.

95

Like the rest of the Torah, Genesis is primarily a book of instruction, conveying the idea that the Creator of the universe guides those who trust in him. Israel's ancestors are represented here in their family relations, as husband and wife, parent and child, brother and sister. Great moral truths are woven into the texture of the narratives, which illustrate the qualities of truthfulness, grace and loveliness with a wealth of instructive example.

There is no book in the Bible more impressive than Genesis. Its charm and power are inherent in the personal portraits of Abraham, Jacob and Joseph, breathing and alive in the freshness of the world's dawn. Its language is adapted to the understanding of young and old alike. Children can grasp the outline of its story, while erudite scholars continue to discover fresh meanings in it.

Toward the end of the book of Genesis, Joseph sums up the great lesson of his career to the effect that God brings good out of evil, though evil is not to be done in order that good may come. Hence, Rabbi Isaac Abravanel (1437-1508) notes that since the sale of Joseph was the work of divine providence, Joseph's brothers were not deserving punishment; on the contrary, Joseph repeatedly declares that whatever they did was done unwittingly in accordance with the design of divine providence. Excerpt:

"Joseph's brothers thought: Perhaps Joseph will hate us and pay us back for all the evil we did to him. So they sent this message to Joseph: Before he died, your father bade us to ask you to forgive the sin of your brothers and the evil they did to you... But Joseph said to his brothers: Have no fear. Am I in the place of God? You meant to do me evil, but God meant good to come of it, in order that many people should be kept alive. So do not fear; I will provide for you and your little ones. Thus he reassured them and comforted them... When he was about to die, Joseph said to his brothers: I am about to die; but God will surely remember you and bring you out of this land to the land that he promised to Abraham, Isaac and Jacob. When God will remember you, you shall carry up my bones from here."

The name *Genesis*, meaning *origin*, is borrowed from the Septuagint, the Greek version of the Bible, prepared by a group of seventy-two Jewish scholars at Alexandria, Egygt, in the third century before the common era. The Jewish name בראשית is the first Hebrew word (*Bereshith*) in the opening sentence of the Torah. *Bereshith* is also the name of the first of the fifty-four *sidroth*, weekly Torah readings, into which the five books of Moses are divided.

96

BARUKH HU   בָּרוּךְ הוּא

THE customary response ברוך הוא וברוך שמו (blessed be he and blessed be his name) is used upon hearing the benedictory formula ברוך אתה ה׳ (blessed art thou, O Lord). It is applied to the nineteen blessings of the *Shemoneh Esreh* prayer as well as the morning benedictions (ברכות השחר) when recited aloud by the cantor or reader. *Amen* is the concluding response for each of these blessings. The response "blessed be he and blessed be his name" is based on Deuteronomy 32:3.

When, however, one hears the *Kiddush* or the *Havdalah* recited, he is not to use the response "blessed be he and blessed be his name," because this would mean an interruption of benedictions recited on his own behalf. Similarly, the blessings pronounced over the public reading of the *Megillah* on *Purim*, and over the sounding of the *shofar* on *Rosh Hashanah*, do not require the response ברוך הוא וברוך שמו; neither do the blessings before and after the *Shema*, and the blessings over food and the like (ברכות הנהנין).

BLESSED ... FOREVER   בָּרוּךְ ... לְעוֹלָם

THIS passage, which precedes the *Shemoneh Esreh* prayer of the daily evening service, is composed of biblical verses containing the divine name eighteen times, a number corresponding to the eighteen benedictions of the weekday *Shemoneh Esreh*.

This mosaic of biblical verses, connected by similarity of ideas and identity of words, was inserted in the weekday *Ma'ariv* service to take the place of the *Shemoneh Esreh* during the talmudic period when the *Amidah* was still regarded as optional in the evening service. According to Maimonides (Tefillah 1:6), the *Shemoneh Esreh* in the *Ma'ariv* became an obligation as a result of common custom.

The synagogues were often located outside the precincts of the city, since the rulers did not tolerate Jewish worship within the confines of their municipalities. It was dangerous to walk home from the synagogue at night. The people who were afraid to remain till after the *Ma'ariv* would recite this collection of nineteen verses in place of the *Shemoneh Esreh*. When the *Shemoneh Esreh* is replaced by the Sabbath or festival *Amidah*, these verses are omitted.

97

BARUKH SHE-AMAR   בָּרוּךְ שֶׁאָמַר

BARUKH SHE-AMAR (blessed be he who spoke) are the initial words of the hymn which introduces the biblical selections, *pesuké d'zimra*, in the daily morning service. The paragraph is composed of eighty-seven words, a number suggesting the numerical value of the word פז (refined gold), according to medieval sources which include the *Rokeah*, the *Tur*, and the *Hekhaloth Gedoloth*.

Though it is not mentioned in the Talmud, it is known to be of ancient origin. It is included in the ninth century *Siddur* of Rav Amram Gaon. There are indications that it was read responsively by reader and congregation.

The word *barukh* (blessed) is repeated in this benediction thirteen times, reminiscent of the numerical value of the significant word אחד (One). The phrase ברוך הוא (blessed be he) was perhaps a responsive refrain repeated by the worshipers after each clause recited by the reader.

BARUKH SHEM KEVOD   בָּרוּךְ שֵׁם כְּבוֹד

THE expression *blessed be his glorious majesty forever and ever*, accompanying the opening verse of the *Shema*, is traditionally attributed to Jacob. The Talmud (Pesaḥim 56b) relates that when Jacob, on his deathbed, asked all his sons whether they were honest and sincere in the belief that the Lord is One, they replied in unison: "Hear, O Israel our father, the Lord is our God, the Lord is One. Just as there is only One in your heart, so in our heart there is only One." Immediately, Jacob exclaimed: *Blessed be his glorious majesty forever and ever*.

This response, therefore, is recited in an undertone whenever the *Shema* is read throughout the year, except *Yom Kippur*, to set it apart from the text taken from the Torah (Deuteronomy 6:4-9). On *Yom Kippur*, however, it is recited aloud because, according to Yoma 6:2, it was used in the Temple during the *Yom Kippur* service as the people's loud response upon hearing the divine name pronounced by the high priest. Another reason has been suggested to the effect that the angels in heaven chant this response aloud, and on *Yom Kippur* when the people are detached from food and sensual pleasures they figuratively assume angelic traits.

BRAH DODI

BRAH DODI   בְּרַח דּוֹדִי

THREE prayer-poems, composed by three different *payyetanim* or liturgical poets, consist of three, five and six stanzas, respectively, each of which begins with the phrase ברח דודי (make haste, my friend). They are recited in conjunction with the benediction גאל ישראל, immediately before the *Amidah* prayer of the *Pesah* morning service, and are referred to as *Geullah* (גאולה) *piyyutim.*

The first of these, comprising three stanzas to be chanted on the first day of *Pesah*, was written by Rabbi Shelomoh ben Yehudah ha-Bavli, tenth-century liturgist and author of many *piyyutim*. It has been suggested that he was a native of Rome, which medieval Jewish writers included under the designation of Babylon; hence, his surname *ha-Bavli.* Various phrases from the Song of Songs are interwoven in the texture of this poem, pleading for deliverance and liberation of the people of Israel.

The second *Brah Dodi*, recited on the second day of *Pesah* and consisting of four stanzas, is like the preceding one in content, structure and form. It was composed by Rabbi Meshullam ben Kalonymus, a native of eleventh-century Italy. It is a plea for the restoration of Jerusalem and the liberation of Israel, "as at the first month of *Nisan* in days of old."

The third *Brah Dodi*, recited on the Sabbath of *Hol ha-Mo'ed Pesah*, is by Rabbi Simeon ben Isaac ben Abun of Mayence, one of the most prolific liturgists of the eleventh century. He is said to have used his prodigious political influence in preventing persecutions and unfavorable laws inflicted upon his people. Like the preceding two *piyyutim*, it is a prayer for prompt and complete redemption ("Thou who art our only strength, our comforter and liberator, we look to thee to free our captive people").

Each of the three *Geullah* poems concludes with the passage בגלל אבות תושיע בנים, ותביא גאולה לבני בניהם ("For the sake of the fathers thou wilt save the children, and bring liberation to their children's children"). This is directly connected with the *Amidah* prayer, the first benediction of which refers to the merits of our forefathers, for the sake of whom God will bring a redeemer.

For the seventh day of *Pesah*, the famous *Geullah* poem יום ליבשה by Rabbi Judah Halevi (1086-1140) of Spain, whose liturgical poems number more than three hundred, is chanted ("The redeemed

99

sang a new song when the sea was turned to dry land"). The name of the author, יהודה הלוי, is signed in the form of an acrostic at the beginning of the nine stanzas.

CREATION   בְּרִיאָה

The term *creation* is primarily used for the original formation of the universe by God, as described in Genesis 1:1-2:3. The description of the formation of man and his surroundings (Genesis 2:4-25) is supplementary and not contradictory. Though the story of creation has been told in various parts of the world by different writers and at different times, the biblical account of the facts of creation gives us the first definite idea of One God who controls human affairs, maintaining a sympathetic concern over the thoughts and the deeds of his children on earth.

Each of the seven acts of the creation drama covers a period of one day, assumed by some to be a geological period of countless centuries, so that there is no real conflict between the biblical account and the scientific theories of the origination of the universe. Since, however, such a view results in more difficulties than it solves, there are those who think that nothing is gained by making a desperate attempt to force science into the Bible. It is declared unreasonable to expect the first two chapters of the Torah to contain all the facts of astronomy, geology, and biology.

We are told that science is limited to study and observation; it may form hypotheses and theories, but it cannot give a definite answer to the question how the universe was originated. It may discover the laws of nature, but it cannot establish new laws of nature or create life. One scientist, a biochemist writes: "What is a cell? For many years it was thought to be a bag of jelly-like substance. . . Today we know it as a beautifully structured thing, made up of various bodies, of canals and vesicles, of small particles and amorphous material, all arranged and organized as if there were a definite reason for their existence and their placement."

Rabbi Bahya ibn Pakuda, in his famous work *Duties of the Heart:*

"How can one say that the universe came into existence without a wise, purposeful and mighty designer? If ink were poured out accidentally on a blank sheet of paper, legible writing could hardly result. If someone were to bring us a fair copy of script that could only have been written with a pen, and were to tell us that ink had been spilled on paper and these carefully written characters had come of themselves, we would charge him to his face with falsehood. How, then, can one assert that something far finer in its art could have come about without the purpose, power and wisdom of a wise and mighty designer?"

The cosmogony account in the Torah has been an essential part of the Jewish faith, which insists that the world and all it contains is not the product of chance but the handiwork of God, transcendant and almighty, who observes all events and nothing escapes him. Judaism has always emphasized that creation is not spontaneous nor the result of accident, but is the work of the Author of everything in accordance with definite plans and laws.

It has been pointed out that the relationship between God and the world, the belief that his providential activity preserves the universe from collapsing, is the foundation of the meaningfulness of human history and human life. "Contrary to the notion that human life is meaningless, because it is shaped by blind forces, and that man is a puny and helpless creature because he is dependent entirely upon a physical organism, Judaism affirms the creative and life-giving action of the eternal God who is ever at work in his universe, guiding the whole of human existence towards the fulfillment of a purpose. . ." (Isidore Epstein).

BERIKH SHEMEH   בְּרִיךְ שְׁמֵהּ

BERIKH SHEMEH (blessed be the name of the Lord), the prayer recited just before the *Sefer Torah* is taken out to be read during congregational services, is taken from the Zohar, the fundamental book of Kabbalah, first made known in the thirteenth century and attributed to Rabbi Simeon ben Yoḥai of the second century.

The Zohar introduces this inspiring and uplifting prayer in these terms: "When the Torah is taken out to be read before the congregation, the heavenly gates of mercy are opened and the divine love is aroused; therefore one should say: Blessed. . . Thou art he who nourishes and sustains all; thou art he who rules over all. . . Not in man do I put my trust, nor do I rely on any angel, but only in the God of heaven who is the God of truth, whose Torah is truth and whose Prophets are truth. In him I put my trust, and to his holy and glorious name I utter praises. . ."

CIRCUMCISION, BRITH   בְּרִית מִילָה

BRITH MILAH (the covenant of circumcision) is first mentioned in Genesis 17:9-12 as a divine command to Abraham. "God said to Abraham: You shall keep my covenant, you and your descendants after you throughout their generations... Every male among you shall be circumcised ... and it shall be a sign of the covenant between me and you. He that is eight days old among you shall be circumcised."

Circumcision is the characteristic symbol of Judaism, even though it was known to the ancient world long before Abraham and is observed by Muslims and certain sects of our time.

When Antiochus Epiphanus prohibited circumcision more than two thousand years ago, the Jews were ready to die rather than abandon it. It came to be the first condition of any male proselyte to Judaism. It is performed on the eighth complete day after birth, even on Sabbath or *Yom Kippur*. On a doctor's advice the operation may be delayed. Once delayed, the circumcision must not take place on a Sabbath or a major festival.

The *mohel* (circumcisor) is usually subject to regulations which ensure the performance of the operation with adequate precautions. The main participants in the ceremony of circumcision are the father of the child and the *mohel*. The *sandek*, whose privilege it is to hold the child during the operation, is the third participant who is said to have emerged into importance not before the tenth century.

The title *sandek* has been identified with the Greek term *synteknos*, denoting literally *with the child*. German-speaking Jews used the name *Gottvater* or *G'vater* (*Kwater*) for *sandek*. At a later period the title *Kwater* was conferred upon the person handing the infant to the *mohel*. The prophet Elijah is the invisible participant at circumcisions, being referred to as "the angel of the covenant" (Malachi 3:1) and protector of children. The special chair reserved for Elijah is left in position for three days, because the first three days after the circumcision are a dangerous period for the child.

The greeting ברוך הבא (blessed be he who enters) extended to the infant is at the same time a welcome to Elijah. The word הבא is said to be composed of the initials of הנה בא אליהו. The numerical value of הבא is eight, alluding to the infant of eight days.

Maimonides, in his *Guide for the Perplexed* (3:49), speaks of circumcision in the following terms: "It gives to all members of the same

102

faith, to all believers in the Oneness of God, a common bodily sign, so that it is impossible for any stranger to say that he belongs to them . . . and then attack them. . . . If the operation were postponed till the boy grew up, he might perhaps not submit to it. The young child has not much pain. The image of the child has not yet taken a firm root in the parents' minds. The parents' love for a new-born child is not so great as it is when the child is one year old. The father's love for the child might lead him to neglect the law if he were allowed to wait two or three years. . ."

It has been proposed only recently that upon completion of suitable courses, the *mohalim* should be examined and licensed by the state. . . Hospitals should provide isolated, sanitary circumcision rooms with separate facilities for guests invited to be present at the ritual. Hospital personnel should be taught the nature, purpose and significance of ritual circumcision of the newborn.

BARAITHA   בְּרַיְתָא

As A generic term, *Baraitha* signifies all tannaitic statements that were not included in the Mishnah by Rabbi Yehudah ha-Nasi. The largest collection of extra-mishnaic tannaitic teachings is represented by the *Tosefta*, which bears the nearest resemblance to the Mishnah. An individual citation in the Talmud from a tannaitic source other than the authoritative Mishnah is also referred to as *Baraitha*. The *Baraithas* quoted in both Talmuds, the Babylonian and the Palestinian, arc of great use in the study of the origin and development of the traditional law (*Halakhah*).

The Mishnah comprises only a minor portion of the legal material current in the tannaitic schools. The Hebrew equivalent of the Aramaic term *Baraitha* is *Mishnah Hitzonah*, extraneous Mishnah. That the *Tosefta* is identical with the *Baraitha* is the opinion of Rashi and Maimonides, while others regard the *Tosefta* as an independent collection. Michael Higger published the *Baraithoth* cited in the Talmud. The Talmud employs the term מתניתא (*Mathnitha*), which is the Aramaic equivalent of *Mishnah*, to designate the extra-mishnaic *Baraithoth*.

The name *Baraitha* is also attached to special collections of *halakhic* and *aggadic* content, such as *Baraitha d'Rabbi Meir* known as *Kinyan Torah*, which forms the sixth chapter of *Pirké Avoth*; the *Baraitha d'Rabbi Yishmael*, containing the thirteen rules of the talmudic exposition of the Torah, which is included in the daily Prayerbook to complete the daily minimum of Bible and Talmud study that is required of every Jew.

BAREKHU בָּרְכוּ

THE main part of the service, consisting of the *Shema* with its benedictions and the *Shemoneh Esreh*, is introduced with the invocation ברכו את ה' המבורך (bless the Lord who is blessed), derived from Nehemiah 9:5. This is a well-established formula for calling the people to public prayer (Berakhoth 7:3). The additional word המבורך (who is blessed) is in accordance with Rabbi Ishmael, a contemporary of Rabbi Akiva, both of whom are cited in Mishnah Berakhoth 7:3. The congregational response ברוך ה' המבורך is based on Deuteronomy 32:3 ("When I proclaim the name of the Lord, give glory to our God"). The verb "bless" in this and similar passages signifies "praise."

BENEDICTIONS בְּרְכוֹת

THE benedictions pronounced on various occasions are attributed to the men of the Great Assembly (אנשי כנסת הגדולה), the spiritual leaders in the time of Ezra the Scribe, who are considered the successors of the prophets in that they kept alive the knowledge of the Torah and Jewish traditions.

Maimonides writes in his *Mishneh Torah:* "The formulae of all benedictions have come down from Ezra and his counsel. It is improper to change them, to add to or subtract from anything in the phrasing of one of them. Whoever deviates from the form which the sages have given to the benedictions falls into error."

The word ברכה (blessing) is derived from ברך in the sense of bending the knees, worshiping. Compare נברכה לפני ה' (Psalm 95:6) and ויברך על ברכיו (II Chronicles 6:13). The phrase ברוך אתה, therefore, should be understood to mean *worshiped art thou.*

According to Rabbi Meir, who lived during the second century, it is the duty of every Jew to recite one hundred benedictions daily. Before performing a positive commandment, the benediction recited contains the words אשר קדשנו במצותיו וצונו (who hast sanctified us with thy commandments, and commanded us to. . .), as when placing

104

the *tefillin* both on the left arm and on the forehead, or upon lighting the Sabbath lights, or before reciting the *Hallel*.

Three kinds of benedictions are to be distinguished in addition to those connected with the three daily services. They are: 1) blessings pronounced in gratitude for the pleasure we derive from eating, drinking, scenting (ברכות הנהנין; (2 blessings designed to show that certain religious practices are divinely commanded (ברכות המצוות; 3) blessings which express the idea that all tragic or joyous events in private life come from God (ברכות פרטיות.

By means of these benedictions the Jew acknowledges his dependence on God for all things. There are scores of special benedictions to meet every possible occasion, from witnessing an electrical storm to seeing a great sage, Jew or non-Jew; from hearing good news to seeing the wonders of nature; from buying a new house to acquiring new clothes. Those who escape serious danger arising from illness or a perilous voyage recite a special benediction (ברכת הגומל) which reads: "Blessed art thou . . . who bestowest favors on the undeserving. . ."

The blessing ברוך שפטרני, pronounced by the father of a *Bar Mitzvah,* does not signify the father's joy at being relieved of the responsibility for his boy; it merely gives expression to the parent's joy that the son has reached an age when he can distinguish between right and wrong and joins the community as an independent member of Israel.

Abrupt transitions from the second person to the third person occur in the benedictions as in all biblical poetry, for example, . . . ברוך אתה אשר קדשנו (instead of קדשתנו). English syntax does not tolerate such transitions; hence, the benedictions must be rendered consistently in the second person.

In keeping with a talmudic statement (Berakhoth 36a) that the fulness of the earth which belongs to God (Psalm 24:1) may be enjoyed by man after consecrating it with benedictions, there are seven blessings known as ברכות הנהנין (*birkhoth ha-nehenin*).

MORNING BENEDICTIONS   בִּרְכוֹת הַשַּׁחַר

THE morning benedictions, consisting of thanksgivings for the divine benefits bestowed upon us, were originally designed as home meditations to be recited when the Jew awakens in the morning, washes, dresses, respectively. Later on, they were included in the preliminary morning service, containing Bible and Talmud selections. The four-teenth-century Abudarham mentions the blessing שעשני כרצונו said by women in place of שלא עשני אשה said by men, who thank God for the privilege of performing many precepts (שהזמן גרמא) that are not incumbent upon women, owing to their manifold household duties.

In keeping with our duty to engage in the study of the Torah at all times, the readings from the Bible and the Talmud as part of the pre-liminary morning service are meant to enable every Jew to have a daily share in the study of the Torah, written and oral. These read-ings are preceded by a blessing which gives expression to Israel's grat-itude for the privilege of studying God's teachings.

The texts are drawn especially from the Mishnah and the Talmud, in addition to biblical passages concerning the sacrificial system of many centuries ago. The sacrificial system symbolized self-surrender and devotion to the will of God. According to a talmudic statement, God said: "Whenever they recite the order of sacrifices. . . I will for-give all their sins" (Ta'anith 27b).

איזהו מקומן, the fifth chapter of Mishnah Zevaḥim, containing an account of the method in which the sacrifices used to be offered, has been chosen to be included in the preliminary morning service, be-cause it entirely consists of undisputed statements, much unlike other Mishnah selections that are replete with differences of opinion among the tannaitic sages.

The thirteen principles of talmudic logic contained in the *Baraitha d'Rabbi Yishmael* (ברייתא דרבי ישמעאל) have been inserted in this section of the daily Prayerbook to complete the daily minimum of Bible and Talmud study required of every Jew. Since *Baraitha* de-notes a teaching that is external to the Mishnah, it is here regarded as belonging to the *Gemara*, which constitutes the major part of the Tal-mud. Rabbi Yishmael ben Elisha, who was a contemporary of Rabbi Akiva, died as a martyr in the year 135 during the Roman persecutions.

TORAH BLESSINGS   בִּרְכוֹת הַתּוֹרָה

THE two benedictions pronounced over the Torah by the person hon-ored with an *aliyyah* contain forty words, which are said to allude to the forty days spent by Moses on Mount Sinai. These benedictions, each of which consists of an identical number of words (twenty), are quoted in the Talmud (Berakhoth 11b; 49b). Formerly, the worshipers themselves read the Torah selections to which they were called up. Because the whole section is now read by an expert *ba'al keriah* (reader), the persons honored with an *aliyyah* are content with reciting the blessings before and after the reading.

BAREKHI NAFSHI   בָּרְכִי נַפְשִׁי

ON SABBATH afternoons between *Sukkoth* and *Pesaḥ*, Psalm 104 is recited as well as the fifteen psalms that begin with the words שיר המעלות (a pilgrim song). These psalms were sung by the pilgrims as they went up to Jerusalem to celebrate the three pilgrim festivals in the center of national and religious life. Psalm 104, known by its initial words ברכי נפשי (bless, my soul), closely resembles, in its contents, the story of creation as told in the Torah. The psalmist celebrates the divine glory as seen in the forces of nature. The German philosopher-poet of the eighteenth century, Johann von Herder, declared that it is worthwhile studying the Hebrew language for ten years in order to read Psalm 104 in the original.

Psalm 121, belonging to the series recited on Sabbath afternoons, is a perfect expression of trust in God; it has been on the lips of countless people when they felt the need of help beyond that which mortals can offer. "I lift up my eyes toward the hills; whence does my help come? My help comes from the Lord, who made heaven and earth. . . Indeed, the guardian of Israel neither slumbers nor sleeps. The Lord is your guardian, the Lord is your shelter, he is beside you at your right hand, The sun shall not harm you by day, nor the moon by night. The Lord will guard you from all evil; he will guard your life. The Lord will guard your coming and your going, henceforth and forever." This is the song of the pilgrim whose guide is the Lord. The hills around Jerusalem are perhaps meant in the first sentence.

Psalm 128 contains a picture of an ideal homelife. The welfare of the state depends upon virtuous family life. Psalm 131 is a song of childlike humility. As the child that has gone through the troublesome process of weaning can lie happily in its mother's arms, so the psalmist's soul has found contentment and happiness through the discipline of humility.

During the summer season, between *Pesaḥ* and *Rosh Hashanah*, *Pirké Avoth* (Ethics of the Fathers) is read on Sabbath afternoons in place of the psalms headed by *Barekhi Nafshi*.

107

BIRKATH HA-GOMEL בִּרְכַּת הַגּוֹמֵל

Persons who have safely returned from some hazardous voyage or recovered from a serious illness, or been released from unjust imprisonment, must offer thanks to God in the form of a benediction recited in addition to the Torah blessings when called to the public reading of the Torah in the synagogue. This benediction, known as *birkath hagomel*, is derived from Psalm 107, according to a talmudic interpretation (Berakhoth 54b). Psalm 107 begins by calling upon the exiles, brought back to their homes, to give thanks. Then it describes God's goodness in taking care of lost travellers, prisoners, the sick, and sea-voyagers. The refrain at the end of each of the four stanzas reads: "Let them thank the Lord for his kindness and his wonders toward men." As a mnemonic, the four letters of the word חיים have been suggested as the initials of חלי, יסורין, ים, מדבר (illness, torture, sea, desert).

The *birkath ha-gomel*, which is offered within a group of ten men, the minimum required for congregational worship, reads as follows: "Blessed art thou, Lord our God, King of the universe, who bestowest favors on the undeserving and hast shown me every kindness." Upon hearing this benediction, the congregation responds: "May he who has shown you every kindness ever deal kindly with you."

PARENTAL BLESSING בִּרְכַּת הוֹרִים

The blessing of children by their parents on all important occasions, notably on the eves of Sabbaths and festivals, is hailed as one of the most beautiful customs. The *Brandspiegel*, a medieval treatise on morals (published in 1602), speaks of this practice in these terms: "Before the children can walk they should be carried on Sabbaths and festivals to the father and mother to be blessed; after they are able to walk they shall go of their own accord with bowed body and shall incline their heads to receive the blessing." This custom has linked the generations together in mutual loyalty and affection.

The Jewish people have always ascribed great importance to parental blessings. An added significance was attached, in the biblical and talmudic periods, to the blessing given by a dying parent. The custom of blessing the children on the eves of Sabbaths and festivals is of ancient origin.

108

The customary blessing for sons is: "May God make you like Ephraim and like Manasseh (Genesis 48:20). May the Lord bless you and protect you; may the Lord let his countenance shine upon you and be gracious to you; may the Lord favor you and grant you peace" (Numbers 6:24-26). For daughters: "May God make you like Sarah and Rebekah, Rachel and Leah" (Ruth 4:12). These words are followed by the priestly blessing: "May the Lord bless you and protect you. . ." Parents or grandparents also bless the bridal pair under the *huppah*.

NEW-MONTH BLESSING   בִּרְכַּת הַחֹדֶשׁ

BIRKATH HA-ḤODESH (blessing of the new month), recited after the Torah reading on the Sabbath preceding the new Jewish month, is reminiscent of the Temple period when the arrival of a new month was solemnly announced by the Sanhedrin after examining the witnesses who had noticed the appearance of the new moon. The thirtieth day of the expiring month was proclaimed as the first day of the new month if the statement of the witnesses was found to be correct. The proclamation of the new month was signaled from mountain top to mountain top throughout Eretz Yisrael by lighting flares.

In the middle of the fourth century, Hillel II published scientific rules for the computation of the calendar, making the months to alternate between thirty and twenty-nine days. *Nisan, Sivan, Av, Tishri, Kislev* and *Shevat* have each thirty days; the other six months have twenty-nine days each. In leap years, the first *Adar* has thirty days, the second twenty-nine. *Ḥeshvan* is occasionally lengthened to thirty days. When the preceding month has thirty days, its last day is celebrated as the first day of *Rosh Ḥodesh*, while the second day of *Rosh Ḥodesh* marks the first day of the new month.

The petition יהי רצון (may it be thy will), which serves as an introduction to the formal announcement of the new month, is quoted in the Talmud (Berakhoth 16b) as the daily personal prayer of Rav, the founder of the Babylonian Academy of Sura (third century). It was adopted in the eighteenth century as a prayer for the coming month.

The prayer that follows the announcement of the day starting the new month gives expression to the hope that God will grant us "life and peace, joy and gladness, salvation and comfort. . ." The prayer

109

which immediately precedes the announcement reads: "May he who performed miracles for our fathers, and freed them from slavery, speedily redeem us and gather our dispersed people from the four corners of the earth, so that all Israel be knit together. . . Amen."

The expression of messianic hopes contained in these prayers is closely connected with the idea of the moon's monthly renewal, serving as an encouraging symbol of revival and regeneration.

NEW-MOON BLESSING   בִּרְכַּת הַלְּבָנָה

THE blessing of the new moon is recited in the open air when the moon is visible between the fourth and the sixteenth of the month, preferably on a Saturday night, after *Havdalah*, when the observant Jew is in a joyous frame of mind. This festive ceremony of ancient origin is fully discussed in the Talmud (Sanhedrin 42a; Sofrim 20:1-2). The moon, appearing periodically in several phases, has been looked upon as symbolic of the Jewish people whose history consists of varied phases. Also, like the moon, the Jews regularly reappear after being temporarily eclipsed.

The four synonyms referring to the Creator in one of the passages of ברכת הלבנה have as their initials the letters which spell the name יעקב (Jacob), alluding to his descendants, the people of Israel. The passage reads: ברוך יוצרך . . . עושך . . . קונך . . . בוראך.

The expression "Long live David, King of Israel!" refers to Psalm 89:38, which says that David's dynasty shall "like the moon be established forever." The numerical value of דוד מלך ישראל חי וקים (819) is equal to that of ראש חודש. It was the password of Bar Kokhba's army.

The text in the *Siddur* is as follows: "Blessed art thou, Lord our God, King of the universe, who didst create the heavens by thy command, and all their host by thy mere word. Thou has subjected them to fixed laws and time, that they may not deviate from their set function. . . He ordered the moon to renew itself as a gracious crown over those whom he sustained from birth, who likewise will be regenerated in the future. . ."

Kiddush ha-Levanah (Sanctification of the Moon) is another name for *Birkath ha-Levanah* (Blessing of the Moon). The ceremony opens with a benediction praising the Creator of the celestial lights who ordained the monthly renewal of the moon. In the authoritative trac-

110

tate Sofrim (20:1-2), several mystifying details are prescribed in connection with the *Kiddush Levanah* service. They are as follows: "The blessing of the moon must take place at the conclusion of the Sabbath, when one is in a jolly mood and dressed in nice garments. The worshiper should look steadily at the moon, join straight his feet, and recite the benediction... He should say three times *simman tov* (a good sign), and perform three dancing gestures in the direction of the moon while saying three times: Just as I cannot touch thee, may my foes never be able to harm me... Then he should say *shalom* (peace) to his neighbor three times and go home with a happy heart."

GRACE AFTER MEALS   בִּרְכַּת הַמָּזוֹן

BIRKATH HA-MAZON, popularly known as *benshen* (from the Latin *benedicere*), is the grace recited after meals that include bread. It is based on the biblical command: "When you eat and are satisfied, you shall bless the Lord your God for the good land he has given you" (Deuteronomy 8:10). It consists of four benedictions, or paragraphs, three of which are of high antiquity; the fourth, of later origin, was instituted after Bar Kokhba's defeat, about 135 of the common era.

According to a talmudic statement, the first paragraph was composed by Moses, the second by Joshua, the third by David and Solomon, and the fourth by the sages (Berakhoth 48b). The first is an acknowledgment of God as the sustainer of all creatures; the second, a thanksgiving for the grant of the Torah and Eretz Yisrael; the third, a prayer for the restoration of Zion and Jerusalem; the fourth, an expression of gratitude for the general benefits and favors bestowed on man by his Creator. The third paragraph closes with *Amen* so as to mark the end of the three benedictions which are based on Deuteronomy 8:10.

The introductory formula, used when three or more men recite the grace jointly (ברכת הזימון, is taken from the Mishnah (Berakhoth 7:3). The duty of inviting the table-companions to recite grace jointly is based on Psalm 34:4 ("Exalt the Lord with me, and let us extol the Lord together"). The numerous petitions beginning with הרחמן (May the Merciful One) are later additions, including insertions for Sabbath, *Rosh Ḥodesh* and festivals, *Purim* and *Ḥanukkah*.

The last paragraph of *Birkath ha-Mazon* begins with the word יראו, which should be pronounced *y'ru* (revere). It was customary to recite this passage silently out of regard for the feelings of poor guests who used to be invited to the table. Since the passage contains biblical quotations to the effect that those who seek the Lord are not in want of good things, nor are their children begging for food, it might embarrass present company if chanted aloud.

The abridged form of grace, known as מעין שלוש because it is a short summary of the first three paragraphs of the *Birkath ha-Mazon*, is recited after meals that do not include bread, but food consisting of the seven species enumerated in the Torah as descriptive of Eretz Yisrael: "a land of wheat and barley, of vines and fig-trees and pomegranates, of olive oil and honey" (Deuteronomy 8:8). Any food that does not consist of these seven species requires the shortest form of grace, known as בורא נפשות, which reads: "Blessed art thou . . . for all the things thou hast created to sustain every living being. . ."

BLESSING OF LIGHTS   בִּרְכַּת הַנֵּרוֹת

THE lighting of the Sabbath lights has been the special duty of the housewife ever since ancient times (Mishnah Shabbath 2:6). Though there is no biblical command concerning the Sabbath lights, the benediction is worded: "Blessed art thou . . . who hast . . . commanded us to light the Sabbath lights." This is in keeping with the command: "You shall carry out the directions they (the sages) give you."

The traditions of Judaism are regarded as a continuous chain, even though some of its links are not directly to be traced from the Bible. The blessing is not quoted in the Talmud, but is found in the ninth century *Siddur* of Rav Amram Gaon. The custom of lighting a minimum of two lights, then adding one for each of the remaining members of the household, alludes to the two words "Remember" and "Observe" which introduce the Sabbath commandment in the Decalogue (Exodus 20:8; Deuteronomy 5:12). The lights are symbolical of the cheerfulness and serenity which distinguish the Sabbath as a day of delight. The same applies to all Holy Days.

It is customary for the housewife to cover her eyes while reciting the blessing at the lighting of the Sabbath lights. The reason is that she must not enjoy the Sabbath lights prior to the blessing, in keeping with the rule that the benediction ought to precede the act. When she kindles the festival lights, however, she recites the blessing and then she lights the candles.

112

The same procedure cannot be followed in the case of the Sabbath lights, because she must not light a fire after her formal reception of the Sabbath expressed by the blessing of the lights. There has been a deep-rooted belief that all noble prayers uttered during the moments of covering the eyes will be answered. Hence, various supplications have been used by housewives during the performance of lighting the Sabbath lights.

PRIESTLY BLESSING   בִּרְכַּת כֹּהֲנִים

THE priestly benediction, expressed in three biblical verses and chanted at the end of the *Amidah* prayer, was part of the daily service at the Temple. Every morning and evening the priests raised their hands aloft and pronounced the *birkath kohanim* (priestly blessing) from a special platform (*dukhan*).

In Israel, *Kohanim* chant it daily in the synagogues; in the Diaspora, it is chanted only on festivals. Those of priestly descent remove their shoes, wash their hands, and ascend the platform in front of the ark. Then they face the congregation and, with fingers stretched in a symbolic arrangement underneath the *tallith* covering their face, they repeat the priestly blessing word for word after the *ḥazzan*.

The worshipers refrain from looking at the *kohanim* during the repetition of the fifteen majestic words of which the priestly benediction is composed, to indicate that they emanate from the highest spheres. This priestly service is termed "duchenen" from *dukhan* (platform). Taken from Numbers 6:24-26, the benediction reads: "May the Lord bless you and protect you. May the Lord let his countenance shine upon you and be gracious to you. May the Lord look kindly upon you and grant you peace."

BIRKATH SHEVA   בִּרְכַּת שֶׁבַע

THE Sabbath *Amidah* is named *Birkath Sheva* or תפלת שבע because it contains seven blessings. The first three and the last three benedictions are the same in all forms of the *Amidah*, whereas the intermediary benediction varies in all four services of the Sabbath. The thirteen petitions of the weekday *Shemoneh Esreh* are omitted because the worshiper is likely to be reminded of his failings and troubles while

113

inserting his personal requests, and on Sabbaths and festivals, the days of rest, he ought rather to forget his sorrows and be cheerful (Tanḥuma, *Vayyéra*). The special benediction inserted in place of the thirteen intermediate paragraphs deals with the particular day, Sabbath or festival. The *Musaf* service of *Rosh Hashanah*, however, has three intermediate benedictions instead of one, thus constituting a total of nine benedictions.

MEAT-MILK MIXTURE   בָּשָׂר בְּחָלָב

THREE times the Torah declares: "You shall not boil a kid in its mother's milk" (Exodus 23:19; 34:26; Deuteronomy 14:21). This is rendered by the Targum: "You shall not eat meat and milk together." Recently discovered inscriptions of pre-Israelite inhabitants of Syria record the ancient practice of seething a kid in its mother's milk as part of the idolatrous worship of the Canaanites. Archeological discoveries in the Syrian town Ugarit, today known as Ras Shamra, which was destroyed in the twelfth century before the common era, have added much knowledge of ancient Canaanite religion and culture. The Ugaritic cult documents are of special interest to students of the Hebrew Bible.

Meat cooked with milk is a common dish among the Arabs. The context of the biblical passage (Exodus 23:19; 34:26) shows that some ancient form of sacrifice is meant. Many primitive tribes regard milk as an equivalent for blood. To eat, then, a kid boiled in its mother's milk must have been regarded as eating it with the blood, which the Torah forbids along with the bloody sacrifices of the heathen. Hence, Maimonides writes: "Meat boiled in milk ... is also prohibited because it is somehow connected with idolatry, forming perhaps part of the service, or being used on the festivals of the heathen. I find support for this view in the circumstance that the Torah mentions the prohibition twice after the commandment given concerning the festivals ... as if to say: When you come before me on your festivals, do not seethe your food in the manner as the heathen used to do (*Guide*, 3:48).

The prohibition occurs three times, Rashi points out, to signify that the eating, cooking and deriving any benefit from a mixture of milk and meat are forbidden. According to Moses Mendelssohn, the benefit arising from the many inexplicable laws of God is in their practice, and not in the understanding of their motives.

114

BATH KOL   בַּת קוֹל

BATH KOL has been defined as a mysterious voice by which God on occasion communicated to men after the cessation of prophecy. This divine voice is called *bath kol* (echo), to avoid saying that the actual voice of God was heard by men not included among the prophets. According to a tannaitic statement quoted in Yoma 9b, the holy spirit left Israel after the death of the last prophets, but they still availed themselves of the *bath kol* as a substitute for prophecy, offering guidance in human affairs.

The expression *bath kol* is frequently used in the sense of universal sentiment; it is reminiscent of the popular saying: קול המון כקול שדי (the voice of the people is like the voice of the Almighty). The verdict reached by a large majority is assumed to reflect the will of God. We are told that Eretz Yisrael trembled from one end to the other when the prophetical books of the Bible were translated into Aramaic by Jonathan ben Uzziel, and a *bath kol* came forth saying: "Who is he that revealed my secrets to men?" (Megillah 3a).

Yonathan ben Uzziel, we are told further, contemplated preparing a *Targum* for the third division of the Bible, but he was deterred by a *bath kol*, saying: "No more!" The explanation is that he was prohibited from preparing an interpretive translation of the biblical division containing the book of Daniel, because this would enable laymen to speculate on the date of the advent of the Messiah, resulting in devastating disillusionments. Those who made calculations, from biblical verses, as to when the Messiah would come (מחשבי קיצין) were reviled by the sages (Sanhedrin 97b).

LAW COURTS   בָּתֵּי דִין

THROUGHOUT the long period of Jewish homelessness and *galuth*, the Jewish law courts continued to exercise public authority, supervising communal order and safety and using moral pressure. They even had power to appoint inspectors of weights and measures.

Here is a short description of talmudic law concerning judges in Jewish courts, as summed up by Maimonides:

The judge must not permit one of the litigants to state his case fully while telling the other to be brief; nor must he show courtesy to

115

one, speaking softly to him, while frowning upon the other and addressing him harshly. He must not allow one litigant to be seated while keeping the other standing. When he finds that a litigant is at pains to defend himself by a sound argument, he is permitted to assist him somewhat, though he must not appear as playing the part of an advocate.

On leaving court, a judge must not say: "I voted for acquittal, or for condemnation, but my colleagues differed with me; and what could I do, seeing that they were in the majority?" A judge should ever regard himself as if a sword were suspended over his head.

In capital cases, the judges open the discussion with a favorable argument. The decision for acquittal is by a majority of one, whereas a majority of at least two is required for a conviction. In civil cases, however, the decision for or against the defendant is by a majority of one. Unlike civil cases, in which a judgment may be reversed either for or against the defendant, a sentence may be reversed in capital cases only for acquittal but not to convict (*Yad, Sanhedrin* 21:1, 3, 11; 22:7; 23:8).

In Temple times, the *Beth Din ha-Gadol* (supreme court) at Jerusalem comprised seventy-one members and was known as the Great Sanhedrin. It exercised final authority on religious problems and appointed judges for the lower courts, consisting of twenty-three members each, to sit in judgment on criminal cases. The local courts, comprising at least three members each, had jurisdiction over civil cases. In the Diaspora, Jewish courts continued to exist in centers of Jewish population. Presided over by rabbinic authorities, called *dayyanim* (judges), the Jewish courts had jurisdiction over the internal communal affairs. After the breakdown of communal autonomy in the nineteenth century, they were limited to ritual matters and voluntary arbitration. In the State of Israel rabbinical courts have jurisdiction in such matters as marriage and divorce.

GAON was the title applied to the heads of the two major Babylonian academies at Sura and Pumbeditha, who were looked upon as the spiritual guides of the Jewish people from the end of the sixth to the middle of the eleventh century. Thereafter the title *Gaon* has been used to designate any outstanding talmudic scholar, such as Rabbi Elijah Gaon of Vilna (1720-1797) who was consulted by celebrated rabbis even before his twentieth year. The word גאון (excellency) was part of the name גאון יעקב (Pride of Jacob) by which the Babylonian academies were known. The phrase גאון יעקב was borrowed from Psalm 47:5 ("He chose our heritage for us, the pride of Jacob whom he loves").

The Gaon was generally elected by the academy, but occasionally he was appointed by the exilarch, or head of the exile, a dignitary of considerable political importance, of the Davidic dynasty, who served as a secular bond of unity among all the dispersed Jews. The Gaon of Sura ranked above the Gaon of Pumbeditha. He evidently owed his superior rank to the ancient reputation of the academy of Sura, founded by Rav (Abba Arikha) in the third century; there the more prominent scholars taught throughout the geonic period.

The duties of the Geonim were to serve as directors of the academies, continuing as such the educational activity of the talmudic sages, and to answer all questions that were addressed to them as the highest authorities on Jewish lore. Enjoying supreme religious and spiritual sway over all the Jews dispersed in many lands, the Geonim carried on an active correspondence with numerous widespread communities. It resulted in the branch of literature known as תשובות הגאונים (Geonic Responsa), which provides the means of tracing the religious and secular problems of the scattered Jews during the geonic period that lasted more than five centuries.

Because the Geonim did not make it a practice to preserve copies of their replies, or responsa, only a small number of these have come down to us. The Geonim not only disseminated the teachings of the Talmud, explaining its contents and developing its principles, but also maintained Jewish unity; all Jewry looked to them as guides to life in all its aspects. They attracted students to their academies from the entire Diaspora, who in turn eagerly communicated to others the talmudic knowledge they had gained in Sura and Pumbeditha.

117

The *Kallah* months, *Adar* and *Elul*, which were chiefly devoted to foreign students who followed their craft or trade during the remainder of the year, were also used in the Babylonian academies for popular lectures on religious duties in connection with the festivals of *Pesaḥ* and *Sukkoth*, *Rosh Hashanah* and *Yom Kippur*. The word כלה is said to mean *general assembly*, or popular college, at which not only specialists but ordinary laymen were present in large numbers.

The *Letter of Rav Sherira Gaon* (אגרת רב שרירא גאון) has been the basic source for information on the geonic period. Written in 992 in response to an inquiry by the Jews of Kairouan, North Africa, it gives a historical account of the origins of the Mishnah and Talmud and the sequence of the talmudic authorities, the Savoraim and Geonim. More recently, the Cairo Genizah has shed additional light on the history of the Geonim. Rav Sherira lists Mar Ḥanan as the first Gaon who took office in Pumbeditha in 589, and Rav Mar bar Rav Huna as the first Gaon in Sura, taking office in 591. Rav Sherira and his son Rav Hai were the last Geonim of the Pumbeditha academy: Rav Sherira, from the year 968 to 998; and Rav Hai, from 998 to 1038. The two ancient academies of Sura and Pumbeditha, dating from the early amoraic times, moved to Baghdad at the end of the ninth century and retained their distinctive names. The last Gaon of the Sura academy was Rav Azariah ha-Kohen (1034-1038). The two academies then united in Baghdad and continued their existence for another hundred and fifty years.

REDEMPTION

ONE of the most quoted biblical passages is the prophecy that "a redeemer shall come to Zion" (Isaiah 59:20). The redeemer is described as a king who shall reign and govern wisely. "He shall do what is just and right in the land. In his days Judah shall be saved, Israel shall dwell in security" (Jeremiah 23:5-6). The principal features of this expectation are the recovery of independence, an era of peace and prosperity, of faith in God and his Torah, of justice and brotherly love among men, and of the ingathering of the homeless exiles (קבוץ גליות).

The second book of Maccabees (1:27-28) quotes a prayer which reads: "Gather together our scattered people, set at liberty those who are in slavery, look upon those who are despised, and let the nations

118

know that thou art God." The tenth benediction of the *Shemoneh Esreh* prayer reads: "Sound the great *shofar* for our freedom; lift up the banner to bring our exiles together, and assemble us from the four corners of the earth."

GOG AND MAGOG   גּוֹג וּמָגוֹג

EZEKIEL'S vision concerning an attack upon Israel by a violent enemy, Gog and Magog, occupies two chapters (38-39). The prophet foretells the utter destruction of Gog, whose weapons will provide Israel with fuel for seven years and whose corpses will require seven months to bury; then the entire world will acknowledge the power and majesty of the true God. "On that day, when Gog invades the land of Israel . . . mountains shall be torn apart, and cliffs shall topple over. . . I will overwhelm him with utter panic. . . O Gog, I will strike your bow from your left hand and will make your arrows drop out of your right hand. You shall fall upon the mountains of Israel, you and your hordes. . . I will restore the fortunes of Jacob and have mercy on the whole house of Israel. . ."

Traditionally interpreted, this vision refers to a distant future, at the end of days, in which God will eventually defeat the enemies of Israel in the land of Israel. Rav Saadyah Gaon speaks of Gog and Magog in connection with the messianic era: "Then Gog and Magog will hear about the descendant of David and the excellence of his people and country and the abundance of their wealth. . . He will gather people from various nations . . . notorious sinners marked for perdition. . . On that day four types of misfortune will descend upon them. . . Then the spirit of prophecy will descend upon all Israel, young and old. This blessed period will last until the end of time. . ."

GEZEROTH   גְּזֵרוֹת

A RABBINICAL decree issued as a preventive measure is referred to as *gezerah* (גזירה), from the root גזר (to decide). *Gezeroth* are used for prohibitions, while *takkanoth* are enactments of a positive character. On one occasion, eighteen restrictions (י"ח דברים) were enacted that were designed to improve the observance of fundamental laws. These included prohibitions against improper relations between Jews and

119

non-Jews, against assimilation and intermarriage (Shabbath 17a). The Talmud relates that after the destruction of the Second Temple, there were some Pharisees who planned to prohibit the eating of meat and the drinking of wine; but Rabbi Joshua prevented them from carrying out their intention, in consideration of the majority of the people who could not exist without the necessary food (Bava Bathra 60b). Hence the rule: אין גוזרין גזירה על הצבור אלא אם כן רוב הצבור יכולין לעמוד בה. ("We must not impose a restriction on the public which the majority cannot endure").

DIVORCE   גֵּט

THE Bible mentions a bill of divorce (*sefer kerithuth*) on three occasions (Deuteronomy 24:1; Isaiah 50:1; Jeremiah 3:8). While the Prophets use the expression figuratively, the Torah presents a law concerning an actual bill of divorce when it forbids the husband to remarry his divorced wife if, in the meantime, she had been the wife of another man.

Though the Torah does not indicate the contents of a *sefer kerithuth*, the Mishnah gives the following as the essential formula of a *get* or bill of divorce: "Let this serve you as a bill of divorce from me, as a letter of dismissal and deed of liberation, that you may marry any man you wish" (Gittin 9:3).

This bill is handed by the husband to his wife together with a formal declaration in the presence of witnesses. The method of giving a *get*, which requires the sanction of a court (*beth din*) consisting of three men well versed in the religious laws of marriage and divorce, involves proceedings entailing delay, which in turn affords an opportunity of reconciliation.

Here are some regulations that must be complied with: The three *dayyanim* (judges) must not be related to the couple or to one another; the same applies to the witnesses and the scribe who writes the *get*. The bill of divorce must be written in the presence of the three *dayyanim*, and prepared especially for this particular couple. The ink must be clean and black, and the pen must be made from goose-quill.

The *get*, written on parchment or paper which must be in perfect condition without erasures or holes, has to contain the exact names of the husband and the wife and the exact date and place of the execution of the document. It must be written in Hebrew square characters, used in the writing of a *Sefer Torah*, in twelve lines (the numerical value of the word גט is twelve). The writing and the delivering of a *get* must take place in the daytime, but not on days immediately preceding *Rosh Ḥodesh*, Sabbath, or holyday.

Rabbenu Gershom (960-1040) convened a synod of rabbis at Mayence which, among other provisions, prohibited polygamy in European lands and made it unlawful for a Jew to divorce his wife without her consent. According to Maimonides' code, *Mishneh Torah*, if the husband debars his wife from participating in certain joyous functions, or if he prevents her from wearing costly dresses and jewelry that he can afford to buy, she may sue for and be granted a divorce... If she says: "My husband is distasteful to me, I cannot live with him," the court should compel the husband to divorce her, because a wife is not like a captive woman (*Ishuth* 13:4-14:8).

Jewish tradition, however, has always been opposed to groundless divorces, as can be seen from the following talmudic statements: "If a man divorces his first wife, the very altar weeps. He who sends away his wife is a hateful person. When a divorced man marries a divorced woman, there are four minds in the bed" (Gittin 90b; Pesaḥim 112a).

According to the School of Shammai, no man may divorce his wife unless he found her guilty of an immoral act (Mishnah Gittin 9:10). When Malachi addresses himself to those who lack a trace of moral sense, he says: "You drench the Lord's altar with your tears, sobbing and groaning because he never heeds your offerings... You ask, Why? It is because the Lord was a witness at your marriage in youth to the wife with whom you have now broken faith" (2:13-15). The phrase אשת בריתך signifies that there is a covenant between husband and wife.

In certain circumstances, such as leprosy, apostasy, misbehavior and dishonest occupation, the Jewish court may compel the husband to issue a *get*. No marriage can be annulled by a *get* (גט) without prior civil divorce; nor can a civil divorce without a *get* be regarded as valid for the purpose of remarriage. The laws concerning the writing and transmission of the *get* were purposely made exceedingly stringent to prevent possible misuse by the husband of his privilege to annul the marriage tie.

Though the husband may remarry immediately after the divorce, the wife must wait three months after receiving the *get*. This is for the purpose of establishing definitely the paternity of the child she bears after her remarriage.

GEHENNA   גֵּיהִנֹּם

THE phrase גיא בן–הנם (Jeremiah 32:35) is mentioned as the valley of the son of Hinnom, near Jerusalem, where idolaters used to sacrifice human lives. In this valley of slaughter, children were burned in sacrifice to the bloody deity Molech; hence, the entire area took on a sinister aspect and became identified with woe and suffering.

The name גיהנם (Gehenna) passed into use as a designation for the place of punishment in the hereafter. The Greeks and the Romans had their place of woe situated as far below Hades as Hades was below heaven.

According to a tannaitic statement, the doors of Gehenna close behind apostates, informers, promoters of sin and tyrants, for many generations (Tosefta Sanhedrin 13:5). According to the Zohar, sinners are punished in Gehenna for twelve months, half of the time in fire and half in snow. Among those who do not face Gehenna, a talmudic passage includes the very poor and the diseased. Some add: Any man who is afflicted with a shrew for a wife is likewise exempted from future Gehenna (Eruvin 41b).

It has been asserted by some students that it is indeed a mystery how anyone can believe in eternal punishment or in the loss of any soul which God has made and also believe in the love and the justice of God. The Jewish people have rested with confidence upon the goodness and the compassion of God. In days of trial, their belief in the life after death fortified them; it enabled many thousands to undergo martyrdom; it prevented scepticism, and served as a powerful motive for the avoidance of sin.

GHETTO   גֵּיטוֹ

THE term *ghetto* came into use in 1516, when the Jews of Venice were confined in a special quarter of the city. A century before that, in 1416, the Spanish kings ordered the Jews' quarters, as well as those of the Moors, to be surrounded by walls and provided with gates locked at night. The compulsory concentration of Jews in ghettos— in Italy, Spain, Germany and Poland—gave the enemies of the Jewish people a convenient goal to murder and plunder in the event of an outburst. Many of these medieval Jewish settlements have been

122

preserved in Rome, Prague, Amsterdam, and Frankfurt. The communal feeling and the traditional Jewish culture were maintained and nurtured in the ghettoes.

The Nazis set up ghettos in eastern Europe (1939-1942) to concentrate, isolate, and break the spirit of the Jewish people prior to the "final liquidation" and annihilation. They systematically starved the ghettos, which they instituted in over-crowded areas in Warsaw, Lodz, Vilna, Cracow, and elsewhere in Poland, Hungary, Roumania and Russia. On the eve of Passover, April 19, 1943, began the battle of the Warsaw Ghetto. The pre-war Jewish community in Warsaw had been the largest in Europe, close to four hundred thousand. Starvation, disease and deportation had taken the lives of three hundred and thirty-seven thousand. Now, when the Germans marched in to begin the "final liquidation," the Jews fought back. They heroically held out for twenty-seven days. Fewer than eighty escaped alive through the sewers under the ghetto walls.

GEMATRIA   גִּימַטְרִיָא

GEMATRIA is a method of disclosing the hidden meaning of a biblical or other text by reckoning the numerical equivalents of the Hebrew letters. This form of interpretation is used largely in the talmudic-midrashic and kabbalistic literatures.

Here are a few examples: According to Genesis 14:14, Abraham had 318 trained servants. This number equals the sum of the letters spelling the name אליעזר; hence, the number 318 actually refers to Eliezer, the servant of Abraham mentioned in Genesis 15:2 (Nedarim 32a). יין (wine) and סוד (secret) equal each other numerically (70). Hence, the saying נכנס יין יצא סוד, when wine enters, secrets are out.

The ladder Jacob saw in his dream, reaching from earth to heaven, referred to Sinai, since the numerical value of סלם (130) equals that of סיני. This means that the Torah, revealed at Sinai, is the ladder which leads from earth to heaven.

The tetragrammaton, or four-letter name of God, consisting of the numerical equivalents of 10, 5, 6 and 5, the sum of whose squares is 186 (100+25+36+25), is numerically equivalent to מקום, referring to God as the Omnipresent.

Gematria has at times been used also as a form of arithmetical amusement. The kabbalistic literature has made much use of specula-

123

tions based on the numerical values of the Hebrew letters. Since the word תורה amounts to 611, it refers to the 611 commandments transmitted to Israel through Moses, which together with the first two commandments of the Decalogue given directly by God himself on Mount Sinai make up the 613 positive and negative precepts.

The numerical value of the word אחד (One) is equivalent to אהבה (Love) so as to indicate, according to Rabbi Joseph Albo's *Ikkarim* of the fifteenth century, that the highest purpose and goal that we should try to attain is love for God who is One.

METEMPSYCHOSIS   גִּלְגּוּל נְשָׁמוֹת

THE mystic belief in metempsychosis, the passing of the soul at death into another body, was held by the ancient Egyptians and is a tenet in East Indian philosophy. This doctrine has been tolerated rather than approved by Judaism.

The Zohar describes the incarnation of the soul in the following manner: From the beginning, God created all the souls in the very form in which they would afterwards appear in this world... At the time when the soul is to descend, the Lord calls it and says: "Go to such and such a place." The soul submits and descends against its will... If it returns laden with sin, it must obtain purification so as not to be delivered to *Gehinnom*... To be saved from punishment, the soul migrates from body to body.

In the opinion of most Kabbalists, no soul migrates through more than three bodies before it has run its entire course. The sinner expiates his sin in this world in the new existence in which his soul reappears. It may enter the body of a pious man, and by his good deeds he may cleanse the dross still adhering to the soul and facilitate its ascent on high. If pious men suffer, it is only and solely for sins committed in a previous existence; so that suffering is not a punishment for sins now committed, but a "purgatory" for evil deeds of a former life. On the other hand, the sinner may benefit from the good deeds that he performed in his previous existence. He prospers now, so that *all* his reward is eaten up by him in this world, and nothing but punishment is reserved for him in the hereafter.

According to some, a soul which has sunk to the lowest level of contamination becomes an evil spirit in this world, and it is anxious to enter living bodies for torment without recourse for punishment in *Gehinnom*. Such a soul becomes a *dibbuk* (דבוק), well known in kabbalistic books. To expel it by adjuration, to free it from this temporary existence as quickly as possible, is a meritorious deed, a real *tikkun* (תקון), an improvement, playing an important part in Ḥasidic literature. Such exorcism was practised by kabbalistic wonder-workers who were influenced by the mystic teachings of Rabbi Isaac Luria (1534-1572) of Safed, Palestine.

Rav Saadyah Gaon of the tenth century writes in his *Emunoth v'Deoth* (Beliefs and Opinions), one of the standard works of Jewish religious philosophy, to the effect that there are some, calling themselves Jews, who believe in metempsychosis, that the soul migrates from one person to another and even from man to beast, and that in this way it is punished for its sins and purged. They see a confirmation of their view in the fact that some persons exhibit qualities which are characteristic of lower animals. But this is absurd.

EXILE   גָּלוּת

GALUTH (exile) has the connotation of expulsion, as in the case of the Babylonian captivity (גלות בבל), which lasted from the destruction of the First Temple in 586 before the common era to the reestablishment of the Judean Commonwealth in 516, the year of the Temple's rebuilding, namely: seventy years. The second, Roman Exile (גלות אדום) has been the main cause in the extension of the Diaspora or dispersion of the Jewish people in the past nineteen centuries.

The name *galuth* also denotes banishment to a city of refuge for involuntary manslaughter. In a case of manslaughter, *qaluth* was both a punishment and a protection against blood revenge. By fleeing into one of the refuge cities, a manslayer, pursued by a blood avenger (גואל הדם), was protected against the ancient law of life for life. In addition to the six cities of refuge (ערי המקלט), the forty-two Levitical cities served as a protection of the unintentional homicide.

Galuth has come to mean the abnormal life of the Jewish minority in the lands of dispersion. In the words of Ḥayyim Greenberg: "Wherever Jews live as a minority . . . is *Galuth*." Moses ibn Ezra, one of the leading Hebrew poets of the Spanish period (1060-1138), describes *galuth* as "a form of imprisonment . . . the refugees are like plants without soil or water." The conventional connotation of *galuth*, as applied to dispersed Jewish people, is that of degradation and misery.

125

Rabbi Samson Raphael Hirsch writes: "Israel's entire *Galuth* history is one vast altar, upon which it sacrificed all that men desire and love for the sake of acknowledging God and the Torah. . . I would grieve if Israel understood itself so little . . . that it would welcome emancipation as an end of the *Galuth*." In 1906, Solomon Schechter wrote: "The term *Galuth* expresses the despair and helplessness felt in the presence of a great tragedy. . . It is a tragedy to see a great ancient people, distinguished for its loyalty to its religion . . . losing thousands every day by the mere process of attrition. . . It is a tragedy to see a language held sacred by all the world . . . doomed to oblivion and forced out gradually from the Synagogue. . . This may not be the *Galuth* of the Jews, but it is the *Galuth* of Judaism. . ."

GOLEM   גֹּלֶם

T H E word *golem* in the sense of an unformed substance is to be found in Psalm 139:16. In the Mishnah (Avoth 5:9), *golem* is used in the sense of a stupid person, whose habit it is to interrupt the speech of his fellow man and be hasty to answer, without acknowledging the truth or admitting that he does not know what he does not know. The Mishnah uses *golem* as the opposite of a wise person when it says: There are seven characteristics of a *golem*, and seven of a wise man. The wise man does not speak in the presence of one who is greater than he in wisdom. . . The opposite is to be found in a stupid person.

In medieval Jewish legends, the word signified an automaton, an artificial man, created by kabbalistic methods, such as placing in its mouth a piece of paper inscribed with the divine name. When thus created, the automaton became the servant of its creator carrying out his orders, and at times turned into a monster of destruction. It turned into an inert mass when the divine name was removed.

Rabbi Judah Loew (Maharal) of Prague is credited with having created one of the best known *golems* at the end of the sixteenth century. After his death in 1609, numerous legends began to develop about him. The most famous one was the story of the giant *golem* which he had fashioned out of clay and into which he had placed the tetragrammaton, the four-lettered divine name, thus bringing the automaton to life and making it obedient to his will.

The *golem* served its master loyally until at last it became unruly and a danger to the city. The rabbi removed the sacred word, the life principle, and turned the *golem* back again to clay. These legends always describe the *golem* as serving for the protection of the persecuted Jews of that period.

BENEVOLENCE   גְּמִילוּת חֲסָדִים

GEMILUTH ḤASADIM (practice of kindness) is a virtue which includes every kind of help: visiting the sick, comforting those who mourn, escorting the dead to the grave. The Mishnah counts it among the things for which no limit has been prescribed by the Torah (Peah 1:2). Since *gemiluth ḥasadim* consists of personal acts of kindness, it can be practised by rich and poor alike.

Commenting on Genesis 47:29, where Jacob asks Joseph to deal kindly and truly with him after death, the *Midrash Tanḥuma* points out that kindness shown to the dead is indeed an act of true love (חסד של אמת), since there is no prospect of repayment or gratitude: a poor man may one day be in a position to repay his benefactor, but the dead man cannot repay. According to the Talmud, whoever is merciful is certainly of the children of Abraham. The Jewish people are characterized by modesty, mercy, and benevolence (Betzah 32b; Yevamoth 79a).

In his *Mishneh Torah*, Maimonides writes: "The quality of mercy is characteristic of the Jewish people. They are like brothers . . . and if a brother shows no mercy toward a brother, who will? On whom, then, should the poor of Israel depend? . . . Alas, their help must come only from their brethren. . . The highest degree of righteousness (*tsedakah*) is to aid a man in want by offering him a gift or a loan, by entering into partnership with him, or by providing work for him, so that he may become self-supporting."

Gemiluth ḥasadim finds expression in all efforts of goodwill, and is exemplified by receiving all men cheerfully, by loving peace and striving for peace (Avoth 1:12, 15).

GEMARA   גְּמָרָא

THE name *Gemara*, derived from the Aramaic verb גמר (to learn), refers to the second part of the Talmud consisting of discussions and amplifications of the Mishnah which is the first part. The Mishnah

(teaching), which was concluded at the beginning of the third century, covers the whole range of Jewish legislation as well as religious
and ethical teachings transmitted by the Tannaim who were the
authorities on the Oral Law from the time of Hillel to that of Rabbi
Judah ha-Nasi, a period of about two centuries. The Gemara is the
interpretation of the Mishnah by the Amoraim, the bearers of the
oral traditional lore, who were active in Palestine and Babylonia from
the time of the completion of the Mishnah until the redaction of the
Babylonian Talmud.

There is the Babylonian *Gemara* and the Palestinian *Gemara*, referred to as תלמוד בבלי and תלמוד ירושלמי. The former, which is
the more complete, was concluded by the academies of Babylon at
the beginning of the sixth century; the latter was finished during the
fifth century. When the Talmud is spoken of without any qualification the reference is to the Babylonian Talmud; the Palestinian Talmud is only about a fourth the volume of the Babylonian, which
contains about two million five hundred thousand words.

Its vastness has given rise to the expression *Yam ha-Talmud*, "the
ocean of the Talmud." It is often referred to as *Shas* (ש"ס), from the
initials of the Hebrew *Shishah Sedarim* (six orders), alluding to ששה
סדרי משנה. The Babylonian Talmud is a veritable encyclopedia covering the whole gamut of human life. Originally, the name *Talmud*
was applied only to the Gemara, but it now includes also the Mishnah.

The Babylonian Talmud, containing 5,894 folio pages, is usually
printed in twelve large volumes, the pagination of which is kept uniform in all editions. Only thirty-six of the sixty-three Mishnah tractates are included and interpreted in the Babylonian Talmud, though
most of the subject matter of the omitted tractates are treated in the
Gemara of other tractates. The style of the Babylonian Talmud is
mostly brief and succinct; whole sentences are often indicated by a
single word. It is at no time easy reading. The text has no punctuation to mark the groupings and the separation of phrases, clauses and
other structural elements of sentences. Close attention and hard
thinking are required for the understanding of the context. The commentary of Rabbi Solomon Yitzḥaki (1040-1105), known as Rashi,
is a masterpiece of brevity, precision and clearness.

Rashi lived in Troyes, France, where his school rapidly achieved a
wide reputation. Though he was also occupied with the cultivation
of his vineyards, he wrote a commentary on the Talmud which has
never been superseded nor rivalled. This work, in lucid Hebrew, gives

the student just sufficient help to make the text both clear and interesting. It has been observed that Rashi has two of the rarest gifts of a commentator: the instinct to discern precisely the point at which explanation is necessary, and the art of giving or indicating the needed help in the fewest words.

The French talmudic scholars of the twelfth and thirteenth centuries continued Rashi's work on the Talmud by their glosses, known as *Tosafoth* (addenda); hence they are referred to as *ba'ale tosafoth* or *Tosafists*. Initially, supplementary to Rashi's commentary, they soon developed into a new independent mode of Talmud study. All regular editions of the Talmud are provided with Rashi and Tosafoth.

PARADISE   בַּן עֵדֶן

THE exact spot of the Garden of Eden, described as the extremely fertile first home of man, has not been determined. Some authorities suggest that its site is most probably to be sought about the head of the Persian Gulf. The Septuagint used the Greek word *paradeisos* (park) in rendering the biblical *Gan Eden*. Hence, *Paradise* and *Gan Eden* have been used synonymously to designate the abode of sanctified souls after death. Because the Garden of Eden was the abode of man in his state of innocence, it became the dwelling place of the upright in the hereafter. According to Jewish lore, there is a celestial as well as a terrestial Garden of Eden, the earthly one being only a copy of the sublime heavenly Paradise.

Nahmanides, in his commentary on Genesis 4:13, says that the narrative of Eden has a double meaning and that its prototype is in heaven. Talmudic legend reports that the world is one-sixtieth of the celestial garden, which is one-sixtieth of Eden. Since the word *eden* signifies delight and pleasantness, and because of its connection with the Tree of Life, the Garden of Eden has been regarded by Jewish tradition as the eternal home of bliss reserved for the souls of the righteous. One of the books of the Apocrypha speaks of it as being filled with all the delights of the senses, with streams of milk and honey, with trees that are laden with all sorts of fruits, with mountains that are bedecked with lilies and roses (II Esdras 2:19).

According to a talmudic statement, however, there is no eating in the future world . . . but the righteous sit with their crowns on their heads and enjoy the brilliance of the *Shekhinah*, the Divine Presence

129

(Berakhoth 17a). Abravanel, in his commentary on I Samuel 25:29, writes: "The reward of the souls in the world beyond is their ability to attain the true concept of God which is a source of the most wonderful feeling, an attainment impossible for man in this earthly life."

GENIZAH ‎גְּנִיזָה

GENIZAH (hiding space) has been applied to a place in which discarded ancient works and fragments of manuscripts were deposited for the purpose of preserving good things from harm and bad things from harming. The *Genizah* served as a storehouse for timeworn sacred writings, called *shemoth* (divine names) because they contained references to God. The sanctity attached to them forbade willful neglect. Heretical books, too, found their way into the *Genizah*, so that countless Hebrew manuscripts which have survived intact owe their preservation in part to their lodgment in an old synagogal storehouse.

The most famous *Genizah* is that of Cairo, Egypt, where Solomon Schechter found a rich collection of Hebrew manuscripts shedding considerable light on Jewish literature and history. The large majority of the *Genizah* contents were transported from Egypt to Cambridge University, England, in 1898, by Solomon Schechter. About two thirds of the Hebrew text of Ben Sira, the famous apocryphal work that came down to us in its Greek translation, was recovered in manuscripts found in the Cairo *Genizah*, where it had been customary for many centuries to deposit discarded Hebrew books.

The so-called "Damascus Document," a fragmentary manuscript on the constitution and the religious life of a Jewish sect in Damascus, was discovered in two incomplete versions in the Cairo *Genizah*. The tenor of the book is like the "Manual of Discipline" that has come from one of the Qumran caves near the Dead Sea. The "Dead Sea Scrolls" along with many fragments of other books, which have made their appearance in recent years and caused universal discussion, are: 1) the book of Isaiah contained in its entirety in the largest and oldest of the scrolls, and also in part in one of those acquired by the Hebrew University; 2) the Commentary on Ḥabakkuk; 3) the Manual of Discipline; 4) the Lamech Scroll, written in Aramaic; 5) the War of the Sons of Light with the Sons of Darkness; and 6) the Thanksgiving Psalms. The members of the Qumran sect regarded themselves as the chosen "sons of light," fully aware of divine secrets.

130

The practice of Jewish congregations to this day is that all Hebrew writings, when they can no longer be used, are preserved from profanation by being deposited somewhere in the synagogue-building, whence they are taken from time to time to be buried in the cemetery with great pomp. This is based on the *halakhah* which is formulated by Maimonides as follows: "A *Sefer Torah* which has become old or unfit for use is to be laid in an earthen vessel and buried beside a scholar. Its concealment consists in this" (*Hilkhoth Sefer Torah*). The same statement, verbally carried over into the Shulḥan Arukh of Rabbi Joseph Karo, is to be found in Yoreh Deah 282:10. The instruction to bury the *Genizah* was not carried out in all places, and so the Cairo *Genizah* has disclosed its riches to students of ancient Jewish literature.

Genizah studies were advanced by Louis Ginzberg in the talmudic field, by Jacob Mann in the geonic, and Israel Davidson in the liturgical. In the field of Bible, discoveries were made of biblical manuscripts with unique characteristics. They contained vocalization of the Hebrew text strange to modern eyes. It appears that in the seventh and eighth centuries, different systems of vocalizing the Hebrew consonantal text sprang into existence: Yemenite, Babylonian, and Tiberian. Much of the vocalization and grammar of these first two systems differs from the Tiberian, as shown in the revised and enlarged edition of *The Cairo Genizah* by Paul E. Kahle.

The discovery of the Cairo *Genizah* brought to light the forgotten remains of the ancient Palestinian poets, such as the work of the Hebrew liturgical poet Yannai of the sixth century, who was the first known Hebrew poet to employ rhyme consistently and to sign his name acrostically. The discovery of the lost poetic work of Yannai is regarded as the most important single find in the Cairo *Genizah*. Rabbi Elazar ha-Kallir, the most influential and prolific among the early authors of religious poetry (*payyetanim*), is counted among the followers of Yannai.

GESISAH   גְּסִיסָה

JEWISH tradition considers a dying person (*goses*) as a living individual who must not be touched lest his death be hastened thereby. He is compared to a flickering candle which is extinguished by touching it. Even though he has been agonizing for a long time, it is unlawful to hasten his death by removing the pillows from under his head. Those present are expected to recite prayers and psalms instead of engaging in idle talk.

Since "there is not a righteous man on earth who does good and never sins" (Ecclesiastes 7:20), a Jew is expected to make confession on his death-bed (Shabbath 32a). If unable to make a confession verbally, he is expected to do so mentally. A form of confession recorded in the Mishnah (Sanhedrin 6:2) reads: "May my death be an atonement for all the sins I have committed." Like Rabbi Akiva, who was martyred by the Romans in 135, a dying Jew departs with the *Shema* on his lips, uttering Israel's confession of faith: "Hear, O Israel, the Lord is our God, the Lord is One."

PROSELYTES   גֵּרִים

THE name *ger* (stranger) has come to mean in Hebrew a convert to Judaism who performs the duties and enjoys the privileges of a Jew. Anyone who has accepted Judaism out of inner conviction and without ulterior motives is called גר צדק or גר אמת (sincere, true proselyte), in contrast to גרי אריות who, like the Samaritans (II Kings 17:25), have embraced Judaism through fear of punishment.

According to a rabbinic statement, the man who adopts Judaism to marry a Jewess, or because of love or fear of Jews, is not a genuine proselyte (Gerim 1:3). A true proselyte is like a born Jew . . . like a new-born infant (Mekhilta 12:49; Yevamoth 62a). In a letter to a proselyte, Maimonides writes: "All who adopt Judaism are Abraham's disciples. . . There is absolutely no difference between you and us."

There is also a partial proselyte, referred to as גר תושב (sojourning proselyte), who has not adopted Judaism in its entirety, but has agreed to observe the seven precepts imposed upon the descendants of Noah: abstinence from idolatry, murder, theft, blasphemy, incest, eating the flesh of a living animal, and the duty of promoting justice. He is regarded an as honest seeker after truth and, apart from ritual restrictions, he enjoys equal rights before the courts.

There are seemingly contrasting statements in talmudic literature concerning those who are admitted to full membership in the household of Israel. "A would-be proselyte is neither persuaded nor dissuaded. . . Proselytes are as hard on Israel as a sore on the skin. .

132

If one sincerely wishes to adopt Judaism, welcome and befriend him; do not repel him" (Yevamoth 47b; 109b; Mekhilta 18:6). "If one comes to ask for admission to Israel, he is not received at once, but is asked: Do you not know that this nation is downtrodden and afflicted, subjected to many ills, liable to varied penalties for disobedience to the precepts of the Torah?. . . If he persists, he takes a ritual bath and submits to circumcision. . ." (Yevamoth 47a).

Both male and female applicants become proselytes by *tevilah* (immersion) in a *mikveh* or pool of running water. Upon emerging from the water they pronounce this blessing: "Blessed art thou, Lord our God, King of the universe who hast sanctified us with thy commandments, and commanded us about immersion." The reason that proselytes recite the benediction *after* the immersion, and not *before* the performance of this precept, is that prior to the immersion it does not apply to them. To be ritually *kasher* (fit for use), water of the *mikveh* has to come directly from a natural spring or a river.

Maimonides, replying to a question addressed to him by a proselyte, wrote: "You have asked about the prayers and benedictions, whether you should say *our God and God of our fathers*. . . You should pray like any Jew by birth. . . Any stranger who joins us till the end of time . . . is a disciple of our father Abraham and a member of his household. . . You are to say *our God and God of our fathers*, because Abraham is your father. . . You may certainly say in your prayers *who hast chosen us, who hast given us the Torah* . . . and *who hast separated us*, because God has indeed chosen you and separated you from the peoples and given you the Torah; for, the Torah is given alike to us and to the stranger, as it is written: One Torah and one judgment shall be for you and for the stranger who sojourns with you (Numbers 15:16). . . Let not your lineage be light in your eyes. If our lineage is from Abraham, Isaac and Jacob, your lineage is from God himself."

The Jewish system of morals attracted numerous converts during the Roman period. Many Romans attached themselves to Judaism with varying degrees of intensity. The greater number of "those who revered God" renounced polytheism and image worship, abstained from forbidden food, kept the Sabbath, and attended the synagogue on frequent occasions. Judaism acquired converts wherever Jews settled in the Diaspora. According to some, about two million Roman citizens had been converted to Judaism prior to the threat of the death penalty by the emperor Hadrian (117-138) and later Byzantine decrees, which forced the abandonment of proselytizing. There are in-

stances of wholesale conversion to Judaism by tribes, of which the
Khazars of the eighth century are the most notable.

Though the adoption of Judaism by individuals has frequently resulted in great suffering, some have urged the recapture of the "mission of Judaism." The talmudic sages ascribed the sin of the molten
calf in the wilderness to the influence of the Egyptian proselytes.

Judaism was a missionary religion when it was confronted with
paganism, but its missionary activity was of a restricted character.
All that Judaism was concerned with in its missionary work was to
substitute the religion of humanity for the false gods and false morality of the pagan world. Judaism withdrew from the missionary field
when paganism yielded to the two daughter faiths which shared in
common many truths, religious and moral, with the mother faith.

According to rabbinic teaching, any person who regulates his life
by the Seven Precepts of the Descendants of Noah, mentioned above,
fulfills his immediate task as a co-worker with God. But higher in
character must be the contribution of the son of Israel, who is charged
with the duty to promote divine righteousness on earth. The Jew
must be thoroughly obedient to the Torah in which is revealed the
moral will of God.

Even though Judaism opens the door to proselytes, it must long
remain the religion of a minority, keeping the great ideals before the
eyes of mankind. Just because Judaism teaches that every good man,
irrespective of his beliefs, is saved and has a share in the world to
come, it follows that to be a good Jew signifies something ethically
higher than being a good man. Jews must be prepared to defend their
heritage at the cost of their lives, as in the past, and to sacrifice their
material wealth. Many a potential martyr becomes indifferent to the
ideals for which he would offer his life in time of persecution. The
world has need of a minority of idealists, it has been asserted.

RAIN AND DEW   גֶּשֶׁם וְטַל

THE prayer for rain, solemnly recited on the eighth day of *Sukkoth*
as part of the *Musaf* service, introduces the formula מַשִּׁיב הרוח ומוריד
הגשם (Thou causest the wind to blow and the rain to fall) which is
inserted into the beginning of the *Amidah*, or silent devotion, during
the period between *Sukkoth* and *Pesaḥ*, when the rainy season in Eretz
Yisrael arrives. The poems composed by Rabbi Elazar ha-Kallir of

134

the eighth century are chanted; they refer to the biblical miracles that were performed for Israel in connection with water that has a puri-fying significance. It reads in part:

Remember Abraham who followed thee like water,
Whom thou didst bless like a tree planted near streams of water;
Thou didst shield him, thou didst save him from fire and water. . .
Remember Isaac whose birth was foretold over a little water;
Thou didst tell his father to offer his blood like water. . .
Remember Jacob who, staff in hand, crossed the Jordan's water. . .
Thou didst promise to be with him through fire and water.
Remember Moses in the ark of reeds drawn out of the water. . .
He struck the rock and there gushed forth water. . .
Remember the twelve tribes thou didst bring across the water;
Thou didst sweeten for them the bitterness of the water. . .
Turn to us, for our life is encircled by foes like water.

The prayer for dew, chanted on the first day of *Pesaḥ* as part of the *Musaf* service, is a supplication for a season rich in fertility, when the plants in Eretz Yisrael are to be refreshed by the regular descent of dew during the hot period of the year.

Rabbi Elazar ha-Kallir's prayer-poem for dew is one of the most delightful of his numerous *piyyutim*. It conveys the hope for the fer-tilization of the earth and the restoration of Israel. It reads in part:

Let dew fall on the blessed land;
Bless us with the gift of heaven;
In the darkness let a light dawn
For the people who follow thee.
Let dew sweeten the mountains;
Let thy chosen taste thy wealth;
Free thy people from exile.
That we may sing and exult.
Let our barns be filled with grain;
Renew our days as of old. . .
Make us like a watered garden. . .

In the hot, dry months between May and September, the atmos-pheric vapor, condensed in small drops on cool areas between evening and morning, saves the vegetation of Israel. When cool breezes blow across from the Mediterranean, dew is precipitated.

The Bible employs dew to symbolize God's word which has a won-derful reviving power though it falls, like dew, gently and unheard (Deuteronomy 32:2). The freshness of youth, as well as the life-giving power of God, is metaphorically represented by dew (Psalm 110:3, II Samuel 1:21; Isaiah 18:4; 26:19). From about December 5th till *Pesaḥ*, the ninth benediction of the *Shemoneh Esreh* includes the petition for both dew and rain (טל ומטר).

The petition ותן טל ומטר לברכה (bestow dew and rain for a blessing), inserted in the ninth benediction of the *Shemoneh Esreh*, is known as שאלה (request), while the formula משיב הרוח ומוריד הגשם, inserted in the second benediction, is called הזכרת גשמים (a reference to rain). According to a talmudic statement, prayer for rain is one thing, and reference to rain is another thing: שאלה לחוד והזכרה לחוד (Taanith 4b).

In Eretz Yisrael, the plea ותן טל ומטר is first inserted on the seventh of Tishri, the day set by Rabban Gamaliel in Temple times for the benefit of the pilgrims who had come from Babylon to celebrate *Sukkoth* in Jerusalem, so that they might have fifteen days after *Sukkoth* in which to return home without the interference of rain. In countries other than Eretz Yisrael, the petition for rain does not begin before the sixtieth day after the autumnal equinox, that is, December 5th or 6th.

The first three benedictions of the *Shemoneh Esreh* are designed as praise of God the Redeemer, the Omnipotent, the Holy One. Rain is considered as great a manifestation of the divine power as the resurrection of the dead (Taanith 2a); hence, משיב הרוח is inserted, during the rainy season in Eretz Yisrael, in the second benediction, known as גבורות, praising the powers of God. The actual petition for rain, however, is inserted in the ninth benediction, rather than in the second.

CHRONICLES

דִּבְרֵי הַיָּמִים

CHRONICLES, the very last book in the Hebrew Bible, consists of two books which count as one in Jewish tradition. It contains a historical record dating from the creation of the world to the end of the Babylonian captivity. Unlike the book of Kings, which covers the history of the kingdoms of Israel and Judah, Chronicles is confined to the story of the kingdom of Judah only, and completely ignores the northern kingdom of Israel.

In describing David's rule, it differs from the parallel account in the book of Samuel by omitting his misdeeds and adding details of his projects. The religious view presented by the book of Chronicles is the conviction that history is not made by chance. Only those events are treated which illustrate a divine purpose and providence.

The interest of Chronicles is centered in the Temple worship and the liturgical service of the sanctuary. In the account of the reign of Solomon, the building of the Temple is emphasized. According to tradition, Ezra was the author of both books: Chronicles and Ezra. Since the last two verses of Chronicles are identical with the first verses of Ezra, it has been conjectured that these two books constituted originally one continuous history of Judah.

The Hebrew style of Chronicles has numerous peculiarities, not found in other biblical books, which are perceptible even in a translation. It has been pointed out that in addition to numerous idioms, hardly a verse occurs in this book which does not present singularities of style. Among these are the heavy combined sentences by the use of two clauses connected by the word *asher*. Following are several excerpts from the last chapter of the second book of Chronicles:

"King Zedekiah did what was evil in the sight of the Lord his God... The leading priests and the people were likewise exceedingly unfaithful, copying the abominable practices of the pagans and defiling the Temple which the Lord had hallowed in Jerusalem. They mocked God's messengers, despised his words, and scoffed at his prophets, until the wrath of the Lord burst upon the people... He brought down on them the king of the Chaldeans, who killed their young and old and had no compassion... The House of God and all the buildings of Jerusalem were burned; all the costly vessels were destroyed. The Chaldean king carried the survivors off to Babylon, where they became servants to him and to his sons until the establishment of the

137

Persian empire. . . Then the Lord stirred up the spirit of Cyrus, king of Persia, to issue a proclamation throughout all his kingdom, permitting reconstruction of the House of God at Jerusalem."

DEUTERONOMY　　　　　　　　　　דְּבָרִים

DEUTERONOMY, the fifth book of the Torah, is titled in Hebrew *Devarim* (words) after the initial phrase. The Greek word, of which *Deuteronomy* is the English form, is used in the Septuagint to render the phrase *Mishneh ha-Torah*, the repetition of the Torah, in Deuteronomy 17-18, where we read: "When he is enthroned in his kingdom, he shall have a copy of this Torah made from the book that is in the custody of the Levitical priests." But this book is not merely the repetition or copy of laws already given. It is both a review of events and a further interpretation of teachings to be found in Exodus, Leviticus, and Numbers. The entire book of Deuteronomy is permeated with a spirit of fervent and profound religion.

The book of Deuteronomy carries events up to the death of Moses and prepares for the succession of Joshua. The greater part of the book is taken up with the addresses of Moses to the people of Israel as they were about to cross the Jordan to the land of Canaan. In these discourses Moses reviews the events and the legislation of the forty years spent in the wilderness. There are at least three speeches. The first is a summary of the main experiences of Israel in the desert; the second reviews the Ten Commandments and includes the declaration of God's Oneness; the third stresses the duty of loyalty to God.

The final chapters consist of two poems recited by Moses in the hearing of the people; they also tell the story of his death. The moving narrative describing the death of Moses reveals the final experience of the great leader. From the peak of Mount Nebo, Moses surveys the whole extent of the promised land; he dies on Mount Nebo in solitude at the age of one hundred and twenty.

A number of passages from Deuteronomy have been incorporated into the daily prayers, notably the *Shema*, Israel's confession of faith, which expresses the duty of loving and serving God with our whole being. The fifth book of the Torah contains a considerable number of human laws and is one of the most beautiful and profoundly ethical books of the Bible. The long poem *Ha'azinu*, in the thirty-second chapter, is one of the best productions of biblical poetry. Excerpts:

138

"What great nation has laws as just as this Torah which I am setting before you this day? Only take heed lest you forget the things which your eyes have seen. Make them known to your children and to your children's children... You are children of the Lord your God—you must not eat any detestable food... If you happen to come upon a bird's nest when the mother-bird is sitting upon the young ones or the eggs, you must not take away the mother-bird along with her offspring; you must let the mother go and you may take only the young...

"If a man kidnaps a fellow man in order to enslave or sell him, the kidnapper shall be put to death... You shall not defraud your servant; you shall pay him each day's wages before sundown... You shall not violate the rights of the alien or the orphan, or take the clothing of a widow in pledge... You shall not have weights of different sizes in your bag, one large and the other small; you shall have a true and just weight, a true and just measure. Everyone who is dishonest is an abomination to the Lord your God..."

JUDGE   דַּיָּן

THE first judiciary of Israel was organized by Moses on the advice of his father-in-law Jethro. For the adjudication of cases of less moment, he assigned a judge to each thousand, to each hundred, to each fifty, and to each ten (Exodus 18:13-26). Before his death, Moses gave the following instructions to his people: "You shall appoint judges and officers in all your towns ... to administer true justice for the people. You shall not distort justice; you must not be partial. You shall not take a bribe; for a bribe blinds the eyes of the wise and twists the words of the just. Justice and justice alone shall you follow, that you may live and possess the land which the Lord your God is giving you" (Deuteronomy 16:18-20).

The duplication of the word justice (צדק צדק) stresses the importance of even-handed justice to all, whether it is to your advantage or disadvantage, whether in word or action, whether to Jew or non-Jew. It has been suggested that the emphasis of justice in this connection implies that one must not use *unjust* means to secure the triumph of justice. Maimonides sums up the seven qualification of an authentic judge: wisdom, humility, reverence for God, disdain of gain, love of truth, love for his fellow men, and a good reputation (*Yad, Sanhedrin*

2:7). According to a talmudic statement, a judge is a *talebearer* if, after the conclusion of a lawsuit, he says: "I was for acquittal but my colleagues were for conviction" (Sanhedrin 31a).

Courts of three *dayyanim* (judges) each existed in all towns of Eretz Yisrael for the adjustment of civil disputes. The term *dayyan* is now used in the sense of a member of a rabbinical court (*beth din*). The rabbinical *dayyan*, unlike ordinary rabbis, has to be qualified as a judge in money matters and problems of civil law that are brought before a *beth din*.

CIVIL CASES   דִּינֵי מָמוֹנוֹת

TALMUDIC law, civil and criminal, is discussed mostly in the third and fourth divisions of the Mishnah: *Nashim* (women) and *Nezikin* (damages). Of the ten tractates contained in *Nezikin*, the first three are *Bava Kamma*, *Bava Metzia*, and *Bava Bathra* (first gate, middle gate, and last gate). Each of these three tractates consists of ten chapters in both Mishnah and Gemara, which deal with compensation for injury or loss occasioned to person or property.

Bava Kamma contains practically the whole law on the subject of redress, and forms two main sections: injury and misappropriation. Under the heading of injury are included all sorts of damage done by the defendant personally or by any of his chattels and agencies. Misappropriation similarly embraces all kinds of unlawful possession, acquired intentionally or unintentionally.

Bava Metzia treats of lost property, guardianship, usury, and the hire of laborers. The main subject discussed in it is claims arising out of any transaction in which two parties have a share, from a joint finding to wage agreements; it contains much of the talmudic law relating to trade and industry.

Bava Bathra deals with claims of right to do or possess something, or prevent another from doing or possessing something. Broadly speaking, each of the ten chapters deals with a separate class of claim of ownership of immovable property. The third chapter, for example, deals with *hazakah*, the presumption of legal title to property held in uninterrupted and undisputed possession (in case of land, three years).

The three tractates known as *bavas* (gates), which originally formed one large tractate of thirty chapters, show us the talmudic sages in the role of secular judges, regulating the purely worldly affairs of the

140

Jewish people and deciding their business disputes. The Jewish court competent for civil cases was the local *beth din*, composed of three judges (*dayyanim*). A *dayyan* is disqualified from sitting in court if one of the parties or one of his fellow *dayyanim* is related to him, if he feels biased toward one of the litigants, or if he is considered unfit because of his conduct, religious or moral. The *dayyanim* were selected from among ordained rabbis. Reference is also made in the Talmud to a court of laymen (*beth din shel hediototh*), composed of one scholar and two laymen, and a court of arbitration (*borerin*), in which each party chooses a judge and the two judges together choose a third one to preside. Jews who brought their disputes before non-Jewish courts were severely criticised for what was regarded as *hillul ha-shem* (profanation of the divine name), an unworthy action which reflects discredit upon Judaism.

Rabbinic law demands the performance of acts beyond the requirements of the law, *lifnim mi-shurath ha-din;* for the sake of equity and ethical consideration, man is exhorted not to insist on his legal rights. The Talmud relates: Some porters negligently broke a barrel of wine belonging to Rabbah, so he seized their garments to guarantee the payment of the damage for which they were liable according to strict law (*din Torah*). The porters then went and complained to Rav, head of the Sura Academy. "Return their garments," Rav ordered. "Is that the law?" Rabbah inquired. "Yes, it is," Rav replied, "for it is written: Thus you will walk in the way of good men" (Proverbs 2:20). Their garments having been returned, the porters pleaded: "We are poor men; we have worked all day, we are hungry; are we to get nothing?" "Go and pay them," Rav ordered, "for it is written in the above verse: Keep to the paths of the righteous" (Bava Metzia 83a).

One of the basic principles of rabbinic law is *dina d'malkhutha dina:* in civil matters, the law of the land where Jews reside is binding (Gittin 10b). This rule was introduced by Samuel, founder of the Nehardea Academy and colleague of Rav (177-257), whose debates with Rav on *halakhic* problems are frequently cited in the Talmud. Samuel was an authority on civil law, in which his views were accepted as decisive. An expert astronomer, the Babylonian *Amora* Mar Samuel was referred to as *Yarhina'ah* because he was thoroughly versed in the regulation of the lunar year. Since he was very friendly with the Persian king, he was surnamed king Shavor (Bava Bathra 115b; Pesahim 54a). He expressed himself to the effect that the paths of the heavens were as clear to him as the streets of his home town Nehardea.

141

CAPITAL CASES   דִּינֵי נְפָשׁוֹת

IN capital cases, witnesses had to undergo severely strict tests and
cross-examination and were warned of the gravity of their charges.
They were addressed by the court in terms such as these: "Perhaps
what you are about to say is mere conjecture or hearsay, based on sec-
ond-hand information... Perhaps you are not aware that we shall,
in the course of the trial, subject you to close examination and searching inquiry. You must know that cases of capital punishment are not
like trials concerning monetary matters, in which one may make restitution and redeem his guilt by money.

"In cases of capital punishment the witness is accountable for the
blood of the person wrongfully condemned and for the blood of his
potential posterity until the end of time. Adam was created alone to
show that should anyone destroy a single life he shall be called to account as though he had destroyed the entire world.

"Furthermore, all men are fashioned after the pattern of the first
man, yet no two faces are exactly alike. Therefore, every person may
well say: For my sake the world was created" (Sanhedrin 4:5).

False witnesses had at times to suffer the punishment they intended
to inflict on the accused. The sanctity of human life is one of the basic principles of the Torah, according to which deliberate homicide is
punishable by death, and involuntary manslaughter with exile.
There is no difference between the life of an infant and that of an
adult. Though attempted suicide is not punishable, it is strongly
condemned. Since life is not man's own possession, but a trust from
God who creates life, the man who commits suicide is a murderer.

Only a court of twenty-three judges (Sanhedrin Ketannah) was considered competent to try capital cases. The Sanhedrin Gedolah, the
Great Sanhedrin, with seventy-one members, was the Supreme Court
of Appeal on all disputed points of law; it met in the Temple at Jerusalem. Death sentence was pronounced only if there was a majority
of at least two judges. All possible privileges were given to the accused
by the court. Once the accused was acquitted he could not be tried
again. Even though a convict was already on the way to execution,
fresh evidence in his favor had to be heard. A man marched in front
of the procession asking people to give their evidence if favorable to
the convict. He was given a strong drink before the execution; the
period between sentence and execution was kept as short as possible.

142

Banishment to a city of refuge for involuntary manslaughter was both a punishment and a protection against blood revenge. By fleeing into one of the cities of refuge, persons pursued by avengers of blood were protected against the ancient law of life for life. Forty-two Levitical cities, in addition to the six cities of refuge, also served as a protection of the unintentional homicide.

In talmudic literature there is a marked tendency to restrict capital punishment, if not to abolish it altogether. According to a statement in the Mishnah, a court was stigmatized as murderous if in the course of seven years it condemned a human being to death.

Rabbi Tarfon and Rabbi Akiva declared: "Had we belonged to the Sanhedrin, during Judea's independence, no person would ever have been executed," as they would always have found some legal technicalities by which to make a sentence of death impossible (Makkoth 1:10). During the Roman occupation of Palestine, the right to carry out death sentences was taken from Jewish authorities long before the destruction of the Temple.

LAWS OF HEAVEN   דִּינֵי שָׁמַיִם

ACCORDING to a tannaitic statement in Bava Kamma 55b, there are four acts for which the offender is exempt from the laws of man but liable under the laws of heaven (פטור מדיני אדם וחייב בדיני שמים) namely: he who breaks down a fence which encloses his neighbor's animal, so that it goes out and causes damage; he who bends a neighbor's standing corn towards a fire; he who hires witnesses to testify falsely; he who knows of evidence in favor of another but refrains from testifying in his behalf.

In the four instances, the offender cannot be punished by a human court, though he provided others with the opportunity to commit a criminal act. The Torah makes one legally responsible only for injuries and damages directly inflicted, whereas injuries and damages by indirect action are not subject to a suit at law (גרמא בנזיקין פטור), though they are forbidden (Bava Kamma 60a; Bava Bathra 22b).

The concept *laws of heaven* conveys the thought that, to the sages of the Talmud, the Torah is revelation of the divine ideal for the improvement of human character and conduct. Hence, it was their objective to widen the scope of the law in accordance with the spirit of equity and fairness.

143

DEMAI   דְּמַאי

PRODUCE concerning which there is a doubt as to whether the rules relating to the Levitical tithes were strictly observed is known as *Demai* (suspicion, doubt). The term is applied to produce bought from a farmer who happens to be an *am ha-aretz*, ignorant of the rules governing tithes.

The uninstructed of the land (עמי הארץ) were under suspicion of not giving tithes from their produce. They were not, however, suspected of not giving *terumah* (gifts to the priests), because *terumah* had a higher degree of sanctity and was only a light payment, which might be performed by giving the priest the smallest quantity—a single grain of wheat.

Since their produce was *demai*, that is, doubtful whether it had been tithed, a scrupulous observer of the Jewish law (*ḥaver*) who bought grain from an *am ha-aretz* had to set aside *ma‘aser* (a tithe for the Levites) and *ma‘aser min ha-ma‘aser* (a tenth part of that tithe).

The latter, comprising one-hundredth part of the grain, was given to the priests, since it was a deadly sin for a non-priest to take the sacred *terumah*. The second tithe (*ma‘aser sheni*) had to be eaten in Jerusalem, according to Deuteronomy 14:22-27).

As to the first tithe (*ma‘aser rishon*) and the poorman's tithe (*ma‘aser ‘ani*), the Levite or poor man had to prove that the grain was untithed in order to collect, in keeping with the talmudic rule that the claimant must produce evidence (המוציא מחברו עליו הראיה). The Mishnah tractate entitled *Demai* consists of six chapters.

DANIEL   דְּנִיֵּאל

THE book of Daniel, consisting of twelve chapters, is made up of two parts. The first six chapters, written chiefly in Aramaic, tell of the miraculous deliverance of Daniel and his three friends who were exiled to Babylon by Nebuchadnezzar before the fall of Judea; they also include Daniel's interpretations of Nebuchadnezzar's dreams.

The last six chapters are apocalyptic writings, professing to reveal the future. They are said to refer to the persecuting kingdoms of Babylonia, Persia, Greece, and Syria. Daniel lived at the royal court, and survived till the days of Cyrus, the Persian conqueror of Babylon,

144

who authorized the return of the Jewish exiles and permitted them
to rebuild the Temple at Jerusalem in 538 before the common era.

The four Aramaic words, written by a mysterious hand on the wall
at Belshazzar's feast, may have appeared in the form of anagrams.
According to the Talmud, the inscription *mené mené tekel upharsin*,
which could not be read by anyone except Daniel, appeared like this:

```
M  M  T  L  R
E  E  E  U  S
N  N  K  P  I
E  E  E  A  N
```

After the conjunction "u" (and), the letter "p" changes in Hebrew
to "ph". The word *parsin* is the plural of *peres*, which denotes division
and is spelled exactly like the Hebrew word for Persia. Hence, instead of *upharsin*, this word should be transliterated *uparsin*

Cuneiform inscriptions make it clear that Belshazzar was the eldest son of and co-regent with Nabonidus, the last king of the Babylonian empire (556-539). In the Bible, however, Belshazzar is spoken
of as the son of Nebuchadnezzar, because "son" in Hebrew sometimes
denotes "descendant." Excerpt:

"The windows of Daniel's room were opened toward Jerusalem, and
three times a day he bent his knees and prayed to God. Daniel's foes
surged in and found him offering prayers and supplications to his God.
They went before king Darius and asked: Did you not sign an edict
that any man who makes petition to any god or man within thirty
days, except to you, O king, shall be cast into the den of lions? It is
true, the king replied. Then they said to the king: Daniel pays no
heed to you, O king; he recites his prayers three times a day to his
own God...

"So Daniel was cast into the den of lions... At daybreak, the king
went in haste to the den of lions. When he came near the den, he
cried in a tone of anguish: O Daniel, has your God been able to deliver you from the lions? Daniel replied: O king, live forever! My
God has sent his angel and shut the mouths of the lions; they have
not hurt me. He has found me innocent; nor have I done you any
wrong... The men who had accused Daniel were then brought and
cast into the den of lions; and before they reached the bottom of the
pit, the lions crushed their bones."

The book of Daniel exerted a deep influence on Jewish mysticism.
It teaches the absolute supremacy of God, and the ultimate triumph
of what is good in the world after the conflict between good and evil.

D'TSAKH ADASH B'AḤAV   דְּצַ"ךְ עֲדַ"שׁ בְּאַחַ"ב

In the Passover Haggadah, the ten plagues inflicted upon the Egyptians before Israel's exodus from Egypt are given in three words, consisting of a combination of the initial letters of the ten plagues in the order we read about them in the Torah (Exodus 7:8-12:30). This mnemonic device is attributed to Rabbi Yehudah, one of the most eminent Tannaim of the second century. Elsewhere, Rabbi Yehudah suggested a mnemonic of two words, "lest you should make an error" (Menaḥoth 11:4). He stressed the serious responsibility of a teacher when he said: "Be careful in teaching, for an error in teaching amounts to intentional sin" (Avoth 4:16).

In Psalms 78 and 105, the order of the ten plagues differs, as they are enumerated, from the order of the plagues described in detail in the book of Exodus. According to Rabbi Yehudah, quoted in the Midrash (Exodus Rabbah 6:7; 8:3), the initial letters of the ten plagues were engraved on the staff of Moses that he might remember their proper sequence (נוטריקון דצ"ך עד"ש באח"ב). The three-word mnemonic of Rabbi Yehudah is designed therefore, to indicate, the authentic sequence of the events related in the Torah in connection with the liberation of Israel.

The sages of the Talmud maintain that each plague corresponds to a crime committed by the Egyptians against the people of Israel (measure for measure). Some of the plagues were meant to blot out the superstitious beliefs that were cherished by the Egyptians. The first plague, for example, was aimed against the Nile, regarded as a god because its regular overflow between June and November produced fertility of the soil without the benefit of rain. The newborn infants were cast into the Nile as offerings to the river god. One of the most remarkable features of the religion of the Egyptians was their veneration of animals. The number of animals which were deemed sacred was prodigious indeed. The frog, therefore, became the cause of intense annoyance to them. The sacred bull Apis may have been attacked with disease, as well as other sacred animals.

The first plague was not just a discoloration of the water, since we are told that "the fish in the river died" (Exodus 7:21). Apart from the eleven times frogs are mentioned in the eighth chapter of Exodus, they are mentioned twice again in Psalms 78:45 and 105:30 as a reference to the Egyptian plagues.

146

CORRECT BEHAVIOR   דֶּרֶךְ אֶרֶץ

DEREKH ERETZ (the way of the land) signifies local custom, good behavior, courtesy, politeness, etiquette. Rabbinic literature is replete with rules of dignified conduct: A person to be spoken to must first be addressed by his name, just as the Lord first called to Moses and then spoke to him (Yoma 4b). A parent or a teacher should not be called by name (Sanhedrin 100b). The most important message of Moses, to prepare the people of Israel for the reception of the Torah at Mount Sinai, was first addressed to the women and then to the men, according to the rabbinic interpretation of Exodus 19:3 (Mekhilta).

The talmudic sages visited one another very often for the purpose of learning. A student should visit his teacher every holiday (Rosh Hashanah 16b). The answer "yes" to a knock on the door does not mean "enter" but "wait" (Bava Kamma 33a). One must not suddenly enter his neighbor's home, not even his own home (Niddah 16b). Anything that causes an odor should not be eaten in company (Kethubboth 40a). The guests drink wine to one another's health, the formula being *l'ḥayyim* (to your health). A person who drains his cup in one draft is a glutton; in three drafts, a cad; the proper way is to take it in two (Betzah 25b).

Cleanliness promotes holiness (Avodah Zarah 20b). The servant waiting at the table should not wear the clothes in which he did the cooking (Sanhedrin 94a). The Sabbath garment must be distinguished from everyday apparel (Shabbath 113a). "Keep aloof from what is ugly and whatever resembles it" (Ḥullin 44b). Rabbi Joshua ben Levi said: "Never use an indecent expression, even if you have to use more words to complete the sentence" (Pesaḥim 3a). Otherwise, conversation should be concise, especially when speaking to a woman (Avoth 1:5; Eruvin 53b). "Man should always express himself in fitting terms" (Pesaḥim 3a) applies to figures of speech by which a softened expression is sustained for a phrase offensive to delicate ears.

Derekh Eretz is also the title of two lesser tractates appended to the Babylonian Talmud: *Derekh Eretz Rabbah* and *Derekh Eretz Zuta*, each being independent of the other despite their common name. *Derekh Eretz Rabbah* (large) emphasizes many a rule by the use of stories of the private life of the sages.

Derekh Eretz Zuta (small) is not a shorter version of *Derekh Eretz Rabbah*, but rather a collection of ethical teachings consisting of nine

147

chapters, including the section on peace. It contains rules of conduct and urges gentleness, patience, respect for age, readiness to forgive; it finally dwells on the moral and social duties of a rabbinic scholar. Leopold Zunz declared: "*Derekh Ertez Zuta*, which is meant to be a mirror for scholars, is full of high moral teachings and pithy worldly wisdom which philosophers of today could study to advantage."

Examples: If others speak evil of you, let the greatest thing seem unimportant in your estimation; but if you have spoken evil of others, let the least word seem important. If you have done much good, let it seem little in your eyes, and say: Not of mine have I done this, but of the good which has come to me through others. However, let a small kindness done to you appear great.

AMORITE CUSTOMS   דַּרְכֵי אֱמֹרִי

THE Amorites, inhabitants of Canaan who had extended their territory east of Jordan and also dwelled in Lebanon before the Hebrew conquest, are often referred to as masters of witchcraft and impure mysteries by which they contaminated Israel in the time of the Judges. A special section of the Talmud (Shabbath 67a-b) discusses various superstitions called "the ways of the Amorites."

In the Torah, superstition implies a belief in and practice of witchcraft, sorcery and necromancy current among the heathen nations. Maimonides writes to the effect that every witch is an idolater, having her own strange ways of worship offered to deities. In order that we may keep far from all kinds of witchcraft, we are warned not to adopt any of the practices of the idolaters... In those days the belief in the stars was very strong; it was generally assumed that life and death, good and evil depended on the stars... Originators of false and useless principles . . . tell their fellow men that a plague will befall those who will not perform the act by which that idolatrous faith is supported and confirmed forever. . .

The Torah prohibits all heathen customs, called by our sages "ways of the Amorites," because they are connected with idolatry . . . you will find that in certain kinds of worship they turn toward stars, in others to the two great luminaries . . . therefore all practices of those nations have been prohibited in these words: You shall not live by the customs of the nations I expelled before you (Leviticus 20:23. . . It must now be clear . . . that the prohibition of wearing garments of

148

wool and linen, of using the fruit of a tree in the first three years, and of mixing varied species, are directed against idolatry... (*Guide*, 3:37).

Despite all this opposition, many superstitions practices found their way into Jewish life from the surrounding population; they may have quite a Jewish air without being specifically Jewish. The *Mezuzah*, for example, has been used as a good-luck charm, as an amulet to ward off evil spirits. In his *Mishneh Torah*, Maimonides writes: "Those fools defeat in this manner the fulfillment of a great commandment to remember the Oneness of God ... turning the *Mezuzah* into an amulet for their selfish interest, believing in their foolish hearts that it can be made to serve the preservation of transitory worldly goods" (*Yad, Tefillin* 5:4).

LAW AND PROCEDURE   דָּת וָדִין

SEVEN synonyms for law are to be found in the Hebrew Bible (חק, משפט, דין, מצוה, עדות, פקוד, דת). From the beginning, Judaism has been more a religion of doing than of believing. It has placed the main emphasis on the legal rather than on the mystical element. The constitution of Judaism is not a number of creeds, but ten commandments; Moses is not represented as a metaphysician or theologian, but as a lawgiver. No mystic doctrines are communicated at Sinai, but a proclamation of the divine will concerning the function of man on earth.

Yet, the Torah is by no means a lawbook; half of its contents is narrative, appealing to the understanding and the imagination of all ages. Great moral truths are woven into the texture of the narrative portions of the Torah, in which the ancestors of Israel are represented in their family relations, as husband and wife, parent and child, brother and sister. Here are illustrations of truthfulness, grace and loveliness, with a wealth of instructive example.

All the translators of the Torah made a great error indeed when, for want of an exactly corresponding term, they rendered *Torah* by *Law*, giving rise to an utterly false conception of the nature of Judaism. Since the word *Torah* denotes teaching, knowledge, its English equivalent is preferably *Lore*, defined as that which is or may be learned, the whole body of knowledge possessed by a people.

The oral lore, which gradually became written lore, embodied in the vast talmudic-midrashic literature, contains the authoritative inter-

pretation of the Torah by the religious sages of Judaism for many
centuries. It is entirely misleading to describe the Jewish religion as
purely legal in character. The *Halakhah* often presents instances in
which a person cannot be punished according to law though he is
guilty from an ethical or moral point of view (פטור מדיני אדם וחייב
בדיני שמים).

Din (law) applies exclusively to those religious duties which concern definite actions that are prohibited or allowed. The Jewish people ever found joy and satisfaction in the fulfillment of religious
precepts and customs; hence the expression שמחה של מצוה (joyous
mitzvah-performance). In the daily evening service, there is a passage
which reads as follows: "Lord our God, when we lie down and when
we rise up we speak of thy laws and rejoice in thy Torah and in thy
precepts." Judaism has preserved its inner unity in law and custom,
and in the study of the Torah which has been regarded as the highest
religious duty.

Unlike the Mishnah, the two Talmuds are not lawbooks in the strict
sense of the term; they both contain numerous discussions and dissenting opinions placed beside one another, with many debated questions
left undecided. For this reason, the need of codifying the extensive
contents of the Talmuds was felt more and more. The first code collection, *Halakhoth Pesukoth*, was composed by the blind Gaon Yehudai
of Sura during the middle of the eighth century; it served as the basis
of various subsequent codes, attempting to make a better arrangement of the material according to subjects. The most original and
important work of this kind is Maimonides' *Mishneh Torah*, consisting of fourteen books in lucid and superb Hebrew. This gigantic work
penetrated every Jewish community shortly after its appearance in
the year 1180.

In the *Mishneh Torah*, which is indeed the full summary of Judaism
in all its varied aspects, Maimonides condensed the Jewish lore contained in the Bible, the two Talmuds, the Midrash, and the responsa
literature of the Geonim. About four hundred commentaries have
been written on the *Mishneh Torah*, which has exercised the greatest
influence on Jewish life. The numerous commentaries and super-
commentaries are not concerned for the most part with *what* Maimonides says but rather *why* he says it. What he says is incontestably
clear. The questions and arguments raised by talmudic scholars refer
as a rule to the sources of Maimonides' code, since he neither specified his sources nor gave reasons for his decisions.

150

After the *Mishneh Torah*, the *Tur* by Rabbi Jacob ben Asher of the fourteenth century obtained far-reaching influence. It remained the undisputed authority for more than two centuries, inasmuch as its author had used the *Mishneh Torah* as his model while at the same time discussing the contradictory opinions of the post-talmudic authorities. To meet the need of a new code after the expulsion of the Jews from Spain and Portugal, Rabbi Joseph Karo produced the *Shulḥan Arukh* based on the *Tur*, as it is commonly called, or *Arbaah Turim*, containing four parts. Rabbi Moses Isserles (רמ"א) of the sixteenth century provided the *Shulḥan Arukh* with glosses concerning *minhagim* (local customs), accepted by the Ashkenazim as legally valid. The *Shulḥan Arukh* has contributed largely to the consolidation of Judaism by serving as the most authoritative code of Jewish law and general practice.

Though essentially a lawbook, this code, like Maimonides' *Mishneh Torah*, is suffused with a deep spirit of saintliness and wisdom. Here is an example of its style: "Everyone should give to *tsedakah* (charity). Even a poor man who is supported by charity should donate a portion of what he receives... A man who wishes to become worthy of divine grace should curb his selfish impulses and contribute generously... Whatever is given for a noble purpose must be the finest.

"If a man builds a house of worship, it should be more beautiful than his own home; if he provides food for the hungry, it ought to be the best on his table; if he gives clothing to the naked, it should come from among the finest of his clothes... A man should always avoid accepting charity; he should endure misery rather than be dependent on his fellow men... Whoever is so much in need of charity that he cannot live without it, and yet is too proud to accept it, is guilty of bloodshed and suicide..."

T'sedakah, the Hebrew equivalent of relief, is not a matter of philanthropic sentiment, but of legal rightness. It is expected of all men toward all men. The Torah frequently emphasized that men of means are *obligated* to provide for those in want. Hence, the laws concerning charity in the Jewish codes of law.

Rabbi Abraham Danzig of Vilna (1748-1820) summarized the subjects of two sections of the *Shulḥan Arukh's* four sections in his work חיי אדם (the life of man). Rabbi Solomon Ganzfried of Ungvar (1804-1886) is best known as the compiler of an abridgment of the *Shulḥan Arukh*. Both authors, Rabbi Danzig and Rabbi Ganzfried use the following statement as an introduction to their respective works:

"The verse *I keep the Lord always before me* (Psalm 16:8) conveys a high religious-ethical principle. When a man is alone in the house he does not act as if he were in the presence of a great king; his manner of speech is not among his own relatives and friends what it might be in the company of a king. Hence, when a man realizes that the supreme King, whose glory fills the whole universe, is always near him, marking all his actions, he is bound to be inspired with reverence and humility."

Though the works of the Geonim contained important contributions to the codification of the Jewish traditional laws and customs, they were eclipsed by the subsequent codes, chiefly by the *Shulḥan Arukh*.

HAVDALAH

HAVDALAH (distinction), marking the end of Sabbath and festivals, corresponds to the *Kiddush*, which proclaims the holiness of Sabbath and festivals. Both are attributed to the men of the Great Assembly, who functioned during and after the Persian period of Jewish history, about 500-300 before the common era. The *Havdalah*, recited over wine, consists of four benedictions: over wine, spices, light, and the distinction between the sacred and the profane, between light and darkness, between Israel and the nations, between the seventh day and the six workdays.

According to Maimonides, the symbolic use of fragrant spices is to cheer the soul which is saddened at the departure of the Sabbath. When a festival follows immediately after the Sabbath the spices are omitted, because the soul then rejoices with the incoming festival. The wine for the *Havdalah* is allowed to flow over as a symbol of the overflowing blessing expected in the coming week. It is customary to cup the hands around the *Havdalah*-candle and to gaze at the fingernails. The reflection of the light on the fingernails causes the shadow to appear on the palm of the hand, thus indicating the distinction "between light and darkness."

A twisted candle of several wicks is used, because the phrase *meoré ha-esh* (the lights of fire) is in the plural. The custom of dipping the finger in the wine of the *Havdalah* and passing it over the eyes alludes to Psalm 19:9, where God's commands are described as "enlightening the eyes." These usages are not applicable whenever the *Havdalah* is recited as part of the *Kiddush* for festivals. In addition to the *Havdalah* over wine, there is another *Havdalah* inserted in the fourth benediction of the *Shemoneh Esreh*.

In talmudic literature, great importance is attached to the *Havdalah*: future salvation as well as material blessings are promised to those who recite the *Havdalah* over the wine cup. "He who resides in Israel, he who teaches his children Torah, and he who recites the *Havdalah* at the conclusion of the Sabbath will enter the world-to-come" (Berakhoth 33a). According to a talmudic legend, fire was one of the things God had left uncreated when Sabbath set in; but after the close of the Sabbath, God endowed man with divine wisdom. "Man then took two stones, and by rubbing them together produced fire. . ." (Pesaḥim 53b).

153

The Midrash elaborates this as follows: "The light which God created on the first day lit up the world for man from the time he was created until the sunset of the following day; the surrounding darkness filled Adam with dread. . . Then God furnished him with two bricks which he rubbed together until fire was produced; whereupon he offered a benediction over the fire" (Genesis Rabbah 11:2).

Rabbi Isaiah Horowitz, known as the *Sheloh* from the initials of his chief work שני לוחות הברית (the two tablets of the covenant), says that women do not drink of the wine of the *Havdalah*, in allusion to the guilt incurred by Eve when she gave some of the forbidden fruit to Adam, which is said to have been the juice of grapes. Hence, the popular belief among Jews of Russian and Galician origin that a girl will develop a mustache if she drinks of the *Havdalah* wine.

The *Sheloh*, or *Shené Luḥoth ha-Berith*, has been described as a profoundly ethical but unsystematic work of kabbalistic tendencies on Jewish laws and customs. Rabbi Isaiah Horowitz was born in Prague and died in Eretz Yisrael (1565-1630). He served as rabbi in various communities in Poland, Germany, and Bohemia.

HAVINENU   הֲבִינֵנוּ

THE shortened *Amidah*, consisting of one paragraph beginning with the word הביננו, was composed in the third century by Rabbi Samuel of Nehardea, one of the first generation of the authors of the Babylonian Talmud known as *Amoraim*. This prayer, quoted in Berakhoth 29a, is a synopsis of the middle thirteen petitions of the *Shemoneh Esreh;* it is called מעין שמונה עשרה (abstract of the eighteen benedictions). On urgent occasions, it was permitted to abridge the intermediary thirteen benedictions by reciting the *Havinenu* passage, which is preceded by the opening three benedictions and concluded by the last three benedictions of the original *Shemoneh Esreh*.

Translated into English, *Havinenu* reads as follows: "Grant us, Lord our God, wisdom to learn thy ways; forgive us that we may be redeemed; keep us from suffering; satisfy us with the products of thy earth; gather our dispersed people from the four corners of the earth. Judge those who stray from thy faith; punish the wicked; may the righteous rejoice over the rebuilding of thy city, the reconstruction of thy sanctuary, the flourishing dynasty of thy servant David. . . Answer us before we call. Blessed art thou, O Lord, who hearest prayer."

HAGBAHAH AND GELILAH   הַגְבָּהָה וּגְלִילָה

H AGBAHAH (elevating) and *gelilah* (rolling up) refer to the ceremonial raising of the *Sefer Torah* and then rolling it up in the synagogue worship service following the reading of biblical portions prescribed for Sabbaths, festivals and various other occasions. Among the Sephardic Jews, the raising of the Torah takes place before the reading, in keeping with an ancient custom. In Sofrim 14:14, however, this custom is mentioned as being performed after the reading.

When the Torah is raised, the standing congregation sees at least three columns of writing while reciting these verses: "This is the Torah which Moses placed before the children of Israel. It is in accordance with the Lord's command through Moses" (Deuteronomy 4:44; Numbers 9:23). Then come three verses from Proverbs 3:18, 17, 16, in a reversed order from the original text. They are: "It is a tree of life to those who take hold of it, and happy are those who support it. Its ways are ways of pleasantness, and all its paths are peace. Long life is in its right hand, and in its left hand are riches and honor. The Lord was pleased, because of his righteousness, to render the Torah great and glorious" (Isaiah 42:21).

PASSOVER HAGGADAH   הַגָּדָה שֶׁל פֶּסַח

T HE traditional Passover Haggadah, reflecting Israel's constant struggle for life and liberty, is one of the most frequently edited books. Few Hebrew classics are so famous and have attracted the attention of so many Jews as the Haggadah. Since the sixteenth century, the Haggadah has appeared in more than two thousand separate editions. Representing a gradual development, the Haggadah is not the work of any one man nor the product of any one period. Some of its contents have come down to us from ancient times, and were an essential part of the *Seder* service two thousand years ago. *Seder Haggadah* denotes an arrangement of the varied literature that went into the composition of the Haggadah, which has become the standard for all the people of Israel.

The Jewish people have not ceased to lavish their love on the Haggadah, the priceless midrashic collection that has stirred the spirit of freedom in the hearts of young and old through countless generations.

155

Its pages have often been richly ornamented with numerous paintings and drawings depicting memorable events in the history of the Jews. Based upon the idea that he who questions much learns much, the Passover Haggadah is extensively quoted in talmudic literature and widely discussed by great authorities like Rav Saadyah Gaon, Rashi, Maimonides. Its text is permeated with history, folklore, prayer and poetry. The Haggadah is filled with biblical quotations and rabbinic interpretations so that every Jewish family, once a year at least, is afforded an opportunity to comply with the statement that those who discuss Torah at the table are eating at the table of God (Avoth 3:4). Scores of scholars have written significant commentaries on this inspiring anonymous work.

The recital of the Haggadah is the most indispensable part of the *Seder* service. Primarily the narrative of Passover, the Haggadah tells the story of the entry into Egypt and of the liberation of the Israelites from their servitude there. It explains the use of the paschal lamb during Temple times, the *matzoth*, the *maror* (bitter herb). After the hymns of thanksgiving, and the symbolical explanations of the numbers one to thirteen, it ends with the song of divine retribution for the mistreatment of Israel (*Ḥad Gadya*).

Heinrich Heine, in his *Rabbi of Bacharach*, has this to say about the recital of the Haggadah during the *Seder* service: "The master of the house reads the Haggadah with an old, traditional chant; again and again the others at the table join him in chorus. The tune . . . lulls and soothes, and at the same time it rouses and calls, so that even those Jews who long since turned from the faith of their fathers . . . are touched when the well-remembered chants of Passover reach their ears."

CLEANSING OF UTENSILS הַגְעָלַת כֵּלִים

According to the interpretation of the talmudic sages, the Torah refers to the cleansing of the utensils from the forbidden food, which they had absorbed, when it says: "Whatever can stand fire, such as gold, silver, bronze, iron, tin and lead, you shall put into the fire. . . But whatever cannot stand fire you shall put into the water" (Numbers 31:22-23). Vessels used for cooking in hot water have to be purified by means of hot water; those used for roasting in fire must be cleansed by fire; and others used only for cold food-stuffs have to be

156

scoured with cold water (Rashi). Hence, the Mishnah states: "If a man bought utensils from a non-Jew, those which it is the custom to immerse (in order to free them from uncleanness) he must immerse (טְבִילַת כֵּלִים), those which it is the custom to make white-hot in the fire he must make white-hot in the fire . . . a knife needs but to be polished and it is then clean" (Avodah Zarah 5:12).

According to the *Shulḥah Arukh*, clay vessels used for *ḥametz* cannot be fitted for use on *Pesaḥ* by scouring with hot water or by putting them into the fire. Ovens and ranges of stone and bricks can be fitted for *Pesaḥ* by means of fire. Before the purification of a utensil it must be thoroughly cleansed of rust, though not of ordinary stains. A utensil that cannot be thoroughly cleansed cannot be fitted for use on *Pesaḥ*. It is customary not to *kasher* glass utensils for *Pesaḥ* by means of purification. If possible, the cleansing should be performed in the presence of a person who is familiar with the rules of purification.

LIGHTING THE CANDLES   הַדְלָקַת הַנֵּרוֹת

THE Mishnah takes for granted the ancient custom of kindling special Sabbath lights by the housewife (Shabbath 2:6-7). In accord with the cherished Jewish view, considering the home as the woman's sphere and the workaday world as the man's, the lights marking the beginning of the Sabbath are kindled by the wife, while the twisted candle of the *havdalah* marking the resumption of the week's work at the end of the Sabbath rest is kindled by the husband. Since the Bible uses light and joy as synonyms (Psalm 97:11; Esther 8:16), it has been suggested that the Sabbath illuminations were originally intended as symbolical of a day of joy, serenity and good cheer.

The custom of lighting two candles at least is explained by the two synonyms, "Remember" and "Observe," which introduce the Sabbath commandment in the two versions of the Decalogue, respectively (Exodus 20:8 and Deuteronomy 5:12). The benediction pronounced at the lighting is not mentioned in the Talmud but is found in the ninth-century Prayerbook of Rav Saadyah Gaon.

The Karaite practice of sitting in absolute darkness on Sabbath eve has contributed greatly to the removal of the Karaite sect from the main fold of Judaism. In his *Mishneh Torah*, Maimonides writes: "Even if one has no food, and has to go begging for the money to pay for the oil required for the lighting, it is his duty to do so, for this is part of *oneg Shabbath* (Sabbath delight). Prior to the lighting, one should pronounce this benediction: Blessed art thou . . . who hast commanded us to light the Sabbath lights" (Shabbath 5:1); even though this is one of the non-biblical precepts, it is based on the authority of the talmudic sages. All religious duties ordained by the sages, such as the reading of the *Megillah* on *Purim* and the kindling of Sabbath lights and *Ḥanukkah* lights, require the formula "who hast sanctified us with thy commandments and commanded us" in the introductory benediction. "Where in the Torah did God so command us? In Deuteronomy 17:11, where we are told to act according to their judgment. . . This applies to all the *mitzvoth* inaugurated by the sages" (כל המצוות שמדברי סופרים—*Yad, Berakhoth* 11:3).

HOSEA   הוֹשֵׁעַ

THE book of Hosea occupies the first place among the twelve Minor Prophets. The name *Minor Prophets*, as compared with *Major Prophets*, does not refer to value but to volume—the length of the individual books. Since each of these twelve books was very short, they were gathered into a single collection to safeguard their preservation. For this reason, they count as one book in the Hebrew Bible and are commonly known as "The Twelve" (*Tré-Asar*).

Chronologically, the book of Hosea is after the book of Amos, but it is placed first because of its length. The length of the Major Prophets likewise determined that they should be placed before the Minor Prophets.

Hosea the prophet lived after Amos during the eighth century before the common era, and prophesied in the kingdom of Israel before Isaiah did in the kingdom of Judah. Hosea's prophetic work began before the death of Jeroboam II, and he was still living when the kingdom of Israel was destroyed by the Assyrians in 721. Hosea's style is highly poetic and difficult to follow.

Many passages in the book of Hosea are not clearly understood because we are no longer fully acquainted with certain events to which they allude. The problem of Hosea's marriage to Gomer has aroused a great deal of discussion, and many attempts have been made to reconstruct the actual course of events.

According to some scholars, the narrative is an allegorical parable describing God's love for Israel in terms of the prophet's tragic love

158

for the allegedly faithless Gomer. Israel's faithlessness to God is the principal theme of Hosea's prophecy, predicting dire punishment and ultimate deliverance through sincere repentance. Excerpt:

"On that day, says the Lord, I will abolish bow, sword and war from the land, and I will let them lie down in safety. On that day I will answer the heavens, and they shall answer the earth; the earth shall answer the grain, the wine and the oil, and they shall answer Jezreel. . . The Lord has a quarrel with the inhabitants of the land. There is no faithfulness, no kindness, no knowledge of God in the land. There is swearing, lying, killing, stealing, and adultery; one crime follows hard upon another. . . How can I give you up, O Ephraim! How can I hand you over, O Israel! . . . I will heal their faithlessness; I will love them truly, for my anger has turned away from them. . . Once again they shall dwell beneath my shadow; they shall blossom like a vine. . ."

HOSHANA RABBAH   הוֹשַׁעְנָא רַבָּה

THE seventh day of *Sukkoth* is called *Hoshana Rabbah* (the great *hoshana*) because of the seven processions formed round the synagogue (*hakkafoth*) with the *lulav* and *ethrog* amidst prayers for deliverance. In Temple times, the people formed a procession around the altar on each of the first six days of *Sukkoth* while chanting: "We implore thee, O Lord, save us" (Psalm 118:25). On the seventh day of *Sukkoth* they formed seven such processions, following which they would beat willow-sprigs against the ground, symbolically casting off sins as the leaves were beaten off (Mishnah Sukkah 4:5-6). For this reason, *Hoshana Rabbah* cannot occur on a Sabbath, for then the willow-sprigs (*hoshanoth*) could not be used.

When the new calendar was framed by Hillel II and his advisers, about 359, they deemed *Hoshana Rabbah* so important and so much in conflict with the Sabbath that they would not allow the first day of *Rosh Hashanah* to occur on a Sunday. The Mishnah designates *Hoshana Rabbah* as *yom ḥibbut ḥarayoth* (day of striking twigs) and relates: "They used to bring twigs and strike them against the ground at the sides of the altar" (Sukkah 4:6).

Abudarham speaks of the custom of reading the Torah on the night of *Hoshana Rabbah*, out of which has grown the custom of meeting socially on that night and reading the anthology known as *Tikkun*

Lel Hoshana Rabbah, which includes the whole of Deuteronomy and the Psalms, as well as passages from kabbalistic works. Since the book of Deuteronomy is the last of the Five Books of Moses, it is recited during the night of *Hoshana Rabbah* because the annual cycle of Torah readings is completed the next day, on *Simḥath Torah.*

HOSHANOTH   הוֹשַׁעֲנוֹת

THE prayer-poems known as *Hoshanoth,* which are recited during the festival of *Sukkoth* after the *Musaf* service, are pleas for deliverance and liberation. They were mainly composed by Rabbi Elazar ha-Kallir, who lived presumably in Eretz Yisrael during the eighth century. The numerous *piyyutim,* or liturgical hymns, of this illustrious *ḥazzan-payyetan* were introduced in all Jewish communities, where they were imitated by hundreds of inspired *payyetanim* of succeeding generations. The medieval *ḥazzan* was often a combination of poet, composer and singer, many of whose melodies have been preserved down to our time.

Alphabetically arranged, each of the *Hoshanoth* compositions contains as many verses or phrases as there are letters in the Hebrew alphabet. They are replete with historical and midrashic allusions and are constructed in an involved poetic fashion. They consist of many intricate acrostics and a large variety of Hebrew synonyms which, if translated into another tongue, are likely to create a wrong impression and confuse the reader who happens to be unfamiliar with the puzzling intricacies of both Hebrew language and Jewish folklore. One of the *Hoshanoth,* for example, is composed of an interesting alphabetic list of twenty-two Hebrew synonyms referring to the Temple at Jerusalem; another presents an alphabetic description of the qualities attributed to the people of Israel in Jewish literature; a third enumerates destructive forces of nature, such as locusts, mentioned in the Bible on various occasions.

The word הושענא, transliterated *hosanna* in non-Jewish books, is an abbreviation of הושיעה נא (O save) in Psalm 118:25. This invocation was repeated during the days of *Sukkoth* in a solemn procession around the altar; on the seventh day of *Sukkoth,* called *Hoshana Rabbah,* the procession with palm branches occurred seven times. *Hoshana* became a term also for the willows carried in that sevenfold circuit-procession of *Hoshana Rabbah.*

160

MEMORIAL SERVICE   הַזְכָּרַת נְשָׁמוֹת

THE memorial service, known as *Yizkor* (may God remember) from the initial word of the prescribed prayer, was originally confined to *Yom Kippur*, the Day of Atonement, in order to stir the people to repentance. This theory is to be found in the *Kol-Bo*, an abridgment of the fourteenth-century work *Orḥoth Ḥayyim* by Rabbi Aaron ha-Kohen of France. The ancient custom of *Hazkarath Neshamoth* is referred to in the Apocrypha, where we read that Judah Maccabee "took a collection amounting to two thousand silver drachmas, each man contributing, and sent it to Jerusalem . . . to pray for the dead . . . he made atonement for the dead, so that they might be set free from their sin" (II Maccabees 12:43-45).

Furthermore, the Torah reading for *Yom Kippur* begins with the words "after the death." The plural form *Yom Kippurim* was explained by Rabbi Jacob Weil of the fifteenth century as a reference to the atonement required for both the living and the dead. Since the eighteenth century, however, memorial services have been conducted also on the last day of *Pesaḥ*, the second day of *Shavuoth*, and the eighth day of *Sukkoth* or *Shemini Atsereth*.

Yizkor, like the anniversary of a death (*Yahrzeit*), presents a stirring emotional appeal to modern Jews, some of whom are remote from their ancestral faith or any affiliation with other functions of the synagogue. The current intense interest attached to the *Yizkor* services may well be attributable to a desire to recapture a part of one's heritage submerged in the dense traffic of the world. The ceremony is transformed from a commemoration of death into a declaration of spiritual life.

HOSPITALITY   הַכְנָסַת אוֹרְחִים

THE intense feeling of hospitality among the Jewish people is reflected throughout the Bible and the Talmud. A graphic description of Abraham's hospitality and kindness to strangers is to be found in Genesis 18:1-8, where we read: "When he raised his eyes he saw three men standing at a distance from him. As soon as he saw them, he ran from the entrance of the tent door to meet them, and bowed down to the earth and said: My lords, if I find favor with you, do not pass by

161

your servant. Let a little water be brought that you may wash your feet, and then rest yourselves under the tree.

"Since you have come to your servant, I will bring you a little food that you may refresh yourselves; then you may go on. They replied: Do as you have said. Then Abraham hastened into the tent to Sarah and said: Quick, three measures of fine flour! Knead it and make loaves. And he ran to the herd, picked out a good, tender bullock, and gave it to the servant who hastened to prepare it. Then he took butter and milk, and the bullock which he had prepared, and set it before them; and he stood by them under the tree while they ate." The *Ramban* observes that although Abraham had many servants, he himself ran to the herd, because he was eager to show hospitality.

In midrashic literature, Job is represented as a most generous man. He built an inn at the crossroads with four doors opening in four directions, so that transients might have no trouble in finding an entrance. The abuse of hospitality once caused a civil war in Israel, which might have resulted in the extinction of the whole tribe of Benjamin (Judges 19-20).

The duties of hospitality occupy a very prominent position in the ethical teachings of the talmudic sages, who regard hospitality more highly than the reception given to the *Shekhinah* (Divine Presence). And in the *Ethics of the Fathers*, one of the ancient Jewish teachers of Jerusalem tells us: "Let your house be wide open; treat the poor as members of your own family" (Shabbath 127a; Avoth 1:5). Rav Huna observed the custom of opening the door of his house, when he was about to take his meal, and saying: Any one who is hungry may come in and eat" (Ta'anith 20b). To sit long at the table, so as to give an opportunity to the belated poor to enter and partake of the meal, was regarded as a highly meritorious act (Berakhorh 54b). In Jerusalem the custom prevailed of displaying a flag in front of the door, thereby indicating that the meal was ready, and that guests might come in and eat. The removal of the flag was a sign that the meal was finished, and that transient guests should cease entering.

It was the custom with some in Jerusalem to place all the dishes on the table at once, so that the fastidious guest was not compelled to eat something he did not like, but might choose anything he wished (Lamentations Rabbah 4:4). The guest was expected to leave some of the food on his dish, to show that he had more than enough. If, however, the host asked him to finish his portion, it was not necessary to leave any (*Sefer Ḥasidim*, 870-878). The habitual parasite, who took

162

every opportunity to eat meals at the house of another, was very strongly denounced by the sages (Pesahim 49a).

It is the duty of the host to be cheerful during meals, and thus make his guests feel at home and comfortable at the table (*Derekh Eretz Zuta* 9). It is commendable that the host himself serve at the table, thereby showing his willingness to satisfy his guests (Kiddushin 32b). The host is warned against watching his guest too attentively at the table, for thereby the visitor may be led to abstain from eating as much as he would like (*Sefer Ḥasidim*, 105).

FUNERAL PROCESSION   הַלְוָיַת הַמֵּת

THE duty of attending the dead to the grave is considered in Jewish tradition as one of the highest forms of lovingkindness. The man who fails to join a funeral procession for a short distance (six feet) is compared to one who mocks the poor. If, for some reason, a person is exempt from joining the procession, he is expected to rise in deference to those who attend the dead, since they are engaged in the performance of a good deed. The law requires us to rise before anyone who is performing a *mitzvah*.

HALAKHAH   הֲלָכָה

THE term *Halakhah* is used in the sense of talmudic law, guidance, traditional practice, the final decision of the rabbinic sages on disputed rules of conduct. *Halakhah* frequently denotes those sections of rabbinic literature which deal with Jewish legal tradition, in contradistinction to *Aggadah* which includes ethical teachings and everything in the Talmud and midrashic literature that is not of a legal nature. About seventy percent of the Babylonian Talmud is taken up with *Halakhah*.

The first systematic collection of *Halakhoth*, covering the whole field of the oral law, was made by Rabbi Akiva. This served as the basis for the collection made by Rabbi Judah ha-Nasi, known as the *Mishnah*, which became the prime text of discussion in the academies of Palestine and Babylonia. The teachers who lived after the codification of the Talmud, the Geonim in their responsa, interpreted and further developed the traditional law.

163

Distinguished scholars contend that in the *Halakhah* we find the mind and character of the Jewish people exactly and adequately expressed. For more than two thousand years *Halakhah* has been the central factor in Jewish spiritual and national life. It is an inner, independent Jewish product on which little outside influence has been exerted. The codification of Jewish law reached its peak in Maimonides' *Mishneh Torah*, followed by Rabbi Jacob ben Asher's *Turim*, the *Shulḥan Arukh* of Rabbi Joseph Karo with glosses by Rabbi Moses Isserles (*Rema*).

It has been plainly affirmed that the *Halakhah* controls the attitude and behavior of an observant Jew in practically every area of his life. It addresses him as producer and consumer, as worshiper and thinker, as husband and father. It commits the Jew to a divinely ordained discipline and presents a blueprint for an idealized existence within the realities of life. It guides him along the road to sanctification of himself and his environment. It emphasizes that man must always act with a conscious awareness of his relationship to God. In the *Halakhah*, nothing is sacred unless man makes it so. Mount Sinai, sanctified by God's descent to man, has retained no trace of sanctity; its very location is now a matter of archeological dispute, whereas Mount Moriah, which Abraham sanctified by his ascent to meet God, became the site of the Temple, and remains eternally sacred.

HALLEL   הַלֵּל

HALLEL (praise) consists of Psalms 113-118. It is called הלל המצרי (Egyptian *Hallel*) because Psalm 114 refers to the exodus from Egypt and begins with the words: "When Israel went out of Egypt." On *Purim*, celebrating a miraculous deliverance that occurred outside the Holy Land, the reading of the *Megillah* takes the place of *Hallel*. On *Rosh Hashanah* and *Yom Kippur*, the joyous chanting of *Hallel* is omitted because the High Holydays are not intended for jubilation. Nor is the *Hallel* recited in the house of a mourner during *shiv‘ah*. There is a theory that the *Hallel* psalms were assembled for liturgical use at the dedication of the Temple after the Maccabean victory.

On *Rosh Ḥodesh*, a minor festival, *Hallel* is recited in abridged form, the first eleven verses of Psalms 115 and 116 being omitted. *Half-Hallel* is likewise used on the last six days of Passover, because there is a tradition that God restrained the angels from singing his praise upon seeing the Egyptians drowning in the Red Sea on the seventh day of Passover. He said to them: "How can you sing hymns while my creatures are drowning in the sea?" (Megillah 10b). In order not to make *Ḥol ha-Mo'ed Pesaḥ* appear as more important than the seventh day of *Pesaḥ*, the *Hallel* is abridged throughout the last six days. The *full-Hallel* is recited on the first two days of *Pesaḥ*, *Shavuoth*, the nine days of *Sukkoth*, *Ḥanukkah*, and on the *Seder* nights.

When the *full-Hallel* is recited, the Sephardic Jews use the words לגמור את ההלל (to complete the *Hallel*) in the introductory benediction. Three different forms were used originally for the reading of the *Hallel:* 1) The leader intoned the first half verse, which was repeated by the congregation as a refrain throughout the entire Psalm recited by the reader. 2) The leader chanted half-lines, which the congregation repeated after him. 3) The leader chanted the first line, and the congregation responded with the second line of the verse. The last nine verses of Psalm 118 are spoken twice when the *Hallel* is recited, because they do not follow the arrangement of synonymous parallelism of the previous verses. Each of the last nine verses expresses a new thought.

Synonymous parallelism, consisting of a reiteration of similar thoughts in similar phrases with just enough variation to sustain the interest and prolong the mood, is a chief characteristic of biblical poetry. It is best seen by the following illustrative couplets, taken from Psalm 114.

> The sea beheld and fled,
> The Jordan turned backward.
> The mountains skipped liked rams,
> And the hills leaped like lambs.
> What ails you, O sea, that thus you flee?
> Why, O Jordan, do you turn backward? . . .
> Tremble, O earth, at the Lord's presence,
> At the presence of the God of Jacob,
> Who turns the rock into a pool of water,
> The flint into a flowing fountain.

Psalm 136 is called in the Talmud (Pesaḥim 118a) *Hallel ha-Gadol*, the Great *Hallel*, to distinguish it from the Egyptian *Hallel* (Psalms 113-118) sung on festivals. Psalm 136 differs from all other psalms in that each of its twenty-six verses closes with a refrain ("His mercy endures forever"), probably designed to be sung in full chorus by the people. The twenty-six refrains of praise correspond to the twenty-six generations from the creation until the giving of the Torah. The Lord showed kindness to man even before he had given him the Torah (Pesaḥim 118a). Also, the numerical equivalent of the tetragrammaton, the four-lettered name of God signifying the divine quality of mercy, is twenty-six.

HA-NOTHEN TESHUAH   הַנּוֹתֵן תְּשׁוּעָה

THE prayer for the government, recited on Sabbath mornings after the reading of the Torah, has undergone some verbal variations in the course of time. The ancient custom to pray for the welfare of the government is based on Jeremiah 29:7 ("Seek the welfare of the country where I have sent you into exile; pray to the Lord for it, for your welfare depends on its welfare").

Rabbi David Abudarham of the fourteenth century, in his commentary on the Prayerbook, writes: "It is the custom to bless the king and to pray to God that he may give him victory." Though the text varies in the old manuscripts, the general tenor of this prayer is the same. It is composed of excerpts from Psalms 145:13; 144:10; Isaiah 43:16; Jeremiah 23:6; Isaiah 59:20.

According to the Italian Jewish scholar Azariah dei Rossi of the sixteenth century, the dispersed Jews should pray to God for the peace of *all* the inhabitants of the world, that no nation shall lift up sword against nation, and that God may remove from their hearts all strife and hatred, for our peace depends on theirs.

The prayer for the government, recited in American synagogues, reads: "He who granted deliverance to kings and dominion to princes—his kingdom is a kingdom of all ages. . . May he bless and protect the president and the vice-president, and all the officers of this country. May the Supreme King of kings, in his mercy, sustain them and deliver them from all distress and misfortune. . ."

REMOVAL OF LANDMARKS   הַסָּגַת גְּבוּל

LANDMARKS, consisting of stones or heaps of stones which defined the boundary of a man's field, were of extreme importance when there were no fences. Their removal, for purposes of enlarging one's own estate, was equivalent to theft. Hence the Torah declares: "You

166

shall not remove your neighbor's landmark. . . Cursed be he who removes his neighbor's landmark!" (Deuteronomy 19:14; 27:17). Removal of landmarks was an ancient crime more difficult to combat than today when real estate ownership is determined by means of land-measurements.

By way of extension, any unfair methods used in the encroachment upon another person's livelihood are strictly prohibited as *hassagath gevul* (removal of landmarks).

HASKAMAH   הַסְכָּמָה

HASKAMAH (approbation) has several meanings, one being a permit issued by noted rabbis for the publication of a Hebrew book. The primary purpose of these permits (*haskamoth*) was to prevent the publication of a work that was likely to create ill-will on the part of the non-Jewish neighbors.

This semi-imposed censorship was first introduced at the rabbinical conference at Ferrara, Italy, in 1554, one year after the public burning of the Talmud. It was enacted that all Hebrew books had to be approved by three rabbis and a communal representative before they could be published, in order to check utterances which might be misinterpreted by the ruling authorities.

At a later period, *haskamoth* were sought by authors as a form of recommendation of their works. The recommendation of a book by a number of Jewish authorities would greatly enhance its value in the eyes of a larger reading public. Furthermore, the *haskamoth* came, in the course of time, to assume something of the nature of copyright. They would forbid the printing of all or part of the book before the lapse of a decade or so.

Purchasers, too, would be warned against buying books that have been reprinted without the permission of the author or original publisher before the expiration of the period set in the *haskamah*. The *haskamoth* were written in a variety of styles, sometimes persuasive and sometimes threatening; they appeared at the very beginning of the book. At a later period, the *haskamah* was earnestly desired by authors as an indication of piety or scholarship. Books would appear frequently with a number of *haskamoth*, in the form of recommendations by various rabbis of great reputation, printed immediately after the front page.

EULOGY ADDRESS   הֶסְפֵּד

THE term *hesped*, denoting a eulogy in praise of the deceased, has come down from ancient times. There is a talmudic statement that from the way a person is mourned you may learn whether he deserves future bliss (Shabbath 153a).

Following a description of the achievements and good character of the deceased individual, the funeral address usually closes with an expression of faith in immortality, and with an encouragement to the survivors to continue the good work of the person they are lamenting. The Bible preserves David's poetic funeral orations over Saul and Jonathan and over Abner (II Samuel 1:17-27; 3:33-34).

Poetic beauty and striking imagery are to be found in the *hespedim* recorded in the Talmud. Though in the past only individuals of great distinction were eulogized publicly when they died, present-day Jewish practice permits the delivery of *hespedim* for all, inasmuch as they are likely to console the survivors.

The kindness shown by comforting the mourners is a Jewish trait of high regard, upon which great emphasis is placed in Jewish literature. Since, however, we are told not to offer comfort to a mourner "while his dead lies before him" (Avoth 4:23), we are advised to discharge this duty by visiting him in his home during the week of mourning (*shiv‘ah*).

HAFTARAH   הַפְטָרָה

HAFTARAH (conclusion) is the prophetical section recited after the reading of the Torah on Sabbaths and festivals. Usually, though not always, the *Haftarah* contains some reference to an incident mentioned in the assigned Torah reading. On the three Sabbaths preceding the fast of *Tish‘ah b’Av*, the ninth day of *Av* commemorating the destruction of the Temple, prophecies of rebuke are recited, whereas on the seven Sabbaths after *Tish‘ah b’Av* the *Haftarah* consists of prophetic utterances of comfort and consolation.

The person who receives the honor of reading the *Haftarah* is referred to as the *Maftir*, the one who concludes the reading of the Torah. At least three verses from the end of the weekly portion (*sidrah*) are repeated when the *Maftir* is called to the Torah.

168

On the festivals, however, or when *Rosh Ḥodesh* coincides with the Sabbath, the verses read for the *Maftir* are taken from Numbers 28-29, prescribing the various sacrificial offerings for festivals and *Rosh Ḥodesh*. These are read from a second *Sefer Torah*. The blessings before and after the reading of the *Haftarah* are quoted in *Sofrim*, the tractate appended to the Babylonian Talmud in the seventh century.

Rabbi David Abudarham, of fourteenth-century Spain, in his commentary on our liturgy, traces the custom of reading from the Prophets after the Torah reading back to the period of persecution preceding the Maccabean revolt. According to his theory, the *Haftarah* was introduced as a substitute for the Torah reading, prohibited under the severe decrees of Antiochus Epiphanes.

Some authorities suggest that the readings from the Prophets may have been instituted to emphasize the great value of these books to the Torah of Moses. This was done in order to oppose the Samaritans who refused to recognize the sanctity of the Prophets. This sect, which originated in the early years of the Second Temple in the district of Samaria, Palestine, strictly observed the precepts of the Pentateuch, but rejected not only the rabbinic interpretation and tradition but also the prophetical writings.

HEFKER   הֶפְקֵר

THE talmudic term *hefker* (ownerless) refers to property left by a person without heirs, or property unclaimed by an owner, or property confiscated by the court and disposed of by the process of law, in keeping with the rule: הפקר בית דין הפקר (Gittin 36b).

Maimonides defines *hefker* as follows: "All that is to be found in deserts, rivers and streams, is *hefker;* whoever is first acquires title to such things as grass, wood and the fruit of trees. He acquires title to fish, birds and beasts that are ownerless. . . But if fish, birds or beasts are kept in private enclosures . . . they are private property, and anyone who catches them from such a place is guilty of stealing (*Yad, Zekhiah* 1:1).

The property of a proselyte, unless inherited by those children whose conception and birth took place after his conversion, is deemed *hefker*. It may be acquired by the first person claiming it as his own, provided he assumes all the responsibilities and duties connected with the ownership of the property, such as the payment of taxes.

169

Hefker applies not only to abandoned real estate, but also to objects lacking definite marks of identification that have been lost or stolen. The assumption is that the owner of the lost and found articles has given up all hope of recovering them, or else would be unable to prove his ownership. Thus, according to a statement in the Mishnah (Bava Metzia 2:1), newly purchased objects, which the owner cannot yet certainly identify, belong to the finder, without even having to announce that he has found them. According to Bava Metzia 21b, unconscious resignation (יאוש שלא מדעת), that is, an object which is usually given up if lost, if it has not been missed as yet, it is not considered as given up (יאוש), and the finder is obligated to seek out the owner of the lost object in order to restore it to him.

HAKKAFOTH   הַקָּפוֹת

ON THE eve of the *Simhath Torah* festival, all the Torah scrolls are taken out of the *aron ha-kodesh* (holy ark) for the seven *hakkafoth* (processional circuits) around the synagogue. The repeated *hakkafoth* are performed until every adult person in the congregation has been honored with carrying a *Sefer Torah*. At the end of each *hakkafah*, there is a great deal of singing and dancing on the part of all the participants. The *hakkafoth* are repeated during the morning service of the *Simhath Torah* festival. The Hasidim perform *hakkafoth* even after the *Ma‘ariv* service of *Shemini Atzereth*, the eighth day of *Sukkoth*.

The seven processions with the *Sifré Torah* on *Simhath Torah* became customary during the sixteenth century, in order to endear the Torah to the children.

IMMORTALITY   הַשְׁאָרַת הַנֶּפֶשׁ

THE belief in a continued existence after death is variously expressed in such terms as "revival of the dead" and "world to come." An affirmation of immortality is to be found in the beginning of the *Amidah* ("Thou revivest the dead . . . and keepest faith with those who sleep in the dust").

The belief in the resurrection of the body, which Maimonides incorporated into his Thirteen Principles of Faith, may have arisen from Ezekiel's vision of the valley of the dry bones. This prophetic vision

170

is generally taken, however, as a vivid illustration of the hope of restoration of a nation that was given up as dead: "Son of man, these
bones are the people of Israel. Behold, they keep saying: Our bones
are dry, our hope is lost, we are undone! Prophesy therefore to them
and tell them: Thus says the Lord God: O my people, I will open
your graves and bring you back to the land of Israel... I will put
my spirit into you, and you shall live. I will place you in your own
land..." (Ezekiel 37:11-14).

There are some who suggest that the deathlessness of the soul is
implied in Ecclesiastes 12:7, which reads: "The dust returns to earth
and the spirit returns to God who gave it."

The Wisdom of Solomon, the most important book in the Apocrypha for the development of theology, containing a wealth of ideas
concerning the destiny of the righteous and the wicked, associates
immortality with reward and punishment after death: "The souls of
the upright are in the hand of God, and no torment shall reach them.
In the eyes of foolish people they seemed to die, and their decease was
thought an affliction ... but they are at peace ... their hope is full
of immortality, and after being disciplined a little, they will be shown
great kindness" (3:1-5).

Rabbi Yehudah Halevi, the famous philosopher and poet of twelfth-
century Spain, entertains no doubts concerning immortality. In his
Kuzari, which is written in the form of a discussion at the court of
the king of the Khazars, he admits that other religions make greater
promises of reward after death. The Torah does not quote God as
saying: "I will put you in gardens after death and give you pleasures," but: "I will be your God and you will be my people."

The Jewish sages expressed themselves a great deal about the future
world, though the Bible does not emphasize this aspect of the Jewish
faith. There are also allusions to the immortality of the soul in the
translation of Elijah to heaven and in the belief of his second coming.

Maimonides, in his commentary on the Mishnah (Sanhedrin 10:1),
regards immortality as intellectual. The truly virtuous man, he
writes, will pursue good for its own sake. The child has to be encouraged to study by the offer of prizes. As man grows, his desires
become progressively greater, and the prizes have to be increased.
The hope of reward is inducement to the people to live virtuous lives.
The saint requires no inducement. His slogan must be that of Anti-
gonus of Sokho, who used to say: "Be not like servants who serve the
Master for the sake of a reward, but be like servants who serve the

Master not for the sake of a reward" (Avoth 1:3). However, he concludes: A man loses nothing by shaping his conduct with a view to reward and punishment until, by habit and zeal, he arrives at an understanding of the truth and serves purely out of love. Our sages said: "A man should by all means learn Torah and do good deeds, even if it is only to gain a reward or avoid punishment, for eventually he will arrive at a stage of doing good for its own sake" (Pesaḥim 50b).

RESTORING LOST GOODS   הָשָׁבַת אֲבֵדָה

FAILURE to restore to the owner a lost article that has been found by someone is accounted as theft in Jewish law. "If someone commits a sin of dishonesty . . . by retaining his neighbor's goods unjustly, or if, having found a lost article, he lied about it . . . he shall restore the thing that was stolen or unjustly retained by him . . . or the lost article he found, or whatever else he swore falsely about; on the day of his guilt-offering he shall make full restitution of the thing itself, and in addition, give the owner one-fifth of its value" (Leviticus 5:20-24).

Our duty of restoring lost articles applies likewise to any of our neighbor's property that is on the verge of destruction; it is our duty to save it if we can. If the rightful owner of a lost article is unknown, the finder is expected to consult the proper authorities.

PROVIDENCE   הַשְׁגָּחָה

DIVINE providence signifies God's control and guidance of the universe and all it contains. This is expressed figuratively in many biblical passages, as in Zechariah 4:10 where we are told that "the eyes of the Lord range through the whole earth."

Psalm 145 celebrates God's providential care for all his creation, declaring that "the Lord is good to all, his mercy is over all his works... The Lord upholds all who fall, and raises all who are bowed down. The eyes of all look hopefully to thee, and thou givest them their food in due season. Thou openest thy hand, and satisfiest every living thing with favor... The Lord is near to all who call upon him... He hears their cry and saves them..."

In the apocryphal book of Ben Sira we find that "good and evil, life and death, poverty and wealth come from God (11:14). Accord-

172

ing to a talmudic statement, "a man does not even strike a finger here below unless it is decreed on high" (Ḥullin 7b).

The same thought is expressed in midrashic literature: "A snake never bites, a lion never rends, a government never interferes unless so ordered from above" (Ecclesiastes Rabba 10:11.1). "What has God been doing since creation? He has been building ladders for some to ascend, for others to descend" (Tanḥuma Mattoth 9, ed. Buber).

Since divine providence means God's foreknowledge of all events, Jewish thinkers have always made attempts to reconcile the two doctrines that seem to be contradictory, namely: divine omniscience and man's freedom of will (*yedi'ah* and *beḥirah*). Rabbi Akiva declares: Everything is foreseen by God, yet freewill is granted to man (Avoth 3:19), that is to say, God's foreknowledge does not predetermine man's actions, good or bad. In matters of ethical conduct man has the ability to choose between alternative possibilities of action. Hence, the talmudic saying: "Everything is in God's hands, except the fear of God" (Berakhoth 33b). Also: Man possesses the power to defile himself and to keep himself clean (Yoma 39a). He is guided on the way he desires to walk (Makkoth 10b). Practically all Jewish philosophers of the medieval period reject fatalism, pointing out that divine foreknowledge is not identical with causation.

Maimonides writes: "The theory of man's perfectly free will is one of the fundamental principles of the Torah and its adherents. Another fundamental principle taught by the Torah is this: Wrongdoing cannot be ascribed to God. All afflictions as well as all kinds of human happiness are distributed according to justice... I do not believe that it is through divine providence that a certain leaf drops from the tree, nor do I hold that when a spider catches a fly it is the result of a special divine decree in that moment.

"In all similar matters the action is entirely due to chance. It may be by mere chance that a ship sinks with all her contents, or the roof of a house falls upon those within. But it is not due to chance that the men drowned or otherwise injured just happened to be in the ship or the house. It is due to the will of God and his method of justice which our mind is unable to understand. The prophetical books describe God's providence only in relation to human beings...

"Every person has his individual share of divine providence (*hash-gaḥah peratith*) in proportion to his perfection. It is wrong to say that divine providence extends only to the species and not to individual beings, as some philosophers teach... There is an essential distinction between God's knowledge and ours; as we cannot accurately comprehend his essence, so we have no correct notion of his knowledge. . ." (*Guide*, 3:17-20).

Maimonides' theory has been described as showing that man knows what liberty is better than what providence is. Modern Jewish theology has not advanced the subject beyond Maimonides.

HASHKIVENU   הַשְׁכִּיבֵנוּ

THE night prayer *Hashkivenu*, preceding the *Amidah* of the *Ma'ariv* service, ends on weekdays with the words שומר עמו ישראל לעד (who guardest thy people Israel forever), and on Sabbaths and festivals it concludes with the words: "who spreadest the shelter of peace over us and over all thy people Israel and over Jerusalem."

The expression הפורס סוכת שלום, instead of the weekday ending, is used to express the idea of peace which fills the Jewish home on Sabbaths and festivals. However, this version is quoted in the Palestinian Talmud (Berakhoth 4:5) as of daily usage. The compromise between the two competing variations, the Babylonian and the Palestinian, was effected by the Geonim, who introduced one for Sabbaths and one for weekdays.

HASKALAH   הַשְׂכָּלָה

UNDER the influence of Moses Mendelssohn (1729-1786), philosopher and pioneer of German enlightenment, there began to flourish a movement among certain sections of European Jews to acquire western culture, to adopt the language, dress and habits of the non-Jewish neighbors. In 1783, the Society for the Cultivation of Hebrew Literature began publishing the periodical *Hammeassef* for the purpose of fighting the battles of light against darkness, utilizing the Hebrew language as the best medium for the dissemination of western ideas among talmudically trained Jews.

The objective of the Haskalsh movement was a complete transformation in education and habits of life, a revolt of youth against elders, of communities against their leaders. Sympathy was aroused for young people who had spent the best years of their youth in dark rooms over talmudic works. The inadequate Jewish system of educa-

174

tion was generally deplored as one of the main causes for the many evils which beset Jewish life in those days. Rabbi Israel Salanter (1810-1883), whose goal was to disseminate knowledge of the Talmud over the widest possible area, made efforts to improve the method of study so as to achieve greater results with less expenditure of energy and time. He furthermore urged that ethical literature be included in the curriculum of the Jewish schools. As a result, new editions of ethical works were published for the use of the members of a *Ḥevrath Musar* (ethical society), established by Rabbi Israel Salanter.

The followers of the *Haskalah* (enlightenment) movement firmly believed that the only hindrance in the way of Jewish emancipation, social and political equality, was distinctiveness resulting from an exclusively religious education given to the children. Hence they strove to modernize the Jewish schools by introducing a variety of secular subjects into the curriculum.

The Jewish enlightenment movement, which was parallel to the German Aufklaerung movement, soon spread from Germany to Russia and Poland, where the so-called *maskilim* (intellectuals) made every effort to enlighten the Jewish masses. Though self-taught, the *maskilim* often achieved erudition which they proceeded to disseminate by means of literary efforts in the Hebrew language.

The nineteenth century Haskalah movement in Russia produced a rebirth of both Hebrew language and literature that eventually struck deep roots among the people. Although the Haskalah slogan in Russia was: "Be a man outside your house and a Jew inside your home," we find descriptions such as this: "The so-called aristocracy in Russia . . . removed from their homes and their home-life anything that was Jewish at all. . . Like apes they imitated the manners and customs of the non-Jews. . . In the first anti-Jewish outbreaks, the children asked their parents: Why do they beat *us*? Are we, too, Jews?"

The Russian pogroms, with government collusion, during the period 1881-1905, sadly disappointed the *maskilim* in their hopes. They were designed "to force one-third of the Jewish population to emigrate, another third to be converted, and the remaining third to die of starvation and massacre." The Russian term *pogrom*, meaning destruction, is often applied to the anti-Jewish outbreaks from 1881 onward.

The Haskalah movement then gave way to the Zionist movement, proceeding from the assumption that the Jewish people, desiring to retain their identity, cannot and will not assimilate and be submerged in the multitudes of the peoples of the earth. Haskalah in the original sense came to an end, and a new ideology stressing Jewish identity filled the hearts of myriads.

The Enlighenment movement in Russia and Poland culminated, however, in the revival of Hebrew and the production of a goodly number of poets and novelists. Men such as Judah Loeb Gordon (1830-1892) and Abraham Mapu (1808-1867) expressed the longing of their generation for the idyllic life of ancient Israel and the optimism of the past, thus exerting a tremendous influence upon countless Jewish readers.

SUICIDE   הִתְאַבְּדוּת

THE Jewish prohibition of suicide is based on the traditional interpretation of Genesis 9:5 ("Surely I will require an account of your life's blood"). Rabbi Baḥya ibn Pakuda, in his *Ḥovoth ha-Levavoth*, points out that the nearer the relation to the murdered person, the more horrible the crime, and man is closest to himself. A suicide is a sentinel who deserted his post. It has been noted that a person is considered a suicide (מאבד עצמו לדעת) only when there is absolute certainty that he premeditated and committed the act with a clear mind, not troubled by some great fear or worry which might have caused him temporarily to lose his mind (*Ḥatham Sofer, Yoreh Deah* 326).

The laws of mourning are suspended in the case of a suicide: no *keriʻah*, no eulogy, no *shivʻah*, unless it is evident that the act was prompted by madness or fear of torture, as in the case of king Saul.

HATIKVAH   הַתִּקְוָה

HATKIVAH (the hope), the national anthem of Israel, was composed by Naphtali Herz Imber (1856-1909) and published in 1886. It was first adopted as the Zionist anthem at the end of the nineteenth century. The *Hatikvah* hymn, which expresses the Jewish unbounded hope for liberation, has been modified somewhat in recent years.

The origin of the melody has been traced to a Sephardic hymn as well as a tune in Smetana's symphonic poem, *Die Moldau*. Smetana uses a folk theme practically identical with the first half of *Hatikvah*. The words express the Jewish yearning for the restoration of Zion and the hope for freedom and independence.

176

Translated from the Hebrew into English, Israel's national anthem reads as follows:

> As long as deep in the heart
> There still throbs a Jewish soul,
> And along towards the east
> An eye keeps watch upon Zion—
>
> Our great hope is not yet lost,
> The hope of two millennia,
> To be a free people in our land
> Of Zion and Jerusalem.

PERMISSION

THE term התר (hetter) is variously used in the sense of legal permission, legitimate action, and permitted object; it is the antonym of אסור (issur), the contrary meaning of which is prohibition, and also prohibited object. A rabbinic scholar who is qualified to decide on religious questions pertaining to issur v'heller, actions or things forbidden or permitted, is called מורה הוראה (moreh hora'ah) if properly ordained by a superior rabbi, who has authorized him to issue such decisions. Such an authorization is referred to as hetter hora'ah or semikhah.

The term hetter nedarim is applied to the release from vows by the declaration of a moreh hora'ah after finding due reason for their annulment. This belongs to the category of what is known as hetter ḥakham, dispensation by a scholar's decision. Removal of a religious objection by the proper rabbinic authority is called hetter (permission).

WARNING

HATHRA'AH is a warning, by witnesses, given to a person who is about to commit a criminal act, letting him know the penalty which he will incur. Rabbinic law provides that, immediately before perpetrating a crime, the offender must be cautioned of the gravity of his act; otherwise, guilty intention cannot be proved. Guilty intention alone can render a person subject to full penalty for his crime.

This principle is based on the fact that many sins are committed through ignorance and error. The warning must name the particular punishment which the contemplated crime entails, whether corporal or capital; otherwise, the legal penalty attached to the crime cannot be imposed (Sanhedrin 8b; Makkoth 16a).

This does not apply to a burglar, since the very crime of burglary constitutes his warning (Kethubboth 34b; Sanhedrin 72b). Neither are false witnesses exempt from retaliatory punishment when they have not been forewarned, because the nature of their crime does not admit of forewarning.

HATTARATH HORA'AH   הַתָּרַת הוֹרָאָה

The rabbinical diploma known as *hattarath hora'ah* (permission to decide on religious questions) certifies that, after a thorough examination, the candidate has proved himself competent and worthy to be a rabbi. The *hattarath hora'ah* is not a license, but simply a certificate of character and qualifications; it confers no sacred power. Communities often elected rabbis who had no diplomas. A scholar who occupied the position of a *yeshivah* principal was not required to possess a diploma. The *hattarath hora'ah* served as a substitute for the *semikhah* which could be conferred only in Eretz Yisrael by a member of the Sanhedrin. The title *Moreh Hora'ah* is derived from the degree of *hattarath hora'ah*. The title *Morenu* (our teacher and guide) was introduced in the fourteenth century by Rabbi Jacob Moelln (*Maharil*) for one who acquired extensive talmudic learning.

The diploma of the modern *semikhah* is in the form of a certificate of recommendation. Though its phraseology is partly that of the original *semikhah* (*yoreh yoreh, yadin yadin*) to the effect that the recipient may teach and judge, the teaching refers only to dietary and ritual laws (איסור והתר), and the judging only to civil cases. The repetition of the terms emphasizes the ordination. A *hattarath hora'ah* is, as a rule, recognised only when issued by a rabbi of acknowledged authority who has personally examined the candidate.

UVA L'TSIYYON

וּבָא לְצִיּוֹן   ו

UVA L'TSIYYON (a redeemer shall come to Zion) is the opening phrase of the closing prayer of the daily morning service. This prayer, consisting of biblical quotations accompanied by the paraphrase of the Targum, has been designed to enable every Jew to have a daily share in the study of the Torah (*Rashi*, Sotah 49a).

It is referred to as *Kedushah d'sidra* because the threefold repetition *holy holy holy* from Isaiah 6:3 forms here part of a series of other biblical verses. On Sabbaths and festivals, when the Torah and the Prophets are publicly recited at great length, the reading of *Uva l'Tsiyyon* is postponed till the afternoon service. On *Yom Kippur*, however, *Uva l'Tsiyyon* is moved from the *Minḥah* service to *Ne'ilah*, to form a division between the two. A similar division is effected by the Torah reading between the *Musaf* and *Minḥah* services of *Yom Kippur*.

The first two verses of ובא לציון are omitted in the *Ma'ariv* service of Saturday night, because they refer to liberation which is associated with daytime. The liberation from Egyptian bondage is said to have occurred in daytime. The Saturday-night *Ma'ariv* service is prolonged by reciting the remainder of the ובא לציון prayer, beginning with ואתה קדוש, for the merciful reason that the departed souls of the wicked are not tormented as long as the Sabbath continues. The same reason has been suggested for the biblical passages ויהי נועם and ויתן לך.

In addition to the biblical mosaic of verses, several of which are rendered in Aramaic, *Uva l'Tsiyyon* contains the following petition: "Blessed be our God who has created us for his glory and separated us from those who go astray... May he open our hearts to his Torah; may he set in our heart love and reverence to do his will and to serve him with a perfect heart..." This prayer for enlightenment corresponds to Isaiah 59:21, quoted at the beginning of *Uva l'Tsiyyon*.

CONFESSION

וִדּוּי

JEWISH confession, addressed direct to God and not to an intermediary, is of no avail unless it expresses feelings of honest regret and sincere repentance. The one who confesses his sin without repenting has been compared to a man that holds a defiling dead reptile in his hand while seeking ritual purification through immersion in water; no water in

179

the world will cleanse him unless he first gets rid of the defiling object, for it is written: "He who confesses and forsakes his sins obtains mercy" (Proverbs 28:13; Ta'anith 16a).

Nor can the Day of Atonement win atonement for the man who says to himself: "I shall sin and *Yom Kippur* will procure atonement for me" (Yoma 8:9). In Judaism, there is no vicarious atonement: the burden of a man's guilt cannot be thrust on the shoulders of another; the innocent do not expiate the wrongs of the sinners.

Commenting on Proverbs 28:13 ("He who conceals his transgressions shall not prosper, but he who confesses and forsakes them shall obtain mercy"), the sages make the observance that when a man is charged with a crime before a human tribunal he receives punishment when he admits his guilt; if he is charged before the divine tribunal, he receives remission if he confesses with the determination to forsake his sins. The general view in midrashic literature is that it is never too late to mend and repent, though it is pointed out occasionally that there comes a time when, as a result of habitual lapses and uninterrupted sin, the power of repentance is taken from a man.

The most prominent confessions found in the Prayerbook are *Ashamnu* and *Al-Ḥet*, the short form and the long form of confession. *Ashamnu* consists of twenty-four expressions for sin, alphabetically arranged. The round number of twenty-four expressions is reached by the threefold use of the last letter of the Hebrew alphabet. *Al-Ḥet*, alphabetically arranged, is an exhaustive catalogue of sin, unrolling the whole range of human failings and backslidings. Each of its forty-four lines begins with the words *Al ḥet sheḥatanu* (for the sin we have committed).

The sins enumerated include: idle talk, offensive speech, evil thoughts, insincere confession, contempt for parents and teachers, fraud and falsehood, bribery, slander, arrogance, obstinacy, talebearing, groundless hatred, breach of trust. The confessions are phrased in the plural because the entire community regards itself responsible for many offenses that could have been prevented. On the Day of Atonement, they are recited repeatedly to make the people intensely aware of the need of a fuller mastery over the impulses.

Every Jew makes confession on his deathbed, in keeping with a talmudic statement: "When a man is sick and near to death, he is asked to make confession" (Shabbath 32a). Criminals are urged to confess within a short distance of the scene of execution. If they have nothing to confess, they are instructed to say: "Let my death be an atonement for all my iniquities" (Sanhedrin 6:2).

180

Yom Kippur expiates sin against God, but not sin against man, unless the offended party is conciliated (Yoma 8:9). If the injured party refuses to forgive after the third request, he is described as cruel. In the case of slander, one is not duty-bound to forgive.

VEHU RAḤUM   וְהוּא רַחוּם

THE seven somber elegies constituting the long *Vehu Raḥum*, recited during the morning service on Mondays and Thursdays, were composed, according to legend, soon after the destruction of the Second Temple. Leopold Zunz (1794-1886), however, suggests that they were written during the Gothic and Frankish persecutions of the seventh century. It has been said that whoever can read this long prayer without emotion has lost all feeling for what is great and noble. The soul of an entire people utters these elegies and supplications, giving voice to its woe of a thousand years. Here is nothing of make-believe, but everything comes from the reality of suffering and life.

The long *Vehu Raḥum* is recited on Mondays and Thursdays, when the Torah is read during the public service, because on these days the people would come from the suburban villages to attend the markets and other occasions in the cities. Even those who were unable to hear the Torah read on the Sabbaths could hear it read when they came to town during the week. Being part of the *Taḥanun* supplications, *Vehu Raḥum* is omitted on all festive occasions, such as *Rosh Ḥodesh*, *Lag b'Omer*, *Brith Milah*, and the five days preceding *Shavuoth*.

The first sentence of *Vehu Raḥum*, consisting of thirteen words, is held by some interpreters to recall the thirteen attributes of divine mercy, described in Exodus 34:6-7. For this reason, the daily evening service also begins with that sentence, borrowed from Psalm 78:38. "As the evening approaches, man is conscious of having sinned during the day, and thus begins his prayer with this appeal to the divine mercy" (*Maḥzor Vitry*). The verse reads: "He, being merciful, forgives iniquity, and does not destroy; often he turns his anger away, and does not stir up all his wrath." According to the *Sefer ha-Rokeaḥ*, an ethical work by Rabbi Elazar of Worms (1160-1238), the opening supplication for pardon in the *Ma'ariv* service is attributable to the fact that it has no equivalent in the ancient Temple service. In order to differentiate *Ma'ariv* from *Shaḥarith* and *Minḥah*, a petition for mercy replaces a sin-offering which was presented only at daytime.

181

VAYEKHULLU   וַיְכֻלּוּ

THE passage in Genesis (2:1-3), declaring that when God had completed the creation of the universe he hallowed the seventh day, is recited three times as an essential part of the Sabbath-eve service: during the *Amidah* prayer, after the *Amidah* prayer, and introductory to the *Kiddush*. According to a talmudic statement (Shabbath 119b), he who recites this passage on Friday evenings is deemed as if he were God's associate in the creation of the world. It has been pointed out that the last three words of this passage (בָּרָא... לַעֲשׂוֹת) signify that the work of creation continues so long as the conflict between good and evil remains undecided. Ethically, the world is still unfinished and it is the privilege of man to help finish it.

It is in connection with וַיְכֻלּוּ that the Talmud quotes a statement concerning a good and an evil angel accompanying every man home from the synagogue on Friday evening. If they find the house in good order, the good angel says: "May the next Sabbath be as this one." If, on the other hand, they find the house neglected, the evil angel says: "May the next Sabbath be as this one." In each case, the second angel is obliged to respond *Amen* (Shabbath 119b).

LEVITICUS   וַיִּקְרָא

LEVITICUS, the third book of the Torah, is called in Hebrew *Vayyikra* from its initial word, just as the book of Genesis is called *Bereshith* because it begins with that word in the original Hebrew text. Leviticus is primarily a book of laws, most of which concern the priests and Levites. It defines clean and unclean animals for purposes of food, and contains ten chapters (17-26) commonly designated as the Holiness Code, stressing a high moral standard and embracing laws of humanity and charity. Leviticus is almost entirely legislative in character; the few narrative portions are subordinate to the main legislative theme. The people of Israel are taught in this book to keep themselves in a state of purity as a sign of their steadfast adherence to God.

This book presents a system of worship rich in symbolism and lofty in ethical standards. The desire for a visible element in worship is satisfied by numerous sacrifices, each designated to meet a particular need of the worshiper. The sacrificial system symbolized self-surrender and devotion to the will of God. The peace-offering with its communion feast conveyed the idea of fellowship. It served to keep alive the sense of dependence on God for the natural blessings of life, while it had the social value of promoting the solidarity of the nation. The daily offering symbolized Israel's pledge of unbroken service to God. The fragrant smoke of incense rising towards heaven was a natural symbol of prayer ascending to God, as in the words of the psalmist: "Let my prayer rise like incense before thee" (Psalm 141:2).

The well-known verse, "You shall love your neighbor as yourself," meaning love for any human being, summarizes much of the social legislation of Leviticus. The holiness of God requires human holiness, which includes such details as cleanliness and self-discipline. The relation between hygiene and religion is stressed in the regulations about leprosy. Leviticus is the basis for the major part of the Jewish religion. Many Jewish virtues can be traced to the influence of this book and its ideal laws, liberating human beings from brutality and bestiality. Excerpts:

"You shall not steal; you shall not cheat; you shall not speak falsely to one another. You shall not defraud or rob your neighbor; you shall not keep the wages of a hired laborer overnight. You shall not curse the deaf, or place an obstacle in front of the blind. . . You shall not act dishonestly in rendering judgment; you shall not be partial to a poor man nor favor a rich man. You shall not go about spreading slander among your people; you shall not stand by idly when your neighbor's life is at stake. . . Take no revenge and bear no grudge against your people, but love your neighbor as yourself. . . When a stranger resides with you in your land, you shall not molest him . . . you shall love him as you love yourself. . . You shall not act dishonestly when using measures of length or weight or capacity.

V'YITTEN LEKHA   וְיִתֶּן לְךָ

A LENGTHY collection of scattered biblical verses that contain the assurance of deliverance, prosperity and peace, forms part of the Ma-'ariv liturgy for Saturday night; it serves as an encouragement in the face of the new week of toil which follows the Sabbath rest. This collection, known as V'yitten Lekha (God grant you), ends with Psalm 128 that emphasizes the dignity of labor: "When you eat of the toil of your hands, you shall be happy. Your wife shall be like a fruit-ful vine ... your children like olive plants around your table."

According to a talmudic interpretation, happiness in this life and in the hereafter is the reward of one who enjoys what his own hands have produced (Berakhoth 8a). "Love work" (Avoth 1:10) is one of the essential principles in talmudic literature. "Even Adam did not taste food until he had worked, as it is written: The Lord God took Adam and put him in the Garden of Eden to till it and look after it" (Genesis 2:15).

The majority of the talmudic sages were humble workmen. Hence the statement: "Flay carcasses in the market place—if you are in need—and do not say: I am a priest, a great man, and I hate to do this thing" (Pesaḥim 113a). Also: "The man who works for a living is greater than the man who is pious" (Berakhoth 8a). "Labor en-nobles" (Nedarim 49b). "Man dies when he stops working" (Avoth d'Rabbi Nathan, chapter 11). It is significant that the Hebrew word *avodah* denotes both work and worship.

DISPUTATIONS וכּוּחִים

DISPUTATIONS between Jews and non-Jews were frequent in ancient and medieval times. The talmudic-midrashic literature contains ex-amples of disputations between Jews and adherents of various reli-gions. The friendliness and good humor of these religious discussions, at a later period, gave way to remorseless fanaticism that was directed not only against Jews and Judaism but also against Jewish literature. In the middle of the thirteenth century, twenty-four carloads of cop-ies of the Talmud were burned in the public square of Paris. A gen-eration later, a converted Jew by the name of Pablo Christiani induced the king of Aragon to compel Rabbi Moses Naḥmanides (*Ramban*) to join him in a public disputation.

Naḥmanides' disputation with Pablo, which took place at Barce-lona in 1263 and lasted four days, concerned chiefly the Jewish con-cept of the Messiah. It was debated, in the presence of the king and many dignitaries, whether the Hebrew prophets had predicted a Mes-siah of divine or human birth, and whether the Messiah had or had not already appeared. Naḥmanides declared that he could not be-lieve that the Messiah had come as long as the promised cessation of all warfare had not been fulfilled.

184

As to the legendary *aggadoth* (tales) of the Midrash, he argued that of the three types of literature in the hands of the Jews only the Holy Scriptures and the Talmud were authoritative in terms of Jewish religious conduct. The Midrash, which is the third branch of Jewish literature, contains private opinions and individual interpretations, which a Jew is free to accept or reject. Naḥmanides had little difficulty in demonstrating Pablo's misinterpretations.

Although he had been promised immunity and the right of free expression in the course of the debate, Naḥmanides was soon summoned before the king's court again and tried for blasphemy. He was condemned to two years' exile, and his account of the contest, which he had written for the bishop of Gerona, was ordered to be burned. Pablo received permission to intensify his disputations with the Jews throughout Aragon, while the Jews were ordered to listen to his tirades against Judaism and defray his expenses. Leaving his family and friends in Spain, Naḥmanides undertook the dangerous journey to the Holy Land, where he arrived at the age of seventy-three and settled in Acre. He professed great respect for Maimonides and defended him against the anti-Maimonists.

The Tortosa disputation was the most violent of all the medieval religious debates and lasted more than eighteen months (1413-1415). Dramatically organized to settle the question of the relative merits of the two religions, the disputation was conducted before a brilliant assembly in the city of Tortosa in northern Spain. Rabbi Joseph Albo, author of the philosophic work *Sefer ha-Ikkarim* (Book of Principles), was among the twenty-two Jewish representatives. After sixty-nine sessions, the verdict was what had been expected. The Talmud was condemned, and a variety of hostile laws against the Jews were enacted. During the disputation, the pope exerted constant physical and moral pressure upon the Jews to become apostates.

V'LAMMALSHINIM   וְלַמַּלְשִׁינִים

The *Shemoneh Esreh* prayer, originally consisting of eighteen benedictions, was increased to nineteen benedictions when, somewhat before the year 100, an additional petition was inserted against traitors and apostates who instigated persecutions.

Known as *birkath ha-minim* (benediction against the sectaries), it is an imprecation against the harmful tactics of the sectarian propagandists, and reads: "May the slanderers have no hope; may all wick-edness perish instantly; may all thy enemies be soon cut down. . ."

The word *malshinim* (slanderers) is a comparatively late substitu-tion for *minim* (apostates). The wording of the entire passage has undergone various modifications through fear of the official censors.

Rabban Gamaliel II, who was the first to bear the title *Nasi* (prince), officially recognized by the Roman government, was instrumental in adding the prayer against the sectaries, whose activities proved injur-ious to the Jewish people.

U'NETHANNEH TOKEF   וּנְתַנֶּה תֹּקֶף

The prayer-poem *U'nethanneh Tokef*, figuring prominently in the *Musaf* service of the High Holydays, is traditionally attributed to Rabbi Amnon of Mayence, a legendary martyr at the time of the Crusades (twelfth century). Since, however, this prayer was among the finds in the Cairo *Genizah*, it must have been composed at an earlier date. According to some, it was published by Rabbi Kalony-mus ben Meshullam, one of the most eminent liturgical poets of eleventh-century Germany.

This stirring poem, describing in exalted language the heavenly procedure on the day of judgment, has been the subject of a popular story, the oldest mention of which is found in the thirteenth-century work *Or Zarua* by Rabbi Isaac of Vienna; this book contains copious material about Jewish life in medieval Germany. The story reads:

Rabbi Amnon, a wealthy scholar of noble descent, was repeatedly but fruitlessly pressed by the Archbishop of Mayence to change his faith. On one occasion he went so far as to ask evasively for a three-day respite to consider. Upon reaching home he would neither eat nor drink; he was sad at heart and wept bitterly because he had given the impression that he might renounce his belief in the absolute Oneness of God. When he failed to appear at the end of three days, he was arrested and compelled to plead guilty. As a punishment, his hands and feet were cut off. On New Year's day, Rabbi Amnon was brought to the synagogue at his own request. When the reader (*hazzan*) was about to lead the congregation in the recitation of the *Kedushah* (sanc-tification), Rabbi Amnon asked him to pause. Dying from his wounds, Rabbi Amnon recited the prayer-poem *U'nethanneh Tokef* and immed-iately expired. Three days later he appeared to Rabbi Kalonymus

186

ben Meshullam in a dream and taught him this prayer that it might be introduced to all congregations.

The poem depicts *Rosh Hashanah* and *Yom Kippur* as the days of heavenly judgment, when it is decreed "how many shall pass away and how many shall be brought into existence; who shall live and who shall die; who shall come to a timely end, and who to an untimely end; who shall perish by fire and who by water; who by sword and who by beast; who by hunger and who by thirst; who by earthquake and who by plague; who by strangling and who by stoning; who shall be at ease and who shall wander about; who shall be at peace and who shall be molested; who shall have comfort and who shall be tormented; who shall become poor and who shall become rich; who shall be lowered and who shall be raised. But repentance, prayer and charity cancel the stern decree." The *U'nethanneh Tokef* meditation mentions also God's consideration of human weakness and his benevolence.

FOUR-LAND COUNCIL   וַעַד אַרְבַּע אֲרָצוֹת

THE Council of Four Lands was the central body of Jewish autonomy in Poland between 1580 and 1764. The *four lands* were Great Poland, Little Poland, Podolia and Galicia. For nearly two centuries, until it was suppressed by the Polish government in 1764, the Council virtually governed the entire Jewish population of these provinces.

Consisting of representatives of all the main communities concerned, the Council acted as a supreme court to decide on disputes between one community and another; to take measures for the safeguarding of Jewish rights, when threatened by the civil power; and to maintain the strict discipline which was necessary for the self-preservation of the Polish Jews.

The Council adopted ordinances (*takkanoth*) to protect the community against individual Jews, and had, as the means of enforcing its decisions, the *herem* (ban of excommunication), solemnly pronounced and strictly carried out against those who defied its constituted authority. The general Council, consisting usually of thirty men chosen by the four separate councils of the four provinces, met semi-annually, unless an emergency demanded an extra session.

The number of rabbis in the Council was limited to six; the head was always a layman. The purpose of this arrangement was to make sure that matters of finance remained in experienced hands. Follow-

187

ing the Chmielnitski massacres (1648), when many communities were impoverished, the Council cared for countless widows and orphans.

VATTODIÉNU   וַתּוֹדִיעֵנוּ

THE paragraph beginning with the word ותודיענו is inserted in the *Amidah* on a major festival that occurs on a Saturday night. It is referred to as a form of *Havdalah*, describing the distinction in the degree of holiness between Sabbaths and festivals. *Vattodienu* is quoted in the Talmud (Berakhoth 33b) as a precious pearl (*marganitha*) and is attributed to Rav and Samuel, the founders of intensive talmudic learning in Babylonia and heads of the academies at Sura and Nehardea, respectively.

Vattodiénu, a good example of a formula transformed into a poem, reads: "Thou, Lord our God, hast made known to us thy righteous judgments, and hast taught us to perform thy pleasing statutes. Thou, Lord our God, hast given us right ordinances, true precepts, and good laws. Thou hast granted us joyous holidays, holy festivals . . . Thou, Lord our God, hast made a distinction between the holy and the common, between light and darkness . . . Thou hast made a distinction between the holiness of the Sabbath and the holiness of the festival. . . Thou hast distinguished and sanctified thy people Israel with thy holiness." In the course of time, several variations and additions have modified the original composition of this paragraph, which is quoted in the Talmud and by Maimonides somewhat differently.

The paragraph ותתן לנו, which immediately follows *Vattodiénu*, mentions the pilgrim festivals as *haggim* and *zemannim*, namely: our festival of freedom, our festival of *Mattan Torah*, and our festival of rejoicing. Since the terms *haggim* and *zemannim* are employed as synonyms for festivals, the phrase זמן חרותנו does not mean that *Pesah* is "the season of our freedom" but rather our *festival of freedom*, and so on.

ZOHAR

The ZOHAR (Splendor), written in Aramaic in the form of a commentary on the Five Books of Moses, is the fundamental work of the mystic teachings of Judaism. Rich with deep religious inspiration, and containing many mystical interpretations of the Torah that have been in existence for centuries, the Zohar has served ever since its first appearance as the starting-point for every kabbalistic discussion of Judaism.

The Zohar's mystic interpretation of the Torah is based on the principle that the biblical narratives contain deeper and more vital truths than they literally express. According to the conception of the Zohar, mysterious high purposes constitute the very soul of the Torah in all its contents.

Regarding the origin of the Zohar there are divergent opinions. There are those who defend the antiquity of certain sections, while others believe that Rabbi Moses de Leon compiled the Zohar from heterogeneous sources, adding his own contributions; still others champion the early authorship of the entire work. The five full volumes of the Zohar cover about two thousand four hundred closely printed pages. Only fifty percent of its contents is available in an English translation.

The Zohar first became known about the middle of the thirteenth century as the work of the Tanna Simeon ben Yoḥai, who had lived in the second century for thirteen years in hiding from the Roman persecutors after the unsuccessful Bar Kokhba revolt. Hidden in a cave, Rabbi Simeon and his son Elazar are said to have been visited on frequent occasions by Elijah, who instructed them in the esoteric teachings of the Torah, which form a large proportion of the subject matter of the Zohar.

Summing up the kabbalistic ideas that had been developed up to the time of its appearance in Spain through the efforts of Rabbi Moses de Leon, the Zohar has played a great part in the lives and the writings of many saintly rabbis since the end of the thirteenth century. The influence of the Zohar spread among the Jewish people with remarkable speed; the enthusiasm felt for it was shared by many non-Jewish scholars. After the Talmud, the Zohar is said to have exercised the deepest influence on Judaism.

The mystic allegorism of the Zohar has tended to stimulate the imagination of the kabbalistically-minded reader and to enable him to

189

transcend the earthly existence and, by means of prayer and devotion, to unite himself with God. In spite of the disastrous effects of the messianic movements led by Shabbethai Zevi and Jacob Frank, who used the Zohar as their mystic guide, this work is highly revered for its lofty thoughts and refined spiritual motives. It has produced in its readers the zest of saintly worship and of active participation in the betterment of the world; it has attracted students seeking an answer to the problems of God and man.

The Zohar has been described as a work sealed with seven seals. It is a compilation of subject-matter drawn from many strata of mystical thought. Many of its teachings are to be found in the oldest portions of the Babylonian and Palestinian Talmuds. The Zohar mirrors Judaism as an intensely vital religion of the spirit, and contains excerpts from writings entitled 1) *Idra Rabba,* 2) *Idra Zuta,* 3) *Mathnitin,* 4) *Midrash ha-Ne'elam,* 5) *Ra'aya Mehemna,* 6) *Sava,* 7) *Razé d'Razin,* 8) *Sefer Hekhaloth,* 9) *Sifra d'Tseni"utha,* 10) *Sithré Torah,* 11) *Tosefta,* 12) *Yanuka.* Besides the Zohar proper, there is also a collection entitled *Tikkuné Zohar,* consisting of seventy additions to the Zohar on Genesis. The Aramaic diction of the Zohar, blending the styles of the Talmud and the Targum, contains elements of Hebrew.

The Zohar often impresses upon the mind of the reader that the Torah contains higher truths in addition to the literal meaning of the narratives and precepts. "The narratives of the Torah are its garments. . . More valuable than the garment is the body that wears it, and more valuable even than that is the soul which animates the body. Fools see only the garment of the Torah; the more intelligent see the body; the wise see the soul of the Torah. . ."

According to the Zohar, everything in the Torah has a threefold significance: the outward, the inner, and the innermost, which is the most important and the most to be desired. The highest goal of the religious person is to penetrate into the inmost purpose of the precepts and practices. It is with this in view that the Zohar deals with all ethical duties and problems. There is hardly a philosophic or ethical subject with which the Zohar does not occupy itself.

In addition to the mystical ideas about the origin of the universe and the super-terrestrial life, the Zohar tries to show the inner worth and the marvelous nature of actual human beings, who are endowed with sublime potentialities. The Zohar stresses that every human act has its effect upon the universal course; the spiritual forces above depend for their activity upon the energizing influences from below.

190

The stories of the Zohar have fascinated many of its readers. They represent comradeship, love of learning, and a spirit of adventure. The heroes of those stories are constantly travelling afoot while talking with their companions concerning the Torah; they enliven their journeys, discussing the beautiful aspects of the earth and the mysteries of heaven; for "the journey is made perfect only by discussing the words of the Torah."

Following are a few sayings from the Zohar:

The ideal man has a male's strength and a female's compassion.

There is no true justice unless mercy is part of it.

When a dog is hit by a stone he bites a fellow dog.

He who praises no one is an arrogant man.

The man who praises himself shows that he knows nothing.

Grandchildren's love is appreciated more than children's love.

ZUGOTH   זוגות

FIVE *Zugoth* (pairs) of leading scholars, who preceded the tannaitic sages in Eretz Yisrael during a period of a hundred and fifty years, are listed in the *Ethics of the Fathers* (Avoth 1:4-12). Hillel and Shammai, the last of the five *Zugoth*, are regarded as the first of the *Tannaim,* whose interpretations of the Torah are recorded in the Mishnah and in other tannaitic works. Tradition reports that the first named of the *Zugoth* served as president (*Nasi*) and the other vice-president (*Av-beth-din*) of the Sanhedrin in Jerusalem.

They are quoted in the *Ethics of the Fathers* in the following order:

1) Yosé ben Yoezer and Yosé ben Yoḥanan
2) Joshua ben Peraḥyah and Nittai of Arbel
3) Judah ben Tabbai and Simeon ben Shetaḥ
4) Shemayah and Avtalyon
5) Hillel and Shammai

ZEKHUTH AVOTH   זְכוּת אָבוֹת

THE Jewish idea of merit is closely connected with that of good deeds. The ethical idea of merit, according to Jewish thinking, implies the existence of three things: 1) a moral law under which man is placed, 2) a free will which enables him to obey it, and 3) a system of rewards and punishments by which obedience or disobedience to the law is stressed. Conduct is meritorious when it agrees with the law and is at the same time voluntary.

The phrase *zekhuth avoth* (merit of the fathers) implies that the good deeds of the ancestors contribute to the welfare of their descendants. The expression זוכר חסדי אבות (thou rememberest the good deeds of the patriarchs) is repeated three times daily in the opening benediction of the *Shemoneh Esreh* prayer. The *zekhuth-avoth* concept, in Jewish theology, is expressive of the idea that individuals profit in their lifetime by the meritorious acts of their ancestors. The Torah, in the second of the Ten Commandments, clearly indicates that the benefits of a man's good deeds (מעשים טובים) will extend indefinitely, implying that God's mercy in rewarding righteousness infinitely transcends his anger in punishing the sinful (Exodus 20:6; Deuteronomy 7:9).

Zekhuth Avoth has also been interpreted to imply that a person is best able to advance on the road to moral perfection if he starts with the accumulated spiritual heritage of righteous ancestors. The earliest use of the phrase *zekhuth avoth* (merit of the fathers) is in the *Ethics of the Fathers*, where we read: "Let all who work for the community do so from a spiritual motive, for then *the merit of their fathers* will sustain them, and their righteousness will endure forever" (Avoth 2:2). The inspiration drawn from the past will increase the zeal and the achievement of those engaged in doing good work. The intended sacrifice of Isaac (*Akedah*) is often mentioned in the liturgy in reference to the idea of *zekhuth avoth* ("Even as Abraham our father held back his compassion from his only son . . . in order to do thy will, so may thy mercy hold back thy anger. . .")

EXODUS MEMORIAL   זֵכֶר לִיצִיאַת מִצְרַיִם

THE phrase *in remembrance of the exodus from Egypt* occurs frequently in the prayers of the Sabbath and the festivals. The three pilgrim festivals (*Pesaḥ, Shavuoth* and *Sukkoth*) are, of course, directly connected with the exodus from Egypt. As to the Sabbath, we read in the Torah: "Remember that you were once a slave in the land of Egypt, and that the Lord your God brought you out from there by a mighty hand and an outstretched arm; therefore the Lord your God has commanded you to observe the Sabbath" (Deuteronomy 5:15).

The constant reference to the exodus in the Bible is explained by the fact that the redemption from slavery in Egypt was the greatest event in Jewish history. It marked the birth of the Jewish people as a nation and signified God's providence in Israel's struggle for existence.

The Torah connects the exodus from Egypt with every kind of legislation, social as well as religious and ethical. The Ten Commandments begin with the far-echoing declaration: "I am the Lord your God who brought you out of the land of Egypt." In reference to the portable sanctuary (*mishkan*) we read: "They shall know that I, the Lord, am their God who brought them out of the land of Egypt.

In regard to the divine precepts in general, the Torah says: "Be careful to observe the commandments which I, the Lord, give you ... who brought you out of the land of Egypt. . ." Concerning the treatment of fellow men: "Do not act dishonestly. . . You shall have a true scale and true weights. . . I am the Lord your God who brought you out of the land of Egypt. Be careful, then, to observe all my statutes and ordinances." Upon dismissing a servant, "you shall not send him away empty-handed. . . Remember that you were once a slave in the land of Egypt" (Exodus 20:2; 29:46; Leviticus 22:31; 19:35-37).

Israel's venturing forth into the unknown wilderness involved a supreme act of faith, referred to in endearing terms: "I remember your youthful affection, the love of your bridal days, how you followed me in the wilderness, in a land unsown" (Jeremiah 2:2-3). Hence, Israel must never forget the exodus from Egypt and all that this historic event symbolizes.

REMEMBRANCE   זִכָּרוֹן

THE verb *remember* and its derivatives occur frequently in biblical and talmudic-midrashic literature. Thus we are told to think back on the days of old, to reflect on the years of each generation. "Ask your father and he will inform you, ask your elders and they will tell you" (Deuteronomy 32:7). Concerning the attack of the Amalekites, "the Lord said to Moses: Write this down as something to be remembered" (Exodus 17:14). The twelve memorial stones set up by the Israelites at Gilgal to commemorate their passage of the Jordan were likewise designed for the educational advantage of future generations: "When your children ask you what these stones mean to you, you shall tell them. . . These stones are to serve as a perpetual memorial to the Israelites" (Joshua 4:7).

Psalm 137, which represents a lifelike memorial of the bitter experiences of exile, contains the famous expression: "If I forget you, Jerusalem, may my right hand be forgotten! May my tongue cleave to my palate if I remember you not, if I place not Jerusalem ahead of my joy." Hence, the sages introduced various enactments and usages in remembrance of the Temple (זכר למקדש) and in memory of its destruction (זכר לחרבן).

In order to commemorate the destruction of the Temple, they ordained that no Jew should live in royal luxury; that Jewish women should not wear all their jewels; that the veil covering the bride's face during the *ḥuppah* ceremony should contain no silver or gold threads. Similarly, it has become customary to break a clay vessel after the signing of a betrothal contract (תנאים, *tenaim*), and for the groom to break a glass at the conclusion of the *ḥuppah* ceremony. Even in entertaining a bride and groom, which is regarded as a religious function of great merit, we are told that there should be no excess of rejoicing. "No person is allowed to indulge in unrestrained laughter, even when rejoicing in the performance of a *mitzvah* (*Kitzur Shulḥan Arukh* 126:4).

It has been remarked that a scattered people which remembers its past and connects it with the present will undoubtedly have a future as a people, and perhaps even a more glorious life than the one in the past.

ZECHARIAH   זְכַרְיָה

THE book of Zechariah, the eleventh of the Minor Prophets, consists of fourteen chapters. The first eight chapters, generally referred to as part one, contain a series of eight visions, by means of which the prophet expresses his assurance that the Lord will restore Israel's former glory. The last six chapters, spoken of as part two, include prophecies concerning the advent of Messiah, deliverance, final victory, and God's reign of peace.

Some scholars are of the opinion that the last six chapters belong to a much earlier anonymous author, a "Second Zechariah"; others, however, maintain that the so-called Second Zechariah lived at a much later period than the original Zechariah who, like his older contemporary Haggai the prophet, urged the immediate rebuilding of the Temple in Jerusalem during the years 520-518 before the common era.

The introduction to the book strikes the keynote to the visions it contains: "In the second year of king Darius, the word of the Lord came to Zechariah the prophet, bidding him to tell the people: "Turn to me, and I will turn to you; be not like your fathers, who did not listen to me." Chapter eight includes words of encouragement:

"Old men and old women shall again sit in the streets of Jerusalem. The streets of the city shall be full of boys and girls playing there. I will save my people from the land of the east and from the land of the west; I will bring them home to dwell within Jerusalem. They shall be my people and I will be their God. I will sow peace and prosperity; the vine shall yield its fruit; the ground shall give its produce, and the skies shall drop their dew. I will save you, O house of Israel, and you shall be a blessing. Fear not, but let your hands be strong... These are the things you must do: Speak the truth to one another; render judgments that are true and for the common good; do not plot evil in your hearts against one another. . ."

Zechariah's prophecies, like those of Ezekiel, are apocalyptic. The purpose of his night-visions is to teach the future purification of Jerusalem.

ZEMIROTH   זְמִירוֹת

T H E *Zemiroth* (table songs), sung during the Sabbath meals and at the close of the Sabbath, sum up the very essence of holy joyousness that has been the keynote of Judaism. These songs and hymns, composed at a very early date, became particularly popular during the sixteenth century through kabbalistic influence. The love for song gave rise to many Hebrew poets, whose hymns were frequently collected and published by various congregations. Only a small number of the hundreds of *Zemiroth* by many medieval poets may be found in the current editions of the Hebrew Prayerbook.

The custom of singing table songs, adding light and joy to the Jewish soul on the Sabbath, is said to be two thousand years old. Philo, describing the life led by the Essenes, mentions their custom to sing table hymns in appreciation of God's continuous vigilance and goodness. There is a talmudic statement to the effect that when Jewish people eat and drink, they begin with words of Torah and hymns of praise; when idolaters eat and drink, they begin with frivolity and obscenity (Megillah 12b).

The tunes of the *Zemiroth*, reflecting the experiences of Israel, are mostly adapted local folk tunes that eventually became characteristically Jewish. Hymns like *Yah Ribbon* are sung to the same tune everywhere. This hymn was written in Aramaic by Rabbi Israel Najara, one of the most prolific Hebrew writers of the sixteenth century. His *Zemiroth Yisrael*, comprising three hundred and forty-six poems, was published at the end of the sixteenth century, and it soon became the most popular songbook among the Jewish communities in the orient. Rabbi Israel Najara (1555-1628) was one of the prominent members of the kabbalistic school at Safed, Upper Galilee, where he spent most of his life. He died as the rabbi of the community of Gaza. The initial letters of the verses of *Yah Ribbon Olam* (Eternal Master of Worlds) form the name-acrostic ישראל, by which the poet's memory is immortalized.

Though *Yah Ribbon* contains no allusion to the Sabbath, it is chanted on Friday evenings in all parts of the world. After describing the wonders of God's creation, the poet, kabbalistically inspired, concludes with a prayer for the redemption of Israel and the restoration of Jerusalem, "the city of beauty."

Tsur Mishello is the title of another hymn chanted as an introduction to the grace (*Birkath ha-Mazon*) recited after the Sabbath meal. Though this poem bears no relation to the Sabbath, it is not chanted on the busy weekdays. Its four stanzas contain the substance of the *Birkath ha-Mazon*. Like countless other liturgical hymns, this poem is of unknown authorship.

Ha-Mavdil, the hymn chanted after the *Havdalah* which is recited to mark the conclusion of the Sabbath, was composed by Rabbi Isaac ibn Ghayyat of eleventh-century Spain, who was the teacher of Rabbi Isaac Alfasi, author of the famous talmudic compendium known as the *Rif* (initials of Rabbi Isaac Fasi). *Ha-Mavdil*, containing references to atonement, must have been originally written for the *Ne'ilah* service of *Yom Kippur*.

Here are several lines from the hymn: "The day has declined like the shade of a palm; I call upon God who fills all my needs... Open heaven's exalted gate for me... I call for thy help. O grant redemption, in the twilight, the evening of the day... We are like potter's clay in thy hand; pardon our transgressions, both light and grave..." The acrostic of this poem is Yitzhak ha-Katan.

196

ELDER זָקֵן

IN PRIMITIVE times, age was a necessary condition of authority. The Torah speaks not only of the elders among the people of Israel but also among the Egyptians and the Midianites (Genesis 50:7; Numbers 22:7). The Greek term *presbuteros* and the Latin term *senatus* signify an elder. During the biblical period, the elders dispensed justice each within his own circle. They were powerful in both local and national affairs. At their request, Samuel consented to a monarchical form of government; through their intervention, Abner succeeded in appointing David king over Israel (I Samuel 8:4; II Samuel 3:17).

During the tannaitic period, the title *zaken* (elder) was awarded to a scholar. The graduates of the school of Shammai were called זקני בית שמאי (Berakhoth 11a); and in general, the terms זקנים and חכמים were used synonymously. On the other hand, an ignorant and sinful old man would be called זקן אשמאי (Kiddushin 32b). The Mishnah speaks of the ancient elders as the recipients of the traditional teachings from Joshua and as the forerunners of the Sanhedrin (Avoth 1:1).

The term זקן ממרא (*zaken mamreh*) denotes a defying scholar, one who persists in maintaining and asserting a schismatic position against the final decision of the supreme court in Temple times. By rebelling against the majority of the *Sanhedrin Gedolah* at Jerusalem, and in issuing a contrary decision, a judge committed a capital offense, and his punishment was death. He was classed with the individual who incites others to worship false gods (מסית). The severe punishment of a *zaken mamreh* was designed to prevent an increasing series of schisms among the people of Israel (Sanhedrin 88a b).

The law concerning a *zaken mamreh* is derived from the Torah, where we read: "You shall carry out the directions they give you, and the verdict they pronounce for you, without turning aside to the right or to the left. . . Any man who willfully refuses to listen to the priests who officiate there before the Lord your God, or to the judge, shall die. Thus shall you purge the evil from your midst" (Deuteronomy 17:11-12). A *zaken mamreh* was punished only when he decided against a biblical law, the transgression of which entailed the severe penalty of *kareth* (extinction). The *zaken mamreh* could be sentenced only by the Great Sanhedrin, consisting of seventy-one members, when the Temple was still in existence. He was punished only when he rebelled against a decision of the Great Sanhedrin while he was within the *lish-*

197

kath ha-gazith (chamber of hewn stone), which housed the Sanhedrin in the Temple (Sanhedrin 14b; 52a; 87a; Sotah 7b). He was exempted if he rebelled in his hometown.

ZERA'IM   זְרָעִים

THE first of the six divisions of the Mishnah is known under the name of *Zera'im* (Seeds) because it contains agricultural laws, such as the prohibition of mixed planting, and the taxes on the products of the soil. *Zera'im* consists of eleven tractates, as follows:

1) *Berakhoth*, nine chapters, treating of benedictions and prayers, especially the daily prayers.

2) *Peah*, eight chapters, on questions about the corners of fields set aside for the use of the poor (Leviticus 19:9; Deuteronomy 24:19).

3) *Demai*, seven chapters, on the requirements for tithing produce purchased from a person suspected of not having tithed properly.

4) *Kilayim*, nine chapters, on the prohibitions of cross-breeding and mingling varied species of plants, animals, and clothing (Leviticus 19:19; Deuteronomy 22:9).

5) *Shevi'ith*, ten chapters, on the laws of the Sabbatical Year (Exodus 23:11; Leviticus 25:1-7).

6) *Terumoth*, eleven chapters, on the gifts due to the priests from the Israelites and the Levites (Numbers 18:8; Deuteronomy 18:4).

7) *Ma'aseroth*, five chapters, on the tithe given to the Levites (Numbers 18:21-24).

8) *Ma'aser Sheni*, five chapters, on the tithes eaten in Jerusalem (Deuteronomy 14:22-27).

9) *Hallah*, four chapters, on the portion of dough given to the priests (Numbers 15:21).

10) *Orlah*, three chapters, on the forbidden fruits of trees or vineyards for the first three years after planting (Leviticus 19:23).

11) *Bikkurim*, three chapters, on the first-fruits brought to the Temple (Deuteronomy 26:1-11); it contains a vivid description of the first-fruits offering in the Second Temple.

The Babylonian Talmud has *Gemara* commentary on Berakhoth, the first tractate of *Zera'im*. The Palestinian Talmud has *Gemara* on all eleven tractates.

HABAKKUK

THE book of Ḥabakkuk, the eighth of the Minor Prophets, consists of three chapters that contain some of the noblest utterances in the history of religious experience. Nothing is known of the personal life of Ḥabakkuk, the great prophet who, like Job, asked searching questions and received answers from God. Ḥabakkuk complains against the cruelties and inhumanities of the oppressors. Their continued victories and successes seem to him inconsistent with divine justice. The Lord's response is that evil shall ultimately perish from the earth, and the upright shall live by their faithfulness. The book is full of force, thought, and poetic expression. It possesses unique religious values, marking reflective thinking concerning an ethical universe. The language used is that employed by Amos, Isaiah and Jeremiah.

"How long, O Lord, shall I cry for help and thou wilt not hear? I complain to thee of wrongs, and thou dost not help. Why dost thou show me evil and make me look upon misery? Oppression and outrage confront me; strife and contention arise. The law is slack, and justice never appears; the wicked beset the righteous, and justice goes forth twisted. . ." (1:2-4). The prophet stations himself on a watch-tower and looks hopefully for a divine answer. The tower is not a literal tower, but the inner light of revelation whereby he ponders the problems.

"Thy eyes are too pure to behold evil; thou canst not gaze upon wrongdoing. Why, then, dost thou look on faithless men and keep silent when the wicked swallow up the innocent? Thou hast made men like the fish in the sea, like crawling things without a ruler. The foe hooks all of them, drags them out with his net, and joyfully gathers them up. Through them he lives in luxury, and his food is plentiful. Shall he keep on emptying his net, murdering people without pity?. . .

"The good man lives by his faith; the arrogant man shall not abide. His greed is as wide as the netherworld; like death he never has enough. Woe to him who heaps up what is not his own; how long can it last? Woe to him who acquires unjust gain. . . The stone shall cry from the wall, and the beam in the woodwork shall echo the call. Woe to him who builds a city by bloodshed, and founds a town on crime! The toil of nations ends in smoke, and peoples wear themselves out for naught. But the knowledge of the Lord's glory shall fill the earth, as water covers the sea."

Some scholars maintain that Habakkuk was a younger contemporary of Isaiah; others place him later, as a younger contemporary of Jeremiah. It is difficult to know the precise date of his prophecy.

HEVRAH KADDISHA   חֶבְרָה קַדִּישָׁא

HEVRAH KADDISHA (sacred society) is the title applied to the group formed for burying the dead and supervising the burial arrangements. This has always been regarded as a holy duty, a religious act of great merit, a deed of kindliness and of piety. Though societies for this purpose must have existed in talmudic times, the formation of the first *Hevrah Kaddisha* is credited to Rabbi Judah Loew ben Bezalel (Maharal) of Prague (1530-1609), who wrote ethical works and enjoyed a great reputation as a saint, scholar, philosopher and wonder-worker.

Historical records of such societies date back to the beginning of the seventeenth century. Generally, the membership consists of eighteen, the numerical equivalent of חי (alive), or a multiple of eighteen. On the seventh of *Adar*, the anniversary of the death of Moses, it is customary for these groups to celebrate with a banquet following a fast observed in memory of the dead. In the Talmud, *mithassekin* and *gomlé hasadim* are mentioned as supervising the burial functions (Mo-'ed Katan 24b; Kethubboth 8b).

HAGGAI   חַגַּי

THE book of Haggai, the tenth of the Minor Prophets, consists of four prophecies delivered within the space of four months in 520 before the common era. A contemporary of Zechariah and Malachi, Haggai is one of the last three literary prophets. His prophetic activity occurred eighteen years after Cyrus had permitted the exiles to return to Judea. The work of rebuilding the Temple had been at a standstill for seventeen years, because of the hostile Samaritans who interfered with the work of restoration.

Haggai sent four messages urging the returning exiles to rebuild the Temple in Jerusalem. He roused the energies and the aspirations of the people who started a new life in Judea: "You who saw the Temple in its former splendor, what do you think of it now? You think nothing of it? Yet, take courage . . . work, for I am with you.

Once again the treasures of all nations shall come in, and I will fill this house with splendor. The silver is mine, the gold is mine . . . upon this place I will bestow prosperity" (Haggai 2:3-8).

Haggai's unadorned prose reflects the wretched situation of Jerusalem prior to the arrival of Nehemiah, who was twice governor of Jerusalem in 445 and 433 before the common era. His noble character and strong self-reliance, combined with a serene trust in God, contributed to his success in fortifying Jerusalem physically and spiritually against the surrounding enemies of his people. The book of Haggai is deemed of great importance as a historical source, because together with the book of Zechariah it lifts the veil over the obscure period from 561 to 444 before the common era. The revival of Judaism, it is shown, was created by the practical measures of Nehemiah.

FEASTS AND FESTIVALS   חַגִּים וּזְמַנִּים

THE terms חגים and זמנים are frequently used interchangeably in the sense of festivals. In Maimonides' *Mishneh Torah*, the division containing the laws concerning the feasts and festivals bears the title זמנים (*Zemannim*). Hence, the phrase זמן חרותנו means *our festival of freedom* and not, as rendered in some texts and Prayerbooks, "the season of our freedom." Similarly, זמן שמחתנו means *our festival of rejoicing*, and not "the season of our rejoicing."

The seven biblical festivals, occurring within the first seven months of the year, include the three pilgrimage festivals (*shalosh regalim*): *Pesaḥ, Shavuoth* and *Sukkoth;* the High Holydays, known as *Yamim Nora'im* (Days of Awe): *Rosh Hashanah* and *Yom Kippur; Shemini Atsereth*, the eighth-day festival following the seven days of *Sukkoth;* and the most important new moon festival occurring on the first day of the seventh month.

The symbolic significance of the sacred number seven is conveyed in the circumstance that the Sabbath is the seventh day; the sabbatical year is the seventh year; the jubilee, the first after seven times seven years; forty-nine days elapse (7×7) between *Pesaḥ* and *Shavuoth; Pesaḥ* and *Sukkoth* each consisting of seven days.

The three pilgrim festivals, originally pastoral in character, marking the spring (barley), summer (wheat), and autumn (fruit) harvests, respectively, are referred to as *ḥaggim,* implying rhythmic processions around the sanctuary. On *Pesaḥ, Shavuoth* and *Sukkoth,* adult males had to appear in the Temple with gifts showing their gratitude for the divine blessings of the land (Deuteronomy 16:16-17). The term *ḥag* is applied to all the pilgrim festivals, but especially to *Sukkoth;* the term *mo'ed* (appointed season), used interchangeably with *ḥag,* refers to these festive occasions taking place on specified days.

The first and last days of *Pesaḥ* and *Sukkoth* are considered festive days, when work is prohibited somewhat less rigidly than on the Sabbath and *Yom Kippur* (cooking and preparing vital food is permitted, except on *Shabbath* and *Yom Kippur*); the intermediate days between the first and last days of *Pesaḥ* and *Sukkoth,* known as *Ḥol ha-Mo'ed,* are non-festive in the sense that work, the neglect of which would entail a financial loss, is permitted.

Sukkoth, the *ḥag* par excellence, is designated as *zeman simḥathenu* (our festival of rejoicing) in the liturgy. In Temple times, the eve of the second day of *Sukkoth* was proverbial for the rejoicing occasioned by the ceremonial drawing of water (שמחת בית השואבה). The Water Feast began at nightfall and lasted till the following morning. The outer court of the Temple was brilliantly illuminated. Priests and Levites, in stately torchlight procession, accompanied by the playing of all sorts of musical instruments, made the circuit of the Temple court, while the women were looking on from their galleries.

During the day, the great feature was the procession which accompanied the priest who had been allotted the duty of drawing water for the libation ceremony from the pool of Siloam at Jerusalem. Hence the traditional statement: "Whoever has not witnessed this celebration has never seen real rejoicing" (Sukkah 5:1). The Torah is frequently compared to water that purifies. In Numbers 24:7, the constant flow of water is symbolic of numerous descendants. In Isaiah 12:3 we read: "With joy shall you draw water from the fountains of deliverance." Hence the joyous procession to and from the well on the second day of *Sukkoth.*

The post-biblical festivals, regarded as workdays because they are not described as holy days, are: *Ḥanukkah, Purim, Lag b'Omer, Tu Bishvat. Isru Ḥag* (bind the festival) is the semi-festal day after each of the three pilgrim festivals (*Pesaḥ, Shavuoth, Sukkoth*), when the pilgrims left Jerusalem for their homes in the times of the ancient Temple. In biblical times, the first day of the month, *Rosh Ḥodesh,* was celebrated as a holiday (I Samuel 20:18; II Kings 4:23; Isaiah 1:14) with special sacrificial offerings (Numbers 28:11-15).

202

Simḥath Torah (Rejoicing of the *Torah*), celebrated in Israel on *Shemini Atsereth*, the eighth day of *Sukkoth*, and in the Diaspora on the ninth day, was not known in talmudic times. It came into use presumably around the ninth century in Babylonia, where the one-year cycle for the reading of the Torah prevailed. On *Simḥath Torah*, the last section of the Five Books of Moses is read, thus concluding the one-year cycle, and immediately the new cycle is begun by the reading of the first chapter of Genesis.

Ḥathan Torah (bridegroom of the Torah) is the title given to the person who is honored with the reading of the concluding section of Deuteronomy, while *Ḥathan Bereshith* (bridegroom of Genesis) is the title applied to the one who is honored with the reading of the initial section of the Torah. One of the outstanding features of *Simḥath Torah* is the sevenfold procession around the synagogue, referred to as *Hakkafoth* (circuits), which became customary in the sixteenth century. Every adult person in the congregation, bearing a Torah scroll, is given the honor to participate in any one of the processions, often followed by children carrying flags inscribed with expressions like: "Thrill with joy over the Torah!" (שישו ושמחו בשמחת תורה).

ḤAD GADYA   חַד גַּדְיָא

Ḥad Gadya, the song intended for the entertainment of the children so as to keep them awake until the conclusion of the *Seder* service the first two nights of Passover, consists of ten stanzas written in the form of a nursery rhyme and phrased in the simplest style of Aramaic-Hebrew. It was not made part of the *Haggadah* text until late in the sixteenth century, when it was included in the Prague edition of 1590. Many still regard it as an allegorical song, though scholars surmise that it is simply a nursery rhyme based on a popular French ballad.

The principal idea conveyed in this song is, it seems, identical with Hillel's famous utterance concerning measure for measure: "Because you have drowned others, others have drowned you; and those who have drowned you shall themselves be drowned" (Avoth 2:7).

The refrain about the "kid father bought for two zuzim" has been taken to mean the people of Israel whom God acquired as his own by the two tablets of the covenant. The animals and the inanimate objects, as well as the butcher and the angel of death, are employed by God as means of mutual chastisement for wrongs committed.

203

ḤEDER   חֶדֶר

T H E name for the old-fashioned religious elementary school was *ḥeder* (room), because it was held in the room where the teacher and his family lived. The hours of study began early in the morning and lasted to eight or nine in the evening. The instruction started with the mechanics of Hebrew reading and proceeded to Bible, Mishnah and Talmud. The pupils that showed promise kept advancing to ever-higher grades, then to the *beth ha-midrash* and *yeshivah*, where they were grounded in the Talmud and the vast literature which had grown about it.

A minimum of Jewish education was possessed even by the weaker students who dropped out in the lower grades to learn a trade. The *Talmud Torah* (teaching of the Torah) was a community school maintained for poor children whose parents could not afford to pay tuition to the *melammed* (teacher). Thus Jewish education was widely diffused, and ordinary men in moderate circumstances commanded a fund of Jewish learning, which was maintained and nurtured throughout life. The daily congregational services, morning and evening, were always combined with varied kinds of Jewish learning: courses in Rashi's commentary on the Torah, or in Talmud, or in laws and customs.

Elementary schools existed in every Jewish community. The higher schools for advanced students (*yeshivoth*) were supported by the community, while the elementary schools (*ḥadarim*) were private in the sense that the teachers received their fees directly from the parents, though they were authorized by the community. The boys were taught the mechanics of Hebrew reading in three months. In the fourth month the reading of *Ḥummash* was started with the book of Leviticus (*Vayyikra*). During the second three months they read a portion of the weekly *sidrah* in Hebrew. The following six months were used in translating the weekly *sidroth* into the native tongue of the pupils. By the age of thirteen the pupils had studied selections from the Talmud with the commentaries.

The talmudic expression *tinokoth shel beth rabban* (babies of the teacher's house) may well indicate that the custom of giving instruction in the house of the teacher dates back to an early period in Jewish history. Originally, the word תִּינוֹק, derived from the verb יָנַק, was applied to an infant nursed by its mother.

204

MONTHS   חֳדָשִׁים

IN BIBLICAL times the months were commonly distinguished by number: the first, the third, the seventh month. The names of only four Hebrew months are found in Bible narratives relating to the period preceding the Babylonian exile: *Aviv, Ziv, Ethanim, Bul (Nisan, Iyyar, Tishri, Marheshvan)*. After the Babylonian captivity we find the Babylonian names of the months, which are now employed in every Jewish calendar: *Nisan, Iyyar, Sivan, Tammuz, Av, Elul, Tishri, Marheshvan, Kislev, Teveth, Shevat, Adar, va-Adar* or *Adar Sheni*. The accepted Jewish calendar is based on the extremely accurate system published by Hillel II in 359, making the months to alternate between thirty and twenty-nine days.

Nisan, Sivan, Av, Tishri, Kislev and *Shevat* have each thirty days; the other six months have twenty-nine days each. In a leap year, consisting of thirteen months instead of twelve, when *Adar* is doubled, the first *Adar* has thirty days, the second twenty-nine. When the preceding month has thirty days, its last day is celebrated as the first day of *Rosh Ḥodesh*, while the second day of *Rosh Ḥodesh* marks the first day of the new month. Otherwise, *Rosh Ḥodesh* consists of one day, marking the first day of the new month.

The month can contain only whole days, and lunation requires 29 days, twelve hours, 44 minutes, 2.8 seconds, elapsing between two successive new moons; hence the alternation between thirty and twenty-nine days. This does not fully absorb the forty-four minutes 2.8 seconds above the twelve hours. For this reason, *Marheshvan* is as often as necessary lengthened to thirty days. Since *Yom Kippur* may not come on a Friday or a Sunday, on account of the great inconvenience of preparing food, the first day of *Rosh Hashanah* cannot occur on Sunday, Wednesday, or Friday. Nor can *Hoshana Rabbah*, when the willow branches are struck against the ground at the end of the synagogue service, fall on a Sabbath. The adjustment is made at the end of *Marheshvan* and *Kislev* in the preceding year. *Marheshvan* signifies the eighth month in Babylonian; since the letters מ and ו interchange (so also ו and י), מרחשון=ורח שמן (eighth month).

The new-moon benediction, quoted in Sanhedrin 42a, ends with the phrase מחדש חדשים, where the word *ḥodesh* is used to designate the new moon. It should be rendered *renewst the moons*. The name ירח (moon) has been connected with אורח (wanderer).

DUTIES OF THE HEART   חוֹבוֹת הַלְּבָבוֹת

ONE of the most widely read and deeply loved ethical works has been *Ḥovoth ha-Levavoth* or *Duties of the Heart* by Rabbi Baḥya ibn Pakuda of eleventh-century Spain, the most popular Jewish philosopher of the Middle Ages. The first systematic presentation of the ethics of Judaism, Rabbi Baḥya's *Duties of the Heart* describes the Jewish faith as a great spiritual truth founded on reason, revelation, and tradition.

Combining depth of emotion, poetic imagination, eloquence and exquisite diction with a keen intellect, the author appeals to the sentiments and stirs the hearts of his readers. He declares that a man may be as holy as an angel and yet he will not equal the one who leads a fellow man to righteousness.

Baḥya's great personality, rich in piety and touching humility, shines through every line of his *Duties of the Heart*. In his chapter on humility, he declares that humility is expressed in gentle conduct toward fellow men, whether or not they are of equal standing. It springs from a consideration of one's own failings and shortcomings. Humility is shown especially in refraining from finding fault in others.

Faith, he says, must be intellectual, not blind and unreasoning. God's existence is knowable from the fact that non-existent beings cannot create existent beings. Tradition alone, without the support of scientific proof, is sufficient for those who are not able to study. But, "if you are a man of intellect . . . you are obligated to use your own faculties to gain clear and definite knowledge of the truth, so that your faith and conduct may rest on a foundation of tradition, reason, and personal understanding."

He writes: Life and death are brothers that dwell together; they cling to each other and cannot be separated. They are joined by the two extremes of a frail bridge over which all created beings travel. Life is the entrance; death is the exit; life builds, death demolishes; life sows, death reaps; life plants, and death uproots. Know that yesterday shall never come back; nor should you say: "I shall do it tomorrow." Hasten to do your task every day, for death may at any time send forth its arrow-like lightning.

Baḥya's *Duties of the Heart*, written originally in Arabic, was rendered into Hebrew by Rabbi Yehudah ibn Tibbon of twelfth-century Spain, who translated Rav Saadyah's *Beliefs and Opinions* and Rabbi Yehudah Halevi's *Kuzari* from the original Arabic into Hebrew.

206

ḤAZZAN   חַזָּן

THE term *ḥazzan* originates from Assyro-Babylonian in which it denoted *overseer*. In the Amarna tablets, it signifies a governor stationed
in Palestine by the Egyptians. In ancient Israel, the *ḥazzan's* duties
included that of a sexton, taking care of the synagogue and its contents, as well as that of an elementary school teacher. From the roof
of the synagogue the *ḥazzan* announced the beginning and the end of
the Sabbath and the festivals by sounding the *shofar* three times
(Mishnah Shabbath 1:3; Tosefta Sukkah 4:11). In modern usage, the
ḥazzan is primarily the *sheliaḥ tsibbur*, the congregational reader of
prayers, referred to as cantor or precentor.

During the medieval period, the prescribed Hebrew prayers were
amplified by the addition of prayer-poems and hymns, known as *piyyutim*, composed by *ḥazzanim-payyetanim*, such as Rabbi Elazar ha-
Kallir of the eighth century, whose numerous *piyyutim* are to be found
in the current editions of the *Siddur* and the *Maḥzor*. The *ḥazzan* in
the Middle Ages was often a combination of poet, composer, and singer, whose melodies have been preserved down to our time. In the
twelfth-century work *Sefer Ḥasidim* there is a statement which reads:
"If you cannot concentrate when you pray, search for melodies and
choose a tune you like. Your heart will then feel what you say, for
it is the song that makes your heart respond."

As a rule, the *ḥazzan* of the medieval period was a man of extensive
learning and of high esteem. Consideration of character took precedence to consideration of voice quality. It often happened that the
ḥazzan was the only member of the congregation who possessed a
Prayerbook manuscript which included many poetic interpolations.
The congregation was therefore greatly dependent on the *ḥazzan*, and
actually led by him, in the worship services.

Ḥazzanim, in the modern sense, who are influenced by the musical
style of non-Jews, were strongly disliked by *Ḥasidic* leaders. Rabbi
Jacob Joseph of Polonnoye, author of *Toledoth Yaakov Yosef*, which
is the primary source for the teachings of Rabbi Israel Baal Shem Tov,
writes: "Our souls are sick with listening to *ḥazzanim*... They sin
and bring others to sin. When they prolong their melodies without
end, the people gossip in the synagogue, interrupting the silence of
prayer... Originally, the *ḥazzan* sang devoutly ... he was the most
important person in the city, expressing the proper meaning of each

207

word he sang. Hence, our tradition is opposed to the changing of melodies which fit the words of the prayers. In the course of time, however, the *ḥazzan* has ceased to pray at all, stressing only the melody. . .''

This was written in the latter part of the eighteenth century, when the impact of musical progress made itself felt among *ḥazzanim* who, in an earlier period, used to carry melodies and customs from one community to another, thus contributing to the unification of the musical tradition of the synagogue.

ḤAZAK ḤAZAK!   חֲזַק חֲזַק!

At the completion of any of the Five Books of Moses, read publicly in the synagogue, the congregation stands up and exclaims: חזק חזק ונתחזק ("Be strong, be strong, and let us take courage!"). This unanimous response on the part of the congregation is reminiscent of the expression חזק ונתחזק בעד עמנו ("Be strong, and let us be of good courage for our people!") in II Samuel 10:12 and I Chronicles 19:13. This is understood to mean: Let us gather courage to live in accordance with the teachings contained in each of the five books of the Torah. The Sephardim are accustomed to greet the person who is honored with being called up to the Torah by saying חזק וברוך.

ḤAZAKAH   חֲזָקָה

Ḥazakah (taking hold, possession) signifies in talmudic law any claim based on undisturbed possession of landed property during the legal period of three years. If a man has no title-deeds, his claim to rightful ownership can be sustained if he can prove three years' undisputed possession. The term *ḥazakah*, combining the meaning of holding, occupation and presumed ownership, is a title not supported by documents or witnesses, but based on the mere fact of possession.

Such possession creates a presumption of ownership only if the possessor pleads at the time that he obtained the object in a lawful manner, by purchase or gift. If he does not advance this plea, the fact of three years' possession has no legal value. This is expressed by the dictum כל חזקה שאין עמה טענה אינה חזקה (Bava Bathra 3:3), possession without a plea of purchase or any legal acquisition gives no title.

208

The word *ḥazakah* is also used in the sense of inference, such as the presumption that none will marry without first ascertaining the physical condition of the party he marries (Kethubboth 75b).

The term *ḥazakah* has a variety of meanings in Jewish legal literature: 1) the formal taking possession of real property; 2) possession under circumstances giving rise to the presumption of rightful ownership; 3) a legal presumption; 4) reputation. Formal protest by the original owner within the three-year period of possession is, under Jewish law, sufficient to overcome the presumption (*ḥazakah*) of rightful ownership arising from such possession.

SIN   חֵטְא

VARIOUS words are employed in the Bible to denote sin. Though they are often used interchangeably, their primary signification reveals the inner meaning of the biblical conception of sin. The word חטא, used most frequently, connotes missing the mark. That is to say, the good action leads to a positive result, while the sinful action leads to no result. The term עון (sin) denotes something distorted and twisted, while the word פשע is derived from the verb *to rebel*. In order that life should be kept intact, every sin brings its punishment, inflicted by the Author and Guardian of life.

ḤAYYÉ ADAM   חַיֵּי אָדָם

THE books *Ḥayyé Adam* and *Ḥokhmath Adam* by Rabbi Abraham Danzig (1748-1820) represent the most important works on Jewish law and ethics after the *Shulḥan Arukh*, composed by Rabbi Joseph Karo of the sixteenth century. The subject matter treated in both *Ḥayyé Adam* and *Ḥokhmath Adam* coincides with that of the first two parts of the *Shulḥan Arukh*, and is based on the enormous mass of new material which accumulated in the course of two and a half centuries after the appearance of the *Shulḥan Arukh*. The new material, carefully collected and sifted by Rabbi Abraham Danzig, is presented in a simple, easy-to-read Hebrew style, readily understandable by the cultured Jewish layman.

His *Ḥayyé Adam* (human life) and *Ḥokhmath Adam* (human wisdom) contain a remarkably precise and lucid discussion of new details introduced by the more recent rabbinic authorities, referred to as the *Aḥaronim*. These lawcodes represent special emphasis on the ethical bearings of the *mitzvoth* and religious precepts. The famous תפלה זכה (sincere prayer), written for the eve of *Yom Kippur*, is taken from the *Ḥayyé Adam*, where it was first introduced as an anonymous composition.

Rabbi Abraham Danzig was born in Danzig. At the age of fourteen, he was sent to the *yeshivah* of Prague, where he spent four years under the guidance of Rabbi Ezekiel Landau (נודע ביהודה). He then settled in Vilna, Lithuania, where he was offered the salaried position of rabbi which he declined; he preferred to be an independent merchant instead of receiving a stipend on the basis of Jewish scholarship. In his later years, after having lost almost everything he possessed through the explosion of a powder magazine, he accepted the position of *dayyan* or judge of a rabbinical court. He held this office till his death. His books met with unusual success during his lifetime. In many Jewish communities, societies were formed for the purpose of studying his works.

WISDOM   חָכְמָה

WISDOM is used in the Bible as one of the three departments of knowledge among the people of Israel. The other two are Torah and prophecy. The Torah presents the divine commandments to man; the prophets pass judgment on man's conduct in the light of these commands; the wise men, whose wisdom is embodied in the wisdom literature of the Bible (Proverbs, Job, Ecclesiastes), seek by observation and reflection to know things as they stand related to man and God. Wisdom is characterized in the Bible by such qualities as honesty, chastity, sobriety, diligence. In chapter thirty-one, the virtues enumerated by Job are: a blameless family life, consideration for the poor and weak, charity, modesty, generosity, hospitality to strangers, honesty, and just dealings.

Wisdom has been described as one of the five types of writing distinguishable in the Hebrew Bible, the other four being historical, legal, devotional, and prophetic. The practical aspect of wisdom, consisting of sound advice in handling the problems of daily life, is exemplified in the teachings of Proverbs and Ecclesiastes, where the ideal of life is a composite of patience, endurance, discretion, work, helpfulness toward the distressed, and consideration for one's fellow man. According to the teachings of the Jewish wisdom literature, the best aid to the leading of a virtuous life is the Torah, which enables man to check mental disturbance. It proclaims that suffering for a worthwhile cause brings blessedness. Here are a few examples:

Happy is the man who gathers wisdom; no treasure can compare with it. Can a man take fire in his lap without burning his clothes? He who touches a neighbor's wife shall not go unpunished. Reprove a man of sense, and he will love you. The way of a fool is right in his own eyes, but a wise man listens to advice. Worry weighs a man down; a kind word cheers him up. The man who loves his son disciplines him. He who is kind to the poor honors his Maker. Do not eat the bread of a niggardly man. Never talk to a fool, for he will despise your words of wisdom. Go seldom to your neighbor's house; he may grow tired of you and hate you. If your enemy is hungry give him food; if he is thirsty give him water.

Biblical wisdom stresses moderation and the avoidance of extremes. To be wise is to be able to control one's tongue. Silence is the object of much praise in the wisdom texts. According to the book of Proverbs (1:13-22), no wisdom is possible apart from respect for the person and goods of others. The element of knowledge is always secondary, in the wisdom literature, to that of action. To be wise is not so much to be able to comprehend the ultimate secrets of life as the ability to lead a good life.

"Wisdom cannot reside in the evilhearted" is an old Jewish maxim. Character and learning are mutually dependent upon each other. The character of the original thinker generally rises above the level of the commonplace, since great thoughts spring from the heart. "This view grew to be so essential an element of the make-up of the Jew that for him the saint and scholar became identical concepts" (Louis Ginzberg).

SCIENCE OF JUDAISM   חָכְמַת יִשְׂרָאֵל

Leopold Zunz (1794-1886) is described as the founder of the new Jewish learning of the nineteenth century, referred to as *Jüdische Wissenschaft* or *Ḥokhmath Yisrael*. Its object was to reveal Jewish literature and faith to the assimilated Jews as well as to the non-Jewish neighbors. In 1822 he edited the *Zeitschrift für die Wissenschaft des Judenthums*, which resulted in the establishment of his *Verein für*

211

Kultur und Wissenschaft der Juden (Society for the Culture and Science of Judaism).

Heinrich Heine, a fellow student of Zunz, characterized him as a man of word and deed, who created and worked where others dreamed. His monumental history of Jewish homiletics, *Die Gottesdienstlichen Vorträge der Juden*, appeared in 1832. His later works included a history of Jewish liturgy and three books on medieval *piyyutim* and *payyetanim*. The *Literaturgeschichte der Synagogalen Poesie* (History of the Literature of the Synagogal Poetry) presents a record of liturgical creations based on a detailed examination of some five hundred manuscripts. In *Die Synagogale Poesie des Mittelalters* (The Synagogue Poetry of the Middle Ages), Zunz meant to demonstrate the organic structure of medieval Hebrew poetry. He focused his attention on the penitential poetry (*Seliḥoth*) that grew out of the sufferings of the medieval Jews.

WISDOM OF SOLOMON חָכְמַת שְׁלֹמֹה

DESCRIBED as the most important book in the Apocrypha, the Wisdom of Solomon is written in the person of King Solomon, though the probable date of its composition is the first century before the common era. This pseudepigraph, purporting to emanate from Solomon, glorifies wisdom as the guide of mankind and condemns iniquity, pointing out the folly of materialism, skepticism, and idolatry. It has been surmised that the author was an Alexandrian Jew, a man of genius and piety, who believed in the immortality of the soul. He asserts that in this life the ungodly enjoy worldly pleasures, but after death they will vainly repent, while the righteous will enjoy bliss in the hand of God forever (1-5).

He quotes the ungodly as saying: "Our life is short and miserable, and there is no cure when man comes to his end, and no one has been known to return from the abode of the dead. We were born at a venture, and hereafter we shall be as though we had never existed, because the breath in our nostrils is smoke, and reason is a spark in the beating of our hearts; when it is quenched, the body will turn to ashes, and the spirit will dissolve like empty air. And in time our name will be forgotten, and no one will remember what we have done. . .

"So come, let us enjoy the good things that exist. . . Let us have our fill of costly wine and perfumes, and let us not miss the spring flow-

ers... Let our strength be our law of uprightness, for weakness is
proved useless. .." And in reply to these utterances he continues:
"Their wickedness blinded them... For God created man for immortality, and made him the image of his eternity, but through the
envy of Satan death came into the world... The upright souls are
in the hand of God, and no torment can reach them" (2:1-3:1).

ḤOL HA-MO'ED   חֹל הַמּוֹעֵד

ḤOL HA-MO'ED, the half-festive days between the first and the last
days of *Pesaḥ* and *Sukkoth*, on which only essential work may be performed, retains as much as possible of the holiness of the festival.
Though the Torah does not prohibit work during *Ḥol ha-Mo'ed*, it
endows these intervening days with a festive character.

No marriages are performed on *Ḥol ha-Mo'ed*, because one celebration must not be superimposed on another (אין מערבין שמחה בשמחה);
mourning is prohibited; *tefillin* are not put on during the morning services by a large majority of observant Jews; the special festival prayers are recited; the meals are eaten in the *sukkah* during *Ḥol ha-Mo'ed*
Sukkoth, and the eating of *ḥametz* is prohibited during *Ḥol ha-Mo'ed*
Pesaḥ.

ḤALLAH   חַלָּה

THE priest's share of the cake (*ḥallah*), donated in Temple times to the
kohanim, is a biblical law. "When you enter the land into which
I will bring you and when you eat of the food of the land, you shall
present an offering to the Lord. You shall offer a cake of the first of
your dough ... throughout your generations" (Numbers 15:18-21).
This law does not specify what proportion of the dough should go to
the priest; hence the talmudic sages defined *ḥallah* as ½4th of the loaf,
and ¼8th from a baker.

Ḥallah is taken from wheat, barley, spelt, oats, and rye used in the
baking of bread. If the *ḥallah* is not taken from the dough, it must
be taken from the bread. Since *ḥallah* can no longer be observed as
a priestly offering, and in order that this *mitzvah* may not be forgotten,
Jewish housewives in preparing bread are bidden to throw a small
portion of it (the size of an olive) into the fire. This is accompanied

213

by a benediction: "Blessed art thou . . . who hast sanctified us with thy commandments, and commanded us to set aside *ḥallah.*"

This is one of the special religious acts performed by women. The name *ḥallah* is applied to the Sabbath loaves, from which *ḥallah* has presumably been set aside. It is customary to set aside something for charity in conjunction with the removal of *ḥallah.*

ḤILLUL HASHEM חִלּוּל הַשֵּׁם

ḤILLUL HASHEM, the opposite of *Kiddush Hashem*, denotes defamation of the divine name through an act performed in defiance of religious or ethical principles. The term *Kiddush Hashem* (sanctification of the divine name), applied particularly to martyrdom, is extended to any act of integrity which reflects creditably on the Jewish people and the Jewish faith. Both concepts are based on Leviticus 22:32, which reads: "You shall not profane my holy name; I will be hallowed among the Jewish people of Israel."

Any misdeed toward a non-Jew is considered an unpardonable sin, because it gives a false impression of the moral standard of Judaism. Every Jew is described as holding the honor of his faith, and of his entire people, in his hands. According to a statement in the Ethics of the Fathers, "wild beasts come to the world on account of perjury and the profanation of God's name" (Avoth 5:11). This is explained as referring to wild beasts in the shape of human beings who are motivated by blind prejudice and groundless hatred against the Jewish people.

DREAMS חֲלוֹמוֹת

THE book of Daniel is full of dreams which border on prophecy. The interpretation of dreams became a recognized art. The Talmud cites examples of men who received payment for the function. Twenty-four interpreters are said to have practised at the same time in Jerusalem. A certain Bar Hedya shaped his interpretation according to the amount received (Berakhoth 56a-b). Ancient Babylonians had implicit trust in dreams as means of guidance; on the eve of important decisions they slept in temples, hoping for dream counsel. The Egyptians composed elaborate works for dream interpretation. Jo-

214

seph, in Egypt, and Daniel, in Babylonia, were noted for their power of interpreting dreams. Following are several talmudic statements concerning dreams:

"A dream which is not interpreted is like a letter which is not read... Neither a good dream nor a bad dream is ever wholly fulfilled... Just as wheat cannot be without straw, so there cannot be a dream without some nonsense... While a part of a dream may be fulfilled, the whole of it is never fulfilled... Bar Hedya, an interpreter of dreams, used to give a favorable interpretation to the one who paid him; to one who failed to pay him he gave an unfavorable interpretation... If one has seen a dream and does not remember it, let him offer the following prayer during the priestly benediction:

"Lord of the universe, I am thine and my dreams are thine. I have dreamt a dream and do not know what it is... Whether I have dreamt about myself or my companions have dreamt about me ... if they are good dreams, confirm them like the dreams of Joseph... So turn all my dreams into something good..." (Berakhoth 55a-56b). This prayer is included in the Prayerbooks and recited when the kohanim pronounce the priestly blessing. It is recited whether the worshipers have dreamt or not.

Throughout the centuries many have maintained that some dreams are divine communications. The Greek philosopher Aristotle stated: "The fact that all or most men suppose some significance in dreams constitutes a ground for believing that the supposition is based on experience." In the Torah we read: "If there arises among you a prophet or a dreamer ... urging you to follow other gods ... pay no attention to the words of that prophet or that dreamer..." (Deuteronomy 13:2-4). He is regarded as a false prophet who pretends to have received revelations from God in his dreams. Elsewhere in the Bible, dreams are presented as a channel of true prophecy and of genuine revelations (Genesis 20:3-6; 31:10, 25; 37:5, 9). The psychological interpretation of dreams, in modern times, has engaged the attention of many Jewish psychologists.

ḤALITZAH   חֲלִיצָה

ḤALITZAH (untying), the ceremony of taking off a brother-in-law's shoe by the childless widow of a brother, is described in the Torah as follows: "If brothers dwell together, and one of them dies and has no son, the widow must not marry a stranger outside the family; her husband's brother shall marry her ... and her first son shall succeed to the name of the dead brother, that his name may not be blotted out of Israel.

"If the man does not wish to marry his brother's wife ... she must declare to the elders in the public assembly: My husband's brother refuses to perpetuate his brother's name in Israel... Then his brother's wife shall go up to him in the presence of the elders, and pull the sandal from his foot ... protesting: So shall it be done to the man who does not build up his brother's house" (Deuteronomy 25:5-9). Marriage with a brother's childless widow is known as levirate marriage (*yibbum*); the widow is called *yevamah*, and her brother-in-law *yavam*.

The purpose of levirate marriage was to obviate what was regarded as a great calamity when a man's family line became extinct and his property passed on to heirs who were not his descendants. Though the duty of marrying a brother's childless widow was not enforced, the refusal to do so was considered disgraceful in ancient times. *Ḥalitzah*, pulling off the shoe and handing it over, symbolized an act of transfer or renunciation, as described in Ruth 4:7: "To make any transaction valid ... the ancient custom in Israel was that one party would take off his sandal and give it to the other; this was how exchanges were attested in Israel."

In the case of the *yavam's* refusal, *ḥalitzah* was a mark of discredit. With the abolition of polygamy, levirate marriage has disappeared and *ḥalitzah* is the accepted custom, observed by traditional Jews. The *ḥalitzah* shoe, made from the skin of a clean animal, consists of two pieces sowed together with leather threads; it is usually the property of the community.

ḤALUKKAH   חֲלֻקָּה

THE relief system known as *Ḥalukkah* (distribution), which may be traced back to the collections abroad made in ancient times to sustain the academies and the scholars in the Holy Land, has kept alive in the Diaspora the sentimental attachment to Eretz Yisrael through many generations. The new settlement set up in Jerusalem from the thirteenth century onward was sustained by *Ḥalukkah* funds, remitted annually or semi-annually to accredited communal leaders in the

Holy Land for distribution primarily to learned men in needy circumstances, and to widows and orphans. During the nineteenth century, however, *Halukkah* began to be looked upon as degrading; this can be clearly seen from the following declaration by Rabbi Tzevi Hirsch Kalischer (1795-1874), who wrote:

"There are many who will refuse to support the poor of the Holy Land by saying: Why should we support people who choose idleness, who are lazy and not interested in working, and who prefer to depend upon the Jews of the Diaspora to support them?... The people of Palestine are students of the Torah, unaccustomed from the time of their youth to physical labor. Most of them came from distant shores, risking their very lives for the privilege of living in the Holy Land... Their eyes can only turn to their generous brethren, of whom they ask only enough to keep body and soul together, so that they can dwell in the land which is God's portion on earth. Yet, in order to silence this argument once and for all, I would suggest that an organization be established to encourage settlement in the Holy Land for the purpose of purchasing and cultivating farms and vineyards. . ." Until the industrial and agricultural development began in Eretz Yisrael, the Jewish inhabitants there had no other outlook than *Halukkah* relief.

The *Halukkah* collections made in the Diaspora for the support of the poor in Eretz Yisrael played an important part in keeping alive among the dispersed Jewish people an emotional attachment to Eretz Yisrael before the rise of the *Hibbath Zion* movement. Each of the *Halukkah* organizations, in Eretz Yisrael, was called a *kolel* (כולל), or national group maintained by the communities in the countries of origin. The *kolelim* sent *meshullahim*, emissaries, from the four holy cities of Jerusalem and Hebron, Safed and Tiberias, to collect funds abroad. Funds were collected in North Africa, Turkey and the Balkans, by the Sephardic groups who sent most of the *meshullahim*, known also as *shadarim;* later, with the increase of the Ashkenazim, the contributions arrived mostly from Russia and Poland for the support of the respective *kolelim* founded by Hasidim and Mithnaggedim alike.

FIVE SCROLLS   חָמֵשׁ מְגִלּוֹת

THE five biblical books which are known as the Five Scrolls are recited in the synagogue, as part of the liturgy, on the following special occasions: Song of Songs on *Pesaḥ;* Ruth on *Shavuoth;* Lamentations on *Tish‘ah b’Av,* the fast day commemorating the destruction of Jerusalem; Ecclesiastes on *Sukkoth,* the autumn festival; and Esther on *Purim.*

The Five Scrolls, forming a class by themselves, are arranged in the Hebrew Bible according to the sequence of the annual occasions.

PENTATEUCH   חֲמִשָׁה חֻמְשֵׁי תּוֹרָה

THE five books of the Torah are variously referred to by as many as five titles: Torah, Law, Pentateuch, Five Books of Moses, and Five Fifths (*Ḥummashim*). They are Genesis, Exodus, Leviticus, Numbers, Deuteronomy. These names are descriptive of the contents of the books: Genesis (origin) begins with the story of creation; Exodus (going out) tells of the going out from Egypt; Leviticus (pertaining to Levites) contains laws which relate to the priests, members of the tribe of Levi; Numbers derives its name from the census of the Israelites in the wilderness; Deuteronomy (repetition of the law) contains a restatement of the Mosaic laws.

The framework of history, within which the Torah proper is enclosed, extends from the creation of the world to the death of Moses. The five books of the Torah have always been considered as one, single scroll, with a blank space of four lines between adjoining books; although for private study, a single volume for each book has been permitted.

Tradition has it that the events recorded in Genesis were transmitted until the time of Moses by word of mouth and in writing; the subsequent occurrences were witnessed by Moses himself. Writing was used (cuneiform) by the Sumerians in Babylonia long before Moses. Ever since the time of Ezra the Scribe, who arrived in Jerusalem in 450 before the common era, the five books of the Torah have been the basis of religion and education. The study of Torah, including the entire talmudic literature and commentaries, has always been the highest ideal of the Jewish people. The unquenchable thirst for knowledge and education among the Jewish people stems from their traditional veneration of the Torah.

Listed below are the fifty-four Torah sections, known as the weekly portions (*sidroth*), read as part of the Sabbath morning services consecutively. Each week is identified with its current *sidrah* and bears

218

its name. The *sidroth* are named after a key-word in the first verse of each particular portion. The Sephardim refer to the *sidroth* as *parashiyyoth* (פרשיות). The term *sidrah* is frequently used in the Talmud to denote a section of the Bible read either in the synagogue or in the school. Rashi explains *sidrah* in the sense of a section of the Prophets or the Sacred Writings (פרשת מקרא של נביאים או של כתובים— Yoma 87a). In the course of time, the Ashkenazim began to use the term *sidrah* to denote the weekly Torah reading, just as *parashah* is used by the Sephardim. In both Talmuds, *Bavli* and *Yerushalmi*, the term *sidrah* often carries the meaning of a school in which sections of the Bible are read and interpreted.

According to the *Masorah*, the *sidroth* should number one hundred and fifty-four, in keeping with the former triennial cycle of Torah reading. The annual cycle is now universally followed. The chapters and verses of each *sidrah* are indicated in the following pages. The brace, or curved line, indicates the *sidroth* that are combined in regular twelve-month years; they are not combined in leap years, consisting of thirteen months each.

GENESIS   בְּרֵאשִׁית

Bereshith	1:1-6:8	בְּרֵאשִׁית
Noaḥ	6:9-11:32	נֹחַ
Lekh Lekha	12:1-17:27	לֶךְ לְךָ
Vayyéra	18:1-22:24	וַיֵּרָא
Ḥayyé Sarah	23:1-25:18	חַיֵּי שָׂרָה
Toledoth	25:19-28:9	תּוֹלְדוֹת
Vayyétsé	28:10-32:3	וַיֵּצֵא
Vayyishlaḥ	32:4-36:43	וַיִּשְׁלַח
Vayyéshev	37:1-40:23	וַיֵּשֶׁב
Mikkets	41:1-44:17	מִקֵּץ
Vayyiggash	44:18-47:27	וַיִּגַּשׁ
Vayyeḥi	47:28-50:26	וַיְחִי

219

חמשה חמשי תורה

EXODUS שְׁמוֹת

Shemoth	1:1-6:1	שְׁמוֹת
Vaéra	6:2-9:35	וָאֵרָא
Bo	10:1-13:16	בֹּא
Beshallaḥ	13:17-16	בְּשַׁלַּח
Yithro	18:1-20:23	יִתְרוֹ
Mishpatim	21:1-24:18	מִשְׁפָּטִים
Terumah	25:1-27:19	תְּרוּמָה
Tetsavveh	27:20-30:10	תְּצַוֶּה
Ki Tissa	30:11-34:35	כִּי תִשָּׂא
{ Vayyakhel	35:1-38:20	וַיַּקְהֵל)
{ Pekudé	38:21-40:38	פְקוּדֵי)

LEVITICUS וַיִּקְרָא

Vayyikra	1:1-5:26	וַיִּקְרָא
Tsav	6:1-8:36	צַו
Shemini	9:1-11:47	שְׁמִינִי
{ Tazri‘a	12:1-13:59	תַזְרִיעַ)
{ Metsora	14:1-15:33	מְצֹרָע)
{ Aḥaré Moth	16:1-18:30	אַחֲרֵי מוֹת)
{ Kedoshim	19:1-20:27	קְדֹשִׁים)
Emor	21:1-24:23	אֱמֹר
{ Behar	25:1-26:2	בְּהַר)
{ Beḥukkothai	26:3-27:34	בְּחֻקֹּתַי)

220

NUMBERS   בְּמִדְבַּר

Bemidbar	1:1-4:20	בְּמִדְבַּר
Naso	4:21-7:89	נָשֹׂא
Beha'alothkha	8:1-12:16	בְּהַעֲלוֹתְךָ
Shelaḥ	13:1-15:41	שְׁלַח
Koraḥ	16:1-18:32	קֹרַח
{ Ḥukkath	19:1-22:1	חֻקַּת }
{ Balak	22:2-25:9	בָּלָק }
Pinḥas	25:10-30:1	פִּנְחָס
{ Mattoth	30:2-32:42	מַטּוֹת }
{ Massé	33:1-36:13	מַסְעֵי }

DEUTERONOMY   דְּבָרִים

Devarim	1:1-3:22	דְּבָרִים
Vaethḥannan	3:23-7:11	וָאֶתְחַנַּן
Ékev	7:12-11:25	עֵקֶב
Re'ei	11:26-16:17	רְאֵה
Shoftim	16:18-21:9	שׁוֹפְטִים
Ki Thétsé	21:10-25:19	כִּי תֵצֵא
Ki Thavo	26:1-29:8	כִּי תָבוֹא
{ Nitsavim	29:9-30:20	נִצָּבִים }
{ Vayyélekh	31:1-30	וַיֵּלֶךְ }
Ha'azinu	32:1-52	הַאֲזִינוּ
Vezoth ha-Berakhah	33:1-34:12	וְזֹאת הַבְּרָכָה

HANNAH'S SONS   חַנָּה וּבָנֶיהָ

THE narrative of Hannah and her seven children, who were martyred
by the Syrian tyrant Antiochus Epiphanes when they refused to commit idolatry, is recounted in the Second Book of Maccabees (7:1-42)
and condensed in the Talmud (Gittin 57b).

Seven brothers and their mother were arrested and urged by the
king to taste forbidden food. "We are ready to die," one of them cried
out, "rather than transgress the laws of our forefathers." Infuriated,
the king commanded that the boy's tongue be cut out in the presence
of his brothers and his mother. The tormentors asked the second brother: "Will you eat, or have your body torn limb from limb?" When
he refused, he was made to undergo the same torture that his brother
had suffered. And so they tormented each one in turn while the mother stood by surpassingly courageous and encouraging. After the cruel
tortures of her seventh and youngest boy, the mother ascended a
nearby roof top and threw herself to the ground.

In many parts of the non-Jewish world, shrines have been established to the memory of the seven martyred children and their devout
mother, Salomé. The name given them in non-Jewish tradition is
Maccabees, perhaps because of the Maccabean struggles of that period. In some Jewish sources, the name Miriam is given to their mother.

EDUCATION   חִנּוּךְ

THE Torah often emphasizes the importance of teaching the young
diligently in order to inculcate religious and ethical precepts that lead
to happiness and goodness of character. Originally, the education of
children was entrusted to the father, who was commanded to teach
them morning and evening, at home and abroad (Deuteronomy 6:7).
This kind of paternal teaching is reflected in the fourth chapter of the
book of Proverbs, where we read: "Listen, children, to a father's instruction. . . I give you good counsel, do not forsake my teaching.
When I was a son with my father . . . he taught me and told me this:
Keep in mind what I say, observe my commands and you shall live.
Get wisdom, get insight. . ." (4:1-5). For religious education during
the biblical period, the parents could always invite the assistance of
Levites who moved from place to place.

222

Formal education, in the land of Israel, began to develop during the first century before the common era through the efforts of Simeon ben Shetah, brother of queen Salomé Alexandra and president of the Sanhedrin. He is credited with having laid the foundations of an elementary school system by decreeing that children should be taught at school instead of being instructed at home.

About the beginning of the common era, this school system spread from Jerusalem to all parts of the country. The credit for the extension is given to Joshua ben Gamala, a high priest. The Talmud records, commendably, that Joshua ben Gamala should be gratefully remembered, because had it not been for him the Torah would have been forgotten. "In ancient times each father taught his own child. The child who had no father grew up without an education. Then schools were established in the city of Jerusalem, where a father could bring his son for instruction. The fatherless, however, still remained without schooling. Later, schools were established in each district, and boys of sixteen and seventeen were enrolled. But it often happened that a pupil, rebuked by a teacher, rebelled and left school. At last, Joshua ben Gamala established elementary schools in each and every town, and all children of six or seven, including orphans, were enrolled" (Bava Bathra 21a). None was to teach a class of more than twenty-five. Something resembling universal adult education was the *derashah*, a homiletical discourse, delivered in the synagogue.

It has been said that the Jewish religion, because it is a literature-sustained religion, led to the first efforts to provide elementary education for all the children of the community. Writing in the first century, Josephus declares: "Our principal care is to educate our children well." In reference to adult education as part of public worship, he writes: "Moses showed the Torah to be the best and the most necessary means of instruction by enjoining the people to assemble not once or twice or frequently, but *every* week, while abstaining from all other work, in order to hear the Torah and learn it in a thorough manner—a thing which all other lawgivers seem to have neglected."

Here are a few talmudic utterances exemplifying the high value attached to education by Jews in ancient times: "The hope of the world lies in its school children. Their instruction must not be interrupted even for the rebuilding of the Temple. A town that has no school children is headed for ruin. Jerusalem was destroyed because the instruction of its children was neglected. . ." The Talmud interprets the verse "never harm my prophets" (Psalm 105:15) as an allusion to teachers who must not be mistreated (Shabbath 119b). According to a midrashic statement, Israel's enemies cannot prevail so long as there are children in the schools (Bereshith Rabbah 65:15).

First and foremost, the teachers were expected to be of fine character and careful of their dress. They were expected to be patient with their pupils, since "an irritable man cannot teach" (Avoth 2:6). They were advised to maintain their dignity, so that no disrespectful attitude might develop on the part of the pupils. The teachers were deemed worthy of greater esteem than the parents. The extent to which Jewish education was far-spread in talmudic times may well be inferred from this passage: "Is it possible to find anyone without elementary education? Yes, it is possible in the case of a child who was taken captive among non-Jews" (Shevuoth 5a).

The school, where the chief subjects of instruction were the Bible and its rabbinic interpretations, was kept open daily until long after nightfall; even on the Sabbath it was closed for only a small part of the day. A class consisted of twenty-five children on the average; if the number reached forty, an assistant teacher was engaged. The pupils were arranged in a semicircle, so that each of them might see and hear the teacher. Teaching was regarded as a pious deed, performed by the *hazzan* of the synagogue, or by a learned rabbi. The famous academies of Sura and Pumbeditha provided for higher religious study during the Babylonian period of medieval Jewish history. There was no greater disgrace than being called *am ha-aretz* (ignoramus).

The *Sefer Ḥasidim* (Book of the Saintly) of the twelfth century, containing a rich variety of precepts and principles of Jewish living, is replete with sayings concerning the ethical and religious training as the final aim of education. "Children copy their parents; they will be dishonest if their parents are dishonest, and all their study of Torah will prove useless... It is not good to give children much money... Even if a child can only read, he should be made to understand what he reads...

"A teacher must not say: "As I have to teach all day, I will rise early and study for myself." He may be drowsy while teaching, and so neglect his duty... What one teacher forbids should not be allowed by another teacher... The child should be taught the subjects for which he has most aptitude. If he makes good progress in Bible, do not force him to study Talmud... If a child stammers, he should be told to bring his questions to the teacher when the other children have gone away, so that he may not be ridiculed by his fellow pupils..."

224

Maxims of similar import are to be found in all the medieval ethical Jewish literature. The *Menorath Hammaor* by Rabbi Israel al-Nakawa of the fourteenth century has this to say: "If you train your child when he is young, you will enjoy rest and peace later on. You will not have to worry about his forming habits which are hostile to the well-being of society. . . Do not be discouraged if you find that your child is dull; do not give up training and correcting him. Though he may not master all you try to teach him, he will learn a little. . . Try to induce the child to like the process of education. At first you may have to coax him with sweets and toys; then you may have to lure him with the prospects of a higher reward; but, in the end, he will come to love education for its own sake. . . One should make every effort to provide a religious and ethical education for his child, regardless of cost. The education of the young is a communal obligation. Every community must provide teachers for the children. . ."

In his ethical will, Rabbi Judah ibn Tibbon of the twelfth century reminds his son that he travelled far and wide to find teachers for him in science and other secular subjects. He adds: "My son, make your books your companions. Let your shelves be your treasure grounds and gardens. If you are weary, change from garden to garden. Your desire will renew itself, and your soul will be filled with delight. . . Arrange your library in fair order so as not to weary yourself in your search for the book you need. Never refuse to lend books to anyone who can be trusted to return them. Honor your teachers and attach yourself to your friends. Treat them with respect in all places and under all circumstances. . ."

The average Jewish father would deny himself the common necessaries of life in order to provide a good education for his son. As to his daughters, he would concentrate upon their domestic training and upon instructing them in the precepts that are especially important to them as future wives and mothers. In the ethical wills, the daughters received the same attention as the sons with respect to moral conduct. Talmudic law requires that the father shall provide the daughter with a suitable dowry; the obligation to provide the dowry rests upon the father's heirs (Kethubboth 68a).

Joseph ibn Aknin of the twelfth century, giving in detail a number of pedagogic rules, writes that a successful teacher must have complete command of the subject he wishes to teach. He must carry out in his own life the principles he plans to inculcate in his pupils. He must look upon his pupils as if they were his own children, and treat them accordingly. He must train his pupils to lead an ethical life. He must not be impatient but cheerful, and must teach his pupils according to the range of their intellectual abilities.

It has been noted that for some reason the American Jewish community labors under the erroneous notion that Jewish education is good only for young children. A recent national study of Jewish education reveals that seventy-five percent of the pupils attending our weekday classes are found in the first three grades. The *Bar Mitzvah* motive is still predominant as an incentive and ultimate goal for Jewish education. Only two and a half percent are in the high school grades.

Educators of note keep asking: What chances do our pupils have of gaining access to the sources of Jewish wisdom and knowledge? Are our schools preparing their pupils to cope intelligently with their duties and responsibilities as active members of a creative and dynamic Jewish community where fund raising and relief work may not be the major preoccupation? Why should we expect them to be more intelligent and mature in this area when most, if not all, of their Jewish educational equipment has been acquired on a childish level? Many an educator has reached the conclusion that childhood is not the best age for learning. Adults learn much more effectively, when properly motivated. Adult education must claim constantly greater attention.

Some scholars assert that the ignorance of the average American Jew is simply terrifying. If it is to be coped with at all, Jewish education must start with the child and must continue through adolescence to adulthood. Today only an insignificant portion of our Jewish child population receives an intensive Jewish education, the rest either gets a smattering of Jewishness at the Sunday schools, just a little more in the supplementary afternoon schools, or nothing at all. If the Jews are to know more about Jewishness than they know today they should be unceasingly and symphathetically encouraged to learn.

HANUKKAH

HANUKKAH, the post-biblical festival of lights, which is annually celebrated for eight days, beginning on the twenty-fifth of *Kislev*, commemorates the heroic struggle of the Jews against pagan forces at the time of the religious persecutions by the Greco-Syrians, a struggle which proved decisive in forming the character of the Jew-

226

ish people. The Maccabean great victories, in 168-165 before the common era, eventually led to the religious freedom and national independence of the Jews, inspiring many subsequent generations to face persecution with triumphant courage.

The lighting of the candles on the eight days of *Ḥanukkah*, one on the first day and one more on each succeeding day, is linked in the Talmud with the miracle of the cruse of oil: When the Hasmoneans prevailed against the heathen foes, they found in the Temple only one undefiled cruse of oil, intact, with the seal of the high priest. This cruse contained sufficient oil for one day's lighting of the Temple *Menorah*, but, miraculously, its oil lasted for eight days' lighting. The following year, they designated these eight days for giving thanks and praise to God (Shabbath 21b). The rededication of the Temple, after its defilement by pagan worship of Greek gods, occurred in the year 165 before the common era.

It has been pointed out that the Hellenism that reached Judea in common with other oriental countries was not the Hellenism of classical Greece, but a debased kind of Hellenism, decadent and voluptuous, such as was imported by the soldier, the slave-dealer, and the brothel-keeper. The effects of this new civilization upon the moral life in Judea were devastating. All religious precepts were prohibited on pain of death; copies of the Torah were destroyed, and the possession of such a book was made a capital offense. The Temple itself was converted to the worship of Zeus; harlots were brought within its sacred precincts; heathen altars were set up in towns and villages, worship at which was made a test of loyalty.

The Maccabean exploits are told in the two books of the Maccabees, the last books in the Apocrypha. They are filled with stories of defiant martyrdom during a period of fifteen years, and contain descriptions of Mattathias and his five sons: Yoḥanan, Simeon, Judah, Elazar, and Jonathan. It has generally been supposed that the name *Maccabeus* given to Judah denotes hammer, Judah being the striking hammer of the Syrians; but this interpretation is open to objections. Another source for the story of the Maccabees was known in the medieval period under the name of *Megillath Antiochus*, Scroll of Antiochus, which was read in the Italian synagogues on *Ḥanukkah* as the *Megillath Esther* is read on *Purim*.

According to the account in the Second Book of Maccabees, *Ḥanukkah* was patterned after the *Sukkoth* festival: "And it came about that on the very same day on which the sanctuary had been profaned by aliens, the purification of the sanctuary took place [three years later]. And they celebrated it for eight days with gladness, like the *Sukkoth* festival, and recalled how, a little while before, during the *Sukkoth* festival they had been wandering in the mountains and caverns like wild animals. So carrying . . . beautiful branches and palm leaves they offered hymns of praise to him who had brought to pass the purifying of his own place. And they passed a decree that the whole Jewish nation should observe these days every year" (10:5-9). As during the eight days of *Sukkoth*, the entire *Hallel* is recited on each of the eight days of *Ḥanukkah*.

It took eight days to cleanse the First Temple during the reign of Hezekiah, who initiated a series of reforms that eliminated certain idolatrous cults some five centuries before the Maccabean period. The biblical account reads: "They began this purifying on the first day of the first month, and on the eighth day they reached the vestibule of the Lord; then they purified the Temple of the Lord in eight days" (II Chronicles 29:17).

The Torah portions for the separate days are read from Numbers 7:1 to 8:4, because these passages are about the dedication of the Tabernacle in the wilderness and the lighting of the golden *Menorah*. They are called *Parashath Nesi'in*, because they describe the consecration offering, brought on each successive day by the princes of the twelve tribes of Israel when the Tabernacle was dedicated in the wilderness. The offerings consisted of gifts for the transport of the *Mishkan*, such as baggage wagons, as well as sacrificial animals.

The hymn *Maoz Tsur*, which is sung after the lighting of the *Ḥanukkah* lights, was composed presumably in the thirteenth century by one called Mordecai, whose name is given in the initial letters of the five stanzas. *Maoz Tsur* alludes to the deliverance from Egypt, Babylonia, Persia, and Syria.

The condensed story of *Ḥanukkah* is contained in the *Al ha-Nissim* passage, inserted in the *Amidah* and the *Birkath ha-Mazon* to be said during the festival. It reads: "We thank thee for the miracles . . . which thou didst perform for our fathers in those days . . . when a wicked Hellenic empire rose up against thy people Israel to make them forget thy Torah. . . Thou didst champion their cause, defend their rights and avenge the wrongs they endured. Thou didst deliver the strong into the hands of the weak, the many into the hands of the few . . . and the arrogant into the hands of those who were faithful to thy Torah. . ."

228

Since this summary is in the form of a prayer, it passes over in silence the military campaigns that followed the Maccabean reconquest of the Temple that marked the spiritual revival of Judaism and the victory of Torah over Hellenism. The miracle of the Maccabean revolt is likewise conveyed in the prophetical lesson recited on *Shabbath Ḥanukkah*, which contains the verse: "Not by might, nor by power, but by my spirit, says the Lord of hosts" (Zechariah 4:6).

The *Ḥanukkah* event has encouraged many a small group to fight against injustice and oppression. It has been a source of inspiration in the movement to liberate Eretz Yisrael and establish it as an independent State of Israel. It stimulates the Jew to withstand assimilation and the temptation of false gods, to champion the ideals of his heritage in the midst of an overwhelming majority, and to stress Jewish culture in the face of a vast culture that seeks to engulf him.

In addition to the religious practices prescribed for the observance of *Ḥanukkah*, the people introduced various games in which they would indulge particularly while the *Ḥanukkah* lights were burning, since work was forbidden during that half hour or so. They invented, for the amusement of the children especially, a game consisting of spinning a metal or wooden top, on the four sides of which the Hebrew letters גשנה were engraved, presumably forming the initials of נס גדול היה שם (a great miracle happened there). The word גשנה, however, is said to be borrowed from Genesis 46:28, read on *Shabbath Ḥanukkah*, where we are told that Jacob sent Judah to Goshen. The numerical value of גשנה (358) is the same as that of משיח (Messiah).

The last day of *Ḥanukkah* is called זאת חנוכה (*Zoth Ḥanukkah*), because the section read from the Torah on that day begins with the phrase זאת חנוכת המזבח (this was the dedication of the altar). Tradition has it that the construction of the portable sanctuary set up by Moses in the wilderness was completed on the twenty-fifth day of *Kislev*, coinciding with the day commemorating the miracle of *Ḥanukkah*.

Maimonides describes the precept of *Ḥanukkah* lights as "an exceedingly precious one, and one should be particularly careful to fulfill it... Even if one has no food to eat except what he receives from charity, he should beg—or sell some of his clothing—for the purchase of oil and lamps to light... If one has no more than a single *perutah* (small coin) and needs wine for the *Kiddush* and oil to light the *Ḥanukkah* lamp, he should give preference to the purchase of oil for the *Ḥanukkah* lamp over the purchase of wine for the *Kiddush* ... since it serves as a memorial of the miracle of *Ḥanukkah*" (*Yad*, *Ḥanukkah* 4:12-13). Since the lights are intended only for illumination, they must not be used for any other purpose, such as reading.

The *Ḥanukkah* lights, lit in the synagogue as well as in each private home, symbolize the Jewish belief in the gradual progress of spiritual enlightenment. Starting with one light on the first evening of *Ḥanukkah* and increasing the number of lights by one each evening, the Jewish people the whole world over mark thereby the slow but steady victory over the violent storms which have raged against Judaism across the centuries. Hence the *Menorah*, upon which a great deal of Jewish love and artistic expression has been lavished ever since the first century, is looked upon as the symbol of Jewish faith.

The essential feature of *Ḥanukkah* is described by its title: *Ḥag ha-Urim*, the Festival of Lights. The *Ḥanukkah* lights are lit as follows: the first candle is lit on the right side; the next evening, the second candle is placed next to the first candle, the third next to the second, and so on until the eighth and last candle. Each lighting begins with the new candle that has been added, and progresses from left to right, in keeping with the rule that all the turns, made in the Temple, had to be towards the right (Yoma 58b).

The extra candle, serving as a *shammash* (attendant), is used for the lighting of the *Ḥanukkah* lights, concerning which the declaration is repeatedly made: "These lights are sacred; we must not make any use of them other than watching them." On Friday, the *Ḥanukkah* lights are lit before the Sabbath lights; they are lit after the *Havdalah* recitation at the termination of the Sabbath day.

ḤANUKKATH HA-BAYITH   חֲנֻכַּת הַבַּיִת

THE custom of consecrating or dedicating a new house, whether public or private, is based on several biblical passages. In Deuteronomy 20:5, the Torah exempts from service "anyone who has built a new house and has not yet dedicated it." Psalm 30, described as "a song for the dedication of the house," must have been adopted for use at the dedication of Solomon's Temple (I Kings 8), or of the Second Temple, or at the rededication of the Temple after it had been desecrated by Antiochus. In Nehemiah 3:1, we are told that they consecrated one of the several sections of the wall which they built for the protection of Jerusalem.

230

The Mishnah, however, merely states that "if a man built a house or bought new things he should recite: ברוך שהחיינו" (praised be he who has given us life—Berakhoth 9:3). Nor does the Talmud record any form of service for the consecration of a house, or a housewarming. The nearest approach to a consecration is the placing of the *mezuzah* on the doorpost and the appropriate benediction accompanying the act. New synagogues and new cemeteries are consecrated by the use of selected psalms and prayers.

ḤASIDIM   חֲסִידִים

THE term *Ḥasidim*, generally used in the sense of piety, is derived from the noun *ḥesed*, denoting goodness, kindness, affection, godliness. The Mishnah mentions the ancient *Ḥasidim* of the Hasmonean period who observed the divine commandments most meticulously. They are described as the forerunners of the Pharisees. During the Maccabean struggle they suffered martyrdom rather than break the Sabbath. Another type of *Ḥasidim* existed in medieval Germany, who were characterized by a deep awareness of piety and ethical conduct. Their basic teachings and beliefs are contained in the famous *Sefer Ḥasidim*, written for the most part by Rabbi Yehudah he-Ḥasid, who died in 1217.

The essence of *Ḥasiduth*, as defined in the *Sefer Ḥasidim*, is to act in all things not *on* the line but *within* the line of strict justice (לפנים משורת הדין), without insisting on the letter of the law even though it may be to one's advantage to do so. This charitable regard for others as a principle of action is clearly expressed in the *Ethics of the Fathers:* שלי שלך שלך שלך, חסיד—"He who says *What is mine is yours and what is yours is yours* is a *Ḥasid*" (Avoth 5:13). Rashi in his commentaries frequently stresses the idea that the *Ḥasid* does not insist on the letter of the law in a dispute with a fellow man.

Modern Ḥasidism, as a religious and social movement, springs from the teachings of Rabbi Israel Baal Shem Tov (1700-1760), who was born and bred somewhere in the Ukraine. Countless legends attest the profound influence of Rabbi Israel's luminous personality. His striking magnetism, intuitive insight and religious temperament well explain the extraordinary veneration with which he was surrounded soon after his doctrines had become known. The people began to attribute to him unrivalled spiritual authority and miraculous powers. His teachings, transmitted orally from generation to generation, form the groundwork of the vast didactic Ḥasidic literature. Though Ḥasidism at first met with violent opposition on the part of the *Mithnaggedim* (opponents), it soon won the hearts of the Jewish people throughout the East-European countries.

Ḥasidism has been described as a revolt against a one-sided expression of Judaism presented in cold and learned disquisitions, which were understood only by a few. Rabbi Israel Baal Shem Tov taught that all are equal before God—the ignorant no less than the talmudic scholars, and that prayerful devotion and humility are more acceptable in heaven than intellectual attainments. He sought communion with God in the woods and in the fields, emphasizing that life is a divine manifestation.

Rabbi Israel Baal Shem Tov, often referred to as Besht (initials of Baal Shem Tov), furthermore stressed the qualities of optimism and cheerfulness, by teaching that the great principle of serving God is to keep away from sadness as much as possible, and not to yield to paralyzing grief. Man should concentrate his thoughts on God at all times. Let the repentant sinner say: If indeed I have sinned, my Creator will be even more gratified to see that I refuse to let my offense interrupt my joyous service.

The keynote of all his teachings is the omnipresence and immanence of God. All things are pervaded by the divine life; there is nothing which is void of God; in every human thought God is present. Since God is present in all things, there is actual or potential good in all things. Above all, we should realize that the true lover of God is also a lover of man. Every *mitzvah* (good deed) must be done with enthusiasm (*hithlahavuth*); a mere mechanical and lifeless performance of a good deed is not of much value. All men, including sinners and evildoers, must be loved, since they too have in them sparks of divinity. Only the truly humble man is capable of loving one of the wicked, picturing him as better than himself.

Martin Buber, whose attitude to Judaism has been largely influenced by the teachings of Ḥasidism, has endeavored to transform Ḥasidism from a little known movement into one of the recognized great spiritual movements of the modern world. In his *Origin and Meaning of Ḥasidism*, he writes: "Ḥasidism itself wished to work exclusively within the boundaries of Jewish tradition. Yet something hid itself in Ḥasidism that should go out into the world. . . I consider the truth of Ḥasidism vitally important at this particular hour, for

232

now is the hour when we are in danger of forgetting for what purpose
we are on earth, and I know of no other teaching that reminds us of
this so forcibly."

The world's leading authority on Jewish mysticism, Gershom Scholem, has made the following declaration in a critique published in
Commentary with regard to Martin Buber's Neo-Ḥasidism: "The
merits of Buber's presentation of Ḥasidic sayings and legends are very
great indeed. . . But the spiritual message he has read into them in
his more mature works is too deeply bound up with assumptions that
have no root in the texts—assumptions drawn from his own very modern philosophy of religious anarchism. Too much is left out in his
presentation of Ḥasidism, while what has been included is overloaded
with highly personal speculations. These may be of a sublime character and they may appeal deeply to the modern mind, but if we are
searching for an understanding of the actual phenomenon of Ḥasidism
we shall, I am afraid, have to start all over again."

Ḥasidic literature received its impetus from the stories and allegories that were attributed to Rabbi Israel Baal Shem Tov, the founder
of the movement, and his immediate disciples and successors. In retelling the anecdotes, the inspired Ḥasidim would often add embellishments of their own, resulting in abundant artistic creativity. The
courts of the Ḥasidic rabbis were veritable centers of poetry, music
and dance. Saintly leaders, in their sacred passion to bring heaven
and earth closer together, stood out as great poets whose prayers revealed a sense of intimacy with the Creator of the universe and a
feeling of the spiritual dignity of man. The legends and teachings of
the celebrated *Tsaddikim*, as the Ḥasidic rabbis are called because of
their righteous precepts, form the groundwork of a vast didactic literature to which Ḥasidism has given birth. Genuine Ḥasidism represents an authentic part of Jewish tradition.

Directing its appeal to the feelings and emotions, Ḥasidism injected
a new and vital power into Jewish religious life. It showed love and
concern for the uneducated, commonly described as *ammé ha-aretz* (people of the soil), noting that in the soil are to be found gold, silver,
diamonds and all other precious metals and minerals. Rabbi Shneour
Zalman of Liadi (1746-1813), the founder of the *Ḥabad Ḥasidism*,
taught in his philosophic-mystic work *Sefer ha-Tanya*, that man must
gain mastery over his evil impulse by means of wisdom (חכמה), insight (בינה), and knowledge (דעת). The term *Ḥabad* is composed of
the initials of the three Hebrew words, denoting the formation of

ideas, the working out of their details, and the full assimilation of them in the mind. He emphasized intellectual contemplation and study of Torah, stressing the qualities of humility, joy, and melody (*niggun*). *Ḥabad Ḥasidism* spread rapidly and influenced the thinking of Jews in many lands, including chiefly America and Israel.

Artificial stimuli, such as vigorous swaying and dancing, are resorted to by Ḥasidism in order to attain a state of ecstasy and self-forgetfulness during worship. This is in keeping with the Ḥasidic statements: "Forget everybody and everything during your worship; forget yourself and your needs; forget the people of whom you have need. If a man after prayer is conscious of self-satisfaction, he has not prayed to God but to himself. Before you can find God you must lose yourself. In him who is full of himself there is no room for God." Since the divine glory does not rest upon a man when he is depressed but only when he is in a joyous mood, joy is considered to be a higher degree than tears, according to Ḥasidism. Laughter, song and dance are the highest form of worship which must glow like a flame.

Rabbi Naḥman of Bratzlav (1770-1811), the great-grandson of Rabbi Israel Baal Shem Tov, used to say: "Prayer should be said not by rote, but when you feel inspired... Break your anger by doing a favor for the one with whom you are angry... A *mitzvah* that costs money or effort is worth more than one that costs nothing... When a man is able to receive abuse smilingly he is worthy of becoming a leader... If husband and wife quarrel they cannot raise good children... Those whom we influence for good become our spiritual children... Bear in mind that life is short, and that with every passing day you are nearer to the end. How, then, can you waste your time on petty quarrels?... No matter how occupied a man may be, he must snatch at least one hour for daily study..."

Ḥasidism's notable gifts have been made not only to the spiritual and religious life of the Jew, but also to his general cultural life. It has created a rich treasury of allegorical stories, widely admired by poets and writers of fiction. Rabbi Naḥman of Bratzlav is regarded as the greatest master of the parable and the fairy tale in Yiddish literature. His tales, full of rich imagination, are among the most popular of the kind. Ḥasidism has formulated new ethical teachings which have attracted the attention of scholars, thinkers and poets. The *Ḥabad Ḥasidim* of today, known as the "Lubavitcher Ḥasidim," have been described as one of the most intense religious brotherhoods in the modern world.

ḤEREM   חֵרֶם

THE term *ḥerem* denotes property set apart for Temple use, or things consecrated by an extreme form of vow or curse (ban) requiring their destruction. Property of idolaters, for example, is considered *ḥerem* and no enjoyment is to be derived from it. "You shall not bring any abominable thing into your house, lest you be doomed with it; loathe and abhor it utterly as a thing that is doomed" (Deuteronomy 7:26).

The assigning of anything to the Temple, or the private use of priests, was a more solemn act than a mere presentation when it was dedicated in the form of a *ḥerem*-vow. Goods taken from an enemy and placed under the ban were brought into the Temple treasury (Joshua 6:19). "All silver and gold, and the articles of bronze and iron, are sacred to the Lord; they shall be put in the Lord's treasury."

In Ezra 10:8 we read about a proclamation issued throughout Judah and Jerusalem that if anyone failed to appear within three days at the general assembly, convoked for the purpose of abandoning mixed marriages, all his property shall be confiscated and he himself excommunicated. It was a frequent practice of the Jewish authorities to punish certain misdeeds, that were regarded as detrimental to the interests of the community, with excommunication, referred to as *niddui* (isolation), *shammata* (desolation), cutting off all social and business relations for no less than a period of thirty days. During the Middle Ages, the *ḥerem* was a powerful weapon in the hands of the Jewish communities. Since, however, it was frequently abused, it gradually disappeared as a form of punishment or coercion.

SELF-APPRAISAL   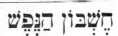 חֶשְׁבּוֹן הַנֶּפֶשׁ

THE most popular Jewish philosopher of eleventh-century Spain, Rabbi Baḥya ibn Pakuda devotes the eighth chapter of his famous work *Ḥovoth ha-Levavoth* (Duties of the Heart) to *ḥeshbon ha-nefesh* or soul-searching. He enumerates a variety of reasons why man should feel grateful to his Creator at all times for all the blessings that surround him from the day of his birth. He writes: When men reach maturity, they foolishly ignore the benefits bestowed on them by the Creator. They may be compared to a little boy found in the desert by a kindhearted person who compassionately took him home and

235

brought him up, feeding and clothing him, and providing him generously with everything he needed till he was old enough to understand
the many benefits he had received... Yet, the foundling did not
realize the value of the benevolence he had experienced even after
the full development of his power of perception, because he had been
accustomed to favors from earliest childhood...

Ibn Pakuda's chapter on *ḥeshbon ha-nefesh* underscores the need
of a world full of praise and gratitude. We must think less of what
we lack, more of what we have. *Ḥeshbon ha-nefesh* is now used in the
sense of soul-searching, self-appraisal and ethical stock-taking.

HOSHEN AND EPHOD   חֹשֶׁן וְאֵפוֹד

THE breastplate, worn by the high priest over his *ephod*, was a square
gold frame ornamented with twelve jewels set in four rows, each stone
being engraved with the name of a tribe of Israel. It contained a
pouch holding the *Urim* and *Tummim*, by means of which divine
judgment was declared; hence the name *ḥoshen mishpat* (breastplate
of judgment).

The *ephod*, to which the breastplate was attached on the front by
means of gold chains and rings, was an apron-like waistcoat, made of
variegated material, supported by straps over the shoulders and
bound round the waist with an embroidered belt. On each of the
shoulder straps was an onyx stone engraved with the names of six
tribes of Israel.

The *Urim* and *Tummim* (light and perfection), serving as one of
the three ways by means of which the divine will might be ascertained,
are said to have been two material objects, two jewels, engraved with
distinguishing characters, used in casting lots.

GROOM AND BRIDE   חָתָן וְכַלָּה

ACCORDING to Ibn Ezra, who interprets the exclamation of Zipporah
in Exodus 4:25 ("you are a bridegroom of blood to me") as referring
to her son after the circumcision, *bridegroom* was a popular title of
honor given by women to a newly-circumcised child. In Arabic, the
verb *hatana* denotes "to circumcize." In biblical Hebrew, the term
חתן means both a son-in-law and a bridegroom, just as כלה signifies

236

either a daughter-in-law or a bride. The familiar expression קול ששון
וקול שמחה קול חתן וקול כלה occurs four times in Jeremiah.

The somewhat poetic designations of *Ḥathan Torah* and *Ḥathan Bereshith* (Bridegroom of the Torah and of Genesis) are given to persons called up to the reading of the chapters ending and beginning the Five Books of Moses, respectively, on the day of the *Simḥath Torah* festival. The honor of *Ḥathan Torah* is deemed greater than that of *Ḥathan Bereshith*.

In the Talmud, the question is debated whether one may or may not exaggerate in praising the bride during her wedding day. According to the School of Hillel, every bride has to be regarded and praised as beautiful and graceful (כלה נאה וחסודה), despite the biblical command: "You shall keep away from anything dishonest" (Exodus 23:7). Similarly, if one has made a bad purchase, the article purchased should be praised rather than disparaged in the presence of the person who has purchased it.

Hence, the sages said that the disposition of each person should ever be pleasant toward his fellow men (לעולם תהא דעתו של אדם מעורבת עם הבריות). The Talmud further reports that in Eretz Yisrael it was customary to sing before the bride: "No powder, no rouge, no hairdo, yet a graceful gazelle" (Kethubboth 17a: לא כחל ולא שרק ... ויעלת חן).

WEDDING　　　　　　　　　　　　　　　　　　חֲתֻנָּה

WEDDINGS have always been joyous occasions among the Jewish people; they were often community festivals, marked by singing, dancing, and lively music. The wedding canopy (*ḥuppah*), under which the bridal couple is married, is reminiscent of the tent ceremony in Bible times, when it was customary to bring the veiled, jewel-decked bride into the groom's tent (Genesis 24:67). The beautifully embroidered *ḥuppah*, supported by four poles which are held by four unmarried young people, is supposed to symbolize the future home of the wedded couple. The use of the portable canopy is attributable to the fact that it was customary for weddings to take place in front of the synagogue, under the canopy of heaven (*taḥath kippath ha-shamayim*). This was considered to be especially auspicious, according to *Minhagé Maharil* and other sources.

In talmudic times, betrothal (*erusin*) and marriage (*nissu'in*) were celebrated as two separate events. The formal betrothal was performed in the house of the bride months before the actual marriage took place in the home of the groom. Hence, two cups of wine are used in modern wedding ceremonies, one for *erusin* and one for *nissu-'in*. The two celebrations are now separated only by the reading of the Aramaic *kethubbah*, the marriage contract specifying the mutual obligations between husband and wife (*Tosafoth*, Kethubboth 7b). The marriage contract, which used to be an important legal protection to the wife, is now used for the purpose of stressing the moral responsibility of the wedded pair: "Be my wife in accordance with the law of Moses and Israel. I will work for you; I will honor, support and maintain you, as it becomes Jewish husbands who work for their wives, honoring and supporting them faithfully. . ."

Since the fourteenth century it has been customary to have a rabbi perform the ceremony. The use of a wedding ring, symbolic of attachment and fidelity, dates from the seventh century. The custom of breaking a glass under the *ḥuppah* is derived from the Talmud (Berakhoth 31a), where it is related that in the course of a wedding feast one of the rabbis broke a costly vase in order to curb the spirits of those present, warning them against excessive joy.

The formula used by the groom, placing the ring on the forefinger of the bride's right hand, is mentioned in the Talmud (Kiddushin 5b): "With this ring, you are wedded to me in accordance with the law of Moses and Israel." This alludes to the traditional interpretations of the Mosaic laws among the people of Israel (the regulations of *erusin* are not directly biblical). The seven benedictions, recited when ten men (*minyan*) are present, are quoted in the Talmud (Kethubboth 8a) as *birkath ḥathanim*. The fourth benediction refers to the perpetual renewal of the human being in the divine form. In the last three benedictions a prayer is uttered that God may comfort Zion, cause happiness to the young couple, and bring about complete exultation in restored Judea and Jerusalem. The marriage service thus combines individual with communal hopes.

Under the *ḥuppah* (canopy), the bride is conducted three times round the groom as part of the wedding ceremony. This custom alludes to Jeremiah 31:21, where the prophet says that a woman encompasses and protects a man. Three times the word (I betroth you) occurs in Hosea 2:21-22, where God addresses his people: "I betroth you to myself forever; I betroth you to myself in righteousness and in justice, in love and in mercy; I betroth you to myself in faithfulness. . ."

238

TEVILAH   טְבִילָה

THE act of taking a ritual bath in a *mikveh* (gathering of water) is called *tevilah* (immersion). A woman in the period of menstruation is regarded as unclean from the moment her menstrual flow begins. After the cessation of the menstrual flow, she counts seven days. At the end of seven days, at night, she performs the precept of *tevilah* by immersing herself in a *mikveh* that contains no less than forty *seahs* of water (about two hundred and forty gallons). The water of a *mikveh* has to come from a natural spring or a river; it entirely loses its effectiveness if it is poured into a vessel; it must be running, not drawn water contained in any kind of receptacle. A *mikveh* is constructed under the supervision of an authoritative rabbi who is known for his piety and learning. He is consulted also about the proper procedure of cleaning the *mikveh* when the water has been removed.

The three types of ritual washing (ablution) mentioned in biblical and talmudic literature are: 1) complete immersion (*tevilah*) in a natural water-source or in a specially constructed *mikveh*, prescribed for married women following their periods of menstruation or after childbirth as well as for proselytes (*gerim*) on being accepted into Judaism; 2) washing of the feet and hands, prescribed for the priests in the Temple service at Jerusalem; 3) washing of the hands (*netilath yadayim*) before sitting down to a meal and before prayer, upon rising from sleep and after the elimination of bodily wastes, also after being in proximity to a dead human body. Apart from ritual purification, the Jewish people have always regarded bathing and physical cleanliness as implicitly important because, as Hillel taught, the human body reflects the divine image of God. In honor of the approaching Sabbath, bathing on Fridays has ever been a universal Jewish custom. Ritual bathing, on the other hand, symbolizes spiritual purification, as well as טהרת המשפחה (purity of married life), and is not necessarily connected with physical cleanliness.

We are told in the Talmud that Rabbi Meir said: "Why did the Torah ordain that the uncleanness of menstruation should continue for seven days? Because, being in constant contact with his wife, a husband might develop a loathing towards her. The Torah therefore ordained: Let her be unclean, even after the least discharge of blood, for seven days, when intimate relations are forbidden, in order that, by being deprived of her intimacy for certain recurrent periods, she

239

should be beloved by her husband as at the time of her first entry into the bridal chamber'' (Niddah 31b).

Maimonides finds a symbolical significance in *tevilah*: "The person who directs his heart to purify his soul from spiritual impurities, such as iniquitous thoughts and evil notions, becomes clean as soon as he determines in his heart to keep apart from these courses, and bathes his soul in the water of pure knowledge" (*Mikvaoth* 11:12).

Associated with the act of embracing Judaism is *tevilah* (טבילת גרות). The candidate, if a male, is first of all circumcised, and when the wound has healed, he is taken to the *mikveh*, in which he makes a complete immersion. The *tevilah* of a proselyte (גר), which must not be performed at night or on a holy day, is regarded as a bath of purification, designed to remove the uncleanness of heathenism. The immersion is always preceded by adequate instruction in religious doctrine and practice.

TEVETH טֵבֵת

TEVETH, the tenth month of the Jewish calendar, consists of twenty-nine days. It occurs during December-January. The tenth day of *Teveth*, known as *Asarah b'Teveth*, commemorates the besieging of Jerusalem by Nebuchadnezzar (II Kings 25:1). It has been observed as a fast day ever since.

PURITY AND IMPURITY טָהֳרָה וְטֻמְאָה

THE biblical laws of purity and impurity are not synonymous with the requirements of physical cleanliness, even though the two types sometimes coincide. The laws of cleanliness have been instinctively observed by religious Jews in their approach to God. Ritual defilement, for which purification was provided in Temple times, was restricted to certain acts and processes. Contact with a human corpse, for example, communicated defilement in the highest degree, and the method of purification is prescribed in the Torah as follows:

"Whoever touches the dead body of any human being shall be unclean for seven days; he shall purify himself with the water on the third day and on the seventh day, and then he will be clean again. But if he fails to purify himself on the third and on the seventh day ...

240

he defiles the *mishkan* of the Lord, and shall be cut off from Israel"
(Numbers 19:11-13).

Even the necessary handling of the ashes of the red heifer (פרה
אדומה), used to cleanse from defilement by contact with the dead,
rendered the priest unclean. "The priest shall then wash his garments
and bathe his body in water. He remains unclean until the evening,
and only afterwards may he return to the camp. . . He who has gathered up the ashes of the heifer shall also wash his garments and be
unclean until evening" (19:7-10).

The mysterious significance of the *red heifer*, purifying the impure
and rendering impure the pure (מטהרת את הטמאים ומטמאת את
הטהורים), has not been explained, despite many attempts at symbol-
ization. Rashi, commenting on Numbers 19:2, quotes a midrashic
statement to the effect that the nations taunt Israel with regard to
the paradoxical institution of the red heifer. For this reason, the Torah employs the term *ḥukkah* (statute), that is, a divine precept which
must be observed even though it defies rational interpretation (Pesikta, *Parashath Parah*).

It has been conjectured that the use of a female, though sacrificial
animals were usually males, symbolized the imparting of new life to
those who had been defiled by contact with death. The color red,
being the color of blood, may have been the token of life. The paschal
lamb could be eaten on the first night of Passover only by those who
had been purified from their defilement.

Hence, the Torah section on the red heifer is read on one of the Sabbaths that precede the festival of *Pesaḥ*, referred to as the Sabbath of
Parashath Parah. This commemorates the practices of purification
that were observed by the Jewish people in ancient days, and at the
same time it impresses on us the need of moral purification, which is
the theme of the *Haftarah* from Ezekiel 36:16-38, recited on that distinguished Sabbath.

TOHOROTH   טָהֳרוֹת

THE sixth of the six divisions of the Mishnah is named *Tohoroth*
(Purities) because it deals with ritual defilement and uncleanliness.
The name *Tohoroth* is euphemistic for unceanliness. This last division of the Mishnah, consisting of twelve tractates, has *Gemara* only
on one tractate (*Niddah*).

1) *Kelim*, thirty chapters, on the ritual uncleanness of utensils (Leviticus 11:33; Numbers 19:15; 31:20). It specifies the laws of impurity affecting utensils of wood, metal, glass, clay.

2) *Oholoth*, eighteen chapters, on the defilement caused by a corpse (Numbers 19:14-16) under the same tent or roof.

3) *Nega'im*, fourteen chapters, concerning leprosy affecting a person, clothes, or dwellings (Leviticus 13:1-59).

4) *Parah*, twelve chapters, containing regulations concerning the red cow (Numbers 19:2-22).

5) *Tohoroth*, ten chapters, on the defilements which continue until sunset (Leviticus 11:24-40).

6) *Mikvaoth*, ten chapters, on the requirements of baths for ritual purification (Leviticus 14:8-9; 15:5-18).

7) *Niddah*, ten chapters, on ritual uncleanness caused by menstruation and by childbirth (Leviticus 15:19-24; 12:1-5).

8) *Makhshirin*, six chapters, on liquids and foods that are susceptible to ritual uncleanness by virtue of the law of Leviticus 11:34, 38.

9) *Zavim*, five chapters, concerning the physical secretions which render a person unclean, precluding him from coming into contact with anything identified with the Sanctuary (Leviticus 15:1-30).

10) *Tevul Yom*, four chapters, on the ritual status of a person who, having incurred any uncleanness that lasts until evening, has taken the required bath known as *tevilah* (immersion) and must now await sunset before he is deemed fully clean.

11) *Yadayim*, four chapters, concerning the defilement of the hands, which are always assumed to suffer second-grade uncleanness unless they are washed with the intention of rendering them clean.

12) *Okatzin*, three chapters, on stalks of fruits and plants susceptible to uncleanness, which is conveyed to the remaining parts; if one part of a fruit suffers uncleanness, it is conveyed to the rest of the fruit.

TU BISHVAT   טוּ בִּשְׁבָט

THE semiholiday *Ḥamishah Asar Bishvat* (fifteenth day of *Shevat*), marking the first day of spring in Eretz Yisrael, occurs six weeks after *Ḥanukkah*. The Mishnah refers to it as *Rosh Hashanah l'Ilanoth* (new year for trees). Since ancient times the Jewish people have observed it by eating fruit grown in Eretz Yisrael, and with the rise of the movement to restore the Jewish homeland *Tu Bishvat*, as the festival is known in brief, has gained new significance as Arbor Day, observed by the planting of trees in Eretz Yisrael.

In Eretz Yisrael, always largely waterless, trees were regarded as special gifts of God. There are many symbolic allusions to trees in the Bible, especially the olive which sends up new shoots to continue the life of the old tree that dies. Trees are represented as symbols of goodness and nobility. The upright person is compared to a tree planted near a stream, that bears fruit in due season, with leaves that never fade (Psalm 1:3). "The righteous will flourish like the palm tree; they will grow like a cedar in Lebanon" (Psalm 92:13-14).

It was customary to plant a tree in Israel when a child was born: a cedar for a boy and a cypress for a girl, who cared for their own trees as they were growing up. Branches from their own trees were used for the poles of the wedding canopy (*huppah*) on the day of their respective marriage ceremony.

Today, when the afforestation of Israel is an absolute necessity, the Jewish children throughout the world are asked to raise funds for the planting of trees for the rehabilitation of the land. Forests are planted in different parts of the country by the generous response to the appeals of the Jewish National Fund. The celebration of *Tu Bishvat* in the Diaspora serves the additional purpose of inducing Jews to use products made in Israel.

TURIM   טוּרִים

THE code of Jewish law known as *Arba'ah Turim* (four rows, alluding to the four rows of precious stones mounted on the high priest's breastplate of judgment) was composed by Rabbi Jacob ben Asher (1270-1343) who died in Toledo, Spain, having spent all his life in poverty and sickness.

The *Turim*, on account of which the author is referred to as *Baal ha-Turim*, is methodically arranged in four parts or rows: 1) *Orah Hayyim* (way of life), dealing with the duties of the Jew at home and in the synagogue, day by day, including Sabbaths and festivals; 2) *Yoreh De'ah* (teacher of knowledge), furnishing instruction in things forbidden and permitted, such as all phases of dietary laws; 3) *Even ha-Ezer*, encompassing the laws of marriage and family matters; 4) *Hoshen Mishpat* (breastplate of judgment), describing civil law and administration. The biblical place name *Even ha-Ezer* (stone of help) is mentioned three times in the first book of Samuel (4:1; 5:1; 7:12). *Ezer* (help) alludes to marriage in Genesis 2:18. The name *Ḥoshen Mishpat* is borrowed from Exodus 28:15.

Based on Maimonides' *Mishneh Torah* in both contents and language, the *Tur*, as the code is commonly called, became so popular that it was regarded as "the people's lawbook of the entire world." Eventually, it became the basis of the *Shulḥan Arukh*, consisting likewise of four parts bearing the same titles. Designed to supply coordinated information for the average Jew, both law codes concern themselves only with laws practised after the destruction of the Second Temple, omitting all precepts which presuppose the existence of the Temple.

Here is an excerpt from the *Tur* on the subject of *tsedakah:* The dispensing of charity according to one's means is a positive precept, which demands greater care and diligence in its fulfillment than all the other positive *mitzvoth* of the Torah. For its neglect may possibly lead to the taking of a life, inasmuch as the denial of timely aid may result in the death of the poor man who needs our immediate help. Whoever closes his eyes to this duty and hardens his heart to his needy brother is called a worthless man, and is regarded as an idolater. . . Man must know that he is not the master of what he has, but only the guardian, to carry out the will of God who entrusted these things to his keeping. . .

Though the *Tur* had become the standard for all Jews, the *Shulḥan Arukh* of Rabbi Joseph Karo (1488-1575), provided with the glosses of Rabbi Moses Isserles (1520-1572), was finally accepted by all as more authoritative.

TALLITH   טַלִּית

THE term *tallith* is derived from the Hebrew-Aramaic verb טלל (to cover). In the Talmud it is frequently used in the sense of a cloak, a loose outer garment worn by men. But the special and most popular significance of *tallith* is assigned to the cloak of honor, adorned with *tsitsith* in keeping with the command to put fringes on the corners of the garments, the sight of which is to remind us to observe all the *mitzvoth* (Numbers 15:38-39).

Rectangular in form, the *tallith*, or prayer-shawl, is worn over the head or thrown round the shoulders by men, usually during morning prayer. Many worshipers prefer to enwrap themselves in a *tallith* reaching a little below their knees. Before beginning his prayers, the worshiper pronounces this benediction: "Blessed art thou . . . who hast sanctified us with thy commandments, and commanded us to enwrap ourselves in the fringed garment." The preferred material is wool, but silk is often used in the manufacture of prayer-shawls.

The blue cord entwined in the *tsitsith* was originally its chief distinction. When, however, it became impossible to procure the special dye required, it was made permissible to use white threads alone. Why blue? "Because this color resembles the sea, the sea resembles the sky. . ." (Menaḥoth 43b). The method of dying the threads sky-blue, kept secret by the inhabitants of Akko (Acre), was lost and forgotten in the dispersion, so that the use of the blue thread in each fringe had to be discontinued.

The *tallith katan*, or smaller form of *tallith*, otherwise known as *arba kanfoth* (four corners), is worn under the outer garment during the entire day.

BIBLE ACCENTS   טַעֲמֵי הַמִּקְרָא

THE primary purpose of the special signs of cantillation or accents (*te'amim, neginoth*), which are placed both above and under the words of the Hebrew Bible, is to regulate minutely the public reading of the holy text. They serve a threefold purpose: 1) as musical notes, 2) as marks of the tone-syllables, and 3) as marks of punctuation, to indicate the logical relations of words to one another. This system of musical notation facilitates a deeper penetration into the meaning of the component parts of biblical verses.

The Hebrew word *ta'am*, denoting accent, essentially signifies both taste and good sense. The phrase *devarim shel ta'am*, for example, means sensible words. The biblical system of accents was primarily designed to indicate the coherence and logical sequence of the sacred text. The distribution of great and small pauses resulted in the singing style known as cantillation, which is frequently heard in the synagogue. The terms *neginah* (melody) and *trop* are used interchangeably with the word *ta'am*.

During the medieval period it was generally believed that the signs of cantillation as well as the signs of vocalization had been originated by Ezra and the members of the Great Assembly, who flourished

245

several centuries before the common era. Aaron Ben Asher, the tenth-century masoretic scholar of Tiberias, who devoted many years to preparing an accurate Bible manuscript with all the traditional marks of vocalization and cantillation, speaks of the accents as the contribution of the prophets to whom the interpretation of every word was revealed. Elijah Levita (1468-1549) was the first to prove the post-talmudic date of the vowels and the accents.

The understanding of the biblical text is readily aided by the signs of accentuation, though it is not always easy to tell just why certain modes of cantillation were chosen. A knowledge of the accents is indispensable in the study of the Hebrew Bible. Rabbi Abraham ibn Ezra of twelfth-century Spain, best known for his penetrating Bible commentaries, declares that one should not accept the interpretation of a biblical passage if it does not follow the guiding accents.

The musical system to which the *neginoth* or *trops* now serve as a notation is said to have existed long before the vowel-signs were invented. The notation which stabilized the traditional pronunciation of each word was possibly introduced at the same period as the notation which perpetuated the traditional modulation. Two systems of accents apply to the Hebrew Bible: the system used in the three poetical books of Job, Proverbs and Psalms (איוב משלי תהלים) is referred to as טעמי אמ״ת, while the system of the remaining twenty-one books of the Bible is called טעמי כ״א. The poetical accentuations are suited to the rhythm as well as to the requirements of sense. The shorter measure of the poetical verses is perhaps responsible for the change of the system of accents.

As marks of punctuation, the accents are divided into *disjunctive*, indicating various degrees of pause, and *conjunctive*, serving to connect words. Thus a twofold system of accentuation exists: 1) the common system used in twenty-one books of the Bible, and 2) the special one used in the books of Psalms, Proverbs and Job, which is richer, more complicated, and musically more significant than the ordinary accentuation.

The *makkaf* (binder), resembling a hyphen which connects two words, indicates that the connected words have only one accent. Two, three, or even four words may be connected in this way. Certain monosyllabic prepositions and conjunctions are almost always followed by a *makkaf*. Longer words are connected by a *makkaf* (מקף) with a following monosyllable, and occasionally two words of more than one syllable.

246

The *metheg* (bridle), a small perpendicular stroke under the consonant, indicates the counter-tone, or secondary accent, as opposed to the principal tone marked by the musical note (*neginah*). It frequently points out that the vowel should not be hastily passed over in pronunciation, but should be allowed its full sound. In the Prayerbooks, the *metheg* indicates words which have the tone on the penultimate (*mil'el*), the last syllable but one. ·

TEREFAH U-NEVELAH   טְרֵפָה וּנְבֵלָה

THE term *terefah*, now denoting any food forbidden by Jewish tradition, is used in the Torah for meat of animals killed by beasts of prey: "You shall not eat any flesh that is torn by beasts in the field" (Exodus 22:31). This prohibition related to the general law which forbids the eating of blood, the principal carrier of life, reserved for a symbolic purpose in the sacrificial system. The flesh of an animal killed otherwise than by *sheḥitah*, or ritual slaughtering, would not be properly drained of blood.

Nevelah is an animal that has died of natural causes. The flesh of such an animal cannot be thoroughly drained of blood. The Torah declares: "Since the life of every living being is its blood . . . you shall not eat the blood of any meat. . . Anyone who eats of an animal that died of itself (*nevelah*) or was killed by a wild beast (*terefah*) . . . shall wash his garments, bathe in water, and be unclean until evening. If he does not wash them nor bathe in water, he shall bear his guilt" (Leviticus 17:14-16)

Rabbi Moses ben Naḥman (Ramban), in his commentary on Leviticus, quotes Maimonides to the effect that the Greeks drank blood in order to communicate with the demons; but he maintains that blood was prohibited because it is the very life of another creature.

The Torah says: "You must not eat any animal that has died of itself. . . You shall not boil a kid in its mother's milk" (Deuteronomy 14:21). The prohibition of carrion is understood to apply to all meat of animals incorrectly slaughtered; the prohibition of animals torn by beasts includes meat of animals revealing diseased or injured parts on post-mortem inspection. Hence, *terefah* refers to an animal afflicted with an organic disease, the discovery of which, after slaughtering, makes it forbidden; *nevelah* denotes whatever has become unfit through faulty slaughtering.

247

The term *tarfuth*, as opposed to *kashruth*, includes also meat-milk mixtures, concerning which the Mishnah states: "No meat may be cooked in milk, except meat of fish . . . and no meat may be served on the table together with cheese, except the meat of fish. . ." (Ḥullin 8:1). The requirement of salting meat is stated in the Talmud (Ḥullin 113a). Meat cannot be thoroughly cleared of its blood unless it is well salted and soaked. The blood found in eggs is forbidden; hence, they are examined before being prepared for a kosher meal. Though the blood of fish is permitted, it must not be eaten when collected into a dish, because of the wrong impression that this is likely to evoke. The rule is: wherever the sages have forbidden a thing in order to avoid the semblance (מראית עין) of wrongdoing, it is forbidden even in strictest privacy (Betzah 9a).

Maimonides writes: "If one has first partaken of cheese or milk, he may eat meat immediately thereafter. He must, however, wash his hands and cleanse his mouth between the cheese and the meat. With what should he cleanse his mouth? With bread, or by chewing fruit and swallowing it or spitting it out... This applies only to the meat of cattle and livestock; but if one eats poultry after milk or cheese, he is not required to cleanse his mouth or wash his hands. If one has eaten meat first, whether the meat of cattle or fowl, he should not partake of milk thereafter until a lapse of time is spent, equal to the interval between two meals, namely about six hours, because the fragments of meat between the teeth are not removed by cleansing" (*Maakhaloth Asuroth* 9:26-28).

Every kosher kitchen is equipped with two sets of dishes, for meat and for milk. Separate tablecloths are used for meat and for dairy meals. Food that contains neither meat nor milk (*parve* food) may always be eaten together with either meat or milk.

Following the ritual slaughtering (*shehitah*), the kashering of meat is as follows: the meat is first soaked in water for half-an-hour. Then it is withdrawn, and coarse salt is sprinkled on all sides until it is well covered. It is left salting for an hour. Then, the meat is rinsed three times in water and prepared for the table. *Terefah* meat can never be kashered. Fish that have fins and scales are kosher.

YIGDAL

THE liturgical poem *Yigdal*, used as an opening hymn in the daily morning service, was composed by Rabbi Daniel ben Yehudah of fourteenth-century Rome. It consists of thirteen lines which summarize the thirteen principles of faith as formulated by Moses Maimonides in his Mishnah commentary (on Sanhedrin 10:1). One rhyme runs through all the thirteen lines, each of which consists of sixteen syllables. In the *Siddur* of the Spanish-Portuguese Jews a fourteenth line is added, which reads: "These thirteen principles are the foundation of the divine faith and the Torah."

The Jewish philosophy of Moses Maimonides (1135-1204), summed up in *Yigdal* as it is in *Ani Ma'amin*, consists of the following fundamental principles: 1) There is a Creator. 2) His Oneness is absolute. 3) He is without material form. 4) He is eternal. 5) He alone may be worshiped. 6) The prophets are true. 7) Moses was the greatest of all prophets. 8) The entire Torah was divinely given to Moses. 9) The Torah is immutable. 10) God knows all the acts and thoughts of man. 11) He rewards and punishes. 12) Messiah will come. 13) There will be resurrection.

The number thirteen is reminiscent of the numerical value of the word אחד (One). Thus there are the thirteen attributes of God; the Torah is interpreted by means of thirteen principles of talmudic logic; the *Bar Mitzvah* age is thirteen; the poem אחד מי יודע (who knows one?) has thirteen stanzas, ending with the thirteen divine attributes.

Though the Bible hardly contains a command bidding us to believe, its whole structure is built upon the belief in the relation of God to man. The Jew belongs to his nationality even after having committed the greatest sin, just as the Englishman does not cease to be an Englishman by having committed a heinous crime. Every article of Maimonides which seems to offer difficulties to us contains an assertion of some relaxed belief, or a protest against other creeds.

The metrical scheme of *Yigdal* is, like that of *Adon Olam*, devised on the basis of a simple sound (*tenu'ah*) and a compound sound (*yathed*). The *yathed* (יתד) consists of a *sheva* (ְ) or *hataf* (ֱ) followed by a regular vowel. The word *yigdal*, for instance, has two *tenu'oth*, while *elo-him* consists of a *yathed* and a *tenu'ah*. The metrical arrangement of *Yigdal* is: twice two *tenu'oth* and *yathed*, followed by two *tenu'oth*:

יגדל אל I הים חי ויש I תבח   נמצא ואין I עת אל מצי I אותו

249

YEDID NEFESH   יְדִיד נֶפֶשׁ

THE mystical poem *Yedid Nefesh* (dearly beloved), breathing the spirit of love between God and his people, was composed by Rabbi Eliezer Askari, who lived in Safed during the sixteenth century and was one of the kabbalistic disciples of Rabbi Isaac Luria and Rabbi Joseph Karo. The acrostic of the four stanzas contains the four-letter name of God (tetragrammaton). The author contemplates God as the cause of bliss and happiness, as the single highest good of all human striving. The object of the poet's prayer is exclusively God and the soul. "Glorious One, thou who art the world's light, my soul is love-sick, pining for thy love... Shed light upon the earth with thy splendor, that we may exult and rejoice in thee..."

The expression אלה חמדה לבי (these things does my heart desire) should be corrected to read אלי, חמדת לבי (my God, the desire of my heart). This is supported by rare editions as well as by context. *Yedid Nefesh* is recited frequently within *Ḥasidic* circles of worshipers.

JUDAISM   יַהֲדוּת

ALTHOUGH the term *Yahaduth* (Judaism) does not occur in the Hebrew Bible or in the Talmud, it is employed in an ancient Midrash (Esther Rabbah 7:11), where it signifies a mode of life based on adherence to the teachings of the Torah given by God. Judaism has been defined as the strictest form of monotheism (belief in one God) and the practical effect of that belief on life. First preached by Abraham, and symbolized by the covenant of circumcision, it is the oldest existing religion, the parent of two faiths that have spread over the major portion of the world.

Judaism believes that man is capable of perfection; he is made in the image of God, therefore he possesses nobility. According to a talmudic statement, God gave the Torah to Moses in the desert, in a no-man's land, so that the people of Israel might not claim exclusive possession of it.

One of the ancient rabbis declared that, as all mankind traces its ancestry to Adam, all men are brothers, the children of one parentage. All men, therefore, are equally capable of achieving the zenith of moral and ethical behavior. The main purpose of Judaism, according

250

to a saintly rabbi of the twelfth century, is to promote mutual understanding and peace among all people. Its function is to keep the great ideals intact before the eyes of mankind.

Judaism lays great stress on reverence for parents, respect for the aged, and benevolence toward the infirm and the weak. In all dealings with men, honesty and truthfulness are absolutely required. Stealing, falsehood, oppression—even the withholding of a man's wages so much as overnight—are forbidden. Talebearing, gossip and unkind insinuation are prohibited, as is hatred of a fellow man in one's heart. The dumb animal has claims upon the kindly help of man, even when it belongs to one's enemy. Justice, truthfulness, care for the weak, regard for the rights of others, love for fellow men and mercy for the beast are the virtues taught by Judaism. "Learn to be good" is the keynote of the prophetic appeal.

The tone of Judaism is optimistic. The world is good and life is precious, for both are the creation of God who is the source and ideal of all goodness and morality. As God is merciful and gracious, so should man be. As a child of God, man has duties toward himself as well as toward his fellow man. He is in duty bound to preserve his health; he who subjects himself to needless fasting and self-mortification is a sinner. The servant of God does not detach himself from secular contacts and does not despise life, which is one of God's gifts.

One of the chief principles of Judaism is the belief in the divine choice of the Jewish people to transmit the divine message to mankind. In the midst of rich and powerful nations, engulfed in passionate idolatry, it was "the smallest of all nations" that preached the unique idea of a universal God to the rest of the world. "He has chosen you from all the nations on the face of the earth to be a people peculiarly his own. It was not because you are the largest of all nations that the Lord set his love upon you and chose you, for you are really the smallest of all nations" (Deuteronony 7:7).

The highest motives working through the history of Judaism have been the strong belief in God and the unshaken confidence that at last the God of Israel will be the God of the whole world, or in the words of the prophet: "On that day the Lord shall be One, and his name One" (Zechariah 14:9). Faith and hope are said to be the two most prominent characteristics of Judaism. Judaism demands belief in a personal God. As to how to live the Jewish life was summarized by Hillel in the famous maxim: "Do not to your neighbor what is hateful to yourself; the rest is commentary; go, learn it."

Some one hundred precepts, out of 613, are practised by observant Jews today; these are largely concerned with festivals, food and prayer, so that the daily life of a Jew, in his business or profession, is not very different from that of his non-Jewish neighbor. Many precepts, connected with the sacrifices, are not in use when the Temple does not exist. The fulfillment of negative precepts, like "you shall not steal" and "you shall not murder," is accomplished by inaction.

In Judaism, it is often declared, religion and morality blend into an indissoluble unity. The love of God is incomplete without the love of one's fellow man. The goal toward which this concept leads is the elimination of man-made misery and suffering, of prejudice and strife, of tyranny and social inequality. Judaism champions the cause of universal peace, the ideal proclaimed to mankind from the days of the prophets, and abhors all violence. It emphasizes the kinship of the human race and the sanctity of human life and freedom. Living in all parts of the world, the Jewish people have been held together by the ties of a common history and particularly by the heritage of faith and culture.

JOSHUA　　　　　　　　　　　　　　　　　　　　　　　יְהוֹשֻׁעַ

THE book of Joshua continues the history of the preceding five books of the Torah and narrates the conquest and settlement of the promised land; it records the completion of the great movement of which the exodus from Egypt was the beginning. Joshua is the first of the four historical books known as Former Prophets or Earlier Prophets (Joshua, Judges, Samuel, Kings), forming a continuous narrative which begins at the death of Moses and ends with the destruction of the first Temple. These writings are classed as prophetic because they were composed by divinely inspired prophets.

As successor of Moses, Joshua defeated six enemy tribes in six years and then proceeded to divide the conquered territory. The final events of his life include the distribution of the land to the tribes of Israel by lot and the appointing of the cities of refuge, designed to shelter anyone who might accidentally commit manslaughter. By fleeing into one of the six cities of refuge, persons pursued by avengers of blood were protected against the ancient law of life for life. Forty-two Levitical cities also served for the protection of the unintentional homicide against blood vengeance.

252

Before his death at the age of one hundred and ten, Joshua delivered two addresses to the people of Israel, urging them to remain loyal to God and live according to the teachings of the Torah. Bible scholars regard the five books of Moses and the book of Joshua as one literary unit, which they designate as Hexateuch (sixfold book). They claim that the book of Joshua was at first an integral part of the so-called Hexateuch. Its contents, dealing with the conquest and distribution of the land, form the necessary conclusion to the Pentateuch.

The miracles found in the book of Joshua convey the idea that without divine intervention the people of Israel could never have conquered the powerful nations occupying the promised land. Those pagans are described as deserving severe punishment for their crimes and moral corruption. Excerpt:

"Thus says the Lord God of Israel: I took your father Abraham from the other side of the Euphrates River and led him through all the land of Canaan. I gave him Isaac, and to Isaac I gave Jacob and Esau. To Esau I assigned the mountain region of Seir to settle, while Jacob and his children went down to Egypt. I sent Moses and Aaron, and I brought your fathers out of Egypt. The Egyptians pursued your fathers as far as the Red Sea, and the Lord engulfed them in it. You lived many days in the wilderness, and I brought you to the eastern side of the Jordan. Then Balak, king of Moab, sent for Balaam to curse you, but he blessed you instead. You crossed the Jordan and came to Jericho, and I put the men of Jericho into your hands. It was not your sword nor bow that defeated them... Now therefore revere the Lord and serve him sincerely and faithfully..."

JOEL יוֹאֵל

THE book of Joel, the second among the Minor Prophets, consists of four chapters, attributed to the prophet Joel about whose personality nothing is known. Even the date of his book is subject to speculation and is greatly disputed among Bible scholars. Joel is placed either in a very early period or in post-exilic times.

The style of the book is fluent, clear and of a high order. Its general subject is divine judgment. A plague of locusts, accompanied by a drought of unusual severity, sweeps in successive swarms over Judea and destroys the produce of the fields and vineyards. Remarkably vivid is the description of the locust swarms filling the entire air;

their destructiveness is compared with that of a mighty army. According to many who have witnessed such a scourge, it is described in Joel with almost scientific accuracy. Excerpt:

"Wake up, you drunkards, and weep for the wine that is snatched from your mouth! An army has invaded our land, powerful and numberless; their teeth are the teeth of a lion, with fangs of a lioness. They have ruined our vines, and splintered our fig trees; they have stripped them clean, till their branches are made white. . . Like blackness spread over the mountains is the huge and powerful army... Before them the land is a paradise, behind them it is a desolate wilderness. Nothing escapes them. They rush on the city, run over the walls, climb into the houses, and enter through the windows like thieves. Before them the earth trembles, the heavens shake; the sun and the moon are darkened, and the stars withhold their brightness."

Joel summons the people to a penitential fast, and promises that God will bring back prosperity and abundance. The fourth and last chapter of Joel describes the future glory of Judea.

"And it shall come to pass afterward, that I will pour out my spirit on all flesh; your sons and your daughters shall prophesy; your old men shall dream dreams, your young men shall see visions. . . For in those days and at that time, when I restore the fortunes of Judah and Jerusalem, I will gather all the nations and bring them down into the Judgment Valley, where I shall enter into judgment with them, because they scattered my people Israel among pagans and divided up my land. Then the mountains shall drip wine, the hills shall flow with milk, and all the stream beds of Judah shall flow with water. Judah shall be inhabited forever, and Jerusalem to all generations."

JUBILEE   יוֹבֵל

THE year of jubilee rests on the same principle as the sabbatical year. The fiftieth year, occurring after seven times seven years had been counted from the last jubilee, the land was to lie fallow, to show that it was not the absolute possession of man. Hence the law: "The land shall not be sold in perpetuity; for the land is mine, and you are but strangers who have become my tenants" (Leviticus 25:23). Just like the sabbatical year, the year of jubilee was designed to give the land a rest from agricultural work. Only the spontaneous produce of that year was to be enjoyed and shared with the poor and strangers.

The sabbatical year began with the first day of *Tishri*, and the year of jubilee with the tenth of *Tishri*. In the sabbatical year, Hebrew slaves were to be set free if they desired their freedom and debts were to be remitted to Israelites. In the year of jubilee, all property was to revert to the original owner who, through poverty, may have been obliged to sell it at some time during the previous years. Hebrew slaves with their families were to be emancipated without price.

According to a talmudic statement (Arakhin 12b), the Israelites counted seventeen jubilee cycles from their entrance into Eretz Yisrael until several tribes went into exile. According to Maimonides, though the jubilees were not observed during the period of the Second Temple, they were counted by the people so as to observe the sabbatical years (*Shemittah v'Yovel* 10:3). Historical evidence is lacking that the year of jubilee was ever strictly observed in actual practice; but in the words of Ewald, "nothing is more certain than that the jubilee was once for centuries a reality in the national life of Israel."

The inordinate accumulation of land in the hands of the few was prevented by means of the jubilee regulations, in compliance with which all property reverted once again to their original ownership. The fiftieth year was marked by the sounding of the *shofar* (ram's horn) on *Yom Kippur;* hence the Hebrew name *yovel* which means ram or ram's horn. The jubilee has been described as a remarkable social law, preventing the acquisition of huge estates, and adjusting the distribution of wealth in the various classes of the community. Some scholars surmise that perhaps the seventh sabbatical year and the year of jubilee were identical, since both the first and the last year of the series were counted.

YOM HA-ATZMAUTH   יוֹם הָעַצְמָאוּת

THE anniversary of Israel's declaration of independence which was signed on the fifth day of *Iyyar*, 5708 (May 14, 1948), is observed annually as a national holiday in Israel and throughout the Diaspora or *Tefutzoth Yisrael*. In Israel, *Yom ha-Atzmauth* (Independence Day) is a festival celebrated in the form of special congregational services in the synagogues, military parades, social parties and festive activities.

The central features of the celebration consist of a special thanksgiving service which includes the reading of the messianic prophecies in the book of Isaiah (10:32-12:6), the chanting of *Hallel* (Psalms

113-118), the reciting of special memorial prayers for the Israelis who fell in battle as well as for the martyrs of the Nazi persecutions, and an invocation to national repentance. The service concludes with the sounding of the *shofar*, followed by the proclamation: "May it be the will of the Lord our God that as we have been granted to see the dawn of the redemption, so may we be granted to hear the trumpet of the Messiah."

According to Israel's proclamation of independence, the State of Israel will be open to the immigration of Jews from all countries of the dispersion; will promote the development of the country for the benefit of all its inhabitants; will be based on the principles of liberty, justice and peace as conceived by the Prophets of Israel; will uphold the full social and political equality of all its citizens, without distinction of religion, race or sex; will guarantee freedom of religion, conscience, education and culture; will safeguard the holy places of all religions; and will uphold the principles of the United Nations Charter.

YAHRZEIT יום הַפְּטִירָה

THE term *Yahrzeit*, which has no adequate Hebrew equivalent, is said to have originated in fifteenth-century Germany, whence it was introduced gradually to all parts of the world inhabited by Jews. Rabbi Joseph Karo (1488-1575) makes no direct mention of *Yahrzeit*, or death anniversary of a parent, in his *Shulḥan Arukh*, the famous authoritative code of Jewish laws and customs. From a passage in the Talmud (Shevuoth 20a) it appears that the death anniversary of a parent was observed as a private fast-day (תענית יחיד).

Rabbi Solomon Ganzfried (1804-1886), in his abridgment (*Kitzur*) of the *Shulḥan Arukh* code, adds a sizable section containing *Yahrzeit* regulations, one of which reads: "It is meritorious to fast on the death anniversary of one's father or mother as a means of repentance and self-examination, which in turn will help his departed parent to reach a higher sphere in *Gan Eden* (Paradise)... It is customary to light a *Yahrzeit* candle..."

It has been noted that Jewish tradition has assigned the day of death, instead of the day of birth, for remembrance because the life of a person can best be evaluated at the end of his journey on earth.

The *Yahrzeit* is observed in accord with the Jewish calendar upon the date of death. Since the human spirit is biblically referred to as

256

"the lamp of the Lord" (Proverbs 20:27), it is customary to light a *Yahrzeit* lamp on the eve of the day; the lamp remains burning until the sunset of the next day. The *Kaddish* prayer, recited on *Yahrzeits*, is often described as a great pillar of Judaism. No matter how far a Jew may have drifted away from Jewish life, the *Kaddish* which he recites in remembrance of parents restores him to his people and to the Jewish way of life. The traditional *Yahrzeit* of Moses (*Adar* 7th) is the occasion of eulogies on great scholars who have passed away during the year. *Ḥasidim* observe the *Yahrzeits* of their saintly leaders with great joy.

YOM TOV   יום טוב

THE term *yom tov* (a good day), applied to all festivals, connotes joy and festivity. The Torah often tells us to rejoice on festive occasions (Deuteronomy 12:18; 14:26; 16:11, 14; 26:11; 27:7). The Jewish codes of law emphasize the idea that it is a *mitzvah*, a religious duty, to be glad at heart and joyful on the festivals. Maimonides writes: "Women should have clothes and pretty trinkets bought for them, according to a man's means... And while one eats and drinks, it is his duty to feed the stranger, the orphan, the widow, and other poor and unfortunate people, for he ... who eats and drinks with his wife and family, without giving anything to eat and drink to the poor and the distressed—his meal is not a rejoicing divinely commanded, but a rejoicing of his stomach ... a disgrace to those who indulge in it" (*Yad, Yom Tov* 6;18). Appropriate passages are read from the Torah and the Prophets as part of the congregational services, which include a *Musaf* describing the festival offerings in Temple times.

In the *Megillath Ta'anith*, an ancient calendar of joyous events in the history of the Jewish people during the Hellenistic and Roman periods, a considerable number of semiholidays are listed when public fasts are not to be observed. Most of them ceased to be kept when the memory of the events they celebrated faded out in the course of time. On the other hand, new semiholidays are declared on rare occasions, such as the *Yom ha-Atzmauth* (Israel's Independence Day) on the fifth of *Iyyar*, proclaimed in 1948 in celebration of the establishment of the State of Israel.

Each of the sacred festivals, except *Yom Kippur*, is celebrated for two days outside Eretz Yisrael, the second day being observed on the

257

authority of the ancient sages as one of the innovations introduced in the Diaspora. The second day is therefore called the *Second Yom Tov of the Diaspora* (יום טוב שני של גליות). It was introduced during the period of the Second Temple, when it was impossible to inform the Jews dispersed in foreign lands concerning the precise dates of forthcoming festivals. By celebrating two days in the Diaspora, all were comfortably certain that the right day was observed simultaneously by all the Jews as a united people. Thus we are told: "Although the second day of a festival is observed only on the authority of the *Sofrim* (sages), whatever is forbidden on the first day is forbidden also on the second day... Only in regard to the burial of the dead is there any distinction between the two days" (*Yad*). As to the festival of *Rosh Hashanah*, it has been celebrated for two days even in Eretz Yisrael, the two days being regarded as one long day. Reform communities do not observe at all the second day of *yom tov*, not even that of *Rosh Hashanah*.

It is highly significant that the Jewish feasts and festivals are chiefly dedicated to the idea of joy. "You shall rejoice at your festival together with your son and daughter, your male and female servants, as well as the stranger, the orphan and the widow" (Deuteronomy 16:14). Joy is the very purpose and goal of the festivals, and it must be shared with the strangers and the poor. You are to be happy with them and they are to be happy with you. This rejoicing is designed to raise man above social afflictions at least during the festival days. The joy which is experienced during the Festival of Freedom celebrates the revelation on Mount Sinai, the legislation of a moral code. The Sabbath represents the first step toward the abolition of slavery.

The study of Torah has always been an essential part of festival rejoicings among the Jewish people. This intellectual joy has never degenerated into sensuality. Though he has been oppressed almost everywhere in the world, there is no room for hatred in the heart of the Jew who believes in peace.

It is indeed remarkable that despite all the sufferings the Jew has endured throughout his history, he has miraculously managed to preserve his equanimity and good humor, without which he would never have been able to rise from deep humiliation to lofty heights. The Jewish festivals are largely responsible for this miracle. Festive joy, being a religious duty, has proved a vital force in the consciousness of the Jew. He could never remain a man of mourning: his festivals and his studies always raised him to the celestial heights of joy.

258

DAY OF ATONEMENT   יוֹם כִּפּוּר

THE Day of Atonement is the climax of the ten-day period of repentance that begins with *Rosh Hashanah*, the Day of Judgment. These ten days of reflection and inspiration bring us the eternal message that it is possible for human beings to improve their characters. They speak to us about our ethical conscience and moral responsibility, about self-examination and spiritual regeneration.

The idea of repentance is regarded as the brightest gem among the teachings of Judaism. Man would be the most unfortunate creature if he had no way to escape from sin. The optimistic spirit of Judaism does not tolerate the idea that a man need ever despair and lose faith in himself. No one can sink so low that he cannot find his way back to God by self-discipline. The very concept of repentance and atonement has made the Jewish outlook on life one of cheerful confidence. The Hebrew term *teshuvah* for repentance signifies return and must not be taken to mean penitence or penance. These words refer to self-castigation. Judaism demands an inner change, and opposes external forms of asceticism for purposes of expiating sin.

There is a midrashic statement that God modelled the world like an architect, and it would not stand until he created repentance. Defined by Maimonides, repentance means that the sinner casts his sins out of his mind and resolves in his heart to sin no more. The atonement prayers, articulating the ideals of human brotherhood and mutual forgiveness, make the worshiper intensely aware of human frailty, reminding him that there is no man who is absolutely free from sin and error. The confessions are recited repeatedly on *Yom Kippur* in the first person plural to emphasize the collective responsibility of the whole community for offenses that can be prevented.

We are repeatedly reminded that *Yom Kippur* brings pardon for sins between man and God, and it cannot bring forgiveness as long as no attempt has been made to repair the injury inflicted upon one's fellow man. God does not clear the guilty in matters touching human beings unless reparation precedes all else (Yoma 8:8). The wrongdoer must first win pardon from the person wronged. Hence the age-old custom of mending quarrels and begging forgiveness of one another for any wrong committed, intentionally or otherwise. This custom is particularly observed on *erev Yom Kippur*. When the offender asks to be forgiven, he should be forgiven wholeheartedly, we are told.

259

Judaism believes in the ability of the worst sinners to improve their ways; without such possibility man's world could not continue. Nothing can withstand the power of sincere repentance, we are told. "Even if a man has been a sinner all his days and he repents in his old age, when all opportunity for sin is gone, though it is by no means the highest form of repentance, it is a valid atonement. Even if he has sinned all his life and repented only on his deathbed, his sins are pardoned" (Maimonides, *Teshuvah* 2:1). The everlasting theme of repentance occupies a very prominent position in all the ethical writings of the Jewish people.

The fast of *Yom Kippur* begins with physical mortification and ends with spiritual exultation. It is a day of self-denial and at the same time a Sabbath of rest (שבת שבתון). The arrangement of the atonement prayers forms a gradual ascent from the sense of guilt to the sense of joy and confident reliance upon divine love and mercy. All human activity gradually unrolls in these prayers and poetic compositions, some of which are literary masterpieces with extraordinary power to elevate and to inspire. The failings and weaknesses of man are contrasted with the well-ordered infinite universe, and he never ceases to be in need of atonement. Hence the admonition: "Repent one day before you die" (Avoth 2:15). But how does a man know on which day he will die? Let him therefore repent every day, for he may die the next day.

The fifty-eighth chapter of Isaiah, recited as the *Haftarah* for *Yom Kippur*, as well as the book of Jonah recited during the *Minḥah* service of that day, reveals the prophetic thinking on this subject. "This is the fast that I esteem precious: loosen the chains of wickedness, let the crushed go free, break all yokes of tyranny! Share your food with the hungry, take the homeless poor to your house, clothe the naked wherever you see them; never turn from your own flesh" (Isaiah 58:6-7). In reference to the book of Jonah, the Mishnah underscores that "it is not written of the men of Nineveh that God saw their sackcloth and their fasting, but that he saw that they turned from their evil ways" (Ta'anith 2:1). Better insight, purer faith, fuller strength is all that is stressed in the Day of Atonement and reconciliation, when those who have been estranged are brought into agreement with God and his precepts.

Tradition reports that on the tenth of *Tishri*, the Day of Atonement, Moses returned from Mount Sinai with the second tablets of the Ten Commandments and announced to the people God's pardon for the

260

sin of the golden calf (Bava Bathra 121a). There is a talmudic saying that on *Yom Kippur* and *Rosh Hashanah* Jews should not appear depressed or in somber clothes, but dressed in festive white, symbolizing cheerfulness (Yerushalmi, Rosh Hashanah 1:3). Cheerfulness has remained a characteristic of the Jewish people to this day.

The first-century Jewish philosopher Philo, who wrote extensively on Judaism as a philosophical system of religion, speaks of *Yom Kippur* as an occasion for self-restraint at a season when the fruits of the earth have just been gathered in and the temptation to indulge is stronger than usual. Abstinence at such a time is likely to raise men's thoughts from the gifts to the Giver who sustains all life.

Reproducing the exact words of the high priest's three confessions during the *Yom Kippur* service at the Temple in Jerusalem, the Mishnah reports that as often as he uttered the tetragrammaton, or the four-letter name of God, the assembled multitudes outside prostrated and responded: 'Blessed be the name of his glorious majesty forever and ever" (Yoma 6:2). In view of the great dread that some mishap might befall the high priest while officiating in the Holy of Holies, he was congratulated at the conclusion of the service and escorted home by his frends, whom he entertained in the evening (7:4).

The traditional melodies with their plaintive tones are designed to give expression to one's awe before the uncertainties of the future. Forgetful of his physical wants, the devout Jew seeks to banish all hatred, ill-feeling and ignoble thoughts, and be occupied exclusively with things spiritual. It has been asserted that so strong is the hold of *Yom Kippur* upon the Jewish conscience, that no loyal Jew will fail to observe it by attending service in the synagogue along with his fellow Jews and by resting from his daily occupation.

Despite the cessation of the sacrificial practices with the destruction of the Second Temple in the year 70, *Yom Kippur* has survived as the great day which symbolizes the importance of repentance. We are told that, though the day itself effects atonement, it avails nothing unless repentance is coupled with it, just as repentance had to accompany a guilt-offering or a sin-offering in Temple times.

In letters written between *Rosh Hashanah* and *Yom Kippur*, one usually concludes with the formula *gemar hathimah tovah*, wishing the recipient that God may seal his destiny for happiness. This is based upon the belief that on the first day of the year the destiny of human beings is determined; hence the *Rosh Hashanah* greeting: "May you be inscribed for a happy year."

Yom Kippur Calendar

1975	5736	Monday	September 15
1976	5737	Monday	October 4
1977	5738	Thursday	September 22
1978	5739	Wednesday	October 11
1979	5740	Monday	October 1
1980	5741	Saturday	September 20
1981	5742	Thursday	October 8
1982	5743	Monday	September 27
1983	5744	Saturday	September 17
1984	5745	Saturday	October 6
1985	5746	Wednesday	September 25
1896	5747	Monday	October 13
1987	5748	Saturday	October 3
1988	5749	Wednesday	September 21
1989	5750	Monday	October 9
1990	5751	Saturday	September 29
1991	5752	Wednesday	September 18
1992	5753	Wednesday	October 7
1993	5754	Saturday	September 25
1994	5755	Thursday	September 15
1995	5756	Wednesday	October 4
1996	5757	Monday	September 23
1997	5758	Saturday	October 11
1998	5759	Wednesday	September 30
1999	5760	Monday	September 20
2000	5761	Monday	October 9
2001	5762	Thursday	September 27
2002	5763	Monday	September 16
2003	5764	Monday	October 6
2004	5765	Saturday	September 25
2005	5766	Thursday	October 13
2006	5767	Monday	October 2
2007	5768	Saturday	September 22
2008	5769	Thursday	October 9
2009	5770	Monday	September 28
2010	5771	Saturday	September 18

YOM KIPPUR KATAN　　　יוֹם כִּפּוּר קָטָן

THE day preceding *Rosh Ḥodesh* is known as *Yom Kippur Katan* (Minor *Yom Kippur*). It is observed as a fast-day by kabbalistically minded Jews, who recite special prayers for forgiveness (*seliḥoth*) during the *Minḥah* service of that day.

The custom to fast on *Yom Kippur Katan* was possibly introduced by Rabbi Isaac Luria (1534-1572), who became renowned for his saintly character and ascetic life. His teaching deeply influenced mystical thought among the Jews throughout the world. Born in Jerusalem and educated in Egypt, Rabbi Isaac Luria spent the last two years of his life in Safed, which had become a most important center of rabbinical and kabbalistic activity.

Rabbi Isaiah Horowitz (של"ה), who died in Tiberias (1630), refers to *Yom Kippur Katan* in these terms: "Following the custom of very saintly men, one ought to repent and make restitution in monetary as well as in personal matters, that he may enter the new month as pure as a new-born infant." The fasting, however, is not obligatory on the day preceding *Rosh Ḥodesh*.

The *seliḥoth* of *Yom Kippur Katan* are recited in the afternoon at the *Minḥah* service. If ten persons are present that have fasted, the Torah section ויחל is read (Exodus 32:11-14; 34:1-10).

JONAH　　　　　　　　　　　　　　　　יוֹנָה

THE book of Jonah, the fifth book of the twelve Minor Prophets (תרי־עשר), records a prophet's experiences rather than his utterances. The story of Jonah, who lived about 750 before the common era, is well known. Ordered by God to prophesy the destruction of Nineveh for its wickedness, Jonah attempted to escape from the divine command by sailing from the land of Israel. After his wonderful deliverance from drowning, he was obedient to a second commission from God. He went to Nineveh, and there proclaimed that it would be destroyed in forty days. God spared the city when he saw the repentance of its people.

The book of Jonah, containing the noblest expression of the universality of religion, is designed to show that kindness of heart and readiness to repent may be found everywhere among men.

263

The episode of the great fish swallowing Jonah has been interpreted figuratively as the captivity which swallowed up Israel. The deliverance from exile has been linked to being disgorged alive from the mouth of the devouring beast. Jonah's reluctance to denounce the heathen city of Nineveh was prompted perhaps by fear of exposing himself to the wrath of the king and the people.

The book of Jonah is recited as the prophetic lesson (*Haftarah*) in the afternoon service of *Yom Kippur*, to show that the compassion of God extends to all his creatures, even those who are as sinful as the people of Nineveh. Jonah, son of Amittai, is mentioned in II Kings 14:25 as having lived during the reign of Jeroboam II. Excerpt:

"Jonah made a tent for himself and sat in its shade, waiting to see what would happen to the city. The Lord God made a gourd grow up over Jonah to shade his head and alleviate his discomfort, and Jonah was exceedingly pleased with it. But next morning, at dawn, God caused a worm to attack the gourd and it withered. At sunrise, God sent a hot east wind and the sun beat on Jonah's head until he fainted... Thereupon God said to Jonah: Are you sorely grieved about the gourd? He replied: I am grieved enough to die.

"Then the Lord said: You would spare the gourd though you spent no work upon it. You did not make it grow—it sprang up in a night and perished in a night. Should I not, then, spare the great city of Nineveh with more than a hundred and twenty thousand human beings, who do not know their right hand from their left?"

YOTSER   יוֹצֵר

YOTSER is the name given to a variety of prayer-poems (*piyyutim*), inserted within the framework of the *Shema* during the morning service of festivals. The term is derived from the phrase יוֹצֵר אוֹר (he forms light), used in the so-called *yotser* benediction that precedes the *Shema;* it emphasizes the goodness of the Creator of light who daily renews the creation. The plural form *yotseroth* is sometimes misapplied to *piyyutim* or liturgical hymns in general.

Because of the inconvenience produced by the numerous traditional melodies that prolong the service, there has been a tendency to omit the *yotseroth*, or else to read them quickly in an undertone, only the concluding stanzas being intoned by the *ḥazzan* or *baal tefillah*. The *yotseroth* are referred to by various titles.

264

EZEKIEL   יְחֶזְקֵאל

EZEKIEL, who lived during the last days of the First Temple and received inspiration from the prophetic utterances of Jeremiah, his elder contemporary, prophesied in Babylon for a period of twenty-two years, having been taken into captivity eleven years before the fall of Jerusalem.

Prior to the destruction of the Temple by Nebuchadnezzar in 586 before the common era, Ezekiel's prophecies were messages of doom; after it, they were messages of hope and assurances of restoration. Dwelling on a prophet's responsibility for the fate of his people, Ezekiel maintains that a prophet is a watchman, responsible for warning his people of the consequences of misdoings.

"Son of man, I set you up as a watchman for the people of Israel. If you say nothing to warn the wicked man from his evil course, that his life may be saved, the wicked man shall die for his iniquity; but I will hold you responsible for his death. . . I have no pleasure in the death of anyone who dies. . . Return and live!" (3:17-19; 18:23, 32).

Ezekiel tells us that each man possesses the power to be good or evil regardless of heredity and predisposition; the individual is master of his own destiny and responsible for his own deeds. "If a man oppresses no one and robs no one; if he feeds the hungry and clothes the naked; if he abstains from crime and observes strict justice between man and man—he is upright and shall surely live. If he has a son who is a violent man . . . that son shall not live . . . he is responsible for his own death" (18:5-13).

Ezekiel stresses the idea that everybody can turn over a new leaf and look hopefully toward the future. His vision of the dry bones vividly illustrates the hope of restoration and revival of a nation that was given up as dead. The final eight chapters of Ezekiel express the prophet's firm belief in a forthcoming restoration, Israel rising to new life from the graveyard of the captivity, rid of its evils and re-established under the rule of God.

The book of Ezekiel is the third of the Latter Prophets, the first two books being those of Isaiah and Jeremiah. Its forty-eight chapters are divided into two equal parts. The first twenty-four chapters contain speeches uttered by Ezekiel prior to the national disaster of 586. The last twenty-four chapters consist of visions that occurred after the destruction of Jerusalem. The final chapters concerning the glorious future of Israel have provided the Jewish people with a beacon of light through the lonely years of exile.

Ezekiel has been described as one of the most interesting figures among Israel's prophets. His famous vision of the dry bones in chapter thirty-seven expresses a firm belief in a forthcoming restoration, Israel rising to new life from the graveyard of the *Galuth*.

"He said to me: Son of man, can these bones live? . . . Prophesy to these bones and say to them: O dry bones, listen to the word of the Lord. Thus says the Lord God: Behold, I will cause breath to enter into you, and you shall live. . . While I was prophesying, there was a rattling sound—the bones came together, bone to bone. And as I looked, there were sinews upon them! Flesh and skin spread over them, but there was no breath in them. Then he said to me: Prophesy to the breath, son of man, and say to the breath: Thus says the Lord God: Come from the four ends of the earth, O breath, and breathe into these lifeless bodies that they may live. . .

"Then he said to me: Son of man, these bones are the people of Israel. Behold, they keep saying: Our bones are dry, our hope is lost. . . Prophesy therefore to them and tell them: Thus says the Lord God: O my people, I will open your graves and bring you back to the land of Israel. . . I will put my spirit into you, and you shall live. I will place you in your own land; then you shall know that I, the Lord, have spoken and performed it."

YEIN NESEKH יֵין נֶסֶךְ

WINE handled by an idolater was called *wine of libation* (יֵין נֶסֶךְ), wine from which a libation to a heathen god was made. The supposition was that the idolater may have dedicated the wine as an offering to his deity; hence it was forbidden to drink it and thus become indirectly guilty of an act of heathenism. This regulation, as well as the dietary laws, made it difficult for a Jew to dine with non-Jews unless they were invited to his table.

We are told that Daniel "resolved that he would not defile himself with the king's food, nor with the wine which he drank" (Daniel 1:8), because the king's food might consist of the meat of unclean animals, or might not be freed from blood, or part of it might have been offered in sacrifice to idols: some of the wine might have been poured out as a libation to the gods.

266

YALKUT SHIMEONI   יַלְקוּט שִׁמְעוֹנִי

THE most comprehensive midrashic collection known as the *Yalkut* (anthology) has been attributed to Rabbi Simeon of Frankfort, who lived in thirteenth-century Germany. It represents a rich treasury of *aggadic*, ethical-historical statements, compiled from more than fifty sources, some of which are no longer in existence, and is arranged according to the twenty-four books of the Hebrew Bible.

The two parts of *Yalkut Shimeoni* contain: 963 paragraphs devoted to the interpretation of the five books of the Torah, and 1,085 paragraphs given to the interpretation of the remaining nineteen books of the Bible. Lengthy quotations from ancient works are often abridged.

AWE-INSPIRING DAYS   יָמִים נוֹרָאִים

THOUGH the Torah does not explicitly indicate the close connection between *Rosh Hashanah* and *Yom Kippur*, the two festivals are represented in Jewish tradition as parts of a unit known as *Asereth Yemé Teshuvah*, the first ten days of the year dedicated to a spiritual regeneration and religious rehabilitation. *Rosh Hashanah* is the beginning and *Yom Kippur* is the culmination of the special ten-day season within which man is offered the opportunity of a spiritual recovery by strenuous personal effort.

According to talmudic tradition, three books are opened on *Rosh Hashanah*: one of the perfectly righteous, one of the completely wicked, and one of the intermediate class which embraces the vast majority of mankind. "The perfectly righteous are immediately inscribed and sealed to life; the completely wicked are immediately inscribed and sealed to death; the intermediate are in suspense (will neither be punished nor acquitted) until *Yom Kippur*. If they repent, they are inscribed to life; if not, they are inscribed to death" (Rosh Hashanah 16b).

In Daniel 7:10 we find mention of books opened in the heavenly court ("the court sat in judgment and the books were opened"). The Mishnah speaks of the record of man's actions in the books of heaven, where "the ledger is open and the hand writes" (Avoth 2:1; 3:20). That the deeds of the righteous and of the wicked are divinely recorded is alluded to in Isaiah 65:6; Malachi 3:16. The book of life is mentioned in Isaiah 4:3; Psalms 69:29; Daniel 12:1. As a result of the pictorial language used by the Talmud in reference to the judgment passed according to merit, it has become customary to greet one another with the blessing: לשנה טובה תכתבו ותחתמו ("May you be inscribed and sealed for a good year").

YA'ALEH V'YAVO   יַעֲלֶה וְיָבֹא

THE prayer beginning with the words *Ya'aleh v'Yavo* (may it ascend and arrive) is added to the *Amidah* or *Shemoneh Esreh* and the *Birkath ha-Mazon* (grace after meals) on *Rosh Ḥodesh* and all sacred festivals. It is not inserted on *Ḥanukkah* and *Purim*, when the prayer *Al ha-Nissim* is added instead. The Talmud refers to this prayer by mentioning the need of remembering the new month in the seventeenth benediction of the *Shemoneh Esreh* (Berakhoth 29b). In Sofrim 19:11, this prayer is quoted as part of the *Birkath ha-Mazon*.

It is based on the following passage in the Torah: "On your feasts and new moon festivals you shall sound the trumpets . . . they will serve as a reminder of you before your God" (Numbers 10:10). In the synagogues, it is customary to call out *Ya'aleh v'Yavo* before the *Amidah* on the eve of *Rosh Ḥodesh* as a reminder to the congregation to insert it in the proper place. Recited for the prosperity of the people and for deliverance and happiness, kindness and mercy, life and peace, *Ya'aleh v'Yavo* refers also to Jerusalem, Messiah, and Israel.

YA'AROTH DVASH   יַעֲרוֹת דְּבַשׁ

THE book *Ya'aroth Dvash* contains the best known collection of the sermons of Rabbi Jonathan Eybeshitz (1690-1764), who was one of the wisest and most learned talmudic scholars of his time. He was very popular as a preacher. He revealed a wide familiarity with the sciences of the day, and was well acquainted with the main works of the medieval Jewish thinkers.

Rabbi Jonathan Eybeshitz taught in part: Judaism imposes no severe restrictions on the flesh. We are not asked to walk barefoot on snow and sleet, to wear coarse garments next to the skin, to torture the body for the good of the soul. In Judaism the duties of religion are calculated to bring joy rather than pain. We are unlike other religious groups who seek to attain saintliness through a dis-

268

cipline of self-mortification. Even the Day of Atonement is ushered in with a festive meal. Heathen philosophers may advance the claim that the divine spirit can rest on a man only when he lives in solitude and in self-abnegation; but our Jewish thinkers justly contend that no such preparations, no such conditions and surroundings, are required for the disclosure of the prophetic visions.

Moderation in all things is with us an essential religious precept. The possession of too much money is superfluous and injurious. Great wealth has often been instrumental in alienating the Jew from his God and his people. Human happiness flows rather from a contented disposition than from the abundance of material possessions. The aim of our religious discipline is to sublimate the pleasures of the senses, to strip them of their grossness and extravagance. Judaism seeks to invest the smallest physical detail with purposefulness and sanctity.

We have always regarded the Torah as the heritage of the entire people. Even one quarter of an hour devoted to the study of some ethical work will bring spiritual refreshment. What medical treatment is to the diseased body, ethical instruction is to the confused soul. God's love for Israel is determined and sustained by the upright life we live. Suffering often serves the purpose of arousing a man from the spiritual stupor into which his folly has cast him. When we violently shake a man who has fallen into a blank stupor, is it our intention to chastise him? We must never surrender our trust in God.

Let us remember always that we have an important role to play in the spiritual regeneration of the world. When a people never tires of affirming the truth for which it stands, an enlightened world cannot but feel impelled to probe the nature of that truth. We must continue to face the world as a separate and indivisible group. Joined one to the other, we gain fullness of stature and become complete, well-rounded personalities.

EXODUS FROM EGYPT   יְצִיאַת מִצְרַיִם

NEARLY all the fundamental precepts of Judaism are linked to the historic event of Israel's exodus from Egypt. The most enduring meaning of the exodus is suggested by the Ten Commandments, which begin with the words: "I am the Lord your God who brought you out of the land of Egypt." The Torah frequently makes use of the remembrance of Egypt as a motivation for the performance of basic ethical precepts: "You shall not molest or oppress an alien, for you were once aliens yourselves in the land of Egypt. You shall not wrong any widow or orphan. . . You shall not oppress an alien; you well know how it feels to be an alien, since you were once aliens yourselves in the land of Egypt. . . You shall treat the alien who resides with you no differently than the native citizen, and you shall have the same love for him as for yourself; for you too were once aliens in the land of Egypt" (Exodus 22:20; 23:9; Leviticus 19:34).

The people of Israel were not permitted to hate even the Egyptians who had enslaved them: "Do not abhor the Edomite, since he is your brother; do not abhor an Egyptian, since you were an alien in his country" (Deuteronomy 23:8). That is to say, since the Israelites had found a home in Egypt even though as slaves, the Egyptians must be remembered with gratitude. The Latin word *hostis*, denoting both stranger and enemy, is significant as indicative of a quite different attitude on the part of the ancient Romans toward strangers.

Jewish tradition has it that the ancient Egyptians were polluted with sin and addicted to both witchcraft and lust. No slave could escape from Egypt. As soon as a fugitive slave met any of the magic dogs and lions and bulls, they would bark, roar, and bellow until the fugitive was captured; but at the time of the exodus none of the animals raised its voice.

The Egyptians who reduced the Israelites to cruel slavery, we are told, made life bitter for them with hard work in mortar and brick and all kinds of field work. "The king of Egypt told the Hebrew midwives . . . if it is a boy, kill him. . . Pharaoh then commanded all his subjects: Throw into the river every boy that is born to the Hebrews. . ." (Exodus 1:16, 22). All this well explains the historic importance of the exodus which led to the creation of Israel as a people with a faith in One God and with a Torah as a guide for civilized man.

The pyramid on the Giza plateau, five miles from Cairo, rises as high as a modern 40-story building. Countless thousands of masons, quarrymen and laborers toiled for thirty years. The stones with which it was built range in weight from about two and a half tons to 15 tons. There are nearly 2,500,000 such blocks in the Great Pyramid, yet the men who quarried them and raised them into position had no mechanical aids except the lever, the roller and the inclined plane. Approximately 100,000 in number were put to manual tasks in the pyramid's construction. Under the direction of overseers they were organized in gangs. Some twenty years of unspeakable toil was thus invested in

270

the erection of one of the eighty pyramids that are scattered along the west bank of the Nile—sepulchers built for tyrannical Pharaohs who longed for immortality.

YATSIV PITHGAM   יַצִּיב פִּתְגָּם

ON the second day of *Shavuoth*, before the reading of the *Haftarah* during the congregational service, an Aramaic *piyyut* (prayer-poem) is recited, named *Yatsiv Pithgam* (true is the word) and composed by Rabbi Jacob ben Meir, a grandson of Rashi. The author of the poem is the famous tosafist *Rabbenu Tam* (1100-1171), whose home at Ramerupt, France, was destroyed by Crusaders in 1147, and he himself narrowly escaped death. He then settled at Troyes, where he headed conferences of French rabbis, the decisions of which are known as the ordinances of Rabbenu Tam. He was the chief exponent of the tosafist method of interpreting the Talmud. He also wrote *piyyutim* and notes on Hebrew grammar. *Yatsiv Pithgam* is the counterpart of *Akdamuth*, which is recited on the first day of *Shavuoth*. According to some scholars, who are quoted in Davidson's *Thesaurus of Medieval Poetry*, *Yatsiv Pithgam* is by an unidentified Jacob ben Meir.

The name of the author and that of his father יעקב ברבי מאיר לוי are indicated in the form of an acrostic at the beginning of the fifteen lines of *Yatsiv Pithgam*, which includes the following prayer: "May the King who lives forever protect his people, whom he destined to be countless. May their valleys be white with flocks of sheep; may their presses flow with wine. . ."

NATURAL IMPULSE   יֵצֶר

THE good impulse (*yetser tov*) and the evil impulse (*yetser ra*) are pictured in Jewish literature as wrestling in perpetual conflict within the heart of man. Satan is usually identified with the *yetser ha-ra*, the evil impulse. In the book of Job, Satan's function is described as that of testing the sincerity of men's characters. In talmudic literature, Satan's function is to strengthen man's moral sense by leading him into temptation. It has been said that every man living shall assuredly meet with an hour of temptation, a certain critical hour, which shall more especially try his mettle.

According to a midrashic statement (Genesis Rabbah 9:9), the existence of the *yetser ha-ra* in the heart of man and the struggle to overcome it lends high value to the good that emerges from the inner battle. The two conflicting impulses, the good and bad tendencies, are said to be implanted in man as a consequence of his having been *formed* (יצר) from the dust and endowed with a soul (Genesis 2:7).

According to rabbinic thinking, the evil impulse is to be found in man at birth; the good impulse begins to develop when he is thirteen years old. The teachings of the Torah are referred to as the antidote to the *yetser ha-ra*. Similarly, Ben Sira (21:11) states: "The man who keeps the Law controls his natural tendency."

In commenting on the two *yods* in the word וייצר (Genesis 2:7), the rabbis declare that God created both the *yetser tov* and the *yetser ra* (Berakhoth 61a). The command to love God "with *all* your heart" they interpret to mean "with both your impulses" (Berakhoth 54a), since both human elements can be employed in the service of God. "Were it not for the *yetser ha-ra*, no man would build a home or get married or follow an occupation" (Genesis Rabbah 9:9). The phrase "very good" (Genesis 1:31) is therefore explained, as alluding to the *yetser ha-ra*, frequently used in the sense of the productive urge.

YEKUM PURKAN

THE Aramaic prayer *Yekum Purkan* (may salvation arise) was composed in Babylonia, where Aramaic remained the daily language of the Jews for more than a thousand years, until the ninth century when Arabic became the popular language.

There are two *Yekum Purkan* prayers, both of which are phrased alike and recited on the Sabbath, following the public reading of the Torah. The first was composed on behalf of Babylonian and Palestinian scholars and leaders; the second is a prayer for the congregation, "great and small, women and children."

In order to make the first *Yekum Purkan* applicable to our own times, Baer suggested to amplify it by the addition of four words to include "all the lands of our Diaspora."

But he refrained from tampering with text itself to remove anachronisms. Curiously enough, *Yekum Purkan* is not included in the Babylonian *Siddurim* of Rav Amram Gaon and Rav Saadyah Gaon, but is mentioned in *Maḥzor Vitry* which has come down to us from France.

272

PIETY   יִרְאַת הַשֵּׁם

THE idea that religion is the foundation of all wisdom is frequently expressed by the sages of Israel. "Reverence for God (יראת השם) is the beginning of wisdom" (Psalm 111:10). "Reverence for the Lord is the beginning of knowledge" (Proverbs 1:7). True morality, that is, must be based on a right relation to God. The talmudic phrase "dread of sin" (יראת חטא), though negative in form, is intensely positive in meaning. It is employed synonymously with יראת שמים (reverence for God) in the sense that it is not enough merely to refrain from wrongdoing, but to be ever ready to do what is right.

In his *Mishneh Torah*, Maimonides conveys the thought concerning true piety in the following terms: When a person contemplates God's great and wondrous works and obtains a glimpse of God's incomparable and infinite wisdom, he will straightway love and glorify him ... even as David said: "My whole being longs for God, the living God!" He will realize that man is a small creature, lowly and obscure, with but limited intelligence, standing in the presence of him who is perfect in knowledge (*Yesodé ha-Torah* 2:2).

Here are several statements on Piety: "Anyone whose dread of sin precedes his wisdom (whose moral conduct means more to him than his learning), his wisdom shall endure. . ." (Avoth 3:11). "A man who possesses learning without reverence for God is like the man who has been entrusted with the keys of an inner court but not with the keys of the outer court; how is he to enter?" (Shabbath 31b). "He who wishes to be pious must first fulfill the precepts of the Ethics of the Fathers" (Bava Kamma 30a). "A man should always find out new ways of piety, always striving to be on the best terms with his fellow men . . . even with the heathen in the street, that he may be beloved above and well-liked below. . . A man who lives from the labor of his hands is greater than one who is pious" (Berakhoth 8a; 37a).

JEREMIAH   יִרְמְיָה

THE book of Jeremiah is the longest of the prophetic books, even though it has fourteen chapters less than Isaiah. Jeremiah's dictations to his faithful secretary Baruch were written down upon a scroll of leather, which the king of Judah slashed with a knife and burned.

But the prophet was not easily discouraged. He ordered his scribe to take another scroll and write therein all the words of the book which the king had burned.

Jeremiah began to prophesy in Jerusalem about twenty years after the death of Isaiah. More is known about his life and teachings than about any other prophet, since the book of Jeremiah contains much historical and biographical material. He was gentle and sensitive, yearning for the comforts of a normal life; yet he felt impelled to speak the truth and be "a man of strife and contention." He delivered messages of doom and foretold the fall of Jerusalem, and was often imprisoned and in danger of his life. Yet he did not flinch. He was cruelly insulted and accused of treason by the people he loved tenderly—those whom he sought to save.

After the fall of Jerusalem in 586 before the common era, he was forcibly taken into Egypt by those who fled the wrath of the Babylonian conqueror. Tradition reports that Nebuchadnezzar, king of Babylon, had instructed his general to treat Jeremiah with consideration and kindness. But the prophet insisted on sharing the hardships and tortures that were inflicted on his people. Afterwards Jeremiah was killed in Egypt, where he had continued his fiery speeches.

Jeremiah also foretold the restoration of Israel, and those who survived the agonies of captivity were promised a safe journey home to Judea. He looked forward to a reunion of deported Israel with the people of Judah, to an ingathering of all the exiles: "Restrain your voice from weeping, your eyes from tears . . . your children shall return to their own land. I will gather them from all the countries where I have driven them. I will bring them back to this place, where I will make them dwell in safety. . ." (31:15 ff).

Jeremiah's influence on his people was greater after his death than before. Arrest, imprisonment and public disgrace were his lot when alive. After his death, the exiled Judeans in Babylon religiously meditated his lessons and were guided by them. Jeremiah's influence is clearly reflected in the visions of Ezekiel, who became a prophet in Babylon and prepared his fellow exiles for Nebuchadnezzar's destruction of Jerusalem, which they believed to be inviolable. Combining prophecy, biography and history, the book of Jeremiah is replete with expressions that are poignant, vehement and meaningful to generations of all time. Excerpts: "Two evils have my people done: they have forsaken me, the source of fresh water; they have dug themselves cisterns, broken cisterns, that hold no water.

274

"Is Israel a slave? Why then has he become a prey? The lions have roared at him, growling loudly. They have made his land a waste; his cities are in ruins, empty of inhabitants... Behold a people is coming out of the northland, a great nation is stirring from the far ends of the earth! They are cruel and have no mercy; the sound of them is like the roaring sea... If you truly mend your ways and your deeds, if you really practise justice between man and man, if you do not oppress strangers, orphans or widows, I will allow you to remain in this place, in the land I gave to your fathers, forever... These are the words of the letter which Jeremiah the prophet sent to the people whom Nebuchadnezzar had exiled to Babylon: Build houses and live in them; plant gardens and eat their fruit; take wives and beget sons and daughters... Seek the welfare of the country where you have been exiled; pray to the Lord for it, since your welfare rests on its welfare.

"I will gather them from all the countries where I drove them; I will bring them back to this place, where I will make them dwell in safety... In this land that you call desolate, fields shall again be bought. Men shall buy fields for money in the places round about Jerusalem and in the Negev..."

INHERITANCE

THE law of inheritance as given in the Torah reads: "If a man dies without leaving a son, you shall let his heritage pass on to his daughter; if he has no daughter, you shall give his heritage to his brothers; if he has no brothers, you shall give his heritage to his father's brothers; if his father had no brothers, you shall give his heritage to his nearest relative" (Numbers 27:8-11).

Unlike modern law, it is not the individual who appoints his heirs, but the law of the Torah, though one may give preference to one rightful heir over the other. He may, however, provide for his property to pass after his death by way of gift. Illegitimate children or children of prohibited marriages have the same rights as their legitimate brothers and sisters.

A firstborn son takes a double share of the father's estate but not of the mother's. It has been suggested that the origin of the double share goes back to the extra expense borne by the firstborn son in bearing the administrative responsibility as the family representative

Later Jewish law developed the following order of inheritance: sons and their descendants; daughters and their descendants; the father; brothers and their descendants; sisters and their descendants; the father's sisters and their descendants; the husband.

While denying the daughters a share where there are sons, the rabbinic law makes adequate provision for their maintenance as long as they remain unmarried. The principle laid down is: "The daughters must be supported, even if the sons are reduced to beggary." Hence, the cost of such maintenance is the first charge upon the estate of the deceased individual.

Though a husband inherits his wife's property, a wife does not inherit from her husband, but her support remains a first charge on his estate until she remarries. A man cannot disinherit his son, though he may, in his lifetime, give his estate to a stranger in the form of a gift. A trustee (*epitropos*) is appointed to take care of the estate until the heirs are of age. There is a moral obligation to pay the father's debts even if they exceed the amount inherited.

YESHIVAH ישיבה

THE terms *yeshivah* and *methivta*, found in the Talmud, are used synonymously for the oldest institution of Jewish learning, devoted primarily to Talmud and rabbinic literature. Originally, these terms signified a meeting of scholars, a council, a session, over which presided an elected *rosh yeshivah* or, in Aramaic, *resh methivta*. The *yeshivoth* that were established in medieval Europe were a direct continuation of the academies that flourished during the talmudic and geonic periods in Eretz Yisrael and Babylonia.

"Nearly all communities in Poland supported a *yeshivah*," writes Nathan Hannover in his *Yeven Metsulah*, which was published in 1653. "They maintained the students and gave them weekly allowances out of public funds. . . In addition to receiving fixed stipends the students were invited as guests, every household having invariably one or more such guests from the *yeshivah*. The number of *hakhamim* (scholars) increased to such an extent that very often there were found twenty *hakhamim* bearing the title of *morenu* or *haver* in a community of fifty *baalé batim* (householders). . ."

The famous *yeshivah* of Volozhin was organized in 1803 by Rabbi Ḥayyim, foremost disciple of Rabbi Elijah Vilna-Gaon, on principles

276

advocated by his great master. His main objective was to make the students independent of private charity. He started with ten students, whom he supported out of his own means, for he was a rich merchant. When the number of students became too large for his means, he appealed for aid to the neighboring communities. When he died in 1828, the *yeshivah* was continued under the leadership of his son Rabbi Isaac, who was succeeded by his son-in-law Rabbi Naphtali Tzevi Berlin in 1854. After Rabbi Berlin's death in 1893, the *yeshivah* was under the management of Rabbi Joseph Baer Soloveichik.

Under the leadership of Rabbi Berlin, known as הנצי"ב, the Volozhin *yeshivah* attained its highest efficiency, having nearly four hundred students. Poor and rich students alike flocked to the Volozhin academy from all parts of Europe and America, thus wandering forth to a home of Torah (Avoth 4:18). The cost of maintenance was collected by *meshullaḥim*, emissaries sent to raise funds for the institution. Rabbi Berlin was one of the first rabbis to support Zionism. In 1887, he was elected a leader of the *Ḥoveve Zion*.

The *yeshivah* system was transplanted in America, where the first talmudical academy, *Ets Ḥayyim*, was organized in 1886 in New York. The Yeshivah University of New York traces its origins to *Yeshivath Ets Ḥayyim* and the Rabbi Isaac Elḥanan Theological Seminary, founded in 1896. When the two merged in 1915, they became first the Yeshivah College (1928) and then Yeshivah University (1945).

The expression ישיבה של מעלה (academy on high) is used in the sense of a heavenly academy, consisting of those who studied Torah on earth and those who supported them. It is another description of *Gan Eden* or Paradise. A euphemism for death is to be called to the *Yeshivah shel Maalah*, in which the study of Torah is continued.

ISAIAH   יְשַׁעְיָה

THE book of Isaiah, containing sixty-six chapters, is the first of the three Major Prophets, the other two being the books of Jeremiah and Ezekiel. The term Major refers to the fact that these prophetic books are longer than the other prophetic books in the Bible.

The fortieth chapter of Isaiah, introducing the great theme of deliverance and restoration, has been credited by scholars to another, second Isaiah. This second Isaiah is referred to as the great unknown

prophet of the exile, because chapters forty through sixty-six are
addressed to the Jews in the Babylonian exile, which occurred more
than a century after the first Isaiah.

The eloquence of the entire book of Isaiah is without parallel in
the literature of the ancient world. Because of the grandeur of his
style and the great power of his personality, Isaiah is considered the
greatest of the Judean prophets.

Isaiah began his prophetic career toward the end of the eighth century before the common era, at a time when there was abundant
prosperity in Judea, vast stores of silver and gold, and a tremendous
variety of treasure. He witnessed the growth of large estates, the
oppression of the poor, the pursuit of wanton pleasure, and the spread
of idolatrous practices.

He was convinced that all this could not continue with impunity.
If it persists, he warned, God will destroy both the kingdom of Israel
and the kingdom of Judah. According to tradition, Isaiah was of
royal blood. He suffered martyrdom by being torn asunder when
King Manasseh persecuted the loyal worshipers of the God of Israel.

Isaiah appeared at a critical moment of his people's history. The
second half of the eighth century, before the common era, witnessed
the collapse of the Kingdom of Israel under the blows of Assyria (722),
while Jerusalem itself, the capital of Judea, was besieged by the army
of Sennacherib (701). Little is known about the last days of Isaiah.
His fiery prophetic utterances, of singular poetic beauty and power,
constantly remind his people of their destiny. Excerpts:

"Strengthen the feeble-handed, make firm the weak-kneed; say to
those with fluttering hearts: Have courage, fear not!... Then the
blind shall see, and the deaf shall hear. Waters shall break forth in
the wilderness, and streams in the desert; the burning sand shall become a pool, and the thirsty ground—springs of waters... Look
around you, look! They all gather together, they come to you, your
sons from far away, your little daughters in arms! See and be radiant,
let your heart thrill and rejoice...

"Loosen the chains of wickedness, undo the bonds of oppression,
let the crushed go free, break all yokes of tyranny! Share your food
with the hungry, take the poor to your home, clothe the naked when
you see them, and never turn from your fellow man... For Zion's
sake I will not keep silent, for Jerusalem's sake I will not rest until
her triumph comes forth clear as light, and her deliverance like a blazing torch... They shall build houses and inhabit them; they shall

plant vineyards and eat their fruit. They shall not build houses for others to live in, or plant for others to eat. . . They shall not toil in vain. . . Before they call, I will answer; while they are yet speaking, I will hearken to them. The wolf and the lamb shall graze together, and the lion shall eat hay like the ox, but the serpent's food shall be dust. None shall hurt or destroy throughout my holy mountain, says the Lord."

ISRAEL   יִשְׂרָאֵל

THE name *Yisrael*, given to Jacob when he was returning from Mesopotamia and expecting to meet Esau, has been interpreted in the sense of striving for God, or "a champion of God." Down to the death of Saul, the designation בני ישראל (people of Israel) comprehended all the descendants of Jacob, without distinction of tribes. When the people had split into two kingdoms, *Israel* was frequently used to denote the ten tribes belonging to the Northern Kingdom. As compared with the Kingdom of Judah in the south, the Kingdom of Israel had twice the population and nearly three times the extent of territory than its rival dominion.

It has been noted that the descendants of Jacob entered Egypt as a group of related families and came out of Egypt as a people with a distinct individuality. "The long sojourn in the land of the Nile failed to submerge them in the great civilization surrounding them or to stifle their native genius. Even when they had spread beyond the narrow confines of Goshen and had penetrated into Egypt proper, and had also been forced into Egyptian economy as laborers . . . they preserved their Hebrew identity. . . The influence of Egyptian civilization on the Hebrew immigrants was slight and, if at all, confined to the handicrafts. . . In the realm of ideas the Egyptian civilization exercised no influence whatever upon Israel. . .

"The Egyptian religion with its devotion to the worship of beasts and reptiles, and with its deification of the Pharaohs, must have aroused in the heart of the Israelites feelings of profound repugnance and contempt. . . Thus Israel formed in Egypt a closed Hebrew community in the midst of a large Egyptian world around it. . . It continued to cultivate as best it could the faith it had inherited from the patriarchs with its few symbols, such as circumcision and occasional worship. . . With the monotheistic faith of Abraham the children of

279

Jacob carried down to Egypt also the traditions embodied in the first two parts of Genesis ... and the patriarchal traditions formed in Canaan before the migration to Egypt. .." (M. H. Segal).

The Talmud characterizes Israel by mercy, modesty, and benevolence (Yevamoth 79a). In the face of unparalleled persecution, Israel as a people has managed to preserve its mental and moral vigor.

YISHTABBAH יִשְׁתַּבַּח

YISHTABBAH and *Barukh Sheamar*, respectively, form the prologue and the epilogue to the biblical mosaic of *Pesuké d'Zimrah* (verses of song), a section of the daily morning service, preceding the *Shema* and the *Shemoneh Esreh*. The concluding benediction *Yishtabbah*, containing fifteen synonyms of praise, is expanded on Sabbath and festivals by the addition of *Nishmath*, known as *birkath ha-shir* (Pesahim 118a).

ORPHAN יָתוֹם

THE Torah repeatedly emphasizes the duty of kindly consideration of the weak, the oppressed and the poor. The widow and the orphan, who are bereft of their human protector, are championed by God who defends their rights. "You shall not afflict any widow or orphan. If ever you afflict them and they cry out to me, I will surely hear their cry, and my wrath will flare up. . ." (Exodus 22:21-23). "The Lord protects strangers; he sustains the fatherless and the widow" (Psalm 146:9). These are typical of all human beings who are too weak to defend themselves against injustice and oppression.

The care of an orphan, who is a minor in need of protection, is regarded as especially meritorious. "He who brings up an orphan is deemed as though he were his real father" (Sanhedrin 19b). As long as the boy cannot manage his own affairs he is treated as an orphan (*Yad, De'oth* 6:10). Maimonides points out that one must deal with orphans gently and kindly, and must not speak harshly to them; their guardian must take greater care of their property than of his own. Even while teaching them the Torah or a trade, which may be done against their will, they must be treated differently from other pupils. In this respect, the fatherless and the motherless are alike. Certain privileges, however, are extended only to the fatherless.

280

HONOR

MARKS of distinction (*kavod*) accorded to individuals are represented in talmudic literature as tokens of self-respect or honor of self. "Let your friend's honor be as dear as your own... Who is honored? One who honors fellow men... Do not despise any man... Cherish the honor of your student as your own" (Avoth 2:15; 4:1, 3, 15).

Rabbi Akiva once sentenced a man to pay four hundred silver pieces as compensation for the embarrassment he had caused a woman by letting down her hair in the street. When the man brought witnesses to testify that the woman lacked in self-respect, Rabbi Akiva said: Even though she is not punishable for disgracing herself, others are for dishonoring her.

A talmudic statement reads: "Be careful about the honor of your wife, for blessing enters the house only because of the wife" (Bava Metzia 59a). And elsewhere: "Love your wife as much as yourself; honor her more than yourself... If your wife is short, bend your head and take her advice." Furthermore, we are told that honor is due to oneself in the form of cleanliness and proper clothes, and work which renders man independent (גדולה מלאכה שמכבדת את בעליה). "It is not the place that honors the man, but the man that honors the place" (Sanhedrin 113b; Nedarim 49b; Ta'anith 21b).

On the other hand, "whoever promotes his own honor at the expense of his neighbor's degradation has no share in the world to come" (Genesis Rabbah 1:5). "Throw yourself into a blazing furnace rather than shame a fellow man in public" (Berakhoth 43b). "God grant that you neither shame nor be shamed" (Mo'ed Katan 9b).

The Talmud states that high position flees from him who hunts for it, and follows him who flees from it (Eruvin 13b). "Great is human dignity, since it overrides a negative precept of the Torah" (Berakhoth 19b). "A man should eat and drink beneath his means, clothe himself within his means, and honor his wife and children above his means" (Ḥullin 84b).

Rabbi Moses Ḥayyim Luzzatto (1707-1747), in his *Mesillath Yesharim*, writes: "Pride is an exaggerated sense of our own importance and an inward belief that we deserve praise... Whoever would attain the trait of cleanness must be free from the taint of pride. He must realize that pride is a form of blindness which prevents even a man of understanding from seeing his own shortcomings."

281

HONORING PARENTS   כִּבּוּד אָב וָאֵם

W E must honor and revere our parents in the same manner as it is our obligation to honor and revere God. Mutual reverence between parents and children has been the basic principle of Jewish family life.

The Talmud refers to parents as God's co-partners in creation, hence the extreme care with which they must be respected by their children. The duty extends beyond the grave: the memory of departed parents must be cherished in many ways. Rabbi David Kimhi, the famous medieval Bible commentator (1160-1235), regularly cites his father as *adoni avi* (my noble father). The works of Rabbi David Kimhi ultimately superseded those of his father, Rabbi Joseph Kimhi.

According to Jewish law, the son is not to occupy his father's seat; he is not to contradict him, or call him by his name. He can be compelled to maintain his parents. He must provide them with all their needs cheerfully; if he supports them with ill grace, he is said to incur divine punishment. He should under no circumstances insult them or display anger towards them. Though a daughter, too, is bound to honor her parents and do for them all she can, she is exempt from certain duties after her marriage, when she comes under her husband's authority and owes him devotion.

On the other hand, a parent is forbidden to be burdensome upon his children; he must not be too exacting. He should rather ignore their shortcomings and forgive them. A parent is forbidden to beat his grown son. The father especially exercises authority over the children during their minority, which ends with the boy at the beginning of the fourteenth year and with the girl at the beginning of the thirteenth. Anyone who beats his grown children is said to deserve excommunication, because in so doing he transgresses the divine command: "You shall not place an obstacle in front of the blind, but you shall revere your God" (Leviticus 19:14). A grown son, if enraged by his father, is likely to strike back.

As the child grows older, his father must be extremely careful not to treat him harshly or overdiscipline him. He must learn to treat him with gentleness and refrain from rudeness or violence in addressing him. He should be very careful about the example he sets to his children both in speech and action. He should be especially careful not to use unclean language. He should treat all his children equally in matters of clothes and presents, so as not to create envy among

282

them. He should not make a big display of his love for his children,
lest they become spoiled. He should love them equally. Sometimes
the favored disappoint, and the neglected make a man happy.

Jewish tradition stresses the performance of good deeds and Torah
study as the best method of honoring parents. A son who does not
follow the right path disgraces his parents; otherwise, people are apt
to say: "Happy are the parents who have brought up such a child!"
A father, too, who is concerned about the welfare of his children,
should engage in the practice of good deeds, so that he may cause his
children to be proud of him. When parents are upright, there is no
limit to the reverence they deserve. Only a parent who leads an ex-
emplary life and gives proper training to his children is entitled to
respect and obedience.

PRIESTS   כֹּהֲנִים

T<small>HE</small> Jewish priest was born, not made. Only those were admitted to
the priesthood who could prove their descent from Aaron. When the
Jews returned from the Babylonian captivity, all those who claimed
priestly rank but were unable to produce documentary evidence of
their descent from Aaron were disqualified (Ezra 2:62).

The principal duties of the priests were those connected with the
sacrificial service of the Temple in Jerusalem, as well as teaching the
people the laws of the Torah. In the course of time, the number of
priests increased to such an extent that it was necessary to divide them
into twenty-four divisions, serving in the Temple in rotation each for
one week. Each division (*mishmar*) was subdivided into several families (בתי אבות), who served one each day.

This gave every priest an opportunity of discharging his duty.
Since the priests were allowed no share in the land, the Torah assigned
certain benefits to them in compensation, which originally formed
their sole source of income. At the three great annual festivals, known
as the pilgrimage festivals (*Pesah, Shavuoth, Sukkoth*), all the twenty-
four divisions are said to have officiated simultaneously.

The high priest, who was the spiritual head of the people, was regarded at times as the secular head of the community as well. During the Hellenistic period, his contact with the foreign rulers, for
whom he collected the taxes of the people, introduced a process of
assimilation among the priests.

In the storm and stress of the times, the real control of priestly pedigrees has been replaced by family tradition. The duties and privileges of priests are now limited to pronouncing the priestly benediction on festival days, the avoidance of contact with a corpse, the redemption of the firstborn males on the thirty-first day after birth (*pidyon ha-ben*), and the precedence of a *kohen* at functions such as the public Torah reading.

KUZARI כּוּזָרִי

THE *Kuzari*, the great philosophic work of the foremost Hebrew poet Rabbi Yehudah Halevi (1085-1142), is regarded as one of the classics of Judaism. Its chief purpose is to show that the continuity of Jewish tradition is the best proof of the validity of the Jewish faith. Written in the form of a discussion at the court of the king of the Khazars, who embraced the Jewish religion in the seventh century, the *Kuzari* vindicates Judaism against the assaults of its various detractors.

The salient teachings of the book are: The good life is the aim of religion. Judaism, the religion of joy, imposes limits on asceticism. "Our Torah as a whole is based on reverence, love, and joy. Your contrition on a fast day is not more effective in drawing you near to God than is your joy on the Sabbath and on holy days." The good man will not shun the world and its activities. Israel is the heart of mankind, filling the same function in the world at large as does the heart in the body of man. "Even as the heart may be effected by the disease of other organs, so Israel is affected by the trouble and wrongs of other nations."

Israel, the martyr-people, feels every pain and disorder of the great body of mankind. The Jewish people has been dispersed throughout the world in order to disseminate the divine truth. Israel has a special aptitude for prophecy by virtue of its Torah and ancestry. In opposition to the fatalistic doctrine of determinism, man possesses free will and is master of his choice. Nor does the idea of divine foreknowledge conflict with this truth. God knows the consequences of human actions, but this is not equivalent to foreordaining them.

In her introduction to the *Selected Poems of Yehudah Halevi*, Nina Solomon refers to Halevi as "God-intoxicated." God, not the physician, is to him the healer; God, not human reason, is the source of truth. The physician is but God's servant. Rabbi Yehudah Halevi

284

had an excellent practice as a physician in Toledo, Spain, when he made a pilgrimage to Jerusalem. According to tradition, he was killed by an Arab horseman.

INTENTION כַּוָּנָה

THE Talmud records opposite opinions on the question whether the performance of meritorious acts requires *kavvanah* (inner disposition) to be considered as the fulfillment of *mitzvoth* (Berakhoth 13a). Conscious intention in the performance of a divine precept is generally held to be of great ethical importance. According to a talmudic statement, if a man thoughful to perform a *mitzvah* failed to do it because he was prevented by force or accident, he is credited as if he had performed it (Berakhoth 6a).

In regard to prayer, the authorities place great stress on *kavvanah* as the chief requirement, and they say: Rather little prayer with intention than much without it. Maimonides, in his code of law and ethics, writes: "*Kavvanah* means that the worshiper must clear his mind of all private thoughts and regard himself as standing before the *Shekhinah* (Divine Presence). If his thoughts are wandering or occupied with other things, he should not pray... He should pray quietly and with feeling, not like one who is trying to unload a burden and departs as soon as he gets rid of it" (*Tefillah* 4:16).

As to the essential parts of the daily prayers, the *Shema* and the *Shemoneh Esreh*, he writes in his *Guide for the Perplexed*: "The first thing you must do is this: Turn your thoughts away from everything while you read *Shema* or during the *Tefilluh*... After some time, when you have mastered this, accustom yourself to have your mind free from all other thoughts when you read any portion of the other books of the prophets, or when you say any blessing... When you are engaged in the performance of religious duties, have your mind exclusively directed to what you are doing" (3:51).

The necessity of inwardness in religion is emphasized by the medieval Jewish philosopher, Baḥya ibn Pakuda, in his famous work *Duties of the Heart*. He says that even the practical outward duties cannot be adequately performed without a sincere and reverent heart. Rabbi Yehudah Halevi of twelfth-century Spain, in his *Kuzari*, points out that contemplation or emotion which ends in itself and is not translated into action is worthless. Since men learn by doing, and moral acts in themselves have social significance, some maintain that God rewards those who do good even when the motive is not unselfish.

Though prayer without inner intent is said to be of little worth, Maimonides, in his Mishnah commentary, writes to the effect that man is accustomed to act or not to act according to the good or the harm which may result; hence, he loses nothing by shaping his conduct with a view to reward or punishment until, by habit and zeal, he arrives at an understanding of the truth and serves purely out of love. This type of service, for its own sake, is termed *lishmah* (לשמה).

In kabbalistic literature, the concept *kavvanah* occupies a highly important position. Rabbi Isaac Luria of the sixteenth century said that prayer means much more than a free outpouring of religious feeling. Mystical intention connected with prayer leads to *dvékuth* or mystical contact with God, which is an ecstasy of silent meditation. Before reciting the morning prayers, the worshiper is expected ever afresh to take upon himself the continuous performance of the divine command: "You shall love your neighbor as yourself." His prayers will then ascend as the expression of all the people of Israel and will prove more effective.

The introductory meditations in the prayerbooks are marked with deep spirituality. For example, the meditation before putting on the *tefillin* contains the thought that by wearing the *tefillin* on the head and near the heart the worshiper is made conscious of his duty to employ his thoughts and emotions in the service of God.

KUTHIM   כּוּתִים

THE Samaritans are called *Kuthim* in tannaitic literature, that is, the people of Kutha and other places of Assyria who were transported to Samaria after the destruction of the Kingdom of Israel and the deportation of the ten tribes. The Kutheans combined their former idolatry with a belief in the God of Israel. The term *Kuthim* is used to denote individuals or groups who oppose Jewish teachings.

The worship of the God of Israel was maintained among them as late as the return of the Judeans under Zerubbabel, whom they approached with a request to be allowed to share in the restoration of the Temple. The descendants of the Kuthim-Samaritans were for a time regarded as suspected Israelites and finally were excluded from the community. The survivors of the Samaritan sect represent a small tribe of people who live in Nablus (ancient Shechem) and call themselves בני ישראל, the people of Israel.

The King of Assyria exiled only a small part of the Israelite population of the country, while the vast majority remained behind in their land and exercised some influence on the settlers, both racially and culturally. According to the Sargon inscription, the number of those whom that king led into captivity was twenty-seven thousand. The arrival of the Samaritans, their amalgamation with the Judeo-Israelite element, played a decisive part in their religious outlook. Under the Moslem rule, the Samaritans gradually declined, and from a great nation, they became a mere sect. On the establishment of the State of of Israel there was a community of fifty Samaritans living under Israel's jurisdiction. Their number in Israel has since increased to a hundred and fifty. When these are added to the two hundred and fifty Samaritans in Nablus, Jordan, we obtain a total of four hundred Samaritans throughout the world.

They earnestly endeavor to adhere to the plain meaning of the ancient laws. They are very strict in their interpretation of the laws relating to the observance of the Sabbath. Not only do they abstain from kindling any fire on that day, but they also refrain from using any light kindled even on the Sabbath eve, and from eating any hot food—restrictions not found among the Jews. On *Erev Pesah*, the fourteenth of *Nisan*, the Samaritans still sacrifice the paschal lamb on Mount Gerizim, and they eat it, in haste, standing, with their loins girded and their shoes on their feet, as it is written in the Torah.

KOL NIDRÉ   כָּל נִדְרֵי

THE Aramaic formula for the dispensation of vows, recited on the eve of *Yom Kippur*, is more than a thousand years old. *Kol Nidré* (all vows) refers to vows assumed by an individual for himself alone, where no other persons or their interests are involved. Though the context of the *Kol Nidré* passage makes it perfectly obvious that no vows or obligations toward others are implied, there have been many who were misled into believing that by means of this formula *all* their vows and oaths are annulled.

The law regarding vows is plainly stated in the Torah: "When you make any vow to the Lord your God, you must pay it without delay... If you refrain from making a vow, you will not be held guilty; but you must be careful to keep any promise you have made with your lips" (Deuteronomy 23:22-24). Since one runs the risk of either breaking or delaying to fulfill the vow made, we are frequently advised to refrain from rash vows even if they are motivated by pious devotion.

On account of its great solemnity, *Yom Kippur* was chosen for the chanting of *Kol Nidré*, which acquired intense significance particularly during the period of persecutions in Spain. Many Jews in Spain and Portugal, who had been forced to forswear their own faith in order to adopt a new religion, attended the synagogues in secret at the risk of their life and used the *Kol Nidré* text as a form of renouncing the vows imposed upon them by the Inquisition.

A *ḥazzan* in Germany, at the beginning of the sixteenth century, composed the stirring tune of *Kol Nidré* which expresses fear, impassioned pleading and hope for ultimate deliverance. This plaintive and touching melody, adopted by the *Ashkenazim* throughout the world, is not used by *Sephardic* and Oriental Jews who recite the passage in the manner of a simple prayer. According to *Maḥzor Vitry*, composed by Rabbi Simḥah Vitry, a disciple of Rashi, the *ḥazzan* chants *Kol Nidré* very softly the first time, like one who hesitates to enter the king's palace and fears to come near him with a request for a favor; the second time he chants somewhat louder; the third time he raises his voice louder and louder, like one who is accustomed to being a member of the king's court. *Kol Nidré* is chanted before sunset because dispensation of vows may not be granted on Sabbaths or holy days.

As a petition for the release of pledges between man and God made forcibly or impulsively, *Kol Nidré* is not part of the *Ma'ariv* for *Yom Kippur;* and yet the popular name of the entire worship service for the eve of *Yom Kippur* is subsumed under the title of *Kol Nidré*, manifesting an attitude of high regard for promises made by man.

In the eleventh century, Rabbi Meir ben Samuel (Rashi's son-in-law) changed the original wording of *Kol Nidré* to make it apply to vows about to be contracted "between this *Yom Kippur* and the next *Yom Kippur*" (מיום כפורים זה עד יום כפורים הבא עלינו). Support for this emendation was provided by a talmudic statement which reads: "Whoever desires that none of his vows made during the year shall be valid, let him declare at the beginning of the year: May all the vows which I am likely to make in the future be annulled" (Nedarim 23b).

This was in consideration of the frailties of human nature and the tragic results of promises too hastily made and pledges inadvertently

288

undertaken. The Hebrew version of *Kol Nidré*, found in the ninth-century *Siddur* of Rav Amram Gaon (page 47), still contains the original reference to vows contracted in the course of the year that has passed (מיום הכפורים שעבר עד יום הכפורים הזה הבא עלינו). This will partly explain the strange confusion in many an English translation of *Kol Nidré*.

MIXED KINDS   כִּלְאַיִם

THE biblical law which forbids mixtures reads: "Keep my statutes: do not breed any of your animals with others of different species; do not sow your field with two different kinds of seed; and do not put on a garment with two different kinds of thread (wool and linen) mingled together" (Leviticus 19:19). On the basis of Deuteronomy 22:11 ("You shall not wear *sha'atnez*, wool and linen woven together"), it has been deduced that, while it is permitted to wear pieces of material consisting of wool and linen which together do not constitute a garment, cloth which is made of wool and linen is not allowed (Rashi). *Ramban* (Naḥmanides) quotes Maimonides that the ancient idolatrous priests wore garments of two kinds of material mingled together.

Maimonides writes: "The Torah prohibits us to mix different species together, to graft one tree to another, because we must keep away from the opinions of idolaters and the abominations of their unnatural sexual relations. In order to guard against the grafting of trees, we are forbidden to sow any two kinds of seed together or near each other . . . the prohibition of grafting holds good for all countries . . . but the sowing of seeds one near the other is prohibited in *Eretz Yisrael* only. . . The Torah prohibits all heathen customs . . . because they are connected with idolatry" (*Guide*, 3:37).

Unnatural mixtures played an important part in the practice of magic. It has been proposed that the word *sha'atnez* for admixture of wool and flax is of Egyptian origin.

KOL-BO   כָּל־בּוֹ

THE comprehensive collection of laws and customs known as *Kol-Bo* (all is in it) is a condensed summary of earlier codifications, and dates probably from the fourteenth century. According to Leopold Zunz,

289

it is an abridgment of *Orḥoth Ḥayyim* (Paths of Life), the compilation of Jewish laws written by Rabbi Aaron ben Jacob ha-Kohen of fourteenth-century France. The anonymous *Kol-Bo* compendium, which includes a wealth of liturgical material, has enjoyed wide popularity. Rabbi Joseph Karo, author of the *Shulḥan Arukh*, was first to indicate that the words of both the *Orḥoth Ḥayyim* and the *Kol-Bo* are identical.

KALLAH   כַּלָּה

KALLAH is the name given to the semi-annual conventions of the Babylonian scholars that were held during the months of *Adar* and *Elul* under the leadership of the heads of the academies (ריש כלה), mentioned in the *Yekum Purkan* prayer. The *Kallah* functioned like a popular university, attracting scholars and laymen from all parts of the country who came to apply themselves to intensified study during the months preceding spring and fall.

Originating during the third century and continuing throughout the geonic period, which lasted until the eleventh century, the *Kallah* gatherings took place during the months when agricultural work was at a minimum.

The Midrash Tanḥuma describes the importance of the *Kallah* conventions in the following terms: "God has designated two academies for the good of Israel. In them day and night are devoted to the study of the Torah; scholars from all places come there twice a year, in *Adar* and *Elul*, to associate with one another and to discuss Torah subjects" (*Noah*, 3).

KELÉ KODESH   כְּלֵי קֹדֶשׁ

THE sacred objects that were used in the Temple service are known as *kelé kodesh*, a term mentioned twice in the Torah (Numbers 4:15; 18:3). In our time, it is applied to the sacred objects (*tashmishé kedushah*) connected with Jewish religious life (*tallith, shofar, Siddur, Maḥzor*). By further extension, the term *kelé kodesh* is applied to individuals who exercise religious functions in the Jewish community.

These include the rabbi (רב), the *shammash* (שמש) or sexton, the cantor (חזן), the *shoḥet* (שוחט), the *mohel* (מוהל), and the *mashgiaḥ* (משגיח) who is appointed to supervise the observance of *kashruth* reg-

290

ulations in a public institution. His function goes under the name of *hashgahah* (השגחה) or supervision. The *sofer* (סופר), or scribe, copies the biblical passages that are inserted in the *tefillin* and the *mezuzoth*, as well as the complete Pentateuch (*Sefer Torah*), on various kinds of qualified parchment.

In smaller communities, several functions are filled by one versatile person, as when the rabbi serves his congregation also in the capacity of *baal tefillah* (בעל תפלה) or *sheliah tsibbur* (שליח ציבור), leading the people in prayer, as well as *baal keriah* (בעל קריאה) or congregational Torah reader, and *baal tekiah* (בעל תקיעה) blowing the *shofar* on *Rosh Hashanah*. As a rule, the qualified *shohet* is likewise a qualified *mohel* who performs circumcisions.

The congregation official known as *gabbai* (גבאי) directs the distribution of *aliyyoth* (עליות) during the public Torah reading on Sabbaths and festivals. The word *gabbai* originally denoted a collector of charitable contributions.

KELAL YISRAEL   כְּלָל יִשְׂרָאֵל

THE concept of *Kelal Yisrael*, signifying the collective conscience of the entire Jewish people, was interpreted by Solomon Schechter: The Talmud, that wonderful mine of religious ideas from which it would be just as easy to draw up a manual for the most orthodox as to extract a vade-mecum handbook for the most sceptical, supports the view that it is not the mere revealed Bible that is of first importance to the Jew, but the Bible as it repeats itself in history, in other words, as it is interpreted by tradition. Liberty was always given to the great teachers of every generation to make modifications and innovations in harmony with the spirit of existing institutions. The norm as well as the sanction of Judaism is the practice actually in vogue. Its consecration is the consecration of general use. It was probably with a view to this communion that the later mystics introduced a short prayer to be said before the performance of any religious ceremony, in which, among other things, the speaker professes his readiness to act *in the name of all Israel*.

Self-exclusion from the general community of Israel is implied by the evil son, who asks in the Passover Haggadah: "What does this service mean to you?" He excludes himself by not saying *to us*. A Jew may be barred from *Kelal Yisrael* by improper conduct.

KNESSET   כְּנֶסֶת

THE term *Knesset* (Assembly) brings to mind the titles signifying the Jewish people (*Knesseth Yisrael*), the Synagogue (*Beth ha-Knesseth*), and the Great Assembly (*Knesseth ha-Gedolah*). The legislative body of 120 men who functioned during and after the Persian period in Jewish history, about 500-300 before the common era, was the supreme parliamentary authority created by Ezra the Scribe. It was considered the link between the last of the prophets and the first of the talmudic sages. In the words of the Mishnah, "the prophets handed down the Torah to the men of the Great Assembly" (Avoth 1:1).

Israel's parliament of the twentieth century likewise bears the title Knesset and consists of 120 members, who are elected by citizens past the age of 18. Candidates for the Knesset must be citizens past the age of twenty-one. The term of the Knesset is four years from the day it is elected. The 120 seats are filled by proportional representation based on the total vote of the country. Members of the Knesset are elected by secret ballot. Each party presents a list of candidates for the 120 seats; its percentage of the total vote determines the number of its representatives in the Knesset.

Members of the Knesset have certain privileges. They are entitled to free travel within the country on all public railway and bus systems. On the other hand, they are forbidden by law to accept any salary from any other source; income from non-salary sources, however, is permitted. The permanent chairman of the Knesset (Speaker) is elected by a majority vote of the Knesset membership. In his absence, one of the Deputy Speakers acts in his place. Two sessions a year are held by the Knesset, consisting of not less than four months each. The Knesset was created in 1949. It meets in the capital city of Jerusalem.

HEAD COVERING   כִּסּוּי רֹאשׁ

JEWISH tradition regards bareheadedness as a form of nakedness, and nudity as one of pagan indecencies and an infraction of propriety in worship. The word עֶרְוָה (nakedness) connotes shameful exposure, indecency, as well as improper behavior in general. In Deuteronomy 23:15, the phrase עֶרְוַת דָּבָר signifies "anything indecent." The Mishnah relates that a man once uncovered a woman's head in the street, and Rabbi Akiva told him to pay four hundred silver pieces as compensation for the embarrassment he had caused her (Bava Kamma 8:6). According to a statement in the Talmud (Yevamoth 63b), there is nothing more abominable in the sight of God than the man who appears naked in public שאין לך משוקץ ומתועב לפני המקום יותר ממי) שמהלך בשוק ערום.

From talmudic statements it appears that the sages did not walk four steps with uncovered head (Shabbath 118b; Kiddushin 31a). This was looked upon as a mark of reverence for God (Shabbath 156b). In Temple times, the priests wore a headdress in the form of a kind of turban while officiating (Exodus 28:37-39).

In view of the religious significance attached to meals by the Jews ever since the period of the Bible, it is conceivable why it is customary to cover the head during meals as well as during prayer.

The skull-cap worn for prayer and meals is called *yarmulke*, a word of Slavic derivation, or *kappel*, (from the Italian *cappelo* for hat), or *kippah* (כפה) in Hebrew. It is looked upon as a distinguishing characteristic of the traditional Jew.

KISLEV   בִּסְלֵו

THE ninth month of the Jewish calendar, *Kislev*, contains as a rule thirty but sometimes twenty-nine days, covering parts of November-December. The twenty-fifth of *Kislev* marks the first day of *Ḥanukkah*. In Temple times, fasts were observed and prayers offered during *Kislev*, if rain had not yet fallen.

According to the Mishnah (Rosh Hashanah 1:3), messengers were sent out on *Kislev* to proclaim the time of *Ḥanukkah*. They were sent on *Nisan*, to determine the time of *Pesah;* on *Av*, to determine the time of *Tish'ah b'Av;* on *Elul*, to determine *Rosh Hashanah;* on *Tishri*, to determine *Sukkoth*.

KAPPAROTH   כַּפָּרוֹת

THE custom of symbolically transferring one's guilt to the fowl on the day preceding *Yom Kippur* is widely known as *kapparoth* (atonements) and related to the use of a scapegoat in Temple times (Maḥzor Vitry, page 373). "This bird is a sacrifice in my stead" is the formula repeated three times as the fowl is held over the heads of adults and children. This practice, first mentioned in the geonic period, was instituted for the purpose of helping the poor, among whom the fowl is distributed.

Religious authorities have differed whether to sanction or prohibit the custom. Some have recommended the distribution of charity instead. "By no means should we imagine that the fowl atones for us; instead, we must reflect that we may deserve dire punishment for our sins, and repent in the hope that God will pardon our sins" (*Kitzur Shulḥan Arukh* 131:1).

Prior to the ceremony of waving a fowl three times around the head, one recites the paragraph *Bné Adam*, consisting of a variety of verses from the books of Psalms and Job concerning God's readiness to deliver "men who sit in darkness and in gloom, bound in misery and iron. . . Fools are they who transgress; they are afflicted because of their iniquities. . . Then they cry out to the Lord in their trouble, and he delivers them from their distress. . ." The initial phrase *Bné Adam* (children of men) has been added to the heart-stirring biblical verses contained in this passage.

WITCHCRAFT כְּשָׁפִים

WITCHCRAFT, a common superstition among primitive peoples, was believed to result from direct contact with evil spirits. The magician's activity was always evil—killing or creating strife. He was never expected to do good; he was the agent for vengeance, hatred, death and destruction. Hence, the biblical law: "You shall not let a sorceress live" (Exodus 22:17). A sorcerer comes under the same law, but because women were more addicted to witchcraft, a sorceress is specified. In Leviticus 20:27, the Torah says: "A man or a woman who acts as a medium or a wizard shall be put to death."

The pretended holding of communication with evil spirits, or sorcery, is regarded as a form of idolatry and rebellion against God. Thus the Torah declares: "When you come into the land which the Lord your God is giving you, you shall not learn to imitate the abominable practices of those nations there. Let there not be found among you anyone who immolates his son or daughter in the fire, nor one that uses divination, soothsayer, charmer, sorcerer or caster of spells, nor one who consults ghosts and spirits or seeks oracles from the dead . . . because of such abominations the Lord your God is driving them out of your way. You must be sincere toward the Lord your God" (Deuteronomy 18:9-13). Human sacrifices are classed here with other pagan superstitions because they were believed to possess magical powers for averting a calamity.

Even though there was no reality in witchcraft, it was an abominable form of idolatry, steeped in imposture, crime and immorality. Since immorality was closely connected with witchcraft, the law of the sorceress is preceded by the section against sexual licence and is followed by the regulation against unnatural vice (Exodus 22:15-18).

Witchcraft persisted throughout Europe well through the eighteenth century. Witches were thought able to change themselves voluntarily into cats or werewolves. Even today this strange belief occasionally crops up in benighted regions. It was believed that domestic misfortunes were brought about by supernatural agents. In magic, forms of words constituted the means by which the demons were compelled to work these evils on unfortunate victims. The *evil eye* of certain persons was believed to possess demonic power.

In his code of laws and ethics, *Mishneh Torah*, Maimonides cites a variety of examples illustrating superstitious beliefs connected with witchcraft, magic and sorcery. It is sinful, for instance, to say: "I will not venture to go to a certain place today, because a piece of bread has fallen out of my mouth, or my cane has dropped from my hand. . . Since a fox ran past me on the right, I will not leave the house today, lest I be confronted by an imposter. . ."

Then he states: "A charmer (הובר) is one who utters words that are not part of any spoken language and are meaningless, foolishly fancying that these words are helpful. The charmers go so far as to say that if one utters certain words over a snake or scorpion, it will become harmless. . . All these strange and uncouth sounds and names have no power to do good, even though they do no harm. . . These practices are all false and deceptive; they were employed by ancient idolaters to deceive the peoples of the world and induce them to become their followers. It is improper for Jews, who are highly intelligent, to be deluded by such absurdities, or to imagine that they are of any consequence. . . Sensible people, who possess sound mental faculties, know by clear proofs that all these practices which the Torah prohibits have no scientific basis . . . only those who are deficient in knowledge are attracted by these follies. . ." (*Yad, Avodah Zarah*).

DIETARY LAWS   כַּשְׁרוּת

THE term *kashruth* (fitness), generally applied to things and persons that meet Jewish religious requirements, is for the most part used in the sense of food ritually clean and edible; *kasher* or *kosher* means fit to eat. Most quadrupeds are nonedible, except oxen, sheep, goats, and certain deer and gazelles. Aquatic animals that lack fins and scales, such as eels, are nonedible. Birds of prey and carrion eaters are unclean and forbidden as food. The Torah gives no reason for any of the restrictions, except the prohibition of blood, which is regarded as the life: "Since the life of a living body is in its blood ... no one among you, not even a resident alien, may eat blood" (Leviticus 17: 11-12). Animals that died of themselves are forbidden chiefly because the blood has not been drained. If improperly slaughtered, they are classified as *nevelah*, a term denoting animals that died of themselves.

Unclean animals are classified as follows: 1) quadrupeds that do not both cleave the foot entirely and chew the cud; 2) carnivorous birds, of which twenty-one are especially named (Leviticus 11:13-19; Deuteronomy 14:12-18); 3) winged insects; 4) fish and other water creatures that do not have both fins and scales; 5) small creeping things (Leviticus 11:29-30).

The meat even of clean animals becomes unclean if dead of themselves or killed by beast or bird of prey or improperly slaughtered. The slaying of animals for food by specially trained men (*shehitah*) is controlled by strictly prescribed regulations ensuring the minimum of pain and the maximum effusion of blood in the animal. The remaining blood is extracted by means of washing, salting and rinsing. It has been suggested that the purpose of all this may be to tame man's instincts of violence.

The term *terefah* includes meat of all animals found, by post-*shehitah* inspection, to contain organic diseases or injuries. The term *nevelah* includes meat of animals improperly slaughtered. Furthermore, the internal fat in quadrupeds, along with the blood, is regarded as the seat of life; it must, therefore, never be eaten (Leviticus 3:17). It is the fat (*helev*) which is attached to the stomach and extends over the intestines. In sacrifices, that fat was burned upon the altar. Also, in quadrupeds, the sciatic sinew (*gid ha-nasheh*), together with other arteries and tendons, must be removed from the slaughtered animal before that portion can be properly prepared for Jewish food.

Three times the Torah repeats the command: "You shall not boil a kid in its mother's milk" (Exodus 23:19; 34:26; Deuteronomy 14:21). According to some, this was part of a Canaanite ritual; hence it is prohibited as a pagan custom. This prohibition may also be intended to preserve the natural instinct of humanity. It is symbolic of that considerate humanity which was to distinguish Israel from the barbarous nations.

In Deuteronomy 14:21, the prohibition is connected with the law of unclean meats; rabbinic tradition has based upon it the law against meat-milk mixtures merely as a biblical support for an ancient Jewish practice. The Aramaic translation of the Torah (Targum Onkelos) renders the verse each time: "You shall not eat meat and milk together" (בשר בחלב). Hence, the law stated in *Kitzur Shulḥan Arukh* reads in part: Meat and dairy foods must neither be eaten nor cooked together; it is forbidden to derive any benefit from such mixture, except in certain instances concerning which a rabbi has been consulted. . . After eating meat one should wait six hours before eating dairy food. . .

During the Passover period, all foods which contain any quantity of *ḥametz* (fermented substance) are prohibited. All utensils which have come into contact with *ḥametz* must not be used throughout the eight days of *Pesaḥ* and the day preceding *Pesaḥ*, beginning at ten in the morning. Wine known, or suspected, to have been handled by an idolater is called יין נסך (wine from which a libation has been poured on the altar) and is forbidden.

The deeply rooted observance of *kashruth* has, among other factors, prevented the Jews from being absorbed by the numerous nations in whose midst they have lived more than two thousand years. Hallowed since the days of Sinai, the dietary laws have been tenaciously kept by the Jewish people in all the lands of the Diaspora. Maimonides states that the dietary laws train us to master our appetites, and not to consider eating and drinking the end of man's existence (*Guide*, 3:35). Though *kashruth* regulations are not directly based on hygienic principles, they have often proved to be hygienic in effect.

The dietary laws have been described as one of the vital resources by means of which Jewish tradition helps to identify the individual Jew with his people.

The Yiddish term *pareveh* or *parveh* refers to food that is neutral, neither *milchig* (dairy) nor *fleishig* (meat), and may be eaten with either meat or dairy foods.

SQUARE SCRIPT   כְּתָב מְרֻבָּע

THE early Hebrew writing, which influenced the square Hebrew script of modern times, was used on Jewish coins from the Maccabean period to the revolt of Bar Kokhba as an archaic form. During the period when the square Hebrew (כתב מרובע) was in common use, the early Hebrew writing (*kethav ivri*) continued to be written in a limited fashion. The Hebrew script which was adopted during the period of the Babylonian captivity was essentially an adaptation of the Aramaic script, hence its name: כתב אשורי, that is, the Aramaic alphabet which had become widespread in Assyria and Mesopotamia and Syria. Aramaic had become the *lingua franca*, the common language of the Near East.

In the course of more than two thousand years, the Hebrew alphabet has developed three fundamental types: 1) *square Hebrew*, which evolved into the well-proportioned printing type of modern Hebrew; 2) *rabbinic Hebrew*, also called *Rashi-writing* (כתב רש"י); and 3) *cursive script*, of which the Polish-German form became the Hebrew cursive script of today. The first Hebrew book printed was *Ḥummash* with *Rashi;* hence the name *Rashi script.*

The so-called Nash papyrus, a fragment of twenty-four broken lines containing in square Hebrew characters the Ten Commandments followed by a portion of the *Shema*, is known to be the oldest extant Hebrew document in the Aramaic script. Discovered in Egypt in 1902 and placed in Cambridge, England, by L. W. Nash, the fragment is dated by some authorities in the late Maccabean period, or the beginning of the common era. The term *kethav merubba* (square script), applied to the Hebrew characters since the thirteenth century, is attributable to the fact that, compared with other alphabets, the Hebrew characters are for the most part square in appearance.

KETHUBBAH   כְּתֻבָּה

THE marriage contract (*kethubbah* or written document), containing the mutual obligations between husband and wife prerequisite to marriage, has been regarded as a safeguard against hasty divorce. The term *kethubbah* is used for the document in which the bridegroom pledges himself to assign a certain sum of money to the bride in the

298

event of his death or of his divorcing her; it is also used for the sum of money so assigned.

The minimum settlement for a virgin is, according to rabbinic law, two hundred *zuz*, and for a widow remarrying a hundred *zuz*. Its origin perhaps goes back to the "marriage price for virgins" which, in biblical times, the bridegroom paid to the father of the bride (Exodus 22:16).

The oldest *kethubbah* that has been preserved was found in Assuan, Egypt, in a papyrus belonging to the fifth century before the common era. The absolute minimum (200 *zuz* = approximately $40) was, as a rule, considerably increased among the well-to-do. The supplementary amount (*tosefeth kethubbah*), promised by the husband in a special clause, assumes the validity of the rest of the *kethubbah*, which is drawn up in Aramaic and bears the signatures of two witnesses.

Traditionally, a marriage performed without drawing up a *kethubbah* is not properly ritualized. It is permanently preserved by the bride. After the reading of the *kethubbah* as part of the wedding ceremony, it is handed over to the bride; its possession by her is deemed particularly important (Kethubboth 57a). Thus the wife is protected in the event of a divorce. Furthermore one of the decrees of Rabbenu Gershom Meor ha-Golah (965-1028) forbade divorcing a woman without her consent.

A new *kethubbah* had to be written and signed by witnesses if the original one had been lost. From the Renaissance period onward, the *kethubbah* formed an important branch of colored ornamentation, especially cultivated by Jews of Spanish-Portuguese origin. Some illuminated early fragments were discovered in the *Genizah* of Cairo.

The printed form of the *Kethubbah*, which is in use today, is couched in the traditional Hebrew-Aramaic of the talmudic authorities. Here is a brief excerpt:

"... Be my wife according to the law of Moses and Israel. I will work for you, and maintain you in accordance with the custom of Jewish husbands, who work for their wives, honoring and supporting them, and maintaining them in truth..."

HOLY SCRIPTURES   כִּתְבֵי הַקֹּדֶשׁ

THE Hebrew Bible, consisting of twenty-four books, is divided into three parts: *Torah, Neviim, Kethuvim* (תורה נביאים כתובים), or תנ"ך

299

(*Tanakh*) by abbreviation. The first part of the Bible, extending from the creation of the world to the death of Moses, is referred to by as many as five titles: Torah, Law, Pentateuch, Five Books of Moses, and Five Ḥummashim (fifths).

The five books of the Torah are: Genesis, Exodus, Leviticus, Numbers, Deuteronomy. These names are descriptive of the contents of the books: *Genesis* (origin) begins with the story of creation and ends with the death of Moses; *Exodus* (going out) tells of the departure from Egypt and the basic laws of the Torah, such as the Ten Commandments; *Leviticus* (pertaining to Levites) contains laws which relate to the priests, members of the tribe of Levi, and is the basis for the major part of the Jewish religion; *Numbers* derives its title from the census of the Israelites in the wilderness; *Deuteronomy* (review of the law) contains a restatement of the Mosaic laws.

The second part of the Bible, the Prophets (*Neviim*), has eight books that are subdivided into Former Prophets (*Neviim Rishonim*) and Latter Prophets (*Neviim Aḥaronim*). The Former Prophets comprise four historical books: Joshua, Judges, Samuel, Kings. The Latter Prophets are also made up of four books: Isaiah, Jeremiah, Ezekiel, the Twelve Minor Prophets (תרי־עשר).

Grouped in one volume, the twelve Minor Prophets are: Hosea, Joel, Amos, Obadiah, Jonah, Micah, Nahum, Habakkuk, Zephaniah, Haggai, Zechariah, Malachi. They are termed Minor Prophets because each of the twelve books is comparatively short.

The books of Isaiah, Jeremiah, Ezekiel are called Major Prophets because they are long. Isaiah, for example, has sixty-six chapters, whereas the book of Obadiah contains only one chapter.

The third part of the Bible, known as Hagiographa or Sacred Writings (*Kethuvim*), consists of the remaining eleven books: Psalms, Proverbs, Job, Song of Songs, Ruth, Lamentations, Ecclesiastes, Esther, Daniel, Ezra-Neḥemiah, Chronicles. Forming a class by themselves, the Five Scrolls (*Ḥamesh Megilloth*) are arranged in the Hebrew Bible according to the sequence of the occasions on which they are recited in the synagogue as part of the liturgy: *Pesaḥ, Shavuoth, Tish-'ah b'Av, Sukkoth, Purim.*

It has been said that a knowledge of the Bible without a college education is better than a college education without a knowledge of the Bible. Translated into many hundreds of tongues, the Bible has been the foremost guide toward the ideal moral life. No other book has done so much to influence mankind. We turn to it again and

300

again, always to discover in it fresh meanings, new approaches to
reality. It speaks to us as it has spoken through the centuries to men
of all generations.

Sunrise and sunset, promise and fulfillment, birth and death, the
whole human drama, everything is in this book that great medicine
chest of humanity. The Jewish people knew very well what they were
about when, in the conflagration of the Second Temple, they left
the gold and silver vessels of sacrifice, and rescued only the Bible. This
was the real treasure of the Temple. They trudged around with it all
through the Middle Ages as with a portable homeland.

Covering a period of time that exceeds a thousand years, the Bible
reflects some of the most interesting epochs of ancient civilizations,
though its object is essentially human instruction rather than scientific or metaphysical speculation. Its lofty ideals are the greatest
spiritual heritage of all mankind. The Jews, however, have become
identified with it to the point best expressed in the proverbial saying:
Israel and the Torah are one and the same thing (ישראל ואוריתא חד).

TATTOO   כְּתֹבֶת קַעֲקַע

INCULCATING reverence for the human body as the work of God,
the Torah prohibits tattooing, declaring: "Do not lacerate your flesh
for the dead, and do not tattoo yourselves" (Leviticus 19:28). Cutting
the flesh and tattooing the skin were closely connected with idolatrous usages among the Canaanites. In their demonstration of grief
and bereavement, they gashed and mutilated themselves, offering
their blood as a sacrifice to the dead.

APOCRYPHA   כְּתוּבִים אַחֲרוֹנִים

THE books of the Apocrypha, representing a substantial and remarkable ethical literature, reflect the developments of social and religious
life among the Jewish people during the period of the Second Temple.
Since they were not included in the Hebrew Bible, the Talmud refers
to them as *Sefarim Ḥitzonim* (outside books); otherwise they are
called *Apocrypha* (hidden away) and *Kethuvim Aharonim* (latter writings), because they were produced after the time of Ezra the Scribe,
when direct revelation had ceased with the passing of the prophets.

301

The book of Tobit is the earliest of all the Apocrypha. In it are enshrined some high ideals of the Jewish people, such as the purity of family life and the duty of kindness to the poor. It has in its plot the framework of a complete novel, introducing the reader to the kind of home in which the Jew lived more than two thousand years ago.

The book of Ben Sira, known as Ecclesiasticus, contains an admirable collection of proverbs covering a wide range of subjects concerning practical affairs, physical health and good manners, which should be read slowly for a true appreciation of their full meaning. The first book of Maccabees describes the rise of the Maccabean revolt and covers the period between 175 and 135 before the common era.

The second book of Maccabees is filled with stories of defiant martyrdom during the Maccabean uprising; it leads us through the heroic struggle of the Jews against pagan forces, a struggle which proved decisive in forming the character of subsequent generations. It contains the story of the martyrdom of the seven youths with their mother.

The third book of Maccabees received its name probably from the fact that its narrative concerns the persecution of the Jews by a foreign king. The fourth book of Maccabees is a philosophic discourse on the supremacy of piety and reason. The only connection this book has with the Maccabees is in the fact that the author's illustrations are drawn from the second book of the Maccabees.

The author of Wisdom of Solomon at times speaks in the person of Solomon, placing his teachings on the lips of the wise king in order to emphasize their value. In the first part, he discusses the destiny of the righteous and the wicked; in the second part, he admonishes against the dangers of materialism and skepticism. The probable date of this book is the first century before the common era. It is generally regarded as the work of a Hellenistic Jew of Alexandria, Egypt, though the date of its composition is placed by some scholars considerably before the first century B.C.E. Wisdom of Solomon was designed to vindicate the principles of the Jewish religion against speculative philosophy and idolatry.

The book of Judith, like the book of Tobit, resembles a historical novel. It tells of the flight of a besieging enemy after a daring act performed by Judith, a pious and beautiful widow, who succeeded in beheading the foe's general, Holofernes. The courage of the besieged was roused to the point that they rushed out and put the enemy to complete rout. Evidently, the purpose of the book of Judith was to confirm the Jewish people in the observance of the Torah and in the

302

resistance of foreign oppression. The story is associated with the festivity of *Ḥanukkah*.

The story of Susannah and the Elders tells how Daniel, by his great wisdom, delivered the virtuous and beautiful Susannah from condemnation to death upon a false charge. This admirably told and edifying folk tale may have been intended to demonstrate that the two witnesses, which the Torah requires, must be examined separately, or simply to extol the wisdom of Daniel in his youth.

The two apocryphal books attributed to Ezra are called I and II Esdras. They reproduce the substance of II Chronicles, the whole of Ezra and part of Nehemiah, with significant omissions, variations, and additions. In I Esdras 3-5:6, Zerubbabel gives such an exhibition of wisdom, in the Persian court, as to win the favor of king Darius, who permits the return of the captive Jews to Judea. The second book of Esdras contains a series of apocalypses, or visions and revelations. It is regarded as a valuable index to the quality of religious thought in the first century. Sometimes I and II Esdras are referred to as III and IV Esdras, the book Ezra-Nehemiah being called I and II Esdras.

Other apocryphal works are: Baruch; Bel and the Dragon; Prayer of Manasseh; Additions to the Book of Esther; Song of the Three Children. Though the books of the Apocrypha were originally produced by Jews, some in Hebrew, some in Aramaic, and some in Greek, they were held under suspicion as being affected by Christian doctrine and later interpolations. According to Rabbi Akiva, he that reads the so-called external books (excluded from the canon of the Hebrew Bible) has no share in the world to come (Sanhedrin 10:1). This explains why, with the exception of Ben Sira, the books of the Apocrypha gradually disappeared and were discredited by Jews, especially in Eretz Yisrael where they suffered religious persecutions.

The synonyms *Genuzim* and *Ḥitzonim* are used in talmudic literature to denote books judged unfit for public use. The word *ganaz* was commonly used in reference to the question whether some book should be withdrawn from the class of sacred writings. Thus there were some sages who wished to *conceal* the books of Proverbs, Song of Songs, and Ecclesiastes, for certain reasons; but the objections in each instance were met, so that these books were not excluded from the Holy Scriptures. *Genuzim* were books which once stood within the cycle of sacred writings. *Sefarim Ḥitzonim*, according to some scholars, included sectarian books known as *Sifré Minim*.

WEST WALL כֹּתֶל מַעֲרָבִי

THE remnant of the Western Wall (*kothel ma'aravi*) of the Temple, destroyed by the Romans in the year 70, was named *Wailing Wall* by non-Jewish travellers who observed pious Jews coming to worship there daily, weeping and lamenting over Jewish hardships throughout the Diaspora. The *kothel ma'aravi* has been regarded with great affection as a reminder of a glorious past and a messianic future. The Arabs did not permit the Jews to pray at the West Wall between the years 1948 and 1967. Ever since the Six-Day War (June 1967) the Wall has been accessible to all Jews. An open plaza has been created and thousands of people come daily as pilgrims, returning to the United City of David. According to tradition, the Divine Presence (*Shekhinah*) has never departed from the Wall of the Holy Temple (מעולם לא זזה השכינה מכותל מערבי של בית המקדש).

CROWN OF TORAH כֶּתֶר תּוֹרָה

ACCORDING to a tannaitic statement, there are three crowns: the crown of Torah, the crown of priesthood, and the crown of royalty; but the crown of a good name excels them all (Avoth 4:17). Another tannaitic statement is quoted in the Talmud to the effect that the third crown, the crown of learning, is not inherited but is available to anyone in the world who is worthy of it (*Sifré* Numbers, 119).

The artistic silver crowns adorning the *Sifré Torah* in the synagogues express the Jewish high regard for Torah in its wide meaning. Another name for the *Kether Torah*, with which the scroll is surmounted, is *Atarah* (עטרה), widely used in geonic times.

The famous tenth-century massoretic text of the Bible, vocalized and proofread by Aaron Ben Asher, is known by the name of כֶּתֶר אֲרַם-צוֹבָה or *The Aleppo Codex*. It was preserved in one of the ancient synagogues of Aleppo, Syria, until it was rescued from a fire and brought to Jerusalem after the War of Independence. It now forms the subject of careful study by well-known Bible scholars as to biblical vocalization and cantilation. The same *Aleppo Codex* is generally referred to by the popular name of כֶּתֶר תּוֹרָה.

304

LAG B'OMER

לַ"ג בְּעֹמֶר   ל

LAG B'OMER, the thirty-third day of the *Omer* period coinciding with the eighteenth of *Iyyar*, serves as a break in the semi-mourning *Sefirah* days between *Pesaḥ* and *Shavuoth*. These days are filled with sad memories of misfortunes that afflicted the Jewish people during the period of Roman domination. In the Middle Ages, too, as well as in later times, they met with overwhelming disasters resulting from the Crusades and hostile movements. Hence the custom to abstain from festivities and rejoicings, such as wedding occasions, during the six weeks that come after *Pesaḥ*.

Lag b'Omer is termed "scholars' festival" and is observed as a semi-holiday, suspending the half-mourning regulations, because on this day, according to the Talmud, a plague that had raged among the disciples of Rabbi Akiva was stayed. In Eretz Yisrael, *Lag b'Omer* is marked by an inspiring pilgrimage of many thousands to the tomb of Rabbi Simeon ben Yoḥai, at Meron. He is believed to have died on this day in the middle of the second century. After the imprisonment of Rabbi Akiba, his teacher, he was forced to hide in a cave with his son Elazar for thirteen years. The authorship of the kabbalistic classic, the Zohar, has been attributed to him.

It has been intimated that the use of bows and arrows by school-children, engaged in games of military character on *Lag b'Omer*, might possibly have been, in previous generations, a commemoration of some military victory on the part of Bar Kokhba who revolted against the Romans and was warmly supported by Rabbi Akiva and his disciples. The cessation of a plague among Rabbi Akiva's disciples may allude to this victory. The use of bows and arrows, customary in some localities also during the day of *Tish'ah b'Av*, after the reading of *kinoth* (lamentations), has otherwise been explained as symbolic of defending the Jewish people against their foes of all generations.

The thirty-third day of the *Omer* falls on the same day of the week as the preceding *Purim* festival. The numerical value of ל"ג is thirty-three. The counting of seven weeks from the day on which the *omer* (measure of barley) was offered in the Temple (sixteenth of *Nisan*) till the Feast of Weeks (*Shavuoth*), serves to connect the anniversary of the exodus from Egypt with the festival that commemorates the giving of the Torah at Mount Sinai. In former times, school children conducted mock-battles with bow and arrow on *Lag b'Omer*.

305

LAMED-VAV TSADDIKIM   ל"ו צַדִּיקִים

THE thirty-six hidden saints (ל"ו צדיקים), described by legend as being extremely modest and upright, concealing their identity behind a mask of ignorance and poverty and earning their livelihood by the sweat of their brow, are generally referred to as *lamedvovniks*. This widely-held belief among pious Jews is based on a talmudic statement to the effect that there are in the world no fewer than thirty-six right-eous men in every generation who "greet the *Shekhinah*," the Divine Presence (Sanhedrin 97b; Sukkah 45b). The biblical verse אשרי כל חוכי לו (Isaiah 30:18), meaning "blessed are all those who wait for him," is used as a proof-text alluding to this idea, since the numerical value of the word לו is thirty-six.

The *lamed-vav tsaddikim* are also called *nistarim* (concealed). In the folk tales, they emerge from their self-imposed concealment and, by the mystic powers which they possess they succeed in averting the threatened disasters from a people persecuted by surrounding enemies. They return to their anonymity as soon as their task is accomplished, "concealing" themselves in a Jewish community where they are unknown. The *lamedvovniks*, scattered as they are through-out the Diaspora, have no acquaintance with one another. On very rare occasions is one of them "discovered" by accident, in which case the secret must not be disclosed. The continued existence of the world depends on their righteousness, it was popularly believed.

CALENDAR   לוּחַ הַשָּׁנָה

THE Jewish calendar in use today is both solar and lunar: the years are reckoned by the sun and the months by the moon. The lunar year, consisting of twelve months averaging twenty-nine and thirty days alternately, contains 354 days, 8 hours, 48 minutes, 34 seconds. The length of the solar year is 365 days, 5 hours, 48 minutes, and 45 seconds.

Since the annual festivals are inseparably connected with the agri-cultural seasons, and a strictly lunar year would cause festivals con-stantly to recede from their appropriate season, it is necessary to adjust the two systems by the intercalation of an additional month (*Adar Sheni* or *va-Adar*) seven times in a cycle of nineteen years. This

306

month falls in the latter part of March and the beginning of April. Nineteen years constitute a lunar cycle, of which the third, sixth, eighth, eleventh, fourteenth, seventeenth, and nineteenth are leap years (שנים מעוברות).

The year begins with the month *Nisan*, the month of ripe grain (*Aviv*), in accord with the command: "This month shall stand at the head of your calendar; you shall reckon it the first month of the year" (Exodus 12:2). But from the earliest times there has been a civil year which begins in the autumn, the season of plowing and sowing, and closes with harvest. In practice they often preferred, in biblical times, to indicate the time of the year by the particular harvest, or agricultural occupation, rather than by the number or name of the month, as in the expressions "the season of early grapes" and "the beginning of the barley harvest" (Numbers 13:20; Ruth 1:22).

As the seventh day of the week is a holy day, so the seventh month, *Tishri*, is the holy month of the year. The *Rosh Ḥodesh*, or new moon festival, of the seventh month, is a festival of special solemnity, celebrated as *Rosh Hashanah*, New Year's Day, in post-biblical times. Since *Rosh Hashanah* must never begin on a Sunday, Wednesday or Friday, so that *Yom Kippur* does not immediately precede or follow the Sabbath, the months *Ḥeshvan* and *Kislev* may consist of thirty days each or twenty-nine days; or, again, *Ḥeshvan* may have thirty days and *Kislev* twenty-nine. A thirty-day month is called *maléh* (full); a twenty-nine day month is called *ḥaser* (defective). *Nisan, Sivan, Av, Tishri, Shevat* are always full, while *Iyyar, Tammuz, Elul, Teveth, Adar* are always defective.

The first day of *Rosh Hashanah* can come neither on Wednesday nor on Friday, because *Yom Kippur* must not fall on Friday or Sunday. This might cause great hardship in terms of food preparation, since all work would then be prohibited for two successive days, Friday and Saturday or Saturday and Sunday. Again, *Rosh Hashanah* cannot come on Sunday, because *Hoshana Rabbah* would then coincide with the Sabbath, when it would be prohibited to observe the ancient custom of striking willow-twigs against the ground as a symbol of casting off the sins.

Rosh Hashanah is postponed for a day if the beginning of the astronomical month (*molad*) occurs on any of the three days mentioned, so that the past lunar year consists of 355 days instead of three hundred fifty-four, while the next year has only 353 days. *Rosh Hashanah* may be delayed if the *molad* of *Tishri* occurs in the afternoon, for

307

which reason there is a one-day postponement of *Rosh Hashanah;* and if the next day happens to be Sunday, Wednesday or Friday, there is a further one-day delay (*dehiyah*). The principle concerning the three days is expressed in three words: לֹא אד"ו ראש; that is, the first day of *Rosh Hashanah* must not occur on Sunday, Wednesday, or Friday. This rule implies that *Pesah* cannot fall on Monday, Wednesday or Friday. The expression לֹא בד"ו פסח means that the first day of *Pesah* cannot fall on Monday, Wednesday or Friday.

A year in which *Heshvan* and *Kislev* are both full (*malé*), consisting of thirty days each, is called *shelemah* (complete), and will contain 355 days (385 if leap year). In a *normal* year (*kesidrah*), when *Heshvan* is defective (29 days) and *Kislev* full (30 days), the total of days will be 354 (or 385), while the defective year (*haserah*), when both months contain only twenty-nine days each, the total of days will be 353 (or 383).

The fixation of the month (קביעת החודש), in Temple times, was determined on the basis of both calculation and observation. When witnesses appeared before the supreme court or the Great Sanhedrin, and reported having seen the new moon, they were thoroughly examined on the thirtieth day of the month. If their testimony was found reliable, the day was declared *Rosh Hodesh* and the preceding month had twenty-nine days. If no reliable witnesses appeared, the day was added to the previous month, making it a month of thirty days, and the following day was kept as *Rosh Hodesh*. The decision of the Sanhedrin was immediately proclaimed in Jerusalem, and messengers were sent out to outlying districts of Eretz Yisrael to announce the day of *Rosh Hodesh*, so that the festivals coming within the month might be observed by all on the same day. Since, however, the messengers could not reach Jewish communities outside Judea in time to inform of the exact day of the new moon, it became customary for the Jews of the Diaspora to observe two festival days instead of one, so as to be certain of observing the proper day.

Rosh Hashanah was observed for two days even in Jerusalem, because even there it was uncertain as to the first day of *Tishri. Yom Kippur* has nowhere been observed for more than one day, because of the hardship of fasting two days in succession. This custom of keeping two festival days in the Diaspora is referred to as יום טוב שני של גליות. Even now when all festivals are fixed and calculated with ease ahead of time, it has the force of law hallowed by time, and cannot be abrogated by any individual community of observant Jews.

The adoption of an astronomically fixed calendar, about the middle of the fourth century, made it possible for the Jews everywhere to determine the first day of the month without actual observation of the lunar phases. It has been noted that the Jewish calendar is the most brilliant achievement of its kind. It was during the administration of Patriarch Hillel II (330-365) that this extremely accurate system of intercalation, equalizing the solar and lunar years, was published in order to preserve the uniform observance of the festivals in the face of persecutions, which prevented Jewish communication with the Babylonian communities.

The scientific rules for the computation of the Jewish calendar, published by Hillel II, make the months to alternate between 30 and 29 days. The months that are distinguished by memorable dates have each thirty days (*Nisan, Sivan, Av, Tishri, Kislev, Shevat*). The other six months have 29 days each. In leap years, the first *Adar* has thirty days, the second twenty-nine. *Heshvan* is occasionally lengthened to thirty days. When the preceding month has thirty days, its last day is celebrated as the first day of *Rosh Hodesh*, while the second day of *Rosh Hodesh* marks the first day of the new month. Reminiscent of the Temple period, when the arrival of a new month was solemnly announced by the Sanhedrin after examining the witnesses who had noticed the new moon, the coming of *Rosh Hodesh* is now announced in the synagogues on the preceding Sabbath after the reading of the Torah.

Originally, the Jewish year had no number of its own. The Bible has no uniform system of dating but employs, for its chronology, important events like the exodus from Egypt, an earthquake, the beginning of a king's reign. During the period of the Second Temple, use was made especially of the Seleucidan Era, which began in 312 before the common era. It was called *minyan shetaroth* (era of documents) because, perhaps, all documents during the Syrian rule and after had to be dated according to this method in order to be legally valid.

From the Greek conquest of Judea (312 B.C.E.) to the middle of the seventh century, about a thousand years, the *minyan shetaroth* was in vogue for all practical purposes. The method of counting from the traditional date of creation (ליצירה) is first mentioned in the earliest post-biblical Hebrew chronicle, *Seder Olam Rabbah*, of the second century, but did not become popular until the tenth century. This era, referred to as *anno mundi* (in the year of the world), begins 3760 years before the common era; thus, the year 5,724 corresponds

309

to 1964. To find the Jewish calendar year (*anno mundi*) subtract 240 from the general calendar year; if, for example, 240 is subtracted from 1964, the corresponding Jewish year is found to be 724 (תשכ"ד), disregarding the thousands in either calendar. By adding 1240 to 724, the corresponding general calendar year is found (1964).

In talmudic times, the Jewish calendar was referred to by such terms as fixation of the month (*kevi'a d'yarḥa*), sanctification of the month (*kiddush ha-ḥodesh*), and principle of intercalation (*sod ha-ibbur*). The name *luaḥ* (לוח) has been applied for calendar since the medieval period.

The days of the week on which the principal festivals, and *Tish'ah b'Av*, will fall may be ascertained by combining the first and last letters of the Hebrew alphabet (א"ת, ב"ש) as follows:

א"ת—*Tish'ah b'Av* (ת) falls on the same day of the week as the first day (א) of *Pesaḥ.*

ב"ש—*Shavuoth* (ש) falls on the same day of the week as the second day (ב) of *Pesaḥ.*

ג"ר—*Rosh Hashanah* (ר) falls on the same day of the week as the third day (ג) of *Pesaḥ.*

ד"ק—*Simḥath Torah* (קריאת התורה) falls on the same day of the week as the fourth day (ד) of *Pesaḥ.*

ה"צ—*Yom Kippur* (צום) falls on the same day of the week as the fifth day (ה) of *Pesaḥ.*

ו"ף—*Purim* (פ) falls on the same day of the week as the sixth day (ו) of the preceding *Pesaḥ.*

ז"ע—*Atzmauth* Day (ע), celebrating the anniversary of Israel's declaration of independence (*Iyyar* 5, 1948), falls on the same day of the week as the seventh day (ז) of *Pesaḥ.*

LEVITES   לְוִיִּם

THE men of the tribe of Levi were granted the privileges of priestly rank, while Aaron and his descendants, who were Levites as well as priests, were set apart for the hereditary priesthood. From the age of twenty to fifty, Levites were entitled to serve at the sanctuary as assistants to priests. It has been suggested that at thirty years of age the Levites became eligible to full service of every sort that pertained to Levites at the sanctuary, including the offices of custodians of the sanctuary and its furniture, and musicians, judges, scribes, teachers.

310

Forty-eight towns in various parts of Israel were assigned for their residence, since they were excluded from any territorial inheritance. Those who found no employment in the Temple earned their livelihood through teaching as they travelled throughout the country. For the maintenance of the Levites, a tenth (tithe) of all the yearly produce was set aside for them. They in turn were to contribute to the priests a tenth part of that which they had received from the people (מעשר מן המעשר).

LULAV   לוּלָב

THE palm branch (lulav), decked with sprigs of willow and myrtle, and the festive citron (ethrog), serving as symbols of the entire realm of vegetation, are the characteristic feature of the morning service at the feast of Sukkoth. The myrtle and willow sprigs tied together with the palm branch are held in the right hand, while the citron is held in the left hand, when the following benediction is recited: "Blessed art thou ... who ... hast commanded us concerning the waving of the palm branch." The reference is to the command regarding the celebration of Sukkoth (Leviticus 23:40), traditionally interpreted as follows: "You shall take the fruit of a beautiful tree (ethrog), branches of palm trees (lulav), boughs of leafy trees (hadassim), and water-willows (aravoth), and rejoice before the Lord your God for seven days."

Since the lulav is the most prominent of the four plants (arba'ah minim), it is held in the right hand and mentioned in the benediction. The four species are waved during the recitation of the Hallel in the direction of the four points of the compass, forward and backward as well as upward and downward (na'anu'im), to symbolize the stream of abundance which comes from the heavens and the four directions of the earth. A procession with the lulav and ethrog is made round the synagogue every day of the feast of Sukkoth (except on the Sabbath when the precept of lulav and ethrog does not apply), culminating in the seven processions (hakkafoth) on Hoshana Rabbah.

The lulav and ethrog, required to be flawless because they symbolize God's abundant blessings on earth, have inspired various interpretations in Jewish tradition. No expense is spared by strictly observant Jews to obtain the finest ethrog, the shape of which suggests the human heart, and the perfect palm branch or lulav representing the spinal cord, as well as the myrtle and willow sprigs, the leaves of which

resemble eyes and lips, respectively. The general thought intimated
by the four species is said to be that of harmony and unity between
the various parts of the human body in doing the will of God.

Furthermore, the *ethrog* and the palm branch represent fruit-bear-
ing plants or, metaphorically, men that are eminently productive;
while the myrtle and willow sprigs represent trees that do not bear
fruit, or men that are least productive. But to do the will of God
with a perfect heart, they all must blend into one brotherhood. Most
synagogues provide several sets for worshipers who have not purchased the *arba'ah minim* (four species) for their own use.

SHOWBREAD

THE command concerning the showbread, in Exodus 25:30, is given
in brief: "On the table you shall always keep showbread set before me."
In Leviticus, however, instruction is prescribed as follows: "You
shall take fine flour and bake it into twelve loaves, using two tenths
of an ephah of flour for each loaf. These you shall place in two rows,
six in each row, on the pure gold table before the Lord... On each
Sabbath day, regularly, this bread shall be set out afresh before the
Lord on behalf of the people of Israel as a covenant forever" (24:5-8).
The twelve loaves, representing the twelve tribes of Israel, symbolized
man's constant indebtedness to God who is the source of every
material blessing. The showbread was a special form of meal offering,
which was eaten by the priests in the sanctuary. The *lehem ha-panim*
(bread of the presence) was so named because it was placed before
God, as a permanent expression of gratitude.

The presence-bread, or showbread, was required to be constantly
in the presence of the Lord. Each Sabbath fresh loaves replaced the
old, which then belonged to the priests who ate them in a holy place
because they were regarded as a holy offering. The preparing of these
loaves involved certain information which was kept as a secret by a
priestly set. They were baked on Friday and were placed on the holy
table on Sabbath morning, six in a row, one loaf leaning against the
other. On the top of each row two golden cups of frankincense were
placed. They remained there till the next Sabbath, when the fresh
loaves were brought and the old loaves were given to the priests. The
frankincense was burned in the sacred fire, and a new supply was
placed upon the fresh loaves.

312

LEKHAH DODI

לְכָה דוֹדִי

THE song *Lekhah Dodi* (come, my friend) has been described as perhaps one of the finest pieces of religious poetry in existence. This poem, written by Rabbi Solomon Alkabets (1505-1584), has become universally popular as a hymn welcoming the Sabbath. It spread to all Jewish communities and was the favorite text for synagogal composers, so that a vast number of melodies were set to it.

The name of the author, Shelomo ha-Levi, is found in the form of an acrostic at the beginning of the stanzas. Each stanza consists of four parts, three of which have the same rhyme, while the fourth part ends in the common rhyme *la* throughout the poem. Combining the language of Holy Scriptures into a rare mosaic, the poet employed phrases from the books of Judges, Isaiah, Jeremiah, Psalms. There is scarcely a phrase in the entire hymn which is not borrowed from the Hebrew Bible.

In vivid figures of speech, the poem gives expression to the hope of Israel. Personifying the Sabbath and comparing it to a bride, in the same sense as Israel is likened to a bride (Jeremiah 2:2), the poem starts out with a refrain: "Come, my friend, to meet the bride; let us welcome the Sabbath." This is based on a talmudic passage (Shabbath 119a), where Rabbi Ḥanina and Rabbi Yannai are quoted as having used this expression in saluting the Sabbath. Referring to Israel, the poet exclaims: "Come forth from thy ruins! Long enough have you dwelt in the vale of tears! Shake off your dust, arise! Awake, awake, utter a song! Why are you downcast? Why do you moan? Your God will rejoice over you as a bridegroom rejoices over his bride."

The title *Lekhah Dodi* is borrowed from the Song of Songs (7:12), where an intense delight in rural life breathes through the lines: "Come, my beloved, let us go into the field, let us stay in the villages; let us go early to the vineyards. . ." Following the example of the famous Kabbalist Rabbi Isaac Luria, his disciples used to go outside the city limits of Safed into the open fields to welcome the Sabbath with the psalms and hymns which are now the component parts of the *Kabbalath Shabbath* service on Friday evenings. The name of the author forms the acrostic of *Lekhah Dodi*, each stanza beginning with a letter of his name. The expression "Last in creation, first in God's plan" means that, though the Sabbath came after the creation of the world, it had been designed by God long before he created the entire universe.

LEKHU NERANENAH   לְכוּ נְרַנְּנָה

Psᴀʟᴍ 95, which begins with the words לְכוּ נרננה (come, let us sing), is the first of the six psalms that introduce the Sabbath-eve service. Together with the hymn welcoming the Sabbath bride (לכה דודי), they form what is termed *Kabbalath Shabbath*, the service immediately preceding the *Maʻariv* on Friday evenings. The six psalms, selected by the Kabbalists of the sixteenth century in Eretz Yisrael, are said to symbolize the six workdays of the week. The seventh psalm follows *Lekhah Dodi*, since it is "a song for the Sabbath day" (Psalm 92).

The reason given for the selection of Psalms 95-99 and 29 is that the initial letters of these six hymns, in the Hebrew text, have the numerical value of four hundred and thirty, equaling that of the word נפש (soul). Furthermore, Psalm 29 contains the divine name eighteen times, corresponding to the eighteen benedictions of the *Shemoneh Esreh* prayer, and the eighteen times God is mentioned in the *Shema*. Psalm 29 ends with an assurance of God's favor to his people.

L'OLAM Y'HÉ ADAM   לְעוֹלָם יְהֵא אָדָם

Iɴ ᴛʜᴇ daily preliminary morning service, there is a passage which forms an impressive setting for the *Shema*, the acknowledgment of the Oneness of God, that is recited after it. It reads: "Man should ever be God-fearing in private as well as in public. He should acknowledge the truth, and speak the truth in his heart. . ."

During the fifth century, it was made unlawful for the Babylonian Jews to recite the *Shema* as being a challenge to the Zoroastrian religion, which is based upon the idea of a conflict between the powers of light and those of darkness. Persian dualism was in opposition to Jewish monotheism, according to which One God creates both light and darkness (Isaiah 45:7). Special government officials were posted in the synagogues to watch the services during that period of religious hostilities and persecutions.

The rabbis of the time impressed upon the people the duty of reciting at least the first verse of the *Shema* privately, in their homes, before proceeding to the synagogue for the morning service. The passage לְעוֹלָם יהא אדם is an exhortation to the effect that Judaism must be practised in secrecy during religious persecutions. On the

314

Sabbath, the initial and concluding words of the *Shema* were inserted in the *Kedushah* of the *Musaf* service, when the government spies had left, and the *Shema* was recited congregationally in an abridged form: (שמע ישראל... להיות לכם... אני ה' אלהיכם).

HIGHER MORAL LAW   לִפְנִים מְשׁוּרַת הַדִּין

THE talmudic expression *lifnim mi-shurath ha-din* refers to a man's duty not to insist on the legal rights accorded to him in a lawsuit, such as compensation and damages, but to renounce them in favor of his litigant who happens to be economically weak. Though it literally means *inside the line of the law*, as opposed to *strict law* (דין תורה), it is interpreted in the sense of *beyond the line of the law*.

In regard to Exodus 23:3 ("You shall not be partial to a poor man in his lawsuit"), it has been noted that the biblical view of justice is remarkable for its unbending insistence on the strictest impartiality. If the matter in dispute is a question of money between a rich man and a poor man, the judge is not to give a wrongful verdict in favor of the poor man out of antipathy to the rich and powerful. Sympathy and compassion are great virtues, but even these feelings must be silenced in the presence of justice.

GLEANINGS   לֶקֶט, שִׁכְחָה, פֵּאָה

FOR the benefit of the poor, the fatherless, the widow, and the stranger, the Torah instructs the owner of a field or a vineyard not to gather the grain which the reapers have failed to remove, or the grapes which remain after the vintage: "When you reap the harvest of your land, you shall not reap the field to its very edge, nor shall you glean the stray ears of grain. Likewise, you shall not pick your vineyard bare, nor gather up the grapes that have fallen. You shall leave these for the poor and the stranger" (Leviticus 19:9-10).

The term gleaning refers to the ears of corn which fall from the hand of the reaper. One or two ears, but not three, come within this law. As to the grapes, the reference is to single grapes which drop in the gathering. The whole subject of the rights of the poor to the produce of the land is discussed in Mishnah Peah, the technical term for the corner of the field which must be left for the poor.

The law regarding the gleanings is expressed in substantially the same terms in Deuteronomy 24:19-21, where a similar provision is extended to the olive garden: "When you reap the harvest in your field and overlook a sheaf there, you shall not go back to get it; let it be for the stranger, the orphan or the widow... When you knock down the fruit of your olive trees, you shall not go over the branches a second time; let that be for the stranger, the fatherless and the widow. When you pick your grapes, you shall not go over the vineyard a second time; let what remains be for the stranger, the orphan, and the widow." According to tradition, the minimum of *peah* (part of the crop which the owner was required to leave for the benefit of the poor) was one-sixtieth of the harvest (Mishnah Peah 1:2).

The owner of the crop, who could derive no benefit from the gleanings, was forbidden to discriminate among the poor. He was considered a robber of the poor if he prevented them from coming into his field by keeping dogs to frighten them away. If, however, there were no poor in the place, the owner was not obliged to seek them elsewhere but might appropriate the gleanings to himself (*Yad, Mattenoth Aniyyim* 4:10).

LESHON HA-KODESH　　　　　　　　לְשׁוֹן הַקֹּדֶשׁ

THE Mishnah refers to the Hebrew language as *leshon ha-kodesh*, the holy tongue, to distinguish it from the Aramaic vernacular or other "secular languages" spoken by the Jewish people (Sotah 7:2-4; 8:1).

According to Maimonides, the reason for calling Hebrew *leshon ha-kodesh* lies in the fact that it falls short of indecent expressions and "has no special name for the organ of generation ... nor for the act of generation itself ... it only describes them in figurative language and by way of hints, as if to indicate thereby that these things should not be mentioned, and should therefore have no names; we ought to be silent about them, and when we are compelled to mention them, we must manage to employ for that purpose some suitable expressions, although these are generally used in a different sense..." (*Guide*, 3:8).

Others have affirmed that Hebrew is God's language, in which he gave us the Torah. It was the Hebrew language in which the prophets expressed their lofty ideas and our fathers breathed forth their sufferings and joys. One cannot understand the people of Israel without understanding Hebrew.

316

EVIL GOSSIP   לְשׁוֹן הָרָע

THE vice of slander is condemned in all Jewish writings. "You shall
not go about spreading slander among your people; nor shall you
stand by idly when your neighbor's life is at stake" (Leviticus 19:16).
The connection between the sin of slander which destroys a man's
reputation and any conduct imperiling a man's life is found to be
significant. According to the Talmud, slander is a hideous capital
crime; a slanderer is like one who denies God; God says of the slanderer: "He and I cannot live together in the world" (Arakhin 15b).

We are told that he who covers up a misdeed fosters friendship,
but he who gossips about it separates friends. For lack of wood the
fire dies out; and when there is no talebearer, strife subsides (Proverbs
17:9; 26:20). "If you hear something said, let it die with you; have
courage, it will not make you burst!" (Ben Sira 19:10). "Be not like
a fly, seeking sore spots; cover up your neighbor's flaws, and reveal
them not to the world" (Orḥoth Ḥayyim).

The term slander has been defined as the utterance or dissemination
of false statements or reports concerning a person, or malicious mis-
representation of his actions, in order to defame or injure him (מוֹצִיא
שֵׁם רָע). In Jewish tradition, the law in Leviticus 19:16 is understood
to forbid the peddling of gossip, even if the report is true and told
without malice (Yad, Deoth 7:2).

The offense is much greater if the report is circulated with malicious intent to injure a man's reputation or to expose him to contempt
or derision. According to the Rabbis, evil gossip (לשון הרע) kills
three: the man who tells it; the one who accepts it, the one about whom
it is told. Hence it is referred to as לישנא תליתאי (the triple tongue
or the talk about third persons).

According to Saul Lieberman the only correct explanation of the expression לישנא תליתאי is the three-forked, triple tongue of the snake.
The serpent's tongue gives the impression that it is three-forked.

Uncharitable comment on fellow men is classified as a shade of
slander (אבק לשון הרע), or more literally, "dust of evil speech"
(Bava Bathra 165a). The strongest terms are used in the prohibition
of slandering the dead (Shulḥan Arukh, Oraḥ Ḥayyim 606:3).

The Midrash describes the spreading of malicious reports in four
words: אמור ברומא וקטיל בסוריא (what is spoken in Rome may kill
in Syria—Genesis Rabbah 98:23).

317

LISHMAH   לִשְׁמָה

THE sixth chapter of the *Ethics of the Fathers* begins with the statement that whoever engages in Torah for its own sake merits many
things; nay more, the whole world is worthwhile for his sake. He is
described as a beloved friend, who loves God and mankind; he pleases
God and mankind. The Torah invests him with humility and respect.
Men are benefited by his counsel and sound wisdom, by his understanding and strength.

Another tannaitic expression on the subject of Torah study, for pure
unselfish ends (תורה לשמה), is quoted in the Talmud to the effect
that whoever engages in Torah for its own sake, it becomes to him an
elixir of life (סם חיים); but if a man studies the Torah not for its own
sake, it becomes for him a deadly poison (Ta'anith 7a). His learning
will harm him, as a heavy rain harms the crop. Another talmudic
statement, however, reads: By all means let a man engage in the
study of Torah and in the practice of good deeds, even if not for their
own sake; eventually he will arrive at the stage of doing good for unselfish purposes (Pesaḥim 50b).

In his Mishnah Commentary, Maimonides points out: Since man
is accustomed to act according to the good or the harm which may
result, he loses nothing by shaping his conduct with a view to reward
and punishment until, by habit and zeal, he arrives at an understanding of the truth and serves purely out of love. The human spirit is
narrow and, while acquiring wisdom, hopes for other, more material
advantages. In searching for truth, the goal is truth itself.

L'SHANAH HA-BAAH   לְשָׁנָה הַבָּאָה

THE formula לשנה הבאה בירושלים (next year in Jerusalem) is liturgically used twice a year: at the end of the *Seder* service and at the
end of the *Ne'ilah* service. This custom is explained on the basis of
the well-known difference of opinion that prevailed between the tannaitic sages Rabbi Eliezer and Rabbi Joshua. According to the one,
the future deliverance of Israel will take place during *Nisan* just as
they were liberated from Egyptian slavery during *Nisan* (בניסן נגאלו
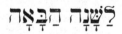ובניסן עתידין להגאל); according to the other, the future deliverance
will occur during *Tishri* (בניסן נגאלו ובתשרי עתידין להגאל).

318

THE Torah declares: "All the creatures that swarm on the ground are loathsome and shall not be eaten... Do not make yourselves loathsome or unclean with any swarming creature... You shall be holy, because I am holy" (Leviticus 11:41-45). The holiness spoken of here is physical in the sense that in keeping themselves free from defilement and contamination, the people learn to avoid what is morally impure.

In addition to forbidden meats, there are some laws concerning vegetable and tree plants, such as: 1) *Orlah* (uncircumcised), that is, unconsecrated; the fruit of a tree forbidden during the first three years after its planting. In the fourth year the fruit is to be dedicated to God, after which the owner is free to enjoy the use of it (Leviticus 19:23). 2) *Ḥadash* (new grain) was forbidden until the second day of *Pesaḥ*, when the *omer* was offered in the Temple in celebration of the grain harvest; a sheaf of new barley was waved before the Lord, as an acknowledgment of his bounty and a consecration of the harvest to him (Leviticus 23:9-14). 3) *Kilayim*, produce of two species of grain or of other vegetables sown in a vineyard; the sowing of mixed seeds in gardens or in fields was also prohibited (Leviticus 19:19; Deuteronomy 22:9). Such mixtures are forbidden in the Torah, as opening the door to the unnatural sins mentioned elsewhere.

Meat permissible for food must come from mammals that chew the cud and also have divided hoofs, and from birds that are not specifically prohibited in the Torah (Leviticus 11:13-19; Deuteronomy 14:11-18). These must be ritually slaughtered and free from such a defect in a vital organ that might have caused their death had they not been slaughtered.

Careful examination, therefore, is enjoined before and after the slaughtering of animals to ascertain their general condition of health. *Shehitah* and *bedikah* (slaughtering and examination) are the two essentials that are spoken of together in connection with the observance of *kashruth*. The term *kashruth* literally means fitness (as food). Since the identification of the birds mentioned in the Torah is now impossible, the list of clean birds, permissible as food, is limited to chicken, goose, duck, pigeon, pheasant, partridge, quail, and turkey. Even in all these, blood is prohibited; all the blood which remains after *shehitah* must be drained by a process called *melihah* (salting).

319

All fish that have fins and scales are permitted. Though the eggs and milk of unclean birds and mammals are equally unclean, honey of bees is regarded as transformed pollen and is permitted to be eaten.

The sages of the Talmud based the prohibition against eating meat and milk together on the law, repeated three times in the Torah, against boiling a kid in its mother's milk (Exodus 23:19; 34:26; Deuteronomy 14:21). From this the rabbis derived three distinct prohibitions: cooking meat and milk together; eating such mixture; deriving any benefit from such mixture. The regulations concerning this law against meat-milk mixture (בשר בחלב) are to be found in the Talmud and the codes. The Yiddish adjectives *milchig* and *fleishig*, describing milk and meat products, are familiar terms.

FLOOD מַבּוּל

THE biblical flood story, unlike frequent flood stories in the ancient literature of the Babylonians and others, possesses the power to stir the conscience of the world. It proclaims the message that unless human society is based on justice and mercy it will perish. The incident of the flood, as related in the Torah, possesses ethical and spiritual significance. God is merciful and interested in the welfare of humanity. Righteousness is rewarded; the wicked are punished.

"Noah was a just man, blameless among the people of his generation... The earth was corrupt in the sight of God, and it was filled with violence ... all men lived corruptly on the earth. God said to Noah: I will destroy them with the earth... God blessed Noah and his sons, saying to them: Be fruitful and multiply, and fill the earth. The fear and dread of you shall be upon all the wild animals of the earth..." (Genesis 6:9-9:2).

SELECT PEARLS מִבְחַר הַפְּנִינִים

ORIGINALLY composed in Arabic, Ibn Gabirol's *Mivḥar ha-Peninim* has survived in a Hebrew translation made in the twelfth century. Rabbi Solomon ibn Gabirol, the famous poet-philosopher who lived in Spain during the eleventh century, began to compose Hebrew poetry at an early age and, during his short life, won for himself a place among the greatest Hebrew poets.

320

Judah Alḥarizi of the thirteenth century, writing on Ibn Gabirol, says: "The poets who succeeded him strove to learn from his poems, but were unable to touch even the dust of his feet. . . He was snatched away when still young . . . his light was extinguished before he had completed his thirtieth year."

In his long philosophic poem *Kether Malkhuth* (Royal Crown), skill-fully dealing with the problem of sin, Ibn Gabirol gives "one of the most beautiful descriptions ever penned of the truth of the divine in-dwelling." Ibn Gabirol may well refer to his *Select Pearls* when he writes: "I gather stray phrases into strings of thought, and from scat-tered words I collect pearls of wisdom." Here are several excerpts:

"A man is wise when he pursues wisdom, but if he is conceited by his attainment of it he becomes a fool. Wisdom gained in old age is like a mark made on the sand; wisdom gained in youth is like an engraving on stone. None is more deserving of sympathy than a wise man who is subjected to the judgment of a fool.

"The mark of an intelligent man is humility; the mark of a fool is impudence. Silence is the best answer to a fool. He who craves more than he needs cannot enjoy what he has. There are three types of friends: one type is like food without which you cannot exist; another is like medicine, which you need only occasionally; a third is like a disease, which you can dispense with altogether.

"If you want people to dislike you, visit them frequently; if you wish them to like you, visit them rarely. None is so poor as the man who is afraid of becoming poor. Everyone can enjoy life except the man who envies others: only the misfortune of others pleases him.

"Accept the truth from whatever source it comes, even from your inferiors. If you keep a secret it is your prisoner; but if you disclose it, you become its prisoner. Why are the wise more often at the doors of the rich than the rich at the doors of the wise? Because the wise appreciate the advantage of wealth, while the rich do not know the value of wisdom."

In Gabirol's כתר מלכות (Royal Crown), which has been part of the *Sephardic Maḥzor* for the eve of *Yom Kippur*, the biblical verses are introduced with extraordinary artistic skill. Following are several expressions culled from Gabirol's long poem: ". . . Thou art One, and at the mystery of thy Oneness the wise are perplexed, for they know not what it is. . . Thou art existent, but the hearing of the ear and the sight of the eye cannot perceive thee; nor can the *how*, the *where-fore*, or the *whence* be applied to thee. . . Thou art existent, and hadst

321

been before time was, and didst abide without space. Thou art existent, but thy mystery is hidden—who can reach it? . . . Thou art wise, but thou didst not learn from another. . .''

TOWER OF BABEL מִגְדַּל בָּבֶל

THE Torah relates that the descendants of Noah, after the flood, said to one another: "Let us build ourselves a city and a tower with its top in the heavens; let us make a name for ourselves lest we be scattered all over the earth... So the Lord scattered them all over the earth, and they stopped building the city. For this reason it was called Babel (בבל), because there the Lord confused (בלל) the speech of all the earth" (Genesis 11:4-9).

The phrase וראשו בשמים (its top in the heavens) has been interpreted as a Babylonian figure of speech in the sense of a very high tower, similar to the description of the Canaanite cities as "great and fortified to the heavens" (Deuteronomy 1:28). Ibn Ezra's comment on Genesis 11:4 reads: "It is probable that they were neither so foolish as to believe that they could ascend to heaven, nor were they afraid of another flood. They merely wanted a central and conspicuous city which would ensure them fame."

Modern scholars generally assume that the reference is to a Babylonian temple tower, a step-temple or ziggurat. An ancient ziggurat in Babylon existed already in the second millennium before the common era. It had eight stories, and was referred to as the "house of the foundation stone of heaven and earth." It was like a step-pyramid, about three hundred feet high above the foundation. The top was reached by a stairway leading from terrace to terrace. It was begun by Hammurabi and developed by a number of other kings; Nebuchadnezzar completed it in the sixth century before the common era. The tower-temple has been regarded by architects as a stage in the development of minaret and spire.

It has been observed that the biblical story cannot mean that the erection of the tower was the only cause of the diversity of languages. It shows rather the futility of human attempts to maintain unity by material means alone, excluding God. From the earliest times the splendid buildings of Babylonia were among the most remarkable achievements of human power and pride. Hence Babylon was seen as the emblem of grandiose ambition and despotic arrogance.

MAGGID　　　　　　　　　　　　מַגִּיד

THE expression "speaking the truth and declaring what is right" (דובר צדק מגיד מישרים) is found in Isaiah 45:19, whence the term *maggid* for one who preaches sermons in which Jewish stories and moral lessons are embodied. The midrashic literature has preserved much of this type of popular lectures referred to as *derashoth*. The regular form for the sermon consisted of three parts during the talmudic-midrashic period: 1) the introduction or opening (פתיחה), 2) the exposition proper (דרוש), and 3) the conclusion. The preacher began by quoting a biblical verse, interpreting it by illustration and parable that would gradually lead up to the text that he was particularly trying to explain to his audience. Having derived from his text various ideas linked or associated with it, by the use of parable, story and allegory, the preacher concluded with words of comfort followed by the *Kaddish* prayer. As a rule, the *maggidim* inspired the people with expressions of encouragement and hope amidst all suffering.

Beginning in the seventeenth century, there were two kinds of *maggidim* in Germany and Poland: the stationary *maggid*, often appointed by the *Kehillah* (Jewish community), and the itinerant *maggid*, who occasionally delivered his *derashah* in smaller communities and rural localities. Since the *maggid* was also known as *darshan* (homiletical lecturer), the title was corrupted often to *baldarsher* in popular speech. The *maggid*, as a rule, made extensive use of aggadic, midrashic and ethical writings, making his *derashah* a religiously enriching experience for hundreds of people who came to listen and be edified. The *derashah* frequently contained not only words of comfort and an expression of hope for a better future but also stern reproof and admonitions, which moved the audience to sobs and tears. Hence, the *maggid* was also called מוכיח (one who exposes, reproves).

Rabbi Jacob Kranz, known as the Dubner Maggid (1740-1804), was the most famous Jewish preacher of his time. His sermons were extremely popular, eloquent, and permeated with a rich variety of parables (*meshalim*) and illustrations taken from human life. The Khelmer Maggid (1828-1900), was one of the wandering preachers who visited hundreds of Russian and Polish Jewish communities, bringing them tidings of the world without, as well as his homiletic talents; he was the envoy and preacher of the moralist movement founded by Rabbi Israel Salanter in the nineteenth century. The title of

323

Maggid was also applied to various *Tsaddikim*, or saintly leaders in the Ḥasidic movement, such as the Great Maggid of Meseritsh, the Kozienitzer Maggid, and the Turisker Maggid.

DEAD SEA SCROLLS מְגִלּוֹת יָם הַמֶּלַח

A PROLIFIC literature has sprung up in many languages since 1947, when a number of manuscripts were found in the desert of Judah, not far from the Dead Sea. It soon appeared that this was only the beginning of what was described as the greatest manuscript discovery of modern times. In addition to the scientific and scholarly works written on the discovery and significance of the world-famed Dead Sea Scrolls, much has been said in periodicals, newspapers, television and on the radio. This lively activity has been directed at all who are concerned with religion and archeology, as well as those who relish one of the most momentous news stories in the twentieth century.

Solomon Zeitlin, however, has vigorously maintained in a growing series of articles, published in the *Jewish Quarterly Review*, that the scrolls are neither so old nor authentic as is generally admitted. One scholar has attempted to prove, from the grammatical and other peculiarities of the texts, that they are only from the early Middle Ages. Another, in England, has asserted that the authors and copyists of the texts were Jewish-Christians, not Jews. Archeological exploration discovered in the neighborhood of Khirbet Qumran, where the scrolls had been found, some eight miles from Jericho: a cemetery of over a thousand graves, a central building, and central caves containing fragments of old manuscripts.

The men at Qumran occupied themselves with writing, reading and studying. Ink-wells have been found in the remains of the buildings at Ain Feshkha on the northwest shore of the Dead Sea. It has been speculated that if all the books of which the remains have come to light in the caves of Qumran were now in the kingdom of Jordan, the community must have possessed an extensive library, consisting of many hundreds of volumes. But possibly members of other groups hid their books in the surrounding caves along with those of Qumran in the hour of danger. Fragments have been found of all the biblical books, except the book of Esther. Among the fragments of the Apocrypha and Pseudepigrapha were two Hebrew manuscripts of Ben Sira (Ecclesiasticus), one Hebrew and two Aramaic texts of Tobit, the Hebrew version of the book of Jubilees, the Aramaic version of the book of Enoch. Some Greek biblical texts have also been found at Qumran, as well as sectarian books and commentaries on Habakkuk, Micah and Nahum, explaining the prophetic writings in relation to the history of the sect.

The so-called *Manual of Discipline* deals with the sect's organization and teachings. Another scroll, called *The War of the Sons of Light with the Sons of Darkness,* is about nine feet in length and six inches wide. It describes a conflict between the righteous and the wicked. The *Scroll of Thanksgivings* is to a great extent reminiscent of the style of the biblical psalms, that is to say, the poets of the sect composed mosaics of expressions from the book of Psalms. The *Lamech Scroll,* in Aramaic, contains chapters from the book of Genesis, embellished and expanded by the introduction of aggadic material. Manuscripts of Deuteronomy, Isaiah and the Psalms, are the most numerous.

The most widely-accepted conjecture is that the Qumran community belonged to the Essenes, described by Philo of Alexandria as a sect of Jews, over four thousand in number, called *Essenes* because of their saintliness.

SCROLL OF ESTHER   מְגִלַּת אֶסְתֵּר

T H E scroll of Esther, known as the *Megillah,* is chanted in the synagogues at the eve of *Purim* and again the next morning. In derision of Haman, the arch enemy of the Jewish people, children have been accustomed to stamp their feet or turn their noise-makers (*greggers*) at the mention of his name. The custom of stamping the feet has been explained as symbolizing the erasing of Haman's name. The names of Haman's ten sons are however, recited in one breath, so as to lessen the apparent gloating over their deserved execution, for it is written: "Do not rejoice when your enemy falls, do not exult when he is overthrown" (Proverbs 24:17).

The last of the five scrolls that form part of the third division of the Bible, *Megillath Esther* tells the story of a Jewish girl who used her influence as queen of Persia to save her people from a general massacre which Haman had plotted against them. It is a tale of plot and counterplot, showing the downfall of the arrogant and the vindication of the innocent. Haman's vanity, malice and cruelty are graphically described; his fate reminds us that "pride goes before a fall." Ahasuerus is painted as a pompous and feeble-minded monarch, who agrees to Haman's plot without a thought. Though the name of God is not mentioned in the *Megillah*, the story clearly implies that God used Mordecai and Esther as instruments for the deliverance of a persecuted people.

HASMONEAN SCROLL   מְגִלַּת הַחַשְׁמוֹנָאִים

THE Scroll of the Hasmoneans, known also as the Scroll of Antiochus (מגלת אנטיוכוס), has come down to us both in Aramaic and Hebrew. The Hebrew version is a literal translation from the Aramaic original, which is said to have been composed in the seventh century.

Rav Saadyah Gaon of the tenth century attributed its authorship to the five sons of Mattathias. It still forms part of the liturgy of the Yemenite Jews. During the medieval period, the *Megillath Antiochus* was read in the Italian synagogues on *Ḥanukkah* as the *Megillath Esther* is read on *Purim*.

The author of this *Megillah* apparently drew largely upon the midrashic interpretations of the *Ḥanukkah* story, although the first book of the Maccabees was not unknown to him. It served as the chief source for a knowledge of the Maccabean struggle known to the medieval Jews. Its legendary nature, and the many stories graphically depicted in this scroll, contributed to making it popular and acceptable to many Jewish congregations.

MEGILLATH TA'ANITH   מְגִלַּת תַּעֲנִית

THE *Megillath Ta'anith* (scroll of fasting) enumerates thirty-five eventful days in Jewish history which were celebrated as festivals, when public fasting was forbidden. Written in Aramaic, this early tannaitic work is flanked by a Hebrew commentary composed not earlier than the seventh century. The many quotations from the *Megillath Ta'anith* in the talmudic literature are taken from the Aramaic text and are introduced by the term *kethiv* (it is written), as in the case of quotations from the Bible (Ḥullin 129b; Megillah 5b; Ta'anith 12a and 18b). The marginal Hebrew comments and annotations, known as scholium, are distinct in form and in value as a historical source from the original Aramaic text, which must have been compiled before the destruction of the Second Temple.

326

The Mishnah, quoting from the Aramaic text of *Megillath Ta'anith*, treats it as an ancient source in the following passage: "Any day concerning which it is written in *Megillath Ta'anith* that *one must not mourn*, it is also forbidden to mourn the day before. Rabbi Yosé says: It is forbidden both the day before and the following day. Where it is written that *none may fast*, it is permitted to fast both the day before and the following day. . ." (Ta'anith 2:8). Unlike the original Aramaic text, the scholium contains traditional accounts and legendary material in addition to some old *Baraithoth*, or tannaitic statements, which are deemed historically reliable.

Extant in many editions, the *Megillath Ta'anith* has had many commentaries. Solomon Zeitlin and others have dealt with the historical themes of *Megillath Ta'anith* and elucidated them as well as the contents of the appended Hebrew glosses. It has been proposed that *Megillath Ta'anith* must have been composed at the beginning of the common era, when Judea was made a Roman province to the great indignation of the Jews. This calendar of victories was intended to fan the spark of liberty among the people and to fill them with confidence and courage by reminding them of the Maccabean victories.

MAGEN AVOTH   מָגֵן אָבוֹת

MAGEN AVOTH is the abridged form of the *Amidah* prayer for Sabbath-eve. It is called *me'en sheva* because it contains the substance of the seven benedictions constituting the *Amidah*. *Magen Avoth* was originally added in order to prolong the service for the convenience of late-comers.

The synagogues were often located outside the precinct of the city, since the rulers did not tolerate Jewish worship within the confines of their municipalities, and it was dangerous to walk home alone at night. By prolonging the Sabbath-eve service, which was far better attended than weekday services, the late-comers were given an opportunity to finish their prayers with the rest of the congregation (Rashi, Shabbath 24b).

In his *Siddur* (page 243), Rashi points out a similar reason for the addition of the Mishnah chapter *Bammeh Madlikin* which, in his opinion, should be recited after the Sabbath-eve service, so as to enable the late-comers to complete their prayers and leave the synagogue together with their fellow worshipers. Accordingly, the foregoing additions are omitted on festival occasions when late-coming is unlikely.

The Sabbath *Amidah* contains only seven benedictions, omitting thirteen petitions that are included in the weekday *Shemoneh Esreh*, because no personal requests are permissible on Sabbaths and festivals. Upon reciting the eliminated thirteen petitions, the worshiper's attention is directed to his failings and troubles; on the days of festive repose one is expected to maintain a cheerful mood and refrain from dwelling upon sad thoughts.

MAGEN DAVID מָגֵן דָּוִד

LIKE the seven-branched *Menorah*, the *Magen David*, composed of two triangles, has been a symbolical ornament of Judaism for many centuries. It was found in the Capernaum synagogue of the third century and on a Jewish tombstone in southern Italy, likewise dated as early as the third century of the common era. Since the *Magen David* (David's shield) is not mentioned in rabbinic literature, and has been found on Roman mosaic pavements, it is assumed that the star formed of two superimposed triangles is not of Jewish origin.

The earliest literary source which mentions the *Magen David* is the Karaite work *Eshkol ha-Kofer* of the twelfth century. The first Zionist congress adopted it as a symbol, with the word Zion in the center. During the first World War it was used by Jewish organizations doing military relief work and describing themselves as the Red Magen David (*Magen David Adom*).

In Israel, the *Magen David Adom* corresponds to the Red Cross. Part of its annual budget is provided by friends outside Israel in the form of gift ambulances.

Franz Rosenzweig (1886-1929), who developed his Jewish philosophy in his main work *Stern der Erlösung* (Star of Redemption), describes the universe as consisting of three fundamental concepts, God-World-Man, represented by the three points of the upper triangle of the *Magen David*, and three basic actions, Creation-Revelation-Redemption, represented by the three points of the lower triangle of the hexagram. The six points of the two inverted triangles are interwoven in the same manner as the six concepts of the universe are interwoven. The points of the hexagram allude to the relationship of God to man and world, on the one hand, and to redemption afforded to God's creation by means of obedience to his revelation. God, having fashioned the world, chose man for a special task. The world is man's laboratory; man must strive eternally; in life he finds God. Judaism holds the completed star; it is Israel's symbol. Through inward growth, Israel can fashion the star for all of humanity.

MID'ORAITHA   מִדְאוֹרַיְתָא

A DISTINCTION is made between biblical precepts which are directly prescribed in the Torah (מדאוריתא) and rabbinic precepts (מדרבנן). The total number of precepts that have been directly traced to the Torah is six hundred and thirteen. Of these, two hundred forty-eight are affirmative (מצוות עשה); three hundred sixty-five are negative (מצוות לא־תעשה). The two categories of precepts, affirmative and negative, are said to be numerically equivalent to the two hundred forty-eight bones in the human body and the three hundred sixty-five days in the solar year, respectively.

MEASURE FOR MEASURE   מִדָּה כְּנֶגֶד מִדָּה

THE concept of *measure for measure*, described as one of the great principles underlying the divine rule, is frequently illustrated in talmudic-midrashic literature. Striking examples from Jewish law and history are cited in Mishnah Sotah (1:7-9), where we are told that as a man deals he will be dealt with (במדה שאדם מודד בה מודדין לו): "Samson followed the desire of his eyes, therefore the Philistines gouged out his eyes. Absalom gloried in his hair, therefore he was hanged by his hair. . ." According to Mishnah Avoth 2:7, Hillel saw a skull floating on the surface of the water, and he addressed it: "Because you have drowned others, you have been drowned by others; and those who have drowned you shall themselves be drowned." That is to say, God always requites measure for measure.

The law of retaliation (like for like) was abandoned by Jewish tradition in favor of fines and penalties. The law known as *lex talionis* ("life for life, eye for eye, tooth for tooth, hand for hand, foot for foot, burn for burn, wound for wound"—Exodus 21:23-25) is in the spirit of even-handed justice. The sages of the Talmud maintained that "life for life" signified monetary compensation, since there was no intention to kill. The rule "eye for eye" has been interpreted to mean that a fair and equitable relation must exist between the crime and the punishment and that all citizens are equal before the law, so that the injuries of *all* must be regarded according to the same standard.

STANDARDS, TRAITS מִדּוֹת

THE word *middoth*, from the Hebrew verb מדד (to measure), represents a variety of related meanings. It signifies dimensions, proportions, rules, standards, attributes. The phrases מדת הדין and מדת הרחמים refer to divine justice and divine mercy, respectively. The thirteen divine attributes (Exodus 34:6-7) are called שלש עשרה מדות. The Mishnah employs the term *middoth* in a description of types, temperaments, characteristics, and dispositions. Thus we read:

"There are four types of men: He who says, *What is mine is mine and what is yours is yours*, is the ordinary type (מדה בינונית), though some say this is a Sodom type (מדת סדום). *What is mine is yours and what is yours is mine*, is ignorant. *What is mine is yours and what is yours is yours*, is saintly. *What is yours is mine and what is mine is mine*, is wicked" (Avoth 5:13).

The first of the four types mentioned neither gives nor takes; he is neither good nor bad, but intermediate. Since, however, he is indifferent to the welfare of others, there are some sages who regard him as a type of Sodom, notorious for corruption and selfishness. The second type is characterized as ignorant, because he does not know the Jewish law, according to which one must do good to others unconditionally, without a view to recompense.

In the same connection, four types of students are described in Avoth 5:15, by these similes: the sponge, absorbing indiscriminately everything, the true and the false; the funnel, retaining none of the subjects learned; the strainer, retaining what is useless and forgetting what is useful; the sieve, retaining what is best.

A man possessing good traits is called *baal middoth* (בעל מדות), meaning *middoth tovoth* (good qualities). In the *Ethics of the Fathers*, two types of people are briefly defined: "Whoever possesses the following three qualities is of the disciples of our father Abraham, namely: generosity, humility, and modesty. Those who belong to the followers of wicked Balaam, however, possess an evil eye, a haughty spirit, and excessive desire (Avoth 5:22).

330

Conceit (גאוה) is condemned as stupid and devastating: "Woe to those who are wise in their own eyes. . . Be not wise in your own eyes. . . You see a man wise in his own eyes—there is more hope for a fool than for him. . . The man of haughty eyes and puffed-up heart I will not endure. . . Pride goes before disaster, and a haughty spirit before a fall" (Isaiah 5:21; Proverbs 3:7; 26:12; Psalm 101:5; Proverbs 16:18). "Do not exalt yourself, or you may fall, and bring disgrace upon yourself" (Ben Sira 1:30).

There is a tannaitic statement that if a person becomes conceited let him remember that a mosquito preceded him in the divine order of creation (Tosefta, Sanhedrin 8:8). In his work *Imré No'am*, Rabbi Meir Hurwitz expresses himself that he is glad he is guilty of some sins, else he might be guilty of the greatest of all sins—conceit.

RULES OF INTERPRETATION   מִדּוֹת

THE thirteen rules (*middoth*), by means of which the Torah is interpreted in talmudic literature, are expounded in the *Baraitha d'Rabbi Ishmael* which serves as an introduction to the tannaitic commentary on the book of Leviticus, the *Sifra*.

Tradition has it that the rules according to which the oral law is derived from the written law were handed down from Sinai. It is for this reason that the *Baraitha d'Rabbi Ishmael* has been included in the daily Prayerbook as part of the daily minimum of study required of every Jew. The unity of written and oral law is the pillar upon which Judaism rests. The term *Baraitha* means a tannaitic collection of teachings that has not been included in the Mishnah. Rabbi Ishmael died as a martyr in the year 135, after the defeat of Bar Kokhba.

In order to form a correct idea of the talmudic interpretation of the Torah, one must be acquainted with the thirteen rules (*middoth*), formulated by Rabbi Ishmael on the basis of the seven *middoth* of Hillel. Following are the thirteen rules, each of which is accompanied by an illustration; these usually reflect the logic of the Talmud.

1) Inference is drawn from a minor premise to a major one, or from a major premise to a minor one (קל וחומר).

If, for example, a certain act is forbidden on an ordinary festival, it is so much the more forbidden on *Yom Kippur;* if a certain act is permissible on *Yom Kippur*, it is so much the more permissible on an ordinary festival.

2) From the similarity of words or phrases occurring in two passages it is inferred that what is expressed in the one applies also to the other (גזרה שוה).

The phrase "Hebrew slave" (Exodus 21:2) is ambiguous, for it may mean a heathen slave owned by a Hebrew, or else, a slave who is a Hebrew. That the latter is the correct meaning is proved by a reference to the phrase "your Hebrew brother" in Deuteronomy 15:12, where the same law is mentioned (... "If your Hebrew brother is sold to you...").

3) A general principle, as contained in one or two biblical laws, is applicable to all related laws (בנין אב).

(a) From Deuteronomy 24:6 ("No one shall take a handmill or an upper millstone in pledge, for he would be taking a life in pledge") the Rabbis concluded: "Everything which is used for preparing food is forbidden to be taken in pledge." (b) From Exodus 21:26-27 ("If a man strikes the eye of his slave ... and destroys it, he must let him go free in compensation for his eye. If he knocks out the tooth of his slave ... he must let him go free ...") the Rabbis concluded that when any part of the slave's body is mutilated by the master, the slave shall be set free.

4) When a generalization is followed by a specification, only what is specified applies (כלל ופרט).

In Leviticus 18:6 the law reads: "None of you shall marry anyone related to him." This generalization is followed by a specification of forbidden marriages. Hence, this prohibition applies only to those expressly mentioned.

5) When a specification is followed by a generalization, all that is implied in the generalization applies (פרט וכלל).

In Exodus 22:9 we read: "If a man gives to his neighbor an ass, or an ox, or a sheep, to keep, or any animal, and it dies..." The general phrase "any animal," which follows the specification, includes in this law all kinds of animals.

6) If a generalization is followed by a specification and this in turn by a generalization, one must be guided by what the specification implies (כלל ופרט וכלל).

In Exodus 22:8 we are told that an embezzler shall pay double to his neighbor "for anything embezzled [generalization], for ox, or ass, or sheep, or clothing [specification], or any article lost" [generalization]. Since the specification includes only movable property, and objects of intrinsic value, the fine of double payment does not apply

332

to embezzled real estate, nor to notes and bills, since the latter represent only a symbolic value.

7) When, however, for the sake of clearness, a generalization necessarily requires a specification, or when a specification requires a generalization, rules 4 and 5 do not apply (כלל שהוא צריך לפרט ופרט שהוא צריך לכלל).

In Leviticus 17:13 we read: "He shall pour out its blood, and *cover* it with *dust*." The verb "to cover" is a general term, since there are various ways of covering a thing; "with dust" is specific. If we were to apply rule 4 to this passage, the law would be that the blood of the slaughtered animal must be covered with nothing except dust. Since, however, the general term "to cover" may also mean "to hide," our present passage necessarily requires the specific expression "with dust"; otherwise, the law might be interpreted to mean that the blood is to be concealed in a closed vessel. On the other hand, the specification "with dust" without the general expression "to cover" would be meaningless.

8) Whatever is first implied in a generalization and afterwards specified to teach us something new, is expressly stated not only for its own sake, but to teach something additional concerning all the instances implied in the generalization (דבר שיצא מן הכלל ללמד).

In Deuteronomy 22:1 we are told that the finder of lost property must return it to its owner. In a next verse the Torah adds: "You shall do the same . . . with his *garment* and with anything lost by your brother . . . which you have found . . ." *Garment*, though included in the general expression "anything lost," is specifically mentioned in order to indicate that the duty to announce the finding of lost articles applies only to such objects which are likely to have an owner, and which have, as in the case of clothing, some marks by which they can be identified.

9) Whatever is first implied in a general law and afterwards specified to add another provision similar to the general law, is specified in order to alleviate, and not to increase, the severity of that particular provision (דבר שהיה בכלל ויצא לטעון טוען אחר שהוא כענינו, יצא להקל ולא להחמיר).

In Exodus 35:2-3 we read: "Whoever does any work on the Sabbath shall be put to death; you shall not light a fire on the Sabbath day." The law against lighting a fire on the Sabbath, though already implied in "any work," is mentioned separately in order to indicate that the penalty for lighting a fire on the Sabbath is not as drastic.

333

10) Whatever is first implied in a general law and afterwards specified to add another provision which is not similar to the general law, is specified in order to alleviate in some respects, and in others to increase the severity of that particular provision (דבר שהיה בכלל ויצא לטעון טוען אחר שלא כענינו, יצא להקל ולהחמיר).

According to Exodus 21:29-30, the proprietor of a vicious animal which has killed a man or woman must pay such compensation as may be imposed on him by the court. In a succeeding verse the Torah adds: "If the ox gores a slave, male or female, he must pay the master thirty shekels of silver." The case of a slave, though already included in the preceding general law of the slain man or woman, contains a different provision, the *fixed* amount of compensation, with the result that whether the slave was valued at more than thirty shekels or less than thirty shekels, the proprietor of the animal must invariably pay thirty shekels.

11) Whatever is first implied in a general law and is afterwards specified to determine a new matter, the terms of the general law can no longer apply to it, unless Scripture expressly declares that they do apply (דבר שהיה בכלל ויצא לדון בדבר החדש . . .).

The guilt-offering which a cured leper had to bring was unlike all other guilt-offerings in this, that some of its blood was sprinkled on the person who offered it (Leviticus 14:13-14). On account of this peculiarity none of the rules connected with other offerings would apply to that brought by a cured leper, had not the Torah expressly added: "As the sin-offering so is the guilt-offering."

12) A dubious word or passage is explained from its context or from a subsequent expression (דבר הלמד מענינו ודבר הלמד מסופו).

(a) The noun *tinshemeth* occurs in Leviticus 11:18 among the unclean birds, and again (verse 30) among the reptiles. Hence, it becomes certain that *tinshemeth* is the name of a certain bird as well as of a certain reptile. (b) In Deuteronomy 19:6, with regard to the cities of refuge where the manslayer is to flee, we read: "So that the avenger of blood may not pursue the manslayer . . . and slay him, *and he is not deserving of death*." That the last clause refers to the slayer, and not to the blood avenger, is made clear by the subsequent clause: "inasmuch as he hated him not in time past."

13) Similarly, if two biblical passages contradict each other, they can be harmonized only by a third passage (הכתוב השלישי מכריע).

In Exodus 13:6 we read: "Seven days you shall eat unleavened bread," and in Deuteronomy 16:8 we are told: "Six days you shall eat unleavened bread." The contradiction between these two passages is explained by a reference to a third passage (Leviticus 23:14), where the use of the new produce is forbidden until the second day of Passover, after the offering of the *omer*. If, therefore, the unleavened bread was prepared of the new grain, it could only be eaten six days of Passover. Hence, the passage in Exodus 13:6 must refer to unleavened bread prepared of the produce of a previous year.

MIDRASH   מִדְרָשׁ

THE term *Midrash* (investigation) signifies study and interpretation; hence, *Beth ha-Midrash* denotes a talmudic school. For the most part, the purpose of the midrashic literature is to explain the biblical text from the ethical and devotional point of view. It is then referred to as *Midrash Haggadah*, in contrast to *Midrash Halakhah* which is mainly concerned with the derivation of laws from scriptural texts.

Rabbi Akiva developed the science of *Midrash Halakhah* to a point where no biblical phrase or word or even letter was insignificant. The results of *Midrash Halakhah* are embodied in the tannaitic Midrashim: *Mekhilta* on Exodus, *Sifra* on Leviticus, *Sifré* on the books of Numbers and Deuteronomy.

Midrash Haggadah is a form of teaching that seeks to admonish and edify. "If you wish to know the Creator of the world, learn *Haggadah;* from it you will come to know God and cling to his ways" (Sifré Deuteronomy, 49). The historical themes of the Bible are midrashically interpreted in such a sense that the entire story of Israel becomes a continuous revelation of God's love and justice.

The Midrash has proved an unfailing spring with the power to sustain and strengthen the Jewish thirst for the word of the living God. Ever since the third century, the most flourishing period of haggadic activity in the Holy Land, the Midrash has represented an important medium for the expression of Jewish thought.

Midrash Rabbah consists of a series of sizable Midrash collections on the Torah and the Five *Megilloth* (Song of Songs, Ruth, Lamentations, Ecclesiastes, Esther). It has been shown by scholars that these collections, referred to as Large Midrash, are divergent in character and originate from various circles and periods.

Genesis Rabbah, the Midrash on the book of Genesis, is called in Hebrew *Bereshith Rabbah*. It consists of a hundred sections, each containing a chain of interpretive *aggadoth*. Scholars consider it as one of the earliest Midrashim that was edited not later than the sixth century. *Exodus Rabbah,* or *Shemoth Rabbah* in Hebrew, dates from the eleventh century even though it includes extracts from ancient Midrashim. *Leviticus Rabbah,* or *Vayyikra Rabbah,* dates from the sixth century as one of the earliest Midrashim. *Numbers Rabbah,* or *Bemidbar Rabbah,* was compiled not earlier than the twelfth century. Much of it greatly resembles *Midrash Tanḥuma.* The last eight sections (15-23) are essentially *Midrash Tanḥuma. Deuteronomy Rabbah,* or *Devarim Rabbah,* was compiled in the tenth century.

Midrash Tanḥuma, exists in two different compilations. It derives its name from Rabbi Tanḥuma bar Abba who is frequently quoted in the various introductions of halakhic character. It is also known as *Midrash Yelammedenu,* because the introductions often begin with the formula *yelammedenu Rabbenu* (instruct us, our master). The work contains a great deal of messianic contemplation, characteristic of rabbinic sermonising, and has always been popular.

The *Pesikta* homilies, comprising two separate collections (*Pesikta d'Rabbi Kahana* and *Pesikta Rabbathi*) revolve around the festivals and other special occasions. The great collection *Yalkut Shimeoni* is a compilation from a large number of midrashic works on all the books of the Bible. In it are numerous passages saved from books that have been lost in the course of many centuries.

In addition to the principal *Midrashim* there are scores of smaller *Midrashim* which have been assembled by Jewish scholars. Eisenstein's *Otsar Midrashim* represents a library of two hundred Midrashim, annotated. *Midrash Abkir,* on Genesis and Exodus, derives its name from the initial letters of אמן בימינו כן יהי רצון, with which each chapter ends.

Following are a few midrashic maxims and aphorisms: "Man enters the world with closed hands, as if to say: The world is mine. He departs from it with open hands, as if to say: I take nothing with me.

"It is easy to acquire an enemy, but difficult to win a friend. He who turns his enemy into a friend is the bravest hero. He who hates a man is as if he hated God.

"There is no absolute good without some evil in it. The greater the man, the humbler he is. He who has nothing to do quickly dies. At first, sin is like a thin thread; but in the end, it becomes like a thick rope. Man's friends are: children, wealth, and good deeds. Do not despise a man who abandons his wickedness and repents.

336

"A person can forget in two years what he has learned in twenty. Bad neighbors count a man's income but not his expenses. When you come into a town, follow its customs.

"In prosperity, people feel brotherly to one another. Slander is as bad as murder. A man's love goes to his parents before he is married; his love goes to his wife after he is married. Every man is a king in his home. The greater the man, the humbler he is."

MAH TOVU   מַה טֹּבוּ

A MOSAIC of five biblical verses, beginning with the words *mah tovu ohalekha* ("how goodly are your tents"), forms the opening passage in the Hebrew daily Prayerbook. Since, according to talmudic interpretation, the phrase "your tents" refers to the synagogues, it has become customary to recite these words upon entering the house of God.

The entire passage conveys the feelings of reverence and joy experienced within the synagogue ("O Lord, I love the house of thy habitation, the place where thy glory dwells. . . I offer my prayer to thee, O Lord, at a time of grace. O God, in thy abundant kindness, answer me"). The expression *time of grace* (עת רצון) is taken to mean the time of public worship (Berakhoth 8a). The five verses are borrowed from Numbers 24:5; Psalms 5:8; 26:8; 95:6; 69:14.

MAH YAFITH   מַה יָּפִית

ONE of the table songs for Sabbath (*Zemiroth*), *Mah Yafith* begins with the words: "How beautiful and delightfully sweet you are, O Sabbath. . ." Its author, Rabbi Mordecai ben Isaac of thirteenth-century France, was a talmudic scholar of great fame. His hymn is largely based on halakhic-midrashic material, and has four rhymed lines to the stanza. It became very popular in both Germany and Poland, having received a set tune which the Polish tyrannical overlords, or *Paritzim*, regarded as symbolic of Jewish song. They used to urge the subservient Jews to sing it and dance to it in a comical fashion. Hence, the expression *Mah-Yofis-Yid* applied to those who bend or crouch in a degrading manner. For obvious reasons, the hymn *Mah Yafith* has lost its popularity and is no longer chanted at the Sabbath table, nor is it included in the Prayerbook editions.

MAH NISHTANNAH   מַה נִּשְׁתַּנָּה

The four questions asked at the *Seder* service on *Pesaḥ* are quoted in
Mishnah Pesaḥim 10:4 with one variation. Instead of asking why
all the participants recline during the *Seder*, the question in the Mishnah reads: "On all nights we eat meat roasted, stewed or boiled—
why do we eat only roast this night?" The questions asked by the
young child at the *Seder* table date back to ancient times when the
paschal lamb was offered and roasted in Jerusalem. With the destruction of the Temple and the cessation of the sacrificial offerings there
naturally came a change in the formula, and the question about the
paschal lamb was replaced by the question about reclining.

The number *four* is prominent throughout the *Seder* service: four
cups of wine, four sons, Rabbi Akiva entertains four guests at his
Seder in Bné Brak. The first sentence of the reply slightly varies from
Deuteronomy 6:21 and is phrased in groups containing four words
each (עבדים היינו לפרעה במצרים, ויוציאנו ה' אלהינו משם, ביד חזקה
ובזרוע נטויה). The masoretic text does not have ובזרוע נטויה in Deuteronomy 6:21. The paragraph contains four synonyms signifying
wisdom and scholarship (חכמים, נבונים, זקנים, יודעים). The passage introducing the four sons contains the word ברוך four times. According
to a talmudic statement, *four* symbolizes the fourfold promise of liberation contained in Exodus 6:6-7.

The introductory line of *Mah Nishtannah*, not counted as one of
the four questions, reads: "Why is this night different from all nights?"
This is followed by the four questions: 1) Why do we eat *matzah*?
2) Why do we eat bitter greens? 3) Why do we dip the greens twice?
4) Why do we recline? The question relating to the twofold dipping
refers to the eating of parsley and bitter herbs dipped in salt water
and *ḥaroseth*, respectively, as a first course to whet the appetite. Rabbi Isaac Abravanel, religious philosopher of the fifteenth century,
says that the answer to the third and fourth questions is that the
people of Israel were liberated from Egypt; that is, the festive meal
and the reclining are both symbolic of well-being and freedom.

Based upon the idea that he who questions much learns much, the
traditional Haggadah contains a variety of passages which are styled
as questions followed by answers on points of Jewish history, faith
and observance. The preservation of the religious significance of the
Passover *Seder* is attributable to these annual questions and answers.

338

MODIM D'RABBANAN   מוֹדִים דְּרַבָּנָן

THE prayer recited in an undertone, while the reader repeats aloud the eighteenth benediction of the *Shemoneh Esreh*, is a composite of several phrases suggested by several sages of the Talmud (Sotah 40a); hence, it is referred to as *Modim d'Rabbanan*: the prayer which begins with the words "We thank thee" (מודים אנחנו לך) as composed of the variant readings reported by a number of talmudic rabbis.

In order to link the people closely together, the sages sought to bring varying forms of Hebrew prayer into harmonious union. The formula "who healest all creatures and doest wonders" (רופא כל בשר ומפליא לעשות) is a combination of two readings (Berakhoth 60b). As a compromise between two competing phrasings, אהבה רבה is recited in the morning service and אהבת עולם in the evening service (*Tosafoth*, Berakhoth 11b). Similarly, a reconciliation was effected between the versions שים שלום and שלום רב. The purpose of all this co-ordination and unification of the prescribed prayers was to prevent the formation of separate religious factions among the dispersed people of Israel.

According to Rabbi David Abudarham of Seville, who wrote a commentary on the Prayerbook in the year 1340, *Modim d'Rabbanan* is recited by the congregation while the reader repeats the eighteenth benediction known as הודאה (thanksgiving), because an expression of thanks is authentic when made in person rather than through a messenger or *sheliah tsibbur*. Petitions, however, may well be conveyed by an intermediary. Hence, the mere response of *Amen* to the rest of the benedictions of the *Shemoneh Esreh* is sufficient.

MUSAF   מוּסָף

MUSAF is the additional service in commemoration of the additional sacrifice offered at the Temple on Sabbaths, festivals and *Rosh Ḥodesh*. Besides the regular morning and afternoon offerings (*tamid*), the Torah provides for additional sacrifices (*musafim*) on the foregoing festive occasions, including *Rosh Hashanah* and *Yom Kippur*. The *Musaf* service takes the place of these *musafim*. It is recited soon after the Torah reading, which follows the morning service (*Shaharith*).

The structure of the *Musaf* consists of the three introductory and the three concluding benedictions of the *Amidah*. Between these is inserted an intermediate benediction in which the additional offering for the day is described and the appropriate biblical passage is quoted from Numbers 28. The priestly blessing is pronounced by the *kohanim* at the conclusion of the *Musaf* service for festivals.

The *Musaf* service for *Rosh Hashanah* is the longest of all *Amidahs*. It includes nine benedictions and three central sections named *malkhuyyoth*, *zikhronoth*, and *shofaroth*, each of which contains ten biblical quotations concerning God's kingship, providence and revelation, respectively. The *Musaf* service for the first day of *Pesaḥ* is known by the special name *Tal* (dew), because prayers for dew are recited when the *ḥazzan* repeats the first two benedictions.

The *Musaf* service for the eighth day of *Sukkoth* (*Shemini Atsereth*) is called *Geshem* (rain), because prayers for rain are recited on that occasion. The *Musaf* service for *Yom Kippur* includes a recital of the *Avodah*, a description of the procedure in Temple times. The *Musaf Kedushah* is more elaborate than the regular one. According to talmudic tradition, the *Musaf* service was in use even in Temple times (Tosefta, Berakhoth 3:3; Sukkah 53a).

MORAL DISCIPLINE   מוּסָר

WHEREVER something is left to conscience, the Torah adds: "You shall revere the Lord your God" or "I am the Lord" (Leviticus 19:3, 10, 11, 14, 16, 18, 34, 37). We are told that the instances recorded in the Torah of God's direct communion with the Patriarchs are designed to teach us how to act. "Just as God clothes the naked (Adam and Eve), so should man clothe the naked; just as God visits the sick (Abraham), so should man make it his duty to visit the sick; just as God buries the dead (Moses), so must man bury the dead; just as God comforts the mourners, so must man comfort the mourners" (Genesis Rabbah 8). All acts of charity and benevolence, prompted by the human heart, are closely connected with the concept of hallowing God's name. The biblical phrase "a pure heart" (לב טהור) is understood to mean a clean conscience.

Psalm 15 sets forth the character and conduct expected of the virtuous man. "The blameless man acts uprightly, and speaks the truth in his heart. He neither slanders nor hurts nor insults his fellow man. He has contempt for a rogue, and honors those who revere the Lord. He keeps his word at his own risk, and does not retract. He lends

340

money without usury, and accepts no bribe against the innocent. He who does these things shall never be disturbed."

The essence of moral perfection is expressed by one of our prophets: "What does the Lord ask of you? Only to do justice, to love mercy, and to walk humbly with your God" (Micah 6:8). Subjects left to the discretion of the heart, which is the seat of self-imposed duty, are spoken of in talmudic literature as דברים המסורים ללב, injunctions that are entrusted to the heart, over which human authorities have no control.

The wrong we do by means of words, such as wounding a person's feelings, is considered even worse then defrauding in money matters, because money can be restored, but mental agony can never be made good. "If a man repents, he must not be reminded of his sins; a proselyte must not be told of his heathen ancestry; nor is a man to ask for the price of an object unless he intends to buy it. One should always be on his guard not to wound his wife's feelings, for just as her tears are frequent so is her sense of wrong deep" (Bava Metzia 58b).

The biblical word *musar* is often used in the sense of moral instruction: "Hear, my son, your father's instruction, and reject not your mothers' teaching. . . He who loves correction loves knowledge, but he who hates reproof is stupid. . . Listen to counsel and receive instruction, that you may eventually become wise" (Proverbs 1:8; 12:1; 19:20). More severely, *musar* occurs in the sense of chastisement, disciplinary punishment (Job 5:17; Jeremiah 30:14; Hosea 5:2).

During the medieval period, the term *musar* gradually acquired the connotation of moral principles which tend to improve the relation of man to man. Since the earliest times, ethics and religion have been closely connected in Judaism. The nineteenth chapter of Leviticus is a typical example of the combination of ethics and religious practice: both elements are contained side by side. Among the chief exponents of ethics in the Middle Ages are Baḥya ibn Pakuda, Maimonides, Naḥmanides, Israel al-Nakawa.

According to Rabbi Akiva, "You shall love your neighbor as yourself" (Leviticus 19:18) is the most comprehensive precept in the Torah (Sifra). According to Ben Azzai, there is a still broader principle expressed in the words: "This is the record of the descendants of man" (Genesis 5:1)—not black, not white, not great, not small, but man. Reverence for the divine image in man, the concept of mankind's unity, is of wider scope than love to our fellow man. Since all mankind traces its ancestry to Adam, all men are brothers, the children of one parentage. All men, therefore, if given the opportunity, are capable of achieving the zenith of moral and ethical behavior.

The ethical work *Sefer Ḥasidim* by Rabbi Yehudah he-Ḥasid of Regensburg, who died in 1217, contains a rich variety of moral principles and precepts, such as the following: "Do not purposely mislead anyone, Jew or non-Jew. Do not say that a certain price has been offered for your merchandise if that is not true. Call attention of a non-Jew to an error that he has made in overpaying you, for it is better that you live on charity than that you disgrace the Jewish name by cheating.

"When a non-Jew comes to you for advice, tell him frankly who is honest and who is dishonest among the people with whom he wishes to deal. If a murderer seeks refuge with you, give him no quarter even if he is a Jew. If a non-Jew observes the laws of civilized men, hold him in higher esteem than a Jew who transgresses the divine commands.

"If you are in debt, pay your debts before you contribute to charity. Expel all envy and hatred from your heart. Anyone who supplies weapons of destruction to a murderer, or provides him with food, is as guilty as though he were an accomplice."

Rabbi Elazar Rokeaḥ, a disciple of Rabbi Yehudah he-Ḥasid, experienced great suffering during the Crusades. In 1196, two crusaders entered his house and killed his wife, his two daughters, and his son. He wrote: "No monument bestows as much glory as an unsullied name. To forgive is the most beautiful thing a man can do. Do not let your sensuous nature control your life. Do nothing of which you are likely to be ashamed. Never speak meaningless words. Do not get into quarrels with anybody.

"Do not crave honor and glory; do not be too eager for money. Make peace among people whenever you can. If you are poor, be thankful for the air you breathe; if you are rich, do not exalt yourself above your poor brother. Both you and your poor brother came naked into the world and will eventually sleep in the dust together."

Rabbi Moses ben Naḥman or Naḥmanides, called *Ramban* from the initials of his name and that of his father, represented Judaism from the side of emotion and feeling, as Maimonides did from the side of reason and logic. In his famous *Iggereth Musar* (Letter of Instruction) which he addressed to his son Naḥman, he wrote from the Holy Land shortly before he died in 1270: "Learn to speak gently to all persons at all times. Regard every person as greater than yourself,

342

If you are richer and wiser than another, you must know that you are charged with greater responsibility. If another commits a sin, it is from error; if you commit one, you are guilty.

"When you address a man, do not keep staring in his face. Always consider yourself in the presence of God. Purify your thoughts, and think before you speak. You should continually examine your deeds, in order to depart from evil and to do good."

Rabbi Yehudah ibn Kalaaz, who lived in Algeria at the beginning of the sixteenth century, wrote in his *Sefer ha-Musar* (book of instruction): "Reverence for God is the thread upon which the various good qualities of men are strung like pearls. When this string is severed, the pearls scatter in all directions and are lost, one by one.

"Man who is made in the image of God should keep his body immaculately clean. He who always prefers his own ideas to those of others cannot make progress. Never be ashamed to learn even from those who seem less important than you. Always be grateful for being spared suffering and distress. Men marvel at the sun's eclipse while failing to notice the daily sunrise. If someone tells you something you already know, keep quiet until he has finished."

From the fourteenth-century ethical work *Menorath ha-Maor*, which is a summation of all phases of Jewish life, the Jew learns the things he must do to show that he is truly a friend: "Be first to greet your fellow man; invite him to your joyful occasions; call him by complimentary names; do not give away his secrets; help him when he is in trouble; look after his interests when he is away; overlook his shortcomings and forgive him promptly; criticize him when he has done wrong; respect him always; do not deceive him, do not lie to him; pray for him and wish him happiness, attend to his burial if he dies."

Rabbi Israel Salanter (1810-1883), founder of the *Musar* Movement, who set up special *Musar* houses for the study of Jewish ethical literature, taught: "The sensual desire in man often makes him mistake momentary pleasure for the true happiness which he craves, and he succumbs to the pressure of his passion. Frequent yielding to his sensual desires finally produces in man an impure spirit—the decay of his spiritual energy—with the result that he becomes a slave to his evil habits.

"The moral clearsightedness commands man to struggle against the temptation of sensual desires, and to be guided in his actions not by the immediate pleasures which they produce but by their remote consequences. Without deep sincerity we would find little to criticize in ourselves; self-love would blind our judgment. Repentance is not re-morse, but a serious attempt to profit from past mistakes.

"Man must not be discouraged if he fails to see any improvement in his moral qualities after much self-discipline. We must train our-selves so that we no longer obey the ethical teachings reluctantly, but follow them quite naturally. We must never allow ourselves to be ruffled even when the greatest misfortunes befall us."

Rabbi Israel Meir ha-Kohen (1835-1933), best known by the title of one of his books—*Ḥafetz Ḥayyim* (desiring life), has been described as one of the prime guardians of the moral genius of the Jews in Po-land and Russia during many decades of his long life. This saintly talmudic author of many books on morals and *Halakhah*, notably the משנה ברורה, a six-volume commentary on the first part of the *Shulḥan Arukh*, discusses at length such misdemeanors as slander. He writes:

Those who listen to slanderous gossip are just as guilty as the tale-bearers. Repeated use of the evil tongue is like a silk thread made strong by hundreds of strands. The slanderer separates husband from wife, brother from brother, and friend from friend. One sinful Jew can do harm to all his people, who are like a single body sensitive to the pain felt by any of its parts. When a group of people are sailing in a boat, none of them has a right to bore a hole under his own seat, for this may cause the sinking of all his companions.

INFORMERS   מוֹסְרִים, מַלְשִׁינִים

THE talmudic sages compared informers to serpents, because death and destruction frequently resulted from acts of denunciation. In-formers were regarded as the worst of all evil-tongued men. The Hebrew term *malshin*, used in Psalm 101:5 and Proverbs 30:10, is de-rived from the noun *lashon* (tongue): "Whoever slanders his neigh-bor in secret, him I will destroy." "Slander not a servant to his master."

It has been noted that if the informer's motive is merely to gratify personal resentment or to secure the reward offered, then, while his act may be to the welfare of the social organism, he himself is ethically to be condemned. The Jewish people suffered severely during the Roman persecutions by reason of malicious informers in their own ranks. Hence the warning: "Do not be intimate with the ruling authorities" (Avoth 1:10). In the Middle Ages, historians tell us, the punishment of the informer was always severe. A price was set upon

344

the head of every informer who was convicted and executed; the blood money was paid by the community to the royal treasury. Execution of informers continued as a frequent occurrence in all the provinces of Spain.

MO'ED   מוֹעֵד

THE second of the six divisions of the Mishnah is called *Mo'ed* (Set Time) because it contains the laws concerning the Sabbath, festivals, and public fasts. *Mo'ed* consists of twelve tractates in the following order:

1) *Shabbath*, twenty-four chapters, on the rules and regulations of Sabbath observance, dealing with each of the thirty-nine categories of prohibited work.

2) *Eruvin*, ten chapters, on the amalgamation of Sabbath bounds, which may not be overstepped without certain formalities, referred to as *eruv hatzeroth, eruv tehumin*, and *eruv tavshilin*.

3) *Pesahim*, ten chapters, on the observance of the *Pesah* festival.

4) *Shekalim*, eight chapters, on the annual tax to the Temple treasury (Exodus 30:12-16), which consisted of a half-shekel for the maintenance of the sanctuary. The Babylonian Talmud has no *Gemara* commentary on *Shekalim*.

5) *Yoma*, eight chapters, on the observance of *Yom Kippur* and the Temple worship.

6) *Sukkah*, five chapters, on the observance of the *Sukkoth* festival.

7) *Betzah*, five chapters, on the laws applicable to festivals. The title *Betzah* (egg) is derived from the first word in the tractate, which is also called *Yom Tov* (festival day).

8) *Rosh Hashanah*, four chapters, on the observance of *Rosh Hashanah* which marks the New Year.

9) *Ta'anith*, four chapters, on communal fasts.

10) *Megillah*, four chapters, concerning the public recital of the book of Esther on *Purim*, listing regulations for the care of synagogues and sacred objects.

11) *Mo'ed Katan*, three chapters, concerning the intermediate days of *Pesah* and *Sukkoth*, referred to as minor festivals (*mo'ed katan*). It also deals with mourning during festivals.

12) *Hagigah*, three chapters, concerning the sacrifices offered during the three pilgrimage festivals (*Pesah, Shavuoth, Sukkoth*).

GUIDE FOR THE PERPLEXED   מוֹרֵה נְבוּכִים

MOSES MAIMONIDES (1135-1204) completed his *Guide for the Perplexed* at the age of fifty-five. A few years later it was translated from the original Arabic into Hebrew, first by Samuel ibn Tibbon and then by Judah Alḥarizi. Acknowledged to be one of the greatest philosophical works of the medieval period, the *Guide* has exerted a profound influence on the thought of Jews and non-Jews. Its purpose was to reconcile reason with faith and to harmonize Judaism with philosophy.

At the outset of his book, Maimonides declares: "When I have a difficult subject before me, when I find the road narrow and can see no other way of teaching a well-established truth except by pleasing one intelligent man and displeasing ten thousand fools, I prefer to address myself to the one man and to take no notice whatever of the condemnation of the multitude."

Following are several random excerpts from Maimonides' *Guide:*

"By *faith* we do not understand that which is uttered by the lips, but that which is apprehended by the soul: the conviction that the object of belief is exactly as it has been apprehended... The human race contains such a great variety of individuals that we cannot find two persons who are exactly alike morally or physically. While one person is so cruel that he kills his own child in his anger, another is too delicate and fainthearted to kill even a fly...

"When great troubles befall us, our eyes become dim and we cannot see clearly; on the other hand, when we are full of gladness we feel as if the light has increased. Thus, Isaiah concludes the good tidings with these words: The light of the moon shall be like the light of the sun, and the sun shall shine sevenfold strong, when the Lord heals the bruised people and binds up their wounds. Jeremiah, in describing the destruction of Jerusalem, says: I looked at the heavens, and they had no light.

"Joel describes the multitude of locusts that came in his days as follows: At their advance the land is quaking, the heavens are shaking, sun and moon are dark, the stars have ceased to shine. Amos, speaking of the destruction of Samaria, says: I will make the sun go down at noon, I will darken the earth in the clear day. Micah, in recounting the fall of Samaria, makes use of these rhetorical figures of speech: The Lord descends from his place, he strides on the heights of the earth! Mountains melt under him, valleys split asunder, like

346

wax before fire. . . The account given of the creation is not intended to be literal in all its parts.

"Men frequently think that evil things are more numerous than good things. They judge the whole universe on the basis of what happens to some individuals. Indulgence in food and drink brings disease and affliction to body and soul. Mental suffering often results from desiring things that are not necessary.

"Men expose themselves to great danger in order to obtain what is non-essential. The more essential a thing is, the more abundant it is in nature; the less essential it is, the rarer it is. Since air is most necessary, it is found most easily. Water, being more necessary than food, is more abundant than food. . . Cleanliness in body and dress is included among the various aims of the Torah, but only if it is associated with purity of action. . .

"The food which the Torah forbids to eat is unwholesome. The Torah forbids pork principally because the habits and the food of swine are extremely dirty and loathsome. The fat of an animal's intestines impedes one's digestion and makes for thick blood. Blood is indigestible and harmful as food, and so is the meat of an animal that has died a natural death (*nevelah*). A diseased animal (*terefah*) is close to becoming *nevelah*, hence harmful and forbidden. The best meat comes from animals that are permitted as food.

"It is impossible for man to be entirely free from error and sin. If we were convinced that our ways cannot be corrected, we would forever continue in our errors. Our belief in the efficacy of repentance causes us to improve and become even better than we were before we sinned. . . Our intellect which emanates from God is the link that joins us to God. You have it in your power either to strengthen or weaken that bond. It will become strong only when you make use of it in a spirit of love for God; it will be weakened when you direct your thoughts to other things. . .

"All ethical principles concern the mutual relations between man and his fellow man, and are given for the benefit of society. Imagine a person who is alone and has no connection whatever with any one else; none of his ethical qualities would be exercised or needed. They are necessary and useful only when a man comes in contact with others. Having acquired the knowledge of God, and seeing in what manner God provides for his creatures, man will be forever determined to practise kindness, justice and goodness, so as to emulate the ways of God." This is referred to as *Imitatio Dei* (imitation of God).

ALTAR   מִזְבֵּחַ

THE literal meaning of the Hebrew term *mizbeah* is place of sacrifice.
More than four hundred references to altars are contained in the Hebrew Bible. The Torah specifies unhewn stones or mounds of earth
for altar construction. In patriarchal times, worshipers constructed
altars wherever they pitched their tents or had special occasion to
offer a sacrifice. David erected an altar on Mount Moriah, Jerusalem,
at a threshing floor of natural stone which he bought from Aravnah
the Jebusite (II Samuel 24:15-25). This rock became the central
place of sacrifice in Solomon's Temple.

The use of iron in the construction of the altar was unlawful, hence
the stones had to be of unhewn natural rock. "An altar of earth you
shall make. . . If you make an altar of stone for me, do not build it
of cut stone (*gazith*), for by putting your tool to it you desecrate it"
(Exodus 20:21-22). This is explained in the Talmud to the effect that
iron weapons shorten life while the altar, symbolizing peace between
God and man, prolongs it.

In Solomon's Temple there was an altar of brass for burnt-offerings
and a golden altar for the burning of incense. The small, gold-plated
altar of incense stood in front of the flight of steps leading up to the
Holy of Holies (*Devir*), whereas the great altar for burnt-offerings was
in the outer court.

Seizing the horns of the altar gave asylum to a person having committed an act of unintentional homicide. If intentional, even a priest
officiating at the altar could not escape his punishment. "When a
man kills another maliciously, you must take him from my altar and
put him to death" (Exodus 21:14). The use of the sanctity of the
altar as an asylum, limited to cases of accidental homicide, was based
upon the idea that the suppliant fugitive placed himself under the
immediate protection of God. The horns of the altar were esteemed
the most sacred part of the whole.

The two and a half tribes who settled east of the Jordan built an altar designed, not for sacrifices or incense burning, but as a reminder
of their close relationship with the other tribes across the Jordan,
west (Joshua 22:10-34). As a symbol of the unity of the Jewish people, the altar of the Temple had a special sanctity. According to a
talmudic statement, the altar sheds tears for the man who divorces
his first wife (Gittin 90b).

348

MEZUZAH   מְזוּזָה

THE *Mezuzah* (doorpost), serving as the distinctive mark of the Jewish home, consists of a small roll of parchment on which is written the *Shema* and the two biblical passages concerning the love for God and his precepts (Deuteronomy 6:4-9; 11:13-21).

Enclosed in a metal or wooden case, the *Mezuzah* is fastened in a slanting position to the upper part of the doorpost on the right side of the entrance of each room, the upper end of the case pointing inward and the lower one outward. The attaching of the *Mezuzah* to the doorpost is accompanied by a special benediction.

The word שדי (Almighty), written on the back of the parchment, is made visible through a small opening near the top of the case. Maimonides declares that those who look upon the *Mezuzah* as an amulet to ward off evils are ignorant, failing to understand its real purpose which is to keep us constantly aware of the divine Oneness and moral duties (*Yad, Mezuzah* 5:5).

The slanting position of the *Mezuzah* is the result of a difference of opinion between Rashi and his grandson Rabbi Jacob ben Meir, known as *Rabbenu Tam* (1100-1171). According to Rashi, the *Mezuzah* should be attached vertically; but according to Rabbenu Tam, it should be in a horizontal position. As a compromise, it has become customary to put it up slantwise. The word שדי has been explained to represent the initials of שומר דלתות ישראל.

Upon entering the house or leaving it, it is customary to touch the *Mezuzah* with the fingers and then kiss the fingers.

MAZZAL   מַזָּל

THE biblical word *mazzal*, occurring in II Kings 22:5, has been taken to mean either planet or sign of the zodiac. In talmudic literature, *mazzal* signifies star of fortune or fate or destiny; hence the formula *mazzal tov* (good luck), and conversely *mazzal ra* (ill luck) rendered *shlim-mazzal* in the Yiddish language.

The formula of congratulations has been described as a survival of the old belief in astrology, as is the rejection of certain days in the week or the month for weddings or new ventures. Maimonides opposes astrology most energetically when he writes: "Pay no attention to the view held by the ignorant, whether non-Jews or Jews, that at man's birth God decrees whether he shall be righteous or wicked. That is not so!..." (*Yad, Teshuvah* 5:2). He declares that the practice of astrology is forbidden, as bordering on idolatry, in Leviticus 19:26, where the Torah says: "Do not practise divination or soothsaying" (*Avodah Zarah* 11:8).

In a letter to the men of Marseilles, he referred to astrology as "a disease, not a science, a tree under the shadow of which all sorts of superstitions thrive, and which must be uprooted in order to give way to the tree of knowledge and the tree of life."

MIZMOR L'TODAH   מִזְמוֹר לְתוֹדָה

Psalm 100 was recited in the Temple in connection with the thanksgiving offering, which was presented on weekdays only. Hence, it forms part of the weekday morning service (before יהי כבוד). Since the thanksgiving sacrifice was not offered up on *Erev Yom Kippur*, *Erev Pesaḥ* and *Ḥol ha-Mo'ed Pesaḥ*, מזמור לתודה is omitted on these days. The *Korban Todah* (thanksgiving sacrifice) was not presented during the *Pesaḥ* festival because of the *ḥametz* that was involved with this offering. On *Erev Yom Kippur* it could not be offered up because the twelve loaves of bread were not likely to be consumed before the *Yom Kippur* fast. Nor was it presented on Sabbaths and festivals, since it was not included among the communal offerings. The psalm מזמור לתודה invites the whole world to join Israel in the worship of God and to acknowledge him as the merciful Father of all mankind. *Mizmor l'Todah*, like all passages directly dealing with the sacrificial system (קרבנות), is recited standing.

MIZRAH   מִזְרָח

Mizraḥ literally means sunrise or place of sunrise, namely, east. By extension, *Mizraḥ* has come also to mean a decorated plate or inscribed card hung on the east wall of the house or synagogue to indicate the direction of Jerusalem for correct orientation in prayer.

At worship, the congregation faces east where the ark is located in the synagogue. The custom of turning toward the east while at prayer, observed by Jews living west of Eretz Yisrael, dates back to great

350

antiquity. We are told that Daniel prayed to God three times a day in the direction of Jerusalem (Daniel 6:10).

According to the Talmud, the Jews in foreign lands turn in prayer towards the land of Israel, those in the land of Israel towards Jerusalem, those in Jerusalem towards the Temple, and those in the Temple towards the Holy of Holies (Berakhoth 30a).

In places east of Eretz Yisrael, the ark is placed in the west (Tosefta Megillah 3:14). Biblical verses like "I set the Lord ever before me" (Psalm 16:8) are used as mottoes appearing on the *Mizrah* plate in a network of tendrils and flowers, a product of popular Jewish art.

MAHZOR   מַחֲזוֹר

THE term *Mahzor*, originally designating the yearly cycle, was later applied to the *piyyutim* or prayer-poems that were composed for the entire cycle of the year. Finally it became the title of the prayerbook for the festivals of the year. The *Mahzor* contains only a portion of the thirty-five thousand metrical compositions that were inspired by the synagogal worship services.

Much of the synagogal poetry was composed by supremely gifted *hazzanim* or cantors, who provided the worshipers with ever-new forms of religious expression and stimulating song. Before long the divine services gained an inner richness and the voice of song, which had been silent since the destruction of the Temple, was heard once again in the synagogue.

Concerning the countless *piyyutim* yet to be found in unpublished manuscripts, Israel Davidson writes in his introduction to the *Thesaurus of Medieval Hebrew Poetry:* "Many years will yet pass and much labor will have to be spent before the contents of the innumerable manuscripts will be made accessible." In his preface to the last volume of the *Thesaurus*, Davidson states that "a rough enumeration brings up the number of poets to 2,843." The religious and secular Hebrew poems listed in Davidson's monumental work total 35,200.

The *Mahzor* passed through a long process of evolution until it finally emerged as a rich anthology of Israel's literary classics. It embodies the visions and aspirations, the sorrows and joys of countless generations. The whole gamut of Jewish history may be traversed in its pages. The liturgical poets borrowed language and meter from the Hebrew Bible and drew their material from Talmud and Midrash.

The *Maḥzor* is a mirror that reflects the development of the Jewish spirit throughout the ages. Interwoven into the texture of its prayers and hymns are passages from the Bible, the Mishnah, the Talmud, and the Zohar. The poetic and philosophic creations of numerous known and unknown authors constitute an integral part of the Prayer-book. No other book so thoroughly expresses the creative genius of our people and so completely unites the dispersed of Israel.

The *piyyutim* were added to the ancient formulas of prayer in a desire to give expression to the intense emotions and aspirations of the people. They show us the Jewish heart laid before God in all its moods: in penitence, in fear, in triumph. The worshiper will always find something in the *piyyutim* in sympathy with his own spiritual condition. Varied as life, their freshness is never lost to those who are imbued with midrashic lore.

MAḤZOR VITRY מַחֲזוֹר וִיטְרִי

THE liturgical work known as *Maḥzor Vitry* was compiled by Rabbi Simḥah of Vitry, France, a pupil of Rashi. It contains the prayer texts, many *piyyutim* and *zemiroth* for Sabbaths and festivals, as well as *Pirké Avoth* and several talmudic selections concerning religious behavior. Its fundamental importance for the history of Jewish liturgy cannot be minimized. *Maḥzor Vitry* has been the basis of *Nusaḥ Ashkenaz*, or the Ashkenazic version. In 1893, the work was edited with notes by S. Hurwitz and published by the Mekitzé Nirdamim Society, founded in 1864 for publishing old Hebrew manuscripts.

MI SHEBBERAKH מִי שֶׁבֵּרַךְ

THE well-known Hebrew prayer for the community, which begins with the words מי שברך (He who blessed), is recited on Sabbaths following the reading of the Torah and the Haftarah. It contains an invocation of divine blessing for the members of all congregations—"their wives, their sons and daughters, and all that belong to them. May he bless those who dedicate synagogues for divine worship ... and those who provide food for needy guests and charity for the poor. as well as those who faithfully occupy themselves with the requirements of the community... May he bless and prosper their work and the work of all the people of Israel their brethren. . ." This prayer is found in the oldest liturgical manuscripts.

Variations of *Mi Shebberakh* are included in the daily Prayerbook for such individual occasions as naming a new-born daughter, and on behalf of persons called to the Torah or those who are sick.

MICAH   מִיכָה

THE book of Micah is the sixth of the Minor Prophets. Although Micah's prophecies refer especially to the southern kingdom of Judah, they concern all Israel. The abrupt transitions indicate that the book is rather a summary of the prophet's teaching than a series of complete discourses.

Micah, speaking for the people against the ruling authorities and threatening them with destruction and exile, was a younger contemporary of Isaiah who began his poetic career toward the end of the eighth century before the common era. Both envisioned the messianic future when war among nations would be no more. The fact that the prophecy concerning universal peace is phrased alike in both Isaiah and Micah has raised the question whether Micah quotes from Isaiah, or Isaiah from Micah, or both quote the same prophecy from an earlier unknown author.

It was Micah who set forth the perfect ideal of religion when he said: "The Lord requires of you only to do justice, to love mercy, and to walk humbly with your God." He declared: "Woe to those who devise iniquity and work evil. They covet fields and seize them; they covet houses and snatch them . . . It shall come to pass in the latter days that . . . nation shall not lift up sword against nation, neither shall they learn war any more. . ." It has been underscored that Micah's classic definition of a simple practical religion has not been surpassed. Each of the three parts of Micah's prophecy begins with the threat of punishment and ends on a note of hope and promise.

HERETICS   מִינִים

IN BIBLICAL Hebrew, the word מִין means kind, species. In talmudic Hebrew, it sometimes denotes a heretic, and often describes a member of an early denominational sect. Since the so-called *minim* were regarded as secret apostates who openly professed the Jewish faith, they were resented even more than all other classes of unfaithful Jews.

They were not an open enemy, but a foe within the camp; they were more dangerous because more secret. The twelfth benediction in the *Shemoneh Esreh* prayer was composed against them (*birkath ha-minim*) at the end of the first century. When, however, they ceased to be a menace to the Jewish faith after separating themselves completely from the Jewish community, the formula was modified to apply to other varieties of sectarians within the synagogue. The term *minim*, therefore, should be defined according to the date of the talmudic passage in which it occurs.

The term מומר (changed, converted) is employed in talmudic literature with regard to a Jew who does not conform to the Jewish law. A מומר להכעיס (a provoking *mumar*), one who shows his contempt of the Jewish law, is contrasted with a מומר לתאבון (a *mumar* who breaks the law to gratify his appetite). The term *mumar* sometimes designates a person who transgresses a biblical command in general. The word *meshummad* (from שמד), denoting an open apostate opposing the Jewish faith, has been explained to mean one who deserves extinction. *Mumar* and *meshummad* are often used interchangeably.

The term אפיקורוס (epicurean) is used in talmudic literature to denote one who treats the traditional teachers of the Torah with disdain; an insolent scoffer; also one who denies the divine origin of the Torah. Another type of heretic is described as כופר בעקר (a denier of the fundamental principle, the existence of the One God). The Karaite heresy, which came into being during the post-talmudic period, was essentially the same as the heresy of the Sadducees, who opposed the Pharisees and rejected the Oral Law (תורה שבעל פה).

The feeling against heresy has always been weaker among the Jewish people than the dislike of separatism. Unbelief or false doctrine was not punishable as was rebellion against civil law. In 1656, Spinoza was excommunicated by the Jews of Holland, who were not strong enough to be tolerant of scandalous notions concerning religion, having too recently acquired the right of freedom of conscience after escaping the tortures of the Spanish Inquisition. Even so, had Spinoza consented to conform outwardly, and not endanger the existence of his fellow Jews who had just found refuge in Holland, he would not only have been safe but even pensioned. The talmudic rule has always prevailed among the Jewish people: אף על פי שחטא, ישראל הוא. That is, once a Jew always a Jew (Sanhedrin 44a).

DEATH מִיתָה

THE verse, "the day of death is better than the day of birth"
(Ecclesiastes 7:1) is understood to mean that a man's life cannot be
judged happy till its end is reached. According to a midrashic statement, birth and death are like two ships in a harbor. There is no
reason to rejoice at the ship setting out on a journey (birth), not
knowing what she may encounter on the high seas, but we should rejoice at the ship returning to port (death) safely (Exodus Rabbah
48:1). Most of the Jewish customs connected with death are based
upon the respect for the mortal frame of the departed.

Burial was the regular mode of disposing of the dead in ancient
Israel. Embalming was not a Jewish practice. Jacob and Joseph
were embalmed (Genesis 50:2, 26) because they were treated as Egyptians, among whom embalming was the regular custom. The bodies
of king Saul and his sons were cremated to prevent their falling into
the hands of the Philistines (I Samuel 31:12). Rock-hewn tombs,
closed with stone slabs, are found grouped in one or more chambers
in natural or artificial caves. In post-biblical times, such tombs were
referred to as *kukhim* (כוכים).

In ancient times, each family had its own burying-place on the
family estate. Manasseh was buried in the garden of his own house,
and so also his son Amon (II Kings 21:18, 26). Usually, however,
the kings of Judah were buried in a royal burying-place in the city of
David. Poorer people would have no family burying-place, hence we
read of "the graves of the common people" (II Kings 23:6) and "the
public cemetery" (Jeremiah 26:23). A measure of disgrace was apparently attached to a so-called pauper's grave. Men desired to sleep
with their fathers, that is, to be buried in the family tomb.

The use of shrouds, or special grave clothes and wrappings known
as *takhrikhin*, originated in the days of Rabban Gamaliel II, president
of the Sanhedrin at Yavneh, who lived during the early part of the
second century. He laid such emphasis upon the use of the simplest
linen shrouds at burial that it became universally accepted by the
people, who to this day avoid gaudy displays at funerals. Coffins
were not used by Jews in ancient times, except in the case of Joseph
whose remains were placed in a chest (*aron*) according to an Egyptian
custom. The bier or couch (*mittah*), upon which the Jews laid their
deceased, was not buried. Early burials, soon after death or within

355

twenty-four hours, became customary as a result of the hot climates where rapid decomposition was probable. This is still observed as a sacred custom even where the same necessity does not exist.

Funeral orations, in honor of the dead rather than a consolation for the living, became known during the talmudic period. If the deceased specified in his will that he desired no funeral oration, his request was heeded (Sanhedrin 46b). The body of a learned and pious man was occasionally brought into the synagogue where the eulogy was delivered (Megillah 28b). According to later authorities, the body of no person should be brought into the synagogue (*Ḥokhmath Adam* 155:18).

The thorough cleansing and washing of the body (*tohorah*) and the continuous watching (*shemirah*) of it till it is interred, for fear of disrespectful treatment, are essential death customs of great antiquity. The presence of numerous guests at a funeral necessitated a funeral feast, referred to as "bread of mourners" (*leḥem onim*) in Hosea 9:4, and as *seudath havra'ah* in talmudic literature, signifying the meal of bracing comfort given the mourners after the funeral. It was provided for the mourners by their friends at the close of the fast during the day of the funeral (II Samuel 3:35; Jeremiah 16:7).

During the seven days of strict mourning (*shiv'ah*), the closest relatives abstain from work and remain at home, sitting on a low bench or low stools, reading the book of Job and receiving visits of condolence. Bereaved children abstain for a year from music and social entertainment.

The *Kaddish*, which is repeated by sons for eleven months after the death of a parent and also on the *Yahrzeit* (anniversary of the death), is in no sense a prayer *for* the dead but an expression of loyalty to the heritage of Judaism; it is regarded as a proof of the ethical life of the deceased, as remembered by affectionate survivors.

MEKHILTA   מְכִילְתָּא

THE *Mekhilta*, one of the oldest halakhic Midrashim of the tannaitic period, deals with the laws contained in the book of Exodus, chapters 12 to 23, though it is for the most part haggadic in nature. In view of the fact that the book of Exodus contains more narrative than law, the midrashic exposition on the book is necessarily less halakhic than haggadic. According to Lauterbach, who edited the *Mekhilta* in three volumes, only two-fifths of its contents are of a halakhic nature. Its haggadic material includes lofty ethical teachings, frequently illustrated by beautiful parables.

The meaning of the Aramaic title *Mekhilta* is measure, rule, analoguous to the Hebrew term *middah* which is used also in the sense of rules how to interpret biblical law. Two other halakhic Midrashim are referred to as *Mekhilta:* 1) by Rabbi Ishmael; 2) by Rabbi Simeon ben Yoḥai.

MALACHI   מַלְאָכִי

THE name Malachi, signifying "my messenger," does not occur elsewhere in the Bible. Hence, it has been questioned whether it is the personal name of the prophet. The Targum identifies Malachi with Ezra the Scribe. As a pseudonym or fictitious name, מלאכי alludes to the promise: "Behold, I will send my messenger to clear the way for me" (Malachi 3:1).

This unidentified prophet, who was active about the middle of the fifth century before the common era, stresses personal religion and emphasizes mercy and faith. He analyzes the proper way of life and deals with questions which have to be faced repeatedly.

The Socratic method of developing an idea through question and answer is a prominent feature of the style of Malachi: "A son should honor his father, and a servant should honor his master. Now, if I am a Father, where is my honor? If I am a Master, where is my reverence? . . . Have we not all one Father? Has not one God created us? Why, then, are we faithless to one another?"

The book of Malachi, the twelfth and last of the Minor Prophets which is regarded as the finale of the Bible from a chronological point of view, contains the firm belief that ultimately all wrongs will be righted. "Behold, I will send you Elijah the prophet, and he will turn the hearts of fathers to their children and the hearts of children to their fathers."

The people addressed throughout the book of Malachi are divided into two classes: 1) the sincerely devout who are beginning to question the divine goodness in view of the prevailing evil; 2) the greedy men who are devout only in name. The message of Malachi paved the way for Nehemiah, who came to Jerusalem to rebuild its walls and was twice governor, in 445 and 433 before the common era.

ANGELS   מַלְאָכִים

THE angels in the Hebrew Bible are messengers conveying the divine
commands and promises, rewards and punishments. They are regarded as superhuman beings dwelling in heaven, who form the divine council and choir surrounding the celestial throne; occasionally,
however, they assume human form and reveal to man God's will and
execute his judgments. According to Psalm 104:4, God makes the
winds his messengers, and flaming fire his ministers. Being immater-
ial, they are not subject to the limitations of time and space. They
are endowed with wisdom and with knowledge of all earthly doings;
when their duties are not punitive, they are beneficent to man. The
psalmist addresses them as follows: "Bless the Lord, all you his angels, you mighty in strength, who do his bidding, obeying his spoken
word. Bless the Lord, all you his hosts. . ." (Psalm 103:20-21).

The names Michael and Gabriel occur in the book of Daniel for the
first time. Michael is described as Israel's representative in heaven,
where other nations are also represented by angelic princes. Among
the Essenes, the Jewish sect with communistic and ascetic tendencies
that originated during the Maccabean period and disappeared with
the destruction of the Second Temple, angelology was a highly developed system of theological thinking. A still more mystical character was given to it by the Kabbalists in the medieval period.

The medieval philosophers, treating the belief in angels in a spirit
more rationalistic than that of Philo, who spoke of the *Metatron* as
the great archangel with seventy-two names, claimed for man a rank
higher than that of the angels (Saadyah Gaon). According to Maimonides, the term *angel* applies to human beings, to animals, as well
as to prophetic ideals: "*Angel* means messenger; hence, every one
that is entrusted with a certain mission is an angel. . . There is no
doubt that the word *angel* is used of a messenger sent by man (Genesis 32:4); of a prophet (Judges 2:1; Numbers 20:16); it is also used
of ideals perceived by prophets in prophetic visions. . . Every appearance of an angel is part of a prophetic vision, depending on the
capacity of the person that perceives it" (*Guide*, 2:6).

Like all angels, the angel of death (מלאך המות) has been described
as a divine messenger and a personification of a particular divine will
or function who, in midrashic-kabbalistic literature and Jewish folklore, has been associated with the negative and destructive aspects of

358

death and evil. In Genesis 6:2, the divine beings (בני האלהים) have been declared to signify "distinguished men" of the ante-diluvian generations, who enjoyed happy and long lives like the angels, since the idea of intermarriage of angels and human beings is altogether foreign to Jewish thought. In poetic Hebrew, *elohim* means *mighty*. However, the phrase בני האלהים occurs in other passages (Job 1:6; 38:7) where the angels are meant. Some interpreters think that Genesis 6:1-4 is an example of primitive ideas concerning unions between angels and the women of the earth, which resulted in gigantic and corrupt races. Ginzberg quotes the two sages of the Midrash who expressed themselves most decisively against the myth of the angels' intercourse with the women (*Legends*, V, 156). The myth of the fallen angels has been degraded in midrashic literature because of their sensuality. The Persian idea of two opposing empires, with Satan as God's enemy, has persisted only in non-Jewish literature, in which Lucifer is identified with the rebel archangel, Satan. The so-called "fallen angels" appear in the Midrash under seven designations: *Nefilim, Eimim, Refaim, Gibborim, Zamzumim, Anakim* and *Avvim*, all of which characterize their gigantic size and limitless boldness.

MELAVEH MALKAH   מְלַוֶּה מַלְכָּה

AT THE conclusion of the Sabbath, known as *Motzaé Shabbath*, the outgoing Queen Sabbath is honored with special festivity hymns and songs, bidding farewell to the holiness of the day and ushering in the new week with a plea for deliverance, health and sustenance. The meal eaten on this occasion amidst songs and hymns is known as *Se'udath Melaveh Malkah*, meaning that the outgoing queen is being accompanied by those who honor and cherish her.

According to a talmudic statement, even the poor who received their daily rations from the communal kitchen had to be provided with three meals (*shalosh se'udoth*) for the Sabbath and one meal for Saturday night's *Melaveh Malkah*.

Prophet Elijah figures prominently in the hymns chanted on Saturday night because, according to popular tradition, he is to appear as the forerunner of the Messiah at the beginning of a new week. Such a plea for deliverance through the appearance of Elijah as the forerunner of the Messiah is expressed in the poem במוצאי יום מנוחה, composed by Rabbi Jacob Menuy who lived in the thirteenth century:

"At the close of the day of rest, O grant relief to thy people; send Elijah to the distressed, that grief and sighs may flee away ... The bereaved city of Zion, held today in utter contempt, may she soon be populated—a happy mother of children... May the vision of the great seer, Jeremiah, come to pass this month; may in this household be heard the sound of mirth and gladness..."

Under kabbalistic influence, the Ḥasidim are accustomed to delay the conclusion of the Sabbath as much as possible by means of the prolonged *Melaveh Malkah* observance.

SALTING מְלִיחָה

THE various ways in which salt was used in ancient times clearly explain why it was regarded as a most important necessity of life. Eating a man's salt came to mean receiving pay from him. The Latin word salarium (salary) denoted salt money, given to the Roman soldiers for salt, which was part of their pay. Hence the expression "we eat the salt of the palace" (Ezra 4:14). Just as salt was absolutely necessary at meals, so it was indispensable at the offering of sacrifices.

The Torah expressly declares: "Every meal offering that you present to the Lord shall be seasoned with salt" (Leviticus 2:13). After the destruction of the Temple, the table set for a meal was considered as an altar, upon which salt must be placed before the blessing is recited. The rabbis likened the Torah to salt without which the world could not get along (Sofrim 5:8). A meal without salt is considered no meal (Berakhoth 44a).

Because of its decomposing action on the blood, salt has been used for draining the blood from meat. Blood cannot be thoroughly extracted from meat unless the meat is well salted (Ḥullin 113a). Among the laws for salting meat, given in the *Shulḥan Arukh*, there are the following rules:

The layer of salt must be neither too thin, for then it is lacking in strength, nor too thick, for then it does not adhere to the meat; and it must remain on the meat not less than twenty minutes. It has no effect on the blood of meat three days old, as the blood is then considered to have coagulated, unless the meat has been previously rinsed in water (*Yoreh De'ah* 69:3, 6, 12).

Salt has no effect on liver on account of the large quantity of blood contained in it. Liver must be cut open, and broiled over a fire with

360

the open parts downward so that the blood may drain from them; while being broiled, it must be lightly sprinkled with salt. After broiling, it should be rinsed three times of the blood which has been discharged. After that it may be boiled. It must be broiled over a flame, and must not be wrapped in any kind of paper. After remaining in the salt for one hour (or at least 24 minutes), the meat must be rinsed three times.

MOLECH   מֹלֶךְ

THE fire-god Molech was a Semitic deity whose worship was characterized in early times by the practice of child sacrifice. The underlying idea was that of appeasing the angry God by offering to him the most valued possession. The Torah makes this crime punishable by death in the following enactment: "Anyone, whether an Israelite or an alien residing in Israel, who gives any of his offspring to Molech shall be put to death" (Leviticus 20:2).

Palestinian excavations have revealed vestiges of infant skeletons in cemeteries around heathen altars. The Ammonites regarded Molech (king) as the ruler and champion of his people; he was an aspect of Baal, whose name likewise signifies lord. The detestable feature of the Molech worship was the burning of children to him in fire; they were first slain, then cremated, as evident from the piles of ashes discovered near the ancient altars.

DIVINE KINGSHIP   מַלְכוּת שָׁמַיִם

THE universality of the true religion is implied in the concept of *malkhuth shamayim*, the kingship of God. There can be only one religion if there is but one God. Hence the prophetic declaration: "The Lord shall be King over all the earth; on that day the Lord shall be One, and his name One" (Zechariah 14:9).

God's kingship means the reign of justice and mercy, to be furthered by means of spiritual efforts to improve the life of mankind on earth. This is the wide, universal application of *malkhuth shamayim* (מלכות שמים) in the Hebrew prayers. The expression עול מלכות שמים (the yoke of God's kingship), which one is to assume, is related to the expressions עול תורה and עול מצוות (the yokes of Torah and *mitzvoth*).

Rabbi Neḥunya, who lived until the end of the first century, said: "Whoever takes upon himself the yoke of the Torah will be relieved from the yoke of a foreign government and the yoke of the daily cares. . ." (Avoth 3:6). "Kingdom of heaven" is an incorrect rendering of *malkhuth shamayim*.

BIBLE VERSES   מַלְכִיּוֹת, זִכְרוֹנוֹת, שׁוֹפָרוֹת

THE *Musaf* service for *Rosh Hashanah* includes the three central sections named מלכיות, זכרונות, שופרות, each of which contains ten biblical quotations concerning God's kingship, providence and revelation, respectively. Three quotations are from the Torah, three from the Psalms, three from the Prophets, and the closing one, the tenth, is again from the Torah. At the conclusion of each of the three sections, the *shofar* is sounded in accordance with an ancient custom discussed in the Mishnah (Rosh Hashanah 4:5-6).

Each section is accompanied by a prologue and an epilogue, written in the purest style of Hebrew and inserted by Rav, the third-century founder of the Sura Academy in Babylonia. The first section, for example, consisting of ten biblical verses in which God is presented as King, has the *Alenu* Adoration as its prologue, and the following passage as its epilogue: "Our God and God of our fathers, reign over the whole universe in thy glory. . . May each being know that thou hast made it, may every creature realize that thou hast created it, may every breathing thing proclaim: The Lord God of Israel is King, and his majesty rules over all."

KINGS   מְלָכִים

THE two books of Kings, which tell the story of the kingdoms of Judah and Israel, are treated as one book in the Hebrew Bible. They cover a period of about four hundred years, extending from the last days of David to the destruction of the first Temple. It is the period of Israel's glory, division, decline, disintegration, and fall. The prophets who appeared in the course of history that is contained in the books of Kings were statesmen as well as ethical teachers.

According to a talmudic statement, the books of Kings were written by the prophet Jeremiah. Indeed, the book of Jeremiah, largely bio-

362

graphical, is very much like them in its make-up. The anonymous writer of Kings, aiming to set forth the lessons which the history of his people affords, traces the dire results of disobedience and the happy consequences of loyalty to the precepts of the Torah. He characterizes the kings of Judah and Israel according to their faithlessness to the divine teachings. Kings I and II consists of three parts: 1) the reign of Solomon; 2) a synchronistic account of Judah and Israel; 3) Judah until the Babylonian captivity.

Judah survived by nearly one hundred and fifty years the rival kingdom of Israel, which was the larger and more powerful of the two. The accumulation of large estates in the hands of a few holders, oppression of the poor, perversion of justice, luxury and over-indulgence undermined the kingdom of Israel and hastened its end. In the story of Naboth's vineyard we have the beginnings of the transition from small peasant ownership to that of large estates in the kingdom of Israel. Excerpt:

"Now Naboth of Jezreel had a vineyard close to the palace of Ahab, king of Samaria. Ahab said to Naboth: Give me your vineyard that I may have it for a vegetable garden, since it is near my house. I will give you a better vineyard for it, or I will give you its value in money.

"But Naboth said to Ahab: The Lord forbid that I should part with the inheritance of my fathers. Ahab went home angry and sullen... His wife Jezebel came and asked him: Why are you so depressed that you cannot eat... Are you not in command of Israel's kingdom? Get up, take some food and cheer up. I will get you the vineyard of Naboth... Two evil men came and brought charges against Naboth, saying: Naboth cursed God and the king. So he was taken outside the city, and they stoned him to death... Ahab then went to take possession of Naboth's vineyard.

"But the word of the Lord came to Elijah, saying: Arise go down to meet Ahab king of Israel, who is in the vineyard of Naboth. Say to him: You have murdered and now you inherit? Thus says the Lord: Where dogs licked up the blood of Naboth, there shall dogs lick up your blood also. Behold, I will bring evil upon you; I will utterly sweep you away... When Ahab heard these words, he rent his garments and put on sackcloth. He fasted and went about quietly..."

In II Kings 3:4-27 we read concerning Mesha, king of Moab, who had rendered to Ahab, king of Israel, the tribute of one hundred thousand lambs and as many rams, that is, their wool. But after the death of Ahab, the king of Moab rebelled against the king of Israel, who asked the king of Judah to join him in making war upon Moab. Now, on hearing that the kings had marched to attack them, all the Moabites had been mustered and were posted on the frontier. When the king of Moab saw that the battle was too disastrous, he took his eldest son, the heir to the throne, and sacrificed him on the wall. It brought such a storm of indignation against Israel, that the Israelites had to leave him alone and return home.

A Canaanite inscription, known as the Moabite Stone or Monument of Mesha (מצבת מישע), turned up, in 1868, in the Arab village of Dhiban, Jordan, and was placed in the Louvre Museum, Paris, where it has remained to this day. When the inscribed stone was discovered by F. Klein, it was a slab of black basalt, three feet ten inches high, two feet broad, and a foot and $2\frac{1}{2}$ inches thick, rounded at the top and the bottom to nearly a semicircle. The inscription consisted of thirty-four lines of Canaanite writing. Although the Arabs broke the stone into fragments, and parts here and there are missing, the inscription is in the main quite intelligible and clear. According to it, Mesha regained the land he had lost and even captured the territory of Reuben and part of Gad. Historians have generally concluded that the Hebrew and Moabite accounts tended to ignore their own losses and setbacks.

MANNA מָן

THE food on which the people of Israel mainly subsisted during the forty years of wandering in the wilderness is described in the Torah: "In the morning a dew lay all about the camp; and when the dew evaporated, there on the surface of the desert were fine flakes like hoarfrost on the ground. On seeing it, the Israelites asked one another: What is this? (מן הוא). They did not know what it was. But Moses told them: This is the bread which the Lord has given you to eat" (Exodus 16:13-15).

The manna was miraculously supplied to the Israelites until they entered Canaan and the fruit of the land was available (Joshua 5:12). According to talmudic tradition, many miracles occurred in connection with the daily descent of the manna. No one could keep it for the next day, or possess more than one *omer*, for it bred worms; yet, the Sabbath portion, which came down on Friday, remained fresh for the sacred day. "It was like coriander seed, but white, and it tasted like wafers made with honey" (Exodus 16:31). *Coriander seed* refers to the size and shape, not to the taste or color of the manna. The coriander is a small, round, aromatic seed of bright brown color.

CUSTOMS   מִנְהָגִים

THE *minhag*, or usage handed down orally from generation to generation, has been described as a most important element in Jewish life. Although the *halakhah* was developed in great detail by the talmudic authorities, the *minhag* always assumed the character of binding law. "Everything should follow local usage" is an oft-quoted tannaitic statement (Bava Metzia 7:1). "Custom overrules law" (מנהג עוקר הלכה) is a well-known statement in Sofrim 14:18). Similarly: "One must not change the custom" (Bava Kamma 117b). "If you come into a city, guide yourself according to its customs" (Genesis Rabbah, 48:16). Since the sages of the Talmud aimed at unanimity and uniformity, they tolerated new customs but did not encourage them.

Whenever codified usage and popular usage come into conflict, the talmudic ruling decides in favor of popular usage. This priority of custom stems from the fact that people are emotionally attached to *minhagim*, cherished from earliest youth, and adhere to them more devotedly than to express commands.

Philo of Alexandria, famous philosopher of Hellenistic Judaism, writing on the *Special Laws*, pointed out: "Customs are unwritten laws, the decisions approved by men of old, not inscribed on monuments or leaves of paper, which the moth destroys, but on the souls of those who are partners in the same society."

Maimonides advises: "Man should try to understand *why* he is asked to observe precepts and customs; but even when he fails to fathom their reason he should not hastily pronounce them as trivial. For customs of religious import are not to be equated with those of a mundane nature; they are in a category by themselves" (*Yad, Me'ilah* 8:8).

The *Sefer ha-Manhig* by Rabbi Abraham ha-Yarḥi (1155-1215) is of historical importance for its description of special synagogal customs in medieval Europe (France, Germany, England, Spain). The author, in the course of his travels through various Jewish communities, noted in his *Guide (Hammanhig)* all the usages prevalent in the synagogues that he visited, citing the talmudic-midrashic sources from which they were derived.

365

The power of communities to establish new customs is severely limited by Jewish law, which requires the consent of the great scholars in the vicinity. Rabbenu Tam, Rashi's grandson (1100-1171), characterized some offensive customs as גיהנם למפרע, that is, when the letters of מנהג (*minhag*) are transposed, they can be made to read גהנם (*gehinnom*).

A large number of *minhagim* were collected by Rabbi Moses Isserles (1520-1572), who added them in the form of glosses to the *Shulḥan Arukh*, the famous code of Jewish law written by Rabbi Joseph Karo (1488-1575). These are accepted as binding by the *Ashkenazim* and not by the *Sephardim*, who also differ in many small details as to the exact wording of certain prayers; hence, the two versions of the Hebrew Prayerbook, *Minhag Ashkenaz* and *Minhag Sephard*.

Rabbi Jacob Halevi Moelln, known as *Maharil* (1360-1427), is regarded as a leading authority on Jewish customs and largely responsible for the synagogal ritual in use among *Ashkenazim* to the present day, even though his work (*Sefer Maharil*) is not mentioned in Rabbi Joseph Karo's *Shulḥan Arukh*.

MENORAH מְנוֹרָה

THE seven-branched candelabrum, used in the portable sanctuary (*Mishkan*) set up by Moses in the wilderness as well as in the Jerusalem Temple, consisted of a base and a shaft with six branches, beaten out of solid gold. The six branches curved to the height of the central shaft, so that all the seven lamps, symbolizing the ideal of universal enlightenment, were in a straight line. They were provided daily with fresh olive oil of the purest quality, and they burned from evening to morning (Exodus 27:21).

Josephus states that three of the seven lamps were allowed to burn by day; according to tradition, however, only the center lamp was left burning all day; it was called Western Lamp (*Ner ha-Ma'aravi*) because it was next to the branches on the east side (Rashi, Shabbath 22b). The Western Lamp is also referred to as *Ner Elohim* (the lamp of God), mentioned in I Samuel 3:3, which is represented in the synagogue by the *Ner Tamid*, the perpetual lamp burning before the ark.

The *Menorah* also symbolizes the creation of the universe in seven days, the center light representing the Sabbath. The seven branches are also said to allude to the continents of the earth as well as the seven heavens, guided by the light of God. Frequently used as a symbol of Judaism and the Jewish people, a representation of the seven-branched candlestick has been found on tombs and monuments dating from the first century.

The earliest preserved and the most authentic representation of the Temple *Menorah* is depicted on the arch of Titus commemorating the triumphal parade following the destruction of Jerusalem in the year 70. According to a talmudic statement (Menahoth 28b), it is prohibited to use a seven-branched *Menorah* outside the Temple. The *Ḥanukkah Menorah* is an eight-branched candelabrum.

MENORATH HAMMAOR   מְנוֹרַת הַמָּאוֹר

THE ethical work *Menorath Hammaor* (the Lamp of Illumination), by Rabbi Israel al-Nakawa of fourteenth-century Spain, contains chapters that have rarely been equalled for depth of penetration into the Jewish soul. It has been proved that the popular *Menorath Hammaor* by Rabbi Isaac Aboab of the fifteenth century is merely a recasting of al-Nakawa's original ethical work, which was edited and published in the original Hebrew by H. S. Enelow.

Rabbi Israel al-Nakawa, who died a martyr's death during the religious persecutions of 1391, drew upon the entire range of talmudic literature for his brilliant work, which is a summation of all phases of Jewish life, both ethical and religious. Following are a few random passages from *Menorath Hammaor:*

"The world is a revolving wheel: one who is rich today may be poor tomorrow, and one who is poor today may be rich tomorrow. Let a man therefore give charity before the wheel has turned. It should be given with a generous spirit and a feeling of compassion. The humble person is loved by his fellow men because he is close to them and takes part in their joys and sorrows. He forgives injuries and bears no grudges against those who have wronged him.

"The Torah is a crown which is not reserved for a chosen few. Any man can earn it for himself if he cares to try. By placing a learned man ahead of others we honor the Torah, which ranks higher than royalty. A man should not allow his occupation to crowd the Torah out of his life, but he should make definite provision for study. Readiness to undergo all manner of privation in the pursuit of learning has always been a characteristic of Jewish students. Even a learned scholar must not think that he has reached his goal; he can always add to his knowledge. There is no pleasure greater than the study of the Torah.

"Marriage is not a onesided affair. The man has obligations as well as the woman. First, he must have as high a regard for his wife as he has for himself. He should sacrifice his personal needs in order to provide more abundantly for his wife and children. Above all, he should treat his wife with love and sympathy, for she is part of him and depends on him. Children of a loveless marriage are likely to be of inferior quality. Faithfulness is one of the essential conditions of an ideal marriage.

"One should make every effort to provide a religious and ethical education for his child, regardless of cost. Every community must provide teachers for the children. A town without pupils is doomed. A man should not make a big display of his love for his children, lest they become spoiled. He should treat all his children equally, so as not to create envy among them. He should be very careful about the example he sets to his children both in speech and action. He should be especially careful not to use unclean language. He must learn to treat his child with gentleness and refrain from rudeness or violence in addressing him.

"The ethical person is content with what he has; the unethical one is never satisfied. If a man is satisfied with his lot, he is likely to live a happy life. None is so rich as one who is content with little. In order to have contentment one must have faith. If a man has no faith he is likely to worry constantly. He will be afraid to spend even a little of what he has lest he lose everything and become poor. Contentment frees a man from greed and envy. Greed leads to many evils; if you are envious, you court all kinds of trouble and ailments. Be generous toward your neighbor; be as concerned about his welfare and reputation as you are about your own.

"The common descent of man, taught by the Torah, implies the obligation of mutual friendship. Association with good people is useful in itself, even though one may never receive a favor from them. To show that you are truly a person's friend, be first to greet him; invite him to your joyous occasions; call him by complimentary names; do not give away his secrets; visit him when he is sick and take care of his affairs; look after his interests when he is away; overlook his shortcomings and forgive him promptly; criticize him when he has done wrong; respect him always; do not lie to him; pray for him and wish him happiness. True friendship means judging your neighbor favorably even when circumstances seem to point against him. The quarrelsome person who constantly complains about others, claiming that he is being persecuted and wronged, cannot hope to keep his friends. To publish the secrets of your fellow man is like killing him; a man's life is actually endangered sometimes by the disclosure of a secret. A sage once declared: When anyone entrusts me with a secret, I dig a grave in my heart and bury it there."

MINḤAH   מִנְחָה

THE term *minḥah* occurs in the Bible in the sense of gift and meal-offering. It is only in talmudic literature that the word denotes afternoon service. *Shaḥarith* and *Minḥah* correspond to the daily sacrifice (*Tamid*) that was offered in the Temple each morning and each afternoon beginning at 12:30. Hence, *Minḥah* may be recited at any time from 12:30 p.m. to sunset. For the sake of convenience, the *Minḥah* service was postponed in the nineteenth century to very near sunset, so that it might be followed by the *Ma'ariv* service after a short interval. Since the recitation of the *Shema* is obligatory only "when you lie down and when you rise up" (Deuteronomy 6:7), it is not included in the afternoon service.

The afternoon service known as *Minḥah* is one of the three daily services mentioned in Daniel 6:11. It consists of *Ashré* (Psalm 145), *Amidah*, and *Alenu*. When there is a *minyan* (a quorum of ten adult males), the leader repeats the *Amidah* (standing prayer) aloud, reciting the *Kedushah* and the *Kaddishim*. On Sabbaths and on fast days a section of the Torah is read before the *Amidah*. The term *Minḥah* has been connected with Elijah's prayer at the hour of the "evening offering" (I Kings 18:36); hence its importance is stressed in the Talmud (Berakhoth 6b).

According to traditional lore, the patriarchs Abraham, Isaac and Jacob were the authors of *Shaḥarith*, *Minḥah* and *Ma'ariv* (morning, afternoon and evening prayers), respectively. The Talmud distinguishes between *Minḥah Gedolah*, *Minḥah Ketannah*, and *Pelag Minḥah:* from 12:30 to sunset, from 3:30 to sunset, and from 4:45 to sunset, respectively (Berakhoth 26b). The third meal on Sabbaths is eaten between *Minḥah* and *Ma'ariv*. On urgent occasions, when time presses, the *Shemoneh Esreh* is not repeated by the *ḥazzan* after the *Kedushah*.

369

MINYAN מִנְיָן

THE number (*minyan*) of ten Jews above the age of thirteen is the minimum required for congregational worship, public Torah reading, the reci ation of *Kedushah* and *Kaddish*. Rabbi Naḥman Bratzlaver said: "Nine *tsaddikim* do not make a *minyan*, but one common man, joining them, completes the *minyan*.

The Mishnah states: If fewer than ten are present, the *Shema* and its accompanying benedictions may not be recited with the reader who leads in the prescribed congregational prayers. Nor may the priestly benediction be pronounced by the *kohanim*, nor may the pre-scribed portions of the Torah and the Prophets be read . . . nor may the seven benedictions over the newly-wed be read. . . (Megillah 4:3).

From Numbers 14:27, where the ten spies (exclusive of Joshua and Caleb) are referred to as an *edah* (congregation), it has been tra-ditionally deduced that a congregation for prayer must consist at least of ten adult males. The worship service held by a *minyan* (quo-rum) or more together is termed *tefillah b'tsibbur*, which includes additions such as are enumerated in the foregoing Mishnah.

MASORAH מְסוֹרָה

THE term *Masorah* is derived from the root מסר (to transmit) and signifies the work of preserving the integrity of the text of the Hebrew Bible. The text of the Hebrew Bible, known as the Masoretic Text, has been transmitted from generation to generation with scrupulous uniformity and unparalleled accuracy of transcription.

As early as the second century, the oral tradition had established the consonantal text and its pronunciation so firmly that no change is known to have occurred in it since. It was at that period that Rabbi Akiva, who died as a martyr in 135, declared: מסורת סייג לתורה (Avoth 3:17), "the Masorah is a fence to the Torah."

Great attention was paid to the exact wording of the biblical text, the source of all Jewish law. During the tannaitic period, traditional laws were deduced from an extra word, an extra letter. Hence the great task of the Masorites of many ages to achieve the textual sta-bility of the Hebrew Bible, and to protect it against any misunder-standing or misinterpretation.

370

With the fall of Jerusalem in the year 70, and the dispersion of the Jews to all parts of the world, it became unavoidably necessary to remove all ambiguity from the consonantal biblical text, which was considered complete and intelligible to Hebrew-speaking scholars but not to Jews who had adopted other vernaculars in the Diaspora.

When Hebrew had ceased to be a spoken language it became imperative to devise a system of vowels, in the form of dots and dashes, so as to enable anyone to learn the mechanics of reading and pronouncing Hebrew correctly. This was accomplished by the Masorites whose activity extended from the sixth to the tenth centuries chiefly in Tiberias.

Originally, the Bible text was in continuous script, without breaks. Earlier Masorites divided it into words, phrases, verses, paragraphs, and books. The division into larger sections (*sidroth*) and smaller sections (*parashoth*), as well as into verses, was already known in ancient times, though the chapters and verses were not designated by numbers until the thirteenth century. A complete system of vowel and accent marks came into existence toward the end of the eighth century.

The Masorah represents the body of countless traditions connected with the biblical text. The Masorites noted anything that was unusual in Bible manuscripts, as when a large letter is used to mark the beginning of an important passage or to prevent the possibility of error. Examples: the first letter of the Torah ('ב' רבתי); the letter ד in אחד (Deuteronomy 6:4), so as not to read אחר; the large ו in גחון (Leviticus 11:420) marking the middle of the Torah according to the number of letters.

Irregularities in the text are often indicated by the Masorah, as when to read words otherwise than they appear in the text (קרי) and when to omit reading a word that is written (כתיב ולא קרי); also, when to supply a word that is not found written in the text (קרי ולא כתיב). These variants number over thirteen hundred.

Addressing themselves to careful watchfulness over the received text of the Bible, the Masorites counted every word and letter; they drew up lists of irregular or unusual spellings, and built up the safeguards for the preservation of the sacred teachings.

The last and most renowned Masorite was Aaron ben Asher of the tenth century, who lived in Tiberias where he spent many years preparing an accurate manuscript of the Bible, provided with vocalization and accentuation in accordance with his school of tradition.

371

Maimonides recommended Ben Asher's work as the best to be followed by all copyists (*Yad, Sefer Torah* 8:4).

Moses Ben Naphtali, a contemporary of Ben Asher, was likewise a member of the Tiberian school of Masoretic scholars. He wrote upon the punctuation and accentuation of the Bible text, differing from Ben Asher in small details totaling about 900. The presently accepted text is according to Ben Asher's version with some minor influences by Ben Naphtali. With these scholars the Masorah activities are regarded as concluded.

The collection of critical Masoretic notes is found either in separate works or in the form of marginal notations. The notations on the side margins and between the columns are referred to as Small Masorah (*Masorah parva*); those on the lower and upper margins of the biblical books are called Large Masorah (*Masorah Magna*); the Masorah Finalis, found in nearly all the printed editions at the end of the various books, indicates the number of chapters, verses, the middle point of the book, full and defective spellings, and abnormally written letters. On account of its obscure terminology and extreme brevity, the Masoretic sign language is a study in itself.

TAXES   מִסִּים

BEFORE the establishment of the kingdom in Eretz Yisrael, when there was as yet no army and no royal court to support, the Sanctuary (*Mishkan*) and the priesthood were maintained by the tithes and other offerings. After the establishment of the kingdom, revenues for its support were obtained from various sources. During the reign of Solomon, the people were oppressed by taxation; this burden was the immediate cause of the division of the kingdom. The people pleaded with king Rehoboam, son of Solomon: "Your father made our yoke heavy. Now therefore lighten the hard service of your father and his heavy yoke upon us, and we will serve you" (I Kings 12:4). The inexperienced young king refused to yield to their request, saying: "Whereas my father laid upon you a heavy yoke, I will add to your yoke. My father chastised you with whips, but I will chastise you with scorpions" (12:11). This response precipitated the revolt of the ten northern tribes.

The first poll tax (מס הגולגולת) mentioned in the Torah was the levy of half a shekel imposed on all men after the exodus from Egypt:

"Everyone who is included in the census must pay a half-shekel . . . everyone of twenty years or more. . . The rich shall not give more, and the poor shall not give less, than the half-shekel (Exodus 30:14-15) In addition to the half-shekel (מחצית השקל) tax, imposed annually on rich and poor alike for the maintenance of the Temple, the citizens had to provide for the maintenance of the government and the support of the poor; when they were subject to a foreign ruler, they had to pay tribute to him.

After the destruction of the Temple, the half-shekel levy for the upkeep of the Sanctuary was converted by the Roman authorities into the so-called *Fiscus Judaicus*, which continued to be collected with great harshness until the fourth century. The collectors visited each town of Judea annually at a fixed time, and in foreign countries, in the Diaspora, places were designated where the *Fiscus Judaicus* was to be paid. Many tried to avoid paying this *Fiscus Judaicus*, the shame of which was unbearable to some.

The Mishnah lists tax gatherers among murderers and robbers (Nedarim 3:4). The publicans, who under the Romans contracted to gather taxes in the provinces and to supervise subordinates empowered with squeezing as much public revenue as possible from the people, reserved a good margin of profit for themselves. They erected toll gates on roads and at bridges; they collected duty on goods carried to market, and on merchandise transported from one town to another; they taxed many such common articles, as salt. Hence they were among those despised by the sages and were grouped among the worst sinners.

TRACTATES   מַסֶּכְתּוֹת

THE talmudic tractates are called *massekhtoth* (מסכתות) from the biblical word מסכת (*massekheth*) denoting web, texture (Judges 16:13-14). The Mishnah comprises sixty-three tractates, each of which is divided into chapters and paragraphs. The same applies to the Tosefta. Each *massekhta* or tractate is named after the principal subject with which it deals. Examples: *Massekhta Berakhoth, Massekhta Shabbath, Massekhta Sanhedrin.* The Hebrew name *massekheth* is interchangeable with the Aramaic equivalent *massekhta*.

The Babylonian Talmud, known as *Talmud Bavli*, has *Gemara* on thirty-seven *massekhtoth* (tractates); the Palestinian Talmud, known as *Talmud Yerushalmi*, has *Gemara* on thirty-nine *massekhtoth*. *Seder*

373

Zera'im, for example, is without *Gemara*, with the exception of its first tractate Berakhoth. A large part of the contents of the tractates without *Gemara* is discussed in other tractates. The *Ethics of the Fathers*, or *Mishnah Avoth* has no *Gemara* in either Talmud.

The *Minor Massekhtoth* (מסכתות קטנות) are the extra-canonical tractates which are included in the editions of the Babylonian Talmud in the form of addenda. They are: 1) *Avoth d'Rabbi Nathan*, 2) *Sofrim*, 3) *Evel Rabbathi* or *Massekheth Semahoth* on mourning, 4) *Kallah* on marital relations, 5) *Derekh Eretz Rabbah*, 6) *Derekh Eretz Zuta*, 7) *Gerim*, 8) *Kuthim*, 9) *Avadim*, 10) *Sefer Torah*, 11) *Tefillin*, 12) *Tsitsith*, 13) *Mezuzah*. The Minor Tractates are of a later date than the rest of the Talmud. One of the sayings contained in *Derekh Eretz Rabbah* is quoted in the Palestinian Talmud as found in *Derekh ha-Aretz*.

MESILLATH YESHARIM מְסִלַּת יְשָׁרִים

THE *Mesillath Yesharim* (Path of the Upright) by Rabbi Moses Ḥayyim Luzzatto (1707-1747) is a classic in contemporary Hebrew literature. In the middle of the nineteenth century it was adopted as the ethical text of the Moralist Movement founded by Rabbi Israel Salanter.

According to the thinking of Rabbi Moses Ḥayyim Luzzatto, who was an ardent follower of the mystic teachings of the Kabbalah and a thorough master of biblical Hebrew, good conduct is the road to God. In order to find out what good conduct is, one must study and then try to follow the guidance offered by sage and saint.

His *Mesillath Yesharim* became a favorite pocket-companion with all Jewish men striving after the higher life. It starts out with the premise that moral conduct is not something naturally given, but rather a stupendous effort to overcome all that thwarts it; it can be acquired by training and education. Several random excerpts follow:

The Torah lays down a general rule: "You shall love your neighbor as yourself"—as yourself, without difference or distinction, without subterfuge or mental reservation, literally *as yourself*. Lying is a most prevalent disease. It exists in various degrees. There are those who actually make it their business to tell lies. They go about inventing stories without any foundation in truth, in order to have material for gossip or because they wish to be considered clever. There are others less corrupt, who are in the habit of introducing some element of untruth into everything they say. Such liars are never believed.

"The liar is punished by not being believed even when he speaks the truth" is a proverbial saying of our sages.

Pride is an exaggerated sense of our own importance. There is the proud man who thinks that because he possesses some superiority, everyone should tremble before him. How dare an ordinary man speak to him, or ask anything of him! He overwhelms people with his arrogant replies, and he scowls all the time. Another behaves as though he were humble and goes to extremes to display modesty and infinite humility, saying to himself: "I am so exalted and so deserving of honor, that I need not have anyone do me honor. I can well afford to forego visible marks of respect." This type of humility is soon recognized as insincere, hypocritical and nothing but pretense.

"He who is envious injures only himself. There are people so foolish that when they see a neighbor in luck, they begin to brood and are so upset and distressed that even the good which they possess no longer affords them pleasure. Akin to envy is greed, which wears out a man's heart until the day of his death. Even worse than greed is the lust for honor. The craving for honor is irresistible. How many are there who would rather starve than engage in work which they consider beneath their dignity, for fear that their honor might be compromised! They submit to idleness which leads to melancholy, theft, and all the cardinal sins, in order not to lower their dignity nor spoil what they regard as their reputation.

In order to possess the trait of cleanness, a man must exert himself a great deal; yet it does not require as much effort as appears on the surface.

NUMBER TERMS   מִסְפָּרִים

THE symbolical use of round numbers occurs frequently in Hebrew literature. The sacredness of the number seven is enhanced by its connection with the creation of the world and the institution of the Sabbath. The number seven appears in the institution of the seventh year of release (*shemittah*), the forty-nine years between jubilees, the seven branches of the Menorah, the forty-nine days between *Pesaḥ* and *Shavuoth*, the seven days of *Pesaḥ* and of *Sukkoth*. The number ten is reminiscent of the ten generations before the flood and the ten generations between Noah and Abraham, the ten plagues in Egypt, the ten commandments, the ten divine utterances by which the world was created, the ten trials of Abraham, and the expression: "They have put me to the test ten times" (Numbers 14:22).

The number forty is often used in the Bible. At the time of the flood, it rained for forty days; Israel wandered in the wilderness for forty years; David and Solomon each reigned for forty years; Elijah journeyed for forty days to flee from Jezebel to the mountain of God. The number seventy, made up of the factors seven and ten, has a symbolical significance. The descendants of the three sons of Noah, repopulating the world after the flood, were seventy in number. Jacob came into Egypt with seventy persons; Moses chose seventy elders to assist him in his duties; Israel was exiled into Babylonia for a period of seventy years; the Septuagint version of the Bible was prepared by seventy scribes.

The sages frequently grouped themes of traditional teaching according to numbers. Many instances are to be found especially in *Ethics of the Fathers:* "They said three things... The world is based upon three things... Ten miracles were performed for our fathers in Egypt, and ten at the Red Sea... Ten miracles were done for our fathers in the Temple... Ten things were created on the eve of Sabbath... There are seven characteristics of a stupid person, and seven of a wise man... There are four characters among men... There are four dispositions... There are four types of students... There are four types of contributors to charity..." Such numerical groupings were an aid to memory.

MAOZ TSUR   מָעוֹז צוּר

THE hymn *Maoz Tsur*, or "Rock of Ages," sung after the kindling of the Ḥanukkah lights, recounts the wonders of the exodus from Egypt and the deliverance from Babylonia, Persia, and Syria. It was composed by a thirteenth-century poet, whose name (מרדכי) is revealed in the acrostic of the initial letters of the five stanzas.

The tune, bright and stirring, has been regarded as traditional since the sixteenth century; it has been identified as an adaptation from an old German folksong, widely used among German Jews as early as 1450. The paraphrase "Rock of Ages" is by Gustav G. Gottheil (1827-1903), who was active in the promotion of Zionism in America. It has been suggested that the author of *Maoz Tsur* may have been the Mordecai ben Isaac who wrote the Sabbath hymn *Mah Yafith*.

The entire Maccabean struggle, as well as the traditional interpretation of *Ḥanukkah*, is summed up in the twenty-four Hebrew words of the fifth stanza, which reads as follows: "Greeks gathered to attack me in the Hasmonean days. They demolished my towers, and polluted all the oils. From the last remaining flask a miracle was wrought for Israel. Men of wisdom decreed eight days for hymns of praise."

MAOTH ḤITTIM   מָעוֹת חִטִּים

SINCE the days of the Talmud, *Maoth Ḥittim* (wheat money) was looked upon as a compulsory community tax collected annually before the festival of Passover, to provide a supply of *matzoth* and wine for the poor and the needy, enabling them to celebrate the festival of freedom properly. The term *Maoth Ḥittim* has, in the course of time, acquired broader significance of assuring a supply of all the Passover essentials for the less fortunate.

MA'AMADOTH   מַעֲמָדוֹת

MA'AMAD (post) is the name given to a group of representatives of the lay people who were deputed to accompany the daily offerings in the Temple at Jerusalem. There were twenty-four *ma'amadoth* in the outlying districts, corresponding to the twenty-four divisions of priests and Levites who served in the Temple in rotation each for one week. But the entire division of priests, Levites and lay representatives could not be expected to go to Jerusalem each time; it was therefore arranged that those who remained at home should gather in their respective cities and towns on the days they were supposed to be in the Temple. The *ma'amadoth* throughout the land held services during the time coinciding with the time of sacrifice in the Temple (*Shaharith, Musaf, Minhah*).

This is the origin of the synagogue, in which the various daily services are called by the names made familiar in the routine of the Temple. Those who went up to the Temple to represent the lay Israelites not only witnessed the offering of public and private sacrifices, but four times daily held a service of their own, consisting of Torah readings and prayers. The same type of service was held by the *ma'amadoth* in the various towns. Hence the name *ma'amadoth* which has been given to an anthology of biblical and talmudic passages, the reading of which is prescribed seriatim for each day of the week, respectively.

All of Israel was divided into twenty-four sections. The priests and Levites within each section formed each a special division or *mishmar* (Numbers 18:1-7), which had to do service in the Temple of Jerusalem one full week every half year; forty-eight weeks of the year were thus distributed between twenty-four divisions, the remaining weeks being festival weeks (*Pesaḥ, Shavuoth, Sukkoth*) during which all Israel made pilgrimage to Jerusalem (Exodus 34:23). Owing to the multitude of the visitors and their offerings, the priests of all divisions had to be present. Josephus estimates a staggering total presence of about three million pilgrims (*Wars*, 6:424).

Every division of priests was subdivided into seven smaller groups, or families (בתי אבות), each of which had to serve one day of the week assigned to the respective division (Chronicles 24:4-18). The representative laymen, who witnessed the sacrificial rites, recited prayers on behalf of those left at home. They, like the priestly division to which they were attached, had to change every week. They were known as אנשי מעמד, while the priests were referred to as אנשי משמר (men of the lay post and men of the guard, respectively). The subdivisions of priests, doing one day's service, were called אנשי בית אב (men belonging to a family).

MA'ARIV מַעֲרִיב, עַרְבִית

THE evening service, known as *Ma'ariv* or *Arvith*, does not correspond to any sacrifice in the Temple, since the offering of sacrifices occurred only twice a day, morning and afternoon (*shaḥarith* and *Minḥah*). For this reason, the *Shemoneh Esreh* was omitted from the evening service in talmudic times and in a greater part of the geonic period. To replace the Eighteen Benedictions of the *Amidah* prayer, eighteen scattered verses, each mentioning the name of God, were introduced at the end of *Ma'ariv*.

According to *Maḥzor Vitry* (page 78), this passage, beginning with ברוך ה' לעולם, was arranged by the heads of the Babylonian Acaemies. It is followed by half-*Kaddish* because at one time it marked the end of the evening service, as may be seen from the ninth-century *Siddur* of Rav Amram Gaon. Maimonides, however, asserts that since the Jews everywhere have consented to recite the evening prayer regularly, it is equivalent to an obligation (*hovah*). By prayer he means the *Shemoneh Esreh*.

The controversy in the Talmud as to whether the evening prayer is optional or obligatory refers to the *Shemoneh Esreh* and not to the *Shema*, which it is obligatory to recite morning and evening. Since the *Maʿariv* prayer was considered by some talmudic authorities to be optional, the *Shemoneh Esreh* is not repeated by the leader and the *Kedushah* is not recited in the evening.

The time for the *Maʿariv* service begins when three stars are visible in the skies; it usually follows immediately after *Minhah* in the synagogue, to avoid the trouble of a second gathering of a congregational quorum or *minyan* of ten adult males. The time may be extended to midnight, and in case of an emergency until the rise of dawn (Berakhoth 1:1).

On Friday evening, the *Maʿariv* service is preceded by *Kabbalath Shabbath*, consisting of six psalms symbolizing the six working days of the week, and Psalm 92 in honor of the Sabbath. *Vehu Rahum* is then omitted because, as a day of joy, the Sabbath is not to be disturbed with supplications for merciful pardon of sin and iniquity.

On Saturday night, called מוצאי שבת (*Motzaé Shabbath*—the outgoing of the Sabbath), *Maʿariv* is preceded by Psalms 144 and 67. Psalm 144 is a prayer for protection. The psalmist marvels at the thought that God who is so great should condescend to care for man who is so insignificant. The short and joyful Psalm 67 expresses the idea that the divine goodness to Israel reveals God also to the other nations on earth and calls forth their praise and their worship. Then the regular *Maʿariv* service begins with והוא רחום, two verses (Psalm 78:38; 20:10) consisting of thirteen words, held by some to correspond to the thirteen attributes of divine mercy (Exodus 34:6-7).

Immediately following the *Shemoneh Esreh* prayer on *Motzaé Shabbath*, Psalm 91 is recited. The Talmud describes this psalm as a song against evil occurrences (שיר של פגעים). It speaks of the safety of those who trust in God amid the perils of their journey through life. The number of verses of this psalm is equivalent to the numerical value of טוב (17), alluding to a "good" week. The number seventeen is reached by repeating the last verse ("With long life will I satisfy him, and will show him my saving power").

In the entire Psalm 91, the letter ז (=7) is not found. This psalm is omitted seven times each year, when festivals occur during the ensuing week. The reason given for its omission is that it is preceded by the verse: "Prosper the work of our hands for us" (Psalm 90:17), and work is not permissible during the seven sacred festivals of the year. The passage ואתה קדוש and ויתן לך then follow, just to prolong the service connected with the outgoing of the Sabbath (מוצאי שבת), thus expressing the Jewish reluctance to part from Queen Sabbath and from the נשמה יתירה (additional soul), the festive cheerfulness that accompanies the Sabbath.

CAVE OF MACHPELAH   מְעָרַת הַמַּכְפֵּלָה

THE cave acquired by Abraham for use as a hereditary burial place (Genesis 23:17-20) is found in a locality that was called Machpelah at Hebron, nineteen miles south of Jerusalem. According to some authorities, the present mosque standing over the cave is successor of a magnificent structure erected by Herod. It is most religiously guarded by the Arabs, who regard Abraham as the founder of their race through Ishmael. Entrance is forbidden to non-Moslems unless they secure permission under special circumstances. The foundations of the building that surrounds the cave date bac to the period of the Second Temple.

The cave consists of two storeys, hence it is referred to as a double cave. Visitors are permitted entrance only to the upper storey, where "there is little to see except counterfeit tombs." One European, an Italian architect succeeded at the risk of his life in entering the lower cavern. "He noticed there sarcophagi of white stone . . . in striking corroboration of the statement of Josephus, that these were of fair marble, exquisitely wrought." Benjamin of Tudela, twelfth-century traveler, relates n is *Itinerary:* "At Hebron there is a large place of worship, which was previously a Jewish synagogue. The natives erected there six sepulchers, which they tell foreigners are those of the patriarchs and their wives. . ."

It is generally admitted that the cave of Machpelah, the original burying-place of Abraham and Sarah, Isaac and Rebekah, Jacob and Leah, is in the area of the great mosque at Hebron, one of the oldest continuously inhabited towns in Palestine. Abraham is closely associated with Hebron, as Isaac is with Beersheba, and Jacob with Bethel, the town mentioned in the Bible more frequently than any other except Jerusalem.

380

MAASÉ BERESHITH   מַעֲשֵׂה בְרֵאשִׁית

The biblical account of the creation, referred to as *Maasé Bereshith*, and the prophetic description of the chariot-throne in Ezekiek 1:1-28, called *Maasé Merkavah*, are spoken of in the Mishnah as mystic speculations which must not be transmitted to any individuals other than those showing themselves worthy, and never more than one or two at a time (Ḥagigah 2:1). The exact nature of *Maasé Bereshith* and *Maasé Merkavah* is not known, but Maimonides is of the opinion that these mysterious doctrines denote physics and metaphysics, respectively. Since he discusses these very subjects in his *Guide for the Perplexed*, he informs us that, in keeping with the instructions of the talmudic sages, he must not be expected to offer more than bare allusions, scattered among other subjects which he explains.

He writes: "You must not suppose that these mysteries are known to anybody completely. By no means... With those who never see light at all, namely the multitudes of the people, we have nothing to do in this book... Heaven knows, I hesitated long before writing this book, because it contains unknown matters, never before treated by any Jewish writer in the *Galuth*" (*Guide*, Introduction). According to Maimonides, the story of creation in Genesis contains a treatment of theoretical physics. Similarly, the first and tenth chapters of the book of Ezekiel contain allusions to profound ideas of theology and metaphysics.

GOOD WORKS   מַעֲשִׂים טוֹבִים

Jewish ethics finds the aims of life in the teachings of Judaism. It lays great stress on reverence for parents, respect for the aged, chastity, charity, honesty and truthfulness. Stealing, flattery, falsehood and oppression—even the withholding of a man's wages so much as overnight—are banned. Talebearing, gossip and unkind insinuation are prohibited, as is hatred of one's neighbor in one's heart. The dumb animal has claims upon the kindly help of man, even though it belongs to one's enemy. Care for the weak, regard for the rights of others, love for fellow men and mercy for the beast are the virtues taught by Judaism. As a child of God, man has duties toward himself as well as toward his fellow man. Hence, he is in duty bound to

381

preserve his health as well as that of others. The world is good and
life is precious, for both are the creation of God who is the course of
all goodness and morality.

The book of Tobit, written some two centuries before the common
era, contains the golden rule: "Do not do to anyone else what you
hate" (4:15). The entire talmudic system of ethics is based on humanitarian rules of conduct. Hillel pronounced the golden rule as the
cardinal principle of the Torah. Rabbi Akiva declared: "Whatever
you hate to be done to you do not to your neighbor; hence, do not
hurt him; do not speak ill of him; do not reveal his secrets to others;
let his honor and his property be as dear to you as your own" (Avoth
d'Rabbi Nathan). Benevolence is included in the Jewish idea of
righteousness, since the owner of property has no right to withhold
from the poor their share; if he does, he acts like an idolater, or like
a thief.

The talmudic sages assert that God punishes those who do not
abide by their word (Bava Metzia 4:2). "He who deviates from the
truth is like one who worships an idol instead of the God of truth"
(Sanhedrin 92a). "One should be careful not to deviate from the
truth even in conventionalities or in fun" (Kethubboth 17a; Sukkoth
46b). "God hates him who speaks with his tongue what he does not
mean in his heart" (Pesaḥim 113b). "It is forbidden to take advantage of the ignorance of any fellow man, Jew or non-Jew" (Ḥullin 94a).
"No one can be called righteous before God unless he is good to his
fellow man" (Kiddushin 40a).

Obscene speech (*nibbul peh*) is regarded as a most detestable trait
(Shabbath 33a). The name for marriage in Hebrew, *kiddushin* = consecration, conveys the idea of the holiness of the marriage relation.
God placed the reverence and honor due to parents in the same category as those due to himself, since parents are for the child the representatives of God (Kiddushin 30b). In this spirit are written numerous
ethical works (*sifré musar*) that have come down from the ancient
and medieval periods of Jewish history.

TITHES   מַעֲשֵׂרוֹת

UNLIKE all others in Israel, the Levites and priests were not to own
hereditary land; in the allotment of the land of Israel they received
no portion of it, except certain cities which were assigned to them for

their residence. Hence, the Torah tells us: "To the Levites I have assigned all tithes in Israel as their heritage for the service they perform in the sanctuary" (Numbers 18:21). The term *ma'aser* (tithe) denotes a tenth part.

Three categories of tithe are mentioned in the Torah: 1) first tithe which must be given to Levites, who, in their turn, must give a tenth of it (*terumah*) as a contribution to the priests; 2) second tithe which the owner must consume in Jerusalem (Deuteronomy 14:22-27); 3) poorman's tithe which takes the place of the second tithe in the third and sixth year of the seven-year cycle culminating in the sabbatical year.

The actual second tithe of produce could be converted into money, plus a fifth of its value, and reconverted into food in Jerusalem (Deuteronomy 14:24-27). The three tithes are called in Hebrew: *ma'aser rishon, ma'aser sheni, ma'aser 'ani,* respectively.

The lay Israelites were required to contribute *terumah* (gifts to the priests) from the fruits of their fields before they paid their tithes to the Levites. The priest's share of the crop, though known as *terumah gedolah,* had no prescribed limit; the smallest quantity would suffice. The Levite's contribution to the priest, however, consisted of a tenth part of the tithe he received; it was called *terumath ma'aser* or *ma'aser min ha-ma'aser.*

The sages asserted that the lay Israelite who contributed to the priests one-fortieth of his crop as *terumah gedolah* showed himself to be a generous person; on the other hand, one who contributed only one sixtieth proved himself to be of a niggardly type; the average person would contribute one-fiftieth.

It has been observed that the history of the European peasants would have been a happier one had the priesthood been debarred from ownership of land.

BIBLE COMMENTATORS   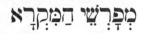

THE Jewish commentators of the Bible, who regarded the Book of Books as an inexhaustible storehouse of wisdom to which one can always resort for guidance and inspiration, frequently read into the text the knowledge which they derived from a variety of sources. They made use of Talmud and Midrash, philosophy and mysticism for a deeper understanding of the biblical message. The fourfold method of Bible interpretation, known as *pardes* (‎פרד"ס) from the initials of ‎פשט רמז דרוש סוד, consisted of the literal, allegorical, homiletical and mystical construction ascribed to the scriptural text by expositors of various bents. The general rule, however, was not to admit any interpretation that was incompatible with the plain meaning of the passage (‎אין המקרא יוצא מידי פשוטו).

Rashi (1040-1105), who had an encyclopedic knowledge of talmudic-midrashic literature and a brilliant gift of both clarity and terseness, selected gems from the Midrash and inserted them with matchless skill in his famous commentary on the Torah. His exposition of the Torah in particular became the most popular and widely used. "What made for the popularity of his commentary was its intermediate attitude between the traditional interpretation of the rabbis and the more modern rational exegesis. . . Interspersed in Rashi's commentary are renditions of difficult Hebrew words and phrases in French. . . Rashi's commentary was excerpted in Latin by the apostate Nicholas de Lyra (died 1340) whose *Postillae Perpetuae*, printed in 1471-2, exercised a potent influence on Luther's translation of the Bible" (Margolis).

Ibn Ezra (1092-1167), profound scholar, poet and philosopher, who traveled extensively away from Spain, where he had lived until 1140, has been described as a born wanderer. He journeyed through North Africa to Italy, France and England, "sojourning everywhere, composing works and laying bare the secrets of knowledge." Ibn Ezra's appearance in the Provence was heartily welcomed, as reported a hundred and fifty years later by a scholar of France who describes the indelible impression made by Rabbi Abraham ibn Ezra (‎ראב"ע): "Our fathers told us of the joy with which the great of our land, its pious men and rabbis, received Ibn Ezra when his wanderings brought him to them. He opened the eyes of the inhabitants of these regions, and wrote for them commentaries and other works." Ibn Ezra's commentaries, replete with references to older Bible scholars, are for the most part written in a succinct and at times obscure style. They are largely concerned with questions of diction, grammar, and the exact intention of the text; they testify throughout to an exquisite perception of the biblical Hebrew and the subject matter. Though his influence extended primarily to scholars, his popularity was second only to that of Rashi (Rabbi Shelomo Yitzḥaki) as Bible commentator.

Rashbam (Rabbi Shemuel ben Meir), Rashi's grandson (1085-1174), in his commentary on the Torah, placed emphasis on the *peshat* (plain meaning) of the text, often differing from his grandfather's exposition.

384

The aged Rashi confessed to his grandson, the *Rashbam*, that he would have liked to revise his own commentary in accordance with the newer interpretations making their appearance daily. Like his grandfather, Rabbi Samuel ben Meir, lived in France and was a Talmud commentator. He completed Rashi's commentary on Bava Bathra and Pesaḥim, though he was unable to match his grandfather's concise style.

Ramban (Rabbi Moshe ben Naḥman), generally referred to as Naḥmanides (1194-1270), was born in Spain, where he became known as an illustrious talmudic authority and Bible commentator. He died in Eretz Yisrael at the age of seventy-six. His principal work, a commentary on the Torah, contains halakhic interpretations, ethical lessons, kabbalistic allusions, as well as literal explanations in which he frequently disagrees with either Rashi or Ibn Ezra. Naḥmanides professed great respect for Maimonides and defended him against the anti-Maimonists. In his opinion, Maimonides' *Guide for the Perplexed* was intended not for those of unshaken belief, but for those who had been led astray by the teachings of the Greek philosophers. It has been noted that Naḥmanides represented Judaism from the side of emotion and feeling, as Maimonides did from the viewpoint of reason and logic.

Sforno (Rabbi Ovadiah ben Yaakov), Italian physician and Bible commentator (1475-1550), who taught Reuchlin Hebrew in Rome and founded a *yeshivah* in Bologna, became known chiefly for his commentary on the Torah, which is marked by wide learning and deep insight. Primarily interested in discovering the plain meaning, he rejects mystical interpretations, making use of every opportunity to develop the ethical implications of the biblical text.

Redak (Rabbi David Kimḥi), the author of a masterly Hebrew grammar and dictionary (*Mikhlol* and *Sefer ha-Sharashim*), was born in Narbonne and died in Narbonne (1160-1235). His commentary on both the Prophets and the Psalms was translated from Hebrew into Latin, during the Renaissance period, for the benefit of non-Jewish students of the Bible. Kimḥi's influence may be traced in every line of the King James Bible translation, as well as many other versions. He was on the side of Maimonides in the controversy on the study of philosophy.

Ralbag (Rabbi Levi ben Gershon), commonly known as Gersonides (1288-1344), was philosopher, mathematician, astronomer, and Bible commentator, who practised medicine. Like Maimonides, he excelled in mathematics, was a great talmudic scholar and an extreme rationalist. He is known mainly for his *Milḥamoth Adonai* (Battles of the Lord), in six books, on theology, astronomy, and philosophy. His commentaries on most of the biblical books presented his philosophy in a more moderate form. Though the *Ralbag* enjoyed widespread popularity, he was often severely criticised for his outspoken observations and opinions. His religious philosophy was supplementary to Maimonides' presentation of Judaism. Rabbi Levi ben Gershon is also widely known as *Gersonides* or son of Gershon.

The popular Bible commentary *Metsudath David* was begun by Rabbi David Altschuler and completed by his son Rabbi Yeḥiel Hillel Altschuler, who lived in Yavorov, Galicia, at the end of the seventeenth century. This commentary consists of two parts: 1) מצודת דוד (Fortress of David), a lucid exposition of the biblical text; and 2) מצודת ציון (Fortress of Zion), a glossary explaining difficult words as they occur. This commentary does not cover the Pentateuch, but the Prophets and the Hagiographa (*Kethuvim*).

The Bible commentary known as *Malbim* (מלבי"ם) was written by Rabbi Meir Leib ben Yeḥiel Michael (1809-1879), who held office as rabbi in several Russian, Roumanian, and German towns. At Bucharest, his opposition to the reform movement led to his imprisonment. He spent his last years at Königsberg. His commentary is replete with interesting thoughts concerning the unity of *Torah she-be'al peh* and *Torah she-bikhthav*, the written and the oral Torah. Special significance is attached to each biblical synonym, so that the biblical text in its entirety is made meaningful to the students.

TALMUD COMMENTATORS מְפָרְשֵׁי הַתַּלְמוּד

MANY commentaries were written on the Babylonian Talmud prior to the eleventh century. They were the chief sources used by Rashi (1040-1105), whose masterly commentary on thirty tractates of the Talmud eclipsed all of them. Every edition of the Babylonian Talmud contains Rashi's commentary. Nowhere is the Babylonian Talmud studied without Rashi. His commentary on Bava Bathra and Pesaḥim, left unfinished, was completed by his grandson Rabbi Samuel ben Meir (רשב"ם), who excelled in learning and lucidity but lacked the terseness, coherence and cogency of Rashi. The *Rashbam*, who supplemented Rashi's work to some extent by writing a commentary on the Torah according to the primary type of biblical interpretation, known as *peshat* or literal meaning, was guided by his fine sense of Hebrew diction and his intuitive knowledge of Hebrew grammar.

Similar to the *Rashbam's* commentary on Bava Bathra and Pesaḥim is that of Rabbi Nissim Gerondi of the fourteenth century, known as ר"ן (*Ran*), on the tractate Nedarim. The surname Gerondi is indicative of persons whose families originated in Gerona, northern Spain. The foremost halakhist of his time, he wrote also a commentary on the tractate Niddah as well as responsa and commentaries on the writings of Alfasi (רי"ף). He was a talmudist, astronomer and physician, who played an important part in the Jewish community of Barcelona, where he was referred to as Magister Nescim.

The commentaries on the Babylonian Talmud have been classified as: 1) *pérushim* (פירושים), running commentaries accompanying the text; 2: *tosafoth* (תוספות), additions to Rashi's commentary; 3) *ḥiddushim* (חידושים), elucidations on certain passages of the talmudic text; and 4) marginal glosses (הגהות). The tractates that are included in Mo'ed and Nashim, which turned into special subjects of study and instruction owing to their particularly religious contents, have been more frequently commentated than Seder Kodashim, for example, which deals with the sacrificial system and all that concerns the Temple of the distant past.

Following are the titles of several best known commentaries on a variety of tractates, in addition to such works on the Talmud as were written by *Ramban, Meiri, Rashba,* and *Maharam* Lublin.

Pérush Rabbenu Ḥananel (פירוש רבנו חננאל), by Rabbi Ḥananel ben Ḥushiel, North African talmudist of the eleventh century (990-1055). This commentary, on Seder Mo'ed and Seder Nezikin (except Bava Bathra), is distinguished for its brevity and clarity. It is printed on the outer margins of the standard editions of Talmud Bavli.

Yam shel Shelomo (ים של שלמה), by Rabbi Solomon Luria, known as מהרש"ל (*Maharshal*), who also wrote *Ḥokhmath Shelomo* (חכמת שלמה) on nineteen tractates. The *Maharshal* (1510-1573) headed the *Yeshivah* at Lublin and was one of the greatest talmudic authorities.

Shittah Mekubbetseth (שיטה מקובצת), by Rabbi Bezalel Ashkenazi of sixteenth-century Jerusalem. It is a valuable collection of commentaries on most of the Talmud, assembled from medieval sources and entitled *Asefath Zekenim* (אספת זקנים).

Maharsha (מהרש"א), by Rabbi Samuel Edels (1555-1631). The full title of the Maharsha's principal work is *Ḥiddushé Halakhoth va-Aggadoth* (חידושי הלכות ואגדות). It is replete with clarifications of talmudic passages that appear to be contradictory and difficult, and contains rational interpretations of aggadic statements.

Tselaḥ (צל"ח = ציון לנפש חיה), by Rabbi Ezekiel Landau (1713-1793), known by the title of his responsa, נודע ביהודה (*Noda Bihudah*), who was the rabbi of the Prague community.

Haggahoth (הגהות), by Rabbi Elijah Vilna-Gaon (1720-1797), glosses and elucidations on both Talmud Bavli and Talmud Yerushalmi.

Ḥatham Sofer חתם סופר = חידושי תורת משה סופר), by Rabbi Moses Schreiber (1762-1839), who founded the famous *Yeshivah* at Pressburg, Slovakia. Consisting of six volumes, the *Ḥatham Sofer* contains both responsa and *ḥiddushim*.

Paḥad Yitzḥak (פחד יצחק), by Rabbi Isaac Lampronti of Ferrara, Italy (1679-1756), who was physician, rabbi, and head of the *Yeshivah* at Ferrara. His talmudic encyclopedia *Paḥad Yitzḥak* is especially valuable for its countless quotations from the unpublished works of Italian rabbis. Embracing the entire field of talmudic learning, the *Paḥad Yitzḥak* has all the halakhic material arranged alphabetically.

GRAVE MONUMENT   מַצֵּבָה

The Torah tells us that Jacob erected a monument (*matzevah*) over Rachel's grave, "and this *matzevah* marks Rachel's grave to this day" (Genesis 35:20). Rachel's tomb has been one of the holy places in Eretz Yisrael throughout the centuries. In II Samuel 18:18 we are told that Absalom, during his lifetime, erected a *matzevah* for himself because he had no son to keep up the memory of his name, "and it is called to this day *Yad Avshalom*" (Absalom's monument).

The Mishnah (Shekalim 2:5) mentions a *nefesh* (monument) built over a person's grave, though there is a talmudic statement to the effect that "no monuments should be put up for the upright, because their oft-repeated words are their memorial (אין עושין נפשות לצדיקים; דבריהן הן זכרונם). According to Rabbi Isaac Luria, however, the *matzevah* has a lofty spiritual significance.

The custom of setting up the tombstone after the first twelve months is explained by the fact that the dead are not forgotten within the first year. Originally, in Eretz Yisrael, ossuaries and sarcophagi were used in place of tombstones in the catacombs and tomb caves; they bore brief inscriptions, indicating the name of the deceased and that of his father.

Gradually, the inscriptions have been extended to include the date of death and words of praise, marking the love and the esteem in which the deceased was held by those who mourn his departure. During the medieval period the inscriptions were phrased in modest terms. Rabbi Jonathan Eibeschütz (1690-1764), one of the greatest talmudic scholars of his time, composed the following epitaph for himself: "Every passer-by should see what is engraved here. The man who stood as a model . . . returned to dust. Pray, take it to heart to repent sincerely. . . Learn to despise vainglory, and flee from it . . ."

MATZAH   מַצָּה

THE unleavened bread, eaten during the eight days of *Pesaḥ*, is made from flour and water, kneaded hastily and baked quickly in order to prevent all fermentation. The separate cakes known as *matzoth* are perforated to keep them from rising in the baking, and then put one at a time into the oven.

The *matzah*, symbolizing the haste with which the people of Israel had to leave Egypt, is rich in ethical significance. It reminds us of the poverty and affliction of our forefathers while under the yoke of tyrants. It is simultaneously the symbol of servitude and of liberation. It also serves as a reminder of poverty-stricken fellow men whom it is our duty to help. It is the bread of those who are in a state of stress and hardship (*leḥem 'oni*), who cannot wait long for sustaining aid. Since the offering of leaven on the altar is forbidden (Leviticus 2:11), the unleavened bread alludes to the purity of heart, essentially connected with bringing a sacrifice, as opposed to the fermenting leaven which is a symbol of decay.

On the *Seder* nights of *Pesaḥ*, the three *matzoth* used are styled *Kohen, Levi, Yisrael;* they are also referred to as *mitzvoth* (precepts) because, in Hebrew, the plural of both *matzah* and *mitzvah* happens to consist of the same consonants and is spelled מצות. Two of the three *Seder matzoth* represent the *leḥem mishneh* (Exodus 16:22) used on Sabbaths and festivals; the third represents the *leḥem 'oni* (bread of poverty); hence it is broken in two.

The *matzah shemurah* (guarded *matzah*) is specially prepared from wheat watched from the moment of harvesting so that no moisture should touch it. For the *matzah shemurah*, every process must be under the strict supervision of observant Jews.

MITZVAH   מִצְוָה

In the plural, the term *mitzvoth* (divine precepts) signifies specific commands contained in the Torah, and is used biblically as a synonym of *toroth, ḥukkim, mishpatim, edoth*. In talmudic terminology, *mitzvoth* is the general term for the divine commandments, computed to be 613. They are classified as being either affirmative or negative: 365 negative precepts, corresponding to the 365 days of the solar year; and 248 affirmative precepts, corresponding in number to the parts of the human body (Makkoth 23b).

611 *mitzvoth*, numerically equaling תורה, are said to have been given through Moses; while the first two commandments of the Decalogue were given directly by God at Mount Sinai. Many of these laws are classified as being bound up with the land of Israel and concern kings, priests, Levites, nazirites, sacrificial offerings, agricultural regulations, ritual cleanliness. These are referred to as מצוות התלויות בארץ. The *mitzvoth* are further divided into duties between man and God (בין אדם לםקום) and duties between man and his fellow man (בין אדם לחברו).

In addition to the *mitzvoth*, designed for the people of Israel alone, the Torah contains seven precepts which are incumbent on all human beings, descendants of Noah. The seven Noachian precepts are: 1) to establish courts of justice, 2) to refrain from idolatry, 3) blasphemy, 4) incest, 5) murder, 6) robbery, and 7) eating flesh cut from a living animal (Sanhedrin 56a-b).

A *mitzvah* which can be fulfilled only by the transgression of another precept (מצוה הבאה בעברה) is deemed unlawful. *Mitzvah* is another word for charity. It refers to any particular opportunity to fulfill the comprehensive duty of men toward their fellow men.

According to Jewish tradition, all ethical and moral laws are essentially divine commandments. The first commandment, given to Adam, was intended to awaken his moral consciousness. Colloquially, the word *mitzvah* has come to express any act of human kindness.

Albert Einstein once declared: "With the affairs of human beings, knowledge of truth must continually be renewed by ceaseless effort, if it is not to be lost. It resembles a statue of marble which stands in the desert and is continually threatened with burial by the shifting sand. The hands of service must ever be at work in order that the marble continue lastingly to shine in the sun." Whereupon it has been added: "A musician must practise by prearranged schedule, regard-

390

less of his inclination at the moment. So with the ethical spirit. It cannot rely on caprice or chance or mood or convenience. We must labor constantly until it becomes *second nature* in the heart of man. Ritual is thus the instrument for giving ethical ideals a grip on our conscience. . . A worship service offers the opportunity to sing; the Passover *Seder*—a chance to reenact a drama; a *Havdalah* service at the close of the Sabbath—a bit of pageantry not found elsewhere. What poetry is to language, ritual is to life . . . even secular groups feel impelled to formalize many of their practices into rites and rituals" (Robert Gordis and David M. Feldman).

MIKVEH

THE Torah requires a purifying bath to remove uncleanness caused by leprosy, discharge of semen, menstruation, childbirth, or contact with a corpse (Leviticus 12:2; 15:5-13; Numbers 19:19; Deuteronomy 23:12). Before officiating at the *Yom Kippur* services, the high priest had to bathe in a *mikveh* (gathering of water) in order to be ritually fit for his tasks.

The water of a *mikveh* has to come from a natural spring or a river; the water entirely loses its effectiveness if it is poured into a vessel; it must be running, not drawn (מים שאובין). In order to cover the entire human body, the *mikveh* must have a minumim capacity of one hundred and twenty gallons of water, coming from a natural spring or from a river that has its source in a natural spring. Some authorities forbid the use of a pool which is full of water in the rainy seaso and dried up in the summer (*Yad, Mikvaoth* 3:1-3). In cities where the water-supply comes through underground pipes, many technicalities must be observed in the construction of a *mikveh*, in view of the rule that the water contained in the *mikveh* must not have passed through a vessel that can hold objects.

From ancient times until the present day, the *mikveh* prescribed for special occasions has played a most important part in maintaining Jewish family purity (טהרת המשפחה). In every Jewish community there has always been a *mikveh* conforming to the requirement of Jewish law.

Maimonides stresses the symbolical significance of ritual baths, quoting from Ezekiel 36:25 ("I will pour clean water over you to cleanse you from all your uncleanness and from all your idols").

MUKTZEH מָקְצָה

Observant Jews refrain from handling on the Sabbath anything per-taining to work, that they may not forget the holiness of the day. This precautionary measure is referred to as *muktzeh* (set aside or stored away); it designates all objects the use of which is essentially for acts that are forbidden on the Sabbath, such as tools, money, candlesticks in which Sabbath candles were lit on Friday at sunset, discarded utensils. Wood, stones, metal are considered *muktzeh* and may not be handled if they are not of permanent use. *Muktzeh* may be touched if it is not moved by the touch. Thus it is forbidden to touch a hanging chandelier, since a mere touch may shake it.

Fruit picked on the Sabbath by a non-Jew is called *muktzeh*, be-cause it has involved an act that a Jew is forbidden to perform on the Sabbath; so also, fish caught on the Sabbath. Highly expensive ob-jects, the owner of which is reluctant to use for fear of material loss (חסרון כיס), are likewise counted as *muktzeh* (stored away).

These regulations extend to holy days which differ from the Sabbath only in one thing, namely: the cooking of food that is essential on the festivals is permitted. *Muktzeh* regulations belong to the class of rab-binic enactments designed to preserve the biblical laws, which are described as a protective fence for the Torah (סייג לתורה).

MARḤESHVAN מַרְחֶשְׁוָן

The eighth month of the Hebrew calendar, counting from *Nisan*, is called *Marḥeshvan*, from the Akkadian ורח שמן (eighth month), the equivalent of the Hebrew ירח שמיני, due to the interchange of the letters ו and מ. Hence, the abridged *Ḥeshvan* is regarded as erroneous.

The name *Marḥeshvan* is not found in the Bible, since it was intro-duced after the Babylonian captivity along with the names of the other months now in use. The biblical name for *Marḥeshvan* is *Bul* (בירח בול הוא החדש השמיני—I Kings 6:38).

It consists of either twenty-nine or thirty days, an extra day being occasionally added so as to prevent the next *Yom Kippur* from occur-ring on Friday or Sunday and causing thereby great hardship in terms of food preparation, since all work would then be prohibited for two successive days.

MARANAN V'RABBANAN   מָרָנָן וְרַבָּנָן

THE Aramaic word *mar* (master) was used as a synonym of *rav* in addressing the sages of the Talmud. It was a title preceding the name, in place of the title רב. The great contemporaries of Rav (Abba Arikha, founder of the Sura Academy in Babylonia) were Mar Samuel and Mar Ukva. Rav Ashi's son (Tavyomi) is designated in the Talmud as *Mar bar Rav Ashi*. In the geonic period, the terms *Mar* and *Rav* together were employed as a title of Babylonian scholars. The double title *Mar Rav* was also combined with the pronominal suffix of the first person plural (מרנא רבנא or מרנן ורבנן=our masters and teachers). The title מרן (*maran* = our master) was later applied as a mark of respect to men like Rabbi Joseph Karo, author of the *Shulḥan Arukh*. The title מורנו, which originated in the fourteenth century, is said to have developed from מרן.

Rav Sherira Gaon of the tenth century, in his letter to the community of Kairawan in northern Africa, writes to the effect that the title רבי (*Rabbi*) is borne by the sages of Eretz Yisrael, who were ordained by the Sanhedrin and received authority to judge in penal cases. The title רב (*Rav*) belongs to the Babylonian sages, who received their ordination in their colleges. The more ancient generations, however, which were far superior, had no such titles as *Rabban, Rabbi*, or *Rav*. Hillel had not the title *Rabban* prefixed to his name. This title is not met with prior to the period of the patriarchate. It was first used by Rabban Gamaliel I, Rabban Simeon his son, and Rabban Yoḥanan ben Zakkai, all of whom were presidents of the Sanhedrin. Now the order of these titles is as follows: *Rabbi* is greater than *Rav; Rabban* is greater than *Rabbi;* while the simple name, without title, is greater than *Rabban* (Moses, Isaiah, Jeremiah, Ezra are generally spoken of without honorary titles). The term רבי (*rabbi*) came into vogue after the destruction of the Second Temple.

MASHSHIV HA-RUAḤ   מַשִׁיב הָרוּחַ

FROM the eighth day of *Sukkoth* until the first day of *Pesaḥ*, the second benediction of the *Amidah* prayer is augmented by the addition of four words: משיב הרוח ומוריד הגשם (Thou causest the wind to blow and the rain to fall). This reference to God's control of the forces

393

of nature is added in winter, during the rainy season in Eretz Yisrael, in connection with the divine power to revive the dead (מחיה המתים). Rain is considered in the Talmud as great a manifestation of the divine power (גבורות) as the resurrection of the dead (Ta'anith 2a), since the periodic revival of nature is brought about by means of rain. The Sephardim, but not the Ashkenazim, insert a different phrase in the summer, namely: מוריד הטל in place of משיב הרוח.

The insertion of the formula ותן טל ומטר לברכה (Bestow dew and rain for a blessing), in the ninth benediction of the *Shemoneh Esreh*, is made in winter, from the sixtieth day after the autumnal equinox (December 5) until the first day of *Pesaḥ*. The Mishnah informs us that while the *praise* of God as raingiver is to be inserted in the second benediction, the actual *petition* for rain is added to the ninth benediction known as *birkath ha-shanim* (blessing of the years).

MESSIAH   מָשִׁיחַ

ORIGINALLY, the term משיח was applied to any person anointed with the holy oil and consecrated to carry out the purposes of God, as the high priest or the king (Leviticus 4:3, 5, 16; I Samuel 12:3, 5; II Samuel 1:14, 16). The title was given to the Persian king Cyrus, chosen to liberate Israel from Babylonia (Isaiah 45:1).

When David received the divine promise that the throne would remain in his family forever (II Samuel 7:13), the title acquired a special reference and signified the representative of the royal line of David. The prophetic vision of the eventual establishment of the divine kingship on earth came to be identified with the restoration of Israel under the leadership of the Messiah, the Lord's anointed.

The traditional outlook of Judaism is that the Messiah will be the dominating figure of an age of universal peace and plenty; through a restored Israel, he will bring about the spiritual regeneration of humanity, when all will blend into one brotherhood to perform righteousness with a perfect heart; "on that day the Lord shall be One, and his name One" (Zechariah 14:9). The Jewish prayers are replete with references to the messianic hopes and aspirations. There is hardly a prophet of note who does not mention the Messiah and the messianic age.

The prophetic view is that nature itself will be transformed in the messianic days, when the power of death will be limited. In the golden age of humanity, there will be a return to longevity, and those who die at a hundred will be reckoned as but children, prematurely cut off for their sins. "No sound of weeping, no voice of crying, shall ever be heard in it; no child shall die there anymore in infancy, nor any old man who has not lived out his years of life; he who dies youngest lives a hundred years. . ." (Isaiah 65:19-20).

The signs heralding the advent of the Messiah at the end of the time of captivity are described in the Mishnah (Sotah 9:15) in such terms as these: "With the footprints of the Messiah, insolence will increase . . . the vine will yield its fruit but the wine will be costly ... scholarship will degenerate, piety will be rejected, and truth will nowhere be found; youth will be impudent . . . and a man's enemies will be the members of his own household."

A midrashic statement says that three days before the advent of the Messiah, Elijah will appear on the mountains of Israel and exclaim: "O mountains of Israel, how long will you remain waste and desolate? ! " Then he will proclaim world peace, and God will redeem Israel (Pesikta Rabbathi, chapter 35).

In Malachi 3:23-4, Elijah is introduced as a type for all times, occupying a prominent place in Jewish lore as the prophet who "will turn the hearts of fathers to their children and the hearts of children to their fathers" before the coming of the great day of the Lord. This has led to Elijah's being described in Jewish tradition as the forerunner of the Messiah.

Since the Messiah may appear at any time and from any parentage, Elijah's name is associated with every circumcision celebration or *brith milah*. The invisible presence of Elijah at the *Seder* celebration is derived from the idea of the Passover of the Future as contrasted with the Passover of Egypt.

Throughout the period of post-biblical Jewish history, numerous false messiahs made their appearance; they claimed divinity or semidivinity, as in the case of Theudas who, in the year 44, announced to his followers his intention to divide the Jordan. The Romans, however, massacred him and his followers even before his miraculous powers could be put to the test.

The most notorious false messiah was Shabbethai Tzevi (1626-1676), who proclaimed himself in 1648 as the משיח and won wide acceptance. Some of his many believers suspended their occupations and sold their property in preparation for greeting the messianic era in Jerusalem. He was finally arrested and given the alternative of

Islam or death. Followed by many of his adherents, he chose Islam. The Judeo-Moslem sect of *Donmeh*, still surviving in Turkey, is the offshoot of these converts.

There is a talmudic statement which reads: "Blasted be the bones of those who calculate the end, for when the calculated time comes and the Messiah does not appear, people despair of his ever coming" (Sanhedrin 97b). Hence, Maimonides writes: "All these matters concerning the coming of the Messiah will not be known to anyone until they happen. . . In the messianic days there will be no hunger or war, no jealousy or strife; prosperity will be universal, and the world's predominant occupation will be to know the Lord" (*Yad, Melakhim* 12:2, 5). This is based on the prophecy which envisions the eradication of evil from human society and a corresponding regeneration of the rest of creation: "Then the wolf shall live with the lamb, and the leopard shall lie down with the kid. . ." (Isaiah 11:6-9).

TABERNACLE מִשְׁכָּן

THE portable sanctuary in the form of a tent, set up by Moses in the wilderness to accompany the Israelites on their wanderings, is known as *Mishkan* (dwelling) and *Ohel Mo'ed* (tent of meeting). It consisted of the outer court, enclosed by curtains, and the sanctuary proper, which was divided by a hanging curtain into two chambers.

The first chamber, known as the *holy place*, contained the *shulḥan* (table), the *menorah* (seven-branched candelabrum), and the *mizbaḥ ha-ketoreth* (altar of incense). Only the priests might enter here. The second chamber, known as *Holy of Holies*, was entered once a year by the high priest—on *Yom Kippur*. The Ark of the Covenant, designed to hold the two stone tablets, was the only object placed here.

Four centuries later, King Solomon placed the Ark of the Covenant in the First Temple, after the destruction of which there is no further record of it. The ark made by Moses contained no image but, instead, the tablets of the moral law, signifying the spiritual nature of the Jewish religion.

The *Mishkan* served as a visible emblem to the people of Israel that God dwelt in their midst, being near to all who call upon him in truth. According to Maimonides, the main purpose of the sanctuary was to wean the people from idolatry and turn their attention towards the one and only God.

PROVERBS   מִשְׁלֵי

THE book of Proverbs, together with the books of Job and Ecclesiastes, belongs to the Wisdom Literature of the Bible. It contains maxims and aphorisms for a better conduct of everyday life. In the book of Proverbs, the ideal of life is a composite of honesty, diligence, helpfulness toward the distressed and consideration for one's fellow man. The authors of these books, together with the prophets, strive to foster among the Jewish people a life of uprightness and seek to mitigate the sufferings of oppressed fellow men.

Throughout the book of Proverbs the young man is warned of the spiritual and physical consequences of evil conduct. Reverence for God, as the highest motive for moral duties that are left to conscience, is repeated seventeen times here. At the end of the book there is the poem which describes the perfect wife, trusted by her husband and admired by everyone. She is kind to the poor and gentle to all. She is self-respecting and dignified. Husband and children prize her as the source of their happiness.

Some of its teachings are: "Reverence for the Lord is the first thing in wisdom. He who controls his tongue is a wise man. A wise man listens to advice. Reckless words wound like a sword. He who guards his lips guards his life. Wealth won in haste will dwindle. Associate with wise men and you will be wise.

"The man who loves his son disciplines him. He who is kind to the poor honors his Maker. A soft answer turns wrath away. Even a fool may pass for wise if he says nothing. Reputation is better than riches. Do not eat the bread of a niggardly man. Never talk to a fool. Do not rejoice when your enemy falls.

"Go seldom to your neighbor's house, for he may grow tired of you and hate you. If your enemy is hungry, give him food; if he is thirsty, give him water. Never boast about tomorrow; you never know what the day may bring. He who gives to the poor will not come to want. A fool gives full vent to his temper. Defend the rights of the poor and the needy."

Bible students often mention the striking similarities between the maxims contained in the book of Proverbs and those found in the wisdom literature of the ancient Egyptians as well as the Babylonians and Assyrians. Some have gone so far as to say that Proverbs 22:17-24:34 represents a Hebrew rendering of the Egyptian collection of

397

Amenemope, a contemporary of the prophet Jeremiah. Others are of
the opinion that Amenemope wrote his work under the influence of
Jewish sages and prophets. As to the parallel maxims that are included in the *Story of Aḥikar*, the Aramaic version of which dates back
to the beginning of the fifth century before the common era, authoritative scholars have suggested that they stem from Jewish sources.

In the opinion of some scholars, the similarities do not necessarily
indicate a conscious borrowing of one source from the other. The
universality of these general truths makes them applicable to all generations and environments. By precept and concrete example, the
ancient teachers seek to establish in our minds an attitude to right
thinking, correct action and right living.

MISHNAH   מִשְׁנָה

THE Mishnah, compiled and edited by Rabbi Yehudah ha-Nasi and
his colleagues at the beginning of the third century, has been defined
as a deposit of four centuries of Jewish religious and cultural activity
in Palestine. This collection of Jewish law and ethics, ranking second
only to the Hebrew Bible (*Mikra*) and forming the basis of the Talmud, is divided into six parts known as *sedarim* (orders), each of which
is subdivided into tractates or books.

The Mishnah comprises sixty-three tractates, including the most
popular tractate *Avoth* (fathers), which deals with the ethical principles formulated by seventy-two sages mentioned by name. The fathers of Jewish tradition, *Sofrim* and *Tannaim*, flourished over a
period of nearly five centuries, from the time of the last prophet to
the end of the second century.

The authorities quoted in the Mishnah and the tannaitic-midrashic
literature are referred to as *Tannaim* (שנה=תני); the scholars and
teachers who preceded the tannaitic period are referred to as *Sofrim*,
from *sefer* (book).

Each of the sixty-three tractates (*massekhtoth*) of the Mishnah consists of chapters subdivided into paragraphs. There are five hundred
twenty-four chapters in all, including the sixth chapter of *Pirké Avoth*,
which is a later addition. Since the Mishnah is contained in six orders
(ששה סדרים), it has been customary to call the Talmud, which embodies and interprets the Mishnah, by the name of *Shas* (ש"ס), an
abbreviation of *shishshah sedarim*. The Mishnah is arranged as follows:

398

1) *Zera'im* (seeds), regulations dealing with agriculture; eleven tractates, beginning with *Berakhoth* on benedictions and the daily prayers.

2) *Mo'ed* (festivals); twelve tractates, beginning with *Shabbath* on prohibited work during the Sabbath.

3) *Nashim* (women); seven tractates on marriage and divorce, beginning with *Yevamoth* covering levirate marriage (Deuteronomy 25:5) and forbidden marriages (Leviticus 18:6).

4) *Nezikin* (damages); ten tractates on civil and penal laws, beginning with *Bava Kamma*, *Bava Metzia* and *Bava Bathra*, on damages to property and injury to persons; found articles, bailment, sales and hiring; real estate and inheritance.

5) *Kodashim* (sacred things); eleven tractates, beginning with *Zevahim* on sacrifices that were offered in the Temple at Jerusalem.

6) *Tohoroth* (cleanness); twelve tractates, beginning with *Kelim* on articles susceptible of ritual uncleanness, the name *Tohoroth* being euphemistic for uncleanness, just as סגי נהור (rich in light) is a euphemism for blind. Instances of euphemism are frequent in talmudic-midrashic literature. The sages often stressed the rule that "man should at all times express himself in fitting terms" (Pesaḥim 3a).

The best commentary on the Mishnah was written by Rabbi Obadiah Bertinoro (1450-1510), who served as rabbi in Bertinoro, Italy. Before emigrating to Eretz Yisrael in 1485, he was rabbi in Palermo and then in Castello. He arrived in Jerusalem after a long journey that lasted two years and a half. The letters he wrote to his father, describing his long journey and the conditions in Eretz Yisrael, are of great cultural and historical importance. They have been translated and published in German, French, Italian and English. His commentary on the Mishnah is generally called ברטנורה (Bertinoro) in brief. It is couched in a lucid, precise and easily intelligible Hebrew style, and incorporates the best interpretations found in the commentaries of Rashi and Maimonides.

The Tosefta (Supplement) is similar to the Mishnah and, in many respects, runs parallel to it; it contains, however, additional subject matter, whence its name. It treats the subjects in greater detail than the Mishnah, quite frequently giving biblical proof and reason for the *halakhah*, which the Mishnah does on rare occasions only.

The compilation and redaction of the Tosefta must have taken place in the first part of the third century by Rabbi Ḥiyya, a disciple of Rabbi Yehudah ha-Nasi. This is the opinion of medieval authorities, stated by Rav Sherira Gaon (906-1006). Rabbah and Oshaya, of the third century, are considered by present-day scholars as the editors of the nucleus of the Tosefta.

MISHNEH TORAH   מִשְׁנֵה תּוֹרָה

MAIMONIDES' code of law and ethics, called *Mishneh Torah* (a copy of the Torah), a phrase used in Deuteronomy 17:18 and Joshua 8:32, covers the entire field of the *Halakhah* in fourteen books written in lucid and superb Hebrew. This gigantic work, on the writing of which Maimonides spent ten years, penetrated every Jewish community shortly after its appearance in 1180.

All rabbinic writings have been greatly affected by the *Mishneh Torah*, which is also known as *Yad ha-Ḥazakah*. It is universally acclaimed as a masterpiece in construction and the greatest product of post-talmudic literature. About four hundred commentaries have been written on the *Mishneh Torah*, which is the full summary of Judaism in all its varied aspects. For the most part, they are not concerned with *what* Maimonides says but rather *why* he says it. What he says is admirably clear. The questions and arguments raised by the numerous commentaries refer to the sources of Maimonides' code. In one of his letters, Maimonides points out that his Hebrew style is so easy that it will take the student only a short time to grasp it.

Following are a few random passages from Maimonides' *Mishneh Torah* or *Yad:* "A man should be neither easily provoked to anger nor should he be like a corpse that has no feeling. He should not close his hand nor be too lavish; he should be neither hilarious nor gloomy. He should always be quietly cheerful. He who avoids extremes and follows the middle course in all things is a wise man He should avoid the things that are injurious to the human body, and cultivate habits that will preserve his health. He should eat only when he is hungry; he should not gorge himself, but leave the table before his appetite is fully satisfied.

"Whoever sits idle and takes no exercise, even though he eats wholesome food, will suffer all his life from declining health. Excessive eating is like deadly poison to the human body, and is the root of all diseases. A wise man talks gently with all people and judges all men favorably. He neither makes overstatements nor understatements, unless a matter of peace is involved. He loves peace and strives for

400

it. If he finds that his words are helpful and heeded, he speaks; otherwise, he keeps quiet.

"The manner of a man's walking shows whether he is wise and sensible or foolish and ignorant. A wise man should dress neatly; he should not dress flashily to attract attention, nor shabbily to suffer disrespect. He must be honest in all his transactions, saying *no* when he means no and *yes* when he means yes.

"A wise man must never mistreat anyone; he should prefer to be among the offended rather than among the offenders. Whoever glories in the humiliation of others has no share in the future world. Slander has caused the slaughter of many Jews.

"A talebearer is one who carries gossip from person to person, even though what he says is the truth. Evil gossip, motivated by a desire to injure someone's reputation, kills three persons: the one who circulates it, the one who listens to it, and the one of whom it is spoken. Intelligent people realize that worldly matters are vain and void and unworthy of vengeance.

"Every Jew, poor or rich, healthy or ailing, young or old, is obligated to study Torah. None of the divine precepts equals Torah study in importance. Knowledge of the Torah, unattainable by the indolent, demands self-sacrifice, painstaking effort, sleepless nights.

"A teacher should not be angry when his pupils fail to understand a subject; he should review it with them many times until they finally grasp it. Just as it is required that pupils respect their teacher, so it is the duty of the teacher to be courteous and friendly to his pupils. One of the sages said: I have learned much from my teachers, more from my colleagues, but most of all from my pupils. A young pupil can sharpen the mind of a teacher by means of questions, stimulating him to glorious wisdom.

"Charity should be given cheerfully, compassionately, and comfortingly. He who induces others to contribute to charity is more deserving than the contributors themselves. The highest degree of charity is to aid a man in want by offering him a gift or a loan, by entering into partnership with him, or by providing work for him, so that he may become self-supporting. One should ever strive not to be dependent on other people. If reduced to poverty, even a distinguished scholar must not disdain manual work, no matter how unworthy of him, in order to avoid dependence on others.

"Some of the great sages derived their livelihood from chopping wood, carrying lumber, watering gardens, and asked no help of the community. A father is forbidden to impose too heavy a burden upon his children, nor should he be too exacting with them regarding their duty to honor him, lest he may cause them to rebel. He should pardon and overlook many things. . ."

In his *Mishneh Torah*, or *Yad ha-Ḥazakah* (strong hand), Maimonides condensed the entire Jewish lore contained in the Bible, the Mishnah, the two Talmuds, the midrashic literature, and the responsa of the Geonim (*Teshuvoth ha-Geonim*).

MISHNAH OF ELIEZER   מִשְׁנַת רַבִּי אֱלִיעֶזֶר

This tannaitic work is also referred to as the Midrash of Rabbi Eliezer. It was discovered in 1932 by H. G. Enelow while examining some manuscripts at the Library of the Jewish Theological Seminary of America. It was edited and published by Enelow in 1933.

The first two chapters of the book are devoted to the enumeration of the thirty-two rules of biblical interpretation; hence its sub-title מדרש שלשים ושתים מדות.

Particular emphasis is placed in this Midrash on the remembrance of the destroyed Temple. It includes various thoughts about the reciprocal duties of fathers and sons, as well as the benefits they may confer on one another. The parents are saved by the virtue of their children. Prayer must not be offered by false lips. The prayers of those who use their tongue either for slander or flattery are not accepted in heaven.

Only by combining work with the pursuit of Torah, we are told, can the Torah be fulfilled. One must not exploit the Torah for selfish ends. Examples are cited of how the sight of the *tsitsith* (ציצית) led men to recall their religious and moral obligations and so served to safeguard their spiritual existence. Several halakhic rules on the observance of the Sabbath are included in the twentieth and last chapter of the book.

METH MITZVAH   מֵת מִצְוָה

It is a religious duty to arrange for the burial of a corpse lying unattended. The duty of burying it devolves upon any person who discovers it. Even a high priest was expected to perform the last offices

402

for the unburied dead. The phrase *meth mitzvah*, strictly speaking, denotes the dead body of a person whose relatives are unknown and whose burial is obligatory on everybody. The unwritten law about the burial of the neglected dead was regarded as a duty of the highest obligation in ancient Israel, as it is in talmudic law.

In the book of Tobit, we read: "If I saw one of my people dead and thrown outside the wall of Nineveh, I would bury him. . . I buried them secretly, for he killed many in his anger. . . My neighbors laughed at me and said . . . here he is burying the dead again" (1:17-18; 2:4-8). By extension, *meth mitzvah* is the equivalent of הלווית המת, which means attending the dead to their last resting-place. This is regarded in Jewish tradition as the most disinterested of all deeds of kindness and man's humanity to man. There is hardly a Jewish community in the world without a burial society, known as *Ḥevrath Kaddisha* (holy association), specially organized for these purposes: 1) to conduct the burial service without charge; 2) to be present at the death of a fellow Jew; 3) to watch over the dead body; 4) to cleanse and shroud it; 5) to bury it with religious services. The members are called *mithassekim* (מתעסקים), attendants.

MATTAN TORAH   מַתַּן תּוֹרָה

T H E revelation at Mount Sinai is referred to as *Mattan Torah* (giving of the Torah) or *Ma'amad Har Sinai* (מעמד הר סיני), the presence at Mount Sinai. According to the Midrash, the souls of all generations were present when God concluded his covenant with Israel. The sages of all generations have received their wisdom from Sinai, because the souls that were yet to be created were present when the Torah was given. When God proclaimed the Torah at Sinai, no bird twittered, no fowl flew, no ox lowed, no angel stirred a wing; the sea did not roar, the creatures did not speak, the whole world was hushed into breathless silence, and the divine voice went forth: "I am the Lord your God" (Exodus Rabbah 28:6; 29:9). The Torah was given publicly in the wilderness, in no man's land, so that Jews may not say to others: "You have no share in it!" Anyone wishing to accept it is welcome to it (Mekhilta 19:2).

In his commentary on the book of Exodus, Ibn Ezra expatiates on several questions in connection with the Decalogue or Ten Commandments. He discusses the variations in the version of the Decalogue as it is repeated in Deuteronomy 5:6-18. Though the first two commandments are identically the same in wording in both versions, the remaining eight vary in form and detail. He concludes that in Exodus 20:1-14 we have the exact wording as it was originally spoken at Mount Sinai, whereas the version in Deuteronomy 5:6-18 is reported by Moses with some slight variations designed to remove possible misinterpretations.

According to the *Ramban* commentary, *You shall not have other gods beside me* extends the prohibition to belief in the divinity of angels or any of the heavenly hosts. The punishment God inflicted on the children for the sins of the fathers is interpreted to mean that the effects of the penalty imposed upon sinners are felt up to and including the fourth generation. Ibn Ezra explains that *You shall not covet* is repeated because the first use of *covet* relates to action by robbery; the second to a feeling in the heart. Hence, in Deuteronomy 5:18, Moses substituted לא תתאוה בית רעך for לא תחמד.

MITHNAGGEDIM מִתְנַגְּדִים

Tʜᴇ opponents of Ḥasidism became known as *Mithnaggedim* after the ban issued by the Vilna Gaon against the Ḥasidim in 1772. In their thinking, Ḥasidism was a serious threat to Jewish life. They particularly attacked the Ḥasidic belief in tsaddikism, according to which the saintly leader (*Tsaddik* or *Rebbe*), irrespective of his knowledge of the Torah, has the power to dispense the divine blessings by virtue of his very personality. The Mithnaggedim reviled the Ḥasidim for the use of the Sephardic liturgy, the establishment of separate houses of worship, and the neglect of Torah study.

The Ḥasidim and the Mithnaggedim were largely reconciled during the nineteenth century, even though they occasionally continued to poke fun at one another. At long last they realized that, essentially, there was little difference between them. Both sections observed the traditions of Jewish life with equal devotion. In our time, the bitterness of the previous generation of Ḥasidim and Mithnaggedim is gone. Tragically, the numbers of both were sharply reduced during the Second World War.

404

PROPHECY נְבוּאָה נ

THE Hebrew word for prophet **(נביא)** signifies a spokesman, or one who speaks for a divine power to human beings. The idea of prophecy is based on the belief in a God on whom the destiny and the well-being of men depend. The Hebrew prophets, who were primarily concerned with current situations and interfered directly with the government of the state, vividly realized that tomorrow is inherent in today.

Foreseeing the outcome of national crises and evil practices, they fearlessly criticized the morals of their own day while teaching a nobler way of living. Their message was usually one of warning and exhortation, including a prediction of coming events in the near or distant future. The wealth of religious and ethical teaching found in the prophetic messages has led Bible scholars to conclude that the true function of the Hebrew prophets was to be teachers of ethical and religious truths. Their boldness could have been possible only in a country where freedom of speech was a fact.

Their severe judgment of the moral condition of the people of Israel resulted from their lofty ethical conception of the God of Israel. Addressing themselves to the people of their own time on things of spiritual importance, they always sought to arouse in them a feeling against social suffering and injustice, urging them to relieve the oppressed, to champion the cause of the weak and the defenseless, to hate the evil and love the good. They never stood aloof from their people, whom they loved intensely and were scornful of all who would invade their land. While protesting and complaining about the absurd extremes of sacrificial activity that lacked in sincere homage, they never failed to plead for human mercy, justice and uprightness.

There were, however, false prophets who stood on the same level with the rest of the people. They were easy-going preachers who confirmed the people in their downward course, and opposed those mighty heroes of the spirit who stood like isolated rocks when all about them was tumbling—the true prophets. According to Maimonides, prophecy rests only upon the wise man who is distinguished by a strong moral character. "The prophets are of various degrees. Just as one sage is greater in wisdom than another, so, in the gift of prophecy, one prophet is greater than another" (*Yesodé ha-Torah* 7:2). "Every one should be a prophet, who is well built physically and has been duly educated and trained . . . fools and ignorant people are not fit

405

for this distinction ... prophecy is impossible without study and training" (*Guide*, 2:32). Striving to express their thoughts clearly, the prophets walk through the world of Judaism like living geniuses.

The prophets were men dedicated to God's service, who retired at times to their watchtower and looked hopefully for divine guidance. As in Habakkuk, the prophetic tower was the inner light of revelation, whereby the prophet pondered the problems of his people.

NIGGUN נִגּוּן

THE Hebrew word *niggun*, from a verb denoting "to make music," generally means melody, tune, or prayer-motif to which a service is traditionally rendered. Each festival, for example, has *niggunim* that are particularly associated with it.

Professor Baron relates that the sixteenth-century Rabbi Mordecai Jaffe, famous author of the rabbinic lawcode *Levush*, complained that his efforts to correct certain errors in the text of the *Kol Nidré* prayer proved unavailing because the cantors were unable to change the text during the services on account of the tune to which they had become accustomed. Memory was at times aided by a uniformly accepted tune. Once a melody became associated with a particular prayer, most changes in phrasing, willful or erroneous, caused a noticeable alteration also in the melody.

Speaking of the Ḥasidic songs, called *niggunim*, an expert of Jewish folk-song, had this to say: They are the most original in form and character of all the Jewish folk-songs, and they are richest, too, in regard to the form and variety of the musical coloration. They are entirely without words, and the people regard them as the *highest* of all songs. They are usually expressive of a prayerful mood, or of religious exultation, and they are generally mystical in character. The Ḥasidic song, this highest wordless melody, is a conversation, a communion with God. In it the singer asks God questions, and is answered; he gives expression to supplications and hopes, his sorrows and his profound belief in God. To the Ḥasid, God is simultaneously both near and far; he is everywhere... The Ḥasid sings his song in the middle of, or before, prayer, in order to put himself in a prayerful mood, and during the singing of his song-prayer he lives so profoundly that he passes into ecstasy... In executing the song, the most important thing is the sincerity of the feelings (Sussman Kisselhof).

406

DOWRY

נָדָן, נְדוּנְיָא

IN EZEKIEL 16:33, the term נדן is found in the sense of gift ("you gave your gifts to all your lovers"). The Assyrian word *nudnu* signifies *dowry*. Hence the Aramaic noun *nedunya*, used in the Talmud for a bride's outfit, wedding equipment given by her father, (Bava Metzia 74b; Kethubboth 54a; Ta'anith 24a). The Bible makes frequent mention of property brought by the bride to her husband at marriage. Rebekah, Leah and Rachel brought maid servants as gifts from their respective parents (Genesis 24:59, 61; 29:24, 29). Solomon received a city from his father-in-law, Pharaoh, as a *parting gift* (שלוחים) or dowry to his daughter (I Kings 9:16). The Talmud speaks of *nedunya* as a long-established custom. The sages instituted the regulation that each father must give some of his property to his daughter who is about to be married. The amounts varied in accordance with the means of the parents. Poor brides were given their dowries out of the charity funds of the community. The Talmud includes dowering the poor bride (הכנסת כלה) among the most meritorious acts.

In the Roman ghetto, during the seventeenth century, two charitable societies specialized in providing trousseaus and dowries for poor brides. These societies were often the cause of serious abuse. Indigent parents promised their daughters large dowries, and when the bridegroom refused to proceed with the wedding unless the dowry was forthcoming, the parents went in tears to the managers of the society and demanded help. "In 1618 this society resolved that no father who promised his daughter more than two hundred scudi was eligible for help. It was also found necessary to limit the number of cases dealt with annually to twelve. In societies of this kind, the girls often drew lots to decide which should receive dowries. The lucky maidens were in much demand..." (Abrahams, *Jewish Life in the Middle Ages*).

The dowry that the bride brought to her husband was recorded in the *kethubbah* (marriage contract). In case of death or divorce, the widow or divorcee could collect from the man's estate the amount stipulated in the *kethubbah* and the value of her dowry. The ancient custom of providing dowries enabled youthful couples to get married long before they were economically independent. The *nadan*, or *nedunya*, sometimes included board and maintenance (*kest*) for a specified time to make it possible for a young student to continue his studies in a talmudic academy.

407

VOWS   נְדָרִים

THE Torah does not prescribe vows; it only regulates them. Since ancient days men have shown a tendency to make a vow to God, in time of anxiety or earnest desire, to be carried out when the desired object is obtained or the danger is over. Vows were assumed voluntarily, but once made they were regarded as compulsory. Only in special cases, as in those of Samson and Samuel who had special missions to fulfill, was the Nazirite vow prescribed.

That vows must not be taken rashly is shown by the example of Jephtah and his daughter. Ben Sira advises: "Let nothing prevent you from paying your vows in time... Prepare yourself before you make a vow" (18:22-23). Philo says: The word of the good man should be his oath, firm and unchangeable... Therefore vows and oaths should be superfluous... Once made, a vow should be sacred, particularly if made with deliberate purpose and sober reason.

The sages of the Talmud generally disapproved of self-imposed abstinences. One of them, Rabbi Isaac, is reported to have said: "Are not the things prohibited in the Torah enough for you, that you wish to deny yourself other things?!" According to a talmudic interpretation of Numbers 6:11, the nazirite was ordered to make atonement for his vow to abstain from drinking wine, an unnecessary self-denial touching one of the permitted pleasures of life. Such a man is called a sinner, how much more one who denies himself the enjoyment of everything (Nazir 22a). Rav is reported as having said: "On the judgment day, a man will have to give strict account of every good thing which he might have enjoyed and did not" (Yerushalmi Kiddushin 66b).

The latest of the great Jewish law codes, the *Shulḥan Arukh* by Rabbi Joseph Karo of the sixteenth century, devotes a great deal of space to the laws on vows. This in itself is an indication of the great importance that was attached to vows in Jewish life centuries ago. It was natural that those who had seen the sad consequences of drinking should have vowed never to touch wine or abstinence for a year.

The following monition, borrowed from the Talmud, opens the chapter on vows in the *Shulḥan Arukh:* "Be not habituated to make vows; he that makes a vow is called wicked... Even vows for charitable purposes are not desirable; if one has the money, let him give it without a vow; and if not, let him defer his vow until he has the

408

money. . . He that takes a vow in order to strengthen his good resolves and to improve his way of life is worthy of praise. . . But, it is
well that a person should not make many vows of self-denial. . ."
The Jewish spirit looks askance at asceticism, which causes inefficiency
in the great struggle of life. The true man takes his full share of the
worldly activities. Philo wrote: "If you see anyone not taking food
or drink . . . refusing baths and oils, neglecting his clothes, sleeping on
the ground . . . pity his self-deception and teach him true temperance."

The Torah states the law on vows as follows: "When you make any
vow to the Lord your God, you must pay it without delay. . . If you
refrain from making a vow, that is no sin for you; but you must be
careful to perform any promise you have made with your lips" (Deuteronomy 23:22-24). The rabbis of the Talmud warn the people that
their very Yea and Nay must be truthful, and that it is even more
sinful to deceive a non-Jew than a Jew (Ḥullin 94a).

The popular expression בלי נדר (without vow), accompanying any
statement concerning some future action contemplated by the speaker,
is in keeping with the idea that we are expected to carry out everything we say, unless we specify that it is not a solemn promise but a
mere thought expressed in words.

NOTARIKON נוֹטָרִיקוֹן

THE Greek term *notarikon* (shorthand-writer) is used in rabbinic literature to denote a shorthand system which employs single letters to
signify whole words. Among the Romans, a *notarius* belonged to a
class of writers-abbreviators. *Notarikon* is primarily used in aggadic
interpretation and in kabbalistic literature. Every letter of a word is
taken as an initial or abbreviation of a word. For example, every letter of the word בראשית, the first word in the Torah, is made the initial of a word, and we obtain בראשית ראה אלהים שיקבלו ישראל תורה
(in the beginning God saw that Israel would accept the Torah).

Also, בראשית is said to allude to ברא רקיע ארץ שמים ים תהום (he
created the sky, the earth, the heavens, the sea, and the abyss). The
first word in the Torah is resolved by means of *notarikon* into many
other significant words and phrases, such as שבת ברית א"ש (=אל שדי)
ירא: (the Sabbath, covenant of the Almighty God, you must revere).

Among the most frequently used abbreviations are: the Hebrew
name for Bible: תורה נביאים כתובים=תנ"ך; אל מלך נאמן=אמן (God is

409

a faithful King); רש"י (Rashi) = רבי שלמה יצחקי; רמב"ם (Rambam) = רבנו משה בן מימון; רמב"ן (Ramban) = רבנו משה בן נחמן. *Notarikon* is one of the exegetical rules (*middoth*), according to which the sages of the Talmud interpret the Torah. The three letters of the word שבת are the initials of the three words שנה בשבת תענוג (Sabbath sleep is a delight).

NEZIKIN   נְזִיקִין

THE fourth of the six divisions of the Mishnah is called *Nezikin* (Damages) because it treats of all damages which are decided by the courts.

1) *Bava Kamma*, ten chapters, on damages to property and person.

2) *Bava Metzia*, ten chapters, on lost and found property, embezzlement, fraud, usury, rights of hired laborers, partnership.

3) *Bava Bathra*, ten chapters, concerning real estate, inheritance, partnership, drawing up legal documents. Originally the first three tractates of *Nezikin* were regarded as one tractate, divided into three sections or gates (*bavoth*); hence, the titles: *Bava Kamma* (first section), *Bava Metzia* (middle section), and *Bava Bathra* (last section).

4) *Sanhedrin*, eleven chapters, concerning the courts of justice and judicial procedure, especially with reference to criminal law.

5) *Makkoth*, three chapters, on crimes punished by lashes and on cities of refuge (Numbers 35:10-28).

6) *Shevuoth*, eight chapters, on the oaths made privately or administered by the court.

7) *Eduyyoth*, eight chapters, a collection of one hundred *halakhoth* (traditional laws) reported under the names of the tannaitic sages who transmitted them in the form of testimonies.

8) *Avodah Zarah*, five chapters, on prohibitions connected with various types of idolatry and heathen superstitions.

9) *Avoth*, five chapters, a collection of religious-ethical teachings of the sages, the fathers of Jewish tradition, who flourished over a period of nearly five centuries. A sixth chapter, called *Kinyan Torah* (Acquisition of Torah), is a later addition. The six Chapters of the Fathers (*Pirké Avoth*), included in the Prayerbook because of their great ethical importance, are recited on Saturday afternoons during the summer, one chapter each Sabbath. This collection of maxims imparts practical rules of wisdom while it demonstrates the continuity of Jewish tradition. Why is *Avoth* inserted as one of the ten trac-

410

tates of *Nezikim* (Damages)? Because "he who desires to be virtuous must fulfill the precepts of *Avoth*" (Bava Kamma 30a).

10) *Horayoth*, three chapters, on misdirections in matters of religious law, originating from religious authorities such as the high priest and the Sanhedrin (Leviticus 4:1-21).

The Talmud has no *Gemara* commentary on the tractates *Eduyyoth* and *Avoth*.

NAZIRITE   נָזִיר

THE Hebrew term *nazir* signifies one dedicated to God by vow involving abstinence from intoxicants and from cutting one's hair. The person who took a Nazirite vow for a certain specified period did not become a hermit; he continued to live in human society without being necessarily an ascetic. He was under obligation to abstain from wine and from all produce of the vine, and to let his hair grow long, during the period of his vow when he was forbidden to touch a dead body.

From the time of the nomadic Hebrew ancestors, the vine was the symbol of a settled life and a culture removed from the ancient simplicity of manners, though quite right in themselves. The free growth of the hair represented the Nazirite's consecration to God in the most visible form; the hair was the glory (*nezer*) of the head. If the period of the vow was not specified, rabbinic law fixed it at thirty days. At the end of the period, the Nazirite appeared at the Temple before the priest, made certain prescribed offerings, and shaved off his hair and burned it; following this, he was again permitted to drink wine (Numbers 6:2-21) and return to ordinary life.

Nazirites evidently existed long before the divine revelation at Mount Sinai, but their mode of life was regulated by the Torah. The Nazirite vow was often taken by men and women alike to express thanks for recovery from illness or for the birth of a child. Though the vow of abstinence was at times undertaken for private and personal reasons, it was often the expression of religious and national zeal, attempting to protect the simplicity of Israel from the corrupting influences of heathen civilization and religious practices.

Thus, the Nazirites had much in common with the followers of the prophetic teachings. "I raised up sons of yours as prophets, and young men to be Nazirites. . . But you gave Nazirites wine to drink, and prophets you forbade to prophesy" (Amos 2:11-12). Whence we

411

see that they were regarded as men of God like the prophets. The Bible records life-long Nazirites who were not bound by all the regulations of temporary Nazirites (Samson, Absalom).

NAHUM נַחוּם

THE book of Nahum, containing three chapters, is looked upon as a permanent expression of the cry of humanity for justice. It is the cry of outraged mankind in the face of brutal oppression. The prophet foretells the fall of Nineveh, "the bloody city," resembling a den of lions, and sees the directing hand of God in history. For centuries Assyria had oppressed all the peoples of western Asia.

Nahum, whose name signifies consolation, limits himself to the graphic description of the downfall of the Assyrian empire. His book is one of the best productions of biblical literature in terms of style and sublimity of thought. His breathless account of the destruction of Nineveh, the Assyrian capital, in the year 612 before the common era, must have been written during or immediately after this historic event. Unlike other prophets, Nahum does not allude to the sins of his own people.

Here are several verses from Nahum, the seventh of the twelve Minor Prophets:

"I am against you, Nineveh, says the Lord of hosts. I will burn your chariots, and the sword shall devour your young lions; I will wipe your prey from the earth, and the voice of your envoys shall be heard no more. O city, bloody throughout, full of lies and plunder! I will expose you to nations; I will show kingdoms your shame. Everyone who sees you will flee from you and say: Nineveh is ruined; there is none to lament her, none to comfort her. . ."

CONSOLING THE MOURNERS נָחוּם אֲבֵלִים

THE act of consolation, consisting of words of sympathy and encouragement offered to persons in distress, is frequently mentioned in the Bible as one of the ancient customs in Israel (Genesis 37:35; II Samuel 12:24; Psalm 119:50, 82). In the book of Job we are told that when Job's friends heard of all the misfortune that had come upon him, they came together to give him sympathy and comfort.

"They sat down upon the ground with him seven days and seven nights, but none of them spoke a word to him; for they saw how great was his suffering" (2:11-13). This is used by the rabbinic authorities as biblical proof that the comforters are not allowed to say anything before the mourner begins to speak. Nor are the comforters permitted to remain any longer than necessary.

We are advised in the Mishnah (Avoth 4:23) not to comfort a mourner while his dead relative lies before him, when his grief is overwhelming. Silence in the company of a heartbroken mourner expresses deeper sympathy and condolence and is much more effective than any words can be. The Talmud stresses silence as meritorious in a mourner's house (Berakhoth 6b: אגרא דבי טמיא שתיקותא).

The usual formula of comfort addressed to the mourners upon their return from the burial service is: "May God console you among the other mourners for Zion and Jerusalem" (המקום ינחם אתכם בתוך שאר אבלי ציון וירושלים). A meal prepared by friends or neighbors for the mourners is called *seudath havra'ah*. The seven-day period of mourning (*shiv'ah*) begins from the day of burial, and applies to seven relatives: father, mother, husband, wife, child, brother, and sister (including a half-brother and a half-sister). The symbol of mourning is the *keri'ah* (tear) in the garment, on the left side opposite the heart for a parent, and in all other cases on the right side. The *keri'ah* is performed standing, and is accompanied by the blessing ברוך דיין האמת ("Blessed be the true Judge"), thus expressing an acceptance of the divine judgment.

NAḤEM   נַחֵם

THE passage נחם אבלי ציון (comfort the mourners of Zion), which is inserted in the *Shemoneh Esreh* recited in the afternoon of *Tish'ah b'Av*, is quoted in Talmud Yerushalmi (Berakhoth 4:3; Ta'anith 2:2). It contains a reference to the Roman legions (לגיונות), employed by Titus during the siege of Jerusalem. According to Rabbi Joseph Karo, this paragraph is added during the *Minḥah* service because the Temple was set on fire toward evening, the time of *Minḥah* (*Beth Yosef*).

The passage reads: "Comfort, Lord our God, the mourners of Zion, the mourners of Jerusalem, and the city that is in mourning, laid waste, despised and desolate... She sits with her head covered like a barren, childless woman. Legions devoured her; idolaters took possession of her; they put the people of Israel to the sword. . . How my heart grieves for the slain! Thou, O Lord, didst consume her with fire, and with fire thou wilt rebuild her. . . . O Comforter of Zion and Builder of Jerusalem."

WASHING THE HANDS נְטִילַת יָדַיִם

THE Talmud (Berakhoth 46b) speaks of מים ראשונים (washing the hands before the meal) and מים אחרונים (washing the hands after the meal). Before eating bread that requires the blessing known as *ha-motzi*, the observant Jew washes his hands and rubs them together; then, lifting them up, he recites Psalm 134:2 (שאו ידיכם—"lift up your hands in prayer and bless the Lord") and, before drying them, he says: "Blessed art thou, Lord our God, King of the universe, who hast sanctified us with thy commandments, and commanded us concerning the washing of the hands" (על נטילת ידים).

The blessing המוציא ("who bringest forth bread from the earth") is derived from the biblical expression להוציא לחם מן הארץ (Psalm 104:14). Before eating pastry, the blessing בורא מיני מזונות is recited instead of *hammotsi*. The abridged form of grace על המחיה, instead of the regular *birkath hammazon* (grace after meals), is recited after eating pastry. Before such light repast, no *netilath yadayim* is required.

At the end of the nineteenth century, we are told, the finger bowl, or glass for rinsing the fingers at the table, came to be used also by non-Jews, even though the original founders of Christianity had ridiculed the Pharisaic observance of *netilath yadayim*. No special blessing is recited when rinsing the fingers (מים אחרונים) before *birkath ha-mazon* (grace after the meal).

The religious discipline of Judaism demands washing of the hands on other occasions too, such as when getting up from bed, or before offering daily prayers. Hygienic habits, resulting from this practice, have been cultivated even among the poorest of the Jewish people.

The verb נטל, used in the phrase נטילת ידים, has several related meanings, so that נטילה denotes taking, lifting up, carrying. The phrase נטילת לולב, for example, signifies *taking up the festive lulav;* נטילת רשות, *taking leave of absence.* Hence, it has been suggested that the biblical phrase שאו ידיכם ("lift up your hands"), mentioned above, is alluded to at the invocation recited when washing the hands before meals (נשיאת ידים = נטילת ידים).

414

WAVING THE LULAV   נְטִילַת לוּלָב

WE read in the Torah: "On the fifteenth day of the seventh month, when you have gathered in the produce of the land, you shall celebrate a feast in honor of the Lord for seven days. . . On the first day you shall take the fruit of a beautiful tree (*ethrog*), palm branches (*lulav*), boughs of a leafy tree (*hadassim*), and water-willows (*aravoth*), and rejoice before the Lord your God for seven days" (Leviticus 23:39-41).

This traditional interpretation is supported by Josephus (30-100), who reports that on *Sukkoth* "we carry in our hands twigs of myrtle and willow together with a palm branch and a citron." It has been suggested, however, that originally the palm branches were used for constructing the booths or *sukkoth*, in which the people lived during the festival.

Since the *lulav* (palm branch) is the most prominent of the four plants, referred to as four species (*arba'ah minim*), it is held in the right hand and mentioned in the benediction (עַל נְטִילַת לוּלָב) "concerning the taking of the *lulav*," with the other three species adjoining it. Maimonides writes: "The normative method of fulfilling the commandment is to lift up the bunch of three species in the right hand and the *ethrog* (citron) in the left hand, and to move them to and fro and up and down, shaking the *lulav* three times in each direction . . . during the recital of the *Hallel*" (*Yad, Lulav* 7:9-10).

The wavings toward all directions (*na'anu'im*) symbolize the stream of abundance which comes from the heavens and the four corners of the earth. The use of the four species is prohibited on the Sabbath for fear they might be carried four or more cubits in a public domain (רְשׁוּת הָרַבִּים); for the same reason, the sounding of the *shofar* (ram's horn) is prohibited on the Sabbath coinciding with *Rosh Hashanah*.

HEBREW EXPRESSIONS   נִיבִים עִבְרִיִּים

THE phrases בָּרוּךְ הַשֵּׁם (thank God) and בְּעֶזְרַת הַשֵּׁם (with the help of God) are frequently on the lips of religious Jews, even though they may speak a language other than Hebrew or Yiddish. Similarly, the expressions חַס וְשָׁלוֹם (*has v'shalom*) and חַס וְחֲלִילָה (*has v'halilah*) in the sense of "God forbid" are of high frequency.

415

The phrase לֹא עֲלֵיכֶם (*lo alekhem*), used in the sense of *may such a calamity never come upon you*, accompanies the report of bad news. The Yiddish term *nebich* is often used in the place of *lo alekhem*. It is a contraction of *nie bei euch* or *nisht bei eich gedacht*.

Following is a list of Hebrew expressions included in the numerous vernaculars of the Jewish people.

שָׁלוֹם, שָׁלוֹם עֲלֵיכֶם, עֲלֵיכֶם שָׁלוֹם, שַׁבַּת שָׁלוֹם, חַג שָׂמֵחַ,

מוֹעֲדִים לְשִׂמְחָה, לְחַיִּים, לְחַיִּים טוֹבִים וּלְשָׁלוֹם, יִישַׁר כֹּחֲךָ,

מַזָּל טוֹב, תִּתְחַדֵּשׁ, לְשָׁנָה טוֹבָה תִּכָּתֵבוּ, גְּמַר חֲתִימָה טוֹבָה,

גְּמַר טוֹב, לִרְפוּאָה, לַבְּרִיאוּת, רְפוּאָה שְׁלֵמָה, בְּרָכָה וְהַצְלָחָה,

חַס וְשָׁלוֹם, חַס וְחָלִילָה, חֲזַק, חֲזַק וֶאֱמָץ, חֲזַק חֲזַק וְנִתְחַזֵּק, גַּם

זוּ לְטוֹבָה, אִם יִרְצֶה הַשֵּׁם, לְמַעַן הַשֵּׁם, הַלְוַאי, עַד מֵאָה שָׁנָה,

עָלָיו הַשָּׁלוֹם, עָלֶיהָ הַשָּׁלוֹם, זֵכֶר צַדִּיק לִבְרָכָה, לִפְנִים מְשׁוּרַת

הַדִּין, קִדּוּשׁ הַשֵּׁם, חִלּוּל הַשֵּׁם, עֶרֶב שַׁבָּת, עֶרֶב יוֹם טוֹב, מוֹצָאֵי

שַׁבָּת, מוֹצָאֵי יוֹם טוֹב, שָׁלֹשׁ רְגָלִים, יָמִים נוֹרָאִים, עֲשֶׂרֶת יְמֵי

תְשׁוּבָה, רִבּוֹנוֹ שֶׁל עוֹלָם, יִרְאַת שָׁמַיִם, כִּבּוּד אָב וָאֵם, רֹאשׁ

חֹדֶשׁ, חֹל הַמּוֹעֵד, הַכְנָסַת אוֹרְחִים, בִּקּוּר חוֹלִים, בַּר-אוֹרְיָן,

לַמְדָן, מְסִירַת נֶפֶשׁ, פִּקּוּחַ נֶפֶשׁ, חֶשְׁבּוֹן הַנֶּפֶשׁ.

NISAN   נִיסָן

THE month of *Nisan*, corresponding to March-April, is the first month of the Jewish sacred year. In the earlier books of the Bible, *Nisan* is referred to as *ḥodesh ha-aviv* (the month of spring). In the post-exilic books, however, the Babylonian name *Nisan* is used (Nehemiah 2:1; Esther 3:7).

During the thirty days of this month it is not permissible to observe public mourning and public fasts; the *taḥanun* supplication in the daily morning service is omitted, as well as the *tsidkathekha tsedek* in the Sabbath *Minḥah* service: nor is *tsidduk ha-din* recited at a burial. The Passover festival, which celebrates the exodus from Egypt, begins on the fifteenth day of *Nisan*.

416

MIRACLES   נִסִּים

EXTRAORDINARY phenomena, distinguished from normal and usual events, are frequently referred to as miracles. In the Bible, such extraordinary occurrences are called wonders and signs performed by God in times of great crisis. It has been suggested that the belief in miracles is based on man's unscientific tendency to regard as miraculous all that is incomprehensible, all that contemporary knowledge cannot explain. Rabbi Levi ben Gershon (*Ralbag*), known as Gersonides (1288-1344), states that miracles cannot be of regular occurrence; if natural phenomena and laws were regularly changed by miracle, it would signify a defect in the natural order. There can be no miracles in reference to mathematical truths, nor in matters relating to the past. An event that has already taken place cannot be reversed miraculously as if it has not taken place.

In the ancient world, the miraculous was a popular thought-pattern, according to which God intervened in the ordinary course of events in order to express his will and purpose. Some biblical miracles have been construed as natural phenomena; the Egyptian plagues have been explained as disasters peculiar to Egypt under certain climatic conditions. The parting of the Red Sea and the Jordan is said to have occurred as a result of a wind blowing in a particular direction.

Rav Saadyah Gaon and Maimonides consider the narrative in Numbers 22:23-34, concerning the mule speaking to Balaam, as enacted in a dream or vision of the night. The poetical setting of the inspired passage in Joshua 10:12-14 is widely interpreted as describing a miraculous lengthening of the day by an obscuration of the sun, impeding Israel's enemies in their flight homewards, a darkness relieved only twenty-four hours later, well into the next day. The story of Jonah has been interpreted figuratively. The episode of the great fish swallowing Jonah is explained as an allusion to the captivity which swallowed up Israel. The deliverance from exile has been likened to being disgorged alive from the mouth of the devouring beast.

According to Maimonides, when a prophet describes the ruin of a kingdom or the destruction of a great nation in such expressions as "the stars have fallen, the heavens are overthrown, the sun is darkened, the earth is waste and trembles," he speaks in metaphors alluding to the defeated. For them the light of the sun and the moon is darkened, in the same sense that the victorious are said to enjoy light

417

and gladness. "When great troubles befall us, our eyes become dim and we cannot see clearly . . . whereas in a state of gladness and comfort . . . man feels as if the light had increased. Thus the good tidings that the people shall dwell in Zion and Jerusalem, and shall weep no more, conclude as follows: The light of the moon shall glow like the light of the sun, and the sunlight shall be sevenfold strong. . ." (Isaiah 30:26).

Speaking on the figurative language of the Bible, Maimonides (*Guide*, 2:29) cites Psalm 77:17-19 as referring to the death of the Egyptians in the Red Sea: "The waters saw thee and were afraid, the depths trembled . . . the earth shook and was confounded." He asserts that a miracle cannot prove what is impossible; it is useful only to confirm what is possible (*Guide*, 3:24). We pay no heed to one, who, by miracles and wonders, seeks to refute Moses, whose prophecy was established not by signs but by revelation. . . (*Yad, Yesodé ha-Torah* 8:3).

Though not denying the possibility of miracles in general, medieval Jewish philosophers made attempts at explaining biblical miracles as natural occurrences. Nahmanides (*Ramban*), however, contends that no man can share in the Torah of Moses unless he believes that all our history consists of miracles (Introduction to Ramban Commentary).

The attitude of the talmudic sages toward miracles is discussed by Solomon Schechter, who writes: "In the whole of rabbinic literature there is not one single instance on record that a rabbi was ever asked by his colleagues to demonstrate the soundness of his doctrine, or the truth of a disputed halakhic case, by performing a miracle. Only once do we hear of a rabbi who had recourse to miracles for the purpose of showing that his conception of a certain halakhah was a right one. And in this solitary instance the majority declined to accept the miraculous intervention as a demonstration of truth and decided against the rabbi who appealed to it. Nor, indeed, were such supernatural gifts claimed by all the rabbis . . . not a single miracle is reported, for instance, of the great Hillel, or his colleague Shammai, both of whom exercised such an important influence on rabbinic Judaism. On the other hand, we find that such men as, for instance, Honi ha-Meaggel, whose prayers were much sought after in time of drought, or Rabbi Hanina ben Dosa, whose prayers were often solicited in cases of illness, left almost no mark on Jewish thought, the former being known only by the wondrous legends circulating about him, the latter being represented in the whole Talmud only by one or two moral sayings. . ."

418

NE'ILAH   נְעִילָה

THE term *Ne'ilah* (closing) today signifies the concluding service on *Yom Kippur*. In Temple times, it was the name of the service conducted "at the closing of the gates" (Ta'anith 4:1), that is, shortly before the gates of the Temple were closed in the evening, on the days of fasting, at the *ma'amadoth*, and on *Yom Kippur*. When the term *Ne'ilah* was restricted to the fifth, concluding service of *Yom Kippur*, it was taken to mean the closing of the gates of heaven, when the sentences passed upon human beings are divinely "sealed."

The *Ne'ilah* service on *Yom Kippur* has been described as sublime in its simplicity, directness of appeal, and purity of style. The *aron ha-kodesh* (holy ark) remains open while the service is chanted in an extraordinarily solemn mood. In the *Amidah*, the phrase "seal us" is used in place of "inscribe us," and in place of the confession litany (עַל חטא) the passage אתה נותן יד is recited.

This paragraph, which depicts in clear language the Jewish conception of forgiveness of sin, reads in part: "Thou dost reach out thy hand to transgressors; thy right hand is extended to receive repentant sinners. . . Thou hast taught us to confess all our iniquities, ceasing to do violence, so that thou mayest graciously receive us into thy presence. . . Thou hast abundantly provided us with means of pardon. . ."

At the end of *Ne'ilah*, three principal declarations of faith are uttered by the *ḥazzan*, who leads in the service, each to be repeated by all the worshipers present: the *Shema*, once; "Blessed be the name of his glorious majesty forever and ever," three times; and "The Lord is God," seven times. The three times allude to the threefold biblical expression: "The Lord is King, the Lord was King, the Lord shall forever be King." The seven times allude to the proverbial seven heavens created by God (*Tosafoth*, Berakhoth 34a). The *Shema* is recited once to emphasize the Oneness of God.

SOUL, BREATH, SPIRIT   נֶפֶשׁ, נְשָׁמָה, רוּחַ

THE Hebrew word *nefesh* (soul) is used in many senses; it has different shades of meaning at different times. It denotes the principle of life, the thing that constitutes a living being. "Man became a living being"

419

(*nefesh ḥayyah*) when God had "breathed into his nostrils the breath of life" (*nishmath ḥayyim*—Genesis 2:7). The Torah applies *nefesh ḥayyah* to animals as well as men, "since the life of a living body is in its blood" (כי נפש הבשר בדם היא), "for blood is life" כי הדם הוא הנפש—Leviticus 17:11; Deuteronomy 12:23). Though life and blood are not quite identical, the blood is the principal carrier of life.

Since the term *nefesh* is related to the verbs *nashaf* and *nashav* (to blow), as in Exodus 15:10 and Isaiah 40:7 (נשפת ברוחך) and רוח ה' נשבה בו), it is defined as that which breathes, the breathing substance or being, the soul, the inner being of man. Hence, the expression נפחה נפשה (Jeremiah 15:9), *she breathed out her soul. Nefesh* is used for life itself as well as for an individual person, as in Exodus 21:23 ("life for life") and Numbers 23:10; Judges 16:30. The verb ינפש (Exodus 23:12; II Samuel 16:14) is employed in the sense of taking breath, refreshing oneself.

The terms רוח and נשמה are used synonymously to denote spirit and breath. The dualism of human nature, consisting of body and soul, is frequently mentioned in talmudic-midrashic literature. All beliefs about souls are related to the doctrine of the revivification of the dead. The souls of all generations are said to have been created at the beginning of the world, and kept till the time of their birth in a heavenly repository called *guf* (body). One of the daily morning prayers, borrowed from the Talmud (Berakhoth 60b), reads as follows:

"My God, the soul which thou hast placed within me is pure. Thou hast created it; thou hast formed it; thou hast breathed it into me. Thou preservest it within me; thou wilt take it from me and restore it to me in the hereafter. So long as the soul is within me, I offer thanks before thee . . . Lord of all souls . . . who restorest the souls to the dead."

In this devout meditation, the term *neshamah* is used repeatedly for *soul*. The talmudic sages hold that the body is not the prison of the soul but its medium of development and improvement. Jewish spirituality combines heaven and earth, as it were. It does not separate soul from body or mind from nature, but understands man and history in the unity of man's physical and spiritual life. Accordingly, the soul must not boast that it is more holy than the body, for only in that it has climbed down into the body and works through its limbs can the soul attain its perfection. The body, on the other hand, may not brag of supporting the soul, for when the soul leaves, the flesh falls into decay.

420

According to the kabbalistic teachings, the destiny of every soul is to return to the source whence it came. Those who in their earthly existence failed to develop that purity and perfection necessary for gaining access to their heavenly source above must undergo incarnation in another body, and even repeat that experience more than once until they are permitted to return to the celestial region in a purified form. Maimonides describes the soul as a unit possessing five faculties: the nutritive; the sensitive, by which one perceives; the imaginitive, by which it has the power to form images of the things impressed on it by the sense; the appetitive, or the ability to feel either desire or aversion; and the rational, by which it acquires knowledge and discerns right and wrong (*Shemonah Perakim*).

The נשמה יתרה (additional soul) denotes the extra measure of delight experienced by the strictly observant Jew on the Sabbath day. The symbolic use of fragrant spices during the recital of the *Havdalah* on *Motzaé Shabbath* is to cheer the soul which is saddened at the departure of the Sabbath and the *additional soul*.

The *ner neshamah*, the lamp lit in memory of a departed soul, is reminiscent of Proverbs 20:27—"a lamp from the Lord is the soul of man" (נר ה' נשמת אדם). The custom of studying Mishnah in memory of the departed is derived from the fact that the word משנה consists of the letters of נשמה, transposed.

PUNCTUATION   נִקּוּד

THE word *nikkud*, signifying the vocalization of the biblical consonantal text, is derived from the term *nekudoth* (dots). Originally, the method of reading the biblical text was entrusted to oral tradition (*Masorah*), which was preserved by scholars and teachers. Rav Saadyah Gaon of the tenth century, as well as his contemporary Aaron ben Asher, regarded the vowel signs as a long-established Hebrew system of vocalization. It has therefore been assumed that Hebrew *nikkud*, having originated in the sixth and seventh centuries, was incorporated into the text of the Bible by the middle of the eighth century as an indispensable aid to its study. The oldest vocalized Bible manuscripts in existence date from the ninth century.

The innovation of *nikkud* was opposed by the Babylonian Geonim only with respect to the texts used in public worship, such as the *Sefer Torah* and the *Megillath Esther*. In a responsum preserved in

Maḥzor Vitry, the great work on liturgy compiled by Rabbi Simḥah of Vitry, a pupil of Rashi, we read the following reply to the question whether it is forbidden to vocalize the *Sefer Torah:* "We have not heard that the *Sefer Torah* was vocalized when it was given to Moses. The punctuation was not given at Sinai, but was introduced by the scholars (החכמים) as an external aid for the reading of the Bible. The prohibition against adding anything to the Torah (Deuteronomy 13:1) would be transgressed by adding the punctuation to the *Sefer Torah.* Although the division of verses and the cantillation according to the meaning have been transmitted from Sinai to this day, it is nevertheless an oral tradition, not conveyed by marks of punctuation" (סימני נקידה).

Originally confined to the biblical text, vocalization or *nikkud* has been used for other works of Jewish literature written with Hebrew characters. It has been employed not only in Hebrew and Aramaic books, such as the Mishnah and the Targum as well as liturgical and poetical works, but also in Yiddish, even though the vowels in Yiddish are designated by vowel-letters. In addition to the current system of vocalization, referred to as Tiberian, two other systems have been discovered: the Babylonian and the Palestinian. The main difference between the Tiberian system and the two other is in the position of the vowel signs. The Tiberian *nikkud* is *sublinear*, that is, the vowels are placed *under* the letters (except two), while the other two are *superlinear*, with the vowels *above* the letters. The Tiberian system has superseded its rivals.

With the introduction of *nikkud* began the period of the *nakdanim*, who furnished the consonantal Hebrew manuscripts with vowel signs and accents (טעמים) as well as with masoretic glosses. The activity of the *nakdanim* continued to the invention of printing.

NER TAMID נֵר תָּמִיד

T H E term *ner tamid* (perpetual lamp) is borrowed from Exodus 27:20 and Leviticus 24:2, where the people of Israel are commanded to keep a lamp burning in the *Mishkan* (portable sanctuary) continually. Symbolizing the permanence of the Torah and the radiance of the Jewish faith, the *ner tamid*, the ever-burning lamp hanging in synagogues before the *aron ha-kodesh* (holy ark), was as a rule an oil lamp, but now the use of electricity is preferred for the sake of convenience and safety. The *ner tamid* has been interpreted also as a symbol of Israel, whose destiny it was to become "a light of the nations" (Isaiah 42:6).

The custom of a *"yahrzeit* light," lighted on the anniversary of the death of a close relative, is based on Proverbs 20:27, where the soul of man (נשמת אדם) is called "light of the Lord." This verse has been interpreted to the effect that conscience is a searchlight, piercing the depths of the heart. In addition to the terms *ner tamid* and *ner neshamah*, there is the *ner shabbath*, the Sabbath lamp, lit in Jewish homes on Fridays before sunset.

MARRIAGE   נִשׂוּאִין

IN talmudic times, the usual age of the bridegroom was eighteen to twenty. Girls were treated as marriageable from the beginning of their thirteenth year. A Jewish court would often compel a man to take a wife. Such pressure, however, was not applied in the case of students. A contemporary of Rabbi Akiva, Simeon ben Azzai was never married, because he was enamored of the Torah; he said: "The population of the world can be kept up by others" (Yevamoth 63b).

It was a generally accepted opinion that the world was created for the multiplication of the human species. In modern times, all attempts at compulsory marriages have become obsolete in Jewish circles, since a man must be able to support a wife before he takes one, and no fixed age can be set for the fulfillment of that condition.

Twelve months was the normal interval between the betrothal (*erusin*) and the marriage (*nissu'in*), when the bride was taken to her husband's house (Kethubboth 5:2). Since the sixteenth century the two ceremonies of betrothal and marriage have been performed on the same day. The talmudic term *shiddukhin* refers to the arrangements preliminary to the legal betrothal, which has been gradually replaced by the engagement.

The performance of a wedding includes the use of a ring and a canopy (*huppah*), the breaking of a glass, the reading of a marriage contract (*kethubbah*), and the recital of the seven benedictions. The ring is said to have been introduced in the seventh century; it replaced the ancient gift of money or an article of value. It need not be of gold, and must not contain gems; it is put on the forefinger of the bride's right hand; afterwards she places it on the customary finger of the left hand.

Originally, the *ḥuppah* was the marriage chamber, into which the bridal couple were conducted after a procession; but now it is merely symbolical. A regular preliminary of the marriage ceremony is the bridegroom's signing of the *kethubbah*, which sets forth the amount payable to the wife in the case of the husband's death or the wife's divorce. The *kethubbah* was designed to protect the rights of the wife and her personal property; it was also intended as a strong restraint against rash divorces. The *kethubbah* is still retained, though it hardly has any legal significance. It is carefully preserved by the bride, and was often engrossed in parchment with illuminated borders.

The bridegroom breaks a glass as a symbol of the mourning for Zion, which is frequently recalled in the Hebrew wedding hymns. The Talmud relates: "When the son of Ravina was married, the father took a costly vase of white crystal, worth four hundred *zuzim*, and broke it before the rabbis present, who were in an uproarious mood, in order to curb their spirits" (Berakhoth 30b). The custom, then, arose from a desire to keep men's joys tempered by serious thoughts and the memory of Zion.

The term for the betrothal ceremony is *kiddushin* (consecration), indicating the religious significance of Jewish marriages which are described as a divine covenant (Proverbs 2:17). Hence the ceremony is usually conducted in the synagogue and is hallowed by the seven blessings, which are recited when a quorum of ten males (*minyan*) is present. They are quoted in the Talmud as *birkath hathanim* (Kethubboth 8a). The fourth benediction refers to the perpetual renewal of the human being in the divine form. In the last three benedictions a prayer is uttered that God may comfort Zion, cause happiness to the young couple, and bring about complete exultation in a restored Judea and Jerusalem.

Since the betrothal ceremony is now combined with the wedding ceremony, two glasses of wine are used. The blessing for the betrothal reads: "Blessed art thou, Lord our God, King of the universe, who hast sanctified us with thy commandments, and prohibited illicit relations; thou hast forbidden the cohabitation of those who are merely betrothed, permitting it to those who are married through consecrated wedlock. Blessed art thou, O Lord, who sanctifiest thy people Israel by consecrated wedlock." This is followed by the groom's placing the ring, symbolic of attachment and fidelity, on the forefinger of the bride's right hand, and saying: "With this ring you are wedded to me in accordance with the law of Moses and Israel."

424

The phrase "in accordance with the law of Moses and Israel" signifies the traditional interpretation of the laws of Moses, since the regulations of betrothal (*erusin*) are not directly biblical. After the reading of the *kethubbah*, the aforementioned seven blessings are chanted over a second cup of wine. Then comes the groom's breaking of the glass in memory of unrestored Jerusalem. The two cups of wine are said to represent cups of joy and sorrow; the bride and groom drink of both, expressing their intention to share one another's joys and sorrows. The plain ring of pure gold is symbolic of the purity of marital fidelity. Since the fourteenth century the wedding ceremony has been conducted, as a rule, by a rabbi, although any Jew is qualified to perform a wedding.

The term *tenaim* (conditions) signifies the engagement, which consists of certain conditions entered into by the parents of the couple as to the dowry (*nedunya*) and other details stipulated in a written document. This contract includes a provision that the party withdrawing from the agreement before marriage must pay to the other party a fine (*kenas*); hence, the Yiddish word *farkenast* denoting *engaged*. It is customary to break a dish at this engagement ceremony (*tenaim*) for the reason given above, or else: to warn the guests against excessive hilarity.

NESIATH KAPPAYIM   נְשִׂיאַת כַּפַּיִם

THE formula of the priestly blessing, which is chanted in the synagogues by those of priestly descent, consists of three Hebrew verses composed of three, five, and seven words, respectively. It mounts gradually from the petition for material blessings and protection to that for divine favor as a spiritual form of happiness, culminating in the request for *shalom*, peace, in which material and spiritual well-being is combined. The priestly blessing, taken from Numbers 6:24-26, reads: "May the Lord bless you and protect you. May the Lord let his countenance shine upon you and be gracious to you. May the Lord look kindly upon you and grant you peace."

Before pronouncing the *birkath kohanim* (priestly benediction), the *kohanim* wash their hands, just as the priests did in the Temple at Jerusalem, where the priestly blessing was one of the most impressive features of the daily service. The term נשיאת כפים (raising the hands) is derived from Psalm 134:2 ("Lift up your hands in holiness and bless"). This verse is also recited when washing the hands before eating (נטילת ידים). Those of Levitical descent (Levites), as in Temple times, pour the water on the hands of the *kohanim* following the removal of their shoes outside the place of worship. In the absence of a Levite, a firstborn son pours the water.

After ascending the platform (*dukhan*), the *kohanim* face the holy ark (*aron ha-kodesh*) and remain standing until the *ḥazzan*, who is reciting the *Amidah* aloud, utters the word כהנים (priests!). Thereupon the *kohanim* turn their faces to the congregation, raise their hands to the level of their shoulders, and separate their fingers in a way that there are five open spaces between them. This is done symbolically in allusion to the expression מציץ מן החרכים (peering through the lattice) in the Song of Solomon (2:9), which has been interpreted allegorically. The word for *lattice* is made out to mean *hé ḥarakkim* (five windows). The fingers are joined in a manner that each of the two hands presents two spaces, making a total of four spaces; there is another space between the thumbs of the two hands when joined together.

The fifteen Hebrew words of the priestly blessing are recited each separately by the *ḥazzan* and repeated by the *kohanim*. At the conclusion of each of the three verses, the congregation responds *Amen*. The congregation listens attentively to each word chanted by the *kohanim*, who do not relax their fingers until they have concluded the blessing and turned their faces from the congregation.

In Eretz Yisrael, the *birkath kohanim* is still recited by *kohanim* every morning and afternoon toward the end of the *Amidah* prayer. Outside Eretz Yisrael, however, it is chanted at the end of the *Musaf* service on major festivals only.

NASHIM   נָשִׁים

THE third of the six divisions of the Mishnah bears the name *Nashim* (Women) because it consists of laws dealing with marriage, divorce, and general relationships of husband and wife. The seven tractates of *Nashim* are as follows:

1) *Yevamoth*, sixteen chapters, concerning the law of levirate marriage and *ḥalitzah*, stated in Deuteronomy 25:5-10. One of the purposes of levirate marriage, or marriage of a childless widow with her brother-in-law (*yavam*), was to keep the property of the deceased within the family. The man who refused to comply with this law of

426

family loyalty granted the widow *ḥalitzah*. Today, *ḥalitzah* rites take the place of levirate marriage which is contracted no more.

2) *Kethubboth*, thirteen chapters, concerning the marriage-settlement for the protection of the wife in case of widowhood or divorce, and the mutual rights and duties of husband and wife.

3) *Nedarim*, eleven chapters, on the making and annulment of vows, particularly with regard to women (Numbers 30:3-17).

4) *Nazir*, nine chapters, concerning the biblical prescriptions in connection with Nazirite vows (Numbers 6:1-21).

5) *Sotah*, nine chapters, concerning the biblical laws relating to the wife suspected of adultery (Numbers 5:11-31).

6) *Gittin*, nine chapters, dealing with the laws of divorce and the annulment of marriage (Deuteronomy 24:1-4).

7) *Kiddushin*, four chapters, dealing with the regulations concerning the marriage status.

USURY   נֶשֶׁךְ, רִבִּית

THE terms *neshekh* and *ribbith* denote anything given on loan upon interest. The Torah forbids to lend anything to a fellow Israelite on condition of receiving back more than the amount of money or quantity of food lent. The distinction made today between usury and interest is unknown to Judaism, which regards mutual loans merely as a means of relieving the temporary distress of a fellow Jew.

The supposition underlying the biblical law is that the people of Israel are linked together in one brotherhood; each Israelite is therefore expected to help his brother Israelite, who is in need of a loan, without taking advantage of his poverty. Many poor Israelite farmers, in Bible times, would have been in a desperate plight if left without occasional free loans in commodities or in money. According to Jewish law, loans are acts of pure charity. The basic assumption is that the borrower is poor and needs money to satisfy his personal wants.

The Torah states: "You shall not demand interest from your brother on a loan of money or of food or of anything else on which interest is usually demanded. You may demand interest from a foreigner, but not from your brother. . ." (Deuteronomy 23:20-21). Since the foreign merchant could not very well be expected to lend to an Israelite trader without interest, some differentiation in law was unavoidable. An equal basis for trading between Israelites and foreigners could be attained only bilaterally. The Babylonian bankers often charged as much as twenty percent interest on loans. The caravan trade was very extensive in ancient Israel.

When the ancient agricultural society was succeeded by a commercial society, the borrowing and lending of money became legitimate by means of a *hetter iska*, a kind of partnership agreement between borrower and lender. The prevailing laws of medieval Europe precluded the Jews from investing funds in landed property, so that they were practically forced into money-lending as the only occupation open to them. Since the church law against usury did not apply to the Jews, they became indispensible to the impoverished princes and monarchs, who squeezed the wealth amassed by Jewish money-lenders in a sponge-like manner during the owners' lifetime or after their death.

NISHMATH   נִשְׁמַת

THE well-known hymn *Nishmath*, recited as part of the *Shaharith* service on Sabbaths and festivals, belongs to the prayers that were composed in remote antiquity. A portion of this poem is quoted in the Talmud as part of a prayer for rain (Berakhoth 59b; Ta'anith 6b). The phrase "countless millions of favors" probably refers to the drops of rain, each drop being considered as a separate favor. The Talmud, indeed, suggests that thanks should be given for every drop of rain. *Nishmath* is identified in the Talmud (Pesaḥim 118a) with *birkath hashir*, recommended by the Mishnah for the closing of the *Haggadah* service on *Pesaḥ*. Many biblical phrases are interwoven in the texture of this beautiful hymn, which has been modified and expanded in the course of many centuries. The first paragraph was known in mishnaic times, the second was composed during the talmudic period, and the concluding part was added during the geonic period. *Nishmath* reads in part as follows:

"The soul of every living being shall bless thy name, Lord our God; the spirit of all mortals shall ever glorify and extol thy fame, our King. From eternity to eternity thou art God. Besides thee we have no king who redeems and saves, ransoms and rescues, sustains and shows mercy in all times of woe and stress. . ."

428

SAVRÉ MARANAN　　　　　　　　　　　　סָבְרִי מָרָנָן　ס

THE phrase סברי מרנן (attention, gentlemen) is inserted in the *Kid-dush* recited over wine on Sabbaths and festivals. It is designed to call attention to the benediction which is about to be pronounced over the wine, so that all who are present may answer Amen.

According to a midrashic source (Tanḥuma, *Pekudé*), this phrase was originally used in the form of a question, signifying: "Gentlemen, what is your opinion?" That is, is it safe to drink of this wine? The response was לחיים (for life and health). Eventually, the term *l'ḥay-yim* came into popular use as a toast over alcoholic beverages at a festive table. The response to the toast of *l'ḥayyim* comes in three words: לחיים טובים ולשלום (for a happy life of peace).

SIDDUR　　　　　　　　　　　　　　　סִדּוּר

THE arrangement of the traditional *Siddur* (Prayerbook) is practically the same in all editions, old and new. The three daily services (*Sha-ḥarith, Minḥah, Ma'ariv*) come first, then the Sabbath and festival services, followed by other liturgical compositions, such as Sabbath hymns. The *Ethics of the Fathers* (*Pirké Avoth*), to be recited on Sabbath afternoons, and the Song of Songs, chanted before the *Kabbalath Shabbath* service, are also included in the more complete editions. The daily Prayerbook contains, in addition, services pertaining to a variety of occasions: *Brith Milah, Pidyon ha-Ben*, marriage, and the like.

It has been said that no religion in the world can be thoroughly understood if its normal daily worship of God is left out of account, for here is where the real pulse-beat of every genuine religion is to be felt. This applies particularly to Judaism as reflected in the *Siddur*, which is the most popular book in Jewish life. If any single volume can tell us what it means to be a Jew, it is the daily Prayerbook, embodying the visions and aspirations, the sorrows and joys of many generations. The *Siddur* is a mirror that reflects the development of the Jewish spirit throughout the ages. The poetic and philosophic creations of numerous known and unknown authors constitute a considerable part of the Jewish prayerbook. Interwoven into the texture of the prayers are meaningful passages from the Bible, the Talmud, and the Zohar.

Passing through a long process of evolution, the *Siddur* has developed in a way that enables every worshiper to become familiar with the various forms of Jewish learning and religious expression. Its diversified authorship proclaims that all Israel has a share in its making. For nearly two thousand years, the Hebrew prayers have saved the Jews from losing their language and their identity. Israel's sages constantly emphasize the importance of uniformity in synagogue service, so as to link the people closely together and prevent them from forming separate religious factions. They have reconciled variant expressions of prescribed prayers and sought to bring them into harmonious union, so as to lessen the danger of rising sects that might weaken still more a harassed people.

Modifications of the contents of the *Siddur* have been urged by men opposing such features of the traditional prayers as the restoration of Israel, the concept of the chosen people, and the distinction between the people of Israel and the nations. Reiterating that no modern person could pray for all the restoration of sacrifices, they proceeded to eliminate with these prayers all petitions for the restoration of the Jewish homeland. The objection to sacrifices served as a cloak for eliminating the hope of a reestablishment of Israel in its ancestral home (Gordis).

Prayers in the vernacular, Gordis points out, have created a new and unexpected complication. Hebrew prayers chanted in the traditional manner can be repeated at almost every occasion without producing a sense of monotony in the worshiper. The collective chanting of the traditional congregants may not be very decorous, but it has virtue of being alive. The characteristic musical modes and scriptural cantillations, which differ with the varying occasions of the year, serve to create a distinct mood appropriate to the day and add variety and interest, even when the text remains the same. Responsive and unison readings in the vernacular are the cause of a marked monotony in the service.

It has been pointed out that Hebrew has always acted as a bond uniting the Jewish people throughout the world. The substitution of English for Hebrew in the synagogue services will never solve religious difficulties. Words of the earlier centuries may not always appear apt for minds of today, but the spirit behind them is the same; the retention of these old formulae and prayers has great value in preserving the long continuity of Jewish worship and tradition. We realize how absurd and impious it is for each of us to go off into his

430

separate nook and corner and there exercise his own private judgment. No man can evolve a satisfactory religion solely out of his own inner consciousness.

Rav Saadyah Gaon (882-942), who was one of the first compilers of a systematic prayerbook with instructions, wrote in his introduction: "I have decided to assemble in this book the authoritative prayers, hymns and benedictions, in their original form as they existed before the exile and after... I shall also mention what I have learned about additions or omissions according to the arbitrary opinions of individual groups residing in a village or city, a district or country... I have pointed out that they were unsupported by tradition" (*Siddur Rav Saadyah Gaon*, page 11). Trying to use his prayerbook as a means of unifying all the Jews, Rav Saadyah attempted to reduce local practices to a common denominator.

Renowned scholars are often quoted to the effect that at a time when all Jews prayed, one Prayerbook sufficed their needs; now when fewer Jews pray, more and more Prayerbooks are required. Modern editors of the *Siddur* must realize that they are dealing with a classic similar to the Bible and the Talmud, to which the terms orthodox, conservative or reform do not apply. They should not take liberties with the original, eliminating a phrase here and adding one there, each according to his own beliefs. Such a procedure is liable to breed as many different kinds of Jewish congregational worship as there are synagogues and temples. The ever-increasing modifications of the text of the *Siddur* are apt to destroy this unique source book of Judaism, which is designed to unify old and young, scholars and laymen, past and future.

It has been noted that you may modernize the Prayerbook as much as you please, you may remove all its anachronisms, its supplications for the restoration of the sacrificial rite, its petitions for Zion, its anthropomorphisms, but you will not thereby insure prayerful feeling. This only the worshiper himself can supply. Many a modern mind feels that some of the prayers in the traditional *Siddur* need reinterpretation, but this can be done without difficulty by each individual Jew. The words of the Prayerbook, used throughout by *Kelal Yisrael* and hallowed by generations as a means of uniting all the divergent elements of scattered Jewry, can still be retained by us with a modified interpretation and explained as expressing our age-long desire for restoration of a concerted form of worship in our ancient homeland. The traditional Jew is conscious of the fact that the language of the liturgy is not expected to be scientifically exact; he prefers to leave something to the imagination, since the function of religion is to appeal to the imagination. Many ethical concepts are to be found in talmudic-midrashic literature in connection with the Hebrew prayers.

SEDER   סֵדֶר לֵיל פֶּסַח

THE power of tradition is clearly demonstrated by the Passover *Seder* service in Jewish homes everywhere. Even the least observant Jews heed its ancient symbolism. The night commemorating the exodus from Egypt has become a history feast, uniting all the generations of the Jewish people. Hence, the sages of old aimed at unanimity and uniformity. It was a matter of principle with them that there should not be division in custom and observance. The national and religious significance of the *Seder* has been successfully preserved chiefly through the effective use of the indispensable *Seder Hagaddah shel Pesah*. The very name *Seder* (arrangement) is borrowed from the title of this famous book. It has stirred the spirit of freedom in the hearts of young and old across the centuries.

The recital of the traditional *Haggadah* is the most essential part of the *Seder* service. Primarily the narrative of Passover, the *Haggadah* tells the story of the entry into Egypt and of the liberation of the Israelites from their servitude. It explains the use of the paschal lamb during Temple times, the *matzoth*, the bitter herb (*maror*). After the hymns of thanksgiving, and the symbolical explanation of the numbers one to thirteen, the *Haggadah* ends with the song of divine retribution for the mistreatment of Israel (*Ḥad Gadya*). Heinrich Heine, describing the effect of the old, traditional chant, the tune that lulls and soothes and at the same time rouses and calls, concludes that even those Jews who long since turned from the faith of their fathers are touched when the well-remembered chants of *Pesaḥ* reach their ears.

The fifteen terms indicating the sequence of the *Seder* service are written in rhyme, devised as a mnemonic. Rabbi David Abudarham of the fourteenth century, famous for his rich commentary on Jewish liturgy, quotes a variety of mnemonic verses which he found in *Haggadah* manuscripts. The mnemonic verse in our printed editions (קדש ורחץ) has been attributed to Rashi, who lived in France during the eleventh century.

432

The number *four* is prominent throughout the *Seder* service: four questions, four sons, four cups of wine. The most quoted reason for the four cups of wine is that they symbolize the fourfold divine promise of liberation contained in Exodus 6:6-7 ("I will free you from the burdens of the Egyptians; I will deliver you from their bondage; I will redeem you; I will take you as my people"). The extra cup of wine, called Elijah's cup, which remains untouched during the *Seder* service, is said to convey the thought that Elijah, forerunner of the Messiah, will eventually decide whether a fifth cup is really needed for the *Seder*, a question that has not been solved by the talmudic authorities. Commonly, Elijah's cup is regarded, symbolically, as the glass of wine ready for any stranger who may seek hospitality.

The curious practice of spilling drops of wine when the ten Egyptian plagues are enumerated stresses the thought that we must not rejoice over the misfortunes that befell our foes and made the cup of our deliverance incomplete. This is in keeping with the following talmudic tradition: When the Egyptians were drowning in the Red Sea, God restrained the angels from singing his praise, saying: "How can you sing while my creatures are drowning in the sea?" (Megillah 10b). It all goes back to the biblical warning which says: "Do not rejoice when your enemy falls; do not exult when he is overthrown, lest the Lord see it and be displeased. . ." (Proverbs 24:17-18).

Since the order of the ten plagues mentioned in Psalms 78 and 105 differs from the order of the plagues detailed in Exodus 7:8-12:30, the tannaitic sage Rabbi Judah of the second century suggested a mnemonic, דצ״ך עד״ש באח״ב, a combination of the initial letters of the ten plagues, assisting the memory of their proper sequence. The Midrash quotes Rabbi Judah to the effect that the same *notarikon* was engraved on the staff of Moses which was used as an instrument for inflicting the plagues (Exodus Rabbah 6:7; 8:3).

The *matzah*, which is most essential in the *Seder* service, is rich in ethical symbolism. It is a reminder of the joyous eagerness which marked the departure from slavery into freedom; it also suggests purity of heart, since leaven is a symbol of decay. In the Zohar, *matzah* is called celestial bread (נהמא עילאה) in the sense that it served as an antidote to Egyptian bondage and corruption.

In order to indicate that the *Seder* night is twice mentioned in the Torah as a *night of vigil* (ליל שמורים), the door is opened toward the end of the service as a symbol of divine protection against all harmful forces. The opening of the door also symbolizes the awaited ap-

433

pearance of Elijah as the forerunner of the Messiah, according to the
view held that the messianic era will begin during the Passover season (בניסן נגאלו ובניסן עתידין להגאל). Past memories and future aspirations thus blend into a serene harmony through the *Seder* service, which
begins with the invitation extended to the poor to share the food,
and ends with: *Next year in Jerusalem* (לשנה הבאה בירושלים).

SEDER AVODAH   סֵדֶר עֲבוֹדָה

T<small>HROUGHOUT</small> the ages, the part of the *Yom Kippur* service known as
the *Avodah* (divine service) has been regarded as the full expression
of Israel's longing for freedom and restoration. Many medieval liturgical poets (*payyetanim*) composed *Avodahs*, some of which were embodied in various *Maḥzor* editions.

In the current *Maḥzorim*, both *Ashkenazic* and *Sephardic*, respectively, the poet begins with a cursory review of the biblical history from
the time of creation down to the time of Aaron the priest. Then he
minutely describes the procedure of the Temple service conducted by
the high priest on *Yom Kippur*. Utilizing the account given in Mishnah Yoma, he relates about the preparation of the high priest, the
appointment of a substitute to meet the emergency of the high priest's
becoming disqualified, the various offerings, the baths and ablutions
of the high priest and his changes of garments.

In the *Nusaḥ Ashkenaz*, the *Avodah*, beginning with the words
אמיץ כח, is one of the most intricate *piyyutim* by Rabbi Meshullam
ben Kalonymus of tenth-century Italy. In the *Nusaḥ Sephard*, the
Avodah, beginning with the words אתה כוננת, was written by an
anonymous author in a flowing, easy-to-understand Hebrew.

SIDRAH, PARASHAH   סִדְרָה, פָּרָשָׁה

T<small>HE</small> Torah is divided into fifty-four sections, which are read in the
synagogue on Sabbath mornings consecutively, so that in the course
of each year the public reading of the entire Pentateuch is completed.
The section of the week, referred to as *sidrah* (order), is often called
parashah, denoting a biblical passage dealing with a single topic.

Though *sidrah* and *parashah* are used interchangeably, each *sidrah* nevertheless consists of seven *parashiyyoth*, one for each of the

434

seven men who are called up to the reading of the Torah at the congregational service of every Saturday morning.

The term *parashah* is also used in the sense of *paragraph*, described as open or closed (פתוחה, סתומה). In the *Sefer Torah*, a *parashah* is open (*pethuḥah*) if it is begun on a new line; a *parashah* is closed (*sethumah*) if it does not begin a new line. In the printed texts of the Torah, the Hebrew letters פ and ס, for פתוחה and סתומה, indicate the traditional manner in which a given *parashah* is written in the *Sefer Torah*. A triple פ, or a triple ס, indicates the paragraph with which a new weekly section (*sidrah*) is begun.

Out of every nineteen-year cycle in the Jewish calendar there are seven leap years, consisting of thirteen months instead of twelve. For this reason, the number of *sidrahs* varies from fifty to fifty-four. Furthermore, some of the Sabbaths during the year coincide with festivals that require special Torah readings in place of the regular weekly portion, so that the ordinary Sabbaths total between fifty-two and forty-seven per year. Hence, the arrangement of the *sidroth* is made conveniently elastic by having some of them double up on occasion. The number of *sidrahs* in the five books of the Torah is as follows: Genesis, 12; Exodus, 11; Leviticus 10; Numbers 10; Deuteronomy 11. Total: fifty-four.

SCRIPTURES   סוֹפְרִים

SCRIBES   סוֹפְרִים

THE term *Sofrim*, derived from *sefer* (book), is employed in talmudic literature as the title of the great authorities on the interpretation of the biblical text, who functioned during and after the Persian period in Jewish history. Their organization began with Ezra the Scribe and terminated with Simeon the Just, who was one of the last survivors of the Great Assembly (Avoth 1:2).

The activity of the *Sofrim* began as a continuation of prophecy which ended with Malachi, of whom nothing is known except his utterances in the last book of the Prophets. The *Sofrim*, or sages, who preceded the later Tannaim and Amoraim of talmudic-midrashic literature, were the first to establish the vast system of Jewish traditional lore.

It has been suggested that originally the Hebrew word *sofer* signified a learned man, knowing how to read and write; as the art of writing was known only to the intelligent, the term *sofer* was used in the sense of scribe and sage interchangeably. The phrase דברי סופרים is often used in the Talmud, where the reference is to the traditional law as transmitted by the Jewish sages (חכמים).

SIYYUM   סִיּוּם

THE completion of the writing of a *Sefer Torah* is celebrated as *Siyyum ha-Sefer;* likewise, when the study of a talmudic tractate is completed, or one of the six divisions of the Mishnah, it is regarded as a joyous occasion. When the whole Talmud has been studied from beginning to end, the attending conclusion ceremony is referred to as *Siyyum ha-Gadol.* We are told that Abbayé (273-339), the famous Babylonian *Amora* who was the head of the Academy in Pumbeditha, was accustomed to make a feast whenever one of his students concluded the study of a tractate (Shabbath 118b).

The concluding *Hadran* (may we return), which is a brief prayer against forgetfulness and a kind of tender farewell to the tractate completed, is recited in Aramaic. This is followed by a discourse on the logical relation between the last statement of the volume ended and the first statement of the volume next in order. Being a festive occasion, the *Siyyum,* generally held on the morning preceding the first day of Passover, exempts the firstborn from their traditional fasting (תענית בכורים) that day.

As a rule, every talmudic tractate ends with a joyous expression. This is in keeping with the rule that all readings must be concluded with something cheerful. Compare the books of Lamentations and Ecclesiastes, Isaiah and Malachi, where more cheerful sentences are repeated at the end. For the same reason, the psalm of the day which is recited on Wednesdays (Psalm 94) ends with "Come, let us sing to the Lord. . ." (לכו נרננה), the first three verses of Psalm 95.

SIVAN   סִיוָן

THE month of *Sivan,* consisting of thirty days, coincides approximately with the month of June. The three days' preparation (שלשת ימי הגבלה) preceding the receiving of the Torah on Mount Sinai (Exodus 19:15) is commemorated on the third, fourth and fifth days of the month of *Sivan.*

436

These days, together with *Lag b'Omer* and *Rosh Ḥodesh*, are distinguished from other days of the *Sefirah* period in that marriages are permissible on them by reason of their festive aspect. On the sixth and seventh days of *Sivan*, the festival of *Shavuoth* is celebrated, commemorating the giving of the Torah (*Mattan Torah*).

SUKKOTH   סֻכּוֹת

THE autumn festival of *Sukkoth*, commemorating the protection afforded the Israelites throughout their wanderings in the wilderness, is described in the Torah as the feast of ingathering at the end of the agricultural year (Exodus 23:16). Concerning the manner of celebrating the seven days of *Sukkoth*, which begins on the fifteenth of the month *Tishri*, we read: "You shall dwell in booths seven days ... that your generations may know that I made the Israelites dwell in booths. . ." (Leviticus 23:42-43).

The eighth day of *Sukkoth*, called *Atzereth* (closing day of the festival season), is regarded as a separate holyday, characterized by the special prayer for rain (*Geshem*), by *Yizkor* services in memory of the departed, and by the recital of the book of Ecclesiastes which contains reflections on the purpose of life and man's ceaseless strivings.

According to Maimonides, the moral lesson derived from the festival of *Sukkoth* is that man ought to remember his bad times in his days of prosperity; he will thereby be induced to lead a modest life. Hence, we leave our elegant homes to dwell in booths that are reminiscent of desert life lacking in all convenience and comfort. On the other hand, *Sukkoth* is kept in the autumn season when the produce has been gathered in from the fields and the farmers are free from pressing labor, when there is neither great heat nor troublesome rain and it is possible to dwell in booths, even though they are hastily constructed and unsubstantial.

The four species, of which the *lulav* (palm branch) is the most prominent, are a symbolical expression of our rejoicing over the change from life in the wilderness to life in a country replete with fruit-trees and rivers. These particular four species (*lulav, ethrog, hadassim, aravoth*) were plentiful in Eretz Yisrael, and were easily obtainable by everybody. Besides, they have a good appearance; two of them, the citron (*ethrog*) and the myrtle (*hadas*), diffuse excellent fragrance; they keep fresh and green for seven days. . . (*Guide*, 3:43).

437

The frail *sukkah*, which must not exceed the height of twenty cubits (thirty feet), is said to convey the idea that man should never be haughty. The walls of the *sukkah* must be sufficiently strong to withstand ordinary gusts of wind. The shade, which is the root-meaning of the word *sukkah*, must exceed the rays of the sun. This signifies that man is to be steadfast in his beliefs and humble in his behavior. The stars must be visible through the roof-covering (סכך) of twigs and leaves as a constant reminder that all blessings reach us from our heavenly Father. The four species symbolize the four types of people who, though different in character, must live in unity and mutual understanding in order to form a happier human society.

The first and second, eighth and ninth days of *Sukkoth* are full holydays; the five middle days of the festival, including *Hoshana Rabbah*, are semi-festivals called *Ḥol ha-Mo'ed*. The eighth day, called *Shemini Atzereth*, is regarded as a separate festival and explained in Talmud and Midrash, as follows: "A king invited his children to a feast. After a few days, when the departure finally arrived, the king said to his children: I beg of you, stay another day; it is hard to separate from you" (Rashi on Leviticus 23:36).

The joyful note characterizing the seven days of *Sukkoth*, which are in the liturgy denominated זמן שמחתנו (our festival of rejoicing), is extended to *Shemini Atzereth*, coinciding with the *Simḥath Torah* festival in Eretz Yisrael. In the Diaspora, however, *Simḥath Torah* is celebrated on the ninth day.

The name *Simḥath Torah* was not known in talmudic times. It came into use presumably around the ninth century in Babylonia, where the one-year cycle for the reading of the Five Books of Moses prevailed. The seven processions with the Torah-scrolls on *Simḥath Torah* (*Hakkafoth*) became customary in the sixteenth century.

SELAH סֶלָה

THE untranslatable term *selah*, which occurs seventy-one times in the book of Psalms and three times in the book of Habakkuk (3:3, 9, 13), is universally interpreted to be a musical or liturgical sign, though its exact meaning has not been ascertained. In Psalm 68:5, the word סלו is used synonymously with שירו and זמרו in the sense of "extol, exalt." Hence, it is safe to assume that *selah* is a direction to the singers to raise their voices before certain pauses; or to the musicians, to protract the tone of the instrumental accompaniment at the moment that the vocal part fades into silence.

Some have taken *selah* as an abbreviation (סימן לשנות הקול), meaning: *sign to change the voice;* or סב למעלה השר (*go back to the beginning, O singer*). The Septuagint renders *selah* by *diapsalma,* implying the intervention by musical instruments at a particular place. Accordingly, it may be a direction to the orchestra; the instruments would be heard with full effect after the cessation of the voices of the singers. In the writings of medieval Hebrew poets, סלה often denotes *forever.* In translating medieval Hebrew texts, *selah* should be rendered *forever,* as the authors understood the term to be when they used it.

SELIḤOTH   סְלִיחוֹת

THE penitential prayers (*seliḥoth*) belong, in part, to the age of the Talmud. Essentially based upon biblical poetry, they are a continuation of the Psalms. The suffering of Israel in the various lands of the dispersion is their principal theme. For about fifteen centuries the liturgical poets continued to enrich the *seliḥah* literature, the earliest examples of which go back to the first century.

Tormented by merciless persecutions, the authors of these prayer-poems described the misery of their people with the blood of their hearts. The recital of the heroic deeds described in the *seliḥoth* helped, consciously or unconsciously, strengthen the solidarity of the Jewish community the world over. Hence, many penitential poems were incorporated into the liturgy to be recited on such special occasions as *Tish'ah b'Av* and the days preceding *Rosh Hashanah.*

The *seliḥoth* reveal the saintly character of past generations, who in profound humility sought the reason of their misfortune in themselves rather than in a divine injustice. The *seliḥah* (forgiveness) is a prayer for pardon in the strict sense of the term, for it gives utterance to the feelings of the worshiper who repents and pleads for mercy.

It is customary to begin the recital of *seliḥoth* on Saturday midnight, four days before *Rosh Hashanah.* If, however, the first day of *Rosh Hashanah* occurs on Monday or Tuesday, so that four days are not left in which to recite the penitential prayers, it is customary to begin a week earlier. The idea of a midnight service is based on Psalm 119:62 ("At midnight I rise to praise thee").

The elegies and supplications contained in the *Taḥanun* for Mondays and Thursdays, known as the long *Taḥanun*, likewise belong to the *seliḥah* literature.

ORDINATION   סְמִיכָה

THE Torah tells us how Moses symbolically transferred his authority to Joshua, his successor, by placing his hands (*semikhah*) on him in the presence of the whole community and investing him with some of his own dignity (Numbers 27:18-23). The custom of *semikhah*, whereby the ancient sages conferred on their disciples the title *Rabbi* (רבי) or *Rav* (רב), thus permitting them to give decisions in matters of civil and religious law, was practised in the manner described in the Torah: the master, in the presence of two other teachers, transferred his authority to his disciple who was to be the future teacher by placing his hands on him.

The principle prevailed that "everyone ordained may ordain." The title *Rabbi* was conferred in Eretz Yisrael; in Babylonia, however, the title *Rav* only could be conferred, so that the recipient was restricted to give decisions in certain specified categories of the law.

In our times, when ordination in the ancient sense no longer exists, the certificate of admission to the rabbinate is termed *hetter hora'ah*, or *semikhah* in a figurative sense; it is issued, following a thorough examination in the field of *halakhah*, by an outstanding authority in Talmud and *Poskim* (law codes). The Hebrew phrases יורה יורה, ידין ידין are essential in such a certificate. *Yoreh yoreh, yadin yadin* are here employed in the sense that the candidate may surely give a decision, may surely pronounce judgment. American and European seminaries grant rabbinical diplomas to students who are trained for the rabbinate and its present functions.

SANDEK   סַנְדָק

THE term *sandek* has been identified with the Greek word *synteknos*, denoting "with the child." The *sandek*, whose privilege it is to hold the infant boy on his knees in the course of the circumcision operation, is likewise synonymous with the German Gottvater, abridged to *G'vater* and *Kwater*, widely in use where Yiddish is spoken. The title

440

Kwater is conferred nowadays upon the person handing the infant to the *mohel*, who performs the circumcision.

Holding the child while the operation is performed is regarded as a great *mitzvah* and honor. Next to the chair upon which the *sandek* is seated, the special chair reserved for Elijah (כסא של אליהו) is placed.

Referred to as "angel of the covenant" and protector of children, Elijah is said to be the invisible participant at circumcisions. His chair is left in position for three days, because the first three days after the operation are a dangerous period for the child.

SANHEDRIN

THE Greek name *Sanhedrin*, signifying the higher courts of law which administered justice in Eretz Yisrael during the period of the Second Temple, denotes two kinds of councils of ordained scholars: 1) *Sanhedrin Gedolah*, consisting of seventy-one members, whose function as a legislative body was to interpret the biblical laws and to enact new laws (*halakhoth*); it was presided over by a president (*Nasi*) and a vice-president, called father of the court of justice (*Av-beth-din*); it had jurisdiction over all religious matters. It met in Jerusalem daily, except on Sabbaths and festivals, from morning until mid-afternoon. 2) *Sanhedrin Ketannah* (lesser council), consisting of twenty-three members, who had jurisdiction over civil and criminal cases in various parts of Eretz Yisrael.

Solomon Zeitlin and others contend that there were two parallel bodies of seventy-one, one for political affairs and one for religious matters, the Great Sanhedrin (*Beth Din ha-Gadol*) never tried capital cases, since it was a legislative body only. All capital cases were tried by the Lesser Sanhedrin in Eretz Yisrael. The political Sanhedrin directed public affairs and administered the criminal law under the control of the Roman procurator, while the religious Sanhedrin regulated and supervised the religious life of the people. Commonly described, the Great Sanhedrin was the Supreme Court of Appeal on all disputed points of law or religious practice.

In addition to the president and vice-president, there was the *Mufla*, the distinguished expert adviser. The personnel of the Sanhedrin varied in different periods. During the Maccabean period, Sadducean or Pharisaic elements predominated according to the disposition of the ruling authorities. The learned members of the Sanhedrin sat in

441

a semicircle with the accused in front of them; they were observed by three rows of disciples who might be candidates for the council.

According to talmudic tradition, only those were appointed to the Sanhedrin who had stature, wisdom, good appearance, maturity, familiarity with languages. . . (Sanhedrin 17a). The Mishnah mentions divergent views among the Tannaim of the second century with regard to capital punishment: "A Sanhedrin that effects one execution in seven years is branded a destructive court. Rabbi Elazar ben Azaryah says: one in seventy years. Rabbi Tarfon and Rabbi Akiva say: Had we been members of a Sanhedrin, no one would ever have been put to death. Rabban Simeon ben Gamaliel says: They would have multiplied murderers in Israel" (Makkoth 1:10).

During the sixteenth century, an attempt was made to revive the Sanhedrin in the land of Israel. A fresh demand for a Sanhedrin has been growing ever since the establishment of the new State of Israel in 1948. Napoleon, in 1806, brought about a curious revival of a Sanhedrin when he convened an assembly of Jewish notables for purposes of Jewish legislation. The seventy-one members of the Napoleonic Sanhedrin consisted of forty-five rabbis and twenty-six laymen.

SEFIRAH   סְפִירָה

THE counting of seven weeks from the sixteenth day of *Nisan*, on which the *omer* offering of the new barley crop was brought to the Temple, until *Shavuoth*, serves to connect the anniversary of the exodus from Egypt with the festival that commemorates the giving of the Torah on Mount Sinai. In talmudic literature the festival of *Shavuoth* is invariably termed *Atzereth*, because it is regarded as the conclusion of the Passover celebration.

Tradition has it that it was announced to the Israelites in Egypt that fifty days after the exodus the Torah would be given to them. As soon as they were liberated, they were so eager for the arrival of the promised day that they began to count the days, saying each time: "Now we have one day less to wait for the giving of the Torah."

Hence, it is explained, the Torah prescribes that the days from *Pesaḥ* to *Shavuoth* are to be counted; the counting symbolizes and commemorates the eagerness with which the Torah was received by Israel. In a similar vein, Maimonides points out that the counting of the *omer* (*sefirath ha-omer*), between the anniversary of the liberation from

442

Egypt and the anniversary of the Torah gift, is suggestive of one who expects his most intimate friend on a certain day: he counts the days and even the hours.

The *Sefirah* period between the two spring festivals, *Pesaḥ* and *Shavuoth*, has long been observed through certain restraints, because most massacres recorded in Jewish history took place in the spring months, beginning with the martyrdom of Rabbi Akiva and his disciples and continuing through the three Crusades (1096-1192).

With the exception of *Lag b'Omer*, the thirty-third day of the *Sefirah*, the period is dedicated to national mourning in order to perpetuate the memory of the great martyrs, who might serve as an inspiration for many generations. Jewish martyrology became an enormous source of strength and means of preservation of the Jewish people.

SEFER HA-ḤINNUKH   סֵפֶר הַחִנּוּךְ:

THE famous medieval classical work *Sefer ha-Ḥinnukh* (Book of Education) was designed by its anonymous author to present in simple form the principles of Judaism by means of an analysis of the six hundred and thirteen divine precepts (*mitzvoth*), arranged in the order of the weekly *sidroth* of Torah readings. In his profound humility, the author concealed his identity and, in the introduction to this important work, referred to himself as the least in his family, a Jew of Barcelona (ברצלוני ... איש יהודי מבית לוי ... הדל באלפי). In the edition which appeared in 1523, however, his name אהרן is given on the frontpage of the *Sefer ha-Ḥinnukh*. It is now generally held that the *Sefer ha-Ḥinnukh* was composed by the illustrious Talmudist Rabbi Aaron ha-Levi of Barcelona, Spain, at the end of the thirteenth century. He deals with the halakhic and ethical aspects of the *mitzvoth*, and quotes Alfasi, Maimonides and Naḥmanides as his outstanding authorities.

Concerning the prohibition in Deuteronomy 25:4 ("You shall not muzzle an ox when treading out grain"), we read in the *Sefer ha-Ḥinnukh:* "It is the duty of man to accustom himself to show kindness, compassion, and consideration to his fellow creatures. When we therefore treat considerately even the animals given for our use, and do not withdraw from them some of the fruits of what their labor obtains for us, we educate ourselves thereby to be all the kinder to our fellow men, accustoming ourselves not to withhold from them

443

what is their due, but to allow them to enjoy with us the result of their contribution."

Deep religious sentiment is attached to *sefirath ha-omer*, the counting of the *omer* during the seven-week period between *Pesaḥ* and *Shavuoth*. It is intended, we are told, to induce us to meditate on the real and deeper meaning of the two festivals. Israel's liberation from Egypt was only the beginning of true freedom for the people; its full measure was not attained until the event of *Mattan Torah*, the giving of the Torah at Sinai, which is commemorated by the festivities of *Shavuoth*. Hence, the genuine Jew is called upon to count the very days intervening between *Pesaḥ* that produced physical freedom and *Shavuoth* that perfected it by the addition of spiritual liberty.

The *Minḥath Ḥinnukh*, by Rabbi Joseph ben Moses of Tarnopol, is a very extensive and learned commentary on the *Sefer ha-Ḥinnukh*.

BOOK OF JUBILEES סֵפֶר הַיּוּבְלוֹת

THE Book of Jubilees is a midrashic commentary and amplification on Genesis and part of Exodus. It contains views and religious practices of a sect that sprang up in Judea during the second century before the common era. A fragment of this book in Hebrew was discovered among the Dead Sea Scrolls. The title of this pseudepigraphical work is attributable to its chronological system, in which all events from the creation to the exodus from Egypt are dated by jubilee periods of forty-nine years, subdivided by sevens. The anonymous author proposes a solar calendar of three hundred and sixty-four days, or fifty-two weeks, divided into four quarters of thirteen weeks each. There would be eight months of thirty days each and four of thirty-one days, or else twelve months of thirty days, and an unnumbered day at the beginning of each season.

Following this system, the 365th day of the solar year would not be counted immediately, but would be retained for a period of forty-nine years, the fiftieth being the year of jubilee. The forty-nine days, or seven weeks, left uncounted in the course of forty-nine years, would then be inserted in the calendar, so that the succession of weeks would remain intact and the Sabbath would not be disturbed; nor would the seasonal calendar be obliterated.

According to the Book of Jubilees, the festival of *Shavuoth* comes on the fifteenth day of *Sivan*, in the middle of the month, as in the case

444

of the other two pilgrim festivals, *Pesah* and *Sukkoth*. It claims to be a divine revelation made to Moses at Mount Sinai, a secret tradition entrusted to the saints of each generation, in addition to the written Torah which must be imparted to all. Much of the legendary embellishment presented in the Book of Jubilees must have been drawn from a common source of *Aggadah;* it sometimes follows the biblical narrative closely, and occasionally deviates from it freely, as when we are told that *Shavuoth* was observed by Noah in commemoration of the eternal divine covenant that the world should not be flooded again, or that *Sukkoth* was first kept by Abraham for seven days.

The Book of Jubilees has been preserved as a whole only in Ethiopic, and about one-third of the book is in Latin. Both were translated from the Greek version, which in turn had been prepared from a Hebrew original. The Ethiopic version was discovered in Abyssinia about the middle of the nineteenth century.

SEFER ḤASIDIM   

THE *Sefer Ḥasidim* (Book of the Saintly) by Rabbi Yehudah he-Ḥasid of Regensburg, who died in 1217, is not a uniform book nor is it the product of one author. It is a compilation of ethical principles and precepts based chiefly on the writings of Rabbi Yehudah he-Ḥasid, who was a philosopher and poet, scholar and mystic. The thoughts of his disciple, Rabbi Elazar Rokeah of Worms, and the ideas of his father, Rabbi Samuel, are well represented in the *Sefer Ḥasidim*. It contains a rich variety of teachings on the virtues that constitute a Jewish saintly life. Following are several examples:

"Never shrink from declaring that you are a Jew. Do not purposely mislead anyone, Jew or non-Jew. In your business dealings, do not say that a certain price has been offered for your merchandise if that is not true. Do not wear an amulet as a charm against evil, but put your implicit trust in God alone. Accept nothing from others if you can support yourself with the little you have.

"It is better to spend money on poor people than to lavish funds on useless trifles and idle luxuries. Ingratitude is the rankest evil, even with regard to dumb animals. Anyone who loads excessive burdens on a draft beast, or plunges his spurs too deeply into a horse's flanks, should be punished. A sick animal is to be treated with tenderness. Call the attention of a non-Jew to an error that he has made in over-

445

paying you, for it is better that you live on charity than that you disgrace the Jewish name by cheating.

"Do not listen to slander; instead, try to restrain the person who bitterly complains about the misdeeds of another. Be intimate with an uneducated man who has a generous soul rather than with a scholar who is closefisted. Expel all envy and hatred from your heart.

"If a man has two sons, one of whom is averse to lending his books while the other does so willingly, he should have no hesitation in leaving his entire library to the second son, even though he is the younger. . . If a man is in reduced circumstances and forced to sell his property, he should disperse first of his gold and jewelry and houses and estates, and only at the very end, when no alternative is left, he should divest himself of his library. . . When a man is travelling on business and finds books that are unknown in his own city, it is his duty to purchase them in preference to anything else and bring them back with him, so that he may cause the diffusion of knowledge."

SEFER YOSIPPON   סֵפֶר יוֹסִיפוֹן

THE most popular history book current among the Jews in the Middle Ages was the book of *Yosippon*, an abridgment of Josephus' history of the Jewish people from the time of their return from Babylonia to the downfall of the Jewish state in the year 70. Though the medieval rabbis believed it to be the original work of Josephus Flavius (first century), Leopold Zunz advanced the theory that the so-called Pseudo-Josephus or *Yosippon* was compiled in the tenth century.

Yosippon, written in pure Hebrew, dates from the third or fourth century. Because of its great popularity, it was frequently recopied by a variety of scribes who inserted interpolations in the text. Every scribe thought it proper to add stories, phrases, local legends, and ideas in vogue at the time, and these very additions increased the popularity of the book, read by scholars and populace alike. Aside from the Bible, it was without rival in Hebrew literature as a narrative book unfolding a great dramatic theme in free, transparent Hebrew, easily understood by the people. The universal demand for the book caused it to pass through the hands of numerous scribes who were not always noted for meticulous accuracy in transcription. Scribes in ancient and medieval times were frequently more than literal copyists. They were often men endowed with knowledge and

446

imagination and would, on occasion, embellish the text with their own comments.

Yosippon was made available in Arabic, Latin, Slavonic, Ethiopic, German, and English. A complete English translation of the book appeared in 1688. *Yosippon* has the Greek ending *on* to the Hebrew name Joseph. This may point to an early date when the Jews still used Greek as their vernacular. The book concentrates especially on the history of the Hasmonean dynasty, the Jewish war against Rome, and the siege of Jerusalem.

SEFER ROKEAH

T H E *Book of Rokeah* (ספר הרוקח) is an ethical work by Rabbi Elazar of Worms, who died in 1238. In 1196, two crusaders entered his house and killed his wife, his two daughters, and his son. Nevertheless, his writings are permeated with spiritual joy soaring above personal disaster. The best known of his works on *halakhic* as well as mystical subjects is *Sefer ha-Rokeah*. The title of the book is explained by the author to the effect that the numerical value of the word רקח (308) is identical with that of his name אלעזר. Rendered into English, the title is *Book of the Perfumer*. Among the things emphasized in the book are the following precepts:

No monument bestows as much glory as an unsullied name. The highest wisdom is found in the Torah. Modesty is the noblest ornament. To forgive is the most beautiful thing a man can do. Do not inquire too much concerning your Creator. Do not seek to know the origin of things. Instead, see that God is never far from your thoughts. Do not let your sensuous nature control your life. Do nothing of which you are likely to be ashamed. Make peace among people whenever you can. If you are poor, be thankful for the air you breathe; if you are rich, do not exalt yourself above your poor brother. Guard yourself against the assaults of envy, which kills sooner than any fatal disease. A contrite heart is the highest sacrifice. A person who is always aware of the presence of his Creator talks gently to everyone and teaches his children to lead a worthy life. He infuses love and kindness into all his actions, and reveres his wife. He loves his neighbors and friends; he lends to the needy and gives charity in secret. Let no oath pass your lips. Never speak meaningless words. Do not be too eager for money. Do not crave honor and glory.

447

SEFER TORAH סֵפֶר תּוֹרָה

THE *Sefer Torah*, containing the Five Books of Moses written on a scroll of parchment, specially prepared to render it durable, is kept in the holy ark (*aron ha-kodesh*) of the synagogue as the most sacred object in the religious life of the Jew. The parchment is of a clean animal (בהמה טהורה); it is composed of separate parts sewn together with threads of sinew. The text is copied by a professional devout scribe (*sofer*), who uses only the best black ink and a quill-pen.

A sheet of parchment (*yeri'ah*) must contain no less than three and no more than eight columns of writing. On the average, the size of a Torah scroll is seventeen inches, numerically equaling טוב (good). Every line is long enough to contain thirty letters. If too long, the lines would involve the shifting of the body when reading from beginning to end.

In the *Sefer Torah* described by Maimonides each column measured four fingers (four inches) in width, and consisted of fifty-one lines. The total number of columns was 266 (*Yad, Sefer Torah* 9:10).

Maimonides informs us concerning the three kinds of parchment designed for the writing of a *Sefer Torah, Tefillin* and *Mezuzoth*, respectively, and he states: "It is a rule dating back to Moses, who received it from Sinai (הלכה למשה מסיני), that a *Sefer Torah* should be written on *gevil* (whole parchment) and the writing should be on the side which was next to the hair of the original hide. The *Tefillin* should be written on *kelaf* (the exterior part of a split hide) and the writing should be on the side which was next to the flesh of the animal. The *Mezuzah* should be written on *dukhsustus* (the inner part of the split hide), on the side nearer the hair" (*Yad, Tefillin* 1:6-8).

The scribe must not write even a single word from memory; he must pronounce every word before copying it from a correct text. Every letter must have space around it and must be so formed that an ordinary schoolchild can distinguish it from similar letters. If the scroll contains vowels or accents it is, like any printed text, unfit for congregational reading in the synagogue.

Decorative crownlets (*taggin*) are added to the tops of thirteen letters, seven of which require three crown strokes each (שעטנז גץ) and six (בדק חיה) one *tag* on the left. The *taggin* are referred to as tittles. The nine letters of the alphabet that are left without any of these crownlets compose the phrase מלאכת סופר.

448

Tradition has it that the *taggin* appeared on the twelve stones that Joshua set up in the Jordan and in Gilgal (Joshua 4:9, 20). Mention is made of a special ancient manual, known as *Sefer ha-Taggin*. Their significance is veiled in kabbalistic mysticism. It has been suggested, however, that they are scribal flourishes designed to ornament the text of the Torah with so many crownlets.

The skilled *sofer* (scribe) is expected to be clean of hand and thought and filled with reverence for the Torah and its contents. He is required to prepare himself by silent meditation whenever he is about to perform his holy work. As a rule, he is careful to begin all columns of the *Sefer Torah* with the letter *vav* (ו), except, of course, the first column which begins with the word *bereshith* (in the beginning). Carefully executed Torah texts, therefore, are referred to as וֵוֵי הָעַמּוּדִים (the *vav* columns). *Vav* (ו) is the most frequent letter in the Bible.

During the thirteenth century, however, the great talmudic authority Rabbi Meir (*Maharam*) of Rothenburg strongly disapproved of the *vav* columns and even sought to forbid them. He wrote: מַה שֶּׁנָּהֲגוּ סוֹפְרִים בּוֹרִים לְהַתְחִיל כָּל עַמּוּד בְּוָי"ו . . . נִרְאָה שֶׁאִסּוּר גָּמוּר יֵשׁ בַּדָּבָר . . . (See Kahana's edition of *Maharam's Responsa*, II, 150; קֶסֶת סוֹפֵר by Rabbi Solomon Ganzfried, 9:8). Nevertheless, to this day the scribes have adhered to what has become an established custom in copying the Torah text.

The poetic verses of *shirath ha-yam* (Exodus 15:1-18) are metrically arranged in thirty lines, like bricks in a wall (Shabbath 103b). The poetic verses of the section *Ha'azinu* (Deuteronomy 32:1-43) are placed in seventy double rows.

The Torah is divided into open and closed sections, *pethuḥoth* and *sethumoth*. The open section begins a new line; the closed section either begins on the last line of the previous section after an intervening space of nine letters, or on the next line sufficiently indented by a nine-letter space. In the printed texts, the *pethuḥoth* and *sethumoth* are indicated by the initials פ and ס.

The Torah scroll is attached to two wooden rollers, each of which is called *etz ḥayyim* (tree of life). The *kether Torah* or Torah crown, made of silver and adorned with little bells, is placed over the upper ends of the *etz ḥayyim* rollers. A mantle, shaped to slip over the Torah when it is rolled up, is made of embroidered silk or satin for the protection of the scroll from dust or harm. A silver breastplate (*ḥoshen*), variously decorated, is suspended by a chain from the top of the *etz ḥayyim* rollers, as is the silver pointer (*yad*), intended for the guidance of the Torah reader. The *rimmonim* (pomegranates), silver ornament, are likewise placed over the *atzé ḥayyim* as headpieces. Reminiscent of the curtain before the *ark of the covenant* (ארון הברית) is the richly embroidered *parokheth* (פרוכת), made of velvet or satin, in front of the *aron ha-kodesh*, the receptacle containing the Torah scrolls.

SIFRA, SIFRÉ   סִפְרָא, סִפְרֵי

THE tannaitic Midrash on Leviticus, known as *Sifra*, was originally referred to as *Sifra d'vé Rav* (the book of the school). The same applies to the tannaitic Midrash on the books of Numbers and Deuteronomy, known as *Sifré*, abridged from the full title *Sifré d'vé Rav* (the books of the school). Originally, this was the comprehensive designation of the tannaitic Midrashim to the books of Exodus, Leviticus, Numbers, and Deuteronomy, all of which contain the laws of the Torah. In the course of time, the midrashic expositions of the laws in Exodus and Leviticus formed separate books called *Mekhilta* and *Sifra*, respectively, so that the title *Sifré* was left for the remaining two books of Numbers and Deuteronomy.

The *Sifra* is a continuous legal commentary on Leviticus, following the biblical text almost clause by clause. It deals with many of the laws which regulate the religious life of the individual and the family, and with basic ethical precepts. The *Sifra* is regarded as one of the most valuable sources for the Jewish religion of the tannaitic period. The idea of the holiness of the people, in imitation of the divine holiness, finds its full expression in this Midrash Halakhah on Leviticus.

450

SERVANT OF GOD

 עֶבֶד הַשֵּׁם

VARIOUS biblical personalities were given the title *eved ha-shem*, servant of God. Abraham, Isaac, Jacob, Moses, Joshua, David, the prophets, were referred to as servants of God. The same epithet is applied to the entire people of Israel in many prophetical passages (Ezekiel 28:25; 37:25; Jeremiah 30:10; 46:27; Isaiah 41:8; 42:19; 43:10; 44:1; 45:4; 48:20). The destiny and duty of Israel are indicated in this designation. In Isaiah 41:8, Israel is addressed: "Israel my servant . . . whom I have chosen." In the prophetic vision, Israel is destined to teach the divine truth to the nations: "Here is my servant whom I uphold, my chosen one with whom I am pleased; I have put my spirit upon him, he shall bring forth justice to the nations. He will not cry nor shout, he will not make his voice heard in the street. A bruised reed he shall not break, and a smoldering wick he shall not quench; he shall faithfully bring forth justice. He will not fail or be discouraged until he establishes justice on the earth; the coastlands will wait for his teaching" (Isaiah 42:1-4).

Isaiah presents ideal Israel as a martyr, who has endured great suffering because of the nations; they regarded him as a sinner and therefore as one to be spurned: "Behold, my servant shall prosper, he shall be raised high and greatly exalted. Many were astonished at him, his appearance was so marred, beyond human semblance . . . he shall startle many nations; kings shall shut their mouths because of him, for that which has not been told to them they shall see . . . who would believe what we have heard? . . . He was spurned and avoided by men, a man of suffering, accustomed to infirmity. . . Yet it was our infirmities that he bore . . . while we thought of him as stricken, as one smitten by God and afflicted. But he was pierced by our offenses, crushed by our sins. . . We had all gone astray like sheep, each following his own way; but the Lord punished him for the iniquity of us all. . . Like a lamb led to the slaughter, and like a sheep that before its shearers is speechless, he opened not his mouth . . . though he had done no wrong nor spoken any falsehood. Yet the Lord was pleased to crush him with infirmity" (Isaiah 52:13-53:1-10).

Rabbi Yehudah Halevi (1085-1142), philosopher-poet, expressing his view of Israel, writes in his famous work *Kuzari:* Israel among the nations is like the heart among the organs of the body. Israel is at one and the same time the weakest and the healthiest of them all.

451

Even as the heart may be affected by the diseases of other organs, so Israel is affected by the troubles and wrongs of other nations. The tribulations which we experience are meant to cleanse us and to remove all taint of evil from us.

SLAVERY   עַבְדוּת

IN THE biblical period, slaves were obtained through warfare. If cities surrendered peaceably, the inhabitants were taken into the service of the victors; but if they resisted and fought, the males at least were put to the sword. In many respects, slavery in ancient times has been regarded as a moral advance. The foreign slave was the property of his owner, who could treat him as he pleased. In the course of time, however, a more humane attitude developed, and the rights of the owner were restricted.

The master was allowed to chastise his slave, but not in a brutal manner; there was a penalty for beating him to death: "When a man strikes his male or female slave with a rod so hard that the slave dies under his hand, he shall be severely punished" (Exodus 21:20). Rest on the Sabbath and the privilege of participating in the religious life of the family circle were not to be denied by an Israelite owner. Fugitive slaves were given asylum, and were not to be surrendered to their owners. The slave went free, if the master destroyed his eye or tooth. Freed slaves had the status of proselytes in every respect.

The Hebrew slave, on the other hand, was in a much more favorable position. He became a slave either by selling his services in order to obtain maintenance or through inability to pay his debts. The male worked for a six-year period and then was released. The female slave, in the age of polygamy, became one of the secondary wives of the owner or his son; hence, she could not claim the privilege of the six-year period. If she had not become a wife of second rank in the house of her master, the owner was obligated to let her be redeemed by her relatives; he could not sell her as a slave (Exodus 21:7-8).

An Israelite who sold himself, or was sold by the court of justice because he was not able to make restitution for a theft which he had committed, remained a slave for a six-year period unless he expressed a desire to continue in that condition; he was then liberated when the year of Jubilee arrived. All Hebrew slaves, both those who had chosen to remain with their masters when the seventh year had come and

452

those who had served six years, were released at the year of Jubilee (Leviticus 25:40), whether or not they preferred to serve their masters.

There is no evidence that slave markets ever existed in Israel. Kidnapping a man or selling him as a slave was a capital offense. A fugitive slave law, that once permitted in America the act of tracking runaway slaves by bloodhounds, would have been unthinkable in ancient Israel, where the relationship between master and slave was often cordial. The slave sometimes inherited the property of his master (Genesis 15:2-3) and was sometimes admitted into the family as a son-in-law (I Chronicles 2:34-35).

According to Mishnah Gittin 4:6, it was forbidden to sell a Jewish slave to a non-Jew, lest he might be driven into apostasy. Unlike Athens, where the ratio of slave to citizen was five to one, the land of Israel was not founded upon a slave system.

According to a talmudic statement, the Hebrew slave was to be regarded as his master's equal. "You should not eat white bread, and he black bread; you should not drink old wine, and he new wine; you should not sleep on a featherbed, and he on straw. Hence, it has been declared that whoever acquires a Hebrew slave acquires a master" (Kiddushin 20a). "A son or pupil may, but a Hebrew slave may not wash his master's feet or help him put on his shoes. . ." (Mekhilta, Exodus 21:2). "Though the Torah permits us to impose hard work on a Canaanite (non-Jewish) slave, piety and wisdom command us to be kind and just" (*Yad, Avadim* 9:8). Freed slaves were considered proselytes, converts to Judaism, in every respect.

IDOLATRY עֲבוֹדָה זָרָה

THE Second Commandment is directed against idolatry, forbidding man to bow down to images and sculptures. The prophets struggled incessantly against the foreign gods and idolatrous practices. The literal meaning of *avodah zarah* is foreign worship or heathenism, which violates the fundamental principle of the divine Oneness, proclaimed by the Jew every time he recites the *Shema* ("Hear, O Israel, the Lord our God is One God").

According to J. B. Pritchard, in his *Archeology and the Old Testament*, the most frequently recurring likeness of anything that is in heaven above, or that is on earth beneath, is the clay plaque of a nude female figure no larger than a man's hand. "These terracottas

453

are far from being works of art. They are generally crude, but always emphasize, sometimes through exaggeration, the distinctively feminine aspects of the human figure. The widespread use of these objects is attested both by the fact that they were sometimes mass-produced through the use of a clay mold and by the great number of them found in almost every major excavation of remains dating from the eighteenth to the sixth centuries B.C... Just what use these objects had remains a mystery to this day. Were they worshiped as a goddess? Were they charms to assist women in childbirth or as an aid to fertility? Or were they representations of the sacred harlots connected with Canaanite shrines. . ."

It has been affirmed that men have worshiped everything on earth, including themselves, stones, hills, flowers, trees, streams, wells, ocean, and animals. Yet with all this bewildering jumble to their discredit, men have never really worshiped anything other than what they imagined behind these phenomena, the thing they feared, power.

The Torah forbids the worship of the true God under any external form, because God is not like anything that human hands can fashion. The worship of the divine in a material form was almost universal in all ages and is still practised by the majority of the human race. The strange behavior of the people in the story of the golden calf is attributable to their close familiarity with the Egyptian iconolatry. The golden calf that was made in the wilderness, and later reproduced by Jeroboam, was also the emblem of a Syrian-Mesopotamian deity. Symbolic representations of deities in a visible and tangible form were produced in the shape of countless animals, hence the prohibition which greatly interfered with the free development of plastic arts in ancient Israel.

Many prohibitions are traceable to idolatrous trends in ancient times. "The idolatrous priests had the custom of removing the beard. The Torah, accordingly, forbade this practice... Tattooing, mentioned in the Torah (Leviticus 19:28), consists in cutting the flesh and filling up the cut with pigment, ink or other printing matter which leaves an indelible mark. This was the custom of the pagans who used to mark themselves for purposes of idolatry, as much as to say that the tattooed was a slave sold to the idol and marked for its service. . ." (*Yad, Avodah Zarah* 12:7, 11).

The three cardinal crimes are: idolatry, adultery, and murder (*avodah zarah, gilluy arayoth,* and *shefikhath damim*). To save his life, a Jew may ignore any command when compelled to do so except for

454

these. It has been pointed out that if Zeus is a god, licentiousness is no sin; if Aphrodite is a goddess, chastity cannot be a virtue. The Mishnah records that, when asked why God did not exterminate all idols, the sages replied: Men worship the sun, moon, stars and planets. Shall God destroy the world because of fools? (Avodah Zarah 4:7). In the ancient world, Judaism was the only religion to oppose idolatry.

HEBREW LANGUAGE   עִבְרִית

Being a branch of a family of Semitic languages, Hebrew was written in the common Semitic alphabet used alike by Moabites, Phoenicians, and Arameans. The Phoenicians transmitted it to the Greeks; the modern European alphabets, in turn, are derived directly, or indirectly through Latin, from the Greek alphabet. The modern English alphabet, for example, is generally traced through Latin, Greek, and Phoenician.

The earliest Hebrew examples occur on the calendar of Gezer, the oldest known Hebrew inscription containing an incomplete list of agricultural seasons and the work associated with them, written in Canaanite script some three thousand years ago. It was found on a limestone tablet in Gezer, eighteen miles north of Jerusalem. The Siloam inscription is another one of the oldest Hebrew inscriptions known (about 700 before the common era). The six lines, beautifully cut in classical Hebrew, are preserved in the Archaelogical Museum at Istanbul.

The transition to the square script (kethav merubba) was effected first in Aramaic, which is closely related to Hebrew. This script is referred to as כתב אשורי, because the Jews adopted it from the Arameans or Syrians. Tradition has it that Ezra introduced the change from the ancient Hebrew script to the Assyrian, or square script. From a study of ancient inscriptions, however, it has been proved that the transition was a gradual process which was completed in Hebrew about 400 before the common era.

The Hebrew alphabet, consisting of twenty-two letters, is purely consonantal; the small marks below and above the consonants, serving as vowels, were invented not earlier than the sixth century to represent to the eye the exact pronunciation of the words. For the practised reader, however, these are not necessary and therefore are omitted in most printed texts. The Sefer Torah must not be vocalized.

455

The Hebrew noun has only two genders, masculine and feminine. The possessive pronoun is attached directly to the noun in the form of a suffix, for example: אב (father); אבי (my father). Pronominal suffixes appended to the verb express the accusative of the personal pronoun, as in שמרני (he watched me). The whole Jewish Bible, with the exception of several sections in the books of Daniel and Ezra and a few verses elsewhere in Aramaic, was written originally in Hebrew, which has remained the language of religion and Jewish literary creativity throughout the generations of the dispersion of the Jewish people. Modern Hebrew now represents a combination of all previous stages of the language: biblical, mishnaic and rabbinic Hebrew, including words for modern concepts derived from old forms as well as internationally accepted terms. It is used as the official language of Israel and is freely spoken by many thousands in the Diaspora. Throughout the medieval period Hebrew continued as a learned tongue, but now there are myriads who speak it even before learning how to read and write.

Hebrew grammar (דקדוק) has for many centuries been a fascinating subject of study among Jewish and non-Jewish scholars. During the medieval period, Hebrew grammatical knowledge was regarded as a measure of Jewish learning and scholarship. Rabbis Abraham ibn Ezra and David Kimḥi, summing up the great achievements of men like Saadyah Gaon, Ibn Gabirol, Ibn Janaḥ, were studied assiduously for a better knowledge of the Bible.

The Karaites, who emphasized the diligent scrutiny of the Bible as a basis for their sectarian religion, were a significant factor in centering the attention of medieval Hebrew scholars on a searching study of the Hebrew Bible by the use of a scientific and grammatical approach. The father of Hebrew philology among non-Jews was John Reuchlin of the sixteenth century who, like the non-Jewish Hebrew grammarians after him, adhered to Jewish findings. From the middle of the seventeenth century the field of investigation gradually widened in the various branches of Hebrew grammar and lexicography.

It has been asserted that anyone with a sense of language and history, irrespective of religious or national sentiment, is thrilled to hear the majestic sounds of ancient Hebrew roll off the tongues of little children in modern Israel. The modern revival of the Hebrew language is an unprecedented phenomenon. Yet, one must not forget that the Hebrew language, though it ceased to be spoken more than two thousand years ago, has persisted as a functional organ, and not as a museum exhibit, under the most adverse conditions. The Hebrew language has always been an integral part of the Jewish make-up. In many instances, the Jewish people modeled upon Hebraic constructions a variety of expressions in the vernacular. In his traditional environment, the Jew was steeped from early childhood in the study of the Bible, the Talmud and later Hebraic sources. The Hebrew language must have become to him something like second nature.

AGUNAH   עֲגוּנָה

A WIFE separated from her husband who has not been heard from for some time is prevented from re-marrying unless she can provide evidence of his death. If she has no proof of her husband's death, or if she has not obtained a Jewish bill of divorce (*get*) from her husband who has deserted her and disappeared, her status as a wife remains unchanged and she is legally barred from remarriage. She is referred to as *agunah*, a term derived from the verb meaning to be *shut off, restrained* (Ruth 1:13). Since early talmudic times, efforts have been made to mitigate the hardship arising from cases of desertion or a suspected death of a husband. According to the Talmud, the testimony of one witness is sufficient to prove a husband's death, so that the woman may not become an *agunah* (Yevamoth 122b). Even hearsay evidence, as well as the testimony of an otherwise incompetent witness, is acceptable (*Yad, Gerushin* 13:29).

Maimonides sums up the subject of *agunah* in the following terms:

"Be not surprised that the sages have permitted remarriage of an *agunah* upon the testimony of a woman, or a male or female slave, or an idolater, or upon hearsay or documentary evidence, and without cross-examination. The Torah insists upon the testimony of two witnesses and upon the other rules of evidence only when the matter cannot be otherwise determined—as, for instance, to prove murder or to prove a loan—but where the matter can be otherwise determined and the testimony of a witness can be refuted, as in the case where he testifies that some one is dead, it is not to be presumed that he will bear false witness. Hence, the rule is relaxed so that Jewish women shall not be *agunoth*."

In the Middle Ages, wife-desertion was very hard to deal with. Under continuous persecution, the husband was frequently bound to leave home in search of a livelihood. In the twelfth century it became necessary to protect the wife by limiting the absence to eighteen months, an interval which was only permitted to husbands who had obtained the formal sanction of the communal authorities. On his return the husband was compelled to remain at least six months with his family before again starting on his involuntary travels. A husband on leaving home would hand to his wife a *conditional divorce*, which would only take effect if he failed to reappear within a certain term. The conditional divorce preserved the wife from the lamentable position of being neither maiden, nor wife, nor widow.

WITNESSES   עֵדִים

THE Torah demands at least two witnesses in trials involving the possibility of capital punishment (Numbers 35:30; Deuteronomy 17:6). Circumstantial evidence of the most conclusive kind was not admitted in the Jewish superior courts of twenty-three judges that had jurisdiction in capital crimes. There was no torture of the accused to compel confession, since this would not be in keeping with an essential principle of Jewish law according to which "no man can by his own testimony incriminate himself in a capital charge" (Sanhedrin 9b: אין אדם משים עצמו רשע).

Since the trial was based completely upon the testimony of eyewitnesses, their qualifications were of utmost importance. Among those excluded from giving testimony in capital cases were women, minors, slaves, deaf-mutes, professional gamblers, and all those who knowingly transgressed the laws of the Torah or were ignorant of them. If the two witnesses were related to each other, they were disqualified. At the opening of the court the witnesses were solemnly cautioned against testifying to anything they knew at second hand.

The twenty-three judges occupied their seats in a semicircle, and examined the witnesses by questions relating to date, time and place, as well as queries pertaining to the circumstances accompanying the criminal act. These questions and cross-examinations are referred to in talmudic literature as חקירות ובדיקות. Even if there were a hundred witnesses, and one of them could not answer a question concerning date, time and place, the testimony of all was disregarded.

If the testimony given by the witnesses was found to agree, the presiding judge began by encouraging the prisoner to refute it by producing contradictory witnesses; he also appealed to the members of the

458

court to advance arguments in favor of the prisoner. If one of the judges pleaded for the defense, he was not allowed to change his mind in favor of the prosecution; if he pleaded for the prosecution, however, he was permitted to vote for the defense.

OBADIAH   עוֹבַדְיָה

CONTAINING one chapter of twenty-one verses, Obadiah is the shortest of all prophetical books. It is the fourth of the twelve Minor Prophets. The unknown author predicts the destruction of Edom, representing the forces of evil. He severely condemns the Edomites for having refused to assist Jerusalem in the day of calamity, and expresses the conviction that they will be treated measure for measure, for they helped the Babylonians to bring about the downfall of Judea. From their mountainous strongholds, south of the Dead Sea, the warlike and cruel Edomites, the archenemies of the Jews, looked down upon their neighbors in Jerusalem.

Obadiah's prophecy brings to mind Psalm 137, containing an outburst of hatred against the enemies of Jerusalem who rejoiced at its fall: "Remember, O Lord, against the Edomites the day of Jerusalem, when they said: Raze it, raze it down to its foundation!"

The confidence that Edom shall not ultimately triumph over Israel is an expression of a spiritual conviction of permanent value that Judaism cannot be extinguished by the forces of evil. The invaders shall be expelled from the lands that they have unjustly seized, and the people of Israel shall occupy their ancient territory.

OLELOTH EFRAYIM   עוֹלְלוֹת אֶפְרַיִם

THE sermonic work *Oleloth Efrayim* by Rabbi Ephraim Luntshitz, who was born in Poland about the middle of the sixteenth century and died in Prague in 1619, contains ethical teachings of high literary quality and deep spiritual depth. Rabbi Luntshitz was the author of the famous commentary *Keli Yakar* on the Torah as well as a number of books of ethical sermons. He was the chief rabbi of Prague from 1604 to 1618 when he was relieved of his duties.

He wrote in part: Money is comparable to fire; one can hardly do without it, yet one does well not to get too close to it. There is no

459

justification for this mad pursuit after the material things of the world. In most instances the rich are too close-fisted to heed the cry of the poor; and when they do respond to some pitiable appeal they invariably publicize their generosity, thus revealing the true motive of their beneficence. Some of them, when about to answer the call of death, do bequeath to charity part of their hoarded treasures. But to surrender to others what a man can no longer enjoy himself is more an act of despair than of conscience.

When we are interested in things of immediate benefit to ourselves only, such as money and power, we are forgetting that in such matters the victorious are always the vanquished. Judaism teaches that love of God and love of man are intertwined. Our acquisitive instinct is rather too strong; it crowds out all other interests from our hearts. The heights of learning can be scaled only by those who follow the path of humility. Men of true learning will endeavor to diffuse the light of the Torah among those who dwell in darkness. A knowledge of the essence of Judaism will tend to direct the flow of our energies into channels of pure and exalted living.

Prayer is the most potent spiritual exercise open to man. The efficacy of our prayers is conditioned by *kavvanah*, the complete concentration of the interests and powers of the worshiper on the act of devotion. When this is absent, prayer ceases to have any spiritual significance; it degenerates into the meaningless chirpings of the birds. The cantors who chant prayers with excessive elaboration cannot concentrate on the thought of the prayers. Indeed, many of them think of nothing else but the good impression they are bent on making.

The sermons should deal with themes of ethical import, and not with midrashic interpretations from which the people can derive no special benefit. The perfection of man is the chief aim of all existence. We shall, of course, frequently stumble and fall, but through sincere repentance we shall rise again and continue the march onward. Though subject to repeated backsliding, every man becomes, when truly repentant, a veritable Moses mounting the Sinai of his spirit where the eternal God dwells.

Rabbi Ephraim Luntshitz, who had filled the office of *Rosh Yeshivah* at Lemberg before he was appointed rabbi of Prague in 1604, was the author of annotations on the Pentateuch, entitled שפתי דעת, forming the second part of his work. In addition to his homilies and ethical sermons, Rabbi Ephraim composed three liturgical poems celebrating the victory over a hostile army that had entered the city of Prague.

OLAM HA-BA   עוֹלָם הַבָּא

THE indefinite expression *olam ha-ba* (the future world) as opposed to *olam ha-zeh* (the present world) is frequently found in talmudic-midrashic literature to signify a new order of things. It is sometimes used interchangeably with *athid lavo* (the future), a vague phrase referring to the messianic era (*yemoth ha-mashiah*) as well. It is described as follows: "In the future world there is no eating, drinking, propagation, business, jealousy, hatred or competition, but the righteous sit, with their crowns on their heads, enjoying the brilliance of the *Shekhinah*" (Berakhoth 17a). "In the hereafter, God will prepare a banquet for the righteous, and there will be no need of balsam or choice spices, for the north and south breezes will waft all the perfumes of *Gan Eden* or Paradise (Numbers Rabbah 13:2). "In the world-to-come there is no death, sin, affliction, but everyone delights in wisdom and understanding" (*Seder Eliyyahu Rabbah*).

Rabbi Isaac Abravanel (1437-1508), in his commentary on the Bible, notes that the reward of the souls in the world-to-come is their ability to attain the true concept of God, which is a source of the most wonderful felicity, an attainment impossible for man in this earthly life because of the disturbances on the part of matter (on I Samuel 25:29). In a letter to Hasdai Halevi, Maimonides writes: "Every man who ennobles his soul with excellent morals and wisdom, based on faith in God, certainly belongs to the men of the world-to-come."

It has been pointed out that, in view of the keen intellectual pleasure and the truly religious spirit of the ancient sages and their successors, it is not strange that they should have envisioned their occupation of mind and heart with religion as continuing in the future world. They could not imagine themselves in another life without the intellectual interests of the present life. As religious men, they obeyed the divine statutes without question; as reasonable men they could not help wanting to know the reason of them.

EZRA-NEHEMIAH   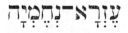

IN THE Hebrew Bible, Ezra and Nehemiah are counted as a single book, because they owe their existence to a single compiler. This combined work is called *Ezra* in the Talmud. A considerable part of

461

Ezra-Nehemiah contains the memoirs left by the two leaders who organized Jewish life in Judea in the beginning of the Second Commonwealth. The main authority for that period of Jewish history is preserved in Ezra-Nehemiah. According to biblical scholars, the books of Ezra, Nehemiah and Chronicles were composed by one author.

The book of Ezra describes the activities of a new figure in Judaism—the scribe, who took the place of the prophet after the return of the Jews from the Babylonian captivity. The scribes (*sofrim*) made available copies of the Scriptures, and carefully interpreted and taught them to the people. They were the Jewish sages and teachers who preceded the *Tannaim* of the Mishnah period.

Accompanied by fifteen hundred exiles, Ezra *ha-Sofer* (the scribe) arrived in Jerusalem in 450 before the common era. According to tradition, Ezra was the founder of the Great Assembly (כנסת הגדולה), a body of spiritual leaders, described as the successors of the prophets in keeping alive the knowledge of the Torah.

The book of Nehemiah, written mostly in the first person singular, tells of the experiences of Nehemiah who was twice governor of Jerusalem, in 445 and 433. The noble character of Nehemiah, his strong self-reliance combined with a serene trust in God, are vividly portrayed in the story of his zealous endeavors to restore the ruined city of Jerusalem and rebuild its walls.

WOMEN'S SECTION עֶזְרַת נָשִׁים

THE women's section at the Temple is referred to in the Mishnah as *ezrath nashim* eight times. During the *Beth-Shoevah* festivities and other religious occasions, the women occupied their separate section in order to avoid any possible frivolity (קלות ראש) resulting from contact with the men. We are told: "As this still led to levity, it was instituted that the women should sit above, and the men below" (Sukkah 51b-52a). This is followed by a biblical quotation to the effect that men and women are to keep apart during religious functions (Zechariah 12:12—בית דוד לבד ונשיהם לבד, בית לוי לבד ונשיהם לבד).

The problem of mixed pews, separate seating and *meḥitzah* (partition) in the synagogue has engaged the attention of many congregations for years. Some prominent rabbis state that a synagogue with mixed pews loses its status as a holy place in the judgment of Halakhah. They declare: It is simply untrue that separate seating in a

462

synagogue, or elsewhere, has anything at all to do with equality or inequality.

Despite some opposition, there has been a great increase in the number of synagogues where men and women sit together in keeping with the concept of *family pews*, which has been described by the opponents as contrary to the Jewish spirit of prayer. They have pointed out that the presence of women among men often evokes a certain frivolity in the group, either in spirit or behavior, and can not contribute to the deepening of religious feeling. The separation of men and women, they have declared, does not imply disrespect for women, but is rather based on the Jewish sense of modesty and reverence.

EVIL EYE   עַיִן־הָרָע

THE terms עין הרע and עין רעה essentially denote envy, jealousy, grudge, greed, ill will. In the Hebrew Bible, we are told not to dine with a man who is stingy (רע עין) and not to desire his delicacies. "Eat and drink," he says to you, but his heart is not with you (Proverbs 23:6-7).

Opposed to the grudging man is the generous man, טוב עין (Proverbs 22:9). In the *Ethics of the Fathers*, we are told that a good eye (עין טובה), or generosity, is the best quality to which a man should cling; and that an evil eye (עין רעה) is the worst quality, which a man should shun (Avoth 2:13-14).

In the course of time, it became a widespread belief that an envious or begrudging glance could work evil upon the person at whom it was directed. According to a talmudic statement, ninety-nine out of a hundred die of an evil eye (Bava Metzia 107b—תשעין ותשעה בעין רעה). Hence the popular expression בלי עין־הרע (without a begrudging eye), which is used when a person's good health or wealth is being admired. Mystical amulets were worn as antidotes counteracting the evil eye.

EN YAAKOV   עֵין יַעֲקֹב

THE well-known aggadic work *En Yaakov*, a compilation of the legendary sections of the Talmud, was first published in Salonica in the year 1516. It soon received wide popularity, was frequently republished, and has eventually become the textbook of special adult study groups. The author, Rabbi Jacob ibn Ḥaviv (1460-1516), was a native of Spain who, after the expulsion in 1492, finally settled in the Turkish seaport city of Salonica where thousands of Marranos sought refuge and were free to revert to Judaism after they had been forcibly baptized in Spain and Portugal.

Rabbi Jacob's annotations are an attempt at a rational interpretation of the talmudic legendary material, as a source of ethics and faith. The *En Yaakov* is available in an English translation.

His son, Rabbi Levi ibn Ḥaviv, who arrived in Salonica at the age of fourteen, soon won distinction among the scholars of the city where he became the head of the *yeshivah* of the Castilian community.

In 1525 he arrived in Jerusalem where he became chief rabbi. He is chiefly remembered for his opposition to the renewal of ordination (*semikhah*), which had been discontinued with the decline of the Palestinian center so that even Palestinian authorities in the Middle Ages were not regarded as fully ordained.

AKKUM   עַכּוּ"ם

THE name *akkum* (עכו"ם) is composed of the initials of the words עוֹבְדֵי כּוֹכָבִים וּמַזָּלוֹת (worshipers of stars and constellations), and refers to ancient idolaters. During the medieval period, at a time when Hebrew books could be retained only if they had been examined by the Christian censor (generally a *meshummad*, an apostate from Judaism), the term *akkum* was used in place of *goy* (גוי) in the sense of a non-Jew. The censor would tear out pages or black out passages which he regarded as objectionable.

The Torah speaks of Israel as *goy kadosh* (Exodus 19:6), a nation destined to be holy. The plural, *goyim*, is employed in the Bible to signify the nations of the world. In the course of time, the singular (גוי) was used interchangeably with נכרי (nokhri) and *kuthi* (כותי) to designate a non-Jew. As a result of the campaign against Hebrew literature, which was followed by the condemnation and burning of the Talmud, the word *goy* was used only by authors who lived in Moslem countries. The name *Talmud*, too, was disliked by the censors. Hence, it gave way to another term—*Gemara*. Hebrew manuscripts, originating from Moslem lands, have תלמוד in place of גמרא, and גוי instead of נכרי and כותי.

464

AL HA-NISSIM   עַל הַנִּסִּים

ON *Ḥanukkah* and *Purim*, the passages which are introduced with the formula עַל הנסים (we thank thee for the miracles) recount the story of both festivals briefly and are recited in the *Amidah* as well as in *Birkath ha-Mazon* (grace after meals). The story of *Ḥanukkah* is a condensed account of the Maccabean struggle, while the story of *Purim* is taken from the book of Esther. Both texts are to be found in the ninth-century *Siddur Rav Amram Gaon*.

AL ḤET   עַל חֵטְא

THE long specification of sins, listed alphabetically with a double acrostic, each line beginning with the words עַל חטא שחטאנו (for the sin we committed), is repeatedly recited in the *Yom Kippur* service, toward the end of each *Amidah*, to make us intensely aware of the need of a fuller mastery over our wandering impulses. The *Al Ḥet* confession is phrased in the plural because it is made collectively by the entire community, regarding itself responsible for many offenses that could have been prevented. A considerable number of sins mentioned in *Al Ḥet* refer to offenses committed with our tongue, such as idle talk, slander and talebearing. In keeping with the spirit of *Yom Kippur*, *Al Ḥet* is intended to bring home to us the consciousness of human weakness and frailty. In the confession we are taught to examine ourselves in the spirit of humility, in the recognition that there is no man absolutely free from sin.

PILGRIMAGE   עֲלִיָּה לְרֶגֶל

THE Torah commands: "Three times a year every male among you shall appear before the Lord your God in the place which he chooses: at the festival of unleavened bread, at the festival of weeks, and at the festival of booths. No one shall appear before the Lord empty-handed, but each of you with as much as he can give" (Deuteronomy 16:16-17). All were under the obligation to appear, except women and children as well as those who were prevented by physical or mental illness (Ḥagigah 1:1).

עליה לרגל

Since women cannot be expected to leave their children and household duties unattended, they are generally exempt from complying with positive religious commands the observance of which depends on a certain time of the day or season of the year (מצוות עשה שהזמן גרמא). Though not subject to the command concerning pilgrimage, women and children in large numbers joined the pilgrims to Jerusalem in Temple times.

For the convenience of the pilgrims, special measures were taken to repair the roads leading to Jerusalem. The pilgrims were received hospitably by the inhabitants of Jerusalem, which was the national center of the scattered people of Israel. They came even from beyond Palestine to be united with their fellow Jews. Some even endangered their lives, during the period of the Second Temple, when they passed the guards posted to stop the pilgrimages (Ta'anith 28a).

ALIYYOTH עֲלִיּוֹת

THE Hebrew term *aliyyah* (ascending) frequently denotes the honor extended to a worshiper to ascend the *bimah* (platform) in the synagogue for the Torah-reading during public worship. The first *aliyyah* is given to one of priestly descent (כהן); the second, to a descendant of the tribe of Levi (לוי); the third, to an Israelite (ישראל). In the absence of a Levite, the *Kohen* is honored by being given also the second *aliyyah* in place of the Levite (במקום לוי). In the absence of a *Kohen*, a Levite or even an Israelite receives the first *aliyyah*. If an Israelite substitutes for the *Kohen*, a Levite is not to be called up after him.

Originally, each person that received an *aliyyah* read his particular section; later, however, a special reader (*ba'al keriah*) was designated for the actual reading; and in our time the persons honored with *aliyyoth* merely recite the appropriate benedictions before and after the reading of the individual parts. The Sabbath reading is divided into seven *aliyyoth* (כהן, לוי, ישראל, רביעי, חמישי, ששי, שביעי).

When, however, more than seven *aliyyoth* are distributed, each additional *aliyyah* is termed *hosafah* (הוספה), and the last of those called up to the Torah-reading (קרואים לתורה) is termed *aharon* (אחרון). The *Maftir* concludes the Torah-reading by reciting the *Haftarah* from a prophetical book. As a rule, the contents of the *Haftarah* bear a certain similarity to the particular *sidrah* of the week.

466

BLOOD ACCUSATION   עֲלִילַת דָּם

As MANY as forty-two cases of blood accusation leveled against the Jewish people occurred in several countries during the nineteenth century. The allegation that the Jews use the blood of a murdered non-Jew in preparation of unleavened bread (*matzoth*) for Passover has been condemned by theologians, historians and scholars as most senseless and stupid. Such an accusation could be hurled only by perverted, bloodthirsty villains, incredibly ignorant and destitute of conscience. Toward the end of the thirteenth century, the blood libel became an almost annual occurrence. The fourteenth-century English poet Chaucer made use of this charge in his *Canterbury Tales*.

The Damascus Affair (1840) is one of the most notorious instances of the blood libel. The news that a charge of ritual murder was brought against the Jews of Damascus, Syria, shocked the civilized world. The trial of Mendel Beilis, who was charged with ritual murder at Kiev, Russia, (1911), was accompanied by violent anti-Semitic propaganda and by a wave of protest in liberal circles throughout the world. During the thirty-four days of the trial, which took place after a relentless investigation pursued by the Russian government for a period of two years, the accused was seldom mentioned. Every effort was made to convict the Jews of blood ritual practices. Beilis was acquitted in 1913 thanks to the profound skill of his defenders. He died in Saratoga Springs in 1934.

ALENU   עָלֵינוּ

THE prayer *Alenu*, proclaiming God as King over a united humanity, has been recited as the closing prayer of the three daily services ever since the thirteenth century. According to an old tradition, Joshua composed it at the time he entered the Land of Promise. It is generally held, however, that it was first introduced by Rav, founder of the Sura Academy (early third century), as an introduction to *Malkhuyyoth*, the section recited as part of the *Musaf* service for *Rosh Hashanah*.

Since the fourteenth century, incessant attacks were concentrated upon *Alenu* on account of the words "they worship vanity and emptiness and pray to a god that cannot save." Hence, this passage was

467

deleted from the Ashkenazic Prayerbooks. The traditional tune of *Alenu* is said to have come down from the twelfth century. In the Middle Ages it was the death-song of Jewish martyrs. It moderated the agonies of their death.

AM HA-ARETZ

In common parlance, the term *'am ha-aretz* denotes a person ignorant of Jewish law and custom. Originally, it was used as a collective noun signifying "the people of the land" or the masses of people (Genesis 23:13; 42:6; Exodus 5:5; II Kings 23:35; 24:14; 25:19). In talmudic literature, the name *'am ha-aretz* is descriptive of Jews who, in Temple times, were ignorant of the traditional law and failed to observe the rules of cleanness and uncleanness, and did not adhere to the strict regulations as regards tithe-separations.

These were mainly of the peasantry, insufficiently acquainted with Jewish lore, or unwilling to recognise the authority of the rabbinic sages. They could not be trusted in matters of ritual purity and tithing; hence, groups were formed by the religious leaders of men who were scrupulous in observing the laws about which there was much laxity. The members of such groups were referred to as *haverim*, in contrast to *'ammé ha-aretz.*

The faithful observants of the prescribed rules and regulations were united in *havuroth* (societies) in every town for common worship and communal acts of benevolence, shunning any contact with the *'ammé ha-aretz*. This exclusiveness tended to intensify the animosity between the masses and the educated. The following expressions adequately illustrate the attitude of the sages: "An ignorant person cannot be pious" (Avoth 2:6). "Do not live near an ignorant man who is pious" (Shabbath 63a). "Disaster comes only because of ignorance" (Bava Bathra 8a). "Who is ignorant? He who does not educate his children" (Sotah 22a).

The Talmud records a favorite saying of the Rabbis of Yavneh concerning the uneducated *'am ha-aretz:* I am God's creature and my neighbor is God's creature. My work is in town, and his work is in the country. I rise early for my work, and he rises early for his work. Just as he does not presume to do my work, so I do not presume to do his work. Will you say that I do much and he does little (in the way of Torah study)? We have learned: One may do much or one

468

may do little—it is all the same so long as one directs his heart to heaven" (Berakhoth 17a; Menaḥoth 110a).

Rabbi Israel Baal Shem Tov, founder of Ḥasidism, frequently showed his love and concern for the uneducated 'am ha-aretz, people of the soil. He is quoted as having declared: "In the soil are to be found all such treasures as gold, silver, diamonds and all other precious and important metals and minerals. So too are the Jewish masses: thay are full of the finest and most precious qualities that man can possess... None should judge his neighbor. Let no one think himself better than his neighbor, for all serve God, each according to the measure of understanding which God has given him."

AMOS   עָמוֹס

THOUGH classed as the third of the Minor Prophets, the book of Amos should come first from a chronological point of view. The earliest known literary prophet, Amos, lived in the village of Tekoa, about twelve miles south of Jerusalem, during the middle of the eighth century before the common era. He left the kingdom of Judah and proceeded to make known the divine warnings in the kingdom of Israel, which had then reached the zenith of its power and prosperity. Though a native of Judah, he addressed himself primarily to the citizens of Israel.

Amos denounces the brutalities and cruel wrongs perpetrated by various nations. He strongly insists upon social justice, respect for the lowly, and the defense of the weak against the powerful. He condemns self-indulgence which breeds cruelty, and compares the pampered women of Samaria to cows grown fat through feeding in the rich pastures of Bashan, east of Jordan. When the idolatrous priest of Bethel tells Amos to go back home and prophesy there, he replies that he is not a professional prophet who tries to please people, but simply a shepherd who has been charged to prophesy to the people of Israel. Here are some of his utterances:

"Seek good and not evil, that you may live. Hate evil and love good, and establish justice in the gate. Let justice roll down like waters, and righteousness like an ever-flowing stream... The days are coming, says the Lord, when I will send a famine in the land; not a famine of bread, not a thirst for water, but of hearing the word of the Lord. Men shall wander from sea to sea, and run from north to east; they

shall run to and fro in quest for the Lord's word, but they shall not
find it. . . The mountains shall drip sweet wine, and all the hills shall
be aflow with milk.

"I will restore the fortunes of my people Israel; they shall rebuild
the ruined cities and inhabit them; they shall plant vineyards and
drink their wine, and they shall make gardens and eat their fruit.
I will plant them upon their land, and they shall never again be uprooted from the land which I have given them, says the Lord."

OMER   עֹמֶר

THE beginning of the grain harvest in the land of Israel was celebrated
on the second day of Passover, the sixteenth of *Nisan*, when a sheaf
of new barley was reaped ceremoniously and the flour offered as a
meal-offering in the Temple. Only after this sheaf (*omer*) had been
offered was the produce of the new harvest permitted for common
use. The *omer*-offering is indicative of the originally agricultural
character of Passover. Another faint vestige appears in the prayer
for dew (*tal*) which is recited on the first day of Passover.

The reaping of the *omer* at the close of the first day of Passover is
described in the Mishnah (Menaḥoth 10:3) as a performance surrounded with unusual formality, in order to counteract the influence
of the Sadducees, who endeavored to maintain their absolute control
over the Temple at the expense of the traditional law (*halakhah*).

The interpretation of the words ממחרת השבת (Leviticus 23:11)
was the subject of heated controversy between the Pharisees, the
spokesmen of the oral law, and the Sadducees who clung to the letter
of the biblical text despite the traditional and internal evidence.

According to the Pharisees, the phrase refers to the sixteenth day
of *Nisan* and should be rendered "the next day after the feast of rest,"
meaning that the counting of the forty-nine days between the *omer*-
offering and Pentecost (*Shavuoth*) should begin the second day of
Passover. The Sadducees, on the other hand, explained the phrase
literally in the sense that the counting should begin on the first Sunday after the feast of *Pesaḥ*, so that Pentecost, which is the fiftieth
day, would always occur on a Sunday.

The traditional interpretation, which is supported by the ancient
Greek translation of the Bible, known as the Septuagint, and by Philo
and Josephus, makes it possible that the Feast of Weeks or Pentecost,

470

like all other Jewish festivals, occurs always on a definite day of the month—the sixth of *Sivan*.

The Sadducees have been followed in this matter by all the schismatic communities, down to the Samaritan and Karaite sects of the present day.

ANENU   עֲנֵנוּ

THE prayer *Anenu* (answer us), which has been provided for fast days, is discussed exhaustively in the Talmud (Ta'anith 11b; 13b). It is inserted in the *Shemoneh Esreh* of both *Shaharith* and *Minhah* during the Reader's repetition, immediately after the seventh benediction which begins with the words: "Look upon our affliction and champion our cause." Individual worshipers omit *Anenu* during the morning service, and combine it with the sixteenth benediction of the *Shemoneh Esreh* during the *Minhah* service. They omit it in the morning for fear that, because of faintness (בולמוס), the fast might be broken before the day is over. The *hazzan*, on the other hand, inserts it when he repeats the *Shemoneh Esreh* on behalf of the entire congregation, and it is held most unlikely that none will complete the fast.

Individuals combine *Anenu* with the sixteenth benediction (שומע תפלה) in the afternoon, because none is entitled to insert a benediction for himself (קובע ברכה לעצמו) (Ta'anith 13b). Combined, the petition reads as follows: "Hear our voice, Lord our God . . . dismiss us not empty-handed. . . Answer us, O Lord, answer us on the day of our fast, for we are in great distress. . . Answer us even before we call to thee. . . Blessed art thou, O Lord, who hearest prayer."

AKEDAH   עֲקֵדָה

THE term *Akedah* (binding) signifies the attempted sacrifice of Isaac by his father Abraham, whose faith was put to the supreme test when he was commanded to present his only, beloved son as a burnt offering on one of the mountains in the land of Moriah (Genesis 22:1-19). This was the tenth and the greatest of the trials Abraham had to face, to prove that he was worthy of being the founder of the Jewish people.

This narrative concerning the binding of Isaac portrays also the faith and obedience of the second Jewish patriarch, Isaac. The will-

471

ingness of Abraham and the readiness of Isaac are symbolic of supreme
trust and devotion as well as Jewish martyrdom followed by divine
mercy. Hence, the *Akedah* is frequently recalled in the liturgy. The
sounding of the *shofar*, or ram's horn, on *Rosh Hashanah* serves as a
reminder of the horn of the ram that was sacrificed by Abraham in
place of Isaac.

The *Akedah* and its saving merit is frequently dwelt upon in the
medieval prayer-poems (*piyyutim*), perhaps as a Jewish counterpoise
to the doctrines of their non-Jewish neighbors. During the Crusades,
the story of the *Akedah* inspired countless parents to offer the lives of
their children as well as their own lives rather than submit to *avodah
zarah* (idolatry). We are told that Israel is the classical people of
martyrdom for truth, conscience, and freedom. The *Akedah* has indeed had a potent and lasting influence on the lives of countless Jews,
who have refused fortune and honors whenever these involved dis-
loyalty to their inherited faith.

In the opinion of Rav Saadyah Gaon, the biblical narrative does
not present an abrogation of the divine command to sacrifice Isaac.
God had told Abraham merely to make ready for the sacrifice of his
son; and as soon as all preparations had been completed, the divine
voice was heard restraining Abraham's hand, saying: "Enough! More
than this I did not desire of you" (*Emunoth v'Deoth*, 3:9). According
to Maimonides, all the trials mentioned in the Bible were designed to
teach man what to do or what to believe; the event which constitutes
the actual trial is but an example for our edification (*Guide*, 3:24).

The sacrifice of the firstborn was a common practice among the
Semitic tribes; it was regarded as the most pleasing service which men
could offer to their gods. Such a sacrificial zeal is mentioned in Micah 6:7 ("Shall I offer my firstborn son for my sin, fruit of my body
for guilt of my soul"?). The offering of a son must have been confined
to occasions when some great offense had to be atoned for or some
great disaster averted, as in the case of Mesha, king of Moab (II Kings
3:27). It was through the supreme test of Abraham's faith that the
people of Israel and all civilized nations learned that God abhors human sacrifice, and that he is to be served only through the practice
of mercy, justice, and humanity. The land of Moriah, which was the
scene of the *Akedah*, is mentioned again in II Chronicles 3:1, where
we read: "Then Solomon began to build the house of the Lord at
Jerusalem in Mount Moriah." The rock which traditionally was the
place of the *Akedah* is beneath the dome of the Mosque of Omar.

AKEDATH YITZḤAK   עֲקֵדַת יִצְחָק

THE biblical commentary *Akedath Yitzḥak* by Rabbi Isaac Arama of fifteenth-century Spain contains sermons on the weekly sections (*sidroth*) of the Torah in the form of philosophic reflections. After the expulsion from Spain, Rabbi Isaac Arama settled in Naples, where he died two years later (1494). He declared that truth is cold until warmed by emotion; thought is dull and drab until tinged with the vivid colors of imagination. His reverence and quenchless thirst for God inspired subsequent teachers and revealed to them the secret of the pulpit's power and influence.

He asserted that those who forever strive to harmonize biblical truth with philosophical thought often so dilute the content of the Torah that it ceases to have any strength or validity. They endeavor to eliminate from the Torah the miraculous and the mysterious, thus undermining the whole structure. It is our task to be a light-giving force in the moral ascent of mankind, even as the sun with its great powers of illumination revives and fructifies the earth. There is much Israel can give to the world. Exposed as we are to many alien influences, we cannot expedite the process of our spiritual transformation. It is becoming increasingly evident that unless we achieve physical liberation, we shall not attain spiritual emancipation.

Thousands are leaving our ranks. . . It is tragically clear that these apostates have found no peace and happiness in the change. They are despised and humiliated everywhere. There are many in our midst who do not show any influence of the teachings of Judaism either in character or mental outlook; they are Jews only in name. They seek to weaken our stamina, to destroy our will to live as Jews by fostering views that are so perilous to our religious discipline.

Yet, Israel need not despair. God's love for his people can never be extinguished. God has not forsaken us; we have forsaken him. We need but return unto him, and his love will be restored to us. Our Torah has become the property of the nations, even though in a distorted form; at least, they subscribe to the essential principles of our faith. We are thus privileged to live in an environment in which the perpetuation of Judaism is assured. We must not become the slaves of greed and pleasure. Our task is to cultivate a love for the simple life, that we may be free for the study of the divine Torah and the performance of its precepts.

473

BASIC PRINCIPLES   עִקָּרִים

SEFER HA-IKKARIM (Book of Roots), by Rabbi Joseph Albo of fifteenth-century Spain, belongs to the last of the philosophical classics
of medieval Judaism. It is counted among the famous works of Rav
Saadyah Gaon (*Emunoth v'Deoth*), Baḥya ibn Pakuda (*Ḥovoth ha-Levavoth*), Yehudah Halevi (*Kuzari*), Abraham ibn Daud (*Emunah Ramah*), Moses Maimonides (*Moreh Nevukhim*), Ralbag (*Milḥamoth
ha-Shem*), and Ḥasdai Crescas (*Or Adonai*). The *Sefer ha-Ikkarim*,
concerned mainly with Jewish dogma, is a vindication of Judaism
particularly directed against the onslaughts of those who used every
method of violence and persuasion to convert the Spanish Jews.

Ḥasdai Crescas, who was the teacher of Albo, reduced the thirteen
principles of faith, formulated by Maimonides, to six; Albo, however,
reduced them to three basic dogmas: Existence of God, Divine Revelation, and Retribution. To deny these three is heresy, according to
Albo, while doubting other beliefs, which he classifies as derivatives
(*anafim*), is not heretical. The derivative beliefs include the creation
of the world out of nothing (*ex nihilo*); the supreme rank of Moses'
prophecy; the resurrection of the dead; the Messiah. Albo maintains
that the three basic dogmas can never be changed, because they are
implied in the first two commandments spoken by God himself. The
rest of the commands may be changed as a temporary measure.

Rabbi Joseph Albo (1380-1444) systematized the fundamentals of
the Jewish religion and influenced the study of Jewish dogmatism of
the later generations. The necessity to establish religious dogmas resulted primarily from challenges to Judaism from the outside. Against
the attitude of those of formulated Jewish dogmas, Rabbi Isaac
Abravanel (1437-1508), statesman and religious philosopher, maintained that there was no need for making distinctions between sets
of Jewish doctrines, declaring that "it is improper to lay down basic
principles, since we should believe everything in the Torah."

According to Rabbi Samson Raphael Hirsch (1808-1888), leader of
Jewish orthodoxy, Judaism embraces six hundred and thirteen precepts, but knows no dogmas (*Nineteen Letters*). Samuel David Luzzatto (1800-1865), many-sided Italian-Jewish scholar, wrote: "The
principal dogma of Judaism is the belief in the divine origin of the
Torah (*Torah min ha-shamayim*) and the acceptance of the yoke of
the *mitzvoth*" (*Peniné Shadal*).

474

ERUV   עֵרוּב

THE literal meaning of the term *eruv* is blending, intermingling. The traditional Jewish law (*halakhah*) concerning a symbolic act of combining several domains for the purpose of making it lawful on the Sabbath to transport things from one to the other is called עֵרוּב רְשׁוּיוֹת (blending of domains). If a courtyard has many tenants, each living in a house of his own, the whole courtyard is regarded as a single private domain in which it is permissible to carry objects from place to place, according to the original biblical law.

The same biblical rule should apply to a city surrounded by a wall, all of which may well be regarded as a single private domain. The rabbinic sages, however, have ruled that if a private domain contains separate residences, the tenants may not carry objects on the Sabbath within its open space unless they have an *eruv* prepared beforehand.

This *eruv* is prepared as follows: All the tenants join in providing an article of food, which is deposited in an appropriate place on Friday, as if to say: "We are all associated together and possess one and the same food, and none of us holds a domain distinct from the domain of the other. Just as we have equal rights in the area which remains a common domain, so have we all equal rights in each of the places held by the various tenants respectively."

This procedure serves to prevent people from mistakenly imagining that it is permissible to transfer articles from a private domain (רְשׁוּת הַיָּחִיד) to a public domain (רְשׁוּת הָרַבִּים), and vice versa. The *eruv* prepared by the residents of a courtyard is called *eruv ḥatzeroth;* the one prepared by all the citizens of a town is called *shilluf* (token partnership). The amount of food required to establish a token partnership is two meals for one person; if the total number of persons involved is eighteen or less, the food requirement for the *eruv* is as little as a dried fig from each resident.

Eruv teḥumin (intermingling of Sabbath limits) renders it permissible, on Sabbath or holydays, to walk a longer distance than otherwise permitted. If food for two meals is placed within the two-thousand yard boundary on the preceding day, the movements are measured from the marked spot which has become a new center from which a two-thousand yard walk is allowed on the Sabbath for the purpose of performing a *mitzvah*, such as attending a *brith-milah* occasion in a nearby town or village.

Eruv tavshilin (blending of dishes) renders it permissible to prepare food on a holyday for the use on the Sabbath which immediately follows it. The permission to prepare food on holydays is restricted to food required for those days; but if the preparation was begun before the holyday, it may be continued on the holyday itself. This is accomplished by symbolically singling out food for the Sabbath on the eve of the festival.

The reason that one may not ordinarily bake or cook on the festival day anything that is to be eaten on the following Sabbath day is explained in the Code of Maimonides: "This prohibition was enacted on the authority of the sages, that one should not be led to cook food on a festival day for consumption on the subsequent weekday, for it follows logically that if one may not cook for the Sabbath, he certainly may not cook for a weekday.

"Accordingly, if one prepares a dish on the eve of the festival intending to rely on this dish, and then cook and bake other food on the festival for the Sabbath, it is permissible. This dish of food on which one relies is known as the *eruv tavshilin* (token mingling of dishes)... The minimum quantity of food that may be used as *eruv tavshilin* is not less than the size of an olive. . ." (*Yad, Yom Tov* 6:1-3).

TOWNS OF ISRAEL   עָרֵי יִשְׂרָאֵל

THE towns of Israel, alphabetically arranged in Hebrew, and their respective populations (in 1974) are as follows:

Elath	12,800	אֵילַת
Ashdod	40,500	אַשְׁדּוֹד
Ashkelon	43,100	אַשְׁקְלוֹן
Beersheba	84,100	בְּאֵר־שֶׁבַע
Beth Shean	11,300	בֵּית־שְׁאָן
Bné Brak	74,100	בְּנֵי־בְּרַק
Bath Yam	99,800	בַּת־יָם
Givathayim	48,500	גִּבְעָתַיִם
Herzliah	41,200	הֶרְצְלִיָּה

Ḥaderah	31,900	חֲדֵרָה
Ḥolon	98,000	חוֹלוֹן
Ḥaifa	218,700	חֵיפָה
Tiberias	28,800	טְבֶרְיָה
Jerusalem	304,500	יְרוּשָׁלַיִם
Kfar Sava	26,500	כְּפַר־סָבָא
Lydda	30,500	לוֹד
Nahariyah	24,000	נַהֲרִיָּה
Nazareth	33,300	נָצְרַת
Upper Nazareth	30,800	נָצְרַת עֲלִית
Nathanyah	70,700	נְתַנְיָה
Akko, Acre	34,400	עַכּוֹ
Afulah	17,400	עֲפוּלָה
Pethaḥ Tikvah	92,400	פֶּתַח־תִּקְוָה
Safed	13,600	צְפַת
Kiryath Ata	27,000	קִרְיַת אָתָא
Kiryath Shemonah	15,200	קִרְיַת שְׁמוֹנָה
Rishon l'Zion	51,900	רִאשׁוֹן־לְצִיּוֹן
Reḥovoth	39,200	רְחוֹבוֹת
Ramlah	34,100	רַמְלָה
Ramath Gan	117,500	רָמַת־גַּן
Tel Aviv	362,900	תֵּל־אָבִיב

Elath, passed by the Israelites on their way north from Sinai (Deuteronomy 2:8), is mentioned in the Bible seven times. The gulf of Elath, at the northern extremity of the Red Sea, is 117 miles long; it is bounded by Saudi Arabia, Jordan, Israel, and Egypt. Elath is being developed as a port; it served as a merchandising port for Solomon's

477

commerce in copper, mined in the nearby desert plain. King Solomon built a navy at Etzyon-Gever near Elath in the land of Edom, on the shore of the Red Sea. Hiram sent his men, expert seamen, to man the fleet along with the men of Solomon; they reached Ophir and brought from there eighteen tons of gold for king Solomon (I Kings 9:26-28).

Ashkelon, one of the five leading Philistine cities during the biblical period, is mentioned in David's lament for Saul and Jonathan: "Tell it not in Gath, proclaim it not in the streets of Ashkelon, lest the daughters of the Philistines rejoice" (II Samuel 1:20). Archeological excavations revealed layers reaching from late Arabic at the top down to the early Canaanite town destroyed some 2,000 years before the common era. In the book of Judges 14:19, we are told that Samson went down to Ashkelon, whence he brought the gala robes to those who had guessed his riddle. The prophets Zephaniah (2:4) and Zechariah (9:5) predicted Ashkelon's destruction. Herod the Great, born in Ashkelon, beautified it with colonnades. Rabbi Benjamin of Tudela, who included Ashkelon among the hundreds of places he visited between 1165 and 1172, notes in his book of travels: "Merchants come here from everywhere to trade... There are about two hundred Jews here." Shortly thereafter, the Jewish community was annihilated by the Crusaders. The town was eventually destroyed by the Moslems. The modern town of Migdal Ashkelon has been developed largely by the Zionist Federation of South Africa.

Beersheba, mentioned in connection with Abraham, Isaac and Jacob, the three patriarchs of Israel, was a favorite dwelling place of the nomadic families because its abundant water supply proved a great blessing for their flocks. Capital of the Negev, modern Beersheba is completely a Jewish town, inhabited for the most part by newcomers from various countries. The Hias House in Beersheba, serving as a boarding place, is primarily intended to provide accomodations for experts who are engaged in developing the Negev for new *olim* (immigrants). Beersheba, on account of its persistent water supply, serves as a key to irrigation projects in this section of the Negev.

Beth Shean, founded three thousand years before the common era, fell into the hands of the Egyptians who garrisoned it for some three centuries. In Joshua 17:16, we are told that the inhabitants of Beth Shean made themselves formidable by the use of iron chariots, "both the natives of Beth Shean and its townships and those who live in the valley of Jezreel." Occupied intermittently for more than five thousand years as the most strategic site in Palestine, a mass of archeological evidence has been produced from its eighteen explored levels. Under king Solomon, Beth Shean became an important commercial center, inhabited mostly by non-Jews. Modern Beth Shean, in the Jordan valley south of Lake Tiberias, was founded in 1949 by new-comers, shortly after the establishment of the State of Israel. The area, which used to be agriculturally rich because of its numerous springs and was therefore known as "the gate of paradise," has been developed recently for cotton-growing. It lies 850 ft. below sea-level.

Bné Brak, mentioned in Joshua 19:45 as one of the cities of the tribe of Dan, became a great center of Jewish learning during the time of Rabbi Akiva. Modern Bné Brak, established in 1924 by pious Jews of Poland, clings to its religious tradition. Its talmudic academies (*yeshivoth*) attract many students from Israel and abroad.

Bath Yam, coastal town with a pleasant sandy beach which attracts numerous vacationers, was founded in 1925. Originally, it was called Bayith v'Gan.

Givathayim, east of Tel Aviv, was created in 1942 by the unification of five suburbs.

Herzliah, named after Theodore Herzl, was founded in 1924 by sons of settlers from established *moshavoth* (agricultural villages). It is one of the leading vacation resorts in Israel.

Ḥaderah, established in 1891 by *Bilu* immigrants, the first *ḥalutzim* (pioneers) in the history of the Zionist movement, is an Arabic name which signifies *green*, alluding to the weeds which used to cover the extensive swamps in northern Sharon. Today Ḥaderah is surrounded by citrus groves; its economy is based on intensive agriculture and industry. Half of its original settlers died of malaria. As a result of the eucalyptus trees that were planted, and the drainage canals that were dug, the dangers to health have ceased.

Ḥolon, less than four miles from Tel Aviv, was established in 1935 on parched sand (*ḥol*). A Samaritan colony in Ḥolon consists of some hundred and fifty persons. The *Lodziah*, textile factory, was built by immigrants originating from the Polish city of Lodz.

Haifa, the second largest city of Israel, has the best sheltered bay on Israel's Mediterranean coast; it serves as the base of Israel's ships, both of the navy and the merchant fleet. It has been conjectured that the name חֵיפָה is a combination of the words חוֹף יָפֶה (*Ḥof Yafeh*, beautiful coast). Built at the foot of Mount Carmel on the narrow stretch of land between the mountain and the sea, Haifa has gradually spread to the mountain top, and also out to the sea on land reclaimed when the deep-water harbor was built (1929-33). The *Technion*, Israel's Institute of Technology, was the first structure erected on *Hadar ha-Karmel* (1912). The Talmud mentions Haifa in Shabbath 26a and elsewhere.

Tiberias, on the western shore of the Sea of Galilee, was founded in the year 26 by Antipas, son of Herod the Great, in honor of the Roman emperor Tiberius. It soon became the seat of great academies of Jewish learning, where the Mishnah was completed in 200 and the Jerusalem Talmud in 400. The famous masoretic scholars, Ben Naftali and Ben-Asher, lived in Tiberias, where the Tiberian system of Hebrew vocalization had been perfected between the sixth and seventh centuries. The tombs of Rabbi Yoḥanan ben Zakkai, Rabbi Eliezer ben Hyrcanus, Rabbi Akiva, the Rambam as well as many other immortal sages rest enshrined here. The tomb of Rabbi Meir, referred to as *Rabbi Meir Baal ha-Nes*, is scrupulously guarded in Tiberias inside the building of Rabbi Meir, to whom miracles have been attributed in aggadic literature. The importance of the town has been further enhanced by the hot springs and the development of colonies around *Yam Kinnereth* (Sea of Galilee).

Jerusalem, the most important city of the Bible, has been the focal point of Jewish religious life and aspirations ever since David made it the City of David. Here David and Solomon, Isaiah and Jeremiah, Ezra and Nehemiah lived and labored for their people.

Shortly after 1000 before the common era, Jerusalem was captured by David, who made it his capital. Solomon enlarged it to the north, and erected the Temple and his palace in the area of the Mosque of Omar, the elegant Moslem prayer place which was built in the seventh century. Described as "beautiful in elevation, the joy of the whole earth" (Psalm 48:2), Jerusalem is higher than almost any other great capital in history; it is situated on a rock plateau at an elevation of two thousand five hundred and fifty feet.

In the Talmud it is noted that "ten measures of beauty came down to earth: nine were taken by Jerusalem, and one by the rest of the world" (Kiddushin 49b). Rabbi Yehudah Halevi, the twelfth-century Spanish Hebrew poet, sang: "Oh, city of the world, most chastely fair, / In the far west, behold, I sigh for thee. . . / Oh, had I eagles' wings I'd fly to thee, / And with my falling tears make moist thine earth. . ."

The etymology of the name Jerusalem is uncertain. Some are of the opinion that יְרוּשָׁלַם signifies *possession of peace* (יְרוּשׁ שָׁלֵם) or

480

a foundation of peace (ירו שלם) or the city of peace. In Jewish thinking throughout the generations, Jerusalem has meant all this and
more. As the capital of Israel today, Jerusalem has entered a new
"era of magnificent achievement which may yet outshine the brilliance of its long and unique past" (Salo W. Baron).

The biblical spelling of the name for Jerusalem is, except in very
few places, without the letter yod (ירושלם). But it is pronounced Ye-
rushalayim in the many passages where it occurs without a yod. The
dual termination ayim is attributable to Jerusalem's situation upon
two hills.

Kfar Sava, popularly called *Kfar Sabba*, has rapidly become a center of citri-culture since 1920. It is based principally on agriculture
and industrial enterprises. Kfar Sava is regarded as the forerunner of
the many colonies in southern Sharon. Beth Berl, a cultural center
for youth movements, is found in the vicinity. It is named after Berl
Katzenelson, leading theoretician of the labor movement in Israel.

Lydda or *Lod*, mentioned in the Bible (I Chronicles 8:12), became
an important rabbinic center after the destruction of Jerusalem. Rabbi
Akiva and other distinguished authorities taught in the Academy of
Lod, which was regarded as second to Jerusalem. Its commercial and
economic status was enhanced on account of its being situated on a
strategic crossroad, in the fertile plain of Sharon, seventy miles south
of Haifa and eleven miles southeast of Jaffa-Tel Aviv. Because of its
airport especially, modern Lydda has become a communications center, where large numbers of immigrants have settled since 1948.

Nahariyyah, on the coast of western Galilee, was established in 1934
by German immigrants as the first Jewish village in the area. They
soon developed it into a seaside resort with a highly intensive garden-
ing and truck-farming economy. At several places in the vicinity of
Nahariyyah, traces of an ancient Canaanite settlement have been
excavated.

Nazareth, in Lower Galilee, is not mentioned in the Hebrew Bible
or the Talmud; it is mentioned several times in the New Testament
as the place where the founder of Christianity was brought up. Secluded within a circular vale and on the surrounding mountain slopes,
Nazareth was unimportant to be spoken of in the Hebrew Bible, the
Talmud, or by the historian Josephus. Since 1948, when Nazareth
was occupied by the Israeli forces, it has been the headquarters of
Israel's northern district. Most of its inhabitants are Catholic, Greek
Orthodox, and Moslem. The new Jewish section, named *Kiryath*

481

Natsrath (קרית נצרת), has been built on the top of the mountain overlooking the town from the east. Most of its inhabitants are newcomers from eastern Europe.

Nathanyah, founded in 1928 and named in honor of Nathan Straus, philanthropist, who was deeply interested in public health and made possible the construction of child welfare stations and a health center under the auspices of Hadassah. Originally, it was planned as a citrus-growing center; it has blossomed forth in the course of a comparatively short period as an important industrial town with a picturesque beach and cool city-parks.

Acre or *Akko*, an important commercial town fifteen centuries before the common era, was not included in the sanctified area of *Eretz Yisrael* even though it had been assigned to the tribe of Asher, since "Asher did not drive out the inhabitants of Akko" (Judges 1:31). Akko was the seat of a Greek colony of merchants before the era of Alexander the Great, and it turned into a hellenistic town which later came under the Romans. At the beginning of the second century, the Jewish inhabitants of Akko were frequently visited by Rabban Gamaliel, who actively combated the spread of *minuth* (heresy) among his people and was instrumental in adding the prayer against the apostates (*minim*) to the *Shemoneh Esreh*. Two thousand Jewish inhabitants were massacred in Akko in the year 66, during the war against the Romans. During the entire period of the Crusades, it served as the capital of the Christian kingdom; it again harbored a Jewish community. In 1799, when Napoleon invaded Palestine, he was forced to leave because he could not reduce Akko. In 1948, it was taken by the Israeli forces. Efforts are being made to restore to Akko its former importance as an economic center.

Afulah, founded in 1925 by the American Zion Commonwealth, has absorbed many immigrants since 1948. Its inhabitants are for the most part farmers and craftsmen. The only sugar factory in Israel is situated in Afulah, which forms part of the Valley of Jezreel (*Emek Yizrael*).

Pethah Tikvah, the oldest of the Jewish agricultural settlements, was founded in 1883 by *Hoveve Zion* (Lovers of Zion), pioneers of the First Aliyyah. They were assisted by Baron Edmond de Rothschild, in 1887, and were subsequently joined by new settlers, so that Pethah Tikvah developed into the largest and one of the most prosperous of the Jewish agricultural settlements. It is referred to as the Mother of Colonies, and depends mainly on orange growing.

482

Safed, in Upper Galilee, near Tiberias, is mentioned in Talmud Ye-rushalmi as one of the places where fire signals announced the new month during the tannaitic period. In the fifteenth century, Safed became a center of talmudic and kabbalistic endeavors; in the six-teenth century, it attracted numerous Kabbalists who desired to be close to the traditional tomb of Rabbi Simeon ben Yoḥai at Meron, an ancient town in Galilee, which has become a place of pilgrimage especially on *Lag b'Omer*. The Zohar, which is the basic foundation of Jewish mysticism, has been attributed to Rabbi Simeon ben Yoḥai, a disciple of Rabbi Akiva. Rabbi Isaac Luria (1534-1572), the famous exponent of Practical Kabbalah, and Rabbi Joseph Karo, author of the *Shulḥan Arukh*, were among those who settled in Safed. The con-quest of Safed in 1948 has been regarded as one of the miracles of the Israeli War of Liberation.

Rishon l'Zion, founded in 1882 by *Bilu* pioneers, was generously assisted by Baron Edmond de Rothschild, who built there wine cellars which are counted among the largest in the world. Wine from these cellars is exported to all parts of the world.

Reḥovoth, several miles southeast of Tel Aviv, was founded in 1890 by Russian Jews under the leadership of Rabbi Samuel Mohilever, who had organized the first *Ḥoveve Zion* society in 1881, in Warsaw, Poland. The name *Reḥovoth* is borrowed from the story of Isaac, who dug another well over which the Philistines did not dispute and called it Reḥovoth, saying: "Now the Lord has made room for us; we shall prosper in the land" (Genesis 26:22). The Weizmann Institute was established in 1944 for applied mathematics, biophysics, electronics, experimental biology, organic chemistry, physics, and atomic research. The Agricultural Experimental Station is under the auspices of the Ministry of Agriculture.

Ramlah, the only town in Palestine founded by the Arabs, was es-tablished in 717; its name is derived from the Arabic word for sand. Until the advent of the Crusaders in the eleventh century, Ramlah served as the capital of the country. The two most important high-ways of Israel converge on this town: the road from Tel Aviv to Je-rusalem and the road from Haifa to Beersheba. About a thousand of its Arab inhabitants remained when Ramlah was occupied by the Is-raeli forces in 1948.

Ramath Gan, founded in 1921, is both a garden city with spacious parks and an industrial center; it has now become the fourth city in Israel. The Bar-Ilan Univserity, named after Rabbi Meir Bar-Ilan was established in 1955, by the *Mizraḥi* World Federation, on the border of Ramath Gan, two miles from Bné Brak.

Tel Aviv, on the coast and immediately north of Jaffa, of which it was originally a suburb, was founded in 1909. It was named after the Hebrew title of Herzl's novel *Altneuland*, which Naḥum Sokolow had borrowed from Ezekiel 3:15. תֵּל אָבִיב is a combination of two words signifying "heap of ruins" (Deuteronomy 13:17) and "spring," respectively. Tel Aviv and the ancient city of Jaffa are combined under one municipal authority.

CITIES OF REFUGE עָרֵי מִקְלָט

IN PRIMITIVE times, the right and duty to avenge a murder belonged to the close relatives of the slain. The six cities of refuge, concerning which we read in the Torah, were designed to shelter anyone who might accidentally commit manslaughter. By fleeing into one of the cities of refuge, persons pursued by avengers of blood were protected against the ancient law of life for life. Forty-two Levitical cities also served for the protection of the unintentional homicide. Anyone killing a man and fleeing to one of those cities was granted a fair trial, and was not put to death unless he had committed actual murder.

In primitive society, shame rested upon the family until its nearest representative, called "blood redeemer" (*go'el ha-dam*), eventually killed the man responsible for the death of one of its members. He slew him without any preliminary trial to settle the actual facts of the case. Then, it often happened, the nearest relative of the second man slain murdered the blood avenger, and a blood feud was established. This system, which prevailed among the Semites and other nations, including the ancient Greeks, was essentially destroyed by the Mosaic legislation, assigning the decision of the guilt or the innocence of the manslayer to an impartial court of justice.

The Torah provides that the principal roads leading to the cities of refuge should be kept open, so that every homicide will be able to find a refuge (Deuteronomy 19:3). Only upon the death of the high priest could the unintentional manslayer leave the city of refuge. This is explained in the Talmud to the effect that the exiled man gains his freedom through the death of the high priest, because the high priest should have prevented the calamity in Israel by virtue of prayer; hence, only his death expiates the homicide's sin (Makkoth 11a).

484

JEWISH VALUES   עֶרְכֵי יַהֲדוּת

In Judaism, religion and morality blend into an indissoluble unity. The love of God is incomplete without the love of one's fellow man. This concept leads toward the goal of eliminating man-made misery and suffering, prejudice and strife, tyranny and social inequality. Judaism champions the cause of universal peace and abhors all violence. It emphasizes the kinship of the human race and the sanctity of human life and freedom. The Jewish people, living in all parts of the world, have been held together by the ties of a common history and a sense of mutual responsibility. The idea that all the people of Israel are knit together (*haverim kol Yisrael*), and are responsible for one another (*kol Yisrael arevim zeh bazeh*), dominates the Hebrew prayers and the entire Jewish tradition.

In Jewish criminal law the defendant before the bar has one great advantage: his guilt must be convincingly proved not only by the public accuser but also by the members of the community. All of them are deemed co-responsible for the offense against property or life. The sins enumerated in each confession recited on the Day of Atonement are phrased in the plural, because the entire community regards itself responsible for many offenses that could have been prevented. The long confession *Al-Ḥet*, containing an exhaustive list of sins which unrolls the whole range of human failings, is based on the idea of social responsibility.

According to a talmudic statement, the severe punishment of an incorrigible son, described in the Torah (Deuteronomy 21:18-21), was never administered and never shall be carried out (Sanhedrin 71a). The biblical law merely stresses the community's interest in the proper upbringing of children; when the authority of parents is powerless, that of the state must be exercised. This law was written merely for the potential reward through studying it (דרוש וקבל שכר). It is indeed rewarding to know the principle underlying the many strictures connected with this law, namely that the entire blame cannot be placed on the incorrigible son. He was left unpunished when his parents were not fit for each other, or when they could not exercise their authority because of defective physical and mental health or lack of harmony and mutual love.

The concept of hallowing God's name is closely connected with all acts of charity and benevolence that are prompted by the human

485

heart. According to a midrashic statement, the instances recorded in
the Torah of God's direct communion with the patriarchs are designed
to teach us how to act: Just as God clothes the naked Adam and Eve,
so should man clothe the naked; just as God visits the sick Abraham,
so should man visit the sick; just as God buries the deceased Moses,
so must man bury the deceased; just as God comforts the mourners,
so must man comfort the mourners. This teaching is contained in the
principle that man is to imitate the merciful qualities of God.

The deeply-rooted observance of the dietary laws has indeed prevented the Jews from being absorbed by the nations in whose midst
they have lived thousands of years. The *kashruth* regulations, though
not directly based on hygienic principles, have often proved hygienic in effect. They have been moreover described as a vital source
helping to identify the individual Jew with his people. According to
Maimonides, the dietary laws train us to control our appetites, so as
not to consider eating and drinking the goal of man's existence. The
animals that are permitted for Jewish consumption represent a concession to the physical human needs, and not a frivolous attitude to
the taking of life. The *shehitah* regulations are designed to reduce the
pain involved in the slaughtering of animals.

Judaism counts cruelty to animals among the most serious of offenses. The Torah describes the Sabbath as a day when the ox and the
mule may have rest, the same as man. An enemy's beast of burden,
lying prostrate under its load, must not be deserted but helped.
One must not plow with an ox and a mule harnessed together, since
they differ greatly in size and in strength. Muzzling an ox when it is
treading out grain is forbidden (Exodus 20:10; 23:5; Deuteronomy
22:10; 25:4). We are told that "the just man takes care of his beast,
but the heart of the wicked is merciless" (Proverbs 12:10).

Hunting was never popular among Jews. Jewish tradition has always regarded unfavorably men like Nimrod, Ishmael and Esau, who
were too fond of the chase. Heinrich Heine, whose relationship to
Judaism varied, had this to say about hunting: "My ancestors did
not belong to the hunters so much as to the hunted, and the idea of
attacking the descendants of those who were our comrades in misery
goes against my grain." Walther Rathenau, who wrote on politics
and philosophy and was assassinated by German anti-Semites in 1922,
stated: "When a Jew says he is going hunting to amuse himself, he
lies." The Jewish trait of compassion, nurtured by a long chain of
tradition, has afforded permanent protection of animals under Jewish

486

control. Hence, the Jews have never organized societies for the prevention of cruelty to animals.

According to Rabbi Akiva, the most comprehensive precept in the Torah is the command: "You shall love your neighbor as yourself." In the opinion of Ben Azzai, a contemporary of Rabbi Akiva, reverence for the divine image in man, the concept of mankind's unity, is of a wider scope—not black, not white, not great, not small, but *man*. Since the Bible traces the ancestry of all mankind to Adam, all men are brothers, the children of one parentage. All men, if given the opportunity, are capable of achieving ethical behavior.

The talmudic-midrashic literature contains an abundance of good counsel in the form of aphorisms and proverbial sayings. Here are several examples: It is easy to acquire an enemy, but difficult to win a friend; he who turns his enemy into a friend is the bravest hero. The greater the man, the humbler he is. He who has nothing to do quickly dies. A person can forget in two years what he has learned in twenty. In prosperity, people feel brotherly to one another. A teacher should give instruction concisely. He who studies but does not review his work is like one who sows but does not reap. Pay special attention to the children of the poor, for it is from them that knowledge will come. Men should be careful not to give their wives any cause for tears, for God counts their tears.

If your wife is short, bend your head and take her advice. A man should eat and drink beneath his means, clothe himself within his means, and honor his wife above his means. The noblest charity of all is that which enables the poor to earn their living. Adversity reveals man's inner strength, but prosperity weakens his will. No man should be held responsible for words uttered in his grief. No man should taunt a reformed sinner about his past. A man notices the weaknesses of others but not his own. Adorn yourself before you adorn or try to improve others. He who seeks a friend without faults will remain friendless. Kindliness is the beginning and the end of the Torah. If two men ask for your help, and one of them is your enemy, help your enemy first. When good people die, they are not truly dead, for their example lives.

The following precepts may well illustrate the moral idealism inculcated by medieval Jewish teachers. Taken at random from several Hebrew works, they read: Expel all envy and hatred from your heart. To forgive is the most beautiful thing a man can do. Do nothing of which you are likely to be ashamed. Do not get into quarrel with anybody. Make peace among people whenever you can. Never speak meaningless words. If you are poor, be thankful for the air you breathe; if you are rich, do not exalt yourself above your poor brother. Both you and your poor brother came naked into the world and will eventually sleep in the dust together.

Learn to speak gently to all persons at all times. Regard every person as greater than yourself. If you are richer and wiser than another, you must know that you are charged with greater responsibility. If another commits a sin, it is from error; if you commit one, you are guilty. Purify your thoughts and think before you speak. Reverence for God is the thread upon which the various good qualities of men are strung like pearls. When this string is severed, the pearls scatter in all directions and are lost one by one. Be first to greet your fellow man; invite him to your joyous occasions; call him by complimentary names; do not give away his secrets; look after his interests when he is away; overlook his shortcomings and forgive him promptly; pray for him and wish him happiness.

In view of the fact that the best and most important part of every man's education is that which he gives himself, the Hebrew verb *hithpallel* (to pray) is reflexive, suggesting identity of subject with object. Thus the Hebrew word for praying connotes self-judgment, self-evaluation, self-instruction. The profound difference between the English verb *to pray* and its Hebrew equivalent is clearly illustrated by the root meaning of *to pray*, which is *to beg, to entreat*. The Hebrew concept of prayer leads to moral conduct and self-fulfillment.

The Hebrew Prayerbook is replete with benedictions directed to the King of the universe who opens the eyes of the blind, clothes the naked, sets the captives free, raises up those who are bowed down, guides the steps of man, gives strength to the weary, and grants us life and sustenance to enjoy many festive occasions. These blessings, numbering one hundred (מאה ברכות), serve as reminders of man's duties to his fellow men, since all actions and attributes which are ascribed to God, the Father of mercies (*Av ha-Raḥamim*), are designed to inculcate in us a moral idealism and a sense of duty toward our neighbors. Hence, the observant Jew repeats them incessantly and fervently, thus concentrating on their full meaning and implication.

The concept of mercy is expressed in many ways throughout Jewish literature. It is best seen in example. Psalm 136 differs from all other psalms in that each of its twenty-six verses closes with a refrain: *His mercy endures forever*. This is probably designed to be chanted in full chorus by the worshipers. According to a talmudic statement, the twenty-six refrains of praise correspond to the twenty-six generations from the creation of the world until the giving of the Torah at Mount Sinai. That is to say, the Lord showed mercy and kindness to man even before he had given him the Torah (Pesaḥim 118a). Moreover, the numerical equivalent of the tetragrammaton, the four-letter name of God that signifies the quality of mercy, is twenty-six.

Similarly, the concept of holiness, often expressed by the formula *asher kiddeshanu* (who hast sanctified us), includes the idea of justice, goodness, wisdom, and truth. The Jewish ideal of persistent and unremitting study and learning is reflected in the blessing which reads: "Blessed art thou . . . who hast sanctified us with thy commandments, and commanded us to study Torah." The lofty ideal of sharing our knowledge with others is expressed in the benediction which addresses God himself as a teacher (*Melammed Torah*). Rabbi Jacob Anatoli of thirteenth-century Naples writes that true wisdom is unselfish. It craves to be shared. The truly wise man will freely dispense what he himself so generously received. Like the prophet of old, he will not be deterred by any timidity or fear from the exercise of his powers. He will speak words of admonition to the strong and weak alike.

The observant Jew of today, in the absence of the Temple at Jerusalem and the numerous precepts connected with the sacrificial system, fulfills approximately one hundred Jewish religious duties out of 613 (*taryag mitzvoth*). The fulfillment of many negative precepts, like *you shall not steal* and *you shall not murder*, is accomplished by inaction. When the anonymous author of the famous medieval work *Sefer ha-Ḥinnukh* states in his introduction that the *mitzvoth* applicable on various occasions total two hundred and seventy, he includes such *mitzvoth* as divorce and *ḥalitzah* which, of course, do not bear upon the daily walk of life. The daily *mitzvoth*, as they are practised by the modern Jew, are largely concerned with *Shabbath*, festivals, food and prayer. The ordinary life of the observant Jew, in his business or profession, is not very different from that of his non-Jewish neighbor.

ORLAH   עָרְלָה

THE Torah forbids the fruit of young trees during the first three years as being *orlah* (uncircumcised) and unclean. In the fourth year the fruit is to be dedicated to God and must be eaten in Jerusalem; or else, its equivalent in money, plus a fifth of its value, must be spent in Jerusalem (Leviticus 19:23-25; Mishnah Peah 7:6).

It is like the second tithe (*ma'aser sheni*), also described as holy (Leviticus 27:30), and must not be eaten outside the walls of Jerusalem except after redemption. For the metaphorical use of *orlah* in the sense of ill-prepared, the phrase עֲרַל שְׂפָתַיִם (poor speaker) is a good example (Exodus 6:12, 30). In Leviticus 26:41, the Torah speaks of humbling "their uncircumcised hearts." In Deuteronomy 30:6, circumcision of the heart means devoting it to noble purposes. The "uncircumcised heart" is closed to divine guidance. The "uncircumcised lips" do not open well in speech.

TEN SEFIROTH עֶשֶׂר סְפִירוֹת

THE term *Sefiroth*, signifying divine emanations or manifestations, first appears in the mystical work *Sefer Yetzirah* (book of creation) which, according to popular tradition, was written by Abraham. Modern scholars, however, maintain that it was composed during the early part of the Middle Ages. The *Sefer Yetzirah*, one of the earliest kabbalistic works, deals with cosmology and stresses the importance of numbers and the letters of the Hebrew alphabet. The numbers from one to ten are represented as the *Ten Sefiroth*, radiating from the *En Sof*, The Infinite Being (God), which is beyond comprehension or description.

According to the mystic teachings of the Kabbalah, every form of existence, material as well as spiritual, is but an emanation of God, who is in everything and everything is in him. The material universe, represented by the tenth *Sefirah* which is called *Malkhuth* (kingship), is the outflow of the other spiritual *Sefiroth* and reflects them; it is the external world, coming in contact with the upper spheres wherein there is a diffusion of the eternal light of the *En Sof*. Then *Ten Sefiroth* represent a transition from the divine to the spiritual, from the spiritual to the moral, from the moral to the physical reality.

The names given to the *Ten Sefiroth* are: 1) *Kether* (crown), 2) *Hokhmah* (wisdom), 3) *Binah* (intelligence), 4) *Hesed* (love), 5) *Gevurah* (power), 6) *Tifereth* (beauty), 7) *Netzah* (victory), 8) *Hod* (majesty), 9) *Yesod* (foundation), 10) *Malkhuth* (kingship). Each of these symbolizes some infinity; the names are arbitrary symbols too. The precise nature of the *Sefiroth* is controversial in kabbalistic writings.

490

TENTH OF TEVETH   עֲשָׂרָה בְּטֵבֵת

THE tenth day of *Teveth*, commemorating the beginning of the siege of Jerusalem by the Babylonian king Nebuchadnezzar in the year 586 before the common era, is a day of fasting. If it falls on a Sabbath, the fast is postponed to Sunday.

Concerning *asarah b'teveth* we read: "In the tenth month, on the tenth day of the month, Nebuchadnezzar king of Babylon came with all his army against Jerusalem, and laid siege to it; and they built siegeworks against it round about" (Jeremiah 52:4; II Kings 25:1).

TEN MARTYRS   עֲשָׂרָה הֲרוּגֵי מַלְכוּת

THE list of the ten martyrs, called עשרה הרוגי מלכות (*asarah harugé malkhuth*), normally includes the following Rabbis: Akiva ben Yosef, Ishmael ben Elisha, Elazar ben Dama, Ḥananya ben Teradyon, Ye-hudah ben Bava, Ḥutzpith *Meturgeman* (interpreter), Yeshevav *Sofer* (scribe), Elazar ben Shammua, Ḥanina ben Hakhinai, Simeon ben Gamaliel, and Ishmael *Kohen Gadol* (high priest). Though these martyrs lived in various periods, tradition has brought them together with the intention of heightening the effect of their tragic death. The history of Jewish martyrdom through the ages is reflected in the portrayal of the *asarah harugé malkhuth*.

The name of the Midrash *Éleh Ezkerah* is derived from Psalm 42:5 (אלה אזכרה ואשפכה עלי נפשי), interpreted to mean: These martyrs I recall, and my soul is melting with secret sorrow. During the Hadrianic persecutions in the year 135, ten sages are said to have been executed on one and the same day because they defied the edict of the Roman government against Jewish religious teaching.

Following the *Avodah* service, recited during the *Musaf* of *Yom Kippur*, an alphabetical poem bearing the title *Éleh Ezkerah* describes the martyrdom of the *asarah harugé malkhuth* both graphically and stirringly. The author of this *piyyut* has not been definitely identified. Mention is made in this composition of a belief that the ten sages of Israel were given over to be slaughtered as a punishment for the sin committed by the ten sons of Jacob who sold their brother Joseph into slavery. In the apocryphal book of Jubilees there is a statement that the sale of Joseph occurred on *Yom Kippur*.

491

Rabbi Ḥananya ben Teradyon was the fourth victim. He was wrapped in the Torah scrolls, from which he had been teaching, and placed on a pyre of green brushwood, and his chest was drenched with water to prolong the agony. His disciples, watching the flames dancing over their beloved teacher, asked: "Master, what do you see?" He replied: "I see parchment burning, while the letter of the Torah soar upward." They advised him to open his mouth that the fire might enter and the sooner put an end to his sufferings; but he refused to do so, saying: "It is best that God who has given life should also take it away; no one may hasten his own death." The executioner removed the wet sponge, fanned the flame, thus accelerating the end, and then plunged himself into the fire. . .

Midrash *Éleh Ezkerah* records Rabbi Yeshevav's last words before martyrdom: There is not a street in all of Rome where someone is not slain by the sword. This wicked nation will continue to shed innocent Jewish blood. My last counsel to you is: Have a care one for the other; love peace and justice. Perhaps there is yet some hope."

DECALOGUE   עֲשֶׂרֶת הַדִּבְּרוֹת

THE Ten Commandments, unequalled for simplicity and comprehensiveness, represent a summary of universal duties that are binding upon the entire human species. They cover the whole religious and moral life, affirming the existence of God and prohibiting idolatry and the profane use of the divine name; stressing the observance of the Sabbath and the reverence due to one's parents; forbidding murder, adultery, theft, false testimony, and predatory desires.

Primarily contained in Exodus 20:2-17, the Ten Commandments reappear in a somewhat modified form in Deuteronomy 5:6-21, where the Sabbath is based upon the deliverance from Egypt, instead of God's resting on the seventh day from the work of creation, and the word "desire" is used in place of "covet." It has been suggested by Bible scholars that, like the last five commandments, each of the first five was originally brief, containing merely the precept without the reason annexed; the elaboration and the minor variations came later. עשרת הדברים means the Ten Words. The Greek term Decalogue is a literal rendering of the biblical *asereth ha-dvarim*. According to a talmudic statement (Berakhoth 12a), the Ten Commandments were recited in the Temple as part of the daily service, before the *Shema*.

492

On account of the heretics, however, who asserted that only the Ten Commanments were divinely given, the custom was abolished outside Eretz Yisrael.

TEN TRIBES   עֲשֶׂרֶת הַשְּׁבָטִים

THE ten tribes of the kingdom of Israel, whose native land was occupied by strangers known as Kutheans or Samaritans, never again formed a distinct community after having been taken into captivity by the Assyrians in 722 before the common era. When the people of the southern kingdom, Judah, were exiled into Babylonia by Nebuchadnezzar some hundred and fifty years later, individual members of the ten tribes attached themselves to them in the course of the captivity, and accompanied them back into Judea when Cyrus the Persian permitted them to return to their homes. In I Chronicles 9:3, people of Ephraim and Manasseh are mentioned, along with those of Judah and Benjamin, as dwelling in Jerusalem after the return. The majority of the ten tribes, however, are assumed to have lost their nationality and assimilated in the country of their captivity. Hence, they are referred to as the lost ten tribes.

In the Apocrypha we are told that the ten tribes "formed this plan among themselves: to leave the heathen population and to go to a more distant region, where the human race had never lived, so that there perhaps they might keep their statutes, which they had not kept in their own country... The Most High then did wonders for them, for he held back the sources of the river until they had passed over. But it was a long journey of a year and a half to that country, and that country is called Arzareth. There they have lived until the last time, and now, when they are about to come again, the Most High will hold back the sources of the river again, so that they can cross over" (II Esdras 13:41-47).

Sabbatyon or *Sambatyon* is the legendary river across which the ten tribes were transported by the Assyrians, and about which so many myths were subsequently accumulated. This river was described by Josephus as the *Sabbatic River*. According to Pliny, the river runs rapidly for six days in the week and stops on the seventh (*Historia Naturalis*, 31:2). When Rabbi Akiva was asked why Saturday is superior to any other day, he answered: "The river Sambatyon proves it" (Sanhedrin 65b). According to the legends disseminated by Eldad

493

ha-Dani, a ninth-century Jewish traveller and scholar, the Sambatyon surrounds the land of the descendants of Moses (בני משה), who have there a powerful kingdom. His story reads as follows:

"The *Bné Mosheh* are surrounded by a river like a fortress which, without water, rolls sand and stones with such a force that if in its course it encountered a mountain of iron it would grind it to powder. On Friday at sunset a cloud envelops the river, so that no man is able to cross it. At the close of the Sabbath the river resumes its torrent of stones and sand." A similar medieval report, current among non-Jews, reads: "One of the wonderful things on earth is a waterless sea of sand... At a distance of three days' journey from this sand sea are mountains, from which descends a river of stones... Beyond this river of stones dwell the ten tribes, who pretend to have kings of their own..."

In the seventeenth century, the fantastic stories of Gershon ben Eliezer Halevi were published in his *Geliloth Eretz Yisrael*, where he describes the Sambatyon River as follows: "It is seventeen miles wide and throws stones as high as a house. On Saturday it is dry ... and it resembles a lake of snow-white sand. The non-Jews who dwell near the river do not drink of its water, nor do they give it to their cattle, considering it a sacred river. The water has, besides, a curative power in leprosy and other diseases. The river ceases to flow on Friday, two hours before sunset..." The Dutch Rabbi Manasseh ben Israel (1604-1657), born of Marrano parentage, wrote his *Mikveh Yisrael* (Hope of Israel) in connection with the reputed discovery of the lost ten tribes in South America. Attempting to prove the existence of the Sambatyon, Manasseh ben Israel asserts that even when its sand is kept in a glass it is agitated during six days of the week and is quiescent on Saturday.

Claiming to be of the tribe of Dan, Eldad ha-Dani travelled through Egypt, Mesopotamia, North Africa and Spain; he aroused very great interest by his strange accounts of the life and laws of the lost ten tribes. The laws and customs which he described as having come from the time of Joshua differed in many details from talmudic tradition. It has been surmised that his reports may have related to tribes of native Jews now known to have lived in the districts he mentioned in his accounts; they have been collected under the title *Sefer Eldad ha-Dani*. He reported that Asher, Gad and Naphtali formed a wealthy and independent state in Southern Ethiopia, and that on their borders was the territory inhabited by the *Bné Mosheh*, encircled by the legendary River Sambatyon.

494

The twelfth-century traveller Benjamin of Tudela, whose book of travels is a major source of medieval Jewish history, heard of the lost ten tribes in Central Asia. David Reuveni, the sixteenth-century adventurer claimed that he was an emissary from the lost ten tribes and forerunner of the Messiah. He asserted that he was sent by his brother, the king of the tribe of Reuben, to obtain help from the European powers against the Moslems. He made a deep impression on Jews and non-Jews. One of the Marranos, who openly returned to the Judaism of his ancestors and assumed the name of Solomon Molcho, attached himself to David Reuveni and made an intensive study of Judaism. He fled to Turkey, where his piety and eloquence attracted a large following, acclaiming him as Messiah. They both were finally arrested by the Inquisition. Molcho was burned at Mantua; Reuveni died a prisoner of the Inquisition in Spain. Shabbethai Tsevi, the pseudo-Messiah of the seventeenth century, appointed rulers over the various lost tribes.

It has been suggested that the legend about Sambatyon is attributable to the confusion of חול (sand) with חול (weekday); the river that throws up sand became the river that "works" on weekdays only. The legend originated with a river of sand and stones which, owing to a volcanic cause, might have been agitated. The Hebrew name was *Nehar Ḥol* (river of sand). This name was later misunderstood to signify *the river of the weekdays*, and this gave rise to the legend of a periodic river which alternated between Saturday and weekdays, whence its name *Sabbatyon* or *Sambatyon*. This ingenious conjecture is held to be quite untenable.

Various peoples have either claimed, or had it claimed for them, that they are the descendants of the missing ten tribes of Israel. Some Afghans, Hindus, Japanese, and North American Indians have pressed this claim. In England, the British Israelites, a Christian organization, believe that the modern Celto-Saxon nations may claim literal descent from the lost ten tribes, who reached the British Isles under the names of Angles, Saxons, and Jutes. Historians, however, assert that some of the ten tribes were included among the Samaritans, others were assimilated while in captivity, while still others were absorbed by the Judean exiles who were deported to areas adjacent to Media and Mesopotamia, where the ten tribes were located.

Manasseh ben Israel's lively correspondence with English puritans and mystics concerning the fate of the tribes resulted in a manifestation of friendly concern for the Jewish cause in England. Oliver Crom-

495

well strongly supported the readmission of the Jews to England, where they had not been permitted to live from 1290 to 1655. This was in response to various petitions presented by Manasseh ben Israel to secure permission for Jews to live in England.

TEN-DAYS REPENTANCE   עֲשֶׂרֶת יְמֵי תְּשׁוּבָה

THE ten days between *Rosh Hashanah* and *Yom Kippur* are known as the penitential season, beginning on the first day of *Tishri* and ending with the close of the Day of Atonement. According to a talmudic statement, three books are opened on New Year's Day: the righteous are inscribed for life, the wicked for death, while the intermediate remain in suspense till the Day of Atonement; by means of good works and repentance they can make the swaying balance incline in their favor, that they may live (Rosh Hashanah 16b).

Repentance is aimed to reinforce the will with a moral dynamic and boundless energy; with the mood of repentance comes new insight and fresh illumination, new aspirations and greater ethical achievement. The ten days between *Rosh Hashanah* and *Yom Kippur* are designed as *yamim nora'im*, solemn days in the Jewish calendar, marked by contrition and prayers for divine forgiveness, and a turning away from the pettiness of our daily life.

Emphasis is placed on the sincerity of repentance, which alone is effective: "If any one says to himself: I will sin and repent, and again I will sin and repent [to escape the consequences], no opportunity is given him to repent. If he says: I will sin, and the Day of Atonement will expiate it, the Day of Atonement effects no atonement" (Yoma 8:9).

PEAH

THE field-corner (*peah*), set aside for the use of the poor, is another example of the kindly consideration of the poor so frequently expressed in the laws of the Torah, championing the weak and the oppressed. "When you reap the harvest of your land, you shall not be so thorough that you reap the field to its very edge, nor shall you glean the stray ears of grain. You shall not pick your vineyard bare, nor gather up the grapes that have fallen; you shall leave these for the poor and for the alien" (Leviticus 19:9-10). This law is part of the Holiness Code, imposed by God as a reflection of his own holiness ("Be holy, for I, the Lord your God, am holy").

Peah is the name of the second tractate of the Mishnah, consisting of eight chapters and dealing primarily with the biblical laws permitting the poor to glean in the fields and vineyards and from the olive trees. It begins with the following statement: "These are the things for which no limit has been prescribed [by biblical law]: the corner of the field, the earliest gathered fruits (*bikkurim* brought to the Temple), the pilgrimage offerings, the practice of kindness, and the study of the Torah. . ."

Though the Torah does not prescribe a limit to the part of the crop which the owner was required to leave for the benefit of the poor, the Mishnah states the traditional law according to which the minimum was one-sixtieth of the harvest.

WIG, SHEITEL

פֵּאָה נָכְרִית

THE term *peah nokhrith* is used in the Mishnah and the Talmud in the sense of false curls or wig (Shabbath 6:5; Nazir 28b). The Yiddish word *sheitel* is applied to the wig worn by Jewish married women in certain circles as an emblem of modesty (צניעות). According to an ancient regulation, married women had to cover their hair, particulary when in the street, so as not to attract the attention of strange men.

Very pious women among the Ḥasidim today do not even wear a sheitel, made of real or artificial hair, but use a kerchief as a head-covering, in view of the *halakhah* which forbids the reading of prayers in the presence of a married woman with her hair uncovered. They cut off their hair on their wedding day and wear thereafter either a

497

kerchief or else a so-called *sterntichel*, resembling a cap which is held together by a circlet or lace studded on the forehead with pearls.

In the Bible, the beautiful hair of a maiden is described as a mark of beauty: "You are beautiful, my love, you are beautiful! Your eyes are dove-like behind your veil; your hair is like a flock of goats, trailing down from Mount Gilead" (Song of Songs 4:1).

EARLOCKS   פֵּאוֹת הָרֹאשׁ

The Torah says: "You shall not clip your hair at the temples or mar the edges of your beard. You shall not lacerate your bodies for the dead or tattoo any marks upon yourselves" (Leviticus 19:27-28). This has been explained as opposing the various mourning customs connected with the ancient heathen worship of the dead.

Any deliberate disfigurement of the body is forbidden as unbecoming the dignity of man: "You are children of the Lord your God. You shall not gash yourselves or make any baldness above your foreheads for the dead" (Deuteronomy 14:1). These practices were commonly employed by the idolatrous nations of antiquity. Cutting the flesh and tattoing the skin were closely connected with cutting the hair in a certain manner as a heathen rite, as indicated in Jeremiah 16:6; 48:37; I Kings 18:28.

This has given rise to the practice among strictly observant Jews not to shave their beards or sidelocks (*peoth*), the length of which is to reach the lobes of the ears (*Kitzur Shulḥan Arukh* 170:1). The beard is described as having five corners (*peoth*) which have not been sufficiently defined, and opinions vary among the talmudic authorities as to precisely what they are. For this reason, the *Kitzur* (abridged code) states: "The man who reveres God should not use a razor on any part of the beard, even on his upper lip or under the chin... Those who remove their beard by means of a salve ... should use a strip of wood."

The Yemenites leave the *peoth* intact when, according to the custom among Oriental Jews, they perform the ceremony of giving the first haircut to a boy of four years. They refer to their long *peoth* as *simmanim* (signs), distinguishing them from non-Jews. Earlocks are now characteristic of Yemenite Jews and Ḥasidim. In 1845, this was one of the Jewish customs which the Russian ruling authorities attempted to abrogate.

498

PIDYON HA-BEN   פִּדְיוֹן הַבֵּן

THE ceremony of redeeming the firstborn son (*Pidyon ha-Ben*) on the thirty-first day after birth has its origin in Exodus 13:13 and Numbers 18:16. This precept was originally designed to counteract the heathen practice of sacrificing the firstborn, of man or of beast, to the Semitic gods.

The firstborn sons in Israel originally belonged to the service of God. Later, the Levites were chosen to replace the firstborn of all the other tribes for service in connection with the sanctuary. In return for this, every firstborn Israelite was to be redeemed by paying five shekels to a *kohen*, descendant of the priestly family belonging to the tribe of Levi.

If the child's father is a *kohen* or Levite, or if the mother is the daughter of a *kohen* or Levite, the ceremony of *Pidyon ha-Ben* does not apply. They are exempt from this duty. If the thirty-first day falls on a Sabbath or a major holiday, the *Pidyon ha-Ben* is postponed to the next day.

With the Sephardic Jews it is customary that the *kohen* officiating at the *Pidyon ha-Ben* performance begins by directing several questions to the mother of the child in order to determine that the child is indeed her firstborn son.

Pidyon ha-Ben does not apply to one born in a Caesarean operation (abdominal delivery) or after a miscarriage. The sum of five shekels or its equivalent, paid to the *kohen*, is generally returned to the father or given to charity. According to the *Kitzur Shulḥan Arukh*, the father should choose a religious-minded *kohen*, who is both well-informed and in need, with the understanding that the redemption money is not to be returned.

RANSOM OF CAPTIVES   פִּדְיוֹן שְׁבוּיִים

THE ransoming of captives is considered to be one of the most sacred obligations of a Jewish community. In Jewish law, it is placed above the important duty of feeding and clothing the poor. Special collections were made for extraordinary communal expenses, such as the support of orphan children and fitting out a poverty-stricken girl with clothing and a dowry (*hakhnasath kallah*), but particularly for the

499

ransom of captives. The Jewish people of ancient and medieval times were frequently subjected to capture by enemies who extorted ransoms from the communities. In the seventeenth century, the Jewish community of Venice organized a society for redeeming the captives (*hevrath pidyon shevuyim*), for the liberation of Jews incarcerated by pirates. Many other communities, following the example of Venice, appointed special *parnasim* (communal wardens) to collect funds for the purpose of ransoming the captives. The community was obliged to pay ransom for any of its members who sold himself into slavery or was taken captive for debts he owed. It was not obliged to pay all that was demanded for the ransom of a scholar.

According to a tannaitic statement, if a man and his father and his teacher were incarcerated, he takes precedence over his teacher in procuring ransom, wnile his teacher takes precedence over his father; that is, he must procure the ransom of his teacher before that of his father; but his mother takes precedence over all of them. A scholar takes precedence over a king, for if a scholar dies there is none to replace him, while all are eligible for kingship (Horayoth 13a).

The Talmud relates that when Rabbi Joshua ben Ḥananya visited Rome, he was told that a handsome-looking boy with curly locks was in prison. He stationed himself at the doorway of the prison ... and said: "I will not budge from here until I ransom him, whatever price may be demanded." He ransomed him at a high figure, and it did not take long before the young man eventually became a great teacher in Israel, namely: Rabbi Ishmael ben Elisha (Gittin 58a).

In the tannaitic period it had been found necessary to enact a law against paying too high a ransom for Jewish captives, lest kidnaping might become a lucrative trade. The Mishnah therefore states: "Captives should not be ransomed for more than their value, as a precaution for the general good" (Gittin 4:6). The price might not exceed the value of the captive if sold as a slave. The talmudic sages forbade the assistance in their attempts to escape, for fear that the treatment of captives in general would be made more cruel. When emperor Rudolph demanded a large sum from the Jews for Rabbi Meir of Rothenburg, who had been seized and committed to prison in 1284, and the Jews were ready to pay any sum the emperor demanded, Rabbi Meir, known as the *Maharam*, refused to be ransomed. He spent the last seven years of his life in prison, revising his literary works. When he died, the emperor refused to surrender Rabbi Meir's body for fourteen years until a large sum was paid for its redemption.

POSKIM   פּוֹסְקִים

THE rabbinic codifiers of Jewish law, known as *Poskim*, whose activity bridged the centuries between the completion of the Talmud and the completion of the *Shulḥan Arukh*, are thought of in terms of two groups: *Poskim Rishonim* and *Poskim Aḥaronim*, or early and latter codifiers. The *Rishonim* include the Geonim and their successors, covering the period between the sixth and the fifteenth centuries; the *Aḥaronim* are the codifiers of a later period. Rav Yehudai Gaon of the eighth century is the first known to have written a law code, entitled *Halakhoth Pesukoth*, of which single quotations have been preserved.

In the year 1950, however, almost the entire work was published by S. Sassoon (Mekitzé Nirdamim, Jerusalem) from a manuscript found in Sana, Yemen. This code has been referred to also as *Halakhoth Ketu'oth*. Rav Yehudai Gaon has been considered as one of the great talmudic authorities responsible for *Halakhoth Gedolah*, the largest and most important work of codification in the period of the Geonim. Some attribute it to Rabbi Simeon Kayyara of the ninth century, who made use of the *Halakhoth Pesukoth* and the *She'eltoth* by Rav Aḥa of Shabḥa, a contemporary of Rav Yehudai Gaon.

The *Halakhoth* by Rabbi Isaac Alfasi, who was born in Morocco and died in Spain (1013-1103), has enjoyed a very wide circulation as a compendium of the Talmud referred to as *Talmud Katan* (abridged Talmud) or *Alfasi*. The *Alfasi*, like the *Halakhoth Gedoloth*, closely follows the Talmud; it retains only what is considered the norm and omits the dissenting opinions and discussions. Several other codes followed, all of which were eclipsed by the most systematic and comprehensive Jewish code of law and ethics, the *Mishneh Torah*, or *Yad ha-Ḥazakah*, written in lucid Hebrew by the *Rambam* (Rabbi Moses ben Maimun) toward the end of the twelfth century. Its influence on many generations has been incalculable. The *Arba'ah Turim* by Rabbi Jacob ben Asher (1269-1340) and the *Shulḥan Arukh* by Rabbi Joseph Karo (1488-1575) were to a great extent drawn from the *Mishneh Torah*. Their very phraseology is borrowed from the code of Maimonides.

The *Turim* and the *Shulḥan Arukh* furnish instruction in the religious duties that are applicable only to conditions existing after the cessation of the Jerusalem Temple, while the *Mishneh Torah* is a repository of all Jewish teachings from the time of the first Moses to the

time of Moses Maimonides. No detail escaped him in the vast talmudic and post-talmudic literature. Unlike his predecessors and successors, Maimonides assembled all the ethical and civil regulations
which the sages had deduced from the Holy Scriptures.

He took no account of whether the entire material which he incorporated in the *Mishneh Torah* was relevant to the conditions of his
time. He dealt with all the laws of Judaism, making no distinction
between those regarding the Temple, the sacrifices, the Jewish kings,
the Sanhedrin, and those which bear on the observance of the Sabbath or the practice of charity and prayer. Maimonides used the historical method, covering all the *Halakhah* literature through all the
phases of its development to his own time.

The *Sefer Mitzvoth Gadol* (large book of precepts) by Rabbi Moses
of Coucy, France (1200-1260), frequently called *Semag* (סמ״ג) after
the initial letters, divides the six hundred and thirteen *mitzvoth* into
two parts: 248 *mitzvoth-aseh* (affirmative precepts) and 365 *mitzvoth-
lo-ta'aseh* (prohibitive precepts). The *Sefer Mitzvoth Katan*, composed
a century later by Rabbi Isaac of Corbeil, called *Semak* (סמ״ק) after
the initial letters, is divided into seven parts designed to be read
through once every week.

The *Or Zaru'a* by Rabbi Isaac ben Moses of Vienna (1180-1260)
is the voluminous code much quoted by later codifiers; it is regarded,
both in size and substance, as the most important product of the German Jews in the field of codification. Rabbi Isaac ben Moses of
Vienna was the teacher of Rabbi Meir of Rothenburg, whose authority throughout Europe gained for him the title *Meor ha-Golah* (light
of the exile).

Rabbi Meir of Rothenburg, known as *Maharam* after the initial
letters of מורנו הרב רבי מאיר, exerted a profound influence on Jewish law and custom; his legal decisions were incorporated in the *halakhic* works of his disciples Rabbi Asher ben Yeḥiel, known as *Rosh*,
and Rabbi Mordecai ben Hillel, author of the famous work entitled
Mordekhai, a talmudic compendium containing quotations from numerous medieval authorities and yielding valuable material on social
and intellectual life. The *Mordekhai* has been described as a veritable
encyclopedia of talmudic literature, comprising many responsa which
represent definite legal decisions. It has served later codifiers as a
source book for legal decisions upon a great variety of subjects.

This compilation of material from over three hundred earlier scholars, includes practically all the halakhic literature in existence up to

502

the time of Rabbi Mordecai ben Hillel, in addition to the author's original notes. The numerous quotations in the *Sefer Mordekhai* are the only source for many works that are no longer available now.

Rabbi Mordecai ben Hillel was martyred in Nuremberg in 1298 with his wife and five children. As a result of the persecutions in Germany during the fourteenth century, his work *Mordekhai* became an authoritative substitute for talmudic studies which had declined. He was greatly admired by the German rabbinic authorities of the fifteenth century, and in the codes of Rabbi Joseph Karo and Rabbi Moses Isserles he is among those who are quoted most frequently.

The lifework of Rabbi Mordecai Jaffe of sixteenth-century Poland was the rabbinic law code known as *Levush* (garment), divided into five sections and classified according to the *Shulḥan Arukh* of Rabbi Joseph Karo. The titles of the work and its parts were derived by the author, Rabbi Mordecai, from Esther 8:15 ומרדכי יצא מלפני המלך (בלבוש מלכות תכלת וחור ועטרת...). Since each part of Rabbi Mordecai's rabbinic code bears reference to the royal garment (*levush malkhuth*) worn by Mordecai in the story of Esther, he is referred to as the author of the *Levushim* (בעל הלבושים).

Though the *Levushim* enjoyed great popularity during the lifetime of Rabbi Mordecai Jaffe, they were eventually superseded by the *Shulḥan Arukh* on account of its brevity and simplicity. As a rabbi of Lublin, toward the end of the sixteenth century, Rabbi Mordecai Jaffe became one of the leaders of the Council of Four Lands (*Va'ad Arba Aratsoth*).

After the completion of the *Shulḥan Arukh* by Rabbi Joseph Karo, who died in 1575, only a few attempts were made to codify the new *Halakhah* material which had increased ever since. The works of Rabbi Abraham Danzig (1748-1820), *Ḥayyé Adam* and *Ḥokhmath Adam*, are regarded as the most important modern contributions in this field; the *Halakhah* of the *Aharonim* is codified in these books.

PURIM   פּוּרִים

In its main outlines, the story of *Purim* is typical of the long chain of persecutions to which the Jewish people in the Diaspora have been subjected. Because of a grudge against Mordecai the Jew, Haman presents the Jewish people as a whole to king Ahasuerus as a dangerous people, "scattered and dispersed throughout the empire ... re-

503

fusing to obey the king's laws." A lot (*pur*) is cast, and the day of the massacre is set for the thirteenth of *Adar*. After the intervention of queen Esther, a cousin of Mordecai, a new act is promulgated by the king, giving the Jews the right to organize for self-defense.

The festival of *Purim* was instituted in commemoration of this event. It derives its name from the word פור (lot) and is celebrated on the fourteenth day of *Adar*, following the fast of Esther which is observed on the thirteenth day when the Jews had to fight for their lives. The annual celebration of *Purim* helped the Jewish people, during the dark days of their history, to maintain their trust in the ultimate deliverance from the dangers and difficulties besetting them. The merrymaking, feasting and masquerading, characteristic of *Purim*, have served a much needed relief from the serious life led during the greater part of the year. It has been supposed that the origin of masquerading is to be viewed as a means of disguise from the evil and coping with it. At the mention of Haman during the public reading of the *Megillah* or the scroll of Esther in the synagogue, it has been customary to stamp with vigor on the floor, thus symbolically erasing the name of Haman. Some would knock two sticks on which the name of Haman was written against one another until it disappeared.

The noise-making instruments, used to blot out the name of Haman, are reminiscent of Deuteronomy 25:19 concerning the merciless Amalekites: "You shall blot out the memory of Amalek from under the heavens." Some were accustomed to have Haman's name written on the soles of their shoes, so that it was worn away through stamping their feet whenever it was mentioned during the reading of the *Megillah*.

The *Megillah* is read aloud in the synagogue at the beginning of the festival in connection with the evening service, and again during the morning service. The names of Haman's ten sons are read in one breath in order to lessen the appearance of gloating over their deserved execution, in keeping with the biblical warning: "Do not rejoice when your enemy falls, do not exult when he is overthrown, lest the Lord seeing it will be displeased. . ." (Proverbs 24:17-18).

The special talmudic tractate named *Megillah* fully discusses all the features of the joyous *Purim* festival, on which the following seven *mitzvoth* are observed. 1) *Megillah* reading, 2) exchange of gifts, 3) distribution of charity, 4) Torah reading, 5) recital of *Al ha-Nissim* in the *Amidah* and in the grace after meals, 6) the festive meal of *Purim* (סעודת פורים), 7) restraint of all mourning or fasting.

504

The *Hallel*, however, is not chanted on *Purim* because, unlike *Ḥa-nukkah*, the miracle of *Purim* occurred outside Eretz Yisrael. The festive meal of *Purim*, reminiscent of Esther's banquet, is begun in the afternoon and carried on well into the night. The day succeeding *Purim* (fifteenth of *Adar*) is regarded as a minor holiday, called *Shu-shan Purim*, referred to in the book of Esther (9:18) as the day when the Jews of Shushan, capital of Persia, celebrated their triumph. No *hesped* (funeral oration), or mourning, is allowed even on *Shushan Purim*.

The two Hebrew phrases ברוך מרדכי (blessed be Mordecai) and ארור המן (cursed be Haman) have numerically the same value, 502. Hence the talmudic statement that, on *Purim*, a man should drink till he cannot distinguish between them, since numerically they are identical. The *Purim* carnival *Adloyada*, which has been extended in Tel Aviv to three days, derives its name from the just quoted talmudic pleasantry in Megillah 7b, where the phrase עד דלא ידע (till he does not know the difference) is used.

PIZMON   פִּזְמוֹן

T<small>HE</small> *pizmon*, chanted by reader and congregation responsively, or alternately, is the central hymn in the arrangement of the penitential prayers known as *Seliḥoth*. It is characterized by a traditional melody according to which all its stanzas are sung. The term *pizmon* is of uncertain etymology, though it has been suggested that it is related to the word *psalm*.

Briefly described, the *pizmon* is a hymn with a refrain; it has no more than four lines to a stanza. The *pizmon* במוצאי מנוחה, for example, has the refrain לשמע אל הרנה ואל התפלה as the fourth and concluding line of each stanza. The *pizmon* אחות קטנה, recited on the first night of *Rosh Hashanah* by those who follow the Sephardic *Min-hag*, consists of four rhymed lines and a refrain (תכלה שנה וקללותיה.

PIYYUT   פִּיּוּט

T<small>HOUGH</small> the name *piyyut* is derived from the Greek term for poetry in general, it denotes specifically religious poetry; hence, *payyetan* signifies a liturgical poet. The festival prayerbook (*Maḥzor*) con-

505

tains only a portion of the thousands of *piyyutim* (metrical compositions) that were inspired by the synagogue services. Much of the
synagogal poetry was composed by supremely gifted *ḥazzanim* (cantors), who devised ingenious methods for the further deveolpment of
the Hebrew language through a variety of new-style formations. Before long the divine services gained an inner richness and the voice of
song, which had been silent since the destruction of the Temple, was
heard once again in the synagogue.

The *piyyutim* were added to the old formulas of prayer in a desire
to give expression to the intense emotions and aspirations of the people. They show us the Jewish heart laid before God in all its moods:
in penitence, in fear, in triumph. The worshiper is always likely to
find something in the *piyyutim* in sympathy with his own condition.

The singing of these prayer-poems together has been regarded as
apt to plant the spirit of the Torah in the minds and hearts of young
and old. Most of the *piyyutim* are composed of biblical phraseology
and midrashic interpretations. The *payyetanim* borrowed language
and meter from the Scriptures and drew their material from the inexhaustible wealth of ideas dispersed in both Talmud and Midrash.

The ceaseless efforts of Rabbi Elazar ha-Kallir, a *ḥazzan-payyetan*
of extensive learning who is said to have lived in Palestine during the
eighth century, are chiefly credited with the promotion and advancement of the *piyyut* literature. His numerous prayer-hymns were introduced in all Jewish communities, where they were imitated by
inspired *payyetanim* of succeeding generations. The *ḥazzan* in the
Middle Ages was often a combination of poet, composer and singer,
many of whose melodies have been preserved down to our time. In
the twelfth century, the author of *Sefer Ḥasidim* wrote: "If you cannot concentrate when you pray, search for melodies and choose a tune
you like. Your heart will then feel what you say, for it is the song
that makes your heart respond."

Repeated expression is given in the *piyyutim* to the undying hope
that God will finally put an end to the misfortunes and sufferings of
Israel and all mankind. They are filled with the prayers of men and
women who have struggled to maintain life and turned to God in
their distress. No other kind of medieval Hebrew literature has been
so popular as the *piyyut*. It has penetrated into every part of the
religious life and entered the synagogue and the Jewish home alike,
cheering the family with table songs (*zemiroth*), welcoming the Sabbath and bidding it farewell, sharing in the joys and the sadness of

the home from birth to death. Indeed, no other medieval poetry has been read so frequently by so many people and with so much approval.

The daily Prayerbook and the holyday Prayerbook, the *Siddur* and the *Maḥzor*, contain only a portion of the thirty-five thousand metrical compositions that were inspired by the standard Jewish prayers. These books merely represent the kind and quality of the vast number of *piyyutim* that were intended to provide the worshipers with ever-new forms of religious expression and stimulating song.

Israel Davidson, in the introduction to his *Thesaurus of Medieval Hebrew Poetry*, writes: "Many years will yet pass and much labor will have to be spent before the contents of the innumerable manuscripts will be made accessible." In his preface to the last volume of the *Thesaurus*, he states that "a rough enumeration brings up the number of poets to 2,843." The religious and secular Hebrew poems listed in Davidson's monumental work total 35,200.

Poetry seldom says directly what it means; it only hints at it under figures of speech. Some *piyyutim* are difficult to understand because they are couched in rare diction and allegorical allusions. Quite often one is likely to miss the *payyetan's* thought by reason of the metaphorical imagery, conciseness and brevity, endless variations of rhyme and acrostics usually employed in the *piyyut*. Biblical expressions are quoted at every turn and talmudic-midrashic themes are continually intimated, so that without frequent reference to the ancient Hebrew classics the reader cannot fully appreciate the *piyyutim*. The best *piyyutim*, however, combine simplicity and clarity and contain noble ideas about the basic problems of life on earth.

Since about the middle of the eighteenth century numerous attempts have been made to render the *piyyutim* of the *Siddur* and the *Maḥzor* into English on the basis of translations which began to appear as early as the fourteenth century. Their defects have been due largely to the word-for-word method and the evident supposition that the translator need not thoroughly understand the Hebrew text in order to translate it. On examining these versions one may detect at a glance the vast jungle of words from which a clear idea only rarely emerges. They are the product of an age that scarcely believed help was needed or desirable for the understanding of the *piyyutim*, giving them to people without note or comment.

Ibn Ezra, who is best remembered for his brilliant commentary on the Bible written in the twelfth century, demands that prayer should be in lucid biblical Hebrew and finds fault with the obscure Hebrew

style of the *payyetanim*. In view of his strong opposition, it is difficult
to explain why Ibn Ezra himself composed scores of *piyyutim*. Quite
obviously, the poet cannot communicate his vision in ordinary language. The music of the sounds plays an important part in attuning
the mind of the reader to receive the message. The nuances and sub-
tleties of expression have to be earnestly studied before their significance is fully unfolded.

PILPUL פִּלְפּוּל

IN CONNECTION with Talmud studies, the term *pilpul* is employed in
the sense of a penetrating theoretical discussion which culminates in
the drawing of conclusions in matters of *halakhah* or traditional law.
It is derived from the Hebrew verb *pilpel* (to spice, to season), signifying to argue a proposition, opinion, or measure.

Since the word *pilpel*, as a noun, means pepper, the suggestion has
been that the argument is as keen as strong pepper. Essentially aiming to clarify a talmudic subject by analysis of its essentials, there
were times when the *pilpul* was made unpopular by its hair-splitting
tendencies serving as an end in itself rather than a means of solving
mooted problems.

Pilpul as a method of training was especially applied in the talmudic
academies (*yeshivoth*) of Poland from the sixteenth century on. Its
object was to sharpen the minds of the students so that they might
see deeper into the difficult talmudic passages. By means of *pilpul*,
the most familiar objects are made to appear in a new light. Hence
the name *ḥiddushim* (original products), or *ḥillukim* (analyses), is
applied to this method of study.

The extreme development of hair-splitting *pilpul*, or talmudic gym-
nastics, dates from Rabbi Jacob Pollak of Prague, who served as rabbi
in Cracow and died in Safed, Eretz Yisrael, about 1532. The talmudic academy (*yeshivah*) which he had founded in Cracow supplied
many of the Jewish teachers of Poland. It was here that the system
of *pilpul* was elaborated, serving the purpose of developing the acumen
of the students. The far-fetched analyses and combinations are often
pursued for their own sake, without distinctive reference to law and
ethics. The mental alertness of the Polish Jews and their inclination to
engage in dialectical debates have often been ascribed to *pilpulism*, a
characteristic acquired through many generations.

PESUKÉ D'ZIMRAH   פְּסוּקֵי דְזִמְרָה

IN KEEPING with a talmudic saying that praise should precede prayer (Berakhoth 32a), the recitation of biblical passages forms the initial part of the daily morning service. They are called *Pesuké d'Zimrah* (verses of song) and consist mainly of Psalms 145-150, ending with the song of Moses (Exodus 14:30-15:18). On Sabbaths and festivals, additional psalms are inserted (19, 34, 90, 91, 135, 136, 33, 93).

The *Pesuké d'Zimrah* also include passages containing mosaics of quotations from various other psalms and the books of Chronicles and Neḥemiah. The benedictions *barukh she-amar* and *yishtabbaḥ* serve as prologue and epilogue, respectively, to the *Pesuké d'Zimrah;* on Sabbaths and festivals, the poem *Nishmath* precedes *yishtabbaḥ*. Psalm 100 (מומור לתודה), in which the whole world is invited to join Israel in the worship of God, is inserted on weekdays. In Temple times it was recited on weekdays while the thank-offerings were being presented upon the altar.

Rabbi Meir of Rothenburg, whose authority among the Jews of the thirteenth century gained for him the title *Meor ha-Golah* (light of the exile), is credited with first introducing the *Pesuké d'Zimrah* as a prelude to the main congregational morning service, which begins with *barekhu* (ברכו) and continues through the *Shema* and the *Shemoneh Esreh.*

PASSOVER   פֶּסַח

THE feast of unleavened bread, instituted in Egypt to commemorate the liberation of the people of Israel more than three thousand years ago, is the first of the three annual pilgrimage festivals at which all men were required to appear in the Temple. The other two pilgrim feasts, *Shavuoth* and *Sukkoth*, likewise commemorate great historic events directly connected with the exodus from Egypt, namely: the revelation at Sinai and the forty-year training toward the conquest of the Holy Land.

Though many residents of remoter regions probably made the long journey to Jerusalem but once in their lives, they participated in spirit in the pilgrim celebrations through the festival services of the synagogue and the home. The *Seder* meal, enjoyed by each Jewish family

on the first night of Passover, has always enshrined the most precious
memories and the most exalting aspirations and hopes of the Jewish
people. Josephus gives the exaggerated number of pilgrims in Jerusalem on one occasion as "not fewer than three million."

Though Passover, like *Shavuoth* and *Sukkoth*, is in certain respects
reminiscent of an agricultural feast (*omer*-offering and prayer for dew),
its historical character as a festival marking the birth of the Jewish
people is frequently emphasized in the Torah. Indeed, the Torah associates the liberation from Egypt with every kind of legislation, religious as well as ethical. The very Decalogue begins with a statement
concerning the exodus. In Deuteronomy 5:15, even the Sabbath, the
most sacred day in the Jewish calendar, is connected with the exodus
from Egypt.

The spring season in which Passover is celebrated is often underscored in the Torah as the month of *Aviv* (Exodus 13:4; 23:15; 34:18;
Deuteronomy 16:1). Spring has always been regarded as suggestive
of the beginning and the survival of the Jewish people. According to
a Jewish tradition, the messianic era will begin in the spring month
of *Nisan*, which marks the historic redemption of Israel from Egypt
(בניסן נגאלו ובניסן עתידין להגאל).

Passover, the greatest of all historical festivals, brings the Jew into
close touch with his people's past, wakening him to the proud consciousness of being free and sharing the glowing aspirations of his liberated ancestors. The predominant feature of Passover has always
been an exuberance of joy. In the darkest days of medievalism the
synagogue and home resounded with song and thanksgiving. As
the springtide of nature fills each creature with joy and hope, so Israel's feast of redemption promises the great day of liberty to those
who still chafe under the yoke of oppression.

In the Bible, the name *Pesah* applies only to the paschal offering
of the fourteenth day of *Nisan* which was consumed on the first night
of the festival, while the entire festival is referred to as *Hag ha-Matzoth*,
the feast of the unleavened bread. The first and last day, in Eretz
Yisrael, are holy days, and the intermediate five days are *Hol ha-Mo‘ed*,
days with a festive character during which work is not prohibited.
Outside Eretz Yisrael, however, the festival is observed for eight days,
in keeping with time-honored tradition. The *Seder* service, with its
ancient symbolism, consists mainly of the reading of the *Haggadah*,
the drinking of four cups of wine, and the meal which has the character
of worship. In the Diaspora, the *Seder* service is conducted twice, on

the first and second nights of *Pesah*, while in Eretz Yisrael only on the first night.

All *hametz* (leaven) is cleared from the Jewish homes before ten o'clock in the morning of the fourteenth of *Nisan* known as *Eruv Pesah*. It is prohibited to eat or possess *hametz* during the eight days of the festival. After burning the *hametz* on *Erev Pesah* morning, the following formal pronouncement is made: "Any kind of leaven in my possession, whether or not I have seen it, whether or not I have removed it, shall be regarded as nonexistent or as mere dust of the earth." If *Erev Pesah* coincides with the Sabbath, the *hametz* is burned on Friday morning. The Jewish code of religious laws and precepts contains detailed rules and regulations for the proper observance of a *kosher Pesah*.

Pesah has meant many things to the Jewish people throughout the ages. From their very beginning, they saw God's outstretched arm in history; they owed their very existence as a people to their faith in divine intervention. The ultimate meaning of the plagues and the other miracles, connected with the exodus from Egypt, is that "the Guardian of Isreal neither slumbers nor sleeps" (Psalm 121:4).

The home observance of the *Seder* and many other *mitzvoth* has strengthened family ties and made Jewish home life beautiful. From the day the Jews left Egypt and were fashioned into a people out of a mass of slaves, they have shared in common memories and hopes, as well as an attachment to their Torah, language and country. They regarded the three of these as holy across the more than thirty centuries of maintaining an existence as a distinct people.

PESIKTA   פְּסִיקְתָּא

THE *Pesikta d'Rav Kahana* is a midrashic collection consisting of thirty-three homiletical discourses for special Sabbaths and for the festivals. It is called *Pesikta* because it is written in *piskoth* or sections. Long before manuscripts of the *Pesikta* were discovered, Leopold Zunz had reconstructed it from quotations and references in other sources.

The *Pesikta Rabbathi*, a midrashic collection containing discourses for the Festivals and the special Sabbaths, was edited in 1880 by Meir Friedman, who was probably unaware of the existence of the Parma manuscript, which among other Midrashim contains the *Pesikta Rab-*

bathi. It is called *Pesikta Rabbathi* (the larger) to distinguish it from the earlier *Pesikta d'Rav Kahana*. It comprises forty-eight sections, and must have been compiled not earlier than the ninth century, while the *Pesikta d'Rav Kahana* dates probably from the seventh century.

What has been erroneously known as *Pesikta Zutarta* (פסיקתא זוטרתא) is a midrashic commentary on the Torah and the *Ḥamesh Megilloth*. It was written by Rabbi Tobiah bar Eliezer early in the eleventh century and is called לקח טוב (good teaching). Each section begins with the word טוב (good).

SAVING A LIFE   פִּקוּחַ נֶפֶשׁ

THE duty of saving an endangered life (*pikkuah nefesh*) suspends the operation of all the commandments in the Torah, with the exception of three prohibitions: no man is to save his life at the price of murder, adultery, or idolatry. The sages of the Talmud interpret the words "he shall live by them" (וחי בהם), in Leviticus 18:5, to mean that the *mitzvoth*, the divine commands, are to be a means of life and not of death. Specifically, the duty of saving a life supersedes the Sabbath laws (פקוח נפש דוחה את השבת). The humanitarian definition of the suspension rule signifies the duty to promote life and health. From a Jewish point of view, it is sinful to observe laws which are in suspense on account of the danger to life or health. One may do any work on Sabbath to save a life (Kethubboth 5a). "The Sabbath has been given to you, not you to the Sabbath" (היא מסורה בידכם ולא אתם מסורים בידה) is a well-known statement in the Talmud (Yoma 85b). It has been noted that the German pessimistic philosopher Schopenhauer could not forgive Judaism for its affirmation of life.

In his *Mishneh Torah*, Maimonides discusses the duty of profaning the Sabbath when failure to do so is certain to endanger human life: "The commandment of the Sabbath, like all other commandments, are set aside if human life is in danger. Accordingly, if a person is dangerously ill, whatever a skilled local physician considers necessary may be done for him on the Sabbath... When such things have to be done ... they should rather be done by adult and scholarly Jews... Similarly, if a ship is storm-tossed at sea, or if a city is surrounded by marauding troops or by a flooding river, it is a religious duty to go to the people's rescue on the Sabbath and to use every means to deliver them" (*Yad, Shabbath* 2:2-3).

512

PROZBUL   פְּרוֹזְבּוּל

THE term *prozbul* is explained as a contraction of the Greek words
pros boulé (before the council). It was a legal instrument drawn up
by the creditor in court, whereby he secured his loans against the
operation of the biblical law of *shemittah* (sabbatical release). By the
law of Deuteronomy 15:1-3, all loans were cancelled at the beginning
of every seventh, sabbatical year.

In order to overcome the reluctance of people to lend money to one
another for fear of forfeiting their claim to it with the arrival of the
sabbatical year, Hillel introduced a method whereby the year of release (*shemittah*) did not affect the debts that had been turned over
to the court.

Appearing before the court (*beth din*), the creditor declared in the
presence of witnesses, who signed the document named *prozbul*, that
he would collect any debt which he might have outstanding with the
person mentioned in the *prozbul* at any time (Mishnah Shevi'ith 10:4).

Hillel's remedy, whereby the lender retained the right to reclaim
the loan at any time he saw fit, was brought about when "he saw that
the people refrained from giving loans one to another and transgressed
what is written in the Torah. . ."

The biblical law concerning the septennial cancellation of debts
was left unchanged by means of a legal fiction, according to which the
court, instead of the individual lender, reclaimed the loan.

PHARISEES; SADDUCEES   פְּרוּשִׁים; צְדוֹקִים

IN THE *Arukh*, the only medieval lexicon covering the talmudic-midrashic literature, Rabbi Nathan ben Yeḥiel of Rome (1035-1106) defines the name *parush* (Pharisee): "one who separates himself from
all uncleanness and from eating anything unclean," unlike the *ammé
ha-aretz*, the ignorant and common people who were not so particular.
There are various attempts at explaining the etymology of the term,
but none of them has won unanimous approval among scholars and
historians.

The best hypothesis advanced seems to be that of the *Arukh* just
quoted. The Pharisees were so called because of their self-imposed
separation from the masses of the less observant Jews during the per-

513

iod of the Second Temple. For the sake of greater strictness they organized themselves in special fraternities (*havuroth*), the members of which were referred to as *haverim* in distinction to the *ammé ha-aretz*, mainly of the peasantry, who were not sufficiently acquainted with the traditional regulations or were unwilling to recognize the authority of the sages.

In contrast to the priestly aristocratic class known as the Sadducees, to whom the written word was the all in all, the Pharisees supplemented the biblical teachings by the traditions and measures introduced in the course of time. The age-long conflict between the Pharisees and the Sadducees was one of the most important factors in the development of Judaism.

While the Sadducees for the most part represented the old conservative positions of the priesthood, the Pharisees were essentially a democratic party in the sense that they were themselves drawn from the people, the lay Israelites; they safeguarded the religious rights and privileges of the laymen as against the exclusive priesthood. Recogizing universal education as basic to Judaism, the Pharisees established schools in all villages in Eretz Yisrael, where instruction was given in the oral law as well as the written law.

The Pharisaic ideal was to bring life more and more under the dominion of religious observance, valued chiefly because of its educational worth. By carefully instilled habits, many religious and ethical precepts were impressed upon the minds and hearts of the people, with whom the observance of Sabbaths and festivals was invested with special sanctity in the home. The progressive tendency of Pharisaism has remained an ever-living force in Judaism, which has proved its strength by withstanding the shocks of time.

It is frequently pointed out that not all Pharisees were alike. Some individuals would cloak themselves in the mantle of Pharisaism and overawe others by a display of insincere piety, by boasting of having left nothing undone in the matter of religious performance. The true Pharisees insisted on inwardness and sincere intent (*kavvanah*), and despised all hypocrites and charlatans, not to be admitted in the presence of God. Hence, it has been concluded that of all the strange ironies of history, perhaps the strangest is that the word *Pharisee* is current as a word of reproach.

The derivation of the name Sadducees, though not quite certain, is generally connected with the high priest Zadok, whom king Solomon installed in place of Abiathar. The name Sadducee or Zadokite evidently designated an adherent of the priestly aristocracy, which served in the same office until 162 before the common era. In time it extended to all who shared the principles current among the rich, well-connected priests for whom religion was primarily the system of worship at the Temple.

Their slavish adherence to the written word led them to interpret "an eye for an eye" (*lex talionis*) literally rather than in the traditional sense of monetary compensation. They rejected the belief in immortality. Since most of their activities and interests centered around the Temple cult, they disappeared soon after the destruction of the Second Temple. The later Karaite sect, opposing talmudic Judaism, regarded itself as the direct successor of the Sadducees.

PIRKÉ AVOTH   פִּרְקֵי אָבוֹת

THE name *Pirké Avoth*, signifying chapters of the fathers, is applied to the five chapters of Mishnah Avoth along with a sixth chapter from another tannaitic source, incorporated in the *Siddur* for recitation on Sabbath afternoons between *Pesaḥ* and *Rosh Hashanah*. These chapters are recited successively, so that in the course of the summer *Pirké Avoth* is repeated more than three times. Originally, however, the reading of *Pirké Avoth* was probably restricted to the six Sabbaths between *Pesaḥ* and *Shavuoth*. Hence, the added sixth chapter, called *Kinyan Torah*, which deals with the methods of acquiring the knowledge of Torah, was to be read on the Sabbath immediately preceding the festival of *Shavuoth*, which is celebrated as the anniversary of the giving of the Torah at Mount Sinai. Though the Ashkenazim recite *Pirké Avoth* every Sabbath afternoon during the summer, the Sephardim read it only on the six Sabbaths between *Pesaḥ* and *Shavuoth*.

Rav Amram Gaon of the ninth century mentions, in his *Siddur*, the custom of reading *Pirké Avoth* on Sabbaths. These chapters, containing tannaitic maxims and aphorisms, have been described as *Ethics of the Fathers*, a title that adequately represents the contents, consisting of the moral and religious teachings of several generations of sages, each new generation contributing of its wisdom and ethical standards. The high level of these sayings, especially applicable to scholars and students, reflects the ethics of the fathers of Jewish tradition. Ideally, Jewish life should be dedicated to the teachings of *Pirké Avoth*. "He who desires to be virtuous must fulfill the precepts of *Avoth*" (Bava Kamma).

PIRKÉ D'RABBI ELIEZER   פִּרְקֵי דְרַבִּי אֱלִיעֶזֶר

THE midrashic work on Genesis and parts of Exodus and Numbers, attributed to Rabbi Eliezer ben Hyrcanus, disciple of Rabbi Yoḥanan ben Zakkai and teacher of Rabbi Akiva, consists of fifty-four chapters. Some parts of it are said to be as late as the eighth century, though they contain older elements. Mainly ethical in its makeup, the *Pirké d'Rabbi Eliezer* comprises a wealth of legends and folklore as well as astronomical discussions in connection with the story of creation. Many ancient customs that are not found in any other source are described in this work.

Reference is made in the *Pirké d'Rabbi Eliezer* to such customs as the contemplation of the finger-nails during the blessing בּוֹרֵא מְאוֹרֵי הָאֵשׁ, the pouring of the wine upon the table after the *Havdalah* and extinguishing the candle in it, and then dipping the hands in it and rubbing the eyes. Also: the blessing of *Tal* on the first day of *Pesaḥ*, the sounding of the *shofar* after the morning services during the month of *Elul*, the banquet after circumcision, the chair of Elijah during circumcision, the performance of the marriage ceremony under a canopy (*ḥuppah*), that the dead may be buried only in *takhrikhin* (shrouds), and that one is to say רְפוּאָה (your health) upon hearing the sneezing of a person. The purpose of *Pirké d'Rabbi Eliezer* is chiefly ethical.

The introduction to the entire work deals with the youth of Rabbi Eliezer and his thirst for knowledge. Against the wishes of his father, who threatened to disinherit him, he began to study late in life and developed into the greatest scholar of his time; he became famous as "Rabbi Eliezer the Great," who possessed a phenomenal memory and was compared to "a cemented cistern which loses not a drop" (Avoth 2:11). The fifty-four chapters of *Pirké d'Rabbi Eliezer* are arranged in seven divisions, which are merely fragments of a larger work.

TSE'ENAH URE'ENAH   צְאֶינָה וּרְאֶינָה

THE most popular Yiddish book, presenting a free translation of the Torah and other biblical selections, has been the famous *Teitsch Ḥummash*, otherwise known as the *Tse'enah Ure'enah*, written by Jacob Ashkenazi (1550-1626) of Janow, Poland. The Hebrew title is borrowed from the Song of Songs (3:11) and signifies: "Come out and see, you women."

The book consists of many traditional commentaries on the Pentateuch, interspersed with legend and ethical teachings, which gained widespread acceptance among Jewish women who had no access to the original Hebrew sources. For generations, the *Tse'enah Ure'enah* has served as a storehouse of Jewish knowledge for women who, in turn, influenced their children by imparting to them the fascinating information contained therein.

Long before the appearance of modern Yiddish literature, Yiddish books served as a vehicle for spreading among the Jewish people proverbs and legends, folklore and allegory, prayers and songs. The wonder stories of Rabbi Naḥman Bratzlaver (1770-1811) and the inspiring Ḥasidic tales were all transmitted in Yiddish. Like modern German, Yiddish is a language derived from Middle High German, with the addition of Hebrew elements.

Jewish immigration into Poland in the twelfth century introduced Yiddish from Germany into the Slav lands; there it assimilated, like all living languages, some local elements and was further enriched in the course of Jewish wanderings. The title *Teitsch Ḥummash* is a combination of the German *Deutsch* and the Hebrew *Ḥummash*; the same applies to the term *Ivri-Teitsch*. Both are reminiscent of the time when the Yiddish language was referred to as Judeo-German.

MILITARY SERVICE   צָבָא

ISRAEL'S army consisted originally of infantry only. It included all the men, from twenty years old and upward, being enrolled for service, except the Levites who were not numbered in the wilderness for military service. King Saul retained three thousand men of all Israel as a standing army to hold the Philistines in check (I Samuel 13:2). David organized the army into twelve divisions of twenty-four thou-

517

sand footmen each (I Chronicles 27:1-24). Solomon added a large force of chariots and horsemen, and distributed them throughout his empire. Jehoshaphat, Uzziah, and Judah Maccabee paid considerable attention to the organization and equipment of their respective armies. The need of military leadership against the Philistines resulted in the Israelite monarchy. Defense was in the hands of a citizen militia in the period of Ezra and Nehemiah. The first battles of the Maccabeans were fought by irregular troops in parts of the country occupied by the enemy.

The Torah contains laws pertaining to the conduct of war. The people of Israel are instructed to show human kindness even in warfare. Exemptions from military service are permitted. Certain categories of able-bodied men are exempted for a time, namely: those who built a new house or planted a vineyard, and men engaged to be married. Newly married men are exempted for a year. Cowards are rejected or discharged. Fear is infectious, and the presence of cowardly persons in the army is likely to cause weakness and danger.

Thus we read: "When you go out to war against your enemies and you see horses and chariots and an army greater than your own, do not be afraid of them, for the Lord your God . . . will be with you. When you are about to go into battle, the priest shall come forward and say to the soldiers: Hear, O Israel! Today you are going into battle against your enemies. Be not weakhearted or afraid; be neither alarmed nor freightened by them. . . Then the officers shall say to the people: Is there anyone who has built a new house and has not commenced to use it? Let him return to his house, lest he die in the battle and another man will dedicate it. Is there anyone who has planted a vineyard and never yet enjoyed its fruits? Let him return home, lest he die in battle and another man will enjoy its fruits in his stead . . ." (Deuteronomy 20:1-8).

Then the Torah declares that war is to be regarded as the last resort, to be used only when negotiations for peace have been tried and failed. The conduct of war is to be guided with reason and mercy. There is to be no wanton destruction of human life and property. Rashi points out that the four expressions of exhortation in Deuteronomy 20:3 correspond to the four tactical devices which hostile armies employed in battle. To strike terror into the hearts of their opponents, they beat their shields one against the other, trampled the ground heavily with their horses and made them neigh, shouted war cries, and blew various trumpets.

518

TSIDDUK HA-DIN   צִדּוּק הַדִּין

THE term *tsidduk ha-din*, signifying the submission to the justice of
God, is mentioned in the Talmud (Avodah Zarah 18a) in connection
with the martyrdom suffered by Rabbi Ḥanina ben Teradyon and his
family. He was burned at the stake, after the defeat of Bar Kokhba
in 135, for his refusal to obey the anti-Jewish decrees of Hadrian.

Before the execution was carried out by the Romans, Rabbi Ḥanina
quoted the first half of the biblical verse הצור תמים פעלו ("He is
God, faultless is his work"); his wife completed it: אל אמונה ("He is
the faithful God . . . just and upright he is"—Deuteronomy 32:4);
their daughter then quoted from Jeremiah 32:19 (גדול העצה: "Thou
art great in counsel and mighty in action; thy eyes are open to the
ways of men, to give to every one according to his conduct. . ." These
biblical passages were later embodied in the rhymed verses of *tsidduk
ha-din*, recited during burial services at the cemetery.

TSADDIK   צַדִּיק

IN THE Hebrew Bible alone, the root צדק, generally translated in the
sense of righteousness, occurs over five hundred times, counting all
its inflections. In the prophetic writings, righteousness is synonymous with ethical conduct. The man who refrains from wrongdoing
and makes an effort to establish what is right is called righteous. The
marks of the righteous man, according to Jewish thinking, are the
sincerity of purpose and the strenuous endeavor to accomplish it. The
righteous man who has fallen into sin is distinguished by his repentance, as in the case of king David.

According to a talmudic observation, in each generation there are
at least thirty-six righteous men in the world, for whose sake the
world escapes destruction. This is based on Isaiah 30:18 (אשרי כל
חוכי לו, blessed are all those who wait for him), where the word לו
has the numerical value of thirty-six (Sanhedrin 97b). Hence the
popular belief that there are, concealed, thirty-six *tsaddikim* (ל"ו
צדיקים), otherwise referred to as *nistarim* (anonymous), who sustain
the entire world wherein they are dispersed. According to Yoma 38b,
one righteous man can ensure the existence of the world (אפילו בשביל
צדיק אחד עולם נברא). No sooner is one righteous man removed from

519

the world than he is succeeded by another righteous man as good as he. The righteous man is he who is saturated with Torah and possesses within himself the instrument of dealing a deadly blow to the evil impulse (*yetser ha-ra*). "The righteous are considered as alive even when they are dead" (Berakhoth 18a).

In the Ḥasidic movement, which came into being during the eighteenth century, the *Tsaddik* is looked upon by his disciples and adherents as the living incarnation of the Torah. The various Ḥasidic groups developed different characteristics in accordance with the particular type of saint to whom they looked for guidance. "When a great *Tsaddik* was asked why he did not follow the example of his teacher in living as he did, he replied: On the contrary, I do follow his example, for I leave him as he left his teacher... Around the lives of the great *Tsaddikim* legends were spun often in their own lifetime. Borrowed ideas and true originality are mixed in this overwhelming wealth of tales which play an important part in the social life of the Ḥasidism. To tell a story of the deeds of the saints has become a new religious value..." (Gershom Scholem).

CHARITY   צְדָקָה

THE biblical term *tsedakah* is often used synonymously with justice, truth, kindness, ethical conduct, help and deliverance. It is applied, in post-biblical Hebrew, specifically to the relief of poverty as an act of justice and moral behavior. The word *tsedakah*, designating any work directed toward aiding the poor, signifies that the poor man's right to food, clothing and shelter, is considered by Judaism as a legal claim which must be honored by the more fortunate.

Concerning the duty to support the poor generously the Torah declares: "Take heed lest ... you grudge help to your needy kinsman and give him nothing... You shall give to him freely, without ill will... Poor people will never cease to be in the land; hence I command you: You shall open your hand to your brother, to your poor and needy in your land" (Deuteronomy 15:9-11).

In Jewish thinking, *tsedakah* is not a matter of philanthropic sentiment, but an act of justice. The Torah contains a variety of laws applying to the tithe for the poor (*ma'aser ani*), the gleaning of the field (*leket*), the year of release (*shemittah*), the field-corner to be reaped by the poor (*peah*). And since the assigned gifts are legally considered

520

as the property of the poor, the owner is not entitled to decide who should receive them. They must be shared by all the poor who happen to come to the fields. The Talmud discusses in detail the Jewish methods of cooperative *tsedakah* enterprise, including the collection of food and money for the poor (*tamhuy* and *kuppah*).

Jewish literature is rich in praise of beneficence and liberality to the poor: Charity equals all the other commandments; a penny for the poor will obtain a view of the Shekhinah; whom God loves, he sends a golden opportunity for charity; by benevolence man rises to a height where he meets God; do a good deed before you begin your prayers; God provides the means, if you really want to do charity. What you give to charity in health is gold; what you give in sickness is silver; what you give after death is copper. . .

In his *Mishneh Torah*, Maimonides devotes ten chapters to *Mattenoth Aniyyim* (gifts to the poor) and the rules and regulations related to this subject. He writes: Anyone who can afford it must give charity to the poor according to their needs. One's first duty lies toward his poor relatives, then toward the needy of his own town, and finally toward those of other towns. Anyone who stays in a town for thirty days should be compelled to contribute to public charity. Any man who gives aid to the poor in a surly manner and with a gloomy face completely nullifies the merit of his own deed. Charity should be given cheerfully, compassionately and comfortingly. He who induces others to contribute to charity is more deserving than they.

Maimonides asserts that, in Jewish religious law, the highest degree of charity is to aid a man in want by offering him a gift or a loan, by entering into partnership with him, or by providing work for him, so that he may become self-supporting. The lowest degree is when one gives grudgingly. The next highest degree is when the donor and the recipient are not aware of each other. In all, he enumerates eight degrees of charity, each one higher than the other.

Following his famous scale of eight types of contributors, he addresses himself to the poor in these terms: A man should ever strive not to be dependent on other people. The sages said: "Rather make your Sabbath a weekday with regard to festive meals than be dependent on human beings" (Shabbath 118a). If reduced to poverty, even a distinguished scholar must not disdain manual work, no matter how unworthy of him, in order to avoid dependence on others.

Rabbi Israel al-Nakawa of fourteenth-century Spain writes in his *Menorath Hammaor* (lamp of illumination), that the world is like a

521

revolving wheel: one who is rich today may be poor tomorrow. Let a man therefore give charity before the wheel has turned. Prominent men in France used to make their coffins out of the tables on which they served food to the poor, to show that a man can take nothing with him except the good he has done.

There are those who like to give ostentatiously; others, who give both for the common good and for the sake of fame; while some contribute to charity secretly and from noble motives only.

But, greater than these is the man who contributes to the common fund (*kuppah*), so that neither the recipient of the gift nor the donor know each other's identity. Still greater is the man who lends to the poor in time of trouble and assists them to support themselves and become independent.

TSIDKATHEKHA TSEDEK צִדְקָתְךָ צֶדֶק

THE three verses from Psalms 36:7, 71:19 and 119:142, are recited in a reverse order at the Sabbath afternoon service, immediately following the *Amidah* prayer. They read: "Thy righteousness is everlasting righteousness, thy Torah is truth (119:142). Thy righteousness, O God, is most high; thou hast done great things; O God, who is like thee? (71:19). Thy righteousness is like the mighty mountains; thy judgments are like the vast deep; man and beast thou savest, O Lord" (36:7). These verses contain the words ה' אלהים אמת (the Lord is the true God), a phrase found in Jeremiah 10:10. The order of the verses in the Sephardic *Siddur*, however, is consecutive. The Ashkenazim use the reverse order, which ends with "O Lord," so that the Reader's *Kaddish* recited after the three verses should appear more logically connected with what precedes it.

Since צדקתך צדק is presumably a substitute for the weekday *Tahanun*, it is omitted on occasions when the *Tahanun* is omitted on weekdays. It is also regarded as a form of *tsidduk ha-din* (acknowledgment of divine justice), said on the occasion of a death. According to the Zohar, the three who died on a Sabbath were Moses, Joseph, and David. Further allusions are found in the three verses, one of which is composed of ten words, corresponding to the Ten Commandments; the other is made up of forty letters, reminiscent of the forty days Moses spent on Mount Sinai; the third consists of five words, bringing to mind the five books of the Torah.

522

WILLS   צַוָּאוֹת

LAST wills disposing of property used to be uncommon among the Jewish people, because inheritance was for the most part regulated by the traditional law, providing a double share for the firstborn son and equal shares for all the other sons. On the other hand, Jewish literature has been greatly enriched by a considerable variety of ethical wills that convey a genuine picture of the life and ideals of the times in which they were written. Long before their death, great Jews began to prepare their instructions to their descendants, revising them from time to time, until their compositions finally emerged as finished ethical dissertations.

One of the earliest ethical wills is to be found in the book of Tobit, the earliest of all the books of the Apocrypha, which introduces the reader to the kind of home wherein the Jew lived more than two thousand years ago. Here are enshrined the high ideals of the Jewish people as to the purity of family life and the duty of kindness to the poor. Several quotations from Tobit are:

"My son, do not neglect your mother; provide for her as long as you live; try to please her; do not be a cause of grief to her. Remember that she faced many dangers for your sake. You will succeed in life if you are truthful. God will not ignore you if you do not ignore the poor. Do not do to anyone else that which is hateful to you."

The *Testaments of the Twelve Patriarchs*, belonging to the apocalyptic literature of the Second-Temple period, are represented as the last instructions of the twelve sons of Jacob. Each in turn asks his descendants to emulate his virtues and shun his vices. The following are a few excerpts from the instructions that are professedly addressed to the descendants of the sons of Jacob:

"My children, pay no heed to the beauty of lewd women. Beware of deceit and envy. Work diligently and acquire wisdom. Lead a life of sincerity. Have pity on the poor and the weak, Be compassionate toward all persons and animals. Anger is blind and does not permit one to see the face of another as it really is. Do not become angry when someone speaks against you; do not become vain when you are praised. Speak the truth to your neighbor, and love each other with a true heart. Hatred is evil; it makes small things appear great. Put envy out of your souls, and love one another with singleness of heart. Be patient with one another's faults and overlook them. A good man

523

shows mercy to everyone, even to sinners. He is neither envious nor jealous of others, but rejoices always in their good fortune. . ."

During the Middle Ages, as well as during the early talmudic period, the spiritual leaders of Israel left ethical wills in a similar vein that had a marked influence on the development of Jewish life and thought. Rabbi Judah ibn Tibbon of twelfth-century Spain writes:

"My son, ability is of no avail without inclination. Exert yourself while still young. Take good care of your health; do not be your own destroyer. Honor your wife to your utmost capacity. If you give orders, let your words be gentle. All I ask of you is to behave in a friendly spirit toward all; to gain a good name; to revere God and perform his commandments.

"Devote yourself to your children; be not indifferent to any slight ailment in them or in yourself. Never refuse to lend books to anyone who can be trusted to return them. Honor your teachers and attach yourself to your friends. My son, make your books your companions. Let your shelves be your treasure grounds and gardens. . ."

FAST OF GEDALIAH צוֹם גְּדַלְיָה

IMMEDIATELY after *Rosh Hashanah*, the third day of *Tishri* is observed as a fast day in commemoration of the murder of Gedaliah, the Jewish governor appointed by Nebuchadnezzar "over the poor of the land" after the destruction of Jerusalem in 587 before the common era. He was treacherously assassinated at his residence by Ishmael of the royal dynasty. Gedaliah shared the views of the prophet Jeremiah with regard to yielding to the Babylonians and serving them.

In Jeremiah 38:17-18, the prophet's message to king Zedekiah reads "If you surrender to the officers of Babylon's king, you shall save your life; this city shall not be destroyed with fire, and you and your family shall live. But if you do not surrender to the officers of Babylon's king, this city shall fall into the hands of the Chaldeans, who shall destroy it with fire, and you shall not escape their hands."

Gedaliah adjured the people, after the Babylonian conquest of Jerusalem, not to be afraid to serve the Chaldeans, to stay in the land and submit to the king of Babylon, for their own welfare (Jeremiah 40:9-10). After the assassination, Gedaliah's followers fled to Egypt for fear of the king's revenge. They took to flight in spite of Jeremiah's warning: "If you remain quietly in this land, I will build you up, and not tear you down; I will plant you, not uproot you... Do not fear the king of Babylon, of whom you are now afraid; do not fear him, says the Lord, for I am with you to save you, to rescue you from his power... But if you disobey the voice of the Lord your God, and decide not to remain in this land ... the sword you fear shall reach you in the land of Egypt..." (42:10-16).

The fast of Gedaliah thus commemorates a tragic event which completed the destruction of the First Commonwealth of Israel.

ZIONISM   צִיּוֹנוּת

THE term *Zionism*, coined by Nathan Birnbaum in 1893, denotes a movement for the re-establishment of an autonomous Jewish community in Eretz Yisrael. It implies a synthesis of the everlasting Jewish longing for the restoration of Eretz Yisrael and the independence of the people of Israel. The objective of Zionism was defined by the Basle Program, adopted in 1897, at the first Zionist Congress, convened by Theodore Herzl. In his famous pamphlet, *Der Judenstaat* (The Jewish State), Herzl had set out to prove that the Jewish people were a nation whose national life should be taken up anew in a territory provided for them by the other nations. He ardently believed that the Jewish State would bring peace and happiness to the rest of the Jewish people in the Diaspora.

The text of the Basle Program reads: "Zionism aims at establishing for the Jewish people a publicly and legally assumed home in Palestine. For the attainment of this purpose, the Congress considers the following means serviceable: 1) the promotion of the settlement of Jewish agriculturists, artisans and tradesmen in Palestine; 2) the federation of all Jews into local or general groups, according to the laws of the various countries; 3) the strengthening of the Jewish feeling and consciousness; 4) preparatory steps for the attainment of those governmental grants which are necessary to the achievement of the Zionist purpose."

The Balfour Declaration, which practically coincided with the entry of the British into Jerusalem in 1917, during the first World War, reads: "His Majesty's Government view with favour the establishment in Palestine of a national home for the Jewish people, and will use their best endeavors to facilitate the achievement of this object, it being clearly understood that nothing shall be done which may prejudice the civil and religious rights of existing non-Jewish communities in Palestine or the rights and political status enjoyed by Jews in any other country."

The Jewish Agency for Israel, created to implement the task of Zionism, has, with the establishment of the State of Israel in May 1948, continued to function as a coordinator of all Jewish overseas efforts in Israel. Its activities include immigration, absorption, and agricultural settlement. Its department of education and culture maintains seminars in Israel and abroad for Hebrew educators and for students of Hebrew, both Jewish and non-Jewish. The Jewish Agency Executive maintains headquarters in Jerusalem and New York.

More than a hundred years ago, Moses Hess wrote in his *Rome and Jerusalem:* "March forward, Jews of all lands! The ancient fatherland of yours is calling you. . . The day on which the Jewish tribes return to their fatherland will mark an epoch in the history of humanity." Twenty years later, in 1882, the pioneer Zionist Leon Pinsker declared in his *Auto-Emancipation:* "In order that we may not be compelled to wander from one exile to another, we must have a place of refuge, a rallying point, of our own." In 1933, Ḥayyim Weizmann, who had grown up in an atmosphere of *Ḥibbath Zion* (Love for Zion) and toward the end of his lifetime served as the first president of the State of Israel, asserted: "If before I die there are half a million Jews in Palestine, I shall be content because I shall know that this saving remnant will survive."

According to Martin Buber, in *Avukah Annual* (1930), "it is not a commonwealth of Jews that should be established, but a truly Jewish commonwealth. A truly Jewish commonwealth can be none other than one in which the precepts of Moses with regard to the equalization of property, the appeals of the prophets for social justice, are translated into reality." Ben Gurion, in 1946, declared: "We established hundreds of new Jewish villages on new soil. . . We didn't merely buy the land, we recreated the land. . . In the swamps of Ḥedera hundreds of Jews died of malaria, and they refused to leave that place until it was made healthy. . . We did it on the sand dunes of Rishon l'Zion. With our toil, our sweat, and with our love and devotion, we are remaking the soil to enable us to settle there. . ."

Aḥad Ha-am (1856-1927), whose collected articles were published in four volumes entitled *Al Parashath Derakhim* (At the Crossroads), maintained that the revival of Jewish nationhood must involve the revival of Judaism through the creation of a spiritual center (*Merkaz*

Ruḥani) in Eretz Yisrael. Zionism, he said, cannot confine itself to the material work of rebuilding Eretz Yisrael. We must advance along both lines at the same time. The establishment of a single great school of learning or art in Eretz Yisrael, or a single academy of language and literature, would be a national achievement of first-rate import-ance, and would contribute more to the attainment of our aims than a hundred agricultural settlements. He believed in the creation of a place for the regeneration of Judaism, from which spiritual influences would radiate into all the lands where Jews continued to live.

TSITSITH   צִיצִית

THE Torah attaches great importance to the wearing of *tsitsith* as a visible reminder of the obligation to keep the divine commandments: "When you look upon it you will remember to do all the commands of the Lord" (Numbers 37:39). The numerical value of the letters in the Hebrew word צִיצִת (fringe) happens to be exactly six hundred. To make this number add up to 613, corresponding to the 613 *mitzvoth* (commands), the *tsitsith* is made of eight threads with five knots.

In this way each of the four fringes on the four corners of the *tallith* (prayer-robe) represents all the teachings of the Torah. Hence, the wearing of *tsitsith* is said to be of equal merit with the observance of the whole Torah (Nedarim 25a). The thirty-nine windings that go into the making of each fringe represent the numerical value of יְ'ה'ו'ה' אֶחָד (the Lord is One).

Jewish women, who are free from all precepts that have to be per-formed at a specified time (מצות עשה שהזמן גרמא), are exempt from wearing *tsitsith*. The blue thread (פתיל תכלת) entwined in the fringe was its principal distinction, "because this color resembles the sea, the sea resembles the sky, and the sky resembles the throne of glory" (Menaḥoth 43b). After the dispersion, the method of dying the threads sky-blue became a forgotten art, and the use of the blue thread was discontinued. Ever since the tannaitic period, the white wool-threads alone have been inserted. The *mitzvah* of wearing *tsi-tsith* is performed by means of the special *tallith* and *tallith katan*, or *arba kanfoth*.

By the thirteenth century it had become unusual for Jews to mark their ordinary outward garments by wearing fringes. . . In 1215, the Jew was compelled to wear a degrading badge; the fringed garment became all the more an honorable uniform, marking at once God's love for Israel and Israel's determination to "remember to do..."

CHASTITY, MODESTY   צְנִיעוּת

THE Hebrew word *tsenuah* (צנועה) denotes a modest woman, careful to carry out her religious obligations. Similarly, צנוע signifies a pious man. "He who fulfills the words of the sages is called *tzanua*" (Niddah 12a). One of the enactments ordained by Ezra, we are told, was that a woman must wear a *sinnar* out of modesty (Bava Kamma 82b). One of the reasons given for the destruction of Jerusalem was the prevalence of shamelessness (Shabbath 119b). Many regulations were introduced to safeguard the purity of the people and to insure chaste living. During the Hadrianic persecutions of the second century, the sages advised the people to suffer death rather than be guilty of adultery (*gilluy arayoth*).

In his ethical work, *Duties of the Heart*, the eleventh-century philosopher Baḥya ibn Pakuda often emphasizes the necessity of chastity. He writes: "Be not one of those who are engulfed in drunkenness and lust, submitting like slaves to evil passions; they think only of the satisfaction of sensual desires and the indulgence of bestial pleasures."

The medieval Jewish writers stressed the great quality of modesty in terms such as these: "The noblest of all ornaments is modesty." "Man's finest virtue is that of which he is unaware." "Modesty is humility and wisdom combined." "A small act done modestly is a thousandfold more acceptable to God than a big act done in pride."

PROTECTION OF ANIMALS   צַעַר בַּעֲלֵי חַיִּים

JUDAISM attaches particular stress to respecting the needs and feelings of dumb animals. The Sabbath is described as a day when the ox and the mule may also have rest, the same as man (Exodus 20:10; Deuteronomy 5:14). The talmudic sages count cruelty to animals among the most serious of offenses. The Torah prohibits muzzling an ox when it is treading out grain (Deuteronomy 25:4).

In view of the feelings of animals, the Torah says: "You shall not slaughter it on one and the same day with its young" (Leviticus 22:28). Maimonides explains this as follows: "The pain of the ani-

528

mals under such circumstances is very great. There is no difference between human suffering and the pain felt by other living beings in a case like this" (*Guide*, 3:48).

The humanitarian motive towards the animal is also evident in the law concerning an enemy's beast of burden that must not be deserted but helped when it is seen lying prostrate under its burden (Exodus 23:5). The Torah also says: "You shall not plow with an ox and a mule harnessed together" (Deuteronomy 22:10), since they differ greatly in size and strength.

Ibn Ezra explains that the uneven steps would cause discomfort to the large animal and distress to the smaller. God is often represented as being constantly concerned with providing for the needs of animals, and we are told that "the just man takes care of his beast, but the heart of the wicked is merciless" (Proverbs 12:10).

Hunting was never popular among the Jewish people. Nimrod and Ishmael and Esau, who were too fond of the chase, have always been regarded unfavorably in Jewish tradition. According to the Talmud, a man should not eat before he has fed the animals (Berakhoth 40a). Age-long Jewish spirituality has built a dike against brutality.

Tradition has it that Moses and David were chosen as leaders because they treated their flocks gently. Rabbi Judah ha-Nasi, editor of the Mishnah, is said to have been punished because he refused to help a calf that was being taken to the slaughter; he was cured of his sickness only when he saved the lives of little kittens (Bava Metzia 85a).

Rabbi Ezekiel Landau (1713-1793), in one of his responsa, writes: "The law against cruelty to animals applies in every case except where an animal is slaughtered outright, or killed for a material benefit to man... In the Torah the sport of hunting is ascribed only to fierce characters like Nimrod and Esau, never to any of the patriarchs or their descendants... I cannot comprehend how a Jew could ever dream of killing animals merely for the pleasure of hunting... We may kill wild animals found in places inhabited by human beings, where the beasts constitute a menace. But it is certainly no act of merit to pursue wild beasts in their haunts. It is rather a lustful occupation... When the act of killing is prompted by sport, it is downright cruelty."

The principle of kindness to animals is extended to a variety of limitations governing the slaughter for food. Because of the cruelty involved, hunting has been prohibited by the rabbinic authorities. According to Jewish law, one is not permitted to eat before feeding the animals; nor may a person buy an animal if he is not sure that he can provide sufficient food for it.

Hence, the Jews have never organized societies for the prevention of cruelty to animals. The Jewish trait of compassion, nurtured by a long chain of tradition, has afforded permanent protection of animals under Jewish control. The minute care and detail how an animal is to be slaughtered for food, prescribed in talmudic literature, stem from the desire to inflict as painless a death as possible by following the strict regulations of the ritual *sheḥitah* method.

ZEPHANIAH   צְפַנְיָה

ZEPHANIAH, an older contemporary of Jeremiah, lived in Jerusalem during the reign of Josiah (640-609 before the common era). He aimed to arouse the moral sense of his people, who had adopted the religious customs of their Assyrian conquerors. Zephaniah, who was one of the first to break the long silence of more than fifty years which followed the death of the great prophet Isaiah, condemned the pro-Assyrian court ministers who served as regents during Josiah's minority. His prophecy, therefore, comes directly before that of Jeremiah, who is said to have been influenced by it in both language and ideas.

The brief book of Zephaniah, consisting of three chapters, stresses the demand for purity of heart and conduct. It contains also the idea that suffering has a disciplinary value. Zephaniah's prophecy was occasioned by the Scythian invasion of western Asia, which marked the beginning of the end to the Assyrian empire. Zephaniah pictures the approaching calamity and predicts the future glory of Jerusalem.

"I will utterly sweep away everything from the face of the earth. I will sweep away man and beast, birds of the air and fish of the sea. I will strike at Judah and all the inhabitants of Jerusalem. I will punish those who enrich the palace by violence and fraud. I will punish those who are at ease, who say to themselves that the Lord will do neither good nor ill. Their goods shall be plundered, and their houses laid waste. They shall not live in the houses they build, nor drink wine from the vineyards they plant...

"Sing, O Zion! Shout, O Israel! Rejoice with all your heart, O Jerusalem! The Lord is in your midst; you shall fear evil no more... I will deal with all your oppressors. I will save the lame, and gather the outcast; I will lift them out of shame to world-wide praise..."

530

BURIAL

THE first territory which Abraham acquired in the promised land was a burial ground. In the Bible, not to be buried is the worst misfortune that can happen to a dead person (I Kings 14:11; 16:4; 21:19). Even a man condemned to death had the right of burial (Deuteronomy 21:23). The Torah is vigorously opposed to pagan funeral rites; it opposes any attempts to communicate with those who have died.

The obligation to the dead, claiming the service of their friends and fellow Jews, is referred to in talmudic literature as מת מצוה. Care of the unburied body of a friendless man takes precedence over all other *mitzvoth*. Cremation has always been opposed by Jewish law. Tobit devoted himself entirely to the task of burying the unclaimed bodies of the slain: "I gave my bread to the hungry and my clothes to the naked, and if I saw one of my people dead I would bury him. . ."

According to Jewish law and custom, interment of a human body follows speedily after death. During biblical times, burial of the dead was the general method practised by the Jewish people; it was regarded as one of the laws of humanity not to let any one lie unburied. The expression וכפר אדמתו (Deuteronomy 32:43), understood to mean that the sacred soil of Eretz Yisrael atones, has been connected with the custom of putting earth of the Holy Land under the body in the coffin.

The proper burial of the dead has been regarded as a sacred religious duty resting upon the entire community. Irrespective of their social status in life, all Jews are regarded as equal in death. The burial clothes are the same for all, and a plain wooden coffin is used for all. The burial society (חברה קדישא) is in charge of the necessary preparations, which include what is known as *tohorah* (purification): washing the body from head to foot in lukewarm water, trimming the nails, combing the hair. The body is then clad in *takhrikhin* (burial clothes) of simple linen. Rabban Gamaliel II (80-110) set the example, when funeral expenses had become common extravagances, by the order he gave for his own funeral, introducing the custom of burying the dead in simple linen dress (Kethubboth 8b; Mo'ed Katan 27b).

In ancient Israel coffins were not generally used, but the body was carried upon a bier (*mittah*) to the grave where it was placed and covered with stones to prevent marauding by beasts. Rocky hillsides were favorite burial places. In medieval France it became customary to use for the coffin boards the table upon which food for the poor

531

had been served, to show that a man can take nothing with him when he dies except the good he has done.

When death occurs, those present recite ברוך דיין האמת (blessed be the true judge). The body is removed from the bed and placed on the floor. A light is lit and placed near the head of the deceased; it is kept burning until after the funeral. The light symbolizes the soul.

KABBALAH קַבָּלָה

THE term *Kabbalah* primarily denotes reception, and then oral tradition. Ever since the thirteenth century it has especially been used to designate the mystic teachings of Judaism, originally handed down orally from generation to generation. The mystical philosophy, or theosophy, of the Kabbalah is hidden and unintelligible to those who have not been properly prepared and instructed in the secret wisdom (חכמה נסתרה), often referred to by the abbreviation ח"ן (grace). The phrase יודעי חן alludes to those who are familiar with kabbalistic literature.

The subjects treated by the Kabbalah concern the essence of the Supreme Being, the origination of the universe, the creation of man, the destiny of man and the universe, and the profound significance of the sacred Torah. Throughout the age of the Tannaim and Amoraim, however, Kabbalah signified the tradition embodied in the prophetical books of the Bible, and not the theosophic tradition to which the name was attached in later centuries.

That Jewish mysticism has its roots in the Bible itself is clearly evident from the miracles performed by the prophets Moses, Elijah, Elisha, and the descriptions of the divine chariot in the first chapter of Ezekiel. All this has been defined as practical mysticism. The theoretical mysticism of the Kabbalah seeks to explain the transition from the Infinite Cause of Causes (אין סוף) to the finite, tangible universe, by means of ten graded emanations (*Sefiroth*), ten classified entities, representing the forms and moulds into which all created things were originally cast.

The Kabbalah teaches that there is an unbroken inter-relation between the supersensual, metaphysical world and the world of humanity. It maintains that the powers of evil can be brought to an end by the triumph of morality among men through the supremacy of man's spirit over his desires. That the two worlds have a reciprocal influence

532

on one another is demonstrated by its doctrine of emanation. It regards prayer as the medium which unites the human life with God, who is the original principle of all being.

First handed down orally to the chosen few and then committed to writing, the mystical interpretation of the Torah is principally embodied in the Zohar (brightness), which made its appearance for the first time in thirteenth-century Spain. It was issued in parts, which were not assembled in one work until near the age of printing. The vast printed literature of mystical texts has been estimated at three thousand. In addition, there exists an even greater array of manuscripts not yet published.

Thus the Kabbalah, originally intended only for the ears of the elect initiates who were not to divulge its secrets before a large reading public, is gradually being made accessible to the scholarly world through translation and interpretation of manuscript material and printed texts. For the most part, the study of the beginnings of mysticism and the Kabbalah among the Jewish people has thus far been influenced by preconceived ideas and biased notions.

Unlike the so-called *theoretical Kabbalah*, which endeavors to explain the connection between God and creation, the existence of good and evil, and the path to spiritual perfection, the *practical Kabbalah* concentrates on intense *kavvanah* or deep meditation for the purpose of linking the soul with the Deity. The practical Kabbalah is identified with the teachings of Rabbi Isaac Luria (1534-1572), who was regarded by his devoted disciples as משיח בן יוסף, the forerunner of the Messiah (משיח בן דוד). He is generally referred to as *Ari*, an abridgment of Ashkenazi Rabbi Isaac, who died at the age of thirty-eight after an intensely religious and highly ascetic mode of life. A knowledge of his teachings is limited to what was written down by his disciple Rabbi Ḥayyim Vital (1543-1620). The Lurianic ideas on the pre-existence and transmigration of souls (*gilgul neshamoth*) are contained in Vital's work עץ חיים (Tree of Life). Rabbi Isaac Luria wrote nothing himself except three Aramaic Sabbath hymns and a few Hebrew poems.

The leading kabbalists of the sixteenth century were concentrated in Safed, Eretz Yisrael, and included Rabbis Moses Cordovero, Isaac Luria, Solomon Alkabets, Joseph Karo, and Ḥayyim Vital. They formulated an attempt to explain the origin of the material world from God who is incorporeal, and referred to it as *Tsimtsum* (contraction); that is to say, God who is omnipresent left a vacuum for the

533

universe by contracting from himself into himself; he constantly sustains it by means of spiritual beams of light emanating from the *En Sof*. Evil and darkness entered the world when the impact of the divine light proved too strong for the *Sefiroth* (Emanations), and seven out of ten were broken (*shevirath ha-kélim*). This brought about endless confusion of light and darkness. But man can release the holy sparks (ניצוצות הקדושה) from defilement by the observance of the divine precepts, Torah study, and deep meditation. The complete restoration (*Tikkun*) will hasten the advent of the Messiah. Some of this thinking was later absorbed in Ḥasidism.

The literature of practical Kabbalah is still concealed in manuscripts. The leading spokesman of practical Kabbalah, Rabbi Isaac Luria (אר״י ז״ל) elaborated the idea of intense concentration (*kavvanah*) to make the performance of every religious act an opportunity for linking the individual soul with the Creator. This mystical piety is known in Ḥasidism under the title of *dvékuth* (דבקות).

Rabbi Shneour Zalman of Liadi, founder of the *Ḥabad* movement in Ḥasidism, compares the mystic teachings of the Kabbalah to salt which adds flavor to food, though it is not itself a food. The Kabbalah adds flavor to the Torah, though it is not comprehensible in itself (*Tanya, Leviticus*). Horodetzky (1871-1957), historian of Kabbalah and Ḥasidism, described the kabbalistic teachings as the core, essence and spirituality of Judaism.

KABBALATH SHABBATH קַבָּלַת שַׁבָּת

THE opening service on Friday evening, preceding the *Ma'ariv* service, is called *Kabbalath Shabbath* (Welcoming the Sabbath). It consists of six psalms (95-99; 29) with the addition of the famous poem *Lekhah Dodi* by Rabbi Solomon Alkabets of the sixteenth century. A seventh psalm (92-93) then follows.

The *Kabbalath Shabbath* service was first introduced by the kabbalists of the sixteenth century who flourished in Safed, Eretz Yisrael. The six psalms, symbolizing the six workdays of the week, were selected by Rabbi Moses Cordovero (1522-1570), who was the head of the Safed school of mystics before the advent of Rabbi Isaac Luria in 1569. According to his kabbalistic view, the aim of morality is to secure the unification of all powers of the soul and place them under the control of divine wisdom

The initial letters of the six selected psalms (ל ש י מ י מ) have the numerical value of four hundred and thirty which in turn equals the numerical value of the Hebrew word for soul (נפש).

Psalm 29, the last of the six psalms selected, contains the name of God eighteen times, a number corresponding to the eighteen times God is mentioned in the *Shema* section, recited in the *Shaḥarith* and *Ma'ariv* services. Eighteen is also reminiscent of the eighteen benedictions of the *Shemoneh Esreh* prayer, and the eighteen times the three patriarchs (Abraham, Isaac and Jacob) are mentioned together in the Hebrew Bible. Rabbi Moses Cordovero was a brother-in-law of Rabbi Solomon Alkabets, whose *Lekhah Dodi* poem is the outstanding feature of the *Kabbalath Shabbath* service.

ANCESTRAL GRAVES   קִבְרֵי אָבוֹת

IN the times of the Talmud, the cemetery was visited on fast days to pray at the graves of the departed, that they may intercede in behalf of the living (Ta'anith 16a: כדי שיבקשו מתים רחמים עלינו). We are told that Caleb, who was one of the twelve men sent to spy out the land of Canaan, went and prostrated himself on the ancestral graves (הלך ונשתטח על קברי אבות), asking for intercession (Sotah 34b).

This has been the Jewish custom throughout the centuries. As a rule, graves are visited during the month of *Elul*, which precedes the Jewish New Year, *Rosh Hashanah*, and upon anniversaries of the death of parents. There is a talmudic saying to the effect that it is pleasant to find rest among one's ancestors.

KIDDUSH   קִדּוּשׁ

BEFORE the evening and morning meals on Sabbaths and festivals, *Kiddush* (Sanctification) is recited over wine, the symbol of joy, for it is "wine that cheers man's heart" (Psalm 104:15). The use of wine in connection with the *Kiddush* is spoken of in the Talmud, where the biblical command "remember the Sabbath" is interpreted to mean "remember it over wine" (Pesaḥim 106a). Wine is metaphorically represented as the essence of goodness. Israel is likened to a vine brought from Egypt and planted in Eretz Yisrael, where it took deep root and prospered (Psalm 80:9-11). When wine is not available, the

Kiddush is recited over two loaves of bread (*leḥem mishneh*) that commemorate the double portion of manna that was gathered on Fridays.

The origin of the *Kiddush* is traced back to the early period of the Second Temple, and is attributed to the men of the Great Assembly, who flourished at that time.

On Sabbath eve, the *Kiddush* begins with the phrase יום הששי (the sixth day) and continues with the words ויכלו השמים (the heavens were completed). The initial letters of these Hebrew words make up the tetragrammaton, the divine name (י'ה'ו'ה') of four letters. This will explain why the *Kiddush* begins with the last two words (יום והששי) of the first chapter of the Torah and immediately continues with the beginning of the second chapter.

The phrase סברי מרנן is inserted in the *Kiddush* to call attention to the blessing about to be pronounced over the wine. Literally it means: attention, gentlemen. By responding *Amen*, and listening with attention to the recital of the *Kiddush*, they fulfill their duty of bearing witness that the universe is the creation of God. Since the *Kiddush* is a form of testimony, all stand up as witnesses who testify standing.

The morning *Kiddush* for Sabbath or festivals is called *Kiddusha Rabbah* (the great *Kiddush*) by way of inversion, since it is of later origin and of less importance than the *Kiddush* that is recited in the evening (Pesaḥim 106a).

On all festivals other than the last two days of Passover, the benediction שהחיינו is added to the *Kiddush:* "Blessed art thou, Lord our God . . . who hast granted us life and sustenance and permitted us to reach this festival." *Sheheḥeyanu* is omitted on the last two nights of *Pesaḥ*, which commemorate the crossing of the Red Sea, to indicate that we must not rejoice over the misfortune that befell our foes.

KIDDUSH HA-SHEM קִדּוּשׁ הַשֵּׁם

THE term *Kiddush ha-Shem* (sanctification of the divine name) is generally applied to situations that call for martyrdom in times of persecutions; it is, however, extended to any act of integrity which reflects creditably on the Jewish people and the religious faith. The Torah declares: "You shall not profane my holy name; I will be hallowed among the people of Israel" (Leviticus 22:32). Hence, the concepts *Kiddush ha-Shem* and *Ḥillul ha-Shem* (defamation of the divine name). Nothing must be done that tarnishes Judaism or the Jew. The Talmud warns against any misdeed toward a non-Jew, because it gives a false impression of the moral standards of Judaism.

It has been stated that if the positive principle of *Kiddush ha-Shem* is an ideal of conduct which only holy men can attain, the corresponding negative principle of *Hillul ha-Shem* imposes an unconditional obligation on every Jew. If any act, though permitted by law, may provoke the defamation of Israel and of God, then, in spite of its abstract legality, it becomes a great sin and crime.

An example of *Hillul ha-Shem* is quoted in the Talmud to the effect that not to pay the butcher at once where it is customary to pay in cash constitutes a defamation of the divine name (Yoma 86a). Another talmudic statement reads: "If you must, sin privately, but do not defame the divine name publicly (Kiddushin 40a).

An example of *Kiddush ha-Shem* is the story told in the Midrash about Rabbi Simeon ben Shetah, president of the Sanhedrin during the early part of the first century. One day his disciples gleefully announced to him that they had found a precious stone in the collar of the donkey he had bought from an Arab. "But I purchased a donkey and not a precious stone," he said and immediately returned the gem to its owner. Upon receiving it, the Arab exclaimed: "Praised be the God of Simeon ben Shetah!" (Deuteronomy Rabbah 3:5).

Kiddush ha-Shem has been defined: to act so as to manifest a sublime faith; to do more than what the formal law requires; to practise goodness not out of fear nor for one's own glory, but for the glory of God. The hallowing of the divine name is in the familiar beginning of the *Kaddish* prayer and in the *Kedushah*, which contains the famous Trisagion "holy, holy, holy is the Lord of hosts" (Isaiah 6:3). The highest standards of Jewish ethics are embodied in the terms *Kiddush ha-Shem* and *Hillul ha-Shem*.

KADDISH   קַדִּישׁ

ORIGINALLY, the famous liturgical doxology known as the *Kaddish* (Sanctification) was used as a short prayer at the close of sermons delivered in Aramaic, the language spoken by the Jewish people for about a thousand years after the Babylonian captivity. Hence it was recited in Aramaic, the tongue in which the religious discourses were held. At a later period the *Kaddish* was introduced into the liturgy to mark the conclusion of sections of the service, as well as the end of biblical and talmudic readings recited or interpreted in public.

Since the merit of studying the Torah was always considered exceedingly potent, the idea must have arisen early that the living might through Torah study benefit the remembrance of the deceased. Hence, such study was assigned to mourners; a study in Talmud or a religious discourse was conducted for them, and this was concluded by the *ḥazzan's* recitation of the *Kaddish* (Sofrim 19:12).

Gradually, though not exclusively, the *Kaddish* became an indirect prayer for the departed. It embodies the messianic hope, but contains no reference to the dead. The earliest allusion to the *Kaddish* as a prayer recited by the mourners themselves is found in *Maḥzor Vitry*, dated 1208, where it is stated plainly: "the lad rises and recites *Kaddish*."

One may safely assume that since the *Kaddish* has as its underlying thought the hope for the redemption and ultimate healing of suffering mankind, the power of redeeming the dead from the sufferings of *Gehinnom* came to be ascribed to the recitation of this sublime doxology.

In the course of time, the *Kaddish* was popularly thought of as a direct petition offered for the well-being of departed parents and relatives. Formerly, the *Kaddish* was recited the whole year of mourning, to rescue parents from the torture of *Gehinnom* where the wicked are said to spend no less than twelve months. In order, however, not to count one's own parents among the wicked, the period for reciting the *Kaddish* was later reduced to eleven months.

The *Kaddish* has become a great pillar of Judaism. No matter how far a Jew may have drifted away from Jewish life, the *Kaddish* restores him to his people and to the Jewish way of living. The observance of the anniversary of parents' death, the *Yahrzeit*, at which the *Kaddish* forms the most important feature, originated in Germany, as the term itself well indicates. Rabbi Isaac Luria, the celebrated kabbalist of the sixteenth century, explains that "while the orphan's *Kaddish* within the eleven months helps the soul to pass from *Gehinnom* to *Gan-Eden*, the *Yahrzeit Kaddish* elevates the soul every year to a higher sphere in Paradise."

The essential part of the *Kaddish* consists of the congregational response: "May his great name be blessed forever and ever." Around this response, which is found almost verbatim in Daniel 2:20, the whole *Kaddish* developed. It has been conjectured that the *Kaddish* prayer was recited after sermons some two thousand years ago. The absence of all references to Jerusalem and the destroyed Temple, as well as its plain, unmystical language points to an early date. The reason that the Talmud does not discuss the *Kaddish* is explained by the fact that in those days the *Kaddish* had not yet been made part of the daily service.

During the geonic period it was affirmed that the ten synonyms of praise, contained in the *Kaddish* that glorifies "God's great name throughout the world which he has created according to his will," correspond to the ten divine utterances by which the world was created (Avoth 5:1). The seven words of the congregational response (יהא שמה רבא מברך לעלם ולעלמי עלמיא) are composed of twenty-eight letters, the numerical value of the word כח (power). This alludes to the first verse of the Torah, which consists of seven words that are composed of twenty-eight letters. It is noteworthy that the concluding three paragraphs of the full-*Kaddish* likewise consist of ten words each, not counting the closing phrase ואמרו אמן.

The concluding Hebrew paragraph of the *Kaddish* (עושה שלום) repeats the thought expressed in the preceding semi-Aramaic paragraph. It was borrowed from the meditation recited at the end of the *Shemoneh Esreh*. The accompanying three steps backwards with the inclinations to the left, right and forward, which symbolize the worshiper's retiring from the presence of the divine King, were likewise transferred from the final sentence of the *Shemoneh Esreh*. On the other hand, the phrase ואמרו אמן (and say Amen), added at the end of the silent meditation after the *Shemoneh Esreh*, must have been transferred from the *Kaddish* which is always recited in the hearing of no fewer than ten men.

The *Kaddish* has five different forms: 1) *Kaddish d'Rabbanan* (scholars' *Kaddish*), recited after the reading of talmudic-midrashic passages in the presence of a *minyan* or quorum of ten men; 2) *Kaddish Shalem* (full *Kaddish*), recited by the reader at the end of a major section of the service; 3) *Ḥatsi Kaddish* (half *Kaddish*), recited by the reader between sections of the service; 4) *Kaddish Yathom* (mourner's *Kaddish*), recited by the mourners after the service and after the recitation of certain psalms, such as the Psalm of the Day; 5) an expanded form of the mourner's *Kaddish*, recited at the cemetery after a burial (קדיש לאתחדתא).

The *Kaddish* prayer, binding the generations together in love and respect, has been described as a sacred thread in Israel. The *Kaddish* makes the hearts of parents and children beat in eternal unison.

KEDUSHAH   קְדֻשָּׁה

THE *Kedushah* (Sanctification), like the *Kaddish* prayer, is one of the liturgical features that are restricted to congregational worship, requiring a quorum of ten men (*minyan*). It is attached to the *Amidah* prayer in the morning and afternoon services, and is recited responsively when the *ḥazzan* or reader repeats the *Amidah* in the hearing of the congregation.

The threefold repetition of *Holy* (קדוש קדוש קדוש) denotes emphasis and intensity. The entire doxology of *Kedushah* is a mosaic of biblical verses (Isaiah 6:3; Ezekiel 3:12; Psalm 146:10).

The introductory words summon the congregation to join in the praise of God in the manner of the angelic hosts, who keep calling to one another: "Holy, holy, holy is the Lord of hosts; the whole earth is full of his glory." The Talmud (Sotah 49a) accentuates the unusual importance of the *Kedushah* by intimating that the entire ethical world of the Jew rests upon the constant emphasis of holiness.

The *Kedushah* is recited only when a *minyan* is present because it is written: "I will be sanctified among the people of Israel" (Leviticus 22:32), implying that the proclamation of the holiness and kingship of God is to be made in public worship only. The same applies to the *Kaddish* prayer.

It is noteworthy that in the passage לדור ודור, immediately following the *Kedushah*, the most characteristic letter *shin* (שׁ) of the word קדוש is repeated six times, alluding to the thrice-repeated *kadosh* in heaven and on earth. The same letter (שׁ) occurs six times in the introductory line of the *Kedushah*, which reads: נקדש את שמך ... כשם שמקדישים אותו בשמי מרום ("We sanctify thy name ... even as they sanctify it in the highest heavens"). The number six may also allude to the six-winged Seraphim chanting *kadosh kadosh kadosh*, according to Isaiah 6:2.

The threefold utterance of *kadosh* (holy) is included in the prayer *Uva l'Tsiyyon*, which is called *Kedushah d'sidra*, because (according to Rashi) it is inserted in the daily minimal biblical lesson designed for all Israel.

In the *Musaf* service for Sabbaths and festivals, as well as in the services for the Day of Atonement, the *Kedushah* is expanded by the inclusion of the first sentence of the *Shema*, consisting of six words, and the concluding six words (להיות לכם לאלהים, אני ה' אלהיכם).

540

This abridged form of the *Shema* was inserted in the *Kedushah* when, in the fifth century, special government officials were posted in the synagogues to prevent the congregational proclamation of God's Oneness. Toward the end of the service, when the spies had left, the *Shema* could be congregationally uttered at least in its abbreviation. The longer form of *Kedushah* is recited during all the repeated *Amidahs* of *Yom Kippur* in order to mark the extra importance of the day. There are three *Kedushoth:* 1) the *Kedushah* forming part of the *Ami-* *dah,* 2) the one included in *Yotser,* and 3) the one in *Uva l'Tsiyyon.*

KODASHIM   קָדָשִׁים

THE fifth of the six divisions of the Mishnah is known under the name of *Kodashim* (Sanctities), because it deals with subjects connected with Temple service and ritual slaughtering (*shehitah*). The eleven tractates of *Kodashim* are as follows:

1) *Zevahim,* fourteen chapters, on the sacrificial system of the Temple period.

2) *Menahoth,* thirteen chapters, on the cereal and drink offerings. A handful of the meal-offering was burnt on the altar and the remainder was consumed by the priests.

3) *Hullin,* twelve chapters, on the slaughter of animals and the dietary laws. The rules prescribed for slaughtering include five things which must be avoided: there must be no delay; no pressure may be exerted on the knife's moving backwards and forwards; the knife must not be allowed to slip beyond a certain area of throat; there must be no thrusting of the knife under the skin or between the gullet and windpipe; the gullet or windpipe must not be torn out of position in the course of slaughtering.

4) *Bekhoroth,* nine chapters, concerning the human firstborn and the animal firstlings, in reference to the command in Exodus 13:2 ("Consecrate all the firstborn to me . . . of man or of beast. . .").

5) *Arakhin,* nine chapters, on vows of valuation (Leviticus 27:1-34) or voluntary contributions to the upkeep of the Temple. By setting a valuation upon himself or any of his family, a person obligated himself to pay a certain amount into the treasury of the Temple.

6) *Temurah,* seven chapters, on the substitution or replacing of one species for another, which is prohibited when a certain animal was dedicated as a sacrifice (Leviticus 27:10).

7) *Kerithoth*, six chapters, on the sins punishable by *kareth*, premature or sudden death, or being cut off from the community of Israel.

8) *Me'ilah*, six chapters, on sacrilegious treatment of property belonging to the Temple.

9) *Tamid*, seven chapters, on the daily offerings, brought every morning and evening (Exodus 29:38-42; Numbers 28:1-8).

10) *Middoth*, five chapters, on the architecture of the Temple.

11) *Kinnim*, three chapters, on the offerings of birds. The title *Kinnim* (nests) refers to the pairs of birds prescribed in the Torah as offerings (Leviticus 5:1-10).

KAHAL, KEHILLAH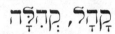

DURING the medieval period, Jewish localities organized themselves into communities having autonomous rights and being responsible for taxation as well as the establishment of educational and charitable institutions. The head of such an organized community was called *Rosh ha-Kahal* or *Parnas* (פרנס). He was assisted by three to seven advisers particularly in money matters, who were referred to as טובי העיר. There were besides several trustees (גבאים), forming committees that were in charge of the public institutions, such as the synagogue, the hospital and home for the aged, charity funds and ransom funds (*pidyon shevuyim*). In the nineteenth century, with the abolition of the ghetto in central Europe, Jewish self-government was reduced to conducting the purely religious affairs of the various communities.

ECCLESIASTES

THE book of Ecclesiastes, traditionally identified with king Solomon, contains twelve chapters of maxims and wise observations on the purpose of life. The author, Koheleth, counsels patience, endurance and discretion, and gives expression to the theory that history and nature move in a circle, an ever-revolving and recurring cycle.

A sense of futility and pessimisn is displayed throughout the book, which deals with the pursuit of wisdom, pleasure, wealth, and evil-doing. Upon examining the value of wisdom, wealth and pleasure, Koheleth finds life unsatisfying. He declares that wealth does not

542

yield happiness, since it is often lost before it is enjoyed. At death, it is left to people who have not toiled to acquire it.

How are we to gain happiness? Shall we follow wisdom or unrestrained pleasure? Human existence is monotonous: there is nothing new in the entire world. We should therefore alternate wholesome work with reasonable pleasures of life while we can, since there is no telling when the end comes.

The book of Koheleth concludes, however, with this counsel: "Revere God and keep his commandments, for this is the whole duty of man." As one of the Five *Megilloth* (scrolls) in the third division of the Bible, Koheleth is recited in the synagogue on the eighth day of the *Sukkoth* festival.

Following are a few maxims excerpted from the book of Ecclesiastes: "A lover of money will never be satisfied with his money. Sweet is the sleep of the worker, whether he eats much or little. But the surfeit of the rich man does not let him sleep. Naked he came from his mother's womb, and naked he must return; for all his toil he has nothing to take with him. A good name is better than precious perfume.

"Let your garments be always spotless. Cast your bread upon the waters; after many days you shall find it. Sweet is the light of life; it is pleasant for the eyes to see the sun. Rejoice in your youth, young man. Remove all worries from your mind, and keep your body free from pain. Remember your Creator in the days of your youth. . ."

It has been said that there is nothing grander than Ecclesiastes in its impassioned survey of mortal pain and pleasure, its estimate of failure and success; none of more noble sadness; no poem working more indomitably for spiritual illumination.

INCENSE   קְטֹרֶת

THE fragrant smoke of burning incense at dawn and sunset was a natural symbol of prayer ascending to heaven from the Temple of Jerusalem. "Let my prayer rise like incense before thee" (Psalm 141:2) distinctly alludes to this. On *Yom Kippur*, the high priest carried a golden censer full of glowing coals, as well as a double handful of finely ground fragrant gums and spices, when he entered the Holy of Holies (*kodesh ha-kodashim*), where he put the incense upon the fire, "so that the cloud of incense covered the ark . . . otherwise, he might die" (Leviticus 16:12-13).

Incense had to be offered on the altar every morning and every evening. The Mishnah tells us that it was the custom to decide by lot which of the priests were to perform the various functions, among which the offering of incense was considered particularly desirable (Yoma 2:4). In offering the incense, fire was taken from the altar of burnt-offerings and carried into the Temple, where it was laid on the incense altar, and then the incense was emptied from a golden vessel upon the fire.

Sweet incense was used extensively as an element in Temple worship. It has been noted that its use was probably due to the worshiper's desire to honor God by offering to him what he enjoyed himself. "Perfume and incense gladden the heart" (Proverbs 27:9). It served also to counteract the smell of blood and burning flesh when animal sacrifices were offered in the courts of the *Mishkan* (Tabernacle) and the Temple. The burning incense doubtless effected a sanitary influence. It neutralized the odors arising from the slaughtered animals and also animated the spirits of the officiating priests. Hence, it was usually presented as an accompaniment of sacrifices. It was offered either in censers or on an altar erected for the purpose (מזבח הקטרת).

Maimonides plainly points out: "Since many animals were daily slaughtered in the holy place ... the smell of the place would undoubtedly have been like the smell of slaughterhouses, if nothing had been done to counteract it. ... All this aimed at producing due respect towards the Sanctuary, and indirectly reverence for God. When a person enters the Temple, certain emotions are produced in him; and obstinate hearts are softened and humbled..." (*Guide*, 3:45). The incense-offering was regarded as most sacred and the sole prerogative of the priests. "Aaron shall burn the incense of fragrant spices on the altar every morning; when he trims the lamps he shall burn it. And when Aaron lights the lamps toward evening, he shall again burn it" (Exodus 30:7-8). A trace of incense forms part of the *Havdalah* service. The daily Prayerbook includes, as part of the preliminary morning service, a graphic description of how the incense was produced. This is taken from several tannaitic sources recounting ancient traditions. The passage פטום הקטרת, recited at the end of the *Musaf* service on Sabbaths and festivals, is an abridgment of the more detailed tannaitic description of the incense preparation which is included in the preliminary morning service. Great mystical importance has been attached to the meticulous recital of this Baraitha which is taken from the Talmud (Kerithoth 6a).

KINOTH   קִינוֹת

THE lamenting elegies recited in the synagogue on *Tish'ah b'Av* (Ninth of *Av*), in addition to the reading of the book of Lamentations, were composed by medieval liturgical poets (*payyetanim*) in sad remembrance of the loss of national independence and the destruction of the Temple. The book of Lamentations is the prototype of all such compositions by Rabbi Elazar ha-Kallir of the eighth century and other *payyetanim*, who described contemporary persecutions and expressed deep sorrow over the mortal sufferings of their people.

Included among the writers of *Kinoth* (lamenting poetry) are Rabbi Solomon ibn Gabirol, Rabbi Yehudah Halevi, Rabbi Moses ibn Ezra, and Rabbi Abraham ibn Ezra. Only a selection of the vast number of these compositions is now recited in the synagogues on the morning of *Tish'ah b'Av* after the Torah reading. One of the most famous poetic compositions by Rabbi Yehudah Halevi is the lamentation אֱלִי צִיוֹן (Lament, O Zion), arranged in alphabetical order and recited on *Tish'ah b'Av* with a traditional chant.

AMULETS   קְמֵיעוֹת

IN THE Mishnah, amulets are mentioned on two occasions as being worn for the curative power they were believed to possess (Shabbath 6:2; Shekalim 3:2). A protective force was attributed to inscribed amulets, folded with mystical writings in them in addition to magical symbols, suggested by kabbalistic works such as the book of Raziel which contains a variety of formulas for *kemeoth*. The writing consisted of a series of divine names and biblical verses of symbolical character, which were to protect the wearer from any attack of illness or evil spirits. Three biblical verses (Exodus 14:19-21) were believed to have the highest mystical significance, because each of then consists of seventy-two letters, corresponding to the seventy-two letters of one of the mysterious names of God. Hence, these verses were assumed to represent the ineffable divine name; they were inserted in the amulets in varied forms as an appeal to God for protection.

The silver or gold containers of amulets, bearing on the outside the divine name *Shaddai* (Almighty), were often artistic achievements. In addition to biblical quotations, the names of angels and combinations of Hebrew letters went into the composition of amulets. The rabbinic authorities, however, emphasized the study of Torah and the performance of good deeds as counteracting all evil.

The mystical word *abracadabra*, derived probably from the Aramaic tongue, was used as a formula of incantation against fever or inflammation. Medieval patients were advised to wear this magic word, written in the following manner on an amulet, in the belief that it would ward off and cure diseases.

ABRACADABRA
ABRACADABR
ABRACADAB
ABRACADA
ABRACAD
ABRACA
ABRAC
ABRA
ABR
AB
A

A similar idea is quoted in the Talmud (Pesaḥim 112a) to the effect that as an incantation against temporary blindness or loss of direction, the person in danger should say: "My mother has told me to beware of *shabriri: shabriri, briri, riri, rir, ri* (רי, ריר, רירי, בריר, שברירי).

In the *Sefer Ḥasidim*, by Rabbi Yehudah he-Ḥasid of the twelfth century, we read: "Do not wear an amulet as a charm against evil, but put your implicit trust in God alone."

KARAITES קָרָאִים

THE Karaite sect, founded by Anan ben David in the middle of the eighth century, regarded itself as an integral part of the Jewish people, though it was read out of the Jewish fold by the adherents of rabbinic Judaism. The struggle between the Karaites and the Rabbanites was both constant and arduous for more than four centuries. It is true that the Karaite movement weakened the Jewish people numerically, but it had a leavening effect on the development of Jewish learning throughout the Arabic-speaking countries, where Karaism flourished for some time and created a variety of controversial issues based on a new, more literal interpretation of the Bible.

Anan ben David was often quoted by his followers as having said: "Make a thorough search of the Torah and do not rely on my opinion." The Karaites, then, rejecting talmudic-traditional authority and basing themselves on individual interpretation of the biblical teachings, frequently attacked rabbinic methods of interpretation and thus compelled great scholars like Rav Saadyah Gaon and Moses Maimonides to devote more time to the study of the Bible according to its literal sense (*peshat*). The Karaite writers, like Yefet ben Ali and Salmon ben Yeruḥam of the tenth century, considered themselves as the intellectuals (*maskilim*) of the time and used their Bible commentaries, each according to his style, to ridicule what they termed Rabbanite superstitions and misinterpretations.

Writing in his Arabic commentary on Isaiah, Yefet ben Ali digresses as follows: "This section refers to the people of the Diaspora and to the best among them as well. They are at present divided into four classes: 1) the exilarchs who pretend to be the possessors of knowledge; 2) the common people who neither desire wisdom nor think about it; they know no more about religion than to go to the synagogues from Sabbath to Sabbath and to say *Amen* and *Shema Yisrael;* 3) the studious among the common people, whom the exilarchs teach the nonsense of the Talmud, and sorcery, instead of what might profit them; 4) the *maskilim* (Karaite teachers) who, endowed with the knowledge of the Torah, are generous with the dissemination of their wisdom, in return for which they accept no recompense."

The Karaites failed to realize that the talmudic-traditional teachings stemmed from the need of adjusting Jewish living to changing conditions. Their watchword "back to the Bible" came to be purely a theoretical one, after all, when they developed a tradition of their own and called it "yoke of heritage" (סבל הירושה). In the course of time, the Karaites held as binding the doctrines and the usages which were regarded as obligatory by their community (*edah, kibbutz*), even though these could not be traced directly to the Bible.

Originally, the Karaites were known as Ananites, from the name of their founder Anan of Baghdad, Babylonia. In his *Book of Precepts* (*Sefer ha-Mitzvoth*), Anan extended the idea of forbidden work on Sabbath by making it unlawful, for example, to light on a Friday a candle that would keep burning on Sabbath eve. His adherents were therefore told to sit in darkness on Friday nights. He forbade them to leave their homes on the Sabbath, except to attend congregational services of their own.

According to Anan, the Jews of the Diaspora were forbidden to eat meat, since such food depended on the existence of a Temple and a sacrificial system. A strain of gloom pervaded Anan's injunctions; bad results followed when he had discarded the traditional prayers in use, substituting for them the recitation of isolated psalms and biblical verses newly put together.

Daniel al-Kumisi of the ninth century, one of the outstanding Karaite scholars who originally was an admirer of Anan, calling him ראש המשכילים (head of the intellectuals), later changed his views and referred to him as ראש הכסילים (the biggest fool). Rav Saadyah Gaon of the tenth century took up the arguments of the Karaites and proved that they were both destructive of Jewish life and illogical. After his onslaughts, Karaism was never again a serious danger to Jewish life.

Karaite attacks on rabbinic Judaism were, however, responsible for the production of immortal works by Rav Saadyah Gaon, who translated the Bible into Arabic, with a commentary based on grammar and usage of words within the compass of the entire biblical literature. His version served as a mine in the hands of successive generations of Bible students. His counter-attacks which appeared in the form of permanent literary achievements finally checked the destructive inroads of Karaism. In the twelfth century, Moses Maimonides was moved to compose his gigantic Jewish Law Code, *Mishneh Torah*, representing a complete synthesis of biblical and traditional lore as Judaism indivisible. This achievement was accomplished in Cairo, Egypt, where Maimonides found the Karaite community to be rich, influential, and fanatically attacking rabbinic Judaism.

Jewish enemies across the centuries hardly differentiated between Karaites and Rabbanites. The Russian pogromists made no distinction between the two opposing factions. Yet, in the Crimea, where the Karaites emphasized their separateness from the rest of the Jews, they obtained certain advantages from the tsars of Russia. One of their Karaite scholars, Abraham Firkovich (1785-1874), who held posts in various communities in the Crimea, forged dates and inscriptions so as to give his own people the appearance of greater antiquity. His falsifications undermined confidence in all his scholarly productions. It was Abraham Harkavy (1835-1919), who published over four hundred studies on various branches of Judaica, that discriminated between truth and fiction in the discoveries of Firkovich.

As a result of the Russian Revolution in 1917, the Crimean Karaites were cut off from the dwindling society of fellow Karaites else-

548

where. Following the Second World War, barely three hundred of them survived. The Karaite communities of Jerusalem and Damascus progressively wasted away; many of their coreligionists migrated to Egypt. Ever since the year 1948, when the State of Israel came into being as an independent State, thousands of Karaites left Egypt and settled in Israel.

Most of the surviving Karaites are now to be found in Israel, where there has been an attempt to integrate them with the Israeli Jewish community. In all, their number is estimated to be around eight thousand souls.

The Karaite population in Israel was doubled soon after the Sinai campaign and the intensification of the persecutions in Egypt. When the Karaites began to flock to Israel in 1950, they received aid from the government in the creation of special Karaite settlements. Religious problems pertaining to marriage, divorce, circumcision, *shehitah*, had to be solved; hence, the Israeli government appointed so-called *hazzanim* to organize the religious life of the Karaites. Several thousand Karaite sectarians are to be found in five villages (Ofakim, Ashdod Yam, Matsliah, Ramlah, and Renen).

The Israeli government yielded to the Karaite request not to take their young daughters into the army, in view of the great emphasis placed by the Karaites on the ideal of chastity. In 1955, the question of intermarriage between the Jews and the Karaites was debated in the Knesset. David Ben Gurion demanded that the rabbinical authorities should help find a solution to this problem of absorbing the Karaites into the Jewish fold; there were others who pointed out that the Karaites themselves are not quite ready for a step like this. Twelve centuries ago, the reputed founder of Karaism, Anan, decreed against any Karaite association with the followers of rabbinic Judaism, in order to avoid intermarriage or the eating of meat prepared not in accordance with the *shehitah* regulations observed by the Karaite sect.

Since the new Karaite generation, trained in the schools of Israel and speaking the language of Israel, is not likely to be at all sensitive to intermarriage with Rabbanite Jews, complete integration is expected before the lapse of many years. There are leading Israelis who think that these "Mourners for Zion," having emerged out of darkness into light, out of mourning into festivity, are an inseparable segment of the *Yishuv*, the Jewish settlement, in Israel. With all the Karaite centers liquidated during the second World War, a new leaf in the history of the Karaite sect is being turned over.

OFFERINGS   קָרְבָּנוֹת

THE word *korban* (sacrifice) occurs about eighty times in the Hebrew Bible, particularly in the books of Leviticus and Numbers. In the prophetical books it is mentioned on four occasions (Ezekiel 20:28; 40:43; Nehemiah 10:35; 13:31). The burnt-offerings, which were entirely burnt on the altar, are more accurately named *holocausts*, meaning: whole burnt-offerings. Only a small portion of thanksgiving sacrifices was burnt on the altar; the remnant was eaten by priests and worshipers. Thanksgiving sacrifices, and the like, gave rise to joyous feasting and banqueting in Temple times.

Sin-offerings (חטאות) and guilt-offerings (אשמות) were distinguishable as follows: guilt-offerings were used in connection with the restitution of stolen goods, for example; sin-offerings were made whenever a person involuntarily violated divine commands, without injuring the property of fellow men. The inherent meaning of the term *korban* is *a means of approach* to God, from the Hebrew root *karav* (to approach).

The sacrificial system in ancient times symbolized self-surrender and devotion to the will of God. The peace-offering (*shelamim*) with the communion-feast showed the idea of fellowship. It served to keep alive the sense of dependence on God for the natural blessings of life, while it had the social value of promoting the solidarity of the nation. The daily offering (*tamid*) symbolized Israel's pledge of unbroken service to God. The fragrant smoke of incense rising towards heaven was a natural symbol of prayer ascending to God, as seen from Psalm 141:2 ("Let my prayer rise like incense before thee").

Anciently, Hebrew worship was essentially social. A sacrifice was a public ceremony; private persons were accustomed to reserve their offerings for the annual feasts, satisfying their religious feelings in the interval by vows to be fulfilled when the festal season came around. Then multitudes of people streamed into the Temple from all directions, marching joyfully to the sound of music, and bearing with them bread and wine to set forth the feast, which meant open-handed hospitality. No sacrifice was complete without guests; portions were distributed freely to rich and poor within the circle of a man's friends and acquaintances (I Samuel 9:13; II Samuel 6:19; 15:12).

Since the blood was considered the seat and sign of life, and therefore something sacred, the ordinary preparation of an animal for meat was looked upon as having a sacrificial character, so that it should be

550

performed at the sanctuary. Though life and blood are not quite identical, the blood is the principal carrier of life; hence it was reserved
for a sacred symbolic purpose. The slaughtering of animals for food
used to be rare, therefore, and only at a family feast. In Deuteronomy
12:20, however, the people of Israel were permitted to have meat for
food in their respective communities throughout the land of Israel.

Sacrificial worship was coordinated with knowledge of the Torah
and with the performance of good deeds. The synagogue was the
sphere of the larger part of religious activity, as being the ordinary
place of worship during the period of the Second Commonwealth. The
teacher and the sage tended to overshadow the priest. An ignorant
high priest was considered inferior to a scholar of illegitimate birth.

There were public and private offerings, according as they were
offered at the expense of the people at large or of an individual. With
the destruction of the Temple, the sacrificial system ceased, and prayer
became its substitute. Even to this day, the Hebrew liturgy includes
sections on the subject of sacrifices, such as אֵיזֶהוּ מְקוֹמָן, which are
recited as a historical study connecting the present with associations
of the past. The *Seder Avodah*, recited as part of the *Musaf* service
for *Yom Kippur*, belongs to this category of public worship.

According to the rationalist view of Maimonides, the sacrificial system as it is outlined in the Torah was designed to wean the people
away from the religious customs of the idolatrous neighbors. Hence
it was restricted to one place, the Jerusalem Temple. This thought is
clearly supported by Leviticus 17:7, where we are told: "No longer
shall they offer their sacrifices to the satyrs, after whom they go
astray." The *Ramban*, however, writing on Leviticus 1:9, emphatically disagrees with Maimonides and rejects the theory that the sacrificial system was ordained as a mere concession to the people who
were forbidden to worship idols or to offer human sacrifices.

The destruction of the Temple created new conditions which gave
rise to the theory that other observances were accepted as a substitute for the sacrificial worship. The study of the Torah took the place
of the rites of the altar and was designated as *avodah* (service). According to a talmudic statement (Megillah 3b), the study of Torah is more
valuable as a religious duty than the daily burnt-offerings (גָּדוֹל תַּלְמוּד
תּוֹרָה יוֹתֵר מֵהַקְרָבַת תְּמִידִין). Thus the offering of the daily sacrifices was superseded by the duty of studying the laws relating to the
subject. Prayer, too, is treated as an equivalent for the abolished service, and is designated as עֲבוֹדָה שֶׁבַּלֵּב, service of the heart.

In the course of time, the slaying of animals for food was relegated to specially trained men, called *shoḥetim*, whose method causes the maximum effusion of blood in the animal, and the remaining blood is extracted by means of the washing and salting of the meat. These injunctions have without a doubt contributed to render the Jews a habitually humane people. It has been suggested that the one circumstance that no Jewish mother ever killed a chicken with her own hand will explain why homicide is rarer among Jews than among others.

KEROVOTH   קְרוֹבוֹת

THE title *Kerovoth* is applied to the *piyyutim* (liturgical poems) that have been incorporated in the *Amidah* prayer for festivals and distinguished Sabbaths. When the Reader repeats the earlier part of the *Amidah* aloud for the congregation, the *Kerovoth* are recited responsively or alternately. The term *Kerovoth* is derived from the verb קרב (to approach), that is, the cantor's approaching the holy ark (*aron ha-kodesh*) and offering petitions on behalf of the worshipers. In midrashic literature the term *kerova* is used synonymously with *payyetan* (poet) and hymnologist. The word is sometimes spelled קרוב"ץ as an abbreviation of קול רנה וישועה באהלי צדיקים ("the joyful song of triumph in the tents of the righteous"), an expression found in Psalm 118:15. The traditional melodies of the *Kerovoth* are distinguished from all other melodies that are associated with the *piyyutim* and have a more ancient character.

These poetical insertions and the accompanying special melodies have helped to create the refreshing atmosphere of each festival. They have awakened in the Jew fervent enthusiasm for his heritage and tradition, and a prayerful desire for restoration and self-renewal.

KERÉ AND KETHIV   קְרִי וּכְתִיב

MORE than thirteen hundred variants in the Hebrew Bible have been recorded by the masoretic experts, who noted anything that was unusual in the sacred text. These variants are known as *keré* (to be read) and *kethiv* (it is written). Some words are always to be read otherwise than they are written. This occurs in the Torah wherever the pronoun הוא stands for the feminine היא and the noun נער for נערה.

552

In order to indicate the correct reading in the vocalized texts, the vowels are simply attached to the word as it should be read. Examples:

נַעַר = נַעֲרָה; יִשָּׁשכָר = יִשָּׂכָר

הוּא = הִיא; יְרוּשָׁלַ ִם = יְרוּשָׁלַיִם

אָנוּ = אֲנַחְנוּ; וִישְׁתַּחוּ = וְיִשְׁתַּחֲווּ

The Masorah indicates when to omit reading a word that is written (כתיב ולא קרי) and when to supply a word that is not found in the text (קרי ולא כתיב).

Something quite different is the expression אל תקרי (do not read), a talmudic device whereby the interpretation of a biblical passage is enriched through a small change in the vocalization of a word, and is not intended to indicate a variant in the text. Example: "Students of the Torah increase peace in the world, for it is written: All your children shall be taught of the Lord, and great shall be the peace of your children (Isaiah 54:13). Do not read here *banayikh* (your children) but *bonayikh* (your builders), that is, scholars who are the true builders of the ideal of peace" (Berakhoth 64a). The play on the two Hebrew words is designed to attract attention to the great significance of peace: בָּנַיִךְ = בְּנַיִךְ.

TORAH READING   קְרִיאַת הַתּוֹרָה

THE public Torah reading at the synagogue has been one of the most powerful factors of education. Originally, the reading was accompanied by translation and interpretation so that the contents of the Torah became known to all the people of Israel. Writing in the first century, Josephus states that Moses showed the Torah to be the best and the most necessary means of instruction by enjoining the people to assemble not once or twice or frequently, but every week, while abstaining from all other work, in order to hear the Torah and learn it in a thorough manner—a thing which all other lawgivers seem to have neglected.

The Torah reading on Sabbath afternoons, when people have leisure, and on Mondays and Thursdays, the market days in early times, is attributed to Ezra the Scribe, who organized Jewish life after Israel's return from the Babylonian captivity. In Eretz Yisrael it was the

553

practice to read the Torah, on Sabbath mornings, in triennial cycles. Hence, the Torah used to be divided into about one hundred seventy-five weekly sections (*sidroth*). Today, the universal custom is to complete the public reading of the Torah each year and to divide the Five Books of Moses into fifty-four larger sections.

Since, however, the ordinary year does not contain fifty-four Sabbaths, it was found necessary, in order to complete the annual cycle, to have two weekly sections combined and read together on some Sabbaths of the year. In leap years, consisting of thirteen months instead of twelve, there is of course no need to combine any of the *sidroth*. Festivals often coincide with Sabbaths, in which case not the *sidrah* (section) of the week is read, but one that has some bearing on the particular festival.

The regular reading of the Torah on Monday and Thursday mornings, and on Sabbath afternoons, is divided into three parts, and the honor to ascend the *bimah* (platform) for the Torah reading is extended to three worshipers. The Sabbath reading is divided into seven parts called *aliyyoth* (ascents). Sometimes, more than seven such honors are distributed, each being called *hosafah* (addition). The Torah reading on *Yom Kippur* morning consists of six parts, and three parts in the afternoon reading. On major festivals, five men are called up to the Torah; on *Ḥol ha-Moʻed*, the intermediate days of *Pesaḥ* and *Sukkoth*, as well as on *Rosh Ḥodesh*, four men are given *aliyyoth;* on *Ḥanukkah* and *Purim*, as well as on *Tishʻah bʼAv* morning and afternoon, three men are called up.

SHEMA READING   קְרִיאַת שְׁמַע

THE first sentence of the *Shema*, consisting of six Hebrew words, has been the keynote of Judaism throughout the ages. It contains two statements, proclaiming the Oneness of God and the loyalty of Israel. Its correct English rendering is: "Hear, O Israel, the Lord is our God, the Lord is One." The last letters of the first word שמע (hear) and the last word אחד (One), if combined, form the word עד (witness); that is to say: he who recites the *Shema* bears witness that God is One, the God of all humanity. For this reason, the letters ע and ד are written large in the unvocalized text of the Torah.

The *Shema* reading, composed of three biblical sections, is the oldest and most essential part of the liturgy. The first paragraph, taken

554

from Deuteronomy 6:4-9, demands that we love and serve God with our whole being. Love goes deeper than fear: love serves unselfishly. The numerical value of אחד (One) corresponds to אהבה (Love) = 13.

The second paragraph, taken from Deuteronomy 11:13-21, demands that we give living expression to our love of God by the careful observance of his precepts which are designed to assure our happiness. The third paragraph, taken from Numbers 15:37-41, speaks of the fringes (tsitsith) as intended to remind us constantly of our duties towards God; it contains a warning against following the evil impulses of the heart.

In the morning service (Shaḥarith) the Shema is preceded by two benedictions and followed by one; in the evening service (Ma'ariv) it is preceded by two benedictions and followed by two. These seven blessings are in keeping with the biblical expression: "Seven times a day I praise thee" (Psalm 119:164; Berakhoth 11b). In the morning service, the first benediction (יוצר אור) praises God for the natural light of the sun; the second benediction (אהבה רבה) is one of the most beautiful prayers in the liturgies of the world, entreating the Merciful Father to enlighten our eyes and our minds to understand his teachings. The third benediction, ending with גאל ישראל before the Amidah, speaks of God as the Redeemer of Israel.

Jewish tradition gives minute directions about the time and manner of the recitation of the Shema. It must be read with the utmost exactness; a slight pause must be made between words separated by repeated letters, such as בכל לבבך, which are liable to be jumbled together; the last word of the first verse (אחד) must be read with greater emphasis and mental concentration. Inscribed in the mezuzah on the doorpost of every habitable room, and forming one of the texts encased in the tefillin, the Shema is the first spiritual lesson a Jewish child is taught, and the last words uttered by or spoken in the hearing of the dying.

Rabbi David Abudarham of fourteenth-century Spain, whose commentary on the Hebrew prayers provides a vast store of explanations culled from a variety of sources, dwells on the word שמע, interpreting it as an acrostic of שאו מרום עיניך (lift up your eyes to heaven); when? שחרית מנחה ערבית (morning, afternoon and evening); to whom? שדי מלך עליון (to the Almighty Most High King); for the acceptance of עול מלכות שמים (the yoke of the divine majesty). As indicated above, the Mishnah refers to the recitation of the Shema as קבלת עול מלכות שמים (accepting the yoke of the divine majesty).

555

NIGHT PRAYER קְרִיאַת שְׁמַע עַל הַמִּטָּה

A special prayer, along with the first paragraph of the *Shema*, is quoted in the Talmud (Berakhoth 60b) to be recited before going to bed at night. It is a petition for peace and protection during the night. "Grant that I lie down in peace and that I rise up in peace. Let not my thoughts upset me—nor evil dreams, nor sinful fancies. . ."

The name *Keriath Shema al ha-Mittah* is attributable to the section of the *Shema*, which is the chief element of the night prayer. Some psalms and excerpts from the *Ma'ariv* service are included. The *Adon Olam* hymn marks the end of the night prayer.

A special, abbreviated night prayer for children reads as follows:

Blessed art thou, Lord our God, King of the universe, who closest my eyes in sleep. May it be thy will, Lord my God and God of my fathers, to grant that I lie down in peace and that I rise again to life. Hear, O Israel, the Lord is our God, the Lord is One. Blessed be the name of his glorious majesty forever and ever.

You shall love the Lord your God with all your heart, and with all your soul, and with all your might. And these words which I command you today shall be in your heart. You shall teach them diligently to your children, and you shall speak of them when you are sitting at home and when you go on a journey, when you lie down and when you rise up. You shall bind them for a sign on your hand, and they shall be for frontlets between your eyes. You shall inscribe them on the doorposts of your house and on your gates.

Blessed be the Lord by day; blessed be the Lord by night; blessed be the Lord when we lie down; blessed be the Lord when we rise up.

The Guardian of Israel neither slumbers nor sleeps. Into thy hand I commit my spirit, O Lord. For thy salvation I hope, O Lord.

KERI'AH

Upon hearing of the death of his son Absalom, king David arose and rent his garments (II Samuel 13:31). Hence, the rite of rending the garments of a mourner is performed while standing. The rent of the garment, made lengthwise and not crosswise, must be made near the front of the neck but not at the seam. For parents, all that the mourner is wearing is rent opposite the heart, with the exception of the under-

556

shirt and the upper garment. For other close relatives, only a small
rent (the size of a handbreadth) is made in the external garment alone.
If informed of their death after thirty days, a person is not obligated
to rend his garments. For parents, however, the duty of rending the
garments applies at all times. In *shiv'ah*, putting on a different garment on a weekday requires rending.

JEWISH NATIONAL FUND

THE Jewish National Fund, widely known in Hebrew as *Keren Kayyemeth l'Yisrael* (Israel's Permanent Fund), was founded at the fifth
Zionist Congress (1901) according to the principles worked out by
Hermann Schapira (1850-1915), professor of mathematics at Heidel-
berg. His recommendation, made at the first Zionist Congress, that
the Jewish National Fund should be based on the biblical principle of
leasing the land and not selling it to individuals, was adopted on the
proposal of Theodore Herzl in 1901. Until 1920 the Jewish National
Fund was the only Zionist colonising fund.

Following the Balfour Declaration (1917), the *Keren Hayesod*
(Foundation Fund) was established as the financial arm of the Zionist
Organization; it was designed to attract not only Zionists to the restoration of Eretz Yisrael, but the entire Jewish people. Since the establishment of the *Keren Hayesod* in 1920, the Jewish National Fund
has devoted itself mainly to the purchase and preparation of land for
purposes of settlement. At the establishment of the State of Israel,
the Jewish National Fund owned 235,523 acres. In 1949-50, the Israeli government transferred to it 606,097 acres of abandoned soil.

In a message delivered by Weizmann in 1951, the first president of
Israel declared: "To bring water to the thirsty earth, shade to the
sun-parched sands, the laughter of children to a countryside where
only jackals howl; to unearth the good soil under the rocks, to push
back the desert, and remove the last swamps—these are among the
tasks of the Jewish National Fund in its second fifty years."

In 1962, the Israeli public was called upon to contribute nine million
Israeli pounds ($3,000,000) to that year's special drive of the joint
Keren Kayyemeth—Keren Hayesod campaign. In conjunction with
this appeal, *The Jerusalem Post* stated: "It is likely that if modern
Israel were a wealthy, self-sustaining country, it would still make
sense to devise projects in which the Jews of the Diaspora could be

partners, with money if not with their persons... An important part of the Keren Kayyemeth's work is its educational activity in connection with its fund-raising in schools here and abroad and in organizations... If further study should indicate that we really cannot afford the loss in water reserves caused by afforestation everywhere, perhaps the Keren Kayyemeth should switch its focus away from agriculture to education and take to financing school scholarships, a project of at least the same immediate appeal as planting trees. Moreover, the critical need for Jewish education abroad might also provide a new challenge... Today the nation's spiritual and cultural soil is badly in need of redemption. Undertaking such a task might also prove to be the redemption of the Keren Kayyemeth."

By 1948, when the State of Israel was proclaimed, we are told, the Jewish National Fund had planted five million trees. In the first ten years of Israel's existence as an independent state twenty-six million additional trees were planted; and hundreds of thousands of acres of arid land in the hill areas and the Negev desert were reclaimed. A total of forty million trees had been planted prior to the new project of planting a Freedom Forest in Jerusalem, under the auspices of the Jewish National Fund, numbering two million trees. The entire forest will be linked by a system of small parks, recreation areas, playgrounds, roads and tree-lined walks.

Between 1948 and 1969, five hundred thirty-two new settlements were set up by the JNF, twice the number that had exsisted when the State of Israel was established. The JNF has emerged as an important factor on the labor market. The number of workdays provided in reclamation and afforestation programs has risen to five hundred thousand annually.

Large expanses in Israel are waiting to be reclaimed. The rock-strewn hills of Judea, Samaria and Galilee, the empty wastes of the Negev, the barren sand dunes along the coast, comprise a vast area of unproductive land which must be settled. Relentless war must be waged against erosion of Israel's soil. The JNF plants rows of trees to serve as windbreaks, preventing sandstorms from creating dustbowls. The land won by reclamation, such as swamp drainage, constitutes 10% of Israel's total agricultural surface. The Hula Valley has become one of the most productive agricultural regions in Israel, when 60,000 dunams of excellent cropland had been gained through reclamation. The idea of national ownership prevents land speculation.

558

ROSH HASHANAH רֹאשׁ הַשָּׁנָה

MARKING the Jewish New Year with which Jewish chronology begins, *Rosh Hashanah* occurs on the first day of the seventh month (*Tishri*), the holy month of the year just as the seventh day in the week is a holy day. The sabbatical year and the year of jubilee were likewise designed to begin on the seventh month, corresponding to September or October, when the annual agricultural cycle began in Eretz Yisrael.

Since early times *Rosh Hashanah* has been regarded as a day of reflection and repentance, essentially concerned with the individual and his ideal way on earth. Unlike the other historical-national festivals, beginning in the spring with *Pesaḥ* and closing with *Sukkoth* in the fall, *Rosh Hashanah* and *Yom Kippur* are characterized by special solemnity and referred to as *Yamim Nora'im* (Days of Awe) when all mankind stands before the divine throne for judgment.

Rosh Hashanah traditionally marks the creation of the world. Medieval writers noted that the letters of the word בראשית, with which the book of Genesis begins the account of creation, could be rearranged to read א' בתשרי (the first day of the month *Tishri*), when the Jewish New Year is celebrated. The Talmud emphasizes the importance of *Rosh Hashanah* not only as the birthday of the world, but also as the festival commemorating some of the most dramatic events in Israel's history. We are told that God remembered Sarah on the first day of *Rosh Hashanah*; Isaac was born on *Rosh Hashanah*; Hannah was remembered on *Rosh Hashanah*, and her son Samuel was the answer to her prayers at the sanctuary of Shilo.

Rosh Hashanah is designated by four names, two biblical and two liturgical. In Leviticus 23:24, it is identified as a day of Sabbath observance (שבתון) and of *shofar* blasts as a reminder (זכרון תרועה); and in Numbers 29:1, as a day of sounding the *shofar* (יום תרועה). Liturgically, *Rosh Hashanah* is called *Yom ha-Din* (Day of Judgment) and *Yom ha-Zikkaron* (Day of Remembrance), when all mankind passes before the divine throne to give strict account of deeds committed during the year and to receive the promise of mercy by virtue of the ancestral kind deeds (זכות אבות) which are being remembered.

In the Bible, the name *Rosh Hashanah* is found only once (Ezekiel 40:1); there it is not clear whether the reference is to the festival celebrated on the first day of the month *Tishri*. One of the Mishnah tractates is named *Rosh Hashanah*. It discusses, among other sub-

559

jects, the regulations concerning the *shofar* and the special arrangement of the worship service for this festival.

The characteristic features of the liturgy for *Rosh Hashanah* are the three sections introduced into the *Musaf* service, known respectively by the titles *Malkhuyyoth, Zikhronoth, Shofaroth*. Each is made up of verses concerning God's kingship, providence and revelation, respectively. Each contains three quotations from the Torah, three from the Psalms, three from the Prophets, and concludes with another from the Torah. From the Mishnah (Rosh Hashanah 4:5-6) it is evident that the custom of sounding the *shofar* at the conclusion of each section dates from ancient times.

The most prominent feature in the observance of *Rosh Hashanah* is the sounding of the *shofar*. It consists of three distinctive notes (*tekiah, shevarim, teruah*), looked upon since ancient times as a call to repentance. Serving as a reminder of the *shofar* blasts at Mount Sinai, they have been interpreted to call: "You who are asleep, wake up! Search your deeds and repent. Look into your souls, you who indulge all year in trifles. Amend your ways; let each one of you give up his evil course and purpose" (Maimonides). On *Rosh Hashanah*, the beginning of the Ten Days of Repentance, the *shofar* warns the people and stirs them to moral rehabilitation. In a similar fashion, Amos the prophet describes the *shofar* as a means of arousing the conscience of the people, summoning them to self-judgment and self-improvement. The *shofar* on *Rosh Hashanah* begins with short, plaintive sounds and finishes on an encouraging. triumphant note.

The *shofar* is made from the horn of any clean animal, except from the horn of an ox or a cow, which might recall the incident of the golden calf in the wilderness, where the people of Israel showed their unworthy weakness and faithlessness. The *shofar* varies widely in size and in form. The average *shofar* is from ten to twelve inches. The Sephardic Jews favor the *shofar* with the spiral curve.

Another feature in the observance of *Rosh Hashanah* is the custom of symbolically casting the sins into a running stream (תשליך). Although the name *Tashlikh* (thou wilt cast) is derived from Micah 7:19, the custom presumably dates from the fourteenth century and is mentioned for the first time in *Sefer Maharil* by Rabbi Jacob Moelln (1355-1427), the leading Jewish authority of his generation. Some, however, have found allusions to the custom of *Tashlikh* in midrashic legend and in the Zohar. In the afternoon of the first day, or on the second day if the first day of *Rosh Hashanah* coincides with the Sabbath, processions are formed to the banks of a river where some verses from Micah (7:18-20) and Psalms 33 and 130 are recited. It is all based on the figurative expression: "Thou wilt cast all our sins into the depths of the sea," meaning that God will readily pardon the sins of sincere repentants. The *Tashlikh* prayers are recited near a stream where there are fish, symbolizing human beings who are caught in nets of sin and punishment.

The custom of casting bread crumbs upon the water as food for the fish is connected with the symbolic emptying of the pockets and casting the sins into the depths. In the words of the Zohar: "Whatever falls into the deep is lost forever." By sending the sins away on the flowing stream, the worshiper figuratively expresses his desire that sins may not distort his personality. The symbolic custom of *Tashlikh* stresses the hope that we may be forgiven, and the yearning to be cleared of sin.

The season why *Hallel* is omitted on both *Rosh Hashanah* and *Yom Kippur* is explained in the Talmud on the ground that the Days of Awe (*Yamim Nora'im*) are not intended for jubilation.

Petitions for a sweet year are symbolized by the use of honey and the avoidance of sour or pickled foods on *Rosh Hashanah*. Very popular is the custom of sending New Year greeting cards containing the words לשנה טובה תכתבו (may you be inscribed for a good year). This is in keeping with the tradition that on *Rosh Hashanah* the destiny of human beings is inscribed in heaven for the ensuing year: "How many shall pass away and how many shall be brought into existence ... who shall come to a timely end, and who to an untimely end ... who shall become poor and who shall become rich; who shall be lowered and who shall be raised."

The book of life (ספר חיים), in which the upright are inscribed and from which the ungodly are blotted out, is mentioned in Psalm 69:20. The Mishnah (Avoth 2:1) tells us that the deeds of every human being are recorded in a book. Rabbi Yehudah he-Ḥasid of the twelfth century points out that God is in no need of a book of records and that the "book of life" is a figurative expression, since "the Torah speaks the language of man" (*Sefer Ḥasidim*, 33).

According to a talmudic statement, on *Rosh Hashanah* and *Yom Kippur* Jews should not appear depressed or in somber clothes, as do suppliants before a human judge, but in a joyous mood and dressed in festive, white garments, symbolizing cheerful confidence (Yerushalmi, Rosh Hashanah 1:3). Hence the emphasis is on white.

Calendar: First Day of *Rosh Hashanah*

1975	5736	Saturday	September 6
1976	5737	Saturday	September 25
1977	5738	Tuesday	September 13
1978	5739	Monday	October 2
1979	5740	Saturday	September 22
1980	5741	Thursday	September 11
1981	5742	Tuesday	September 29
1982	5743	Saturday	September 18
1983	5744	Thursday	September 8
1994	5745	Thursday	September 27
1985	5746	Monday	September 16
1986	5747	Saturday	October 4
1987	5748	Thursday	September 24
1988	5749	Monday	September 12
1989	5750	Saturday	September 30
1990	5751	Thursday	September 20
1991	5752	Monday	September 9
1992	5753	Monday	September 28
1993	5754	Thursday	September 16
1994	5755	Tuesday	September 6
1995	5756	Monday	September 25
1996	5757	Saturday	September 14
1997	5758	Thursday	October 2
1998	5759	Monday	September 21
1999	5760	Saturday	September 11
2000	5761	Saturday	September 30
2001	5762	Tuesday	September 18
2002	5763	Saturday	September 7
2003	5764	Saturday	September 27
2004	5765	Thursday	September 16
2005	5766	Tuesday	October 4
2006	5767	Saturday	September 23
2007	5768	Thursday	September 13
2008	5769	Tuesday	September 30
2009	5770	Saturday	September 19
2010	5771	Thursday	September 9

ROSH ḤODESH   רֹאשׁ חֹדֶשׁ

IN ANCIENT Israel, the day after the crescent of the new moon was
first sighted in the sky was celebrated as a festival with special offerings in the sanctuary and the suspension of everyday occupations
(I Samuel 20:18-34; II Kings 4:23). The prescribed offerings on the
new moon festivals are enumerated in Numbers 28:11-15. The prophets regularly mention the new moon festival and the Sabbath jointly,
naming the new moon festival in the first place. From Amos 8:5 it is
proved that trading was prohibited on both alike ("When will the
new moon be over, that we may sell again? And the Sabbath, that
we may offer corn for sale?"). In Isaiah 1:13-14, the new moon festivals stand at the head of the list of the seasonal holydays, including
the Sabbath.

The new moon marked the beginning of the month, and the day
of the new moon (*Rosh Ḥodesh*), being the commencement of a natural division of time, was observed as a holyday, offering favorable
opportunity for religious instruction. The new moon of the seventh
month was observed as a Sabbath in addition to the usual worship on
the day of the new moon, and was designated as שבתון (Leviticus
23:23). This celebration assumed the character of a new year's festival (*Rosh Hashanah*).

The advent of the new moon was calculated at an early period.
Men watched for it on the evening when it was expected to be seen,
in order to note its appearance. When the evidence of its appearance
was deemed sufficient, the Sanhedrin pronounced the word *mekuddash*
(sanctified), and the day became the first of the new month, leaving
twenty-nine days for the preceding month. The proclamation of the
new month was signaled from mountain top to mountain top throughout Eretz Yisrael by lighting flares. When the Samaritans attempted
to thwart this plan by lighting a beacon fire prematurely, the signals
were discontinued and the announcement of the new moon was made
by messengers.

In the middle of the fourth century, Hillel II published scientific
rules for the computation of the calendar, making it possible to determine the Jewish calendar without actual observation of the lunar
phases. According to this system, the months alternate between
thirty and twenty-nine days. When the preceding month has thirty
days, its last day is celebrated as the first day of *Rosh Ḥodesh*, while

the second day of *Rosh Ḥodesh* marks the first day of the new month.
The blessing of the new month (*birkath ha-ḥodesh*), recited on the preceding Sabbath after the Torah reading, is reminiscent of the Temple
period when the arrival of the new month was solemnly announced
by the Sanhedrin after a thorough examination of the witnesses who
had noticed the appearance of the new moon. The Sabbath preceding
the new month is therefore called שבת מברכין because of the *birkath
ha-ḥodesh* and the prayers recited in connection with the announcement of *Rosh Ḥodesh*.

In addition to *Hallel* and *Ya'aleh v'Yavo*, the morning liturgy includes *Musaf* for *Rosh Ḥodesh*, in which is inserted a prayer based on
the tradition that the *Rosh Ḥodesh* offerings atoned for the sins committed during the previous month. The concluding passage of this
(ראשי חדשים) prayer contains twelve pleas for comfort and forgiveness, corresponding to the twelve months of the year. The thirteenth
plea (ולכפרת פשע) is added during the leap year, which consists of
thirteen months. The day preceding *Rosh Ḥodesh* has been, since the
sixteenth century, identified as *Yom Kippur Katan* (Minor Day of
Atonement), devoted to repentance and penitential prayers (*seliḥoth*)
recited after the *Minḥah* service by Ḥasidim, who observe the custom
of fasting on that day. This custom is said to have been inaugurated
in circles close to Rabbi Isaac Luria, the famous Kabbalist of Safed.

ABBREVIATIONS   רָאשֵׁי תֵבוֹת

INITIAL letters of words (*rashé tevoth*), used in place of words for brevity, are to be found on the Maccabean coins as well as in the tannaitic
literature. The Mishnah (Shabbath 12:5) refers to this system of contraction or omission as *notarikon*, a Greek term originally denoting
shorthand signs. On the Maccabean coins there is no sign to denote
abbreviation; this may be attributable to lack of space. Thus, the
Maccabean abbreviations are: שב שג שד for second, third, fourth year
ישראל for יש ,היהודים for הי and (שנה ב שנה ג שנה ד).

Abbreviations and contractions of words in medieval manuscripts
are marked by various signs, as when the copyist places on the tops
of the letters as many dots as there are words abbreviated; when he
contracts a word he places a dot on the top of the last letter. In modern times, the single and the double slanting lines are employed. The
single line is used at the end of an abbreviated single word (רבי=ר');

the double line is used between the last two letters of an abbreviation: סגן לכהן or סגן לויה=סג"ל; כהן צדק=כ"ץ.

When speaking of a deceased person, the phrases denoting "may he (she) rest in peace" and "may his (her) memory be a blessing" are generally abbreviated in the Hebrew writing: לברכה (וכרונה) זכרונו=ז"ל; עליה השלום) עליו השלום=ע"ה). On *matzevoth*, grave marks, the words פה נקבר or פה נטמן (here lies buried) are abbreviated פ"נ; the inscription תהא נפשו (נפשה) צרורה בצרור החיים=תנצב"ה (may his soul be wrapped up among the living). This expression is borrowed from the Bible. The abbreviation תם ונשלם שבח לאל בורא עולם = תושלב"ע is seen at the end of some rabbinic works, thanking God for his aid.

RABBINATE   רַבָּנוּת

THE titles *Rabban* (our master), *Rabbi* (my master), *Rav* (master) came into use during the first century. The title *Rabban* was applied to three presidents of the Sanhedrin (Rabban Gamaliel, Rabban Simeon ben Gamaliel, Rabban Yoḥanan ben Zakkai). Beginning with the disciples of Rabban Yoḥanan ben Zakkai downward, the title *Rabbi* came into vogue to distinguish the teachers of Torah who received their ordination (*semikhah*) in Eretz Yisrael. Authoritative teachers in Babylonia were addressed as *Rav*. Hence, all the *Tannaim* who are mentioned in the Mishnah and the Tosefta bear the title *Rabbi;* so also, the talmudic sages of a later period, the *Amoraim* of Eretz Yisrael. The Babylonian *Amoraim*, however, are referred to as *Rav*. Since no distinguishing titles of honor were common in the more ancient generations of prophets and sages, the order is as follows: *Rabbi* is greater than *Rav; Rabban* is greater than *Rabbi;* the simple name (Isaiah, Zechariah, Hillel, Shammai) is greater than *Rabban*.

In post-talmudic times, the title *Rabbi* was awarded to anyone qualified to decide questions of Jewish law. The office of *Rabbi*, however, was not salaried before the fifteenth century. The rabbis, whose function was to teach the members of the community, invariably had their private occupations. They were indirectly aided by the preference offered them in their trades and business enterprises. They also had the privilege of exemption from taxes. The honor paid to the rabbis exceeded even that due to parents. They lectured before the Talmud students at the *yeshivah* and spoke in public on rare occasions, as when they informed the people of certain laws and customs.

During the latter part of the eighteenth century, a great change was inaugurated among the Jews of Germany through the influence of Moses Mendelssohn. Congregations began to expect their salaried rabbis to be more than devotees of talmudic studies. The necessity of preaching and defending the Jewish concepts compelled aspiring rabbis to receive a thorough secular training, even at the expense of much talmudic learning. Seminaries for the training of rabbis sprang up in rapid succession, each of which ordained its graduates in the manner that degrees are conferred on graduates of other institution of learning.

In America today, there are various rabbinical schools that confer the title *Rabbi* on the graduates. Traditionally, the authority to act as rabbi may be conferred by another rabbi, on the principle that "everyone ordained may ordain." To be recognized as rabbi, a talmudic student is customarily ordained by receiving *semikhah* from another rabbi who was ordained in a similar fashion. Some rabbis, by virtue of their special distinction in Jewish learning, are accepted as superior authorities on questions of Jewish living. Otherwise, the rabbi and the layman have equal status in Judaism.

The new type of rabbi, produced by modern life with its problems and complexities, is admittedly not so well versed in talmudic lore. He is regarded, however, as more efficient and useful in a larger field of activities, such as the visitation of the sick and the bereaved. He offers consolation and sympathy to persons in distress, promotes Jewish education on various levels, and participates in philanthrophic enterprises of the Jewish community. Though there is no sharp distinction in religious status between the rabbi and the layman, it has been observed that he who accepts a rabbinic position must fulfill the biblical command: "You shall not be afraid of any man" (Deuteronomy 1:17).

We are told that rare indeed is the rabbi of a congregation who is also a scholar. If he is, he will discover that he has to "steal" the time for study. And many rabbis with scholarly pretensions are to be found on the faculties of the rabbinical seminaries and the universities. Thus the rabbinate often attracts men with little interest in Jewish learning. One hears rabbinical students complain: "I want to become a rabbi in order to help people. Why should I waste my time on Aramaic grammar?" And not just Aramaic—the complaint too often extends to students in Bible and Talmud. Here we have a vicious circle. Congregations expect their rabbis to have finished being scholars. Men with no scholarly interests are attracted to the rabbinate. The congregations get the men they have sought. In the process, the rabbinate gradually ceases to be a learned profession. . . In the final analysis, whatever other functions the rabbi might choose to undertake, it is his role as scholar which is the justification of his profession.

It has been pointed out that the service assigned to the modern rabbi is to teach Judaism, and that the teaching must be of a positive nature: the Jewish Bible, the sacred language, Jewish tradition, Jewish law and custom, Jewish faith, and Jewish history. Polemics should entirely be avoided. It is the positive statement which wins the hearts of men in the end.

HOLY SPIRIT רוּחַ הַקֹּדֶשׁ

THE expression רוח הקודש, widely used in talmudic-midrashic literature, means the prophetic inspiration. With the passing of the last three prophets (Haggai, Zechariah, Malachi) the holy spirit departed from Israel, according to a tannaitic statement (Tosefta, Sotah 13:2; Sanhedrin 11a). Subsequent revelations were given by a *bath kol*, a mysterious, heavenly voice. The phrase בת קול (resonance, echo) is used in talmudic-midrashic literature in the sense of an articulate sound proceeding from an invisible source or from the sky, as in Daniel 4:28.

Psalm 51:13 reads: "Cast me not out from thy presence, and take not thy holy spirit from me." Clearly, the reference here is to the holy spirit which enables us to live and prompts us to excel. The books of the Bible were canonized in accordance with the standard of the divine inspiration (*ruah ha kodesh*) they displayed.

RUTH רוּת

THE book of Ruth is recited in the synagogue on *Shavuoth* (Pentecost), the harvest festival commemorating the giving of the Torah on Mount Sinai, because the scene of its story is the harvest field and, too, its leading character embraces Judaism.

Ruth's impassioned declaration of her true-hearted affection for Naomi is one of the most beautiful passages in the book: "Entreat me not to leave you and to turn back from following you; wherever you go, I will go; wherever you stay, I will stay; your people shall be my people, and your God shall be my God; wherever you die, I will die, and there will I be buried. May the Lord punish me time and again if anything but death parts me from you!"

The book of Ruth takes its name from Ruth who clung to her mother-in-law Naomi with all the unselfishness of true-hearted affection. The narrative is one of idyllic beauty. It is the most charming short story in the Bible, and presents a pleasing picture of life in Israel during the period of the judges.

About two-thirds of the narrative is in dialogue. In the Hebrew Bible the book of Ruth is placed among the five *Megilloth* or scrolls (Song of Songs, Ruth, Lamentations, Ecclesiastes, Esther), which are recited in the synagogue on *Pesaḥ, Shavuoth, Tish'ah b'Av, Sukkoth,* and *Purim,* respectively.

The contents of the book of Ruth are well known. Naomi is an example of faithfulness and loyalty, self-sacrifice and moral integrity. Widowed and bereft of her two sons, Naomi returned to Bethlehem from Moab, where they had lived during a famine in Judea. Anxious to provide for Ruth and to see her married, she successfully arranged the marriage of Ruth to Boaz.

Primarily concerned to trace the ancestry of David, the book of Ruth appears to show that the principle of divine reward for good deeds is not confined to one people but is valid for all nationalities. The principal characters of the story are amiable, courteous, unassuming. They all show how a religious spirit may pervade the conduct of daily life.

It has been pointed out that simplicity characterizes alike the noblest and the loveliest poems. There are no better examples of this than Ruth and Esther. There is not a phrase, an image, an accident, too much or too little in either; not a false note of atmosphere or feeling. It was Jews who wrote the magnificent poems called the Psalms, the Song of Solomon, and the books of Job and Ruth. No heritage of modern man is richer and none has made a more brilliant mark upon human thought. Excerpt:

"Whose girl is this?" Boaz asked the foreman of the harvesters. The foreman replied: "It is the Moabite girl who came back with Naomi. She asked to be allowed to glean among the sheaves after the harvesters, and she has been working ever since morning, without resting even for a moment."

Then Boaz said to Ruth: "Now listen, my daughter, do not go to glean in another field; do not leave this one, but stay close to my maid-servants. Keep your eyes on the field they are reaping and follow

568

them. Whenever you are thirsty, go to the water jars and drink.
I have been well informed of all that you have done for your mother-
in-law since the death of your husband, of how you left your father
and mother and the land of your birth and came to a people who were
strange to you. . .'' She answered: "Thank you, my lord, for speaking kindly to me, even though I am not one of your servants."

At mealtime Boaz said to her: "Come here and eat some of our
food; dip your slice of bread in the vinegar." So she sat beside the
harvesters, and he handed her roasted grains. . . Boaz married Ruth,
and she bore him a son. Then the women said to Naomi: "Blessed
be the Lord who has not left you this day without a kinsman. May
the boy's name be renowned in Israel! He will renew your life and
nourish your old age, for he is the child of your daughter-in-law, who
loves you and is better than seven sons to you."

MERCY   רַחֲמִים

Aᴄᴄᴏʀᴅɪɴɢ to a talmudic statement, anyone who shows no mercy
to his fellow man can expect none from God (Shabbath 151b). Throughout the Hebrew Bible, divine mercy includes compassion, lovingkindness, forbearance, grace, patience, and providential deliverance. Psalm
23 portrays God's loving care under the figure of a shepherd's soli-
citude for his sheep ("Only goodness and kindness follow me all the
days of my life"). The kindness and generosity of God are praised in
Psalm 145: "The Lord lifts up all who are falling, and raises up all
who are bowed down. . . The Lord is near to all who call upon him;
he hears their cry and saves them."

The divine justice is inevitably linked with the divine mercy. According to the Midrash, God said: "Sin will abound if I create the
world by mercy alone; but how can the world endure, if I create it by
justice alone? I will therefore create it by both." The qualities of justice and mercy (מדת הדין, מדת הרחמים) are frequently spoken of as the
two primary standards of God's dealing with men. Since man depends
on the mercy of God, he is expected to extend mercy to his fellow men.
"You have been told, O man, what is good, and what the Lord requires
of you: Only to do the right, to love goodness, and to walk humbly
with your God" (Micah 6:8).

God is named חנון ורחום (gracious and full of compassion) as well
as אב הרחמים (Merciful Father) or הרחמן (the Merciful One). These

concepts are the foundation of the ethical teachings of Judaism. We
are told that Jews should be distinguished for their compassionate
disposition; anyone who is merciful is presumed to be a descendant
of Abraham. To praise God means to become merciful like him (Yevamoth 79a; Betzah 32b; Shabbath 133b).

EXILARCH; NAGID   רֵישׁ גָּלוּתָא; נָגִיד

THE Aramaic title *Resh Galutha* is rendered in Hebrew by ראש הגולה
(head of the exile). It was held by the head of the Jewish community
in Babylonia, who was referred to as the Prince of the Captivity or
Exilarch. The institution of the hereditary exilarchate is historically
traceable to the second century. The exilarch, who was believed to
be a direct descendant of the royal house of David, lived in royal state
and was responsible for the internal government of the Jewish community. He acted as chief tax-collector among his own people, who enjoyed a considerable measure of autonomous life until the fifth century.
In addition to collecting the taxes, he appointed the judges, himself
acting as final court of appeal. Some exilarchs, during the geonic period, controlled the selection of the *Geonim*, or heads of the Babylonian
talmudic academies.

Until the eleventh century, the exilarchate was looked upon with
pride as the last vestige of Davidic glory, serving as a bond of union
among all Jews. Nominally, the office continued until the thirteenth
century and was imitated in Egypt and elsewhere under the title of
Nagid (prince, leader). Also Yemen, Syria and Eretz Yisrael had
Nagids, who were responsible for law and order in the Jewish community, and also for the observance of the restrictions imposed by the
Islamic state, such as the wearing of discriminatory badges and the
prohibition of the erection of new houses of worship. They were expected to be pious and learned and men of absolute integrity. David
Maimonides took office in 1237 at the tender age of sixteen. He was
the grandson of Moses Maimonides.

The installation of an exilarch was described by Nathan ha-Bavli, who lived in Babylonia during the tenth century. His famous descriptions of the Babylonian academies are considered as those of
an eye-witness. Following are a few excerpts: "When the community
agreed to appoint an exilarch, the two heads of the academies with
their pupils, and the heads of the community, assembled in the house

of a prominent man... On Thursday they assembled in the synagogue, blessed the exilarch, and placed their hands on him... When the people heard the proclamation, every member of the community sent him a present ... the wealthy members sent him magnificent clothes and beautiful ornaments... The exilarch prepared a banquet on Thursday and on Friday... When he arose on Sabbath morning to go to the synagogue, many of the prominent men of the community met him to go with him to the synagogue. At the synagogue a wooden pulpit had been prepared for him on the previous day... The *hazzan* would begin the prayer *barukh she-amar* (blessed be he who spoke), and the distinguished youths, with melodious and harmonious voices, would respond *blessed be he* after every sentence... When the *Maftir* read the last portion, a prominent man stood near him and translated it. This was a mark of distinction for that man..."

RASHI   רַשִׁ״י

THE great commentator of the Talmud, Rabbi Shelomo Yitzḥaki, or *Rashi,* who found leisure to write a commentary on the Bible, was born in France in 1040, and after spending most of his life in the Rhineland died in Troyes in 1105. Very little is known authentically of his life, except that his chief occupation was the teaching of the Talmud. He sustained himself and his family as best he could by cultivating a vineyard. In addition to his encyclopedic knowledge of the talmudic-midrashic literature, he possessed a marvelous gift of clear and terse writing.

His exposition of the first five books of the Bible, the Pentateuch, in particular, became in time the most popular and widely used. *Ḥummash with Rashi* has meant the average Jewish education everywhere throughout many generations. His commentary on the Torah, homiletical in spirit, is based upon midrashic selections that are attached to the biblical text with great skill. Interspersed in his commentary are explanations of difficult Hebrew words and phrases in French. Men referred to Rashi as *Parshandatha* (פרשנדתא), the Commentator of the Torah par excellence.

Thousands of French glosses, introduced by Rashi under the term of לעז (*la'az*), are preserved in his commentaries on the Bible and the Talmud. Scholars like Blondheim and Darmsteter have engaged in scientific work on *la'az* in Rashi; it represents the earliest existing

specimens of Old French vocabulary. The intrepretation of the word
בלעז as a combination of the initials of בלשון עם זר (in the language
of an alien people) is erroneous. לעז is derived from Psalm 114:1,
where עם לעז is used.

Rashi's commentary on the Torah was the first Hebrew book printed, when it was published in 1475 without the biblical text. Its first
appearance with the text was in 1482. Because of its importance,
Rashi's commentary was made available in Latin translation by non-
Jewish scholars of the seventeenth and eighteenth centuries. The
whole commentary on the Torah was translated into German by
Dukes in 1838. It is now available also in English. Rashi on the Bible
(except the books of Proverbs, Job, and Daniel) is to be found in the
edition known as *Mikraoth Gedoloth.*

Rashi's commentary on the Talmud is more original than that on
the Bible. It greatly extended the knowledge of the Talmud, thereby
increasing the number of talmudic schools which soon came to be of
great importance. His two sons-in-law, Rabbi Judah ben Nathan and
Rabbi Meir ben Samuel, and especially his grandsons (Samuel, Judah, and Jacob), were the first of a succession of *tosafists* who became
closely identified with his work and methods. The name of Rashi is
inseparably connected with Jewish learning; his work has exercised
the widest influence upon scholars and laymen. He has been described
as one of the masterminds of rabbinical literature, on which he has
left the imprint of his terseness and clarity. His work is popular among
all classes of Jews because it is intrinsically Jewish in spirit.

Following are several quotations from Rashi's commentaries: Anyone who brings up a good son is like an immortal (Genesis 18:19). All
the six hundred and thirteen *mitzvoth* are implied in the Ten Commandments (Exodus 24:12). Teachers learn a great deal from the
discussions of their students (Proverbs 13:23). When the heathen
will abandon their idols, God will be One and his name One, since
only his name will be invoked (Zechariah 14:9). Any plan formulated
in haste is foolish (Job 5:13). Students should carefully examine the
underlying reasons and sources of principles taught by their teachers
(Bava Metzia 33b). A student who has not learned to understand
and solve apparent contradictions is but a basket full of books (צנא
מלא ספרי—Megillah 28b). *A basketful of books* is a man full of learning, but without method.

RESPONSA LITERATURE

QUESTIONS and answers (*sheeloth u-teshuvoth*) is the Hebrew designation for the written decisions given by eminent rabbis to questions they received in writing. One of the chief activities of the Babylonian Geonim, heading the two academies of Sura and Pumbeditha, was that of answering questions addressed to them from distant and near Jewish settlements throughout the Diaspora. These responsa represent a special class of rabbinic literature, which is similar in content, though not in form, to the talmudic commentaries and codes.

The much diversified questions touched upon the whole range of Jewish law and custom as well as upon the interpretation of talmudic passages. The answers, carefully cherished by the recipients who permitted transcripts to be made and transmitted from one seat of learning to another, were later on assembled by various men of learning. The Jewish codes of law were subsequently based upon these responsa, composed by the Geonim in the course of five centuries.

The method of exchanging questions and answers between Jewish scholars strengthened the feeling of unity among all Jews in various countries, and played an important part in Jewish survival throughout the Diaspora. The famous *Siddur* of Rav Amram Gaon (ninth century) was composed as a result of a question directed to the Gaon and head of the Sura academy. This liturgical compilation, containing halakhic prescriptions for the whole year, was prepared at the request of a Spanish community seeking to find out the correct order of prayers to be recited daily. Rav Amram's answer was copied by many communities, and became a standard guide in matters of liturgy. Jewish unity was achieved through Rav Amram's *Siddur* for a period of a thousand years; until a century ago, practically all Jewish congregations followed the same liturgical arrangement.

The responsa literature reflects the social and economic conditions of many generations in the Diaspora, and exhibits the ethical standards of the times and the customs practised by the questioners. Hence, the responsa have been used by scholars not only as a great source of Jewish law and tradition, but of historical information concerning the geonic period and the generations that came after it. Indeed, the responsa literature of all periods is replete with incidental information on religious philosophy as well as interesting data of sociological and political interest.

573

SHEELTOTH   שְׁאֵלְתּוֹת דְּרַב אַחָאִי

THE eighth-century work, *Sheeltoth* by Rav Aḥai, has the distinction
of being the first known post-talmudic book of Jewish law (*Halakhah*),
representing the beginning of an uninterrupted tradition of legal codification. Ever since its publication in the middle of the eighth century
it has been studied and quoted on frequent occasions. Serving not
only as a source of Jewish law but also of illuminating textual variations in problematic talmudic passages, the authority of the *Sheeltoth
d'Rav Aḥai* was continually invoked by the medieval talmudic teachers and authors, including Rashi and the Tosafists.

The title *Sheeltoth* (questions) is here used in the sense of inquiries
or discussions of legal subjects. The arrangement of the book is according to the weekly *sidroth* of the Torah. Peculiar to this lawcode
are the frequent digressions into aggadic, or homiletical material. Unlike many other talmudic authorities, Rav Aḥai used a style that was
easily intelligible to laymen; his discussions of various precepts were
written with special reference to moral duties, such as love of truth,
respect for parents, and kindliness to others. They are all based on
the weekly readings from the Torah.

The *Halakhoth Gedoloth*, which belongs to the oldest literature of
the geonic period, contains as many as one hundred and fifty passages
excerpted from the *Sheeltoth*, which is mentioned by Rav Sherira Gaon
and his son Rav Hai Gaon as well as the author of the medieval talmudic dictionary, *Arukh*, Rabbi Nathan ben Yeḥiel who lived in
eleventh-century Rome.

OATH   שְׁבוּעָה

THE term שבועה (oath) is derived from the sacred number שבע (seven). By lifting a hand toward heaven, oaths were made in attestation of the truth of a statement or of the binding character of a promise.
From the narrative concerning Abraham's solemn promise to Abimelech we clearly see the connection between the symbolic number seven
and the taking of an oath: "Swear to me by God that you will not
deal falsely with me... Abraham said: I will swear... So he set
apart seven lambs... Abimelech asked Abraham: What do these
seven lambs mean...? He said: Take these seven lambs from me, to

574

be proof for me that I dug this well. Therefore, that place was called באר שבע (Beersheba), because both of them took an oath there" (Genesis 21:22-31). Thus, *Beersheba* means the *well of the oath* or *the well of the seven.*

The third commandment ("You shall not utter the name of the Lord your God in vain") applies to perjury or false swearing, the breaking of a promise or agreement that has been sealed with an oath in the name of God. Since his name must not be taken heedlessly or lightly, he does not allow it to be associated with an act of falsehood. According to a talmudic statement, "he who deviates from the truth is like one who worships an idol" instead of the God of truth (Sanhedrin 92a). The careless or profane use of the divine name, whereby want of reverence is shown, is prohibited as an extension of the scope of the third commandment. In common conversation, the divine name is not to be uttered unnecessarily. Jewish tradition opposes the use of oaths entirely. Without swearing, "let your *yes* be true and your *no* be true" (Bava Metzia 49a: שיהא הן שלך צדק ולאו שלך צדק).

FEAST OF WEEKS   שָׁבוּעוֹת

THE *Shavuoth* festival, otherwise known as Pentecost (fiftieth day) or Feast of Weeks, was celebrated primarily as a thanksgiving for the wheat harvest; it falls seven weeks after the barley harvest, when an *omer* of the new produce was offered. The Torah refers to *Shavuoth* as *Ḥag ha-Katsir* (the feast of the harvest) and *Yom ha-Bikkurim* (the day of first fruits), observed by offerings of the best ripe produce of the fields (Exodus 23:16; Numbers 28:26). Beginning with the second day of Passover, seven weeks or forty-nine days were carefully counted, and the fiftieth day was celebrated as the beginning of the wheat harvest or the festival of the first fruits. Hence the *Sefirah* (counting) period observed to this day between the second day of *Pesaḥ* and *Shavuoth.*

In the course of time, as a result of the transformation of the agricultural festivals into historical commemorations, the additional significance of *Shavuoth* as the Festival of the Giving of the Torah (זמן מתן תורה) at Mount Sinai completely overshadowed its original significance. Though the Bible does not identify *Shavuoth* with the anniversary of the giving of the Ten Commandments, the tradition, undisputed in the Talmud, has been that the Torah was given on the sixth day of *Sivan*. The name *Ḥag Shavuoth* occurs in Deuteronomy 16:10, where we are told that each pilgrim was to offer what he felt disposed to give.

"You shall count seven weeks, from the day when the sickle is first put to the standing grain. You shall then keep the Feast of Weeks in honor of the Lord your God, and the measure of your freewill offering shall be in proportion to the blessing that the Lord your God bestowed on you. You shall rejoice before the Lord your God with your son and daughter, your male and female servants, and the Levite of your community, as well as the stranger and the fatherless and the widow among you. . ." (Deuteronomy 16:9-11).

Hence, Maimonides writes: "Women should have clothes and pretty trinkets bought for them, according to one's means. . . And while one eats and drinks, it is his duty to feed the stranger, the orphan, the widow, and other poor and unfortunate people, for he who locks the doors to his courtyard and eats and drinks with his wife and family without giving to the poor—his meal is not counted as a rejoicing in a divine command but a rejoicing in his own stomach . . . a disgrace to those who indulge in it" (*Yad, Shevithath Yom Tov* 6:18).

Shavuoth is called *Atzereth* in the Mishnah and the Talmud, in the sense that it serves as a concluding festival to *Pesaḥ*. In the observances of *Shavuoth*, the historical as well as the agricultural aspects are reflected. The Decalogue is read in the synagogue on the first day. Plants and flowers, reminiscent of the slopes of Sinai, decorate the *bimah* and the *aron ha-kodesh*. The first night of the festival is spent in reading an anthology of sacred writings called *Tikkun lel Shavuoth*, a custom not commonly observed these days. The book of Ruth is read for its description of a summer harvest in Israel. The book of Ruth and the famous liturgical poem *Akdamuth* are read before the reading of the Torah on the first day. Milk dishes are the customary foods, symbolizing the Torah which is likened to milk, according to the allegorical interpretation of the Song of Songs ("Honey and milk are under your tongue").

SHEVUTH ‎שְׁבוּת

THE term *shevuth* denotes an occupation, on Sabbath and festivals, forbidden by the traditional *Halakhah* as being out of harmony with the Sabbath laws of the Torah We are told that by the command "you shall rest" (Exodus 23:12), the Torah "implies that one must refrain also from doing things which are not actual work. Such activities, prohibited by the sages on the ground that they conflict with the spirit of Sabbath rest are many, some being forbidden because of their resemblance to prohibited kinds of work, others being forbidden as a preventive measure, lest they should lead to the doing of work that is prohibited under the penalty of stoning" (*Yad, Shabbath* 21:1).

According to Albeck, in the introduction to his Mishnah commentary on Shabbath, the *shevuth* regulations had been observed by the people long before the sages defined them as distinct from the thirty-nine categories of prohibited acts (ל"ט מלאכות). The so-called derivative varieties (*toladoth*) of work were formally prohibited by the sages as a preventive measure, designed to preserve the biblical laws.

SHEVAT   שְׁבָט

THE eleventh month *Shevat*, corresponding to January-February, is mentioned once in the Bible (Zechariah 1:7). It always consists of thirty days, and is counted as the fifth civil month of the Jewish year, beginning with *Rosh Hashanah* on the first of *Tishri*. The fifteenth of *Shevat*, known as *Ḥamishah Asar Bishvat*, was declared by the school of Hillel as the New Year for Trees (*Rosh Hashanah l'Ilanoth*) with respect to tithing (Rosh Hashanah 1:1).

Since most of the annual rains in Eretz Yisrael occur before *Shevat*, the trees that blossom afterwards are considered by the *Halakhah* authorities as belonging to another year. The celebration of *Tu Bishvat*, as the festival is known in brief, has gained new significance as Arbor Day, observed by the planting of trees in Eretz Yisrael.

SEVEN BLESSINGS   שֶׁבַע בְּרָכוֹת

THE seven blessings which are recited over wine during and after a wedding ceremony are quoted in the Talmud (Kethubboth 8a), where they are referred to as ברכת חתנים. When a *minyan* is present, the *sheva berakhoth* (seven benedictions) are recited at meals also during the seven days following the wedding. The fourth benediction refers to the perpetual renewal of the human being in the divine form. In the last three benedictions, a prayer is uttered that God may comfort

Zion, cause happiness to the young couple, and bring about complete exultation in restored Judea and Jerusalem. The marriage service thus combines individual with communal aspirations. It has been customary to prepare a marriage feast for each of the seven days after the wedding, titled *shivath yené mishteh*, during which the seven blessings are repeated at the table. The meal which accompanies a religious celebration such as a wedding is called *seudath mitzvah* (‏סעודת מצוה‏). This includes meals at *Brith Milah, Pidyon ha-Ben, Siyyum ha-Sefer*.

SHIV'AH ‏שִׁבְעָה‏

THE seven-day mourning period (*shiv'ah*) follows the burial of a father, mother, brother, sister, son, daughter, wife or husband. It is observed by abstaining from all ordinary work and diversions. The expression "sitting *shiv'ah*" alludes to the custom of the mourner's remaining at home during the first seven days of mourning, sitting unshod on a low stool. Friends visit the mourner's home for prayer and condolence during the seven-day period.

The Sabbath is included in the count, even though the outward signs of mourning are suspended for the day. If the burial took place an hour before a major festival, the mourner does not have to observe *shiv'ah* after the festival. If, however, the death occurred on *Ḥol ha-Mo'ed*, the full seven-day period of *shiv'ah* must be observed immediately after the festival. If a festival intervenes in the midst of the seven days, the mourning is not continued to completion after the festival. If the death notice reached the relative within thirty days, he must observe *shiv'ah;* but if the news reached him at a later date, the *shiv'ah* mourning is curtailed to one hour.

SHIV'AH ASAR B'TAMMUZ ‏שִׁבְעָה עָשָׂר בְּתַמּוּז‏

THE seventeenth day of *Tammuz* is observed as a fast commemorating the breaking down of the wall of Jerusalem by Nebuchadnezzar and the cessation of Temple worship during the siege of Titus. It ushers in the three weeks of mourning which end with *Tish'ah b'Av*, the fast of the ninth of *Av*. The three weeks between *Shiv'ah Asar b'Tammuz* and *Tish'ah b'Av* are referred to as ‏בין המצרים‏ (between the straits), a phrase borrowed from Lamentations 1:3. The Mishnah

578

mentions five misfortunes that befell the Jewish people on the seventeenth of *Tammuz* and five on the ninth of *Av* (Ta'anith 4:6).

The three weeks are concluded with the so-called Nine Days, from the first to the ninth of *Av*, during which the mourning is intensified to the point of refraining from eating meat (except on the Sabbath).

SABBATH   שַׁבָּת

THE predominant feature of the Sabbath is cessation from labor and business activity. "Remember the Sabbath day to keep it holy" (Exodus 20:8) and unprofaned by workaday purposes is the prescription for this unparalleled institution in the ancient world. The Sabbath is designed to raise man's life to a higher level by affording him a day of rest and imparting to him the idea of human equality. Hence, the commonest epithet applied to the Sabbath is *holy*. The two ideas are closely interwoven. All the aspects of the Sabbath are summed up in the liturgical *Kiddush* (sanctification), recited in the homes and also in the synagogues on Friday nights: ". . . Thou hast sanctified us with thy commandments . . . thou hast graciously given us thy holy Sabbath as a heritage, in remembrance of the creation. . ."

Linked with the creation, the Sabbath has been regarded as a perpetual sign between God and the people of Israel, symbolizing the duty of work and the holiness of rest. The Torah commands· "Six days you shall labor and do all your work; but on the seventh day, which is a Sabbath in honor of the Lord your God, you shall not do any work, neither you, nor your son, nor your daughter, nor your male or female servant, nor your cattle, nor the stranger who is within your gates" (Exodus 20:9-10).

It has been noted that work during the six days of the week is as important to human welfare as is the rest on the seventh, since idleness invariably results in evil. Hebrew has but one word—*avodah*—for work and worship. Man dies when he stops working; work brings us forgetfulness of sorrow, and courage to face it. Hard work is the cure for most ills. There are talmudic statements to the effect that labor ennobles; he who works for a living is greater than he who reveres God (Nedarim 49b; Berakhoth 8a).

The Mishnah defines the main thirty-nine categories of work forbidden on the Sabbath (Shabbath 7:2). They are called אבות מלאכות (principal species of prohibited acts); they were specified or implied in the making of the portable sanctuary (*Mishkan*) in the wilderness. To these were added others, so-called derivative varieties (תולדות), that were liable to result in a breach of the Sabbath laws (שבות). The term *shevuth* signifies an occupation, on Sabbaths and festivals, forbidden by the ancient talmudic authorities as being out of harmony with the celebration of the day. The derivative restrictions are in some way similar to the principal species. No Sabbath laws, however, are permitted to stand in the way of saving human life in cases of illness or danger (פקוח נפש דוחה את השבת). The Talmud interprets Leviticus 18:5 in the sense that the Torah was given that man might *live* by it; the Sabbath, therefore, must not be placed as a reason for permitting a man to die (Avodah Zarah 27b).

Many beautiful home customs have arisen in connection with Sabbath observance. The three Sabbath meals (*shalosh seudoth*) are a religious duty. The Ḥasidim attach special importance to the third meal, which is consumed at sunset, popularly called *shallish seudos* instead of *seudah shelishith*. It is regarded as a symbol of saying goodby to Princess Sabbath; hence the third meal is often terminated long after the close of the Sabbath day. Heine's poem on Princess Sabbath conveys some of the charm which pervaded the Sabbath as a result of its idealization among the Jewish people.

Following are a number of excerpts from Maimonides' code of law, *Mishneh Torah*, concerning the manner in which the Sabbath should be observed:

"In order to honor the Sabbath one should, as a matter of religious duty, take a hot bath on Friday, get dressed in festive clothes, and sit in a dignified manner waiting to receive the Sabbath, just as if one were going out to meet the king. . . One should set his table properly on Friday night, even if he feels the least need for food, and likewise at the end of the Sabbath, so as to honor the Sabbath at both its commencement and its termination. . . There were some sages of old who split firewood for the cooking, lit lamps, or went to market to buy food or drink for the Sabbath. Indeed, the more a man does in this respect the more praise he deserves. . . The more one spends for the Sabbath, the better. However, the sages of old declared: "Make your Sabbath as a weekday, and do not depend upon the charity of others." One should be particularly careful to have no less than three meals on the Sabbath: one in the evening, one in the morning, and one in the afternoon. . . The custom of the righteous men of old was as follows: On Sabbath morning they would go to the synagogue, then return to eat the second meal, then go to the schoolhouse (*beth ha-midrash*) to read Bible and Mishnah until the afternoon service; finally, they would return home and sit down to the third Sabbath meal, eating and drinking until the end of the Sabbath" (*Yad, Shabbath* 30:2-10).

The Sabbath hymn יום זה מכובד (this day is the most precious of all days), composed by an unidentified poet whose name appears in the acrostic as ישראל הגר (Yisrael the proselyte), is based on the talmudic statement that the best food should be prepared for the Sabbath, for "he who delights in the Sabbath is granted his heart's desires" (Shabbath 118a-b). The emphasis on the Sabbath as a day of eating and drinking was meant, according to some scholars, to counteract the ascetic tendencies of the Essenes.

The term *Oneg Shabbath* (Sabbath delight) was made particularly popular by the Hebrew poet Ḥayyim Naḥman Bialik, who introduced the custom of study, refreshment and social recreation, on Sabbath afternoons in Tel Aviv, whence it has spread to many Jewish communities everywhere.

SHABBATH HA-GADOL   שַׁבָּת הַגָּדוֹל

THE Sabbath preceding the *Pesaḥ* festival is designated as the Great Sabbath (*Shabbath ha-Gadol*) in commemoration of the great miracle that occurred on the Sabbath preceding the exodus from Egypt. It is based on the tradition that when God ordered the people of Israel to prepare a lamb on the tenth of *Nisan* for the paschal offering, the Egyptians were paralyzed with fear and could not prevent the offering of the Egyptian deity, the lamb.

Another explanation, given by the thirteenth-century author of *Shibbolé ha-Leket*, is to the effect that there is a long service in the synagogue on the Sabbath preceding *Pesaḥ* on account of the long discourse concerning the rules and regulations pertaining to the forthcoming Passover festival.

Since the Haggadah is recited on the Sabbath preceding *Pesaḥ*, it has been suggested that שבת הגדול is a corruption of שבת הגדה. The most plausible explanation of the name alludes to the *haftarah* recited on that Sabbath, ending with the words: "Behold, I will send you Elijah the prophet before the *great* and awesome day of the Lord. He will turn the hearts of fathers to their children and the hearts of children to their fathers. . ." (Malachi 4:5-6).

The custom of reciting the Haggadah in the afternoon of *Shabbath ha-Gadol* is designed to familiarize the people with its contents before the *Seder* service.

SHABBATH ḤAZON   שַׁבָּת חָזוֹן

The Sabbath preceding the fast of *Tish'ah b'Av* is called *Shabbath Ḥazon* from the opening word of the *haftarah*, consisting of the first twenty-six verses of the book of Isaiah which strike the fundamental notes of the prophet's teaching concerning the inevitable consequences of sinful living. Among the Sephardim this Sabbath is called שבת איכה, from the opening word of the book of Lamentations.

The custom of reading *haftaroth* independently of the *sidroth* on the three Sabbaths before *Tish'ah b'Av* and the seven Sabbaths immediately following this fast day is said to be of very ancient origin. The *Pesikta d'Rav Kahana*, edited by Solomon Buber, enumerates these ten *haftaroth* in the same order in which they are now recited.

SHABBATH NAḤAMU   שַׁבָּת נַחֲמוּ

The opening word of the *haftarah* recited on the Sabbath immediately following *Tish'ah b'Av* is *Naḥamu*, hence the title *Shabbath Naḥamu*. The first twenty-six verses of the fortieth chapter of Isaiah are read, beginning with נחמו, נחמו עמי ("Comfort, O comfort my people"). In accordance with the arrangement of the *sidroth*, the Ten Commandments and the *Shema* are read from the *Sefer Torah* on *Shabbath Naḥamu*, designated as the joyous Sabbath which follows the three weeks of mourning the destruction of the Temple. *Shabbath Naḥamu* is the most important and the most widely observed, being the first of the seven Sabbaths devoted to prophecies of comfort.

SHABBATH SHUVAH   שַׁבָּת שׁוּבָה

The Sabbath between *Rosh Hashanah* and *Yom Kippur* is called *Shabbath Shuvah* from the first word of the *haftarah* read on that day: שובה ישראל (return, O Israel). Since this Sabbath occurs within the ten days of repentance (*asereth yemé teshuvah*) it is often referred to

582

as *Shabbath Teshuvah*, the Sabbath of repentance. The *haftarah* is a combination of three prophetic passages taken from three books (Hosea 14:2-10; Micah 7:18-20; Joel 2:15-27).

SHABBATH SHIRAH   שַׁבַּת שִׁירָה

THE Sabbath on which the victory song of Moses is read in the synagogue is called *Shabbath Shirah*, recalling past triumphs and dispelling the clouds obscuring the promise of a better tomorrow. The song, known as the Red Sea Song (שירת הים), is notable for vivid imagery and poetic fire, giving expression to the mingled feelings of fear, triumph and gratitude, that the people of Israel experienced during the time when they were pursued by the Egyptian foes and rescued.

"My strength and song is the Lord! He has been my savior. This is my God, I glorify him; the God of my father, I extol him. . . Thy right hand, O Lord, magnificent in power, thy right hand, O Lord, has crushed the enemy. . . At a breath of thy anger the waters piled up, the flowing waters stood like a mound, the flood water congealed in the heart of the sea. The enemy said: I will pursue and overtake them; I will divide the spoils and my lust shall be glutted with them; I will draw my sword; my hand shall destroy them! When thy wind blew, the sea covered them; like lead they sank in the mighty waters..."

DEMONS, SPIRITS   שֵׁדִים, רוּחוֹת

PRIMITIVE man accepted the notion that demons and evil spirits, *shédim* and *mazzikim*, are the originators of disaster and disease. The counterpart of demonology is angelology, which deals with spiritual beings that bring good to human beings. In the Torah we find the expression יזבחו לשדים, "they offered sacrifice to demons . . . to gods whom they had not known before. . ." (Deuteronomy 32:17).

It has been surmised that the demons or *shédim*, in this connection, may refer to the divinities worshiped in Assyria in the form of colossal bulls. Similarly, Israel's ancient sin is described in Psalm 106:37-38 as follows: "They sacrifice their sons and daughters to demons, and they shed innocent blood, the blood of their sons and their daughters, whom they sacrificed to the idols of Canaan, desecrating the land with bloodshed."

The Assyrian demi-gods, represented by colossal bulls in front of palaces, were called *shidu*. Surrounded by animistic notions of primitive people, the Jews absorbed some of these and developed a variety of legends of their own concerning evil spirits that can wield a destructive power over human beings. Jewish folklore includes incredible stories about Ashmedai the king of demons, and Lilith the queen of demons. Maimonides completely ignores the subject of demons.

SHADKHAN   שַׁדְכָן

THE term *shadkhan* (marriage broker) is derived from the verb שדך, used in the Talmud (Shabbath 150a) in the sense of stipulating, negotiating a marriage. The profession of the *shadkhan* was well established in the early Middle Ages, especially among the Franco-German Jews. The *shadkhan's* right to compensation is dealt with in medieval Jewish law codes (*Or Zaru'a*, the *Mordekhai*). His work was highly respected. Many prominent rabbis, like the *Maharil* (Rabbi Jacob Moelln), used matchmaking as a source of income, since they refused to accept salaries for their rabbinic functions. The *shadkhan* was entitled to about two percent of the amount involved; when the contracting parties lived more than ten miles apart, the *shadkhan* was entitled to three percent and more.

The *shadkhanim* had widespread acquaintances in the remote parts of the Jewish settlements; many of them had great understanding of human nature, and enjoyed unlimited confidence because of their good character. Some saintly rabbis regarded the business of matchmaking not merely as a source of income, but also as a *mitzvah*, a divine precept, similar to the *mitzvah* of *hakhnasath kallah* (dowering the bride) or aiding young people to marry. Genuinely happy marriages resulted from the direct parental responsibility for the choice of prospective brides and grooms, who were brought to their attention by *shadkhanim*.

In the nineteenth century, however, the *shadkhan* and his profession were used as favorite subjects for humorous descriptions by Jewish and non-Jewish writers. On the other hand, the Jewish matrimonial agent has been described as a prized visitor in the home of every marriageable girl. Special attention was devoted to *yihus*, the family line, which was thoroughly investigated and reported by the marriage broker, in view of the Jewish ambition to marry into a family of a good name and an excellent environment.

SHEHEHEYANU   שֶׁהֶחֱיָנוּ

THE blessing *Sheheheyanu*, normally recited on seventeen occasions in the year, reads: "Blessed art thou, Lord our God, King of the universe, who hast granted us life and sustenance and permitted us to reach this festive occasion." It is recited when tasting fruit for the first time in the season, when putting on a new garment, when moving into a new house, when lighting the first *Hanukkah* candle, when the *shofar* is sounded on *Rosh Hashanah*, the first day the *lulav* and *ethrog* are used on *Sukkoth*, before reading the *Megillah* on *Purim*; and it forms part of the *Kiddush* for festivals, except the last two nights of *Pesah*.

Sheheheyanu is omitted on the last two nights of *Pesah*, commemorating the crossing of the Red Sea, in order to stress the idea that we must not rejoice over the misfortunes that befell our foes. Similarly, only half-*Hallel* is recited on the last six days of *Pesah*, in keeping with the following tradition: When the Egyptians were drowning in the Red Sea, God restained the angels from singing his praise, saying: "How can you sing while my creatures are drowning in the sea?" (Megillah 10b). It all goes back to the biblical warning which says: "Do not rejoice when your enemy falls, do not exult when he is overthrown. . ." (Proverbs 24:17-18).

Though *Sheheheyanu* is recited at the *Pidyon ha-Ben* (redemption of the firstborn son), it is not used at a *Brith Milah* festivity, because of the pain involved to the child circumcised. Nor is it recited at the first counting of the *omer*, which brings to mind the tragic events connected with the *Sefirah* period between *Pesah* and *Shavuoth*. Otherwise it is used on all happy occasions.

SHOGEG; MÉZID   שׁוֹגֵג; מֵזִיד

THE term *shogeg* denotes a person who has sinned inadvertently, as opposed to *mézid* or a person who has committed a wrong willfully. In Jewish law, intent is an important element deciding the guilt or innocence of a wrongdoer. Sincere repentance shows that even willful sins are attributable to ignorance; hence they are treated as errors on the part of those who repent sincerely (גדולה תשובה שזדונות נעשות לו כשגגות—Yoma 86b).

SAMARITANS   שׁוֹמְרוֹנִים

COLONIES of non-Jews from Babylonia, Syria and elsewhere, were settled in Samaria after the deportation of the ten tribes of Israel by the Assyrians in 722 before the common era. In the Hebrew Bible, the name *Shomronim* (Samaritans) occurs only once, namely in the passage which describes the origin and the religious practices of the Samaritan sect: "Israel was exiled from their own land to Assyria until this day. The king of Assyria then brought people from Babylon, Kuthah, Hamath . . . and placed them in the cities of Samaria instead of the people of Israel; they took possession of Samaria and lived in its towns. When they began to live there, they did not worship the Lord. . . The king of Assyria was told that as the nations he had deported to settle in the towns of Samaria did not know the law of the god of the land, he sent lions among them, and that they were being killed because they did not know the law of the god of the land. So the king of Assyria issued orders that one of the priests whom he had carried off should be taken back and allowed to live in the country, to teach them the law of the god of the land. . . But the nations had all made gods of their own, setting up their worship in the shrines made by the Samaritans. . . In worshiping the Lord . . . they also served their own gods. . . To this day they follow their primitive customs. . ." (II Kings 17:23-34).

The religion that prevailed among the Samaritans was a combination of the worship of the Lord, as the God of the land of Israel, with that of various deities worshiped by the different nations from which the settlers were drawn. When, some two centuries later, the Samaritans requested to be allowed to share in the restoration of the Temple, they were refused, being regarded "the enemies of Judah." The Bible records: "When the enemies of Judah . . . came and said to Zerubbabel. . . Let us build along with you, for we worship your God as you do . . . they were told: You have nothing to do with our building a house for our God. . ." (Ezra 4:1-3). It is generally assumed that there must have mingled with the Samaritans a certain number of native Israelites, who had been left behind in the country by their Assyrian conquerors.

Gradually, the Samaritans adopted a form of Judaism based on the Pentateuch alone, rejecting not only the oral tradition but also the prophetical writings. They regarded themselves as continuing the

586

kingdom of Israel, and were in constant political rivalry with the Judeans. In 332, before the common era, they built a temple on Mount Gerizim. Towards the end of the second century before the common era, the temple on Mount Gerizim was destroyed by John Hyrcanus, but it was rebuilt by the Romans after the revolt of Bar Kokhba. This was destroyed again in 484. Josephus says that when the Jews were in prosperity, the Samaritans claimed that they were allied to them in blood; but when they saw them in adversity, they declared that they had no relationship to them, but were descended from the Assyrian immigrants (*Antiquities* 11:8, 6; also 9:14, 3).

Ever since the fourteenth century, the Samaritan sect has gradually declined; it now numbers only a handful of adherents in Nablus, Jordan, and in the State of Israel. The small remnant of Samaritans still offer sacrifices (the pachal lamb) on Mount Gerizim, 2,849 feet above the Mediterranean in the highlands of Samaria. They observe the Sabbath, the sacred festivals, circumcision; they believe in the coming of a redeemer who will convert all nations to Samaritanism. They are devoted to their literature, consisting of the five books of Moses and commentaries, liturgies and treatises on ritual. Of the main daily prayers, they have an abridged version of the *Shema* with the omission of *Hear, O Israel.* They keep repeating: *The Lord is our God, the Lord is One.* Their Hebrew pronunciation, strangely different from either Ashkenazic or Sephardic, preserves an ancient tradition.

Samaritan homes are distinguished by an abridged form of the Ten Commandments inscribed on the doorposts. Their daily prayer includes the first chapter of Genesis and ends with the priestly blessing. They read a portion of the Torah every Sabbath. Some of their oldest hymns they attribute to Moses. They hold three daily services. The Samaritan Pentateuch, quoted by Jerome and Eusebius of the fourth century, differs from the Masoretic Hebrew text in about six thousand places. Most of the variations are unimportant and attributable to scribal errors or to deliberate alterations. In about 1,900 places the Samaritan text agrees with that of the Septuagint, which may suggest that the Greek translators used a Hebrew text much like that possessed by the Samaritans. The Samaritan translation of the Pentateuch must not be confounded with their Hebrew text, written in ancient Hebrew script. The Samaritan version of the Torah was made into their dialect early in the present era. They possess an Arabic translation made in the eleventh or twelfth century. Wilhelm Gesenius made a very careful examination of the Samaritan text of the Torah and, in 1815, declared it to be far inferior to that of the Masoretic text.

Adhering rigidly to the Torah, without admitting any of the prophetical teachings, the Samaritans never developed their religious laws to meet the necessities of changed conditions. They are frequently mentioned in the Mishnah as Kutheans (כותים). The implication is that they are not of pure Israelite origin, but descendants of foreign colonists with whom the district of Samaria was flooded in the eighth century before the common era.

Their strict observance of the precepts relating to *shehitah* and the rules of purification is praised in the Talmud (Ḥullin 4a; Niddah 56b). They never postpone circumcision; they allow no fire on the Sabbath; they compel even children to observe the *Yom Kippur* fast; they make their *sukkoth* of the trees, palm branches and willows, mentioned in Leviticus 23:40, and do not follow the Jewish observance of *lulav* and *ethrog*. In the special talmudic tractate Kuthim, the general rule is that the Samaritans are to be trusted in so far as their own practices coincide with those of the Jewish people. In other respects they are considered as non-Jews.

Though the Samaritan religious observances approximate those of the Karaites in several points, the two sects differ as follows: The Karaites believe in the sanctity of the entire Hebrew Bible as we have it today; the Samaritans have only the five books of the Torah, and the book of Joshua with countless variations, written in an ancient Hebrew script which is no longer in use. The Karaites, calling themselves "Mourners for Zion," believe in the holiness of Jerusalem; the Samaritans regard Mount Gerizim as holy, and not Jerusalem, and consider themselves as the descendants of the Ephraimites who, after the death of king Solomon, declared: "We have no part in David; we have no inheritance in the son of Jesse" (I Kings 12:16). The Karaites believe in the future advent of the Messiah, descendant of David; the Samaritans still retain a grudge against the house of David. The Karaites observe *shehitah* regulations in the slaughter of cattle, and not of fowl; the Samaritans are even stricter than the most observant Jews in relation to the laws of *kashruth*. These are compiled in a special code called *Al-Atbah*.

The entire Samaritan sect, inhabiting both Israel and Jordan, consists of approximately four hundred men, women and children. One hundred and fifty are settled in the Israeli municipality Ḥolon, some two miles south of Tel Aviv-Jaffa. The rest of them live in Nablus,

588

Jordan, near their sacred Mount Gerizim. This small community has succeeded to preserve its identity thanks to the extraordinary devotion of its members to their religious heritage. The Israeli Samaritans are well adjusted to their surroundings. Their children serve in the Israeli army (*Tzahal*); their daughters teach in the Israeli schools, but do not assimilate with the Jewish fellow citizens.

As a rule, the Samaritan calendar is identical with ours, though their leap years differ from ours. In the year 1962-63, their festivals occurred on the same days as ours. Their services on *Rosh Hashanah*, which they observe only for one day, begin at three o'clock before daybreak. Their New Year rejoicings begin after *Yom Kippur*, when they visit one another to express their best wishes. Every Sabbath morning, at three o'clock, they attend services at the house of prayer. At noon they meet again as a congregation of worshipers.

They build their *sukkoth* inside the house, to make sure that they will dwell in them for seven days unhindered by a change in the weather. They spread a net against the ceiling of a room, placing in it a variety of plants and citrus fruits, to which they keep adding new fruits daily. Their synagogue has no benches or chairs. They sit on carpets in the oriental fashion. The women worshipers occupy a separate compartment, in back of the men worshipers. Their *Sefer Torah* is written by a scribe.

JUDGES   שׁוֹפְטִים

THE book of Judges is a story of triumphant faith. It derives its name from the twelve heroic leaders whose deeds and prowess it describes. The Hebrew word for judges (*shoftim*) connotes champions, defenders. The judges, of whom six are described in detail and six are mentioned in passing, were gifted and courageous persons who strengthened Israel's hold of Canaan against a variety of enemies. These champions, including Eli and Samuel who are described in the book of Samuel, inspired the people to fight against those who threatened their existence. The period of the judges lasted about two hundred and thirty years, during the interval between the death of Joshua and the coronation of Saul. The book consists of twenty-one chapters; it is the second in the Prophets.

The book of Judges is replete with character sketches and examples of good traits and bad ones. Deborah, the prophetess who held court and settled disputes among her people, was a dynamic personality in peace and war. The song of Deborah, celebrating the victory over the army of Sisera, is an excellent example of early Hebrew poetry, though the meaning is not clear in some of its verses. It is the outcome of a powerful imagination and reaches sublime heights of religious emotion. Six tribes are praised in the song of Deborah because they formed the Israelite league against Sisera. The tribes of Reuben, Gad, Dan and Asher are rebuked for their non-cooperation. The tribes of Judah and Simeon, who were distant, are not mentioned in the song of Deborah.

Gideon was a man of peace, who succeeded in appeasing the fiery Ephraimites by minimizing his own achievements and magnifying their part in the final destruction of the enemy. His daring modesty and good temper make him a glowing personality.

Jephthah was a man of war and, unlike Gideon, fought the Ephraimites back to their Jordan boundary. He seized the fords of the river and set guards to let no Ephraimites pass over. The identity of Ephraimites was easily detected by the way they mispronounced the word *shibboleth* (stream). They could not pronounce "sh" and said *sibboleth* instead of *shibboleth*.

Samson represents a strange combination of virtue and folly. He is the strong man who is too weak to resist feminine wiles. Delilah has become a symbol of the treacherous woman in whose clutches the strong man is helpless. Excerpt:

Delilah shouted: The Philistines are upon you, Samson! He woke up and thought he might again shake himself free, not realizing that the Lord had left him. The Philistines seized him and gouged out his eyes; they brought him down to Gaza and bound him with bronze chains. He spent his time in prison grinding at the mill. . . Now the Philistine tyrants had gathered for merrymaking and were in high spirits; they shouted: Call for Samson, that he may amuse us!

So Samson was called from prison. He was made to stand between the pillars, and he said to the attendant who held him by the hand: Let me feel the pillars on which the house rests, that I may lean against them. Now the house was full of men and women; all the Philistine lords were there, and on the roof there were about three thousand men and women, looking down in amusement at Samson. He called to the Lord and said: Lord God, remember me; give me strength, I pray thee, only this once, to wreak vengeance upon the Philistines for one of my two eyes.

590

Samson grasped the two middle pillars on which the house rested, one with his right hand and the other with his left, and leaned his weight upon them. "Let me die with the Philistines!" Samson cried. He pulled with all his might, and the temple of Dagon fell on the tyrants and on all the people that were inside.

SHOFAR   שׁוֹפָר

THE *shofar* may be described as the ancient ritual horn of Israel, used to signalize important public events. It is the oldest surviving type of wind-instrument, mentioned frequently in the Bible, the Talmud, and in post-talmudic literature. The revelation at Sinai was introduced by the sound of the *shofar*, causing all the people to tremble (Exodus 19-16). The year of jubilee, designed to emancipate men and their families from slavery and lifelong poverty, was proclaimed by the sound of the *shofar*.

On *Rosh Hashanah*, the notes of the *shofar* proclaim the sovereignty of God and, symbolically, call men to repentance. At the conclusion of *Yom Kippur*, the *shofar* is sounded as a memorial of the jubilee which used to be announced every fiftieth year on the tenth day of *Tishri*. In our days, too, the concluding *shofar* blast following the *Ne'ilah* service of *Yom Kippur* is regarded as a symbolic proclamation of the emancipation from sinfulness.

The sounds produced by the *shofar* are the plain *tekiah*, ending abruptly; the broken *shevarim*, consisting of three short sounds; and the *teruah*, a succession of tremulous sounds equal to three *shevarim*. On *Rosh Hashanah*, these sounds are arranged variously in the following combinations: *tekiah, shevarim, teruah, tekiah; tekiah, shevarim, tekiah; tekiah, teruah, tekiah gedolah*—the considerably prolonged *tekiah*.

The section *Shofaroth*, included in the *Musaf* service for *Rosh Hashanah*, consists of ten biblical verses in which the *shofar* is mentioned, from the revelation at Sinai to the blast that will be the signal for the gathering of the dispersed to worship at Jerusalem (Isaiah 27:13). The Talmud records that, anciently, six תקיעות were sounded at short intervals on Friday afternoons. At the first *tekiah*, the field laborers ceased work; at the second, the stores closed and city labor ceased; and the third *tekiah* was a signal to light the Sabbath lights. After a short pause, the *shofar* sounded *tekiah, teruah, tekiah*, and the Sabbath set in (Shabbath 35b).

591

Many reasons are offered for the sounding of the *shofar* on *Rosh Hashanah*. According to Rav Saadyah Gaon of the tenth century, there are ten reasons: 1) The *shofar* proclaims the sovereignty of the Creator on *Rosh Hashanah*, the anniversary of creation. 2) The *shofar* warns and stirs the people to amend their life during the Ten Days of Repentance, beginning with the New Year. 3) The *shofar* reminds us of the revelation at Mount Sinai, when the people said: "We will do and obey." 4) The *shofar* brings to mind the prophetic warnings and exhortations. 5) The *shofar* is reminiscent of the battle alarm in Judea. 6) the *shofar* brings to mind the attempted sacrifice of Isaac (*akedah*). 7) The *shofar* inspires the heart with awe and reverence. 8) The *shofar* reminds us of the Day of Judgment. 9) The *shofar* inspires us with hope for the final restoration of the people of Israel. 10) The *shofar* is identified with the idea of *tehiyyath ha-méthim* (the resurrection of the dead).

SHOSHANNATH YAAKOV   שׁוֹשַׁנַּת יַעֲקֹב

THE famous *Purim* song *Shoshannath Yaakov* alludes to the biblical verse: "The city of Shushan shouted and rejoiced" (Esther 8:15). The name שׁושׁנת יעקב, therefore, refers to the descendants of Jacob who lived in Shushan. By extension, medieval Hebrew poets referred to the Jewish people in general as *Shoshannah* or *Shoshan* (a rose).

SHEHITAH   שְׁחִיטָה

THE Jewish method of *shehitah*, or ritual slaughtering of animals, though not described in the Torah, was communicated orally to Israel at the time of Moses (Hullin 27a; 28a). That Moses had taught the people the rules of *shehitah* is indicated by the following biblical quotation: "You may slaughter in the manner I have told you any of your herd or flock that the Lord has given you, and eat it to your heart's desire" (Deuteronomy 12:21). Since this is nowhere mentioned in the Torah, it has been assumed that the laws of *shehitah* were transmitted orally.

The slaughtering of animals is entrusted only to eligible and qualified persons versed in the laws of *shehitah* and skilled in their work. The *shohet* must be a religious Jew, possessing the manual skill, who has passed a rigid examination before a competent authority in all the laws pertaining to his task. He must have a written licence, known as *kabbalah*, received from an authoritative rabbi, certifying that he has been thoroughly examined and approved. *Shehitah* may not be performed by an old *shohet* whose hands tremble, for fear that he may press the knife against the throat of the animal instead of gently moving it forward and backward. The *shohet* is instructed to review the laws of *shehitah* at least once in thirty days.

The knife (*hallaf*) with which *shehitah* is performed must be sharp, smooth, and without any perceptible notch; it must be thoroughly examined before the slaughtering. Occasionally, the *shohet* submits his *hallaf* to the rabbi for examination. A special blessing is recited by the *shohet* before the slaughtering. One blessing is sufficient when many animals are slaughtered at the same time. It reads: "Blessed art thou, Lord our God, King of the universe, who hast sanctified us with thy commandments and commanded us concerning *shehitah*.

Soon after the *shehitah* the *shohet* must examine the lungs of the animal to ascertain whether they were not defective when the animal was alive. If certain fatal defects are found in the lungs, the meat is declared unfit for food (*terefah*). On the basis of the extreme care shown by the strict laws of *kashruth*, it has been noted that if the slaughterhouses were placed under the supervision of the Jewish *shohet*, diseases would be less prevalent and the average duration of life would be increased. The charge that *shehitah* is inhumane has been disproved by many physiologists.

As to the prohibition against slaughtering an animal and its young on the same day (Leviticus 22:28), Maimonides points out that the pain of the animals under such circumstances is very great, "since the love and the tenderness of the mother for her young ones is not produced by reasoning but by feeling, and this faculty exists not only in man but in most living things" (*Guide*, 3:48). All other regulations for the lawful slaughter of animals are in harmony with the principle of the prevention of cruelty and are said to have been dictated by it.

The religious requirements in connection with *shehitah* have greatly contributed to the need of organizing self-governing Jewish communities. Regarded as aids to moral conduct, the dietary laws have been rationalized by many Jewish thinkers. In answer to the question: "What difference does it make to God how the animal is slaughtered?" the Midrash states: "The *mitzvoth* were given only to ennoble the people" (Genesis Rabbah 44:1—לא נתנו המצות אלא לצרף בהן את הבריות).

SHAHARITH   שַׁחֲרִית

THE daily morning service, beginning with dawn and ending at noon, is called *Shaharith* (from שחר, dawn). It consists of five parts, namely: 1) *Birkhoth ha-Shahar*, 2) *Pesuké d'Zimrah*, 3) *Keriath Shema*, 4) *Shemoneh Esreh*, 5) *Tahanun*. The *Shema* and the *Shemoneh Esreh* or *Amidah* are the main elements of the daily morning service. The preliminary morning blessings (*Birkoth ha-Shahar*), derived from talmudic sources, are combined with a variety of biblical and tannaitic passages, designed to complete the daily minimum of study required of every Jew.

The biblical selections, called *Pesuké d'Zimrah* (verses of song), consist of Psalms 145-150 and the Song of Moses (Exodus 14:30-15:18). The *Tahanun* (supplication) is recited on ordinary weekdays after the *Amidah;* it is omitted on Sabbaths, festivals, and other festive occasions. The *Amidah*, consisting of nineteen blessings on weekdays and seven on Sabbaths and festivals, is recited by the individual worshipers in an undertone and repeated aloud by the *sheliah tsibbur* or *hazzan* with the addition of the *Kedushah*.

Like all other services (*Minhah, Ma'ariv, Ne'ilah*), the daily morning service is concluded with *Alenu*. Torah reading, from the current *sidrah* of the week, was instituted by the Great Assembly under Ezra the Scribe to be included in *Shaharith* on Mondays and Thursdays.

SATAN   שָׂטָן

IN biblical Hebrew, the term שטן signifies adversary. It is derived from a verb meaning to oppose, to resist, to hinder. King Hadad of Damascus was the Satan of Solomon (I Kings 11:14). Compare I Samuel 29:4; II Samuel 19:23; Numbers 22:22. In the course of time, Satan came to mean pre-eminently *the Adversary*, the incarnation of all evil, whose thoughts and activities are devoted to the destruction of man.

Satan is mostly identified with the evil impulse (*yetser ha-ra*), the lower passions which are a hindrance to man's pursuit of the nobler things in life. He is also identified with the angel of death. He leads astray, then he brings accusations against man, whom he slays eventually. His chief functions are those of temptation, accusation and

594

punishment. Under the control of God, he acts solely with the divine permission to carry out his plots. Though he assumes a will of his own in the book of Job, he keeps within the limits which God has fixed for him (Job 1:12; 2:6).

HYMN OF UNITY   שִׁיר הַיִּחוּד

THE tosafist and philosopher-poet of twelfth-century Germany, Rabbi Samuel ben Kalonymus he-Ḥasid, is credited with the composition of *Shir ha-Yiḥud* (hymn of unity), which is divided into seven parts corresponding to the seven days of the week. This philosophical hymn on the absolute Oneness of God, for which Ibn Gabirol's *Kether Malkhuth* (Royal Crown) seems to have served as a basis, treats of the divine essence from the point of view that God is not like man. Rabbi Jacob Emden, in his *Siddur*, discusses at length the reasons given by some rabbinic authorities who were against the liturgical use of *Shir ha-Yiḥud* while others decided to the contrary. The author employs purely biblical Hebrew, hence there were some who even suspected the author of belonging to the Karaite sect. At the end of the fourth day's section, the words שדי מלכי ואלי (the Almighty is my King and God) begins with letters that suggest the name-acrostic שמואל. *Shir ha-Yiḥud* is included in the High Holyday Prayerbook.

HYMN OF GLORY   שִׁיר הַכָּבוֹד

THE reputed author of *Shir ha-Kavod* (hymn of glory), Rabbi Yehudah he-Ḥasid (died 1200), son of Rabbi Samuel ben Kalonymus, is recited at the close of the Sabbath morning services in responsive form. The hymn is generally referred to by its initial words אנעים זמירות.

  Here are several lines excerpted: "I sing hymns and compose songs because my soul longs for thee... Speaking of thy glory, my heart yearns after thy love... I tell thy praise, though I have not seen thee; I describe thee, though I have not known thee... Thy greatness and thy power they traced in thy mighty work. They imagined thee, not as thou art really; they described thee by thy acts only. They depicted thee in countless visions; despite all comparisons thou art One..." In various American synagogues it is now customary to have a small boy lead the congreagation in chanting *An'im Zemiroth* responsively.

595

SONG OF SONGS   שִׁיר הַשִּׁירִים

THE Song of Songs is the first of the Five *Megilloth* which form, in the Hebrew Bible, a group by themselves because they are read in the synagogue on five great occasions, respectively, namely: *Pesah Shavuoth, Tish'ah b'Av, Sukkoth,* and *Purim.* Throughout the past nineteen centuries, the Song of Songs has been accepted in Jewish tradition as an allegory of the relations between God and Israel. Rabbi Akiva declared it to be the holiest of all the sacred poetical writings.

Since an allegory is a narrative in which the characters and actors are veiled representations, implied but not stated, its virtue is that it leads the reader to think for himself. Indeed, the Bible as a whole is said to possess no single definitive meaning. Its very multiplicity of meanings results in its universal appeal, and marks it a continually relevant book. Some see in the Song of Songs an inspired portrayal of ideal human love, a description of the sacred married union.

According to the paraphrase of the Targum, the poem portrays the history of Israel till the times of the Messiah. It has also been regarded as a representation of the affection of Israel for the Sabbath. The reduplication of the word *song* has a superlative force, intimating that this is a song of the highest character.

Although its meaning has been extended by various methods of interpretation, one cannot miss the beauty of the poem in its literal interpretation. Its author takes us along with him into the open air, to the vineyards, the villages, the mountains. He awakens us at daybreak to catch the scent of the forest trees, to gather the apples and the pomegranates. The verse is fragrant with the breath of spring.

Some interpreters took it to be the story of the author's love for a country maiden, whom he raised to the rank of a queen, himself for a while adopting a simpler mode of life; the poem remained a protest against undue self-indulgence. Another opinion has won wide acceptance among students of the Bible. It contends that the Song of Songs contains a collection of love songs, suitable for marriage festivities.

The Song of Songs has been called a gem of literature; it became an authoritative treasury of word and thought for the mystic's vocabulary. Rabbi Solomon Alkabets, who composed the song welcoming the Sabbath (*Lekhah Dodi*), one of the finest religious poetry in existence, used the theme of the Sabbath bride and borrowed the title of his famous hymn from the Song of Songs (7:12).

596

The Song of Songs, meaning the finest of Solomon's songs, is reckoned among the books known as the wisdom literature of the Bible, even though it contains no direct teaching as in the case of Job, Proverbs, and Ecclesiastes. Some have understood the Song of Songs as an admonition to a married couple to love each other. Excerpts:

"I hear the voice of my beloved! Here he comes, leaping across the mountains, bounding over the hills! My beloved is like a gazelle, like a young deer. There he stands, behind the wall, gazing through the windows, peering through the lattice. . .

"My beloved called and said to me: Rise, my love, my beauty, come away. For, lo, the winter is over, the rain is past and gone; the flowers appear on the earth, the time of song has come! . . . On my bed at night I looked for him whom my soul loves. I asked the watchmen: Have you seen him whom my soul loves? Scarcely had I left them than I found him. I held him and would not let go of him until I had brought him into my mother's house. . .

"I was asleep, but my heart was awake. Hark! My beloved is knocking. . . I opened to my beloved, but he had turned away and was gone. I searched for him, but could not find him; I called him, but he did not answer. . . My beloved has gone down to his garden, to the flowerbeds of balsam, to gather lilies. I am my beloved's, and he is mine. . . How beautiful you are, how pleasing, my love, my delight! Your very figure is like a palm tree. . .

"Come, let us go into the fields, let us stay in the villages. Let us go early to the vineyards, to see whether the grapevine has budded, whether the vine blossoms have opened, whether the pomegranates are in flower. There I will give my love to you. . . Love is strong as death itself; its flashes are flashes of fire, a flame of the Lord. Floods cannot quench love, rivers cannot drown it. If a man offered all his wealth for love, he would be utterly scorned. . . Make haste, my beloved! Be like a gazelle, or like a young deer, on the mountains of spices" (על הרי בשמים).

PSALM OF THE DAY   שִׁיר שֶׁל יוֹם

THE Psalm of the Day is the designation of seven psalms, recited on the respective days of the week at the close of the daily morning service. They are Psalms 24, 48, 82, 94, 81, 93, 92, recited from Sunday through Saturday. According to Mishnah Tamid 7:4, the Psalm of the Day was chanted by the Levites each day during the Temple service. The daily psalms suggest the incidents of the seven days of creation (Rosh Hashanah 31a).

JEWISH MUSIC   שִׁירַת יִשְׂרָאֵל

MUSICAL instruments are mentioned in more than a hundred biblical passages. The most cursory glance at the contents of the Hebrew Bible shows the deep devotion of the Jewish people to the art of music. Dancing and music were practised together under all sorts of conditions in the home and in the fields. The consecration of music to the service of religion contributed to its development and cultivation with zeal and earnestness. In family feasts and religious festivals they sang, played on musical instruments and danced. Marriage processions, as they passed through the streets, were accompanied with music and song (Jeremiah 7:34; 25:10). Women and maidens welcomed the victorious warrior on his return home with music, song and dance (Judges 11:34; I Samuel 18:6). The mind might be quieted and refreshed by music (I Samuel 10:5; 16:16). Psalms were sung to the accompaniment of the harp (Psalm 92:1-3; 137:2).

Percussion, string and wind instruments are mentioned in the Hebrew Bible as follows: תֹּף, a hand-drum, usually played by women on occasions of rejoicing, serving to mark the rhythm for song or dance; מְצִלְתַּיִם, cymbals made of brass, chiefly reserved for religious purposes, such as worship in the Temple, also called צֶלְצְלִים; variously described as bells or castanets, מְנַעַנְעִים, a small metal frame with loose metal bars carrying loose rings, borne and swung or shaken in the hand. Then the wind instruments: חֲצוֹצְרָה, trumpet; חָלִיל, flute; שׁוֹפָר, ram's horn; and עוּגָב, described as made up of several reeds together; hence a pipe organ in modern Hebrew. כִּנּוֹר and נֵבֶל are the only stringed instruments mentioned throughout the Hebrew Bible. Their shape, scope and character have not been ascertained.

The concluding Psalm 150, often described as "the grand finale of the spiritual concert," calls upon all the musical instruments of the Temple service to join in the praise of the Lord: "Praise him with the *shofar* sound, praise him with lute and harp! Praise him with timbrel and dance, praise him with strings and pipe! Praise him with resounding cymbals, praise him with clanging cymbals! Let everything that has breath praise the Lord! *Halleluyah!*"

598

The Bible contains a picture of the musical accompaniment of worship in the Temple as follows: "He placed the Levites in the Temple of the Lord with cymbals, lutes and lyres, in accordance with the regulations of David... The Levites stood with the instruments of David, and the priests with the trumpets... As the offering began, the song to the Lord began also with trumpet blasts, led by the musical instruments of David, king of Israel. The whole assembly worshiped, and the singers sang, and the trumpeters blew blasts; all this continued until the offering was finished" (II Chronicles 29:25-28).

There are scholars who claim that three thousand-year-old Jewish vocal music persists in ancient Hebrew communities of Yemen, Iraq and Iran, where colonies settled after the first exile. To this day certain parts of Jewish sacred music retain evidences of ancient remembered ritual of prayer. The *Avodah*, recited on *Yom Kippur*, is given as a special example. The Temple music involved the use of large orchestral ensembles, very much unlike the unaccompanied singing of modern *hazzanim* or cantors.

The two main categories of Jewish music, religious and secular, go back to the time when our people were still living in Eretz Yisrael. In the course of centuries, however, both Jewish folk and sacred music alike absorbed many elements from the new surroundings. This explains why the music of Jews varies widely in different countries.

SHEKHINAH   שְׁכִינָה

THE term *Shekhinah*, signifying the majestic presence of God among men, is used to express the immanence and the omnipresence of God. We are told that the *Shekhinah* is where men gather for worship, where judges sit as a court, and where even one man studies Torah (Berakhoth 6a). The *Shekhinah* is everywhere (Bava Bathra 25a). This may well be expressed in the famous saying of Hillel: "If I am here, all is here; if I am not here, what is here?" (Sukkah 53a). However, the *Shekhinah* does not rest amidst gloom, laziness, frivolity, levity or idle talk, but only in the joy of performing a *mitzvah* (Shabbath 30b). There is a midrashic statement that he who receives his fellow men kindly is regarded as though he had received the *Shekhinah*.

The terms *Shekhinah* and *Ruah ha-Kodesh* are sometimes used interchangeably in the form of revelation of the Divine Presence or *Ruah ha-Kodesh* (Holy Spirit). In talmudic-midrashic literature, the anthropomorphic expressions of the Bible are avoided as much as possible, and terms like *Memra, Dibbur, Yekara* and *Kavod* (speech, glory) are employed instead. Depicted under the figure of light, the Divine Presence is often presented as coming into intimate contact with human beings. The presence of the *Shekhinah* is felt where sacred study and prayer occur; sin is the cause of its absence. The endowment of a person with special gifts is at times described in terms of the *Shekhinah* or *Ruaḥ ha-Kodesh* resting upon him.

REWARD AND PUNISHMENT   שָׂכָר וָעֹנֶשׁ

ACCORDING to the talmudic sages, man is responsible even for the conduct of others; as such he is liable to punishment if he is indifferent to the wrong that is being perpetrated about him, when an energetic protest from his side could have prevented it. And the greater the man the greater is his responsibility. Thus the righteous man may suffer with justice, though he himself has never committed any transgression. Rabbi Ishmael once explained: "I am the atonement for the Jews," meaning that he took upon himself all their sins to suffer for them. This desire seems to have its origin in a deep sympathy and compassion for Israel. This conduct of suffering *for* or *with* Israel was expected almost from every Jew. "When Israel is in a state of affliction, one must not say: I will rather live by myself, and eat and drink, and have peace of mind. . ." Rav declared in the third century: "He who does not sense the sufferings of his people does not belong to them" (Ḥagigah 5a—כל שאינו בהסתר פנים אינו מהם).

It has been noted that Judaism is satisfied with a mere establishment of the belief in retribution, without concerning itself with the manner in which it would be effected. According to Maimonides, the reward of the righteous in the world to come is spiritual bliss; the punishment of the wicked is exclusion from it, this being a form of extirpation or *kareth* (*Yad, Teshuvah* 8:1).

The following passages, quoted from talmudic-midrashic literature, shed some light on the subject of reward and punishment:

"The wicked who have done some good work are as amply rewarded for it in *this* world as if they were men who have fulfilled the whole of the Torah, so that they may be punished for their sins in the next world; whilst the righteous who have committed some sin have to suffer for it . . . so that they may enjoy their reward in the world to

600

come" (Avoth d'Rabbi Nathan). The responsibility of the individual towards the community is illustrated as follows: "It is to be compared to people sitting in board a ship, one of the passengers of which took an awl and began to bore holes in the bottom of the vessel. Asked to desist from his dangerous occupation, he answered: Why, I am only making holes in my own seat. He was forgetting that when the water came in it would sink the whole ship." The sin of a single person might endanger the whole of humanity. "The world is judged after the merits or demerits of the majority, so that a single individual by his good or bad actions can decide the fate of his fellow men, as it may happen that he is just the one who constitutes this majority."

SHILLUAH HA-KEN   שִׁלּוּחַ הַקֵּן

KINDNESS to animals is an important principle underlying a variety of biblical laws. The law in regard to the sparing of the mother-bird in the nest reads: "If you chance to come upon a bird's nest with young birds or eggs in it . . . and the mother-bird is sitting on them, you shall not take away the mother along with her offspring; you shall let the mother go, although you may take the offspring. . ." (Deuteronomy 22:6-7).

Rabbi Moses ben Nahman (*Ramban*), in his commentary, observes that the reason for this law, as well as for the commandment that an animal and its young must not be slaughtered on one and the same day (Leviticus 22:28), is that it constitutes a cruel act, and the Torah aims at implanting in man the quality of mercy and compassion. Pointing out that when the mother-bird is sent away she does not feel any pain, Maimonides declares: "If the Torah provides that such grief must not be caused to cattle or birds, how much more careful should we be not to cause grief to our fellow men" (*Guide*, 3:48).

SHALOM   שָׁלוֹם

THE Hebrew word *shalom* has a wider meaning than the English equivalent *peace*, for it signifies welfare of every kind: security, contentment, sound health, prosperity, friendship, peace of mind and heart, as opposed to the dissatisfaction and unrest caused by evil (Isaiah 32:17; 48:22). Hillel said: "Love peace and strive for peace" (Avoth

1:12). Among talmudic statements about peace the following may be quoted: "The whole Torah exists only for the sake of peace. For the sake of peace, truth may be sacrificed" (Gittin 59b; Yevamoth 65b):

כל התורה כולה מפני דרכי שלום היא. מותר לו לאדם לשנות בדבר השלום.

The phrase שלום לכם (peace be with you) occurs in Genesis 43:23 in the sense of the usual Hebrew greeting *shalom alekhem*, now generally abbreviated to *shalom*. The inverted order *alekhem shalom* in response to the greeting *shalom alekhem* is a form of emphasis. According to a talmudic statement, he who does not return a greeting is called a robber (Berakhoth 6b). We are told to meet every person with a friendly greeting (Avoth 4:20).

SHALOM ZAKHAR   שָׁלוֹם זָכָר

ON THE Friday night following the birth of a son, relatives and friends of the parents gather for a light feast known as *Shalom Zakhar* (peace, a male!). Various fanciful reasons have been advanced for the term *Shalom Zakhar*. According to an explanation in *Taamé ha-Minhagim*, Friday night has been selected for this celebration because all are at home on Sabbath eve and are at leisure to attend. Since the Sabbath is called *Shalom*, the name *Shalom Zakhar* has been applied. Congratulations and good wishes for the protection and welfare of the mother and the newly-born infant are offered by the visitors. *Shalom Zakhar* has been explained as an allusion to the talmudic saying: כיון שבא זכר בעולם בא שלום בעולם (Niddah 31b). The reference may perhaps be to family peace, when husband and wife live in serene harmony.

SHALOM ALEKHEM   שָׁלוֹם עֲלֵיכֶם

SHALOM ALEKHEM is also the name of a hymn chanted on Friday nights, upon returning home from the Sabbath-eve services. This song of peace, introduced by the kabbalists some three centuries ago, is based on the talmudic passage concerning a good angel and an evil angel accompanying every man home from the synagogue on Friday evenings. If they find the house in good order, the good angel says: "May the next Sabbath be as this one." If, on the other hand, they find the house neglected, the evil angel says: "May the next Sabbath be as this one."

The four stanzas of the hymn *Shalom Alekhem* begin with the following expressions, respectively: 1) Peace be with you, ministering angels. . . 2) May your coming be in peace, messengers of peace. . . 3) Bless me with peace. . . 4) May your departure be in peace. . .

SHULḤAN ARUKH   שֻׁלְחָן עָרוּךְ

THE *Shulḥan Arukh* (prepared table) by Rabbi Joseph Karo (1488-1575) serves as a practical guide in the observance of traditional Judaism throughout the world. It is printed together with the critical glosses of Rabbi Moses Isserles (1525-1572), known as רמ״א, the initials of his name and title.

The arrangement of the *Shulḥan Arukh* is the same as that adopted by the author of the *Arba'ah Turim*, but more concise. It consists of four parts: 1) *Oraḥ Ḥayyim* (way of life) concerning Jewish religious behavior at home and in the synagogue; 2) *Yoreh Deah* (teacher of knowledge) concerning things forbidden and permitted, including all phases of dietary laws; 3) *Even ha-Ezer* (stone of help) concerning marriage and family matters; 4) *Ḥoshen Mishpat* (breastplate of judgment) concerning various phases of civil law. The term *ezer* (help) alludes to marriage in Genesis 2:18. *Even Ezer* is a biblical place-name. The title *Ḥoshen Mishpat* is borrowed from Exodus 28:15.

The ten commentaries on the *Shulḥan Arukh*, usually printed in standard editions, are as follows:

1) מפה (*Mappah*), glosses inserted in the text, by Rabbi Moses Isserles (רמ״א—*Rema*), a contemporary of Rabbi Joseph Karo.

2) טורי זהב (*Turé Zahav* or *Taz*), by Rabbi David ha-Levi Segal (1586-1667). He served as rabbi of the Lemberg community.

3) שפתי כהן (*Sifthé Kohen*) by Rabbi Shabbethai ha-Kohen (1620-1662), on *Yoreh Deah* and *Ḥoshen Mishpat*, referred to as ש״ך (*Shakh*).

4) באר הגולה (*Be'er ha-Golah*) by Rabbi Moses Rivkes (died 1671).

5) באר היטב (*Ba'er Hétev*), on *Yoreh Deah* and *Ḥoshen Mishpat*, by Rabbi Zechariah ben Aryeh of the eighteenth century.

6) באור הגר״א (*Béur Hagra*), notes by Rabbi Elijah of Vilna, known as the Vilna-Gaon (1720-1797).

7) קצות החושן (*Ketzoth ha-Ḥoshen*), on *Ḥoshen Mishpat*, by Rabbi Aryeh ha-Kohen (died 1813).

8) פתחי תשובה (*Pithḥé Teshuvah*) by Rabbi Abraham Eisenstadt (1812-1868) of Bialystok. He was a great-grandson of the *Shakh* (ש״ך).

9) מאירת עינים (*Me'irath Einayim*), on *Ḥoshen Mishpat*, by Rabbi Joshua Falk (died 1614).

10) בית שמואל (*Beth Shemuel*), on *Even ha-Ezer*, by Rabbi Samuel ben Uri of the seventeenth century.

The *Shulḥan Arukh* of Rabbi Shneour Zalman (1747-1813), founder of the *Ḥabad* movement in Ḥasidism, was published in 1810. The product of the greatest scholar and intellect among the Ḥasidim, this *Shulḥan Arukh* is briefly referred to as *The Rav*. It is based upon the *Tur* and other *Poskim* (codifiers), as well as kabbalistic literature.

The *Mishnah Berurah* (משנה ברורה) by Rabbi Israel Meir ha-Kohen (1838-1932), known as the *Ḥafetz Ḥayyim*, is a six-volume commentary on the first part of the *Shulḥan Arukh*, called *Oraḥ Ḥayyim*. Its purpose is to elucidate points of law as well as add new halakhic material. The *Arukh ha-Shulḥan* (ערוך השלחן) by Rabbi Yeḥiel Michael Epstein (1835-1905) is an eight-volume commentary on the four parts of the *Shulḥan Arukh*.

Rabbi Solomon Ganzfried (1804-1886) is best known as the compiler of an abridgment of the *Shulḥan Arukh*, which has been reprinted many times under the title of *Kitzur Shulḥan Arukh*.

SHELIAḤ TSIBBUR   שְׁלִיחַ צִבּוּר

THE term *sheliaḥ tsibbur* (messenger of the congregation), applied to the person leading the congregation in prayer, is often abbreviated to ש"ץ (*shatz*) by combining the initial letter of the two words. According to the Talmud, a suitable *sheliaḥ tsibbur* is "an elderly man whose youth has been spent decently"—זקן ופרקו נאה (Ta'anith 16a); one who is modest and agreeable to the people; one who knows how to chant and has a sweet voice (ויש לו נעימה וקולו ערב).

When the *sheliaḥ tsibbur* recites aloud *Amidah* prayers that contain poetical insertions (*kerovoth*), as in the services for *Rosh Hashanah* and *Yom Kippur*, he begins by chanting an introduction known as *reshuth* (רשות) in solo, requesting *permission* for the insertion of hymns between the ancient benedictions of the *Amidah*. The phrase מסוד חכמים is the preliminary formula for all such introductions. The reader's meditation הנני העני ממעש (I am poor in worthy deeds), recited before the *Musaf* service on *Rosh Hashanah* and *Yom Kippur*, is of unknown authorship. It contains the petition that God accept the prayers on behalf of the congregation. The term חזרת הש"ץ signifies the reader's repetition of the *Amidah* for the benefit of the entire congregation, including those who are not able to read the prayers for themselves.

SHALOSH SE'UDOTH   שָׁלֹשׁ סְעָדּוֹת

THE three meals (*shalosh se'udoth*) that are religiously prescribed for the Sabbath are considered of high importance. One of the talmudic sages asserts that anyone who fulfills the precept of eating the three formal meals will be rescued from three evils (Shabbath 118a). They are to be had on Friday evening, Saturday morning and afternoon. The third meal, commonly known as *shalosh se'udoth* instead of *se'udah shelishith*, is served after the *Minḥah* prayers and continued, among the Ḥasidim especially, till the termination of the Sabbath, when the *Ma'ariv* service begins.

The so-called *Se'udath Rabbi Ḥidka* (סעודת רבי חידקא) refers to a light meal eaten by some in addition to the three Sabbath meals. This is in keeping with the private opinion held by Rabbi Ḥidka that four meals should be eaten on the Sabbath (Shabbath 117b). The *Se'udath Rabbi Ḥidka* is generally eaten after the Sabbath morning *Kiddush* in the form of some pastry (מזונות) and wine.

The Sabbath-afternoon *Oneg Shabbath* (Sabbath Delight) custom, which has become popular in Israel and elsewhere, consists of Sabbath afternoon gatherings to bid farewell to the Sabbath in the form of Torah study and songs (*zemiroth*). The *Oneg Shabbath* movement was first introduced by the famous Hebrew poet Ḥayyim Naḥman Bialik in Tel Aviv. American synagogues and temples have *Oneg Shabbath* gatherings following the late Friday-night services.

THIRTEEN ATTRIBUTES   שָׁלֹשׁ עֶשְׂרֵה מִדּוֹת

THE thirteen attributes of God, referring to the actions emanating from the divine providence, are spoken of in the Torah (Exodus 34: 6-7), according to the following traditional interpretation of the verses: "The Lord, the Lord is a merciful and gracious God, slow to anger and abounding in kindness and truth. He extends kindness to the thousandth generation, forgives iniquity, transgression and sin, and clears [the guiltless]."

605

The repetition of the Lord's name signifies that God is merciful to one about to sin but not yet guilty of sinning, and to the sinner who has repented. This represents the first two divine qualities. The third attribute is inferred from the word *El*, meaning *powerful* to act as his wisdom dictates. The term *merciful (Rahum)* denotes that God acts like a father to his children, preventing them from falling (fourth attribute).

The fifth: He is *gracious (Hannun)* to assist those who have fallen and cannot rise. The sixth: He is *slow to anger*, patient and hopeful that the sinner will repent. The seventh: *Abounding in kindness*, both to the righteous and the wicked. The eighth: *Truthful* and faithful to carry out his promises. The ninth: He extends his mercy to thousands of generations, placing the merits of the fathers to the credit of the children (*zekhuth avoth*). The tenth: He *forgives all iniquity*, sins committed with premeditation. The eleventh: He *pardons all transgression*, sins committed in a spirit of rebellion. The twelfth: He forgives *sins* committed inadvertently. The thirteenth: He *clears* those who repent.

These divine qualities are not an attempt to describe the essence of God philosophically, but rather to represent him as the source and fountain of all ethical behavior. God's attributes are to become the standard of man's morality. This is defined as imitation of God.

SHALOSH REGALIM שָׁלש רְגָלִים

Pesah, *Shavuoth* and *Sukkoth* are known as the three annual pilgrim festivals (שלש רגלים) because of the three pilgrimages which adult Israelites had to make to the Sanctuary. The phrase *shalosh regalim*, occurring in Exodus 23:14 ("Three times a year you shall celebrate a pilgrim feast"), is to be found again in Numbers 22:28, 32, 33). The words פעם and רגל are used interchangeably in the sense of beat, foot and time. In Exodus 22:17, *shalosh pe'amim* (three times) is used in place of *shalosh regalim*.

According to Ibn Ezra, the three pilgrim festivals are called *shalosh regalim* because most of the pilgrims went to Jerusalem on foot. The traditional rule was that every pilgrim had to go on foot at least the final stage of the journey up (*aliyyah*), from the city of Jerusalem to the Temple Mount, since the expression *shalosh regalim* conveys the sense of three times on foot (Hagigah 1:1).

First Days of the Pilgrim Festivals

1975	March 27	May 16	September 20
1976	April 15	June 4	October 9
1977	April 3	May 23	September 27
1978	April 22	June 11	October 16
1979	April 12	June 1	October 6
1980	April 1	May 21	September 25
1981	April 19	June 8	October 13
1982	April 8	May 28	October 2
1983	March 29	May 18	September 22
1984	April 17	June 6	October 11
1985	April 6	May 26	September 30
1986	April 24	June 13	October 18
1987	April 14	June 3	October 8
1988	April 2	May 22	September 26
1989	April 20	June 9	October 14
1990	April 10	May 30	October 4
1991	March 30	May 19	September 23
1992	April 18	June 7	October 12
1993	April 6	May 26	September 30
1994	March 27	May 16	September 20
1995	April 15	June 4	October 9
1996	April 4	May 24	September 28
1997	April 22	June 11	October 16
1998	April 11	May 31	October 5
1999	April 1	May 21	September 25
2000	April 20	June 9	October 14
2001	April 8	May 28	October 2
2002	March 28	May 17	September 21
2003	April 17	June 6	October 11
2004	April 6	May 26	September 30
2005	April 24	June 13	October 18
2006	April 13	June 2	October 7
2007	April 3	May 23	September 27
2008	April 20	June 9	October 14
2009	April 9	May 29	October 3
2010	March 30	May 19	September 23

TETRAGRAMMATON   שֵׁם הַמְפֹרָשׁ

The distinctive name of God (*shem ha-meforash*), consisting of four letters (י'ה'ו'ה'), is not read as written. The avoidance of uttering the sublime name of God is due to apprehensive reverence. An allusion to the rule that the tetragrammaton, the divine name of four letters, should not be pronounced as written is found in Exodus 3:15, where the expression is זה שמי לעלם (this is my name forever). The word לעלם can be read *l'allem* (to conceal), that is, the word *adonai* (Lord) should be substituted for the tetragrammaton, since the Hebrew word *adonai* likewise has four letters (Kiddushin 71a).

In Temple times, the high priest pronounced the tetragrammaton ten times in the course of the *Yom Kippur* service (Yoma 39b), but did this inaudibly so as to keep it concealed from the rest of the people. Since the destruction of the Temple there has remained no trace of knowledge as to the correct pronunciation of the tetragrammaton, which is generally assumed to denote the eternal existence of God.

The quadriliteral name of God is commonly interpreted to signify היה הוה יהיה (he was, he is, he shall be). "Jehovah" is a misreading by non-Jews, who are unaware that the vowel points of the four-lettered name belong to the word *adonai* which is used as a substitute. They are there only to remind the reader about the substitute term.

The meaning of the name was revealed to Moses in the vision of the flaming bush, namely: *the One who is always*. It is derived from the verb הוה, an older form of היה, and is used in the sense of the present tense. Since God speaks of himself in the vision, he calls himself *Ehyeh* (אהיה), that is, *I am*, in the first person. Men, however, speak of him in the third person (יהיה), which has become י'ה'ו'ה' = *He Is*. The four-letter name denotes the absolute self-existence of God, who alone truly exists.

Name (שם) is used in Hebrew in the sense of character and essence. To know the name of God is to know the divine attributes and the relation of God to his people. The divine name is often referred to as equivalent to the divine presence. The distinctive personal name of the God of Israel, the tetragrammaton or the *Shem ha-Meforash*, occurs 6,823 times in the Hebrew Bible while the name *Elohim* occurs much more frequently, having been substituted in some places for the tetragrammaton. The plural form of *Elohim* has been explained as the plural of majesty and excellence. The singular, *Eloah*, occurs only in

608

biblical poetry. The divine name YHWH is variously referred to as *Shem ha-Meyuḥad, Shem ha-Meforash, Shem ben Arba Othiyyoth* (Unique, Distinct, Quadriliteral Name), and simply *ha-Shem* (the Name) or *Yod Hé Vav Hé*, the four letters spelling the name YHWH.

Other divine names are considered as titles signifying perfection and power, or characterizing the divine acts as observed and appreciated in the various stages of human development. This has been illustrated by the example of a man who looks at the sun through various colored glasses; though they change the impressions produced upon the observer, they do not affect the sun.

Generally speaking, the divine name is considered more than a mere designation. It represents the divine relation to the people on earth, characterizing God's essence, his glory and power. Hence, the mystic awe with which its pronunciation was surrounded, and the powers attributed by the kabbalists to its correct manipulation. There is a tannaitic statement that he who pronounces the divine name according to its letters loses his share in the future world (Sanhedrin 10:1).

APOSTASY   שְׁמָד

THE Hebrew word *shemad* denotes both persecution and conversion from Judaism. An apostate from Judaism is called *meshummad*, the passive of the verb שמד, thus alluding to the compulsory conversions in the long history of Jewish persecutions. Some scholars, however, are of the opinion that the word *meshummad* is derived from a Syriac verb meaning to baptize; hence, a convert to Islam, for example, is not described as *meshummad* (baptized) but as *mumar*, a term frequently used in a wider sense to designate an open opponent to Jewish teachings and practices.

The term *meshummad*, meaning a deserter who has forsaken his people, has a much more unfavorable connotation than that of convert. It is felt that the *meshummad* has changed his religion for selfish purposes, and not from conviction or self-protection. An eighteenth-century non-Jewish champion of Jewish emancipation wrote: "What person will not despise the vile being who forsakes the religion of his youth, abandons his kindred and people, and desecrates another faith by externally observing its rites while internally being unconvinced of its divine institution. Rabbi Israel Baal Shem Tov, founder of Ḥasidism, is reported to have said: "Every Jew is an organ of the

Shekhinah. As long as the organ is joined to the body, however tenuously, there is hope; once it is cut off, all hope is lost."

Many *meshummadim*, in order to avoid being confused with their former co-religionists or fellow Jews, developed a super-zeal for their new religion, which they expressed in fanatical hatred of Judaism. They were responsible for the compulsory public disputations, in the Middle Ages, resulting in dire consequences to the Jewish people if the arguments in favor of Judaism proved to be too convincing to the enraged neighbors. The burning of Jewish books, the forcible baptism of Jewish children, the hunting down and then executing innumerable crypto-Jews (Marranos) were some of the activities urged by the zealous *meshummadim*, who served as spies and informers during the medieval period, perhaps in order to remove all suspicion from themselves. The great reduction in the Jewish population during the Middle Ages is attributable to the large-scale conversions.

In 1399, many Jews of Prague were imprisoned because a *meshummad* by the name of Peter (originally, Pesaḥ) charged the Jews with uttering blasphemy in the *Alenu* prayer. He said that the numerical value of the word וריק (and idle) corresponds to that of the name ישו=316, although the phrase הבל וריק was borrowed from Isaiah 30:7. Many were murdered because of this accusation. Through fear of the official censors, the following words were excluded from the *Alenu* prayer: שהם משתחוים להבל וריק ומתפללים אל אל לא יושיע (they, the pagans, bow to vanity and emptiness and pray to a god that cannot save).

A renegade by the name of Peter Schwartz spread the blood-libel, or ritual murder accusation, charging that the Jews used human blood for the preparation of *matzoth* and in the four cups of wine used in the *Seder* service of the *Pesaḥ* festival. This libel known as *alilath dam* (עלילת דם) flared up repeatedly in fourteen European countries. From 1144 to 1940 there were one hundred and fifty-two cases. The notorious *meshummad* John Pfefferkorn, of the sixteenth century, was a butcher by trade, a man of little learning and of immoral conduct; he lent his name to a large number of anti-Jewish writings published by the Dominicans of Cologne. He insisted that all the Jews be either expelled from Germany or employed as street-cleaners and chimney-sweeps; that every copy of the Talmud and rabbinical books should be taken away from the Jews, and that every Jewish house be ransacked for this purpose. But John Reuchlin exposed the Dominicans and the character of Pfefferkorn, their tool.

610

The Spanish Inquisition, established in the thirteenth century, originated for the purpose of preventing the Marranos from practising their ancestral religion in secret. It was to root out this crypto-Judaism that the tremendous machinery of the Inquisition was devised. The sufferers under Torquemada of the fifteenth century were primarily those who relapsed to Judaism. It is generally accepted, however, that Torquemada's personal influence was largely responsible for the expulsion of the Jews from Spain in 1492.

Rabbi Simeon ben Tzemaḥ Duran, known as *Rashbatz* (רשב"ץ), who settled in Algiers after the 1391 persecutions, when Spanish Jews began to settle in North Africa, wrote on the question of the validity of Marrano marriages: "There is no distinction at all to be made in this matter between a Jew and an apostate; for we hold that, although he has sinned, he is still a Jew... Therefore if one of them marries a woman, his marriage is valid... All apostates and children of apostate women are to be considered as full Israelites with regard to marriage." As the years went by, Jewish law tended to be stricter in its judgment of the Marranos and their status; for, why did they not escape sooner? Also, by this time they were of mixed descent.

SAMUEL   שְׁמוּאֵל

THE two books of Samuel are considered as one book in the Hebrew Bible. They continue the history of Israel from the tribal stage to the development of a united nation. They cover a period of about one hundred years (1070-970 before the common era). It was one of the most important centuries in the life of Israel. In the long struggle against its surrounding enemies, Israel learned its own strength and prepared to play its part in the history of mankind. Events during this period are centered about three great personalities: Samuel, Saul, and David.

The books of Samuel, which are among the most instructive and interesting of all the biblical writings, contain the first records of prophecy and represent one of the most important sources for the history of religion. The first book records the life of Samuel and the events that occurred during his administration and that of king Saul. It also describes David's good character and his triumphs, spiritual and material. "King David still lives" (דוד מלך ישראל חי וקיים) is an ancient expression of affectionate admiration (Rosh Hashanah 25a).

The second book describes the career of David and the expansion of his kingdom. It contains a vivid portrayal of the demoralization in David's family, traceable to David's own moral collapse. The story of Absalom's rebellion against David, and of David's mourning over the death of Absalom, is considered to be one of the greatest narratives that has come down to us from ancient times.

It is generally agreed among modern Bible scholars that the book of Samuel is not the work of a single author, but a compilation from earlier written sources, some of which go back in their turn to oral tradition. Many passages are quite untranslatable, and yield no intelligible sense when translated. This will explain the great variety of commentaries on the book of Samuel that have appeared in many languages. Excerpts:

"The Lord sent Nathan the prophet to David. Nathan went to him and said: There were two men in one town, a rich man and a poor man. The rich man had many sheep and cattle; the poor man had nothing but a single lamb. . . Now a traveler came to visit the rich man. But the rich man refused to take from his own flock or his own herd to prepare food for the guest. He took, instead, the poor man's lamb and prepared for the visitor. David's anger blazed against the man, and he said to Nathan: As the Lord lives, the man who has done this deserves to die!

"Then Nathan said to David: You are the man! . . . You have taken Uriah's wife to be your wife, having caused his death by the sword of the Ammonites. Therefore, the sword shall never depart from your house. I will stir up evil against you in your own household. You have acted in secret, but I will act before all Israel. . . The Lord struck the child that Uriah's wife bore to David, and it became sick. David prayed to God for the child, fasting and lying on the ground all night. On the seventh day, the child died. David's servants were afraid to tell him that the child was dead, for fear that he would do something desperate to himself. When David saw that his servants were whispering to one another, he understood that the child was dead. Is the child dead? he asked them; and they answered: He is dead.

"Then David got up from the ground; he washed himself and changed his clothes; he went to the house of the Lord and worshiped; after that he went home, asked for food and ate. What is the meaning of this? the servants asked him; you fasted and wept for the child when it was still alive, but when the child died you got up and ate!

612

He replied: When the child was still alive I fasted and wept because I thought that—who knows?—the Lord might graciously allow the child to live. But now he is dead; why should I fast? Can I bring him back again? I am going to him, but he will never come back to me."

SHEMONEH ESREH   שְׁמוֹנֶה עֶשְׂרֵה

THE *Shemoneh Esreh* prayer is the central element in the three daily services: *Shaharith, Minhah,* and *Ma'ariv.* It is spoken of in the Talmud as *Tefillah,* the prayer par excellence, on account of its importance and its antiquity. According to tradition, it was composed by the members of the Great Assembly who flourished at the early period of the Second Temple.

Originally, the *Shemoneh Esreh,* denoting eighteen, consisted of eighteen benedictions; in its present form, however, there are nineteen. The addition of the paragraph concerning the slanderers and enemies of the people was made toward the end of the first century at the direction of Rabban Gamaliel II, head of the Sanhedrin at Yavneh.

The Talmud offers a variety of reasons for the number eighteen. It corresponds to the eighteen times God is mentioned in Psalm 29 as well as in the *Shema.* The three patriarchs of the Jewish people, Abraham, Isaac and Jacob are mentioned together eighteen times in the Hebrew Bible. The number eighteen is also said to correspond to the essential eighteen vertebrae of the spinal column (Berakhoth 28b).

The *Shemoneh Esreh* is now generally referred to as the *Amidah* (standing), so called because it is recited in a standing posture. The name *Amidah* accurately describes this prayer for Sabbaths and festivals, when it consists of seven blessings only. At the *Shaharith* and the *Minhah* services, the *Shemoneh Esreh* or the *Amidah* is first recited in an undertone by each person in the congregation, and then aloud by the reader on behalf of the congregation. The reader's repetition is designed for the benefit of those who cannot read the *Amidah* for themselves. The *Amidah* is not repeated by the reader during the *Ma'ariv* service, because it was held by the sages of the Talmud that the evening *Amidah* was optional and not obligatory.

On Sabbaths and festivals, the first three blessings and the last three are the same in all forms of the *Amidah.* The thirteen petitions of the weekday *Shemoneh Esreh* are eliminated on the ground that no

613

personal requests may be made during Sabbaths and festivals. Upon reciting these petitions, a person is reminded of his failings and troubles, and on the days of rest one ought to be cheerful and not saddened by worries.

The middle paragraphs of the weekday *Shemoneh Esreh* contain petitions for the fulfillment of our needs. They plead for wisdom, repentance, forgiveness, deliverance, healing, prosperity, ingathering of the dispersed, restoration of justice, suppression of tyranny, protection of the upright, rebuilding of Jerusalem, the messianic era, and the acceptance of prayer. All these petitions are on behalf of the entire community; petitions for personal needs may be inserted in their appropriate place, as when one reaches the eighth benediction which reads: "Heal us, O Lord, and we shall be healed; save us, and we shall be saved. . ."

After the *Shemoneh Esreh*, the following meditation is added: "My God, guard my tongue from evil, and my lips from speaking falsehood. . . Open my heart to thy Torah, that my soul may follow thy commands. . . Save with thy right hand and answer me. May the words of my mouth and the meditation of my heart be acceptable in thy presence, O Lord, my Redeemer." This is taken substantially from the Talmud (Berakhoth 17a).

EXODUS   שְׁמוֹת

THE book of Exodus carries forward the history begun in Genesis and tells of the formation of Israel as a people. It consists of two parts: the liberation of Israel from bondage in Egypt about three thousand two hundred years ago, and the consecration upon Mount Sinai of the so-called kingdom of priests. Exodus contains the idyllic story of the birth of Moses, the divine revelation through the burning bush, and the detailed description of bitter contests between Moses and Pharaoh. Moses is pictured as a man of profound contemplation and decisive action, who finds God in the wilderness and hears his voice in the thunder. Guided by God, Moses takes into the wilderness the hopeless remnant of a despairing people and brings out of it a united nation.

Exodus, the second book of the Torah, is second to no other book of the Holy Scriptures in its interest and religious significance. It describes the oppression and slavery in Egypt as well as the liberation, which came to the people of Israel in the hour of their greatest need

614

and despair. The dramatic account of the giving of the **Ten** Commandments and the basic laws of the Torah are the most outstanding features of the book.

The plagues in the narrative portion of Exodus are miraculously intensified forms of the diseases or other natural occurrences to which Egypt is still liable. Frogs, gnats, flies and locusts are common pests in the country. The Latin historian Pliny, writing in the first century, notes the recurring pests of mosquitoes, frogs, flies and gnats due to the seasonal inundations of the Nile. Epidemics accompanied by a great mortality are frequently mentioned by various writers, both ancient and modern.

The darkness that lasted three days in Egypt was, according to some scholars. the result of the desert sand storms; the hot wind, called *hamsin,* often fills the air with thick clouds of dust and forces people to stay indoors. During the annual inundation of the Nile, the water assumes a reddish color because of the red grass brought down from the Abyssinian mountains. An unusual combination of natural calamities materially facilitated the Israelite departure from Egypt. The terrified Egyptians were finally convinced that they had better set their Hebrew slaves free. Increasing in severity, the plagues brought increasing pressure upon the Egyptians until they yielded.

The book of Exodus is replete with highly ethical concepts and laws. God's deep interest in human affairs is reflected in each of its narratives. He is represented as revealing himself to men and speaking with them intimately. The Ten Commandments, otherwise known as the Decalogue, and the laws contained in the three chapters which are referred to as the Book of the Covenant (Exodus 20-23), are the quintessence of the remaining portion of the Torah. Excerpts:

"You shall not maltreat a stranger or oppress him, for you were strangers yourselves in the land of Egypt. You shall not afflict a widow or an orphan. . . If you lend money to a poor man, you must not act as a creditor; you must not exact interest from him. If ever you take your neighbor's garment in pledge, you shall give it back to him before the sun goes down; for that is the only covering he has. . . You shall not revile the judges, nor shall you curse any of the authorities of your people. You shall not utter a false report. . . You shall not follow a majority to do wrong; nor shall you be partial to a poor man in his lawsuit. You shall not violate the rights of a poor man in his lawsuit. . . You shall never accept a bribe, for a bribe blinds the clear-sighted and perverts a just cause. . ."

NAMES   שֵׁמוֹת

THE relation of name to thing plays an important part in the story of creation. Name and thing are one. "When the Lord God had formed out of the ground all the beasts of the field and the birds of the air, he brought them to the man to see what he would call them; whatever the man called any living creature, that was to be its name" (Genesis 2:19). That is, man would establish his dominion over the creatures of the earth by giving them names. To know the name is to know the essence of a thing; to know is to have power over the object. Adam's utterance of the names of the beasts put those beasts in subjection to him.

The close relationship between man and woman is conveyed by Adam's utterance: "She shall be called woman (אשה), for from man (איש) she has been taken." This sets forth the social and moral relation between man and woman. Since the woman is formed out of the man's rib, she depends upon him; it is her duty to be at hand, ready at all times to be a help to her husband; it is the husband's natural duty ever to defend and cherish his wife as part of his own self. In biblical times, the names of persons were not only significant, but their meaning was known to those who spoke Hebrew.

A large majority of the 2,800 personal names mentioned in the Hebrew Bible convey a special meaning, though the meanings of the remainder have become obscured in the course of time. Frequently the personal names are composite, referring to God either at the beginning or at the end (Jonathan, Elḥanan, Ḥananel, Elyakim, Azaryah, Raphael). Though there was an objection to foreign names among the Jewish people, legend reports that Simon the high priest promised Alexander the Great that all the children of the priestly family born in the year following his visit to Jerusalem would be named Alexander after him (Yosippon). A considerable proportion of Greek and Roman names are contained in the Talmud.

In 1787 the Jews of the Austrian empire were ordered by law to adopt surnames. If they refused, the registration commissioners were empowered to confer names of their own selection. Place-names were turned into surnames. A new settler was often named after the town or country from which he had come during the many wanderings of the Jews in the Middle Ages. Such names as Cohen and Levi, originally descriptive of descent, became surnames. Names like Mendelssohn (the son of Mendel) in the eighteenth century are reminiscent of names like Maimonides (son of Maimon) and Naḥmanides (son of Naḥman) in the twelfth and thirteenth centuries. They are illustrations of the practice of converting the father's personal name into a surname. Occupations suggested many names. Thus Jewish surnames are patronymic, local, occupational, descriptive, and nicknames.

Following is a sampling list of biblical names and various forms of Jewish surnames derived from the original Hebrew.

Aaron: Aarons, Aaronson, Aaronoff, Aaronovich. Abraham: Abrahams, Abrahamson, Abrams, Abramovitz. David: Davidson, Davis, Davison. Jacob: Jacobson, Jacobs, Jacoby. Menaḥem: Mendel, Mendelssohn.

BETH-SHOEVAH FEAST   שִׂמְחַת בֵּית הַשּׁוֹאֵבָה

THE Mishnah reports a proverbial saying to the effect that whoever has not witnessed the *Beth-Shoevah* celebration has never seen real rejoicing (Sukkah 5:1). The reference is to the water-feast which began on the first day of *Sukkoth* at nightfall and lasted till the following morning during the period of the Second Temple in Jerusalem. The outer court of the Temple was brilliantly illuminated for the occasion. A torchlight procession, dances and singing followed while the women were looking on from their galleries. During the day, the great feature was the procession which accompanied the priest who had been allotted the duty and privilege of drawing water for the libation ceremony from the pool of Siloam in Jerusalem.

Beth Shoevah signifies the place of drawing water, alluding to the pool of Siloam. Since the festival of *Sukkoth* falls at the time when the first autumnal rains are due in Eretz Yisrael, it has been suggested that the water-feast symbolized the people's petition for rain. According to a talmudic statement, it alluded to prophetic inspiration. The term water is often used symbolically. In Numbers 24:7, the constant flow of water is symbolic of numerous descendants. The Torah is frequently compared to water that purifies. The prayer for rain (*Geshem*) is recited in the synagogue on the eighth day of *Sukkoth*.

The precise origin of the popular *Beth-Shoeva* celebration is unknown. As soon as the first day of *Sukkoth* came to an end, the people flocked to the outer court of the Temple, known as *Ezrath Nashim* (women's court), where a barrier had been erected across to keep men and women

617

apart. Large golden candelabras were fed from vessels of oil by youthful priests. So bright were the flames that every street in Jerusalem shone with their light. A torch dance took place, in which men of piety and renown participated. At daybreak, the procession left the Temple and proceeded to the Siloam pool. A golden jug was filled from its water and brought back to the Temple. The water was poured upon the altar along with a libation of wine. The libation of water marked the beginning of the rainy season in Eretz Yisrael.

SIMḤATH TORAH   שִׂמְחַת תּוֹרָה

THE name *Simḥath Torah* (rejoicing of the Torah) was not known in talmudic times as the name of a special festival, marking the annual completion of the Torah readings. It came into use presumably around the ninth century in Babylonia, where the one-year-cycle for the reading of the Five Books of Moses prevailed. The seven processions with the Torah scrolls on *Simḥath Torah* became customary in the sixteenth century. In Eretz Yisrael, the *Simḥath-Torah* celebration coincides with *Shemini Atsereth*, the eighth day of *Sukkoth*.

On *Simḥath Torah*, the last section of the Torah is read for the *Ḥathan Torah* (חתן תורה), followed by the *Ḥathan Bereshith* (חתן בראשית), for whom the *beginning* of the Torah is read. This procedure is in keeping with the idea that Torah study is endless. Special attention is paid to the children who come to the synagogue where they receive flags depicting biblical scenes and are given apples and sweets.

At the end of each of the seven *hakkafoth* (processional circuits), joined by children carrying flags with appropriate biblical verses, there is a great deal of singing and dancing on the part of those honored with carrying the Torah scrolls. The *hakkafoth* continue long enough until every man has carried a *Torah* around the synagogue.

SHEMITTAH   שְׁמִטָּה

THE term *shemittah* used in connection with the Sabbatical Year comes from a verb which means to detach, to draw away, let drop. Hence, שנת שמטה (Deuteronomy 15:9; 31:10) denotes the year of a relaxation of debts, the Sabbatical Year during which the land was to lie fallow and be withdrawn from cultivation. The Torah commands: "Six years

618

you may sow your field, six years you may prune your vineyard, gathering in its produce. But in the seventh year the land shall have a complete rest ... when you may neither sow your field nor prune your vineyard. The aftergrowth of your harvest you shall not reap, nor shall you pick the grapes of your untrimmed vines. . . While the land has its sabbath, all the produce will be food equally for yourself and for your male and female servants, for your hired help and the tenants who live with you, and likewise for your livestock and the wild animals on your land" (Leviticus 25:1-7).

As long as the produce of the Sabbatical Year remains on the field, it remains available to everyone. In Exodus 23:11, the Torah says: "But the seventh year you shall let the land lie untilled and unharvested, that the poor among you may eat of it and the beasts of the field may eat what the poor leave; so also shall you do in regard to your vineyard and your olive grove." In Deuteronomy 15:1-3, the Torah commands: "At the end of every seven-year period you shall have a relaxation of debts. . . Every creditor shall release his claim on what he has loaned his neighbor; he shall not press his neighbor for payment. . ." In an agricultural community, where a debt would be contracted only in a case of poverty or misfortune, the loan was considered to be an act of benevolence rather than a business transaction.

When economic life became more complex, debts incurred in business transactions belonged to a different category and could not fairly be cancelled. Hillel instituted, therefore, a method for the adjustment of the law in order to secure creditors against the operation of *Shemittah*. This method was known as *Prozbul*, a legal instrument drawn up by the creditor and attested by the seals of the judges, empowering the court to collect the debt due to him at any time he saw fit. Deuteronomy 15:4 was interpreted by Hillel, who lived in the century preceding the common era, to exclude from the operation of the Sabbatical Year debts that had already been secured by order of the court before the advent of *Shemittah*.

SHEMINI ATSERETH   שְׁמִינִי עֲצֶרֶת

In the Hebrew Prayerbook, both the eighth and ninth days of *Sukkoth* are called יום השמיני חג העצרת, though the ninth day is generally spoken of as the day of *Simhath Torah*. In Eretz Yisrael, where the ninth day is not observed as a feast day, the Torah celebration takes place on the eighth day. The original meaning of the term *atsereth* is festive assembly (Leviticus 23:36; Deuteronomy 16:8), but in talmudic literature it is applied in the sense of conclusion, so that *Shavuoth* is referred to as *atsereth* because it is the concluding festival to *Pesaḥ* just as the *Ḥag ha-Atsereth* is the concluding festival to *Sukkoth*.

The prayer for rain (תפלת גשם) is recited as part of the *Musaf* service on *Shemini Atsereth*; it solemnly introduces the formula משיב הרוח ומוריד הגשם, which is retained in the *Amidah* or *Shemoneh Esreh* prayer until the first day of *Pesaḥ*.

SHEMA YISRAEL שְׁמַע יִשְׂרָאֵל

R<small>ECITED</small> as the confession of the Jewish faith, the verse *Shema Yisrael* (Deuteronomy 6:4) sums up the first and second commandments of the Decalogue, and should be rendered: Hear, O Israel, the Lord is our God, the Lord is One. The Mishnah refers to the reciting of the *Shema* as the acceptance of the yoke of the divine majesty (Berakhoth 2:5). We are told that Rabbi Yehudah ha-Nasi, when preoccupied with his studies, put his hand over his eyes and recited the first verse of the *Shema* in silence (Berakhoth 13b). The reciting of the *Shema* morning and evening is discussed in the Mishnah as an established custom.

The *Shema* was ever on the lips of the Jewish martyrs. Rabbi Akiva endured the greatest tortures while his flesh was being torn with iron combs and died pronouncing the last word, אחד (One), with his last breath. *Shema Yisrael* has been the password by which Jews recognize one another throughout the world. It has been asserted that anyone who has not seen a Jew say *Shema Yisrael* at the *Ne'ilah* service or at the confession before death has never seen religious ecstasy. The last letters of שמע and אחד form the word עד (witness) and are written large in the Hebrew Bible, meaning that he who recites the *Shema* bears witness to the Oneness of God before the entire world. The six words of the *Shema* have become the battle-cry of the Jewish people for more than twenty-five centuries.

The entire passage of the *Shema* has been depicted as a chapter in the Bible which we inscribe on our doorposts and bear on our forehead during prayer. It is a chapter which every mother teaches to her child as soon as it begins to lisp its first words, a chapter which for

620

centuries has sweetened the last hours of dying; so rich in its simplicity, so expressive in its conciseness, that it sums up our principal duties and awakens in us abundant memories and thoughts, all the glories of our past and all the hopes of our future.

The verse *Shema Yisrael*, consisting of six words, is always accompanied by a six-word response which is not found in the Bible. It was used in the Temple daily during the priestly blessing. On *Yom Kippur*, the priests and the people who were standing in the Temple court made this response upon hearing the four-letter name of God pronounced by the high priest ten times in the course of the service. Since it is not taken from the Bible, though it is similar to the expression ברוך שם כבוד לעולם in Psalms 72:19, it is said in an undertone in order to distinguish it from the biblical passages of the *Shema*, which are borrowed from the books of Deuteronomy and Numbers. On *Yom Kippur*, however, it is recited aloud in remembrance of the Temple service.

CHANGING THE NAME   שִׁנּוּי הַשֵּׁם

THE custom of changing a person's name as an aid to his recovery from illness is mentioned in the Talmud as one of the four things which annul the decree sealing a person's fate, namely: charity, prayer, change of name, and change of deeds (Rosh Hashanah 16b). Rabbi Yehudah he-Ḥasid of the thirteenth century states in his *Sefer Ḥasidim*: "If one is dangerously sick, his name should be changed to reverse the decree." The assumption is that the previous name symbolizing the essence of its bearer becomes non-existent when he receives a new name, which transforms him into another person.

Later it became customary to retain the original name and add another to it, one that signifies the recovery of the patient, such as *Ḥayyim* (life), *Raphael* (God heals), *Paltiel* (God rescues), *Azriel* (God helps), *Shalom* (peace). The name is given in the synagogue.

SHAʿATNEZ   שַׁעַטְנֵז

THE wearing of a fabric consisting of a mixture of wool and linen, called *shaʿatnez*, is forbidden in Leviticus 19:19 and Deuteronomy 22:11. Like the interbreeding of different species of animals and the planting together of different kinds of seeds, the wearing of a garment composed of a mixture of wool and linen is regarded as contrary to the divinely appointed order of nature, and as suggestive of the un-natural vice mentioned in Leviticus 18:22-23.

"Nature does not rejoice in the union of things that are not in their nature alike " (Josephus). Since God is not the author of confusion, the natural distinctions he himself has appointed are designed to be respected. *Sha'atnez* may also allude to the unchaste practices con-nected with certain idolatrous rites. According to the Mishnah, the word *sha'atnez* is a compound of the Hebrew equivalents of pressed, woven and twisted (שוע טווי נוז).

SHEKI'ATH HA-ḤAMMAH שְׁקִיעַת הַחַמָּה

Sunset, ushering in Sabbaths and festivals, is often referred to by the Hebrew phrase *sheki'ath ha-ḥammah*, or *sheki'ah* in its shorter form. The lighting of the Sabbath candles is customarily performed eighteen minutes before sunset. According to the *Kitzur Shulḥan Arukh* 75:1, the Sabbath candles should be lit at least half an hour before the stars appear in the sky.

In honor of the Sabbath, as many candles as possible are lit, but never less than two. The two candles allude to שמור (remember) and זכור (observe), which words introduce the divine command concerning the Sabbath (Exodus 20:8; Deuteronomy 5:12). There are some who light ten candles, corresponding to the Ten Commandments, while others light seven, corresponding to the seven days of creation.

SHTADLAN שְׁתַדְלָן

The title *shtadlan*, applied to a representative of the medieval Jewish community with access to high dignitaries and legislative bodies, is derived from the word שדל. It denotes the use of persuasive words making an effort and striving. The *shtadlan* in medieval Germany, Poland and other countries, was chosen by virtue of his eloquence, wealth, good manners and the ability to judge human nature, to plead the cause of his people before the ruling authorities in order to allevi-ate discriminatory measures against the Jewish inhabitants.

622

PSALMS

תְּהִלִּים ת

OVER one-sixth of the Bible is written in poetic form, and about one-half of that has been sung. The Psalms have been on the lips of more people throughout the centuries than any other written compositions. They represent the highest product of the religious poetry of all the nations. They stand out unique among the prayers of the whole world by the majesty of their language and their simplicity.

The word *Psalms* is derived from the Greek version of the Bible, the Septuagint, where it is used in the sense of songs accompanied by the playing of musical instruments. The book of Psalms, consisting of a hundred and fifty stirring hymns, is the first book in the third division of the Bible known as Hagiographa (Sacred Writings). The Hebrew title of this book, *Tehillim*, means praises. The Psalms are, indeed, songs of praise arranged to be sung to the accompaniment of musical instruments.

The keynote of the Psalms is simplicity of heart, faith in God, and good conduct. In the Psalms we find the human heart in all its moods and emotions—in penitence, in danger, in desolation, and in triumph. They are as varied as is human life; they are enlightened in their ethics as they are lofty in their religious spirit. Many of them were used in the Temple services at Jerusalem. The book of Psalms is regarded as a golden treasury of the human spirit, the richest collection of religious poetry in the world.

Tradition ascribes the Psalms to king David. They convey ecstatic expressions of man's trust in God, petitions for personal and national deliverance, reflections upon the moral structure of the universe, and vivid word-pictures of human nature. Psalm 15 has a perfect description of a good man. According to the Talmud, the six hundred and thirteen precepts of the Torah are summed up in this psalm, that is to say, the moral purpose of the Torah is clearly defined here: "O Lord, who may dwell in thy temple, who may reside in Thy sanctuary? The blameless man who acts uprightly, and speaks truth in his heart. He neither slanders nor hurts nor insults his neighbor. . . He keeps his word at his own risk, and does not retract. He lends money without usury, and does not accept a bribe against the innocent. He who does these things shall never be disturbed.

The description of a storm at sea is the part of Psalm 107 often recited by seafaring men. The storm is of exceptional violence, and the sailors realize in terror that they are in extreme danger. Their technical skill has become useless; they are at the mercy of the sea until the roar of the storm dies away, and nothing but a gentle, whispering wind remains.

Psalms 19 and 104 represent the highest human expression of the innumerable wonders of God's creation as they appear every day before our eyes. If only we had the eyes to see and the wisdom to understand, says Emerson, a tree or a star would strike us as the most amazing of miracles ... if only we were given a single chance to observe it. Such psalms help us to open our eyes to the glory of the world as God's handiwork. Psalm 19 has been epitomized in the saying: "The starry sky above me and the moral law within me are two things which fill the soul with ever new and increasing admiration and reverence." It has been declared that it is worthwhile studying the Hebrew language for te ı years in order to read Psalm 104 in the original Hebrew text.

The book of Psalms represents seven types of poetic expression. It contains hymns, thanksgivings, elegies, pilgrim songs, meditations, historical poems, and poems about nature. The hymns, objective in character, are designed for public worship; they are introduced with such opening verses as: "Come, let us sing to the Lord! Praise the Lord! It is good to sing to our God!" The thanksgiving psalms usually begin with an exultant introduction: "I will bless the Lord at all times. . . O give thanks to the Lord, for he is good." The elegies, or psalms of subjective character, are poems of lamentation, outcries against trouble and sorrow, that concern individuals as well as an entire people.

Psalm 114 is historical: "When Israel went out of Egypt . . . the sea beheld and fled; the Jordan turned backward." Psalm 104 celebrates the divine glory as seen in the forces of nature: "Lord my God, thou art great indeed! Thou art clothed with majesty and glory, robed in light as with a cloak. . . Thou makest the winds thy messengers, and flaming fire thy servants. . . Thou sendest forth streams into the valleys; they run between the mountains; they furnish drink for all the beasts of the field. . . Thou raisest grass for the cattle, and vegetation for men's use, producing bread from the earth, and wine that cheers man's heart. . ."

It has been asserted that the Psalms have taught men religion not by precept nor by preachment, but by example. They are religion. They breathe religion. They are religion alive, at work, religion re-

624

flected in the experience of men. It is the soul of religion that speaks in the Psalms, in accents clear and melodious. There is the accent of trust, of joy, of worship, of wonder and of triumph. On all possible occasions, the Psalms have been used as a source of help, inspiration, and spiritual expression. Indeed, they have been the voice, as well as the companion, of humanity. They were the daily food of the Jew. Even before they could become a mainstay and inspiration to others, they were such to the Jew. They sprang from the soul of the Jew, from his experience and his needs. Volumes might be written on what part and influence the Psalms have had in Jewish life as well as in the life of humanity in general.

SINCERITY   תּוֹכוֹ כְּבָרוֹ

SPEAKING against deception and make-believe, Maimonides sums up the Jewish concept of sincerity by declaring that it is unlawful to use flattery and "smooth speech"; one must not say one thing and mean another. Instead, he should possess the quality described in two Hebrew words: תוכו כברו (like heart, like face). He must not urge a person to dine with him, knowing that he will refuse; he must not offer a gift, knowing that it will not be accepted (Ḥullin 94a). Any indirect solicitation of unmerited thanks spells deception and is forbidden (Yad, De'oth 2:6). Regarding those who feign words of friendship, Psalm 5:10 reads: "In their mouth there is no sincerity; their heart teems with treacheries; their throat is an open grave; they flatter with their tongue." Similarly, Psalm 55:22 depicts a cunning flatterer: "Softer than butter is his speech, but war is in his heart, his words are smoother than oil, but they are drawn swords."

Talmudic tradition reports that Alexander Yannai, who reigned in Judea from 103 to 76 before the common era, reversed his inimical policy toward the Pharisees shortly before he died, and told his wife Salome Alexandra who succeeded him: "Fear not the Pharisees or the non-Pharisees, but the hypocrites who ape the Pharisees" (Sotah 22b—

אל תתיראי מן הפרושין ולא ממי שאינן פרושין אלא מן הצבועין שדומין (לפרושין שמעשיהן כמעשה זמרי ומבקשין שכר כפנחס.

Quite different is the kind of deception denounced by Rabbi Samson Raphael Hirsch (1808-1888), who writes: "Why conceal the fact that you are a Jew? Be a real Jew, obeying the law of justice and love, and you will be respected. Be just, truthful and loving to all, as the

תוכו כברו

Torah teaches you. Give food to the hungry and clothes to the naked; comfort those who mourn and care for the sick; give counsel and help to all in sorrow and need... Let us strive with all our power to reach the height of perfection! Let us go back to the sources of Judaism, and study them in order to live by them" (*Nineteen Letters*).

REBUKE   תּוֹכָחָה

IN prohibiting hatred and vengeance, the Torah says: "You shall not hate your brother in your heart; you shall reprove your fellow man, and do not incur sin because of him. Take no revenge and cherish no grudge against your fellow men, but you shall love your neighbor as yourself" (Leviticus 19:17-18). The command הוכח תוכיח את עמיתך has been explained to the effect that if you see that your neighbor has committed misdeeds, you must reason with him and convince him where he is wrong. This should be done privately and gently, for "he who puts anyone to shame in public has no share in the world to come." You should never call him by any insulting name, or say anything that is likely to embarrass him (*Yad, Deoth* 6:6-8).

It has been pointed out, however, that the requirement of admonishing a wrongdoer is applicable only where there is hope that the offender will refrain from transgressing; otherwise, one is absolved from his duty to reprove. "You are not bound to reprove the wicked man who is your enemy, as it is written: He who corrects an arrogant man gets himself abuse... Do not reprove an arrogant man, or he will hate you; reprove a wise man, and he will love you (Proverbs 9:7-8; *Seder Eliyyahu Rabbah*, chapter 19).

PUNISHMENT   תּוֹכֵיחוֹת

THE exhortations contained in various biblical passages are composed of the same ideas. Thus we read in the Torah: "If you live in accordance with my precepts and are careful to observe my commandments, I will give you rain in due season, so that the land will bear its crops, and the trees their fruit; your threshing will last till vintage time, and your vintage till the time of sowing, and you will have food to eat in abundance, so that you will dwell securely in your land. I will establish peace in the land, that you may lie down to rest without anxiety...

626

But if you do not heed me and do not keep all these commandments. . .
I will punish you. . . You will sow your seed in vain, for your enemies
will consume the crop. . ." (Leviticus 26:3-43).

A similar warning (תוכחה) is found in Deuteronomy 27:15-26, where
the blessings for obedience immediately follow the curses for disobedience (28:1-14), and then the rest of the chapter (28:15-68) contains
an enumeration of evils for disobedience (sickness and defeat, exile,
fruitless labors, invasion and siege, plagues). It is now customary not
to call up anyone to the Torah when these passages are read in an
undertone. The Torah reader (ba'al keriah) recites the prescribed benedictions before and after the reading of these terrifying passages,
which are phrased in the second person. The aliyyah is given to the
reader of the Torah himself. In II Kings 19:3, the word תוכחה
occurs as a synonym of צרה (distress).

JEWISH HISTORY   תּוֹלְדוֹת יִשְׂרָאֵל

The biblical books represent an advanced state in the revolution
of historiography, for they aim to present not merely a record of past
events but to construct a philosophy of history. This historic art
was maintained on a high level throughout the prophetic period and
was continued through the Second Commonwealth in the writings of
the Apocrypha, notably in the Books of the Maccabees, and reached
the final climax in the monumental works of Josephus.

Mention must be made of the earliest Hebrew chronicle, the *Seder
Olam* (סדר עולם), dating back to the second century; then the *Seder
Olam Zuta* (סדר עולם זוטא), concerning a branch of the Exilarchate
family; the *Seder Tannaim va-Amoraim* (סדר תנאים ואמוראים) of the
ninth century; the *Iggereth Rav Sherira Gaon* (אגרת רב שרירא גאון) of
the tenth century; and the *Sefer ha-Kabbalah* (ספר הקבלה) by Abraham ibn Daud of the twelfth century. Ibn Daud's *Sefer ha-Kabbalah* is
singularly important for the history of the Sephardic Jews.

The *Sefer Yuḥasin* (ספר יוחסין) by Abraham Zacuto, scientist-
chronicler of the early sixteenth century, who had been forced to flee
from Portugal in 1496 and finally settled in Turkey where he died
after 1510, is an account of Jewish genealogies from the earliest times,
containing much valuable information on Jewish literary history.

Concerning Zacuto's chronological history of the Jews, Isaac d'Israeli (1766-1848), father of Lord Beaconsfield, declared: "The *Book*

of Geneologies of Zacuto is the most important of Jewish histories; but it has not met with the luck of a translator."

The *Shevet Yehudah* (שבט יהודה) by Judah ibn Verga, who died a martyr at the hands of the Inquisition in Lisbon, Portugal, at the end of the fifteenth century, records many of the persecutions undergone by the Jewish people in various times and countries. This work, entitled *Judah's Rod*, was augmented with narratives of later persecutions by his son Solomon ibn Verga and by his grandson Joseph ibn Verga.

The *Emek ha-Bakha* (עמק הבכא) by Joseph ha-Kohen (1496-1576), a physician, who experienced in his own person the miseries of the period, is a martyrology known in the English translation as *The Vale of Tears*, published by Leeser. It covers many centuries of suffering. This work by Joseph ha-Kohen, who practised medicine in Genoa, Italy, is of particular value for the study of the sixteenth-century period in Jewish history.

The *Tzemaḥ David* (צמח דוד) by David Gans (1541-1613), astronomer and historian, who settled in Prague in 1564, comprises a Jewish history and a general history based on earlier sources.

The *Yeven Metsulah* (יון מצולה) by Nathan Hannover, kabbalist and historian, who was killed in 1683 during a Turkish siege, is looked upon as a major historical source for the Cossack pogroms of 1648-1652. More than seven hundred Jewish communities in the Ukraine were annihilated and hundreds of thousands of Jews were murdered. The title יון מצולה (deep swamp) is borrowed from Psalm 69:3; it alludes to the hostile *Yevanim* (יונים) with whom the Russians are denominationally identified. A number of impressive kabbalistic prayers have been taken from Hannover's *Shaaré Tsiyyon* and inserted in the Prayerbook.

Recent Jewish historians (Graetz, Dubnow, Baron, Baer, Zeitlin, Finkelstein, Neuman, Grayzel) have made ample use of the medieval Jewish chronicles as part of their source material for the writing of their respective histories of the Jews.

TOSAFOTH   תּוֹסָפוֹת

A school of talmudic scholars in France and Germany, continuing Rashi's work in the course of two centuries, composed critical and explanatory glosses in the Babylonian Talmud. They are known as

Tosafoth (additions). The first of the *Baalé Tosafoth* were the sons-in-law and grandsons of Rashi as well as his immediate students, whose methods of interpreting the Talmud, by pointing out discrepancies in various parts and then harmonizing them, spread to Spain and England. All the *Tosafoth* include quotations from earlier scholars such as Rabbenu Tam and Rashbam, the grandson of Rashi.

All printed editions of the Talmud are provided, as a rule, with the commentary of Rashi and the *Tosafoth* of the tosafists, whose work extended to the end of the fourteenth century. Unlike Rashi's commentary, the *Tosafoth* glosses are not continuous, but are attached to separate passages which present certain difficulties, including divergent readings of doubtful correctness. As additions to the commentary of Rashi, the *Tosafoth* appear in the usual editions of the Babylonian Talmud on the outer margin of the pages.

TOSEFTA   תּוֹסֶפְתָּא

THE Tosefta is a work closely resembling the Mishnah, hence its name which means addition or supplement. It contains a large collection of tannaitic statements of the traditional law (*Halakhah*). The Tosefta consists of six grand divisions or *sedarim*, each of which is subdivided into tractates, chapters, and paragraphs, analoguous to the Mishnah. Though the subjects treated in both Mishnah and Tosefta are practically the same, and the formulation of the basic *Halakhah* is identical, the Tosefta aims at less terseness than the Mishnah and gives a more detailed version of the tannaitic teachings.

There are many theories concerning the relation between the Mishnah and the Tosefta. It has been suggested that the Tosefta is, from the historical point of view, a richly fertile source owing to the fact that it has escaped the censorship which expunged from the Talmud whatever it found offensive to non-Jewish sensibilities. The nucleus of the Tosefta, which in the main runs parallel with the Mishnah, dates from the third century and is usually attributed to Rabbi Ḥiyya and Rabbi Oshaya, contemporaries of Rabbi Judah ha-Nasi who compiled and edited the Mishnah by the year 200. Many critical studies have appeared on the Tosefta recently, notably the searching work of Saul Lieberman, who has written a comprehensive commentary on the first division of the Tosefta. He has edited *Seder Zera'im* on the basis of various manuscripts and first editions.

629

It has been explained that the Mishnah is written with characteristic brevity as an aid to memory, omitting whatever is not absolutely
necessary as to illustrations and text-proofs. The Tosefta, as a supplementary work, contains whatever is regarded as sufficiently important for further study of the *Halakhah* traditions. Hence, the Tosefta
surpasses the Mishnah in size and contents.

Solomon Zeitlin has pointed out that, despite the various attempts
to explain the composition of the Tosefta, the question of its authorship and compilation is still unsolved. "Many of the *halakhoth* in the
Tosefta are in contradiction to those recorded in the Mishnah; others
are merely elaborations. Many *halakhoth* recorded in the Tosefta are
not found in the Mishnah but in Baraithoth in both Talmuds. . . The
Tosefta, though studied by the sages during the Middle Ages, was
never held to be on a par with the Mishnah in authority. . ."

TORAH   תּוֹרָה

THE term *Torah*, signifying guidance and instruction, is primarily applied to the Five Books of Moses or Pentateuch; also, to the whole
body of Judaism's religious-ethical literature. The inaccurate rendering of Torah by *Law* has all along been a barrier, preventing non-Jews
from understanding the ideal which is summed up in the term *Talmud
Torah*, study of *Torah*, characterized in Jewish tradition as excelling
all things. Indeed, *Torah* comprises every field of Jewish culture—
ethics, justice, religion, education. We are told to "study the Torah
again and again, for everything is contained in it" (Avoth 5:25). Fresh
meanings and new approaches to reality are to be discovered in it by
every earnest and thoughtful student. Rabbi Elijah Vilna-Gaon,
whose all-controlling passion was Torah, demanded the widest secular education. declaring that Torah and science go together. It has
been noted that the title "People of the Book" does not indicate
solely Israel's devotion to the Bible, the Book of Books, but their unquenchable thirst for learning in the broadest sense of the word.

In talmudic literature, the word Torah includes both the written
lore and the oral lore (תורה שבכתב, תורה שבעל פה). The written
lore is contained in the Pentateuch, and the oral lore consists of the
traditional interpretations and amplifications handed down by word
of mouth from generation to generation which are now embodied in
the talmudic-midrashic works. Jewish survival after the destruction of

630

political independence has been attributed to Jewish devotion to Torah, both written and oral, which has served as the center of Jewish life through the ages. The sixth chapter of *Pirké Avoth* is known as *Kinyan Torah* (Acquisition of Torah) because its subject-matter is in praise of the Torah.

Tradition reports that the two forms of Torah, *Torah she-bikhthav* and *Torah she-b'al peh*, have existed side by side ever since the revelation at Mount Sinai. The oral lore, which was not committed to writing during the centuries preceding the redaction of the Mishnah, was transmitted orally by a chain of sages and carriers of tradition. According to modern scholarship, the oral lore, including *Halakhah* and *Aggadah*, was constantly developing in addition to the teachings of the Pentateuch during an extended period. The following observation of Josephus is considered of special importance in this respect: "The Pharisees have made many ordinances among the people, according to the tradition of their fathers, whereof there is nothing written in the laws of Moses; for which cause they are rejected by the sect of the Sadducees, who affirm that they ought to keep the written ordinances, and not to observe those that are grounded upon the tradition of the fathers" (*Antiquities*, XIII, 10:6).

Study of the Torah is expected even if one is extremely poor. "Eat bread and salt, drink water by measure, sleep on the bare ground, and live a life of hardship while you toil in the *Torah*" (Pirké Avoth 6:4). "Every Jew must study Torah, whether poor or rich, healthy or ailing, young or old. Even a beggar who goes from door to door, and a man who has a wife and children to support, must devote time to Torah, for it is written: You shall study it day and night (*Yad, Talmud Torah* 1:8).

The Talmud relates that Rabbi Akiva kept spreading a knowledge of the Torah in the Jewish communities despite the Roman decree against Jewish religious study. When he was asked by a man named Pappus: Akiva, are you not afraid? Are you not aware of the mortal danger of being caught and slain by the Roman authorities? He replied: Let me tell you a story. A fox was walking on the brink of a stream, and saw fish running to and fro in the clear water. Said the fox to the fish: Why do you run so? And they retorted: We run because we fear the fisherman's nets. Come up on the dry land, said the fox, and live with me in safety, even as my forefathers once lived in safety with yours. But the fish said: Water is our natural home. If we are not safe there, how much less safe should we be on land, where we must surely die. It is exactly so with us Jews, Rabbi Akiva continued. The Torah is our life and the length of our days. Though we are in great danger while studying the Torah, we would surely disappear and be no more if we were to give up its study (Berakhoth 61b).

PALE OF SETTLEMENT תְּחוּם הַמּוֹשָׁב

DURING the czarist regime, the Jews suffered restrictions in rights of residence. They were confined in the so-called Pale of Settlement, an enclosed territory comprising certain districts of Russia beyond which they were not permitted to reach out. This resulted in great Jewish suffering from living in crowded cities with limited economic opportunities. At the end of the nineteenth century, the Pale which contained four percent of the Russian empire held ninety-four percent of the Jewish population. The purpose of the Pale, consisting mainly of Polish territory, was ostensibly to free the Russian merchant from Jewish competition. Jews were permitted permanent residence in Poland, Lithuania, White Russia, Ukraine, Bessarabia, and Crimea. There were expulsions, however, from Yalta, Crimea, in 1893, and from various other places as late as 1910. The Pale of Settlement, which was really a large-scale ghetto, was legally abolished in 1917.

TEḤUM SHABBATH תְּחוּם שַׁבָּת

CONCERNING the food eaten by the Israelites during the forty years' sojourn in the wilderness, the Torah declares: "The Lord has given you the Sabbath ... let no man go out of his place on the seventh day" (Exodus 16:29). A double portion of manna was collected on Fridays, so that the people could observe the Sabbath by resting from the labor of gathering food. The law of *teḥum shabbath*, the boundary beyond which one must not walk on the Sabbath, which is two thousand cubits outside the town limits, is based on the traditional interpretation of Exodus 16:29.

The *teḥum shabbath*, or Sabbath limit, is reckoned in every direction of the settlement, and can be extended by another two thousand cubits by means of an *eruv teḥumin* (intermingling of Sabbath limits): a quantity of food, enough for two meals, is placed two thousand cubits from the town boundary, so as to extend the *teḥum shabbath* by

632

that distance. This legal fiction is allowed only when one desires to perform a *mitzvah*, such as *brith milah*, at a place which is distant from the outskirts of his town by a double *tehum shabbath*.

RESURRECTION   תְּחִיַּת הַמֵּתִים

IT HAS been noted that the doctrine of Israel's messianic redemption is connected with the doctrine of resurrection. It is supported by the following biblical utterances: "I will open your graves and bring you out of your graves" (Ezekiel 37:12). "Your dead shall live, their corpses shall rise; awake and sing, you who lie in the dust" (Isaiah 26:19). These verses have been interpreted in the sense of a national restoration, surpassing all expectation. Ezekiel predicts that the dead nation will come to life again. In a striking and beautiful vision, he is transported into a valley full of dry bones. As he prophesies to them they come together into complete skeletons, which become covered with flesh and skin. Then the wind blows upon the inanimate bodies and they come to life. The prophecy refers to a revival of the dead nation, of which the exiles seemed to be the scattered remains.

During the Second Commonwealth, the belief in the resurrection of the body, in contradistinction to the immortality of the soul, became a fundamental doctrine of the Pharisees; they held that the soul and the body would, in the future world, be reunited, reconstituting the original person, who would stand in judgment before God and receive reward or punishment according to his good or bad conduct during life. According to talmudic-midrashic statements, the righteous buried in other lands will roll through subterranean channels to Eretz Yisrael, where God will breathe into them a spirit of life, and they will arise (Kethubboth 11a). It was argued that if a grain of wheat, buried naked, sprouts forth in many robes, how much more so the righteous! (Sanhedrin 90b). According to Mishnah Sanhedrin 10:1, he who says that there is no resurrection of the dead must be counted among those who have no share in the future world.

Ever since the Maccabean period, the pious people of all generations have maintained a firm belief not only in the immortality of the soul but also in the miracle of resurrection, which has been compared to the annual revival of plant-life after winter. Maimonides incorporated the belief in resurrection in his Thirteen Principles of Faith, and wrote a special treatise on the subject to disprove those who accused

633

him of heresy regarding this doctrine. He had been understood to have interpreted the talmudic passages figuratively.

The idea of resurrection is expressed in the *Amidah* prayer, where God's omnipotence is recounted: "Thou revivest the dead... Thou causest the wind to blow and the rain to fall..." Rain is considered as great a manifestation of the divine power as the resurrection of the dead (Ta'anith 2a). In the preliminary morning service, the following talmudic passage (Berakhoth 60b) is to be found in the daily Prayerbook: "My God, the soul which thou hast placed within me is pure. Thou hast created it; thou hast formed it; thou hast breathed it into me. Thou preservest it within me; thou wilt take it from me, and restore it to me in the hereafter... Blessed art thou, O Lord, who restorest the souls to the dead." This prayer is interpreted as an expression of gratitude for awakening from sleep to new life.

TAḤKEMONI   תַּחְכְּמוֹנִי

FLUENT and melodious is the Hebrew style of the *Taḥkemoni*, masterpiece of the famous translator and poet Judah al-Ḥarizi (1165-1235), who was born in Spain. For several years he travelled through various lands, including Eretz Yisrael and Babylonia, and then utilized his experiences in the composition of his celebrated work, the *Taḥkemoni*. It consists of fifty narratives in rhymed prose, describing the communities he visited.

The nineteenth narrative of the *Taḥkemoni*, for example, is about the relative merits of the various virtues: "While I was walking by the riverside, under the shadows of plants and thickets of flowers, I perceived seven pleasant youths of the choicest society... One of them said: I know all good qualities are praiseworthy, but there is none as sublime as humility ... it stirs up love in the hearts of enemies and covers a man's sins and transgressions... His companion said: There is no quality as good and precious as courage and bravery... In truth, there is no precious trait in man like courage blended with strength... The fourth one said: Among all the qualities there is no quality as worthy as faithfulness..."

Al-Ḥarizi's Hebrew translation of Maimonides' *Guide for the Perplexed* has proved, however, less authoritative than that prepared by Samuel ibn Tibbon. He maintains a unique position in medieval Hebrew literature on account of his variety of topics and humorous style.

634

TAHANUN   תַּחֲנוּן

THE *Tahanun* supplication, recited on weekdays after the *Shemoneh Esreh* prayer, is often referred to as *nefilath appayim* (falling on the face) because in the early days of the Talmud it was customary to recite it in the form of prostration with the face to the ground. This custom originated from Moses, who "lay prostrate before the Lord" (Deuteronomy 9:18), and Joshua who "fell to the earth upon his face before the ark of the Lord" (Joshua 7:6).

For this reason, *nefilath appayim* is performed only where there is a *Sefer Torah*. It now consists merely of resting the head on the arm. During the morning service, when the *tefillin* are resting on the left arm, the right arm is used; at the *Minhah* service, however, the left arm is used. The *Tahanun* is recited in a sitting posture. On Mondays and Thursdays, the so-called long *Tahanun* (והוא רחום) is said. It contains heart-stirring elegies and supplications giving voice to the sufferings of the Jewish people over many centuries.

TEHINNOTH   תְּחִנּוֹת

IN KEEPING with the warning of the Jewish sages against regarding prayer merely as a matter of dull routine, but rather as a supplication for divine mercy (Avoth 2:18), men of piety composed their private devotions, or *tehinnoth*, which they recited as meditations during the regular worship services. Examples of such *tehinnoth* are quoted in the Talmud (Berakhoth 16-17).

The *tehinnoth* were created in various Jewish vernaculars (Judeo-Greek, Judeo-Italian, Judeo-Spanish). Since the sixteenth century, many *tehinnoth* appeared in Yiddish, specially designed for women who were not expected to be well-versed in Hebrew, the language of Israel's prayer life. Hence the name *tehinnoth* is used as a general title for the supplementary Prayerbooks published in Yiddish for women. In them are expressed hopes, sorrows and joys, of countless hearts.

The Yiddish devotional prayers, like the Yiddish *Tse'enah Ure'enah*, were most widely read by women and still retain their vogue. They incorporate the essence of a life which is distinctive and unlike any other. Ahad Ha'am asserted: One word, one expression, taken from the Yiddish speech of the people, is more effective than ten abstract ideas.

635

TÉKU   תֵּיקוּ

THE Aramaic word *téku* (let it stand), used in talmudic discussion, occurs at the end of an inquiry when no definite answer is obtainable despite all attempts. *Téku* means: the question remains undecided. According to some, *téku* is not derived from the verb *kum* (to stand), but it is a combination of the initials of four words: תשבי יתרץ קושיות ואבעיות (Elijah the Tishbite will solve all difficulties and inquiries). This is based on an old tradition that Elijah, the forerunner of the Messiah, will settle every doubtful case shortly before the coming of the messianic leader.

BURIAL CLOTHES   תַּכְרִיכִין

THE *takhrikhin* (shrouds), serving as the dress for the dead, are made of white linen cloth. Instead of a single shroud, several articles of clothing are used. For a man's attire, a *tallith* (prayershawl) is added, but with the fringes (*tsitsith*) removed, since the dead are not subject to the law of wearing *tsitsith*.

About fifty years after the destruction of the Second Temple, Rabban Gamaliel II introduced the custom of burying the dead in simple linen garments by the order he gave for his own funeral. He saw that the rich secured fanciful and costly garments in which to bury their dead, thus establishing an extravagant custom which was a burden upon the mourners among the poor, who could not afford the expense and yet were anxious to show high respect for their dead.

The *takhrikhin* are cut and sewed together with long stitches; the ends of the thread are left unknotted, since the *takhrikhin* are intended to last only till the body disintegrates.

TALMUD   תַּלְמוּד

THE name *Talmud* signifies both learning and teaching. The same applies to the titles *Torah, Mishnah,* and *Gemara,* each representing an essential branch of Jewish instruction. The term *Mishnah,* from the Hebrew root *shanah* (to repeat), refers to the study of the traditional law (*Halakhah*) by means of frequent verbal repetition, in keeping

636

with Hillel's proverbial saying that "reviewing a lesson a hundred times cannot be compared with reviewing it a hundred and one times": אינו דומה שונה פרקו מאה פעמים לשונה פרקו מאה ואחת (Ḥagigah 9b). When books were not available, the subjects taught had to be engraved upon memory by means of repeated recitation. The fact that the various branches of Jewish learning bear titles denoting both learning and teaching suggests what is often emphasized in Jewish sources, that knowledge must be shared unselfishly and that we are expected to transmit to others the ideals that have come into our possession.

Both Talmuds, the Babylonian and the Palestinian recensions (*Talmud Bavli* and *Talmud Yerushalmi*), reflect all the beautiful and noble teachings of the Hebrew Bible concerning human life in all its phases, secular and religious. The two Talmuds, consisting of the Hebrew Mishnah and the Aramaic Gemara, represent the academic activities of the Tannaim and the Amoraim who transmitted the tradition, or oral Torah, to the generations, from Hillel and Shammai down to the beginning of the sixth century. Since the middle of the sixth century, the Babylonian Talmud has been the chief source of education for Jews in many lands; its vastness has given rise to the expressive phrase *Yam ha-Talmud* (the ocean of the Talmud). The whole gamut of human life is covered in this encyclopedic work, which is now available in English translation. The Palestinian Talmud lacks the comprehensiveness of the Babylonian Talmud and is less than one-third the size of *Talmud Bavli*.

Marcus Jastrow, in his Talmudic Dictionary, has this to say about the varied contents of the Talmud: "The subjects of this literature are as unlimited as are the interests of the human mind. Religion and ethics, exegesis and homiletics, jurisprudence and ceremonial laws, ritual and liturgy, philosophy and science, medicine and magic, astronomy and astrology, history and geography, commerce and trade, politics and social problems, all are represented there, and reflect the mental condition of the Jewish world in its seclusion from the outer world, as well as in its contact with the same whether in agreement or in opposition."

Because the Talmud concerns itself with every phase of human activity, it has saved the Jewish people from stagnation. The mind of the talmudic student is kept alert; at every point he is in contact with actualities. One of the first requisites of talmudic study is to maintain quick, mental alertness throughout the process of intensive and complicated discussion. Though it is written in a style far removed from modernity, the Talmud breathes with vital freshness and appears as one of the most modern books. The Hebrew liturgy has derived some of its most sublime prayers from the pages of the Talmud.

The following two prayers were borrowed from the Talmud and inserted in the Prayerbook almost word for word: "May it be thy will, Lord our God and God of our fathers, to grant us long life, a life of peace and well-being, a life of blessedness and sustenance, a life of health and piety, a life free from shame and disgrace, a life of prosperity and honor, a life marked by a love for Torah. . ." "My God, guard my tongue from evil, and my lips from speaking falsehood. May I be silent to those who insult me; may my soul be lowly to all as the dust. Open my heart to thy Torah, that I may follow thy precepts soulfully. . ." (Berakhoth 16b; 17a).

The *Talmud Yerushalmi*, known as the Palestinian Talmud, reached its present form in the beginning of the fifth century; large sections of it are now lost. The editing of the *Talmud Bavli*, or Babylonian Talmud, extended for about a hundred years, from 400 to 500 of the common era. It includes the whole Mishnah, even the tractates on which there is no Gemara commentary. The sages known as *Amoraim*, by their interpretation of Jewish tradition, developed the entire lore that comprises the Talmud. Their activities in Eretz Yisrael and Babylonia continued for about three centuries. They were succeeded by the *Savoraim* (reasoners), who completed the redaction of the Talmud in the course of some seventy years. Most of the anonymous passages in the Babylonian Talmud originated from the *Savoraim*.

Here are several proverbial sayings from the Talmud:

The hope of the world lies in its school children. A single light will do for a hundred men as well as for one. I have learned much from my teachers, even more from my colleagues, but I have learned the most from my students. He who studies but does not review his work is like one who sows but does not reap. Love your wife as much as yourself, but honor her more than yourself. If your wife is short, bend your head and take her advice. A man should eat and drink beneath his means, clothe himself within his means, and honor his wife above his means. No man should be held responsible for words uttered in his grief. No one should taunt a reformed sinner about his past. Adorn yourself before you adorn others. A man notices the weaknesses of others but not his own. A little coin in a big jar makes a lot of noise. He who seeks a friend without faults will remain friendless. Kindliness is the beginning and the end of the Torah. If two men ask for your help, and one of them is your enemy, help your enemy first. When good people die, they are not really dead, for their example lives.

Various terms are descriptive of Talmud students. Such are *mathmid* (מתמיד), *illuy* (עלוי), *lamdan* (למדן), *talmid ḥakham* (תלמיד חכם), *ḥarif* (חריף), *baki* (בקי), and *gaon* (גאון).

The *mathmid*, or *masmid*, is deeply devoted to talmudic learning to the exclusion of all else. A young prodigy, who shows extraordinary intellectual aptitude and brilliance of mind in talmudic scholarship, is called *illuy*. A person steeped in talmudic learning is termed *lamdan*. To be a *talmid ḥakham*, a man of learning, has been regarded in Jewish tradition as the abiding ideal which everyone should strive to attain. The talmudic scholar known as *ḥarif* is the quick, ingenious individual, otherwise described as עוקר הרים (*oker harim*), whose dialectical ingenuity is figuratively capable of uprooting mountains. A person well versed in the Talmud is called *baki* and, metaphorically, *sinai* (סיני). A *gaon* is a talmudic scholar of rare genius.

TALMID ḤAKHAM   תַּלְמִיד חָכָם

THE honorific title *Talmid Ḥakham* (disciple of the wise) is given to a person who is well versed in talmudic learning. In medieval manuscripts the singular is תלמיד חכמים; compare the plural תלמידי חכמים. Since knowledge of the Torah has always been prized above worldly goods in the tradition of the Jewish people, the *talmidé ḥakhamim* have been regarded as a kind of aristocracy in Jewish society in terms of both privileges and duties. To enable them to devote themselves entirely to study, they were exempted from the payment of taxes and from performing any specific communal duties.

Maimonides writes: "Even as a sage is recognized by his wisdom and moral principles which distinguish him from the rest of the people, so ought he to be recognized in all his activities: in his food and drink . . . in his talk, walk, dress, management of his affairs and business transactions. All these activities should bear the mark of exceeding refinement and orderliness. . . When speaking, a scholar will not shout or scream. . . He will not raise his voice unduly. His speech with all men will be gentle. But while speaking gently, he will be careful to avoid exaggeration which would make his speech sound affected, like the speech of the haughty. He will be the first to greet every one he meets. . . He will judge every one favorably. He will dwell on the merits of others and never speak disparagingly of anybody. He loves peace and strives for it. If he feels that his words will be effective and heeded, he will speak; otherwise, he will remain silent. . ." (*Yad, Talmud Torah* 5:1, 7).

Harry A. Wolfson, who has been recognised as one of the most influential minds of our time, depicts the method of talmudic study in the following terms: Confronted with a statement on any subject, the talmudic student will proceed to raise a series of questions before he satisfies himself of having understood its full meaning. If the statement is not clear enough, he will ask: "What does the author intend to say here?" If it is too obvious, he will again ask: "It is too plain, why expressly say it?" If it is a statement of fact or of a concrete instance, he will then ask: "What underlying principle does it involve?" If it is a broad generalization, he will want to know exactly how much it is to include. Statements apparently contradictory to each other will be reconciled by the discovery of some subtle distinction, and statements apparently irrelevant to each other will be subtly analyzed into their ultimate elements and shown to contain some common underlying principle. The talmudic student approaches the study of texts in the same manner as the scientist approaches the study of nature. Just as the scientist proceeds on the assumption that there is a uniformity and continuity in nature so the talmudic student proceeds on the assumption that there is a uniformity and continuity in human reasoning.

TAM AND MU'AD   תָּם וּמוּעָד

THE term *tam* (innocuous) is applied in talmudic law to an animal that has inflicted injury not more than twice. Its owner, not having been forewarned, pays only for half the damage. The term *mu'ad* (forewarned) is applied to an animal that has inflicted injury on three successive occasions, so that the owner thus stands *forewarned* and is liable to compensate in full for any damage that has been caused by his animal.

This law of retaliation is otherwise referred to as *lex talionis*. Its purpose is not merely the enforcement of rigorous justice, but also the prevention of greater penalties than would be just. Thus we read in the Torah: "When one man's ox hurts another man's ox so badly that it dies, they shall sell the live ox and divide its price as well as the dead animal equally between them. But if it was known that the ox was previously in the habit of goring and its owner failed to keep it in, he must make full restitution, an ox for an ox; but the dead animal he may keep" (Exodus 21:35-37). The law of retaliation (like for like) is not the same as private revenge. The equivalent penalty is inflicted by the judge, not by the injured person.

The expression *life for life*, where no homicide was intended, has been interpreted to mean *fair compensation*. There is no instance in Jewish history of the literal application of *eye for eye, tooth for tooth* (Exodus 21:24), practised in primitive society. This expression in the Torah has been explained in the sense that the poorest inhabitant has the same rights as his rich and powerful assailant, "the tooth of the peasant is as valuable as that of the noblemen." In Jewish jurisprudence, physical injuries which are not fatal are a matter of monetary compensation for the injured party.

The Mishnah (Bava Kamma 8:1) states: "He who injures his neighbor becomes liable on five counts. He must pay for injury and pain inflicted, for healing and loss of time, and for indignity suffered. According to the *Ramban*, if the culprit was unable to pay the indemnity, he was sold into slavery until the debt was paid.

TAMMUZ   תַּמּוּז

THE month of *Tammuz*, corresponding to June-July, consists of twenty-nine days. The seventeenth of *Tammuz* is the public fast known as שבעה עשר בתמוז, commemorating a number of sad events in Jewish history: the breaking down of the walls of Jerusalem by the Romans in the year 70; the breaking of the two tablets by Moses, the burning of the Torah by a Greek, Apostomos; the cessation of the regular daily offering in the Temple (Megillath Ta'anith 4:6). According to Jeremiah 39:2, Nebuchadnezzar's army made a breach in the city of Jerusalem on the ninth day of the fourth month (*Tammuz*).

The seventeenth of *Tammuz* ushers in the three weeks of mourning, till the end of *Tish'ah b'Av*. During this period the observant Jews abstain from every kind of celebration, in commemoration of the destruction of both the first and the second Temples (586 before the common era and 70). In later times other calamities were associated with this period, such as Bar Kokhba's defeat in 135 and the expulsion of the Jews from Spain in 1492.

TANNA D'VE ELIYYAHU   תַּנָּא דְּבֵי אֵלִיָּהוּ

THIS midrashic work, more correctly called *Seder Eliyyahu*, consists of two parts: *Seder Rabbah* and *Seder Zuta* (major and minor order). They contain thirty-one and twenty-five chapters, respectively. It is a collection of moral discourses, stressing the virtues of repentance, charity, moderation, meaningful prayer, diligent study, chastity and modesty. It is written in pure Hebrew, and seems to have originated in Eretz Yisrael around the tenth century. Its date and place of origin are, however, debated by scholars, some of whom place it in the talmudic period. The name Abba Eliyyahu, occurring in this religious-ethical work, indicates the name of the author, though the book used to be attributed to Elijah the prophet.

TANNAIM   תַּנָּאִים

THE term *Tannaim* (from the Aramaic verb תני = to teach) is applied to the teachers mentioned in the tannaitic literature (Mishnah, Tosefta, Baraitha, Midrash Halakhah). The tannaitic period begins with the death of Hillel and Shammai, the first decade of the common era, and ends with the death of Rabbi Yehudah ha-Nasi, compiler and editor of the Mishnah, at the beginning of the third century. The *Tannaim*, successors to the sages known as *Sofrim*, were active in the course of some six generations or about two hundred and ten years (10-220). Typical *Tannaim* are the five rabbis mentioned at the outset of the Passover *Haggadah*, where we are told that they celebrated the *Seder* together in Bné Brak and spent the whole night discussing the inner significance of the exodus from Egypt. They are: Eliezer, Joshua, Elazar ben Azaryah, Akiva, and Tarfon.

Rabbi Eliezer, famous for his retentive memory, was compared to a cemented cistern which does not lose a drop of water. Against the wishes of his father, who threatened to disinherit him, he began to study late in life and developed into one of the greatest scholars of his time. He is frequently quoted in the Mishnah and spoken of as "Rabbi Eliezer the Great." His teacher, Rabbi Yoḥanan ben Zakkai, used to say: "If all the sages of Israel were in one scale of the balance and Eliezer ben Hyrcanus on the other, he would outweigh them all." Rabbi Eliezer was in the habit of saying: "Let the honor of your fel-

642

low man be as dear to you as your own, and be not easily provoked to anger" (Avoth 2:11, 12, 15).

Rabbi Joshua, one of the five preeminent disciples of Rabbi Yoḥanan ben Zakkai, was held in the highest esteem for his profound scholarship, his love of peace, and his modesty. According to talmudic tradition, his mother used to take him as an infant to the house of learning so that his ears might become attuned to the sound of Torah. He won fame as the representative of Jewish wit and wisdom, having successfully debated with Greek philosophers. He believed that friendliness is the quality which every man should share (Avoth 2:13).

Rabbi Elazar used his great wealth for the welfare of his people during the relentless persecutions that preceded Bar Kokhba's revolt against Roman tyranny. He believed that moral goodness is more essential than speculative thought, and that wisdom is valueless unless it improves a man's character. He used to say: "The person whose wisdom exceeds his deeds is like a tree that has many branches and few roots; the wind comes and plucks it up and turns it over. But one whose deeds exceed his wisdom is like a tree that has few branches and many roots—all the winds in the world, blowing upon it, cannot uproot it" (Avoth 3:22).

Rabbi Akiva, who began his career as a student rather late in life and soon became one of the greatest leaders of his people, trained a vast number of scholars in his academy at Bné Brak, near the city of Jaffa. He is the hero of many stories describing his unselfishness, his loyalty and his devotion. He stressed the idea that man's responsibility is based upon man's unrestricted freedom of choosing between right and wrong. God's foreknowledge does not predetermine man's actions, good or bad. In matters of ethical conduct man has the ability to choose between alternative possibilities of action (Avoth 3:18-19).

Rabbi Tarfon, who had been a priest in the service of the Temple, used his great wealth for charitable purposes. The Talmud relates that his devotion to his mother reached extreme proportions (Kiddushin 61b). Despite his riches, he possessed extraordinary modesty. He used to say: "The day is short; the task is great; the workmen are lazy; the reward is great; the Master is insistent... You are not called upon to complete the work, yet you are not free to evade it. If you study much, you will be amply rewarded." (Avoth 2:20-21). He expressed himself to the effect that the death penalty would have been abolished if he and his colleague Rabbi Akiva had belonged to the Sanhedrin during the Second Commonwealth (Makkoth 1:10).

643

TANḤUMA   תַּנְחוּמָא

THE exegetical Midrash on the Pentateuch, known as *Midrash Tan-ḥuma*, is named after one of the most prolific *haggadists* of the fourth century, Rabbi Tanḥuma bar Abba, who is frequently mentioned in it. It is also referred to as *Midrash Yelammedenu*, from the fact that many of the homiletic interpretations in this Midrash begin with a *halakhic* introduction and open with the phrase *yelammedenu rabbenu* (let our master teach us). Many of the homilies, which include interpretations of a variety of biblical verses, close with messianic hopes for the great deliverance envisioned by the prophets.

The two recensions of the *Tanḥuma* differ widely in Genesis and Exodus, but agree for the most part in Leviticus, Numbers and Deuteronomy. The midrashic collections called *Tanḥuma* or *Yelammedenu* stem from early sources. The thirteenth-century author of the midrashic collection *Yalkut Shimeoni* refers to both *Tanḥuma* and *Yelammedenu* as two distinct works. The *Arukh*, eleventh-century talmudic-midrashic lexicon, mentions the *Yelammedenu* but not the *Tanḥuma*. It is therefore reasonable to suppose that the two works were combined into one by a later compiler.

TANYA

Two famous works bear the title *Tanya:* 1) a collection of laws and customs, described as an abridgment of the *Shibbolé ha-Leket*, a law-code by Rabbi Zedekiah ben Abraham Anav, who lived in Rome in the thirteenth century; 2) a philosophic-mystic text by Rabbi Shneour Zalman of Liadi, founder of Ḥabad Ḥasidism. Both works are known after their initial word, *Tanya*, a term by which a tannaitic statement is introduced from a Baraitha.

The anonymous *Tanya* was first published in Italy in 1514; the ḥasidic *Tanya*, studied daily in Ḥabad circles, was first published in 1797. The original name of the Ḥabad Tanya is *Sefer Likkuté Amarim* (a collection of sayings), "culled from books and saintly sages." It recently appeared in both a Yiddish and an English translation, sponsored by leaders of the Ḥabad movement in New York.

In his preface to *Shibbolé ha-Leket*, Rabbi Zedekiah Anav modestly apologizes for giving preference to opinions and decisions that seem

644

to him true, and relates the following anecdote: A philosopher, who
was asked how he dared to oppose the great men of the past, answered:
We fully acknowledge the greatness of our old authorities and the in-
significance of ourselves. But we are in the position of pygmies that
ride on the shoulders of giants. Pygmies though we are, we see farther
than the giants when we use their knowledge and experience."

HEBREW BIBLE   תַּנַ״ךְ

THE Hebrew Bible, recording the divine relationship with the people
of Israel over a period of more than fifteen centuries, has been the
source of religious ideals for countless millions; it has given impulse
and direction to the cultural progress of mankind by stressing the
dignity of man, whose reason and will remain unchained. It has been
asserted that in the Bible God confers direct with men and men with
angels, face to face, as one friend confers with another. One may add:
In the pages of the Jewish Bible, man stands erect before his God as
befits one in the image of his Creator. This attitude shuts out fatalism
which stops the wheels of human initiative and progress.

One of mankind's debts to the Bible, it has been pointed out, is
the day of rest, one of the greatest blessings to toiling mortals. To us
who know and appreciate the value of the day of rest and recognize
the tribute paid to it by its world-wide acceptance, it must seem
strange that such an institution could ever have had its detractors.
Yet the Greek and Latin writers alike attacked it, and the philosopher
Seneca regarded it as not only valueless, but even pernicious. To remain idle every seventh day, he said, is to lose a seventh part of life.
The Sabbath could never have drawn to itself public attention and
forced its way to general acceptance as a holiday had not its celebration been a strict religious obligation on the Jews formulated in their
Torah. What do we not owe, and what does mankind in general not
owe, to the Bible for this priceless boon, shared by people of all faiths
throughout the world?

The Bible has been the Magna Charta of the poor and of the oppressed; down to modern times no state has had a constitution in
which the interests of the people are so largely taken into account, in
which the duties so much more than the privileges of rulers are insisted
upon, as that drawn up for Israel in Leviticus and in Deuteronony;
nowhere is the fundamental truth that the welfare of the state in the

645

long run depends on the uprightness of the citizen so strongly laid down. The Bible is said to be the most democratic book in the world.

Our great claim to the gratitude of mankind is that we gave to the world the word of God, the Bible. We have stormed heaven to snatch down this heavenly gift, as the *payyetan* puts it. We threw ourselves into the breach, and covered it with our bodies against every attack. We allowed ourselves to be slain in hundreds and thousands rather than become unfaithful to it, and we bore witness to its truth, and watched over its purity, in the face of a hostile world. The Bible is our sole *raison d'être;* and it is just this which the Higher Anti-Semitism, both within and without our ranks, is seeking to destroy, denying all our claims for the past and leaving us without hope for the future. This intellectual persecution can only be fought with intellectual weapons, and unless we make an effort to recover our Bible we are irrevocably lost from both worlds.

The Bible is only one constituent part of Judaism, though the most fundamental one. Who taught the average Jew to understand his Judaism, to love his religion and his God? Without the zeal of the Rabbis, the Bible would never have become the guide of every Jew. They translated it into the vernacular for the people, and expounded it to the masses. They taught them not to despair under the tortures of the present, but to look forward to the future. At the same time they developed the spirit of the Bible and never lost sight of the lofty teachings of the Prophets. It is the immortal merit of the unknown Rabbis of the centuries immediately before and after the common era that they found and applied the proper *fences* for the preservation of Judaism, and that they succeeded in rescuing real morality and pure monotheism for the ages that were to follow.

The accepted view is that the King James translation of the Bible has been a powerful stimulus to English prose, and that it would be hard to find any English writer of stature whose style is completely free from the influence of the Bible.

The chapter divisions and the numbering of the verses in each chapter was introduced into the Hebrew Bible in the sixteenth century, so as to make quoting from it much easier. Prior to the sixteenth century, the Torah was quoted by the weekly portions (*sidroth*); the remaining twenty-one books of the Bible were quoted without specification of the passage. Unless one knew the Bible by heart, it was most difficult and time consuming to locate a biblical verse, when it was cited as follows: "It is written in the Holy Scriptures"; "King

646

Solomon said;" "It is written in Isaiah, Jeremiah, Ezekiel." "King Solomon said" could mean the Song of Songs, Proverbs, or Ecclesiastes. The chapter divisions and the numbering of the verses were originally devised for the Latin translation of the Bible. The Jews were impelled to adopt the same system because of the frequent religious disputations during which numerous biblical textproofs were cited.

The enlarged edition of the Rabbinic Bible (*Biblia Rabbinica*), otherwise known as *Mikraoth Gedoloth*, was published by Daniel Bomberg at Venice in 1525. Like its successors, it consists of the entire standard Hebrew text of the Bible, accompanied by the Targums and by the commentaries of medieval Jewish scholars: Rashi, Ibn Ezra, Ramban, Kimḥi, Ralbag, and others. It is called *rabbinic*, because the commentaries are printed in a modification of the square script known as Rashi script or Rabbinic type. Most rabbinic writings have appeared in this type face. The *Mikraoth Gedoloth* edition was greatly improved under the editorship of a Tunisian Jew, Jacob ben Ḥayyim, who provided masoretic notes and lists of variant readings from the manuscripts he used. His text was soon adopted as the standard Hebrew text of the Bible.

The Kittel-Kahle edition, or *Biblia Hebraica*, which was completed in 1945, is generally quoted in scientific publications of biblical research. A new scientific edition of the biblical text is planned by the Hebrew University Bible Project, initiated in the forties by the late biblical scholar M. D. Cassuto who made a thoroughgoing study of the Aleppo Codex. This manuscript of the Bible, corrected by the famous masoretic scholar Aaron ben Asher of the tenth century, was preserved in the ancient synagogue of Aleppo, Syria, which dated from the fourth century. The Aleppo Codex was rescued from destruction when the synagogue was demolished in the 1947 riots, and has become available for scientific research at Jerusalem. First to make use of the Aleppo Codex while preparing the Jerusalem Bible for publication, Moses David Cassuto developed an approach to Bible research whereby to demonstrate the uniformity of the sacred text.

The Bible quotes fragments from books that no longer exist. The *Book of the Wars of the Lord*, quoted in Numbers 21:14, was an ancient collection of epic poems concerning the battles under the leadership of Moses. The *Book of Yashar*, quoted in Joshua 10:13 and II Samuel 1:18, tells about the exploits of Israel's early heroes. The *Chronicles of the Kings of Israel* and the *Chronicles of the Kings of Judah* are repeatedly cited in I and II Kings.

The Hebrew Bible known as תנ״ך (*Tanakh*), from the initials of תורה
נביאים and כתובים, is arranged in the following masoretic order:

PENTATEUCH	תּוֹרָה
Genesis	בְּרֵאשִׁית
Exodus	שְׁמוֹת
Leviticus	וַיִּקְרָא
Numbers	בְּמִדְבַּר
Deuteronomy	דְּבָרִים

FORMER PROPHETS	נְבִיאִים רִאשׁוֹנִים
Joshua	יְהוֹשֻׁעַ
Judges	שׁוֹפְטִים
I and II Samuel	שְׁמוּאֵל א, שְׁמוּאֵל ב
I and II Kings	מְלָכִים א, מְלָכִים ב

LATTER PROPHETS	נְבִיאִים אַחֲרוֹנִים

MAJOR PROPHETS

Isaiah	יְשַׁעְיָה
Jeremiah	יִרְמְיָה
Ezekiel	יְחֶזְקֵאל

MINOR PROPHETS

Hosea	הוֹשֵׁעַ
Joel	יוֹאֵל
Amos	עָמוֹס
Obadiah	עוֹבַדְיָה
Jonah	יוֹנָה
Micah	מִיכָה
Nahum	נַחוּם

648

Habakkuk   חֲבַקּוּק

Zephaniah   צְפַנְיָה

Haggai   חַגַּי

Zechariah   זְכַרְיָה

Malachi   מַלְאָכִי

SACRED WRITINGS   כְּתוּבִים

Psalms   תְּהִלִּים

Proverbs   מִשְׁלֵי

Job   אִיּוֹב

FIVE SCROLLS

Song of Songs   שִׁיר הַשִּׁירִים

Ruth   רוּת

Lamentations   אֵיכָה

Ecclesiastes   קֹהֶלֶת

Esther   אֶסְתֵּר

Daniel   דָּנִיֵּאל

Ezra-Nehemiah   עֶזְרָא–נְחֶמְיָה

I and II Chronicles   דִּבְרֵי הַיָּמִים א, דִּבְרֵי הַיָּמִים ב

A popular Hebrew saying, to the effect that Bible study should never be neglected, reads: מִן הַתַּנַ"ךְ יָדְךָ אַל תַּנַח.

FASTS   תַּעֲנִיוֹת

T H E only fast day mentioned in the Torah is *Yom Kippur*, described as a day of self-affliction (Leviticus 16:29; 23:27; Numbers 29:7). Traditionally understood, the command "you shall afflict yourselves" signifies abstinence from all food. The term צוֹם (fasting) does not occur in the Five Books of Moses. The first mention of voluntary fasting is in connection with king David, who refused food when he prayed for the child borne to him by the wife of Uriah (II Samuel 12:22). At times, fasts were proclaimed because of calamity. The public fast meant that the people were conscious of guilt, for which they humbled themselves before God. The fasting involved abstinence from iniquity and unlawful pleasures (Isaiah 58:3-10).

In Zechariah 8:19, four fast days are mentioned as occurring in the months of *Tammuz* (17th), *Av* (9th), *Tishri* (3rd), and *Teveth* (10th). They commemorate the Babylonian siege of Jerusalem on *Asarah b'Teveth*, its capture on *Shiv'ah Asar b'Tammuz*, the destruction of the Temple on *Tish'ah b'Av*, and the murder of Gedaliah, and the Jews that were with him, on the third of *Tishri*, called *Tsom* (fast) *Gedalyah*. Concerning these fasts, Maimonides writes: "There are days which are observed by all Israel as fasts because tragic events happened on them, the object being to stir the hearts, and to open paths of repentance. . ." (*Ta'aniyyoth* 5:1).

The fast of Esther (*Ta'anith Esther*), commemorating her fast before she went to plead with the king for her people, is observed on the thirteenth of *Adar*. If it falls on a Sabbath, the fast is held on the preceding Thursday, the eleventh. If one of the other fasts falls on the Sabbath, it is postponed until Sunday. Unlike *Yom Kippur* and *Tish'ah b'Av*, which are observed from sunset to sunset, the fasting on all other fast days begins with daybreak and lasts till sunset, during which time food and drink of any kind is forbidden, but not such physical conveniences as bathing. On fast days, the Torah is read in the synagogue services fron Exodus 32:14; 34:1-10. At the *Minḥah* service, the *Haftarah* is read from Isaiah 55:6-56:8.

A fast deferred to another day, when it happens to coincide with the Sabbath, is called *nidḥeh* (נדחה). *Yom Kippur* is the only fast day that cannot be deferred. *Ta'anith Esther* is the only fast day that is observed on the Thursday *previous* to the thirteenth of *Adar* instead of being *postponed* to Sunday, when *Purim* has to be observed.

The following are included among private, non-communal fasts:

1) On their wedding day, the bride and groom fast while repenting their past misdeeds; they ask forgiveness as on the Day of Atonement.

2) On *erev Pesaḥ*, firstborn sons fast (תענית בכורים) in memory of the deliverance of the Israelite firstborn, who were not stricken in Egypt with the tenth plague. As a rule, a *siyyum* marking the completion of a talmudic tractate, which has been studied in the synagogue, exempts them from fasting that day.

650

3) There are some who fast on a Yahrzeit, the anniversary of a parent's death.

4) Special importance has been attached to a fast resulting from an evil dream (תענית חלום).

5) Adherents of the kabbalistic school fast and recite penitential prayers on *erev Rosh Ḥodesh*, which is called יום כפור קטן (the minor *Yom Kippur*), even though this practice is not mentioned in the *Shulḥan Arukh*.

6) The custom of fasting three days during *Ḥeshvan* and three days during *Iyyar* is referred to as בה"ב (*Bahav*), because it applies to Monday, Thursday and Monday (שני וחמישי ושני). This fasting is associated with the idea that, while celebrating the joyous festivals of *Sukkoth* and *Pesaḥ* of the preceding months, respectively, some frivolity may have been displayed, for which atonement should be sought, as in the case of Job, who offered sacrifices after each feast, saying: "It may be that my sons have sinned and blasphemed God in their hearts" (Job 1:5).

7) Men of piety fast on the Thursdays of שובבי"ם ת"ת, that is, weeks when the following *sidroth* are read: שמות, וארא, בא, בשלח, יתרו, משפטים, תרומה, תצוה.

Here are several talmudic views on fasting: One must not fast excessively, lest he may become a public charge (Tosefta, Ta'anith 2:12). Anyone who indulges in fasting is called a sinner. A scholar may not fast, for it interferes with his study (Ta'anith 11a-b). The merit of a fast is the charity it produces (Berakhoth 6b).

FAST OF ESTHER   תַּעֲנִית אֶסְתֵּר

ON THE thirteenth day of *Adar*, the day preceding *Purim*, the fast of Esther is observed in commemoration of the three days' fast undertaken by the Jews of Persia at the request of queen Esther prior to her pleading the cause of her people before king Ahasuerus. If the thirteenth of *Adar* falls on a Sabbath, the fast is kept on Thursday.

It has been suggested that the institution of *Ta'anith Esther*, is of comparatively late origin, since it is not mentioned in halakhic literature until the eighth century. According to rabbinic tradition, the fasting of Esther occurred during the month of *Nisan*, soon after Haman's casting of lots. It has further been noted that *Ta'anith Esther* was instituted as a counterbalance to the merrymaking of *Purim*.

651

DIASPORA   תְּפוּצוֹת

THE Greek term *Diaspora* (dispersion) was used by the Hellenistic
Jews for all the Jewish settlements that were dispersed outside of
Eretz Yisrael, or *ḥutz la-aretz*. The Septuagint translates the word זעוה
(Deuteronomy 28:25) by *diaspora*: "you shall be in diaspora in all
the kingdoms of the earth." The dispersion of the Jewish people,
which began with the fall of the first Jewish Commonwealth and the
deportation of a large population to Babylonia, reached great proportions under Alexander and the Macedonian rulers. But however widely the Jews were dispersed, they felt themselves firmly affiliated with
the Jewish people in their motherland. The national feeling of the
Jews throughout the world was greatly strengthened by the Maccabean victories and the reestablishment of an independent state, with
boundaries extended to the frontiers of Solomon's kingdom.

In 719 before the common era, when Sennacherib destroyed the
kingdom of Israel in northern Palestine, the first large movement of
Israelites out of their country took place. In the Elephantine papyri
there are indications that in the seventh century before the common
era Israelites settled in southern Egypt as military colonists guarding
the southern frontier. The Jewish military colony was situated on an
island of the Nile, then called Elephantine (the place of elephants).
The Diaspora increased with the fall of Judea. The return from the
Babylonian captivity did not affect the existence of the Babylonian
Diaspora, whence the Jews spread throughout the Persian empire.

During the Greek period, the dispersion grew rapidly. The expand-
ing population of Judea overflowed toward the Greek Isles. In the Roman period, Jewish settlements developed in various parts of Europe.
During the nineteenth century, Jews of Central Europe began to mi-
grate in larger numbers to the United States. By the end of the first
decade of the twentieth century, the United States had the second
largest Jewish community of the world. In the 1960's, close to six
million Jews, representing the largest community in the world, are
nationally and politically associated with the United States as its active citizens. The creation of the state of Israel and the return of
nearly two million Jews are looked upon as small compensation for
the enormous losses under the Nazis who almost annihilated the
European Diaspora. Modern Hebrew writers often refer to the Diaspora as ארצות הפזורה (lands of dispersion).

652

The Hebrew word *golah* (exile) denotes primarily the state of being in bondage in a foreign land. During the biblical period, the Assyrians introduced the practice of deporting at least the leading men of each country they conquered to districts removed from familiar associations and patriotic recollections. The gaps in the population were filled with colonists from other regions. They imported into what used to be the Northern Kingdom of Israel their own religious practices, which they mixed with Jewish beliefs and modes of worship.

The *Shomronim* are called Samaritans, because they inhabited Samaria and its region after the fall of the Israelite kingdom. In the Talmud they are called *Kuthim* after the place of their origin (Kuth) in Babylonia. The Samaritan sect has survived in Israel and in the ancient city of Shechem (Nablus, Jordan) as a small group of four hundred persons.

Unlike the Ten Tribes, exiled by the Assyrians, the Judeans who were deported to Babylonia by Nebuchadnezzar were not assimilated with their new neighbors culturally or religiously. During their stay in Babylonia they struggled to preserve their own culture and prepared for its further development. The brief period of the Babylonian captivity afforded them the opportunity of recalling and deepening their national heritage, hopefully looking forward to their restoration in Eretz Yisrael. Some fifty thousand Judeans wandered back to their homeland when the Persian King Cyrus, for political reasons, permitted them to return and rebuild the Temple. Many Jews, however, who had acquired wealth and position, remained in Babylonia and, together with Israelite survivors of the Ten Tribes, formed what became later known as *Diaspora*. *Resh Galutha* (head of the exile) was the title held by the head of the Babylonian Jewish community, who enjoyed a great measure of self-rule until the fifth century.

Across the centuries, the Hebrew equivalent of Diaspora was *golah* or *galuth* (captivity, exile). In our time, however, there are those who draw a distinction between Jewish life in exile and in Diaspora. *Exile* connotes, they claim, banishment and homelessness; Diaspora, on the other hand, signifies voluntary settlement in a new country where one can live as a free citizen, unmolested. More than ten million Jews live in the Diaspora today, which includes free countries that are not *galuth* but *hutz la-aretz*, other than Eretz Yisrael. Hence the modern Hebrew equivalent of Diaspora is *Tefutzoth*, meaning dispersion.

According to figures published by the World Jewish Congress in 1962, the Jewish population residing in 122 countries totaled

12,915,000. Of this number, ten million lived in three countries, namely: United States, 5,500,000; Israel, 2,200,000; Soviet Russia, 2,300,000 (according to the Russian census of 1959); France 500,000; Argentina, 450,000; England, 450,000; Canada, 250,000; Roumania, 150,000; Brazil, 140,000; Morocco, 125,000; South Africa, 110,000. The eleven countries mentioned contained ninety-four percent of the world Jewish population.

According to the *American Jewish Year Book*, published in 1963, the estimated world Jewish population rose to thirteen million in the year 1962.

PRAYER   תְּפִלָּה

PRAYER is the natural expression of the religious feelings of man. Prayer that is purely selfish is common in pagan religions, reflecting a low conception of the divine. In the Jewish tradition, prayer occupies a central position. The Bible records the prayers of the great men and women in the early history of the people of Israel. Their simple prayers expressed in words the outpourings of the soul. A profound conception of the nature of prayer is revealed in the term *tefillah*, which means invocation of God as a judge. The Jewish prayers are for the most part in the first person plural, because the Jewish people have always been intensely group-conscious. In the synagogue there has been no room for selfish prayers; the watchword of Jewish solidarity and mutual responsibility is to be found in the talmudic statements: "All the people of Israel are companions; all members of Israel are responsible for one another" (Shevuoth 39a; Sanhedrin 27b).

Primarily designed for congregational worship, the Hebrew liturgy was well established in the period immediately following the destruction of the Second Temple. It has given expression to the faith and hopes, sorrows and joys, of the people as a whole. Along with the synagogue, the home also became a place of worship in the form of the customary *Kiddush, Havdalah,* as well as prayers offered at the beginning and end of every meal and at every outstanding event or experience. In the course of time, all activities of life were permeated with thoughts of God; every action was expected to be *l'shem shamayim,* for the sake of God, with pure purpose and good intentions.

Solomon's prayer at the dedication of the Temple contains all the four elements of Hebrew prayers: thanksgiving, praise, confession,

and intercession. It is full of a sense of God's infiniteness, righteousness, omniscience, and forgiveness; it embraces a petition for the
strangers that are not of Israel: "Also, when the alien who does not
belong to thy people Israel . . . comes and turns in prayer towards
this Temple, hear thou in heaven thy dwelling place and do all that
the alien asks of thee. . ." (I Kings 8:41-43). According to a talmudic
tradition, the altar atoned for the nations when the Temple was in
existence. The seventy bullocks that were offered during the seven
days of *Sukkoth* corresponded to the seventy nations which were then
supposed to inhabit the world (Sukkah 55b).

Down to the last days of the First Temple there were no formally
prescribed prayers, not even a general command to pray. However,
the beautiful prayer in Deuteronomy 26:5-10, thanking God for saving Israel from the hardships of the past and giving them a rich and
fertile land, leads us to believe that other offerings at the Temple
were likewise accompanied by prayer. Isaiah (56:7) describes the
Temple as a house of prayer for all peoples. The Hebrew Psalms
stand out unique among the prayers of the entire world by their simplicity, power and majesty of diction. They were widely in use during the period of the Second Temple.

The Psalms have been described as the anatomy of all parts of the
soul. All the sorrows, troubles, fears, doubts, hopes, pains, perplexi-
ties, stormy outbreaks, by which the souls of men are tossed, are depicted in the book of Psalms. The Psalms are the Prayerbook and
the hymnbook of the whole world. They are religion itself put into
speech. The nineteenth Psalm is the most magnificent of sacred songs.
In the Psalms men speak to God and to their own hearts. The book
of Psalms contains the whole music of the heart of man. In every
country, the language of the Psalms has become part of the daily life
of nations, passing into their proverbs, mingling with their conversation, and used at every critical stage of existence. They are the songs
of the human soul, timeless and universal.

The development of congregational worship is a distinct contribution of Judaism to the other faiths that sprang from it. In the first
place the synagogue served the purposes of religious instruction,
whereby the precepts of the Torah entered into the lifeblood of the
people. The reading of the Torah, with accompanying translation and
explanation in the vernacular of the people, which took place on Sabbaths and festivals, and on Mondays and Thursdays (market days),
was introduced by Ezra the Scribe in order to make the Torah the

655

property of all Israel. After the fall of Jerusalem in the year 70, the synagogue became the only center uniting the Jewish people throughout the Diaspora. From this time onward the sages endeavored to establish uniformity in the services.

The interpretation of the passages read from the Torah was designated as *midrash* (exposition), a term occurring twice in the Bible (II Chronicles 13:22; 24:27), though it is common in post-biblical literature. The biblical exposition in the synagogue gradually developed into lectures embracing religious and ethical thoughts and forming the model for later sermons. Some define the term *midrash* as an imaginative development of a thought or theme suggested by Scripture, especially a didactic or homiletic exposition, or an edifying religious story. In his *Gottesdienstliche Vortraege der Juden*, Zunz demonstrates the intimate historical connection between prayers and sermons.

There are two tannaitic statements to the effect that if a person regards his prayer as a perfunctory act, his prayer is not what it should be—a plea for divine grace (Berakhoth 4:4; Avoth 2:18). The Talmud explains this in various ways: Prayer must not be like a burden; it must not be confined to the words of the text, as if one is reading a document; the worshiper must insert his own supplication (Berakhoth 29b). Hence, it has been declared that the Jewish liturgy is a noteworthy endeavor to achieve order without sacrificing freedom (Moore). We are told that Rabbi Yehudah ha-Nasi, editor of the Mishnah, told the Roman emperor, Antoninus, that praying every hour of the day is forbidden, lest a man gets into the habit of calling on God thoughtlessly and thus treating him with disrespect.

The Jewish concept of prayer is summed up by Maimonides when he states: "Prayer without devotion is not prayer... He whose thoughts are wandering or occupied with other things ought not to pray... Before engaging in prayer, the worshiper ought ... to bring himself into a devotional frame of mind, and then he must pray quietly and with feeling, not like one who, carrying a load, unloads it and departs" (*Yad, Tefillah* 4:16). The essential thing in prayer is designated by the sages as *kavvanath ha-lev* (direction of the heart), since prayer must be regarded as "worship with the heart" (עבודה שבלב). *Kavvanah* has been defined as a technical term which includes attention, concentration, and spirit of devotion. "Better is a little with *kavvanah* than much without it" has become a proverbial saying. The term *liturgy*, derived from the Greek *laos* and *ergon* (people and work), essentially denotes public worship.

656

The Hebrew Prayerbook which contains liturgical compositions written over a period of two thousand years, has developed in a way that enables every worshiper to become familiar with the various forms of Jewish learning and religious expression. The diversified authorship of the Hebrew Prayerbook, embracing prophets and psalmists, legalists and poets, proclaims that all the people of Israel have a share in its making. The Hebrew prayers have helped to keep the Jews alive and save them from losing their identity and language.

The ideal dimensions in Jewish history are reflected in the Hebrew prayers; they are permeated with Jewish lore of all ages and serve as a means of uniting a dispersed people with *Kelal Yisrael*. The expression חברים כל ישראל (all the people of Israel are knit together in fellowship) forms part of a prayer recited on the Sabbaths that precede Jewish new months. The element of Torah and tradition pervades the Hebrew prayers; they are designed to make the worshiper ethically sensitive and ever more devout.

It has been observed that the English word *pray* comes from a root meaning *to beg* or *to entreat*, while the Hebrew word for praying (*hith-pallel*) is a reflexive verb meaning *to judge oneself*. The difference is profound. Rabbi Naḥman of Bratzlav (1770-1811), the Baal Shem's grandson, taught: If you are not at peace with the world, your prayer will not be heard. Forget everybody and everything during your prayers; forget yourself and your needs; forget the people of whom you have need. . .

It has been frequently pointed out that our prayers in the synagogue are meant to be community prayers. This attitude has given a universal flavor to Jewish life throughout history. The prayers are not meant primarily to give expression to our own personal feelings. How can millions of Jews feel alike every time they recite the prescribed daily prayers? Instead, prayers are meant to convey to us certain fundamental truths and to prepare us for the trials and complex temptations of daily life. Occasionally, traditional prayer helps us in a purely personal way, when pent-up emotion chokes our power of expression. We cannot speak; it speaks for us, and in it we find repose. Into its classical forms we breathe our feelings and our sentiments. In the synagogue the individual ego is merged in the united chorus of Israel. And nowhere is this merging better expressed than in the congregational melodies. The congregation should not be permitted to deteriorate into a passive audience. As each worshiper adds his fervor to that of his neighbor, he receives in turn the inspiration of his neighbor to add to his own devotion. There is that devotional give and take between him and every member of the congregation— that unfailing sense of intimate brotherhood.

TEFILLAH ZAKKAH   תְּפִלָּה זַכָּה

IN his popular lawcode חיי אדם (Man's Life), Rabbi Abraham Danzig (1748-1820), first published the famous lengthy meditation known as *Tefillah Zakkah* (Serene Prayer), as a confession to be recited by all worshipers on the eve of *Yom Kippur*. He attributed it to ancient sources, from which he copied it. In the *Tefillah Zakkah*, the good impulse (*yetser tov*) and the evil impulse (*yetser ra*) are pictured as wrestling in perpetual conflict within the heart of man. Every man living meets with an hour of temptation, a certain critical hour, which tries the mettle his heart is made of. Excerpts:

"Thou hast created in man two impulses, a good impulse and an evil impulse, that he may have the power of choosing the good or the bad so that thou mayest grant him a goodly reward for choosing well... Now, my God, I have not hearkened to thy voice; I have followed my evil impulse and my heart's desires, refusing the good and choosing the bad. I have not hallowed my limbs, but defiled them. Thou hast given me a mind and a heart to cultivate good thoughts and good ideas ... but I have defiled my mind and heart by entertaining strange thoughts and ideas... Thou hast given me ears to hear the sacred words of Torah; but alas, I have defiled them by hearing lewd language, slander, and all sorts of forbidden talk... I am ashamed, I blush to lift my face to thee, my God, for having abused the faculties with which thou hast endowed me. . ."

The entire *Tefillah Zakkah*, newly edited with an English translation and annotations, is to be found in *Mahzor Ha-Shalem*, Sephardic.

PRAYER FOR THE SICK   תְּפִלָּה לְחוֹלָה

To visit the sick, Jew or non-Jew, is a religious duty incumbent on all Jews (Sotah 14a). The purpose of visiting the sick is to cheer them by pleasant conversation and good advice. Among the tokens of sympathy is the offering of prayer on behalf of the patient. "Whoever visits a sick person helps him to recover" (Nedarim 39b-40a).

658

The following prayer for the sick, representing the first penitential Psalm (6), describes misery and suffering. This is followed by a rejection of all fellowship with wrongdoers.

"O Lord, punish me not in thy anger; chastise me not in thy wrath. Have pity on me, O Lord, for I languish away; heal me, O Lord, for my health is shaken. My soul is severely troubled; and thou, O Lord, how long? O Lord, save my life once again, save me because of thy kindness. For in death no one remembers thee; in the grave who gives thee thanks? I am wearied with sighing; every night I flood my bed with weeping; I drench my couch with tears. My eyes are dimmed with grief; they have aged because of all my foes. Depart from me, all evildoers, for the Lord has heard the sound of my weeping; the Lord has heard my plea; the Lord accepts my prayer. All my enemies shall be utterly put to shame; they shall fall back in sudden shame."

PRAYER FOR ISRAEL   תְּפִלָּה לִשְׁלוֹם יִשְׂרָאֵל

THE Chief Rabbinate of Israel composed the following *Prayer for the Welfare of the State of Israel* soon after the third Jewish independent state in history was established in 1948. On frequent occasions, this prayer is recited in the synagogues of Israel, replacing הנותן תשועה, the customary prayer for the government. It reads:

"Our Father who art in heaven, Protector and Redeemer of Israel, bless thou the State of Israel which marks the dawn of our deliverance. Shield it beneath the wings of thy love; spread over it thy canopy of peace; send thy light and thy truth to its leaders, officers and counselors, and direct them with thy good counsel.

"O God, strengthen the defenders of our Holy Land; grant them deliverance and crown them with victory. Establish peace in the land, and everlasting joy for its inhabitants.

"Remember our brethren, the whole house of Israel, in all the lands of their dispersion. Speedily let them walk upright to Zion thy city, to Jerusalem thy dwelling-place, as it is written in the Torah of thy servant Moses: Even if you are dispersed in the uttermost parts of the world, from there the Lord your God will gather and fetch you. The Lord your God will bring you into the land which your fathers possessed, and you shall possess it (Deuteronomy 30:4-5).

"Unite our hearts to love and revere thy name, and to observe all the precepts of thy Torah. Shine forth in thy glorious majesty over

659

all the inhabitants of thy world. Let everything that breathes proclaim: The Lord God of Israel is King; his majesty rules over all.
Amen" (Ha-Siddur Ha-Shalem).

TEFILLIN   תְּפִלִּין

THE term *tefillin* is reminiscent of the word *tefillah* (prayer). The
quadrangular capsules of the *tefillin* are made of the skins of animals
described in the Torah as clean and fit for Jewish food. They are spoken of as *shel rosh* (head-phylactery) and *shel yad* (hand-phylactery).
Shel rosh consists of four compartments containing four separate strips
of parchment on which are written four passages from Exodus 13:1-10;
11-16; Deuteronomy 6:4-9; 11:13-20. *Shel yad* consists of a single
compartment, containing the same four passages written in four parallel columns on a single piece of parchment.

Shel rosh has on the outside two *shins*, one with three strokes being
to the right of the wearer, and one with four strokes to the left. The
seven strokes of the two types of letter ש equal the number of times
the leather *retsuah* is wound around the left arm upon which the *shel
yad* is placed. The *shin* together with the letters formed by the knots
of the two straps of *shel rosh* and *shel yad* spell the three-lettered divine name שדי (Almighty).

The *tefillin* are worn by Jewish males from the age of thirteen during the daily morning service. They are not worn on Sabbaths and
festivals, which themselves bear witness to the sacred ideas that are
enshrined in the *tefillin*, and are referred to as signs between God and
his people. At one time the saintly scholars wore *tefillin* the whole day.

The four biblical passages that are inserted in both *tefillin, shel rosh*
and *shel yad*, stress the duty of loving and serving God with our whole
being and demand that we give living expression to our love of God
by careful observance of his precepts which are designed to assure our
happiness. We are to subject our thoughts, feelings and actions to the
service of God. This is intimated by wearing the *tefillin* on the head,
symbolizing our mental faculties, and on the left arm next to the heart,
the seat of emotions.

There was a difference of opinion between Rashi and his grandson
Rabbi Jacob ben Meir (*Rabbenu Tam*) as to the order in which the
four biblical paragraphs should be arranged and inserted in the compartments of the *tefillin*. The opinion of Rashi has prevailed. There

660

are, however, some Jews who wear two types of *tefillin* during the daily morning prayers, one pair prepared according to the opinion of *Rashi* and one pair according to the opinion of *Rabbenu Tam*, in order to be certain of performing their duty properly. Hence, we hear of two types of *tefillin*. It is assumed that the difference of opinion existed long before *Rashi* and *Rabbenu Tam;* otherwise the problem might have been solved by examining the contents of a pair of *tefillin* used before the time of *Rashi*.

TEFILLATH HA-DEREKH   תְּפִלַּת הַדֶּרֶךְ

According to a talmudic statement (Berakhoth 29b), one should offer a prayer before starting out on a journey. The following passage, which is included in the daily Prayerbook, is taken from the Talmud:

"May it be thy will, Lord our God and God of our fathers, to lead us on in safety, to guide us in safety, and to bring us to our destination in life, happiness and peace. Deliver us from every lurking enemy and danger on the journey. Let us obtain favor, kindness and love from thee and from all the people we meet. Hear our supplication, for thou art God, who hearest prayer and supplication. Blessed art thou, O Lord, who hearest prayer."

In the Talmud, this prayer is quoted in the singular: "Lord my God . . . lead me, guide me. . ."

TEFILLATH SHEVA   תְּפִלַּת שֶׁבַע

The Sabbath *Amidah* prayer, which is recited in a standing posture in place of the weekday *Shemoneh Esreh*, is called *tefillath sheva* or ברכת שבע, because it contains only seven benedictions. The first three and the last three blessings are the same in all forms of the *Amidah;* the intermediary blessing, ending with מקדש השבת, varies in all four services of the Sabbath as to the introductory parts.

The thirteen petitions of the weekday *Shemoneh Esreh* have been eliminated on the ground that no personal requests, reminding us of human failings and troubles, may be made on the Sabbath and the sacred festivals. Judaism urges its adherents to be cheerful, not saddened, on the days of rest. Hence, the *Amidah* prayer for festivals, too, consists of seven benedictions only, instead of nineteen.

661

TIKKUN תִּקּוּן

THE custom still prevails among strictly observant Jews to spend the first night of *Shavuoth* in reading biblical and post-biblical selections compiled in an anthology called *Tikkun Lel Shavuoth*, which includes also an enumeration of the six hundred and thirteen divine precepts (*mitzvoth*) as well as the Song of Songs. This *Tikkun* is divided into thirteen sections, the numerical value of אחד (One); after each section the *Kaddish* prayer is recited.

The custom of spending the first night of *Shavuoth* in devotional preparation for the anniversary of the giving of the Torah on Mount Sinai, commemorated on the first day of *Shavuoth* by the public reading of the Ten Commandments, has its basis in the preparation made during the three days which preceded *mattan Torah*, the giving of the Torah. Hence, the three days preceding the festival of *Shavuoth* are known as שלשת ימי הגבלה (the three days of setting bounds), alluding to Exodus 19:12, where Moses was commanded to confine the people within certain marked limits in order to impress them with the unapproachable holiness of God. Their outward purifications symbolized the inward purity required in those who draw near to God.

Similarly, the seventh day of *Sukkoth* is ushered in by spending the night of *Hoshana Rabbah* in reciting *Tikkun Lel Hoshana Rabbah*, an anthology containing the whole of Deuteronomy as well as the entire book of Psalms. The book of Deuteronomy, which concludes the Five Books of Moses, is recited because the annual cycle of the Torah readings is completed at the close of the *Sukkoth* festival. The five divisions of the book of Psalms are recited in allusion to the tradition that king David spent his nights in meditation and study.

The name *Tikkun* has been applied also to an unvocalized copy of the Torah, printed in book form, to be used for practice Torah reading. It is commonly known as *Tikkun Sofrim* (תקון סופרים).

TIKKUN ḤATZOTH תִּקּוּן חֲצוֹת

MIDNIGHT prayers, instituted by the Safed kabbalists of the sixteenth century, are known as *Tikkun Ḥatzoth* (midnight service). They were designed to keep alive the memory of the Temple that was destroyed, resulting in *qaluth ha-shekhinah* (exile of the divine glory). The Safed mystics prescribed for *Tikkun Ḥatzoth* the reading of Psalms 137, 79, 42, 43, 111, 51, 126, as well as petitions and lamentations connected with the loss of Jewish independence. The observance of *Tikkun Ḥatzoth* prevailed among the mystically-minded, extremely pious Jews, who adhered to the teachings of Rabbi Isaac Luria, known as *Ari ha-Kadosh* (1534-1572) because of his ascetic life and saintly character. The three-letter name אר"י is composed of the initials of his full designation: *Ashkenazi Rabbi Isaac*, or אדוננו, רבנו יצחק.

Rabbi Isaac Luria's *Siddur*, referred to as *Nusaḥ Ari* (נוסח אר"י), abounds in meditations based upon the idea that no prayer should be recited, no *mitzvah* should be performed without concentrating one's mind upon the act. Most of these meditations (*kavvanoth, yiḥudim*) direct the worshiper's mind to the mystical significance of the religious act he is about to perform.

TEKUFOTH   תְּקוּפוֹת

THE four seasons of the year are known as the four *tekufoth* or cycles. They are: 1) *Tekufath Nisan*, the vernal equinox (March 21), when day and night are equal, the beginning of spring; 2) *Tekufath Tammuz*, the summer solstice (June 21), when the day is the longest in the year; 3) *Tekufath Tishri*, the autumnal equinox (September 23), when autumn begins and the day again equals the night; 4) *Tekufath Teveth*, the winter solstice (December 22), the beginning of winter, when the night is the longest in the year.

According to the famous Babylonian talmudic sage Mar Samuel (177-257), who was an expert astronomer and dealt with problems connected with the Hebrew calendar, each *tekufah* marks the beginning of a period of ninety-one days and seven hours and a half. On account of his skill in regulating the calendar, he is generally referred to as *Yarḥina'ah* (from *yeraḥ*, month). He said: "The paths of the sky are as clear to me as the paths of Nehardea" (Berakhoth 58b).

Mar Samuel Yarḥina'ah was the head of the eminent Nehardea Academy in Babylonia, while his colleague Rav (Abba Arikha) made Sura the seat of an academy destined to achieve exceptional reputation. Mar Samuel's activity in the third century sums up the history of the Nehardean Academy, which was destroyed in 259, five years after the death of Mar Samuel. The city of Pumbeditha replaced Nehardea as seat of the second Babylonian Academy, second to that of Sura.

TAKKANOTH   תַּקָּנוֹת

THE term *takkanah* is used in talmudic literature to signify an enactment or an ordinance of a positive character, while the term *gezerah* (decree) is employed in the sense of a negative regulation, a prohibition. Several examples of *takkanoth*, enacted in various periods and incorporated into current Jewish law, are as follows: Torah reading is to be part of the Sabbath worship services; communities must have elementary schools; a *kethubbah*, or document containing the obligations of the groom toward his bride, is a prerequisite of marriage; a wife may sue her husband for a divorce. These and many others are known as *takkanoth* (improvements).

The famous *takkanah* against polygamy was introduced by Rabbénu Gershom (965-1028), the head of a talmudic academy in Mainz, whose regulations were accepted as binding by the Jews of Europe. These included bans on divorcing a woman without her consent, reading letters addressed to others, and scoffing at converts that returned to Judaism. During the medieval period, the *takkanoth* enforced by the *ḥerem* (ban) were a powerful weapon in the hands of the Jewish leaders, who regulated the internal affairs of the Jewish communities.

The three neighboring communities of Speyer, Worms and Mainz, known by the abbreviation שו"ם, passed the twelfth-century regulations entitled *Takkanoth Shum* (תקנות שום), which were binding on all German Jews. Sumptuary laws, restricting private expenditure in the interest of the community, were frequently drawn up in various medieval towns. Motivated by a desire to prevent ostentation and vulgar showiness, the sumptuary laws regulated the nature and amount of jewelry that women might wear, the maximum number of guests that might be invited to joyous occasions, the kind of dishes that could be served, the kind of wedding gifts that might be presented, the dress of men and women. These *takkanoth* shed light on the social history of the Jewish people during the medieval period.

TARGUM   תַּרְגּוּם

THE name of Onkelos has been given to the Aramaic translation of the Five Books of Moses, perhaps because of some confusion with Aquila who translated the Bible into Greek. Both Onkelos and Aquila are spoken of as proselytes and disciples of Rabbi Akiva who died in 135. *Targum Onkelos* has continued to be read and studied to this day, when Aramaic is no longer spoken by the Jewish people. It became customary to read the weekly *sidrah* each Friday, twice in the original Hebrew and once in the *Targum* (שנים מקרא ואחד תרגום).

Though remarkably faithful to the original Hebrew text as a whole, *Targum Onkelos* occasionally expands somewhat in poetic passages, in order to introduce an ethical idea derived from the talmudic sages. Avoiding anthropomorphic expressions which represent God with human attributes, *Targum Onkelos* uses circumlocutions, as when "the mouth of the Lord" is rendered "the *memra* (word, command) of the Lord." In Genesis 20:3, "God came" is rendered "A word from the Lord came." When God says that he will meet the people (Exodus 25:22), *Targum Onkelos* translates: "I will cause my word to meet you and I will speak with you."

The biblical modes of speech, accomodating the human ear, are thus toned down. Examples: God does not smell the sweet savor of an offering, but accepts it with delight; he does not pass over the people of Israel on the Passover night, but rescues them; he does not go before the people, but leads them; God's feet are his glorious throne; God's staff is the miraculous staff; the finger of God is a blow from before him. Since there cannot be any comparison between the Lord and the pagan gods, Exodus 15:11 is rendered: "There is none but thee ... there is none except thee." The ideas contained in the Targum are closely similar to those met in the talmudic-midrashic literature.

The Targum avoids anything that may appear derogatory at the expense of the ancestors of the Jewish people. Jacob does not steal Laban's heart, but merely hides from him his going away; Rachel does not steal her father's household gods, but only takes them. Jacob does not flee, but simply departs; similarly, Israel does not flee from Egypt, but leaves the country. Leah's eyes were not weak, but pretty; Moses married a beautiful woman, not a Kushite.

The same characteristic applies to the Aramaic version of the prophetical books of the Bible, known as *Targum Yonathan* (ben Uzziel). The Targums to the various books of the Hagiographa or Sacred Writings (*Kethuvim*) are midrashic in character, especially those to the Five *Megilloth* (Song of Songs, Ruth, Lamentations, Ecclesiastes, Esther). The Targum to Proverbs is literal; its Aramaic diction is close to Syriac. The *Targum Sheni* to the book of Esther is additional to the ordinary Targum, but more midrashic and replete with legend.

665

Unlike all other Aramaic paraphrases of biblical books, *Targum On-kelos* to the Pentateuch has long enjoyed sanctity second only to the Hebrew text. The rule of *shenayim Mikra v'ehad Targum* (reading the weekly *sidrah* twice in Hebrew and once in Targum) is to be found in the Talmud (Berakhoth 8a).

The underlying objectives of *Targum Onkelos* may be summed up as follows: 1) elimination of all anthropomorphisms; 2) unquestioned acceptance of the talmudic interpretation of the Torah; 3) use of the translator's own exegetic method. Onkelos inserted qualifying terms, such as the "divine word," to remove any shadow of corporeal action or human quality from God. The Syriac translation of the Bible, known as the *Peshitta* (the Simple) in contrast to the Septuagint, gradually grew out of the early Aramaic Jewish versions, which were originally oral interpretations or translations accompanying the reading of the Hebrew Bible. They became necessary when the Hebrew ceased to be the spoken language of the Jewish people during the Second Commonwealth and Aramaic took its place as their vernacular. In time these extemporaneous paraphrases and translations were written down in the form of the various Targumim.

The three *Targumim* to the Torah are: *Targum Onkelos*, described as the Babylonian Targum; *Targum Yerushalmi*, described as pseudo-Jonathan because it used to be attributed to Yonathan ben Uzziel on account of the initials ת"י (=תרגום ירושלמי); the Fragmentary Targum, fragments of a third Targum.

SEPTUAGINT VERSION   תַּרְגּוּם הַשִּׁבְעִים

THE Greek version of the Bible was prepared by a group of scholars, totaling seventy-two, six from each tribe of Israel. They were sent to Egypt, where the translation of the Torah was to be added to the two hundred thousand volumes in the Museum during the third century (about 250) before the common era. This is according to the fictitious *Letter of Aristeas*, stating that the Torah was translated into Greek by the seventy-two translators in seventy-two days. When the translation was read by Demetrius, the chief librarian, before the Jewish population, it was approved and recommended to be preserved without changes. The king, Ptolemy II, dismissed the translators with costly gifts. Scholars regard this as a fanciful story of the origin of the Septuagint.

666

Those who have made a study of the vocabulary, idioms and syntax used in the Septuagint, have been led to believe that the work gradually developed through the practice of oral translation in the synagogues of Alexandria, though some books were translated and edited by individuals. The Torah was the first and foremost part of the Bible that had to be made accessible to the Greek-speaking Jewish community. It has been suggested that if the initiative proceeded from the Alexandrian Jews themselves, royal sanction was obtained for the translation and a copy presented to the library. Gradually, the other biblical books were translated; by the end of the second century before the common era, all the books of the Hebrew Bible existed in Greek. The various books are generally judged separately as to their individual worth in terms of authentic renderings. Some of them, like the Five Books of Moses, are faithful to the Hebrew text; others, like Jeremiah, vary constantly from the original Hebrew and are paraphrastic. All of them were composed in a popular Hellenistic Greek, much unlike the classical Greek.

A series of new Greek versions of the Bible (Aquila, Symmachus, Theodotion) resulted during the second century from accusations hurled against new religious sects and their interpolations and falsifications of the sacred text. The Septuagint abounds in misreadings, mistranslations, and internal corruptions; hence, there is no single Septuagint version, but every ancient manuscript presents a different text, departing in its own way from the masoretic Hebrew original. Nevertheless, the transliteration of Hebrew names and words in the Septuagint helps us reconstruct the ancient pronunciation of Hebrew.

While the Septuagint was originally intended for the use of the Hellenized Jews, it at the same time transmitted the Jewish teachings to the non-Jewish world and attracted many proselytes to Judaism. The name Septuagint, meaning seventy in Greek, is used as a round number for seventy-two.

Accustomed to the Greek translation of the Bible, Jews of the Roman empire had to be provided with a substitute Greek version to take the place of the Septuagint which was marred by blunders and interpolations; for example, in Psalm 96:10 the phrase "from the cross" was added to the sentence "the Lord reigns," and the word *almah* (young woman) in Isaiah 7:14 was retranslated "virgin" for sectarian reasons. The first substitute for the Septuagint was produced by Aquila, who is identified by some with the Onkelos of the Aramaic version (Targum) of the Five Books of Moses.

Aquila's punctiliously literal translation of the Hebrew into Greek was intended to tell the Jews exactly what the Bible really said. To offset Aquila's literalism, Symachus produced a somewhat free translation into a more elegant Greek than that of the Septuagint. Another contemporary, Theodotian, combined elegance of diction with fidelity to the original when he made a thorough revision of the Septuagint, bringing it into harmony with the masoretic text. Aquila and Theodotion were both converts to Judaism, while Symmachus belonged to the Ebionite sect.

The three last named Greek versions were used simultaneously by scholars who sought authentic information about the contents of the Hebrew original: Aquila served as a dictionary, Symmachus as a commentary, and Theodotion as a translation. Origen (185-254) of Alexandria compiled the Hexapla, a polyglot Bible containing the original Hebrew in square characters, a Greek transliteration enabling the student to pronounce every Hebrew word, and the Greek translations of Aquila, Symmachus, the Septuagint, and Theodotion. The six texts appeared in six parallel columns, hence the name Hexapla. Origen refers to contemporary Jewish authorities in his monumental edition, which was deposited in the library of Caesarea where it was inspected by Jerome (340-420) while preparing his Latin translation of the Bible, known as the Vulgate. Only fragments were found in the Cairo Genizah of some columns copied from Origen's Hexapla; a few leaves of a copy containing the Psalms were discovered in Milan.

TERUMAH   תְּרוּמָה

THE Hebrew term for heave-offering is *terumah*, which signifies a contribution, an offering for sacred purposes, something lifted up and separated as a gift to the officiating priests and the sanctuary. Since the priests and Levites had no inheritance in the Promised Land, they were compensated in the form of tithes given to the Levites, who in turn gave a tithe to the priests (תרומת מעשר or מעשר מן המעשר).

The Levites were to tithe their own tithe and present it to the priests as *terumah*, as the ordinary Israelites did with the produce of their fields. The Israelites, on the other hand, separated one-fiftieth of their crops as *terumah gedolah* to be given to the priests before they separated the tenth part of the produce to be given as tithe (*ma'aser*) to the Levites.

668

Eleven chapters are devoted in the Mishnah to the laws and regulations pertaining to *terumoth* or heave-offerings. The term *terumah* figures prominently in the teachings of the Mishnah; it is referred to nearly six hundred times. The right to eat *terumah* was a guage to priestly status. The portion allotted to the priests from certain offerings in the Temple is also designated as *terumah*. The same term was used also in the sense of half-shekel contributions deposited in the Temple fund for specified sacred needs (*terumath ha-lishkah*).

TARYAG MITZVOTH   תַּרְיַ״ג מִצְוֹת

Ever since tannaitic times, the total number of biblical precepts has been referred to as *taryag mitzvoth*, or six hundred and thirteen commandments, consisting of 248 affirmative *mitzvoth* and 365 negative *mitzvoth* (רמ״ח מצוות עשה and שס״ה מצוות לא תעשה). According to a talmudic statement, the 365 negative precepts equal the number of days of the year, and the 248 affirmative precepts correspond in number to the joints of the human body (Makkoth 23b). The attempt at classifying all the *taryag* (613) *mitzvoth* was made in the eighth-century work *Halakhoth Gedoloth* by Rabbi Simeon Kahira, whose example was followed by others (Rav Saadyah Gaon, Ibn Gabirol) who composed *azharoth* or liturgical poems for the festival of *Shavuoth*, in which they enumerated the *mitzvoth* contained in the Torah. The numerical value of the word אזהרת (exhortations), like the Hebrew letters of the term תרי״ג, happens to be six hundred and thirteen. The *azharoth* are only seldom distinguished by their fine poetic style.

In his *Sefer ha-Mitzvoth*, Maimonides set up fourteen guiding principles for the identification and proper enumeration of the *taryag mitzvoth*. He concludes the introduction to his *Mishneh Torah* with these words: "The total number of precepts mentioned in the Torah that are to be observed for all time to come is six hundred and thirteen. They consist of 248 affirmative *mitzvoth*, reminiscent of the 248 parts of the human body, and 365 negative *mitzvoth*, reminiscent of the 365 days in the solar year." In the introduction to the *Sefer ha-Ḥinnukh*, the medieval anonymous author states that the precepts applicable in our time to all Jews on various occasions total 270: affirmative, 48; negative, 222. The six precepts that are of continuous application concern the belief in the only One God, who is to be loved and revered always.

669

The *taryag mitzvoth* include many precepts relating to sacrifices, Temple service, and ritual purity. These have not been operative since the destruction of the Temple. Other precepts are incidental and pertain only to certain categories of persons. Many negative precepts, like *you shall not steal*, are accomplished by inaction.

REPENTANCE   תְּשׁוּבָה

THE Hebrew term for repentance is *teshuvah*, denoting a return to God after sin, as opposed to *meshuvah* which means backturning, apostasy. Maimonides devotes ten chapters to *teshuvah*. Defining perfect repentance, he offers this illustration: "When an opportunity presents itself for repeating an offense once committed, and the offender, while able to commit the offense, nevertheless refrains from doing so because he is penitent, and not out of fear or failure of vigor. . . If, however, a person only repents in old age, at a time when he is no longer capable of doing what he used to do, though this is not an excellent mode of repentance . . . he is accepted as a penitent. Even if one transgressed all his life and only repented on the day of his death . . . all his iniquities are pardoned. . . Repentance and *Yom Kippur* secure forgiveness only for transgressions against God. . . But transgressions against fellow men . . . are never pardoned till the injured party has received the compensation due to him and has also been conciliated. . . If a person has wronged another by the use of mere words, he has to apologize and beg his forgiveness. . ."

TASHLIKH   תַּשְׁלִיךְ

THE custom of symbolically casting the sins into a running brook on the first day of *Rosh Hashanah*, following the *Minḥah* service, presumably dates from the fourteenth century and is referred to as *Tashlikh* (thou wilt cast), a word borrowed from Micah 7:19 ("Thou wilt cast all our sins into the depths of the sea"). It is mentioned for the first time in *Sefer Maharil* by Rabbi Jacob Moelln (1355-1427), leading authority on Jewish customs and liturgy.

    Rabbi Jacob Moelln (*Maharil*) explains the custom of *Tashlikh* as a reminder of the *Akedah* (binding), the attempted sacrifice of Isaac, concerning which the Midrash relates that Satan, in an effort to prevent Abraham from fulfilling the divine command, transformed himself into a deep stream on the road leading to Mount Moriah. Plunging into the stream, Abraham and Isaac prayed for divine aid, whereupon the place became dry land again. The prayers recited at the *Tashlikh* service are taken primarily from Micah 7:10:20; Psalm 118:5-9; and Psalms 33 and 130.

TISH'AH B'AV   תִּשְׁעָה בְּאָב

THE ninth day of *Av*, mentioned in Zechariah 8:19 as the "fast of the fifth" month, commemorates such national calamities as the destruction of both Temples, the fall of Bar Kokhba's fortress Bethar, and the expulsion from Spain in 1492. According to tradition, the Second Temple, as well as the First Temple, was destroyed on the ninth of *Av*, the day referred to as predestined to misfortune. *Tish'ah b'Av* resembles *Yom Kippur* in its restrictions upon eating and bathing, maintained from sunset to sunset. Unlike *Yom Kippur*, however, which is observed by fasting even on the Sabbath, if *Tish'ah b'Av* happens to fall on the Sabbath, it is postponed to Sunday, as in the case of any other fast. With the exception of *Yom Kippur*, it is forbidden to observe any fast on the Sabbath.

The three weeks between the seventeenth of *Tammuz* and the ninth of *Av* are observed by abstaining from all festivities and joyous celebrations. But, "when the month of *Av* has begun, all enjoyment should be reduced. During the week of the ninth of *Av* and until after the fast, it is forbidden to take a haircut or put on ironed clothing. . . It is forbidden even to wash clothing which is to be put away until the fast is over. It has long been the custom in Israel to eat no meat (except on the Sabbath). . . during this week, until after the fast" (*Yad, Ta'aniyyoth* 5:6).

On the ninth of *Av*, when the book of Lamentations and other dirges (*kinoth*) are recited before congregations seated on low stools as a sign of mourning, the curtain (*parokheth*) is removed from the holy ark (*aron ha-kodesh*), and visits are made to the cemeteries, in order to stress the sense of mourning. The morning service is recited without *tallith* or *tefillin;* these are worn during the *Minhah* service. The elegies known as *kinoth* are descriptive not only of the calamities connected with the destruction of Jerusalem, but also of the Jewish catastrophes that occurred in various lands of persecution.

671

TISHRI   תִּשְׁרִי

THE seventh month of the so-called Jewish ecclesiastical year, which begins with *Nisan*, is the first month of the civil year. *Tishri* corresponds to September-October and consists of thirty days. The first and second days are *Rosh Hashanah;* the third is *Tsom Gedaliah*, the fast commemorating the assassination of Gedaliah, who was governor of Judea after the destruction of the first Temple; the tenth is *Yom Kippur*, the Day of Atonement; the fifteenth begins the feast of *Sukkoth*, followed by *Shemini Atsereth*, the eighth-day festival, and *Simhath Torah*. *Tishri* is referred to as the month of festivals. Its biblical name is *Ethanim* (I Kings 8:2).

TITHHADDESH   תִּתְחַדֵּשׁ

THE popular term *tithhaddesh* (may you ever become refreshed and restored) is applied on the occasion of a new garment acquired or worn by a friend. The expression תבלה ותחדש (*tevalleh u-tehaddesh*) is a similar wish extended to friends upon seeing them wear new garments. Literally, its meaning is: May you wear it out and replace it with a new one.

TUSHLABA   תּוּשְׁלַבָּ"ע

AT THE end of Jewish works on traditional subjects, it has been customary to express humble thanks to the Author of the universe for enabling the author of the book to complete it satisfactorily. The author's permanent gratitude for divine aid is thus expressed in one word, תושלב"ע, which is composed of the initials of the following six words:

תַּם וְנִשְׁלָם, שֶׁבַח לָאֵל, בּוֹרֵא עוֹלָם.

672

מַפְתֵּחַ

מַפְתֵּחַ

677

684

689

690

691

INDEX

INDEX

THE transliterations of Hebrew words here employed follow the accepted Sephardic pronunciation. For the convenience of the general reader, only a few diacritical marks have been used to distinguish between several letters; thus $ḥ=$ ח, $h=$ ה, $kh=$ כ, $k=$ כ and ק, $th=$ ת, and $ṭ=$ ט and ת. Occasionally we have found it necessary to indicate the letter א by an apostrophe ('), and the letter ע by a reversed apostrophe ('), as in *Ma'amin* and *Ma'ariv*.

695

D

E

701

707

TOPICAL INDEX

This index of related topics, grouped into major categories, is designed to be of help in the use of this book in classroom and home study. Acknowledgement is made to Dr. Abraham G. Duker, Chairman of the Department of Judaic Studies of Brooklyn College, New York, and Rabbi Jonathan Porath of the United Synagogue of America, for their helpful suggestions.

The major categories are:

716

719

Topical Index